THE LETTERS OF WILLIAM AND DOROTHY WORDSWORTH

ARRANGED AND EDITED BY
THE LATE
ERNEST DE SELINCOURT

SECOND EDITION

III

The Middle Years

PART II

1812–1820

REVISED BY
MARY MOORMAN
AND
ALAN G. HILL

OXFORD
AT THE CLARENDON PRESS
1970

Oxford University Press, Ely House, London W. 1

GLASGOW NEW YORK TORONTO MELBOURNE WELLINGTON
CAPE TOWN SALISBURY IBADAN NAIROBI DAR ES SALAAM LUSAKA ADDIS ABABA
BOMBAY CALCUTTA MADRAS KARACHI LAHORE DACCA
KUALA LUMPUR SINGAPORE HONG KONG TOKYO

PRINTED IN GREAT BRITAIN

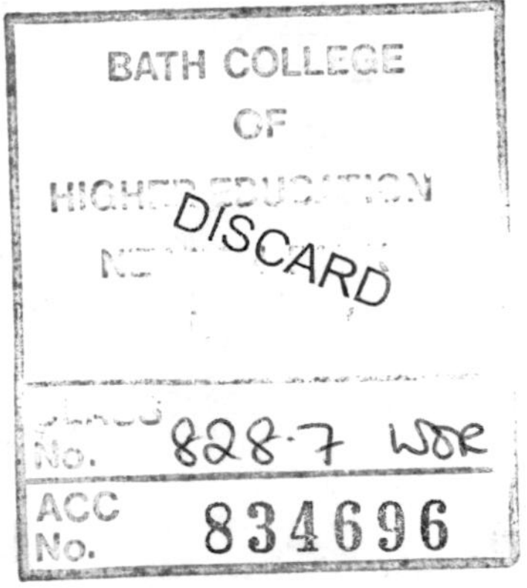

THE LETTERS OF WILLIAM AND DOROTHY WORDSWORTH

THE MIDDLE YEARS

PART II

1812–1820

WILLIAM, EARL OF LONSDALE
by John Opie, from an engraving by S. W. Reynolds

CONTENTS

ABBREVIATIONS

PERSONAL INITIALS

W. W., D. W., M. W., R. W., C. W.: William, Dorothy, Mary, Richard, and Christopher Wordsworth.

S. H.: Sara Hutchinson. S. T. C.: Samuel Taylor Coleridge. C. C.: Catherine Clarkson. H. C. R.: Henry Crabb Robinson,

SOURCES

Broughton *Some Letters of the Wordsworth Family*, edited by L. N. Broughton, Cornell University Press, 1942.

C *Memorials of Coleorton*, edited by W. Knight, 2 vols., 1887.

Cornell Department of Rare Books, Cornell University Library, Ithaca, N.Y.

Curry *New Letters of Robert Southey*, edited by K. Curry, 2 vols., Columbia University Press, 1965.

DWJ *The Journals of Dorothy Wordsworth*, edited by Ernest de Selincourt, 2 vols., 1941.

EY *The Letters of William and Dorothy Wordsworth*, edited by the late Ernest de Selincourt, second edition, I, *The Early Years, 1787–1805*, revised by Chester L. Shaver, Oxford, 1967.

Gillies *Memoirs of a Literary Veteran*, by Robert Pearce Gillies, 3 vols., 1851.

Griggs *Collected Letters of Samuel Taylor Coleridge*, edited by Earl Leslie Griggs, 4 vols., Oxford, 1956–9 (not yet completed).

Grosart *The Prose Works of William Wordsworth*, edited by Alexander B. Grosart, 3 vols., 1876.

Haydon *Correspondence and Table Talk of Benjamin Robert Haydon*, ed. by F. W. Haydon, 1876.

HCR *Henry Crabb Robinson on Books and their Writers*, edited by Edith J. Morley, 3 vols., 1938.

Japp *Memorials of Thomas De Quincey*, edited by A. H. Japp, 2 vols., 1891.

Jordan *De Quincey to Wordsworth, a Biography of a Relationship*, by J. E. Jordan, 1962.

K *Letters of the Wordsworth Family*, edited by W. Knight, 3 vols., 1907.

LY *The Letters of William and Dorothy Wordsworth, The Later Years*, edited by Ernest de Selincourt, 3 vols., Oxford, 1939.

Lamb	*The Letters of Charles and Mary Lamb*, edited by E. V. Lucas, 3 vols., 1935.
Masson	*Collected Writings of Thomas De Quincey*, 14 vols., 1896.
Mem.	*Memoir of William Wordsworth*, by Christopher Wordsworth, 2 vols., 1851.
MLN	*Modern Language Notes*.
MW	*The Letters of Mary Wordsworth*, edited by Mary E. Burton, Oxford, 1958.
MY	*The Letters of William and Dorothy Wordsworth, The Middle Years*, edited by Ernest de Selincourt, 2 vols., Oxford, 1937.
Moorman i, ii	*William Wordsworth, A Biography*, i, *The Early Years*, ii, *The Later Years*, by Mary Moorman, Oxford, 1957 and 1965.
Morley	*Correspondence of Henry Crabb Robinson with the Wordsworth Circle*, edited by Edith J. Morley, 2 vols., Oxford, 1927.
NQ	*Notes and Queries*.
Oxf. W.	*Poetical Works of William Wordsworth*, edited by Thomas Hutchinson, Oxford, 1928 (in one volume).
PMLA	*Publications of the Modern Language Association of America*.
PW	*Poetical Works of William Wordsworth*, edited by Ernest de Selincourt and Helen Darbishire, 5 vols., Oxford, 1940–9.
Rollins	*The Letters of John Keats, 1814–1821*, edited by Hyder E. Rollins, 2 vols., Cambridge, 1958.
S	*Letters of the Lake Poets to Daniel Stuart*, privately printed, 1889.
Sadler	*Diary, Reminiscences and Correspondence of Henry Crabb Robinson*, edited by Thomas Sadler, 3 vols., 1869.
SH	*The Letters of Sara Hutchinson*, edited by Kathleen Coburn, 1954.
Southey	*Life and Correspondence of Robert Southey*, edited by C. C. Southey, 6 vols., 1849–50.
TLS	*Times Literary Supplement*.
TP	*Thomas Poole and his Friends*, by Mrs. Henry Sandford, 2 vols., 1888.
Warter	*A Selection from the Letters of Robert Southey*, edited by John Wood Warter, 4 vols., 1856.
WL	The Wordsworth Library, Grasmere.

LIST OF LETTERS

An asterisk indicates that the letter is here printed for the first time; a dagger that it was not printed by de Selincourt, but elsewhere, subsequently to his edition.

THE MIDDLE YEARS, PART II

1812

1815

1816

513.	*W. W. to Viscount Lowther	14 Oct.	492
514.	D. W. to Jane Marshall	[14] Oct.	494
515.	*W. W. to Viscount Lowther	[15 Oct.]	497
516.	*W. W. to Lord Lonsdale	20 Oct.	497
517.	*W. W. to Viscount Lowther	20 Oct.	498
518.	D. W. to William Johnson	21 Oct.	499
519.	*W. W. to Viscount Lowther	23 Oct.	503
520.	W. W. to Washington Allston	late 1818 or early 1819	504
521.	*W. W. to Lord Lonsdale	6 Nov.	505
522.	*W. W. to Viscount Lowther	8 Nov.	506
523.	W. W. to Lord Lonsdale	28 Nov.	507
524.	*W. W. to Thomas Monkhouse	4 Dec.	509
525.	W. W. to Viscount Lowther	6 Dec.	511
526.	*W. W. to Viscount Lowther	8 Dec.	512

1819

527.	W. W. to C. W.	1 Jan.	513
528.	*W. W. to Viscount Lowther	2 Jan.	515
529.	*W. W. to Viscount Lowther	10 Jan.	516
530.	D. W. to Catherine Clarkson	12 Jan.	518
531.	W. W. to Lord Lonsdale	13 Jan.	520
532.	†W. W. to the Editor of the *Westmorland Gazette*	3 Feb.	522
533.	W. W. to Francis Wrangham	19 Feb.	522
534.	*W. W. to Robert Lumb	27 Feb.	525
535.	*W. W. to John Spedding	1 March	525
536.	*W. W. to Robert Lumb	16 March	526
537.	*D. W. to Sara Hutchinson	*c.* 17 March	527
538.	W. W. to Viscount Lowther	early April	529
539.	*W. W. to Mr. White	3 April	531
540.	*W. W. to Lord Lonsdale	7 April	531
541.	W. W. to J. Forbes Mitchell	21 April	533
542.	*W. W. to Viscount Lowther	25 April	536
543.	*W. W. to Lord Lonsdale	1 May	538
544.	*W. W. to Viscount Lowther	*c.* 8 May	540
545.	*W. W. to Lord Lonsdale	22 May	541
546.	W. W. to Lord Lonsdale	24 May	543
547.	*W. W. to Lord Lonsdale	16 June	544
548.	W. W. to Hans Busk	6 July	546
549.	*W. W. to Viscount Lowther	18 July	548
550.	W. W. to Henry Parry	20 July	549
551.	*W. W. to Viscount Lowther	[28 July]	549
552.	D. W. to Catherine Clarkson	1 Aug.	550
553.	*W. W. to Viscount Lowther	23 Aug.	553

ADDENDA TO PART ONE

LIST OF PLATES

CORRIGENDUM

p. 216, Letter 355. For *MS. untraced* read *MS. Amherst College Library.*

235. D. W. to R. W.

Address: Richard Wordsworth Esqre, Staple Inn, London.
Postmark: C 5 Fe 1812. *Stamp*: Kendal. *Endorsed*: 2 Feb. 1812.
MS. WL.
MY ii. 442, p. 484.

Kendal February 2nd 1812

My dear Brother,

I write to inform you that William drew upon you on the 30th or 31st Janry for 50£ in favour of J G Crump Esqre—and I shall draw on you in the course of a day or two for fifty pounds also in favour of Mr Thomas Cookson; both these Drafts, at one month after date.

William purposes going to London about the middle of April. I hope he will find you there—I was very sorry to give up my visit to Sockbridge at the end of last summer, but I trust I shall be more fortunate this summer but as Mary is going into Wales[1] in the Spring and will not return till the middle of summer—therefore I shall not be able to leave home till she returns.

I am at present at Kendal where I shall remain a few days longer.

I remain, dear Richard,
Your affectionate Sister
D Wordsworth

[1] i.e. to visit her brother Tom Hutchinson at Hindwell, Radnorshire.

236. W. W. to LORD LONSDALE

MS. Lonsdale MSS., Record Office, The Castle, Carlisle.
K (—). MY ii. 443, p. 485.

Grasmere Febry 6th 1812

My Lord,

It is not without considerable difficulty that I can bring my mind to address your Lordship in the present occasion.[1] I shall be brief; while I cannot write at all without a hope that I may be justified in trespassing a few minutes upon your Lordship's time, though in a matter relating wholly to myself. Last autumn I was on my way to wait upon your Lordship at Lowther Castle when I heard that you had left it for the winter. My intention was at that time, with your Lordship's permission, to have represented to you, viva voce, my situation; in order that when you were in possession of a few facts, which it is not likely would ever be known to you unless they came from myself, you might act towards me in respect to the matter in question as to your Lordship's Judgement might seem proper.

I regret that it is not in my power to wait upon you personally; as the experience which I have had of your Lordship's gracious manners would have rendered quite pleasing to me the delicate task, which, through the means of a Letter, I am undertaking not without some reluctance. But to come to the point. I need scarcely say that Literature has been the pursuit of my Life; a Life-pursuit justified (as I believe are those of most men distinguished by any particular features of character) partly through passionate liking and partly through calculations of judgement; and in some small degree through circumstances, in which my Youth was passed; that threw great difficulties in the way of my adopting that Profession to which I was most inclined and for which I was perhaps best qualified.[2] I long hoped, depending upon my moderate desires, that the profits of my literary labours added to the little which I possessed would have answered to the rational wants of myself and my family. But in this I have been disappointed; and for these causes; 1st the unexpected pressure of the times falling most heavily upon men who have no

[1] In this letter Wordsworth explains his financial position to Lord Lonsdale, who about a year later secured for him the Distributorship of Stamps for Westmorland and part of Cumberland. See further Letters 260, 282, etc., below.

[2] Wordsworth means—surprisingly—the Army. He believed that he had 'a talent for command'. Grosart, iii, p. 51. Both his sons later also wished to take up a military career, but did not do so. See Broughton, p. 4; *LY* i, 726, p. 164; 802, p. 280; 804, p. 282.

regular means of increasing their income in proportion; and 2ndly I had erroneously calculated upon the degree in which my writings were likely to suit the taste of the times; and, lastly, much the most important part of my efforts cannot meet the public eye for many years through the comprehensiveness of the subject.[1] I may also add (but it is scarcely worth while) a fourth reason, viz. an utter inability on my part to associate with any class or body of literary men, and thus subject myself to the necessity of sacrificing my own judgement, and of lending even indirectly countenance or support to principles either of taste, politics, morals, or religion, which I disapproved; and your Lordship is not ignorant that except writers engaged in mere drudgery, there are scarcely any authors but those associated in this manner, who find literature, at this day, an employment attended with pecuniary gain.

The statement of these facts has been made, as your Lordship will probably have anticipated, in order that if any Office should be at your Lordship's disposal (the duties of which would not call so largely upon my exertions as to prevent me from giving a considerable portion of time to study) it might be in your Lordship's power to place me in a situation where with better hope of success I might advance towards the main object of my life; I mean the completion of my literary undertakings; and thereby contribute to the innocent gratification, and perhaps (as the Subjects I am treating are important) to the solid benefit of many of my Countrymen.

I have now discharged what I deemed to be a duty to myself; and, allow me to say, what I deem to be a duty I owed to your Lordship. I have been emboldened to make this statement from a remembrance that my Family has for several generations been honoured by the regard of that of your Lordship; and that, in particular, my father and grandfather did conscientiously, I believe, discharge such trusts as were reposed in them through that connection. But *my* situation is a peculiar one; and I have been chiefly encouraged by a knowledge of your Lordship's attachment to Literature, and by the particular marks of kindness with which you have distinguished me.[2]

Having been disappointed in my intention of making the above representation last autumn, I purposed to defer it till I had the honour of waiting upon you in London next spring. But I have this day been informed that, by the recent death of Mr Richardson,[3]

[1] He here refers to *The Prelude* and the uncompleted *Recluse*.

[2] i.e. Lord Lonsdale's repayment of his predecessor's debt to the Wordsworths in 1803, and his assistance to Wordsworth in buying the Broadhow estate in Patterdale in 1806. See L. 35, pt. i, p. 111, n. 2.

[3] Agent at Lowther, d. 25 Jan. 1812.

certain Offices have become vacant, which has awakened my regret at not having made known to you my feelings earlier; as a Letter, at this time upon such a subject, cannot but add to the trouble which must be pressing upon you from many quarters. And, for my own part, I confess that upon this incitement I have written with some reluctance, as I wished that what I had to say should be confined to general representation, and should by no means assume the aspect of particular application; but an opportunity may exist at present which may not soon occur again; and to this possibility and to your Lordship's candour I trust for my excuse.

I have the honour to be
with great truth
my Lord, your Lordship's
most obedient and obliged servant
Wm. Wordsworth

237. D. W. to W. W.[1]

Address: William Wordsworth Esq[re], at Sir George Beaumont's Bart., Grosvenor Square, London.
MS. WL.
MY ii. 445, p. 488.

Thursday 23[d] April 1812

As this letter contains little more than information, to you now useless, I should not think it worth sending but as it is written so plain I can write across, and perhaps it may save you the trouble of enquiring after the writer. Sara and John went to Ambleside this morning not without some hope of finding a letter from you or Mary from Chester, but our expectations were not great; therefore we were not much disappointed, and we conclude that no news is good news. But dearest William I am anxious about your disorder in your Bowels, and I shall look for a letter from Binfield[2] on Friday night. I went to meet John and we came home on the western side of the two Lakes. You will judge from this that the Servants are better. In fact even Fanny is still very weak; but with her mother's help, who milks the cows and with mine in making the

[1] Written across a letter of De Quincey to W. W. which D. W. is forwarding to London. For De Quincey's letter, see Jordan, p. 260. W. W. left Grasmere about 19 Apr. and evidently visited his uncle Canon Cookson at Binfield on the way.

[2] See L. 10, pt. i, p. 18, n. 1.

Beds etc, she is able to do many things, and I can now attend to John's Lessons and have time to sit to my work or read a little, but sewing has hitherto prevented my reading myself, but Sara often reads aloud. You can have no notion how very ill Sarah[1] and Fanny have been; but I think they will soon recover fast, as I every day perceive them to be stronger. Sarah comes down stairs by the help of a stick and leaning upon me. Old Granny is gone home, and we do not expect to see Betty again till the end of the week, but we have no want of further help. It was spread about in the Country that we have a Fever, Mrs King heard it was the Typhus Fever, and durst not even send to inquire after us. The new schoolmaster began last Monday and we sent John on Monday and Tuesday, but yesterday morning he came with John Green[2] to request that we would keep him at home for two or three weeks, as people were afraid to send their children—he being there. This is a great pity, but of course we must quietly submit. Sara saw the master and J. Green, and told them that the disorder was not infectious in the same manner as a fever,—this for our own justification in having suffered him to go to school.—We can get nobody to the garden but Aggy Black, who will come on Saturday to set potatoes. The field is not yet done, nor the walls built. It is a dismal spring thus far. Here, there is not the least appearance of greenness except on the gooseberry Bushes—even the Kings' Larches[3] only shew a faint yellowish haze that just thickens the twigs. The drought is terrible —cold winds hot sunshine and frosty nights. Sara has had a letter from the Luffs[4]—they are still detained in the Isle of Wight and may be so, they do not know how much longer, for the E. India ships with which they were to have gone have sailed, and they must wait for another Convoy. Mrs Luff says that the hedges are green in the Isle of Wight, and pease and Beans in great forwardness in the gardens. It is next to a miracle to us, for every thing looks as if it were dead. The Mountains have lost all the variety which they had in Winter—They are of one cold yellowish colour, with never a cloud to rest upon them. John is certainly much quicker in reading than he was. He has read very hard and taken up the Book frequently

[1] 'Sara' = S. H. 'Sarah' = Sarah Youdell, d. of Jonathan and Betty Youdell of Hackett. See L. 209, pt. i, p. 441, n. 1.

[2] Of Pavement End, Grasmere. See Moorman, i, p. 467.

[3] The Kings lived at the Hollens on the east side of Grasmere. W. W. had a strong antipathy to larches, then beginning to invade the Lake District. See De Quincey's *Works*, ed. Masson, ii, p. 429, and also W. W.'s *Guide to the Lakes*, pp. 117–23. (Rupert Hart-Davis, 1951.)

[4] See L. 6, pt. i, p. 11, n. 4. Captain and Mrs. Luff were on their way to Mauritius.

himself—this with the hope of getting into his new history of England when he has finished Robinson Crusoe. Sara grows thinner —I am very well [and surely] wonderfully strong after what I have had to go through to be no worse for [it. The] Children are in high health and spirits and Catharine speaks up like Mary Keane when she says her lessons, which she does regularly to her Aunt Sara—Willy's face is clear and beautiful—you know he was all covered with scabs when you left home. He continues to be 'Aunty Lad' and 'lub her'. I have not yet seen Mrs Crump; but the Girls have been here—they are enraptured with little Tom—poor Fellow I miss him even more than Dorothy, and I am sure I shall be far more anxious about him if Mary leaves him in Wales. His Merry Andrew hat hangs up for us to look at, and it shall not leave the house till he comes home again. We long to hear from you—your first letter cannot tell us anything of the affair with Coleridge, except you stop at Binfield and in that case you will not write till you have been a few days in Town. Then I hope it will be over. You owe it to yourself to lose not a moment's time. As to Mrs M[1] the more I think of her the more I despise her, and I hope you will not be shy of telling her your mind respecting her conduct between Coleridge and you. Are you likely to see Austin[2]—what does Sir George think of his pictures? I hope you will see them—tell us this and every thing. How is poor Miss Lamb? I hope you will see Henry Robinson ere long—Remember me to him—He lodges at a Mr. Collier's some where in Hatton Garden. Do write as long letters as ever you can. I feel what a comfort they will be, now that I have leisure to think of you. At first whenever the thought of you or Mary came across my mind, I always rejoiced that you were away from our bustle and anxiety, for we had a good deal of *anxiety*, the Lasses were so very ill. Sara has had a letter from Miss Dowling[3]—she is delighted with the expectation of seeing you. She likes Lord and Lady Galway very much. We have had no papers since Saturday—I daresay Mrs Coleridge will not send us them more than twice in the week. Mr Scambler reports of terrible riots. It is my opinion that Mr Whitbread[4] and a few others deserve hanging. Mary Dawson[5] has been

[1] i.e. Mrs. Montagu, third wife of Basil M.; she had interfered unnecessarily in the Coleridge–Montagu affair. See *HCR* i, pp. 80–81.

[2] Samuel Austin of Liverpool (d. 1834), water-colour landscape painter.

[3] See *SH* 44, p. 133. She was a friend of Mrs. Luff's, and in 1818 she took over the school at Ambleside at which for three years Dora W. was a pupil.

[4] Samuel Whitbread (1758–1815), radical M.P. for Bedford. As he was an opponent of the war with France, the Wordsworths would have regarded him with great disapproval.

[5] De Quincey's servant at Dove Cottage. She had formerly been with the Wordsworths.

very kind to us in taking the Children, but she is very poorly, and being so could not amuse them so well as the society they found at the carriers, therefore she could hardly keep them within the garden gate. Jane Dockray[1] is to have a sale on Monday of her household goods. She called to 'settle this business of the stealing before her departure from Grasmere'—but poor Soul! she would not tell us whither she was going. We have not yet been sufficiently settled to read any thing but Novels. Adeline Mowbray[2] made us quite sick before we got to the end of it. Pray give my kindest remembrances to Sir G. and Lady B, and to Mrs Fermor if she be in London. Do not fail to go and see Mr Twining.[3] I wonder if our Brother Richard is in Town. Tell us all about 'Johnsy'[4] and remember us most kindly to him. Our new Master[5] reads prayers to the Boys every night—John says he does not read so well as Mr Johnson; but about like Mr Sewel, which Mr Sewel Sara reports to be the worst Reader in the world.—This is a letter of scraps and bits—I am not settled enough to feel as if I were conversing with you or to write a letter expressive of either thought or feeling. John is just come up to say his lesson to me, he has been new roofing his house, he looks uncommonly well. God bless thee my dearest best Brother, thine evermore

D. Wordsworth.

Tell me if I must direct to Mr. Lambe.[6] I do not like to do it till you have seen him.

[1] Jane or Jenny Dockray.

[2] *Adeline Mowbray or Mother and Daughter*, by Amelia Opie, 1804. A 'problem' novel, based on incidents in the life of Mary Wollstonecraft. (Note by de Selincourt.)

[3] The Wordsworths bought their tea from Twining's. D. W. is probably anxious about the payment of a bill.

[4] i.e. the Revd. William Johnson, the former schoolmaster at Grasmere, now in London, in charge of the Central School, Baldwin Gardens.

[5] Mr. Bamford, a great grandson of Robert Walker, vicar of Seathwaite in Duddon. See C. C. Southey's *Life of Andrew Bell* (1844), ii, pp. 424–5. By the following autumn, however, he was succeeded by Mr. Poolley. See L. 280, p. 79 below.

[6] The Wordsworths often sent letters to each other to Lamb, so spelt.

238. W. W. to FRANCIS WRANGHAM[1]

Address: Revd Francis Wrangham, Hunmanby, near Bridlington, Yorkshire.
MS. Henry Huntington Library.
K (—). *MY ii. 444, p. 486.*

[Early Spring 1812?]

Dear Wrangham,

You are very good in sending one Letter after another to inquire after a person so undeserving of attentions of this kind as myself.—Dr. Johnson I think observes, or rather is made to observe by some of his Biographers that no man delights to *give* what he is accustomed to *sell*. 'For example, you, Mr. Thrale would rather part with anything in this way than your Porter.' Now, though I have never been much of a salesman in matters of literature, (the whole of my returns, (I do not say nett profits but returns) from the worthy trade not amounting to 7 score pounds) yet some how or other I manufacture a letter and part with it as reluctantly as if it were really a thing of price. But to drop the comparison, I have so much to do with writing in the way of labour or profession, that it is difficult to me to conceive how any body can take up a pen but from constraint. My writing desk is to me a place of punishment, and as my penmanship sufficiently testifies, I always bend over it with some degree of impatience.—All this is said that you may know the real cause of my silence, and not ascribe it in any degree to slight or forgetfulness on my part, or an insensibility to your worth and the value of your friendship.—You did well and kindly in giving me a particular account of your family, and your present domestic engagements. It pleases me much to hear that you are so happy. I have also abundant reason to be thankful. My Children amount to five—all affectionate good tempered, and I hope free from vice. As to their intellectual Powers they are none of them remarkable except the eldest, who is lamentably slow: This is to me a mortification as I promised myself much pleasure in rubbing up my Greek with him, and renewing my acquaintance with Nepos and Ovid etc. He is in other respects a very fine boy; and I think will make a sensible man, but he has no quickness of mind.—. I have three Boys and two Girls.—

[1] This undated letter must have been written before June 1812, when Catharine W. died, for he speaks of his *five* children. On the other hand, it cannot have been written before 1812, for the poem of Wrangham referred to must be either *The Sufferings of the Primitive Martyrs* or *Joseph made known to his Brethren*, both of which (Seaton Prize Poems won by Wrangham in 1811 and 1812) were published in 1812. For Wrangham, see L. 49, pt. i, p. 88.

As to my occupations they look little at the present age—but I live in hope of leaving some thing behind me, that by some minds will be valued.

I see no new books except by the merest accident; of course, your Poem[1] which I should have been pleased to read has not found its way to me. You inquire after old Books. You might almost as well have asked for my teeth as for any of mine. The only *modern* Books that I read are those of travels, or such as relate to Matters of fact; and the only modern books that I care for; but as to old ones, I am like yourself; scarcely any thing comes amiss to me. The little money I have to spare the very little I may say, all goes that way.—If however in the *line of your profession* you want any bulky old Commentaries on the Scriptures,[2] (such as not twelve strong men of these degenerate days will venture I do not say to *read* but to *lift*) I can perhaps as a special favour, accommodate you.—.

I and mine will be happy to see you and yours here or any where; but I am sorry the time you talk [of] is so distant; a Year and a half is a long time looking forwards, though looking back ten times as much is brief as a dream.—My writing is wholly illegible at least I fear so. I had better therefore release you. Believe me my dear Wrangham your affectionate Friend

W. Wordsworth.

239. W. W. to J. F. TUFFIN[3]

Address: J. F. Tuffin Esqr., Billeter Lane.
MS. University Library, Davis, California (pasted into John Drinkwater's signed copy of W.'s *Poems*, 2 vols. (1815)).
Hitherto unpublished.

1812
Thursday Night 30 Apl—
past twelve,
Grosvenor Square[4]

Dear Tuffin

Your kind note has just been put into my hand upon arriving from the play. I was very sorry not to find you at home; the more

[1] See previous note.
[2] Wordsworth may have obtained these from his father's library.
[3] See L. 46, pt. i, p. 82.
[4] Wordsworth had gone to London about 19 Apr. to investigate the affair of Coleridge's resentment against him. See *HCR* i, pp. 70–81. He was staying with the Beaumonts in Grosvenor Square.

so because I had heard that you had been suffering from vexatious circumstances.

I have so many calls to make and Friends to see in this part of the Town, that I cannot easily, for some days, find means again to get so far as your present residence; and therefore, if you can continue to look in upon [? me] here I shall take it very kindly. Depend upon it however I will strain a point to wait upon you.

Sir G. Beaumont desires his respects to you and begs me to say that he will be happy to see you. You are very kind in expressing a regret that I am not under your Roof.—

I am most truly
and sincerely your friend
W. Wordsworth

240. D. W. to W. W. and M. W.

Address: Wm. Wordsworth Esqre, Sir G. Beaumont's Bart, Grosvenor Square.
Postmark: 12 o'clock, My 8 1812 Nn. *Stamp*: Twopenny Post, London.
MS. WL.
MY ii. 446, p. 491.

Monday May 3rd [1812]

We went to Ambleside last Night where, my dearest William, we found your short letter, with a long one from the Luffs.[1] We read yours hastily over at Mrs. Ross's[2] and brought Luff's to read by the fire-side, which we will enclose in a Frank by the next post, for they are interesting letters and upon the whole written in better spirits. Luff says that expences have been so great that he fears he shall want the whole of the 100 £. Of course you will settle this with Mr Woodruffe. On Friday evening we sent John to Ambleside and he brought us a letter from Mary M. with a chearful postscript from Mary.[3] Sara has written this morning to Joanna, and I had intended writing to Mary on Wednesday or Thursday; but on second thoughts it seems better to save postage, and after you have read this you may forward it to her in a Frank. My dearest Friends

[1] See L. 6, pt. i, p. 11, n. 4, and p. 5, n. 4 above.

[2] See L. 265 below.

[3] 'Mary M.' = Mary Monkhouse, M. W's cousin, soon to be married to Tom Hutchinson, M. W's brother, who with John Monkhouse, Mary M.'s brother, together kept the farm at Hindwell. 'Mary' = M. W., who was staying at Hindwell.

it was three weeks yesterday since you left us, and we are only now beginning to feel ourselves settled; but we are now thoroughly comfortable. Aggy Black has nearly finished the garden. She has worked for us 7 days. Of course this must be taken from Sarah's wages. As to poor Sarah I am afraid she will not be fit to stand her place for a long time,—perhaps not this summer but the next time we see her we shall be better able to judge. We were at Hacket on Wednesday, and she was then, though considerably amended in her health, so weak as to be unable to walk across the Floor by the help of a stick, without leaning upon her Mother also; yet the last words she said to me were 'You may be sure I will come back again as soon as ever I can'.—Whitsuntide will be here in a fortnight; and if she gives up her place for the half-year it will be best to look out for a Girl who can milk, and will be willing to be under Fanny; and if one very likely should offer we will hire her; but if not, perhaps Sarah may be strong enough before your return, or before hay-time; and at present we can do very well. Fanny though not yet strong, with her Mother's help can do the work with ease—and she is very chearful and happy in her Mother's company; and I find that the old Woman is of very little use at [?] so that it is an advantage to her to be here. In fact she is not of much use here for the work she does except attending the cows; but unless I got up to follow the Children and assist in the mornings Fanny could not do without her or somebody else.—Thank God we are all well. On Thursday Friday and Saturday Fanny and Aggy Black were employed in cleaning the house, and we had the gt parlour coloured by the Ambleside painter, who was to do it for nothing. We have had the furniture scowered and oiled (this dearest Mary is for you, but I do not find it easy, in my random way of telling you all things, to separate into different compartments the different species of intelligence). We expected Mrs Coleridge to have come yesterday but she writes that her Sister Martha[1] and Mr Dawe,[2] the painter who did Coleridge's picture, promised to be here this week, and as they have not contradicted it she expects them and cannot leave home. I hope that Sara will get off her Stockton journey, but Mrs Coleridge insists on the performance of her promise of visiting Keswick, and she *must* go to Kendal, and these two visits will take up five weeks. During that time I shall have the grate set up in William's Study and the passages etc. coloured. We have hung the drawings in this room and both the room and the drawings look

[1] i.e. Martha Fricker, sister of Mrs. Southey and Mrs. Coleridge.
[2] George Dawe (1781–1829), portrait-painter and mezzotint engraver.

much better for it. The two pictures are below stairs.—There is hardly the least shew of greenness upon the earliest pastures of the Vale and we have endless plague with sheep, though all the Fences are mended. There is nothing green but the gooseberry trees—and the Larches—and these last are only green-*ish*.

Catharine is very good and tractable—She never cries. Except today she has never had a real cry since you left us, and today I hurt her very much with washing a sore ear with soap and water—as to Willy he continues the practice of roaring when all things do not go to his mind, but the transitions in his temper are so exquisitely entertaining that except when one is perplexed and busy about something else there is almost as much entertainment as discomfort from his vagaries; the sight of 'My dear [?] Aunt [?]', is sufficient at any time to check the torrent of his most tumultuous distresses. When I began this letter he was sitting upon my knee,—and he says 'Where Pudder?' I suppose he thought I was writing to you—he then turned to fondle me—'Oh Aunty I lub Aunty'. They both look very well. The Coleridges and Algernon were here yesterday and John and A had a happy day of play and reading; for Algernon is very good in reading to John. Poor Derwent had no inclination for Play, and I dare say he would have been very much tired if he had had to *walk* back to Clappersgate last night; but he rode most of the way on the pony. He made no complaints, but his eyes looked very ill—In short he had the appearance of a person who had been drunk over-night. John seems to like the new school very well; at least, inasmuch as he does not like it so well as Mr Johnson's it appears to me to be *so much* better. He began to get off his Grammar on Saturday, and got his task quickly and well. He is reading a Story Book of Algernon's at home and you would be surprized to hear how well he reads it; yet when he is reading a Book that does not interest him he seems to read just as ill as ever.

I have seen the schoolmaster only twice; but we intend to ask him to tea when we have Mrs King and the Crumps. The last time I saw him he told me that John did very well and I believe he takes a great deal of pains while he is in School; but I must say that he appears to us very slow in comprehending what he *reads* in the Grammar. Today we proposed to him to take his History of England to School; but he blushed and said he could not read well enough—I tried him and find he can; but he says 'Nay the Master turns them back if they cannot say well!' I shall therefore go myself today or tomorrow, and if he is a much worse Reader than the History of England Class he had best read it a while by himself—

for if he were frequently turned back from the Class it might dishearten him very much—and I am sure he will, from the fear of being turned back, take pains by himself. He says that the Master told him he had got his task off very well. I have written to Mrs Wilson. The suit of Cloaths is not yet arrived. Charles Stuart was here yesterday—he is going to sell his furniture—Fanny who is working with Aggy Black in the Court calls out that she hears the Cuckow—poor thing! I wonder it thinks of our leafless trees—there is not yet a green hawthorn;—nor a Birch tree with buds visible at 3 yards' distance. We have packed up three Boxes of Coleridge's German Books, and sent him a parcel by coach—You may judge that we had a busy day last Sunday but one in looking over all the German Books, to find out those that were to be sent by coach—and another parcel to be sent to Keswick for Southey. All this we did on the Sunday and packed two chests, and on Friday we packed the third Chest, and Tom Wilson, who was here to put down the carpet, nailed and corded them, and yesterday a Cart which had brought us coals, carried them off. (We have, by the Bye, been obliged to have coals from Keswick, there being none in Kendal.) Coleridge wrote to Mrs C specifying the Books to be sent immediately by the Coach, which he wanted for his present labours —and the next post he wrote again to beg that William would let him have the conclusion of the Essays on Epitaphs; and if he were willing they were to be sent with the other Books by the Coach. Mrs C says he is going to finish the unfinished parts of the Friend.[1] She adds 'perhaps as your Brother is not at home you will not like to send the Essays; but Southey thinks there can be no harm in sending them to Keswick and he will frank them to your Brother, and your Brother may then Do as he pleases.'

To this I replied, that, even if I could have ventured to send the Essays off without your orders, I could not venture to send them to *Coleridge* (he being so careless about MSS.) till we had another Copy transcribed, and I desired Mrs C to tell him that you were in London, and he might ask you for them himself, and we would, in the mean time have a fair copy written out, ready to be sent at a moment's warning, in case we received further orders—but I told Mrs C that I should not inform you that Coleridge had applied for them, because I thought it fit that he should have the trouble of asking for them himself if he wished to have them. Above a week is now elapsed and he has had time enough to ask you—and you are

[1] For the *Essays*, see L. 183, pt. i, p. 388, n. 1. Coleridge did not use them or continue *The Friend*.

now at liberty to make what use you please of this information—and I shall tell Mrs C. that I have now informed you. Southey in reply sent me word that he thought I might have ventured to send the Essays through him to you:—and to this I answered again that you had no person in London to transcribe them for you—I wrote some Memorandums respecting the Books and wrapped the Books in it which we sent to Coleridge—and I therein told him that you were in London therefore he had an opportunity of asking you himself; but that even if I could venture to send off the MS. without your orders I could not do it till another Transcript had been made; which we should do immediately, and have it ready to be sent off at a moment's warning.

Mrs Clarkson tells us, in a letter received last week, that he had told her by letter, that his engagements would bring him in 800£ per Annum, out of which he should allow Mrs C[1] 200£ in addition to what she now has. Besides this he meant to give 2 or 3 courses of Lectures annually, the money arising from which he should keep saved for Hartley and Derwent.

The *Friend* is to be published Quarterly—I suppose as a *part* of the Quarterly publication!!—a pretty Romance truly! — — — And what do you think is the Reason he has assigned for the sudden stoppage of the *Friend*?—He told the Editor of the Eclectic Review that he could not get another sheet of stamped paper, not having money to pay for it—and *we* know that there were loads of stamped paper beforehand.

These things are only worth noticing as additional proofs that he cannot speak truth. The extract from his letter,[2] written since his return to London, I shall transcribe for Mary at the end of this. 'At *Keswick*, forsooth! he satisfied himself that no possibility remained of his being deluded.'—At *Keswick* where the weightiest of his charges was flatly contradicted!—at *Keswick* where nothing *was* done, nothing *could be* done to encrease the offence—whence the insult of total neglect was heaped upon us and received without murmuring [but no doubt he expected some submission on your part].[3] This only proves what we have long been sure of that he is glad of a pretext to break with us, and to furnish himself with a ready excuse for all his failures in duty to himself and others.—

[1] i.e. Mrs. Coleridge.

[2] i.e. Coleridge's letter to Richard Sharp, in which C. enlarged on his estrangement from W. See Griggs, iii, p. 389.

[3] Erased.

Mr Wedgewood[1] is the properest person to be present at your Meeting—At all events—I hope you have had one or more steady respectable persons, for he ought to be put to confusion after speaking of you as he has done—You were his 'vilest calumniator', when you only told a common Friend of some part of his failings, in order to prevent his putting himself into a situation through which he would expose them all, in a tenfold greater degree.—We long for your letter dearest William—I fear this business will harrass you very much, in addition to the first flutter of London—pray tell us all particulars. Consider how much we need your letters.—Thank God Mary is well, and I trust as her appetite is good she will fatten and strengthen.—If Tom does not take to his Book in Wales I think he had much better come home with Mary, unless the effect of Change of air upon his constitution is *very evidently* beneficial. — — —

Mary must not think of touring on horseback—far better take the *Gig* and walk bits where the Gig cannot travel.

No news from France[2]—nor any letters but that have been mentioned to you. I shall be soon obliged to draw upon Richard to pay the Flour Bill—Flour and potatoes are very dear. This week James Fleming is going to plough for potatoes for us in the Low Kirk Field—and next Week we are going to have our 7 weeks' wash—we must hire both Aggy Black and Aggy Ashburner—and Sarah, of course must pay for one of these out of her ½ year's wages. Poor Lass! I hope she will be better when we next see her—It is very well she is at home, because her mind would have been uneasy at giving trouble and not being able to work. — — —

The cows do not give so much milk as they did but very well considering.—We expect to sell butter this week. It is 14d. per lb. As we have plenty of hay it is very well we kept the great cow, as things have turned out. We have already got a guinea's worth of Butter from her—besides the calf—a guinea—and about 4/- new milk at Mr Crump's besides all the blue milk which we have sold—and we have not yet got a pig. The Drive is too dry to be rolled—and besides, Mr King is not yet ready—The place never looked so neat as it does now, but it is far from being what it ought to be. We have only read light books yet. We are going to read the History of the Brazils—I am reading the Cid.[3] God bless you both for ever my

[1] i.e. Josiah Wedgwood (1769–1843), who in 1798 with his brother Tom (d. 1806), had settled an annual payment of £150 on Coleridge.

[2] Possibly from Annette Vallon.

[3] Both these works—the *History of Brazil* and the *Chronicle of the Cid*—were by Southey, published respectively in 1810 and 1808.

dearest Friends—let us hear often and as long letters as possible. Below I transcribe the Copy which William sent us of a part of one of Coleridge's letters to some person in London written since his return from Keswick.[1] After stating many of his vexations—William says that he goes on to say 'And the consummation of all I had scarcely arrived in London last Octbr 12 month before the Conviction was forced upon me, say rather pierced through my very soul with the suddenness of a flash of lightening that he had become my bitterest calumniator who to that very moment I had cherished in my heart's heart. The benumbing despondency alleviated by no gleam of hope and only alternating with fits of (truly may I call it) mental agony I even now dare scarcely look back on. But in the last worst affliction the cure was included. I gradually obtained a conquest over my own feelings and now dare call myself a Freeman, which I did not dare to do till I had been at Keswick and satisfied myself that no possibility remained of my being deluded. The effect of this conquest of my health on my mind and on my very outward appearance have been such that the amiable Family under whose roof I have been sheltered since Octr. 1810 declare that till now they have never seen me as myself.'

241. W. W. to CATHERINE CLARKSON

MS. untraced.
K (—). *MY ii.* 447, *p.* 498 (—).

Grosvenor Square, Tuesday, May 6th [1812]

My dear Friend,

. . . I came to Town with a *determination* to confront Coleridge and Montagu upon this vile business.[2] But Coleridge is most averse to it; and from the difficulty of procuring a fit person to act as referee in such a case, and from the hostility which M. and C. feel towards each other, I have yielded to C.'s wish, being persuaded that much more harm than good would accrue from the interview. I have not seen C., nor written to him. Lamb has been the medium of communication between us. C. intimated to me by a letter addressed to Lamb that he would transmit to me a statement, begun some time

[1] This letter dated 24 Apr. was to Richard Sharp; See Griggs, iii, p. 389. Sharp cannot be excused for showing it to Wordsworth. D. transcribes it for the benefit of Mary who was at present in Radnorshire, where Wordsworth joined her in June.

[2] The misunderstandings between himself and Coleridge were at length clarified, largely through the good offices of Henry Crabb Robinson. This letter was written before Crabb Robinson saw W. on 8 May, and communicated to him the substance of his conversation with Coleridge on 3 May. See *HCR* i, p. 70 ff.

ago, in order to be sent to Miss Hutchinson, but discontinued on account of his having heard that she had 'already *decided* against him.' A very delicate proposal! Upon this I told Lamb that I should feel somewhat degraded by consenting to read a paper, begun with such an intention and discontinued upon such a consideration. Why talk about '*deciding*' in the case? Why, if in this decision she had judged amiss, not send the paper to rectify her error? or why draw out a paper at all whose object it was to win from the sister of my wife an opinion in his favour, and therefore to my prejudice, upon a charge of *injuries*, grievous injuries, done by me to him; before he had openly preferred his complaint to myself, the supposed author of these injuries? All this is unmanly, to say the least of it.

Upon coming home yesterday I found, however, a letter from him, a long one, written apparently and sent before he could learn my mind from Lamb upon this proposal. The letter I have not opened; but I have just written to Lamb that if Coleridge will assure me that this letter contains nothing but a naked statement of what he believes Montagu said to him, I will read it and transmit it to Montagu, to see how their reports accord. And I will then give my own, stating what I believe myself to have said, under what circumstances I spoke, with what motive, and in what spirit. And there, I believe, the matter must end; only I shall admonish Coleridge to be more careful how he makes written and public mention of injuries done by me to him.

There is some dreadful foul play, and there are most atrocious falsehoods, in this business; the bottom of which, I believe, I shall never find, nor do I much care about it. All I want is to bring the parties for once to a naked and deliberate statement upon the subject, in order that documents may exist, to be referred to as the best authority which the case will admit. . . .

242. W. W. to H. C. R.

Address: Henry Robinson, Esq[r], Hatton Garden, No. 56.
Postmark: 12 o'Clock. 15 My. 1812. A.M. *Endorsed*: 15th May 1812. Note W. Wordsworth Autograph.
MS. Dr. Williams's Library.
Morley, i, p. 69.

Friday Morning [15 May 1812]
Grosvenor Square

My dear Sir,

I am just reminded by Lady Beaumont, of an engagement made almost on my first coming here for Sunday next. It is to meet a party of my friends on that day to dinner. This unfortunately I had forgotten. Make the best excuse you can for me to your kind Host and Hostess,—I find that I must provide myself with a regular card to minute down my engagements, or I shall be getting daily into scrapes of this kind. I am very sorry for this; my inexperience in this sort of life is all the excuse I have to offer, with the expression of my regret at not being able to fulfill an engagement from which I expected so much pleasure.

If you can say anything better for me, do. I have never been well since I met your City Politicians. Yet I am content to pay this price for the knowledge of so pleasing a Woman as Mrs Charles Aiken;[1] being quite an Enthusiast when I find a Woman whose countenance and manner are what a Woman's ought to be.

Most truly yours
W. Wordsworth

243. D. W. to W. W.

Address: Wm. Wordsworth Esq[re], at Sir George Beaumont's Bart., Grosvenor Square, London.
MS. untraced.
MY ii. 448, p. 499.

May 17th [1812]

My dearest William,

I have not time for particulars as you will see by what I am going to tell you, but I *must* write by this post, being quite unhappy at the miscarriage of my letters. I know then that I have written five letters to you, all of which but the last ought to have been received when you wrote. The first you *did* receive, the second was written upon one from the French Prisoner at Oswestry,[2] telling you that

[1] Mrs. Charles Aikin was Anne Wakefield, the wife of Dr. Charles Aikin, nephew of Mrs. Anna Letitia Barbauld, the writer of prose and verse and books for children, whom W. considered 'the first of our literary women'. See *HCR* i, p. 8. H. C. R's. MS. Diary for 17 May 1812 has this entry: 'W. wrote on Friday to say a prior engagement which he had forgotten when he accepted Mr. C.'s rendered it impossible for him to come.' 'Mr. C.' is possibly Mr. Carr, Solicitor to the Excise, with whom W. and H. C. R. dined on 31 May, *HCR* i, p. 91. He is described as being 'an old acquaintance of Wordsworth' (ibid., p. 86).

[2] This is apparently a reference to Eustace Baudouin, whose brother Jean-Baptiste married Caroline, the daughter of W. W. and Annette Vallon, in 1816. Eustace subsequently visited Rydal (see L. 330 below). The letter has not survived.

he has no present want of money having received a supply—that he wished much that by applying to the Transport office you could assist him in obtaining his release but seemed to have little hope; and requested to hear again, telling him your address—where he might *always* find you, and saying you might write in English. This to the best of my remembrance is the sum of what he said. The third[1] was written on Mr de Quincey's. The fourth[2] sent under cover to Sharpe was a very long one, to be sent after you had read it under cover to Mary, the fifth was also a very long one sent with the same address and with the same design—so that she will be as much at a loss as you. Never was any thing so unaccountable or so mortifying. It is in vain for me to try to repeat what I then said. The last letters (and I believe *all* of them) were sent from Ambleside. Sara has been at Keswick since last Thursday but one—all this I have told you before. I expected her yesterday—and sent the pony by Anne Dixon who is going to live at Southey's; and this afternoon I have received a letter from her saying that she Mrs Coleridge and Edith[3] are all coming this afternoon—the Girls by the Coach—I suppose to stay about 10 days. This hurries me much—for I must write to Mary also—for she will be uneasy—I did not get yours till this morning—how happy am I that your mind is going to be settled about Coleridge—You have in every part of the arrangement acted wisely and becomingly—and I hope that such intercourse will henceforth take place between you as will be salutary to both parties. When you see him give my Love to him. I suppose he will now receive it, though he has indeed acted to us all, (and Sara and I could not possibly have offended him) as if he intended to insult us. I am sure he does not know the depth of the affection I have had for him. We are all well—except that I have the remains of a very bad cold, and William of a slight one—Catharine's lameness certainly mends; and she is never fretted or unhappy or out of spirits.[4] In my last (which I fain would hope you will receive) I told you all particulars about John and expressed my belief that another school, or rather another manner of life must be tried for him. Sara, Mrs C, and all are come—and I have no time to write more—For God's sake write as often as you can—and I will write again at leisure—this week—but till I have tidings of a *sure* way of sending letters under cover you must be at the expence of postage—What

[1] i.e. L. 237 above, dated 23 Apr.

[2] Probably L. 240 above.

[3] i.e. Edith Southey, Southey's eldest daughter, b. Apr. 1804 at Keswick.

[4] Catharine died only three weeks after this letter was written. See L. 247 below.

can be the cause of the Failure? I told you every thing in my two last.

Kindest Love to the Beaumonts.

God bless thee my dearest William thine ever more

D. W.

My kindest Love to Sir G and L. B.

244. W. W. to CAPTAIN CHARLES PASLEY[1]

MS. E. L. McAdam, Junr. Hitherto unpublished.

Monday, Sir George Beaumont's
Grosvenor Square
[about 25 May 1812]

My dear Sir,

I dined the other day with Dr Stoddart,[2] and was much disappointed in not meeting you; and grieved to hear that I was not likely to see you, as you were gone out of Town.

I learned from Stoddart some particulars of an affair in which you had cause of complaint against a person high in office,[3] in your Profession. It is possible that you might be served in this affair; The person in question is difficult to deal with, but I have perhaps some means of reaching him: at least so strong is my desire to be in any degree useful to one of whom I think so highly as of you, that the mere glimpse of a possibility of serving you tempts me to ask of yourself whether anything said in your behalf to the Man in power by an intimate Friend of mine[4] who is an intimate Friend of his would be of any use to you. If so, do let me know, and also any particulars of the case which would be useful, and which without impropriety I may ask you.

Excuse this Liberty to which I am prompted by an admiration of your character.

And believe me dear Sir
with the highest respect
Your sincere friend
W. Wordsworth

[1] For Captain Pasley, see L. 174, pt. i, p. 370, n. 2.

[2] i.e. Sir John Stoddart (1773–1856), King's Advocate at Malta during Coleridge's stay in the island, 1804–6. He was 'Dr.' in virtue of a D.C.L. taken at Oxford in 1801.

[3] In a letter dated 27 May, now in the Wordsworth Library at Grasmere, Capt. Pasley acknowledged the receipt of a note from W., and spoke of the delay in his promotion owing to army 'red-tape'.

[4] Probably Richard Sharp.

245. W. W. to CATHERINE CLARKSON

Address: Mrs. Clarkson, Bury St. Edmonds.
MS. Harvard University Library.
K (—). *MY ii. 449, p. 501.*

Thursday June 4th [1812]
Grosvenor Square

My dear Friend,

Excuse this Note; it is the only sort of paper I have upon my Table, and if I go down stairs in search of larger I may be detained, and miss the opportunity of this day's post, the morning being already far advanced. Let me tell you then at once which I do with great joy, that on Monday I depart for Bocking[1] with Chrisr: meaning on the Saturday or Sunday following at latest to be with you at Bury.—I should have written to thank you for your last much sooner, but I wished to let you know that this interesting point was settled.

I saw Mr Clarkson for two minutes yesterday; having unfortunately found him at dinner; it was not then fixed when I should take my departure. Mr C. was looking uncommonly well. I shall let him know by twopenny Post tomorrow when I depart for Bocking.— As to public affairs; they are most alarming. The different parties cannot agree; the ——[2] seems neither respected nor beloved; and the lower orders have been for upwards of thirty years accumulating in pestilential masses of ignorant population; the effects now begin to show themselves, and unthinking people cry out that the national character has been changed all at once, in fact the change has been silently going on ever since the time we were born; the disease has been growing, and now breaks out in all its danger and deformity.

—As to the ministry; there is no likelihood at present that the old opposition will come in. An administration, weak in parliament, but strong enough to keep things going in a languid and interrupted course, will be formed of Wellesley, Canning, Moira, and the remains of the Perceval administration; at least such I think will be the issue;[3] but how long this composition will keep together it is impossible to foresee.—I shall have much to say to you upon these things, and the general state of the Country.

[1] The parish in Suffolk of which C. W. was at this time 'Dean'—(i.e. incumbent).

[2] So manuscript. Wordsworth probably means 'Prince Regent'.

[3] Spencer Perceval, the Prime Minister, had been assassinated by a lunatic on 11 May 1812, while W. was in London. He was succeeded by Lord Liverpool (Robert Jenkinson) as Prime Minister, with the various statesmen named by W. occupying posts in the Ministry.

I hear often from Wales[1] and from Grasmere, and nothing but well. This week is employed by Mary and Joanna and T. H. in a Tour in South Wales, chiefly upon the Wye. I however had a Letter from [*name omitted*] dated Hereford and put into the office last Monday evening the day their Tour began.—I shall tell you all that has passed between Coleridge and me. Upon the whole he appears more comfortable and seems to manage himself much better than when he was at Grasmere. I have seen him several times, but not much alone; one morning we had, however a pleasant walk to Hampstead together—I shall [not] advert in the hearing of any body to what you communicated in your last concerning him.

He certainly would not wish to wound you; he is sensible that he has used you ill, and fear, and dislike to encounter disagreeable sensations, a dislike which augments in proportion as it is his *duty* to face them; these are the regulators and governours of his actions to a degree that is pitiable and deplorable—Believe me with an earnest desire to see you

Your most affectionate Friend
W. Wordsworth

I will give you a Line from Bocking.

246. W. W. to THOMAS MONKHOUSE

Address: Thomas Monkhouse, Esq., 21 Budge Row.
Postmark: June 4. 1812.
MS. WL.
LY iii. 449a, p. 1362.

Sir George Beaumont's,
Grosvenor Square.
Corner of South Audley St.
Thursday eleven o'clock.

My dear Sir,

I fear that this note will not arrive in time to answer the purpose for which it is written. If you could carry me to Hampstead this afternoon in your gig, where I am under engagement to drink tea with Miss Baillie,[2] I should be very happy to have so much of your

[1] i.e. from M. W. who was at Hindwell, Radnorshire.

[2] Joanna Baillie (1762–1851), Scottish dramatist and poet, a friend of Scott who greatly admired her work. She lived from 1806 onwards in Hampstead with her sisters.

company; and could you accommodate me with a bed I would return with you to Town to morrow morning. Any time from three to 7 would answer my purpose, or if it suited you to take dinner with your friends, I should be happy to be of the party this day. If this note is not in time for the above pupose, I shall not go to Hampstead at all. Most sincerely yours

W. Wordsworth.

247. D. W. to THOMAS DE QUINCEY

Address: Thomas de Quincey Esq[re], Worcester College, Oxford, *forwarded to* 82 Great Titchfield Street, Oxford Street, London.
Postmark: Oxford, 10 Ju 1812. *Stamp*: Kendal Penny Post.
MS. Miss Maud Craig.
K (—). *MY ii. 450, p. 502.*

[5 June 1812]

My dear Friend,

I am grieved to the heart when I write to you—but you must bear the sad tidings—Our sweet little Catharine was seized with convulsions on Wednesday night at ½ before ten or ½ past 9 o'clock. The fits continued till ¼ after 5 in the morning, when she breathed her last. She had been in perfect health, and looked unusually well—her leg and arm had gained strength—and we were full of hope. In short, we had sent the most delightful accounts to her poor Mother. It is a great addition to our affliction that her Father and Mother were not here to witness her last struggles, and to see her in the last happy weeks of her short life —— She never forgot Quincey—dear Innocent, she now lies upon her Mother's Bed, a perfect image of peace—this to me was a soothing spectacle after having beheld her struggles. It is an unspeakable consolation to us that we are assured that no foresight could have prevented the disease in this last instance, and that it was not occasioned by any negligence, or improper food.[1] This was proved by her evacuations: but we were almost confident it could not be so before we had demonstration of this. The disease lay in the Brain, and if it had been possible for her

[1] See L. 188, pt. i, p. 395. Catharine's first attack of 'convulsions' in 1810 had been brought on as a result of eating a lot of raw carrot while in the charge of the eleven-year-old nursery maid Sally Green. She had remained slightly lame ever since. Her death was probably due to a recurrence of the aneurism. De Quincey, whose favourite she was of all the Wordsworth children, unjustly ascribed her *death* to Sally's negligence, in his 'Memorials of Grasmere' published in *Tait's Magazine* in Sept. 1839. See Masson, xiii, p. 147.

to recover, it is much to be feared that she would not have retained the Faculties of her Mind. God bless you!

Yours affectionately,
D. Wordsworth.

We have written to my Brother, and he will proceed immediately into Wales[1] to impart the sad intelligence to my Sister. You will be pleased to hear that Mary Dawson has been very kind in her attentions to us—we are all pretty well. John has been greatly afflicted, but he has begun to admit consolation. The Funeral will be on Monday afternoon—I wish you had been here to follow your Darling to her Grave.

248. W. W. to CATHERINE CLARKSON

Address: Mrs. Clarkson, Bury St. Edmunds.
Postmark: A J [11] ii 1812. *Endorsed*: W. W. account of little Catharine's death.
MS. Cornell.
Hitherto unpublished.

Bocking Wednesday, June 11th
I believe,[2]

My dear Friend,

You have most probably learned by this time that our dear little Catharine your namesake has been removed to a happier world.[3] I have just been informed of this affecting event; and, I assure you my dear Friend, that it is most painful to me that I shall thereby be prevented from seeing you and your Friends. I arrived here on Monday Evening and purposed on Saturday to take the Coach for Bury; but it is now my duty to turn my face another way. Tomorrow morning I take coach for London and in the evening shall proceed by the mail for Ludlow; hoping still to be at Radnor in time to break the Melancholy News to my dear, I might say, *our* dear Mary. No doubt you will have been written to and will have learned that the sweet Innocent began to be convulsed a little before ten on the night of Wednesday last and died ¼ past 5 next morning; a happy translation for her, for as Mr. Scambler[4] informs me 'from the first

[1] i.e. to Hindwell, Radnorshire, where M. W. was staying.
[2] 10 June 1812 was Wednesday.
[3] See previous letter. W.'s sonnet, 'Surprised by joy—impatient as the wind', *Oxf. W.*, p. 257, was his most moving memorial to Catharine.
[4] Medical adviser at Grasmere.

she appeared quite insensible to her sufferings'; and every attention, he adds, was paid to her that possibly could be.

I left Grosvenor Square on Monday, a short time only before the Letter came with the News; which was forwarded to me and, (by some accident I am unable to explain) instead of reaching Bocking yesterday, has not come till today. My Sister says that they have not written to Mary, wishing that I should be the bearer of the Intelligence. Three days are already lost most unfortunately; and Dorothy says; 'Sara will write to Tom to reach him about the time that we shall reckon upon your arrival in Wales; to inform you how we go on.' This Letter of course will be there before me; and it is possible that Mary may be apprised of the event when I arrive; but still I feel it my duty to go with all expedition possible, for one who cannot well afford to travel but by the Coaches. I shall be at Ludlow on Friday night and at Hindwell on Saturday morning. I cannot conclude without repeating how grieved I am that being so near you we are not to meet, but in this as in every other thing, 'God's will be done.'

Give my best respects to Mr. Clarkson and your Father; I am, my dear Friend and now our only dear living Catharine,

Most tenderly yours
Wm Wordsworth.

I write with a full heart; with some sorrow, but most oppressed by an awful sense of the uncertainty and instability of all human things. — —
I should have come to Bury today, and have returned tomorrow to London had I received the Letter at the usual time of delivery. But Chris and I had taken a long walk and it was nearly two o'clock before we returned, the Bury Coach past and the day so far advanced; and my state of feeling such that I could not face the journey, on a chaise or otherwise.

249. W. W. to CATHERINE CLARKSON

MS. Cornell.
Hitherto unpublished.

Thursday June 18th [1812]
Hindwell near Radnor

My dear Friend,

This with the exception of a short note to Grasmere is the first time I have touched a Pen since my arrival here on Sunday, where I found poor dear Mary in a most disconsolate State from which we have not yet been able to raise her. The suddenness of the shock and her not having been upon the spot have been great aggravations of her distress in losing this beloved child endeared to her by such long and tender anxieties of maternal care and love.—

When I reached London Thursday last, I changed my plan so far as to stay one day, thinking that it would be better that Mr H.[1] should communicate the sad Tidings, and that Mary should have my arrival to l[ook][2] forward to. I wish the thou[ght][2] had struck me at Bocking, [and][2] then I should certainly have seen you for a few hours; but 'tis better perhaps as it is, our meeting and parting must both have been very painful.—

I had hopes to prevail upon Mary to take a little Excursion in this neighbourhood that might beguile her heaviness, but I am now inclined to give this up. She seems so afraid that some of her other Children may be taken from her before she reaches home, and has upon her mind so many tender offices of sorrow to perform for her departed Catharine, that I fear no benefit will be derived from any attempts to turn her attention to other objects . . .[3]

250. W. W. to C. W.

Address: Rev^{d} Dr. Wordsworth at the Deanry [*sic*], Bocking, Essex.
Postmark: 18 June 1812. *Stamp:* Radnor.
MS. Jonathan Wordsworth.
TLS June 5 1959.

Thursday [June 1812]
Hindwell near Radnor

My dear Christopher,

I have but a poor account to give of Mary. I arrived here on Sunday, and she is yet little recovered from the deploreable dejection in which I found her. Her health has suffered: but I clearly see that neither thought nor religion nor the endeavours of friends, can at once quiet a heart that has been disturbed by such an affliction. We must wait patiently and do what we can.—I have no hope of prevailing upon her to turn aside on our way homeward for any object that might amuse or interest her, but she is at present not in a state of health to encounter the fatigues of so long a journey, and

[1] i.e. Tom Hutchinson, M. W.'s brother.
[2] Manuscript torn.
[3] Letter incomplete.

to face the renewal of her anguish which will await her on her first arrival at Grasmere. She suffers more than in the ordinary course of nature from the tender connection and dependence in which this child has long existed with her, or hung upon her maternal care; and I feel that the privation will be a sorrow for life; though I hope at some future period she will be able to draw consolation from her very source of encreased suffering.—

Mr Malcolm,[1] with whom as I said, I was greatly interested, dropped a hint as if the diminution of your chance of success in the affair of the Professorship[2] were likely to abate your efforts to obtain it, do not let this be so on any account. It is your duty to exert yourself to the utmost and surely it would be well to go shortly to Cambridge with this view. Remember us both affectionately to Priscilla, and accept yourself of our affectionate Love. I am happy to have seen your family under your own roof, short and melancholy as was my visit.

Your affectionate Br
W. Wordsworth

My address for at least ten days will be here.

* *For 250a see Addenda.*

251. W. W. to THOMAS DE QUINCEY

Address: Thomas de Quincey Esqr, Great Titchfield Street, London.
Postmark: 20 Ju 1812. *Stamp:* Radnor 164.
MS. New York Public Library, Berg Collection.
Hitherto unpublished.

[Saturday, 20 June 1812]

My dear Friend,

I arrived here on Sunday, after a journey as pleasant as my state of mind would permit. I found Mrs W—in great distress and dejection; nor have we yet made any perceptible progress in raising her mind.—I am therefore much at a loss what to do; whether to return to Grasmere, or continue here awhile with a hope of restoring her to some degree of chearfulness and tranquillity.—At all events we cannot move immediately as she is at present much

[1] Gilbert Malcolm, Fellow of Trinity and Rector of Todenham, Glos. D. W. refers to him as 'my Dr. Christ^r^'s most intimate Friend', see Letters 250a, and 304, p. 110 below. W. W., M. W., and S. H. visited the home of his four sisters, at Burnfoot in Eskdale, 'so Scotch, so merry, and so noisy', on their tour in Scotland in 1814. See *SH* 21, p. 73.

[2] A new Professor of Moral Philosophy was elected in 1813. No chair for which C. W. was qualified was vacant at this time.

reduced, and indeed very weak, too weak to have the fatigues of the journey.—Thomas is very well and looks charmingly.—

I have little hope that Mrs W would derive benefit from any excursion in North Wales, or deviation from the direct route home. Her mind seems too full of fears least she should lose some other of her children during her absence; and she appears too intent upon the thought of performing many tender offices of sorrow to the memory of her departed child to tolerate any proposal of the kind.—

Excuse the shortness of this; I have deferred writing to all my friends with a hope that I might have better news to give. And today I shall write to all. My address for ten days probably will [be] here.—I shall be glad [to] know that you were remembered [at] Grasmere.

Your affectionate friend
W. Wordsworth

Mary had a melancholy satisfaction in thinking of the degree to which you would participate her distress and feel a loss from this same cause. She inquired after this with as lively interest as I have seen her take in any thing.—

252. D. W. to JANE MARSHALL

Address: Mrs. Marshall, Water-Millock, near Penrith.
Stamp: Kendal. *Endorsed*: 1812–21 June—Death of Catharine.
MS. WL.
MY 451, p. 503.

Grasmere Sunday Morning 21st June [1812]

Your letter, my dear Friend, was put into my hands on Friday Evening when I was on my road to Ambleside. I was then in anxious expectation of a letter from my Brother and Sister, which did not arrive, and in consequence our anxiety has in some degree encreased, as the second letter which we have had from our Friends in Wales brought us a very depressing account of my poor Sister. Six hours after the first dreadful shock was communicated to her she was more calm than we had dared to hope; but on the fourth day her Sister[1] wrote to us again, and she said she looked extremely ill and had not eaten a quarter of a pound of food since she heard of her Darling's Death. Very unfortunately my Br had left London when

[1] i.e. Joanna Hutchinson, who was also staying at Hindwell.

my letter to him arrived—he was at Bocking, and did not reach Radnorshire till last Sunday. We had wished that he should be the Bearer of the sad tidings, and had written a letter to Mr. Hutchinson communicating the particulars which we had expected would arrive after my Brother. It so happened that Mary was in the room when that letter was delivered, and it was impossible to conceal the contents from her. If he had been with her from the first, I am sure she would sooner have been rouzed to exertion; and she would also have been spared the agony of meeting him; and the pain and anxiety of expectation.—Oh! that she had been here at the last moments of her sweet Child's life! I am sure she would have borne it better—not that she can ever have a thought that she could have done more for her than *was* done but her heart would have been satisfied and she would have calmly submitted to the will of God. Like us she would have prayed for her release in death; for it was too plain that if she had not been taken from us she would have been a never-ending sorrow—she could not have recovered the use of her limbs, nor most likely of the faculties of her mind; for the seat of the disease lay in the Brain—but never, never can we cease to regret our loss; for she was the sweetest, mildest tempered child that ever was born—the most loving—entirely free from all bad passions: it seemed as if she had not the seed of any evil in her; and even if she had never entirely got rid of the little lameness which remained to the last; it was so very little, that we thought it of small consequence compared with what *might* have been after her first violent attack, and we were thankful it was no worse—being utterly blind and fearless respecting another attack. As I have said, your letter met me on my way to Ambleside— I was then in a very uneasy state of mind concerning my youngest Nephew, William; he was very poorly, and I was going to consult Mr. Scambler, our Apothecary. Thank God! the Child is getting better; but he still looks very ill. With this and other anxieties upon me, my dear Friends, you will not wonder that I *cannot* leave home till after my Brother's and Sister's return. I *cannot* do it. After such a sudden change; from the most promising health, and lively spirits, and blooming looks—I could not be easy to leave the Children for a single night to the care of any others than their Parents. You will say perhaps, 'Miss Hutchinson is here, and what can you do more for them than she can do?' That is very true; and more I cannot do; but I could not bear to leave them; nor I believe, could she consent to be left with them at this time, unless I were called upon to discharge some imperious duty that could not be discharged by another.

We expect a letter tonight, which will most probably fix the time of their return; for though my Brother wishes Mary to consent to stay a little while in Wales, in the hopes that seeing the country may divert her mind from its sorrow, she seems bent upon coming home as soon as possible. I will keep this letter unclosed in order that I may tell you what they say respecting their return; but I hope that if you cannot all come to Grasmere, at least my Aunt and Elizabeth[1] will; we have a bed for them, and a part of your Family might be accommodated at the Inn, which is very near to the Parsonage. I am very much disappointed that my Aunt talks of making so short a stay—we had counted upon having her company for at least a week at Grasmere; but I fear that we must be contented with a shorter visit. I hope that the letter which tonight's post will bring us will fix the time of their return; and I shall then be able to form a notion when I can leave home in case all be well. And in the mean time I hope you will think about coming over to Grasmere. Any time *before* their return; or any time *after* it except the first two or three days would suit us—and you could not come when we should be absent from home more than a couple of hours. I am very glad that Elizabeth is with her Aunt; it will give us great pleasure to see her once again at Grasmere.

So far I wrote before tea. It is now eleven o'clock. I have been obliged to write to my Brother and Sister in consequence of the letter which we have received this evening. Thank God it has brought us a better account of the poor afflicted Mother than the last—but we are convinced that coming home will be the best thing for her, therefore we have written to urge their coming immediately. They cannot be at home before next Tuesday week, therefore if Mrs. Rawson and Elizabeth could come to spend a few days with us before that time, it would be a great satisfaction to us—and as I have said a part of your Family might be accommodated at the Inn. If they do not come till the week after next they would see my Br and Sr, which I should very much wish; but perhaps their time will not allow of this.—It is long since I have been so well pleased, as by the sight of my Nephew John riding behind Mr. Saltmarsh from school. I did not recognize Mr. S., but felt a kindness for the person who had been so very good-natured. When Mr. S. had made himself known we had a few minute's conversation together—and he rode on to Keswick—I was at Mr. de Quincey's cottage at the time. John walks daily to Ambleside School with a Tin Bottle over his shoulder and a Basket on his arm.—We have had one *great*

[1] i.e. Mrs. Rawson and Elizabeth Threlkeld. See L. 19, pt. i, p. 32, n. 3.

pleasure this week in the return of our Niece Dorothy; but that pleasure was sorely mixed with pain—and I never see the dear Children playing together without sad and tender thoughts of what they and we have lost.—You may judge what a comfort it was to me that Miss Hutchinson was with me during our late affliction. She had been at Keswick only a fortnight before, and would have now been at Stockton with Dorothy if Catharine had still been living; but she cannot leave me at this time. I must say no more for the Maids are wanting to carry my letter to the Carrier's. Adieu my dear Friend. My kindest love to my Aunt and Elizabeth and all Friends. Yours truly

D W

253. D. W. to CATHERINE CLARKSON

Address: Mrs. Clarkson, Bury St. Edmonds, Suffolk.
Stamp: Kendal Penny Post. *Endorsed*: account of little Catharine.
MS. British Museum.
MY ii. 452, p. 507.

Grasmere 23rd June [1812]

Assuredly my dearest friend you would have had a letter from one of us, if either had been alone; at least you would have had one from *me*; for poor Sara has been even more inclined than I to shrink from the painful task. If I had not had her beside me to uphold me in my weakness I could not have helped writing, the thought of not doing my duty to you would have been so painful; besides I should have needed your sympathy. It was a hard trial for us when the dear Child was taken from us for ever—and never never can we cease to regret what we have lost; for the purest spirit in heaven could not be more pure and innocent than she was while on earth. She had a temper never ruffled—there seemed no seed of evil in her—and she was so loving that the smallest notice or kindness shewn to her by those with whom she was well acquainted used to draw from her the fondest caress and expressions of love. There was no variety in her ways, she having been kept back by so much illness, and this has made her the most remembrable child that ever I was separated from. When Dorothy is absent it is difficult to call her to mind as she is—she puts on so many shapes; but sweet Catharine is and ever will be the same in our remembrance as when she was alive. This is a comfort now and hereafter will be much more so. Yes, my dear Friend we have many causes for thankfulness, though it is for ever to be regretted that her tender Mother was not here to perform the last sad duties. If she had seen her I am sure she would have found it more easy to contemplate her loss with composure; not that the *shock* would have been less—for I think it was even greater to us than it would have been had we been absent; for the change so visible to our senses was astounding. For several days the Child had been in the most joyous spirits. On the Sunday afternoon and the Monday I had been for several hours with Willy and her in the Churchyard and they had run races and played on the very ground where now she lies. I then particularly noticed how little was to be seen of her lameness, and several persons who came up to speak to us while we were there observed how trifling the lameness was, and how thriving and healthy she looked. That very night on which she was seized she ran up to bed, in such glee striving to get before William, and proud that she was going to sleep in her *Mother*'s bed, an unusual treat. Poor thing she was stretched out there before 7 o'clock the next morning. We returned from our walk at a little after nine and John called me to her at about ¼ before 10, he was going to bed, found that she had been sick. She was lying with her eyes fixed—and I knew what was going to happen and in a fright called Sara. She would have persuaded me that the child was only overpowered with sickness but I had seen her before and knew too well. We lost no time in sending for Mr Scambler and in the meanwhile applied the remedies used before. Mr Scambler gave us no hope—and after we found that there was no cause in the stomach for the convulsions, and that they increased after her Bowels were evacuated, we only prayed for her release in death; for it was plain that had she lived she could not have recovered the use of her limbs, nor probably of her senses; and what a sorrow would this have been for her Mother and every one of us!—We know not how soon we may be deprived of one of the other children; but there is great cause for thankfulness, that if one was to be taken away it was this sweet Innocent; for we now find, a thing of which we had formerly no misgivings, that there was the greatest reason to fear a return of the paralytic affection. We had no fears but that she would get rid of the lameness left by the first attack, but we now learn from others that Mr Scambler always feared the worst, which very wisely he kept from us for nothing could have been done to prevent it[1]—and Oh! how merciful this heavy stroke compared with one that might have left her, helpless, and deprived of her understanding! We have many other Reasons for thankfulness—the child was never

[1] See L. 247, p. 23 above.

so happy in her life as during the last weeks of her existence. Her dependence on her Mother used at times to make her low-spirited when her Mother was not present with her—or she would fret at parting from her; but she had no uneasiness of this kind with her Aunt Sara and me, and was equally delighted to be in our company. She had only one petted fit during her Mother's absence, and then, poor thing! she cried after me. This she did twice in one day and I said she will be as bad after me as her Mother, I must break her of it—and I chid her—and left her to herself. This has given me a pang since her death; but it was better that I did for she had never more any unhappiness. Another comfort was that both the children had been as well attended upon as it was possible, even while the Maids were ill—and afterwards with most unusual care—and that she had never been suffered to have any food likely to disagree with her. Then at the very last—no time was lost; for we have every reason to believe that she was discovered immediately after her seizure—Mr. Scambler was at home, and we were perfectly satisfied with his skill, and his calm confidence that all he did was for the best. His tenderness towards the child was an unspeakable comfort to us. Then what a blessing that Sara was with me!—She had intended going to Stockton, and had been at Keswick only a fortnight before.—She died on Wednesday the 4th of this month and was buried on the 8th. We all three Sara John and I followed to her grave.—She lies at the South West corner of the church yard under a tall and beautiful hawthorn which stands in the wall. It is visible from Robert Newton's cottage, and you, my beloved Friend I daresay have often looked at [it]. We have put a small headstone to mark her grave.—After her death John became a comfort to us, though in deep distress, for he was so very much afflicted; but the thoughtfulness and good sense, and delicate feeling which he shewed, made us lean upon him as on a support, a support for us and his dear Mother, and the other helpless little ones. Poor Willy soon ceased to inquire after Kate; but it was many days before he got the better of his loss; he was fretful and knew not what to do with himself. Dorothy was at Appleby—she was always particularly fond of Catharine, and when she heard of her death was much afflicted for a time; but she is of a volatile nature, and the next day was as happy as ever. She came home last Thursday and we were surprized at her joyfulness, but at night when she went to bed she knelt down before me to say her prayers, and as usual prayed for her Brothers and sister, I suppose without thinking of her. I said to her when she had done—My dear child you have no Sister living now—

and our Religion does not teach us to pray for the dead. We can do nothing for them—our prayers will not help them—God has taken your Sister to himself.—She burst into a flood—an agony of tears—and went weeping and silent to her bed—and I left her after some time still weeping—and so she fell asleep. John goes to Ambleside school with Hartley and Derwent—he walks every morning and returns home at night, with a bottle over his shoulder and a Basket in his hand—he always meets us with smiles—enjoys his school—his play with his school-fellows—and is never tired in Body—a proof that he is very strong. This thought of his strength strikes now suddenly upon me many and many a time—and my heart is humbled—and I fear the more because he is so strong. As to his lessons he is the backwardest Boy I ever knew yet I am convinced that he is not a Dunce in soul. Dorothy is quick and forwarder—much forwarder in everything—but if you read to them both—poetry—history—natural history—stories—whatever it is she yawns and grows sleepy, and his attention would be kept awake, and continually awake if you would read till twelve o'clock at night—and his memory is very good. Willy was very poorly on Friday and Saturday, threw up everything he ate and you can hardly think how anxiously we watched him. I am very thankful that he is now better; so we shall not speak of his illness to his Mother. Dorothy is very industrious on the whole while she is at her work; and fond enough of her lessons; we have begun very steadily and are determined to go on. She is of a disposition that *requires* the utmost strictness. So much for ourselves my dearest Friend; but I must speak of our health. Sara has for some time been growing thin; but she was unusually strong and well before Catharine's death, but since that time she has been rather unwell at times; but upon the whole better than I could have expected, and we have been a great support to each other. I am well—but as you can suppose, have not been constantly so since our loss; but we now, and indeed have long looked at it with calmness; but we have been kept in great anxiety respecting Mary. Owing to the distance letters have been slow and our second account before William's arrival was but a bad one. We are now less disturbed by anxiety for her as we have had a letter from herself, which shews that she is much more composed than when the former account came; but we are extremely desirous to have her at home. William wished her to stay a short time in Wales, thinking that by going about a little she might relieve her mind and be enabled to look back upon Wales with composure in after times and something like pleasure. She yielded because he wished it; but it is very plain to us that she will never be *satisfied* till she gets home, and we have written to urge their immediate return. Poor thing! She sends her best love to you and says she wishes William had now been with you, and should have done so from the first had she not thought that he, like her, would wish to be at home immediately. At the time that her dear Girl was lying a corpse in the house she fondly anticipated the pleasure that you and William would have together in talking of your God-daughter of whom we had sent them such flattering accounts. You do not speak of your own loss in not seeing William—believe me we have bitterly lamented it; but let us not repine, many are the blessings that we have had in common—and let us strive to see each other again. That little child is gone but a few years before us—*our* years of life *must* be few—and let us employ them to the best uses—let us cultivate our best and immortal affections—and do let us see each other again if it be God's will that we live another year. Cannot you come to Grasmere next summer?—You say nothing of Mr Clarkson's coming *this* summer. Oh that you could come with him! We hope to have William and Mary at home next week—Mary Monkhouse will follow them in a few weeks. Poor Mary![1] would that she had not gone from home at that time. I fear she will never dare to go again—and perhaps if she had witnessed the last Days of her Child she might have been induced to go to her Friends in Wales after her mind had been restored to composure—and perhaps she would have gone to see you at Bury!—We sometimes have wished that she could have done so now—but nothing but home will satisfy her. Ours has been a great affliction—and the shock was terrible; but when we look round how much more are others afflicted! Captain [? Tinling's] situation is truly lamentable and I feel very much for that tender-hearted man. Give my kindest love to all your Family. Your Father is always ready to mourn with the afflicted, and I am sure he has felt much for us. I cannot now think of leaving home. Yet I hope I may be allowed at some time or other to see your father and sister again. Give my kindest love to your husband and Tom. I fancy him now almost a full-grown man. Hartley Coleridge grows tall—but he will never reach Tom's size. Mrs Coleridge and Sara and Edith Southey spent a fortnight with us lately. They had left us about ten days when Catharine died. I hope your usual health will be re-established when you write again—and pray write immediately—you cannot think what a comfort your letter was to us. We had not

[1] i.e. Mary W. For Mary Monkhouse see Letters 33, pt. i, p. 60 and 240, p. 10 above.

expected to hear from you—and I had urged Sara to write—and she had urged me—and thus we put it off. God bless you for ever, our own dear Friend—

D. Wordsworth.

254. D. W. to JANE MARSHALL

Address: Mrs. Marshall, Water Millock, Penrith.
Stamp: Kendal Penny Post. *Endorsed*: 1812 July—Crossing Fairfield, Dove Crags.
MS. WL.
MY ii. 453, p. 512.

Sunday 26th July [1812]

My dear Friend,

I know that you are all anxiously expecting news of me and my Friends; and it would have been possible for me to have sent a letter one day earlier, but having caught cold with my journey, but such a cold as I knew would soon pass away, I thought it best to wait till I could send you word that I was no worse for my fatigue. You know that I yielded to my Brother's desire of going over Fairfield, though I was very unwilling to consent to part with your Sister and Mr. Marshall before it was necessary. They will have told you in what a delightful spot we ate our dinners, a spot to which I hope that Mr. Marshall will conduct you before the summer is over. Before we had quitted the woody part of the mountain we discovered a water-fall which after heavy rains must be very grand—there we sate some time; yet long after we had quitted it we saw Mr. M. and your Sister, and I greeted them with my pocket handkerchief, and I fancied that they saw us; for they stopped: and they seemed to linger on the road, from which we hoped that they found it pleasant. Ours was a most grand ascent; but when we had clomb to a considerable height, just above Dove Crag, I unfortunately turned my head round; became giddy and trembled; and if anything had happened to my Brother so as to disable him from assisting me by following close to me and taking hold of me, I must have perished;—at least so I believe. At the top of the Mountain we had the noblest prospect I ever beheld, and when the fear was passed, I felt very glad that we had gone by that road; though I should not be willing to take it again. The descent was very gentle, and if ever I am inclined to go to the Top of Fairfield again, it shall be from this side of the mountain. We reached home at a little after six. I was not much tired, nor at all stiff; but my face burnt so violently that I was obliged to lie down, and take my tea in bed—and the next day it was very much swoln, and so continued till yester evening, when the swelling began to fall; and to day it is almost entirely gone — — I found my Sister in bad spirits, yet on the whole better than I expected, and her appetite is considerably improved; though it is still bad enough; and she looks no better; she does, however, exert herself in the concerns of the house; and at times appears to take part in indifferent matters, so I hope she is in the way of regaining her natural chearfulness. All the Children are well, and all *look* well except Thomas; who I am sure has worms—his looks are quite ghastly and he has an enormous appetite, especially for potatoes and other things unwholesome for a weakly child. John is to go to school again to morrow, which I am very glad of. A month's holiday is far too much for a Boy who is not fond of his Book. This afternoon we are going to drink tea with our neighbours, the two clergymen,[1] who are in Robert Newton's lodgings, the house which I hope your Sisters will occupy for a week or two next summer—and perhaps if they like the place they will stay longer. All the Family have been at Church this morning except my Brother and myself. Our Vicar did duty and the stranger clergymen came from church astonished with the Rector's[2] performance. It is really a melancholy thing that such should be his office—he is a worthy man—very good as a Steward or a Farmer; but totally unfit to preach or read prayers. We have preferred a petition to Mr. Bloomfield, who has promised to preach next Sunday. He gave great satisfaction last week; but I must say the people of our parish are easily pleased, for they think that Mr. Jackson gives 'excellent Sarmons' though he *does* read the prayers rather too fast. — — It was lucky I did not bring my new Bonnet in my hand; for we had a heavy shower before we reached home, which would have entirely spoiled it. I shall send Wilkinson's Prints[3] by the Carrier next Thursday, so they ought to be at Penrith on Tuesday, therefore you will desire the Patterdale carrier to inquire for the parcel. I shall send the 'Curse of Kehama'[4] at the same time.

[1] i.e. Samuel Tillbrooke and C. J. Blomfield. For Tillbrooke, see L. 174, pt. i, p. 368, n. 2. Blomfield (1786–1857) of Trinity College, Cambridge, was a pupil of Porson, who spoke of him as a 'very pretty scholar'. He became Bishop of Chester in 1824 and Bishop of London in 1828.

[2] Thomas Jackson, Rector of Grasmere 1806–21. See L. 193, pt. i, p. 408, n. 1.

[3] i.e. *Select Views in Cumberland, Westmorland and Lancashire, by the Rev. Joseph Wilkinson*, etc. for which W. had written (anonymously) the letterpress in 1809–1810. See L. 176, pt. i, p. 372, n. 1.

[4] By Southey, published 1810.

When you see the Wordsworths[1] pray tell them that we all return thanks for the pig, which was greeted with much joy by the younger part of the Family, and their joy was ten fold when they heard it was to be kept to have young ones. The Pig was set down upon the kitchen floor, and it was impossible to say whether the voice of Willy's raptures, or of [the] Pig's fears, was louder. If Mrs. Wordsworth wish[es] to read my Journal when you have done with it, be so good as to lend it to her; and request her to return it to you when she has finished it. By the Bye its title is not properly a Journal or Tour, but '*Recollections* of a Tour in Scotland, etc., etc.'— —

Tell Jane that her name sake very much admires her pincushion, and yesterday she prevailed upon me to seek her out some silk, and she made an imitation of it. She would be very happy to be acquainted with Jane. I hope you have good accounts from Allonby, and that all are well at home. As soon as the weather is settled again I trust you will venture to let Ellen go to Gowbarrow and that the change will be of service to her. She is a sweet creature; and happy should I be to see her growing fat and strong, when I revisit Watermillock in the Autumn; at present I indulge the hope; but always with fear—after so many sudden changes it is impossible to look beforehand with confidence. I hear that my Brother Richard talked of returning to Sockbridge in the course of a fortnight from this time. My Sister is very much obliged to you for your kind invitation; but at present she can neither talk nor think of leaving home; besides we are this day expecting to see Miss Mary Monkhouse from Wales, and she will stay with us till October; but as she will probably spend a part of that time at Penrith I may seize the opportunity of her absence, to visit my Brother Richard; and *you* if your house is not occupied by other visitors. I often think of Haweswater—and Rawson Bay, and other delightful places which we saw when I was with you. God grant that you may long live to enjoy your present happiness, and to spread, as you do, happiness all around you! Give my kindest love to your Sisters and Mr. Marshall, and Mary Ann and all the dear children — — Do let me hear from you soon. I trust you yourself are quite recovered. We have had no letter from Halifax. Mary was most bitterly disappointed at not seeing Mrs. Rawson. She and my Brother beg their kind love. God bless you my dear Friend. Believe me ever your affectionate

D Wordsworth

[1] i.e. Capt. and Mrs. John Wordsworth, at present living at the Clarksons' old home, Eusemere.

255. D. W. to CATHERINE CLARKSON

Address: Mr. Clarkson, Bury St. Edmonds.
Stamp: Kendal Penny Post. *Endorsed*: R^d Sharp.
MS. British Museum.
K (—). *MY ii. 455, p. 516.*

July 31st [1812]

My dearest Friend,

I received your letter on my return from Ulswater, whither I was obliged to go two days after Mary's return which was a painful necessity as she was so very unhappy, so perfectly cast down. I stayed a fortnight and three days. My motive for going at that time was to see that Cousin of my Mother's who brought me up.[1] You must have often heard me speak of her, and of the fortitude with which she has struggled through the pains of overcoming a lameness produced by breaking her thigh. She was to have returned with me to Grasmere but was summoned home by the illness of her Husband. I stayed four days at Eusemere with the Wordsworths;[2] the rest of my time was spent with a Yorkshire family at Water Millock.[3] How often did I wish for you when I was at Eusemere! The first morning I spent entirely alone (for I found the Wordsworths not at home) in wandering over the grounds—and walking upon the terrace and I also went to the top of Dunmallet. My dear Friend my thoughts were then entirely with you—it was a warm and beautiful day, and I sate upon the stones close to the water at the end of the walk,—a long, long time. The trees near the house are very much grown, and the walks are perfectly shady; but the axe ought to have been used amongst them long ago. I fear that it is now so late that the trees will never forget their early confinement, and perhaps in general it would be better to leave them as they are. Your hops remain and the Virgin's bower; but only one half of the porch is covered, that nearest to Woodside. I hope that your dear Sister's marriage will be a happy one, and I *must* be glad of it, but I cannot help having regrets which I may almost call selfish for your Father and you—yet his happiness will encrease in proportion to hers notwithstanding his great loss. Mr Tillbrook says 'John Corsbie is a noble fellow' and of such qualities I think Tillbrook is capable of judging. We like our neighbours[4] very much. Blomfield is a very pleasing young Man. We spent Tuesday afternoon in a

[1] i.e. Mrs. Rawson of Halifax. See L. 19, pt. i, p. 32, n. 3.
[2] i.e. Capt. and Mrs. John W. W. See p. 38 and L. 195, pt. i, p. 411, n. 1.
[3] i.e. the Marshalls of Leeds, with whom Mrs. Rawson was staying.
[4] i.e. Samuel Tillbrooke and C. J. Blomfield. See L. 254, p. 37, n. 37.

walk to Hacket where we drank tea with our old Servant's Mother. Mr Sharpe[1] was of the party and was very entertaining, and we had a very pleasant afternoon. Tillbrook stationed himself upon a rock and sounded his flute[2] to the great delight of our party—the cows in the field, and a group of rustic children. Dear Mary was the only one who remained at home. She *would* not go to Hacket for the first time—a place which had been so dear to her as that place where Catharine first began to recover after the hooping cough. Her spirits are much mended, and she begins to look better, and has recovered her appetite—but she is very thin. Dear little Tom has worms we think, his looks are miserable. I am sorry to tell you that we still have much trouble with Dorothy. She *can* do anything but she is extremely wayward and is desirous to master everybody. It is a woful thing that so sweet a creature should be capable of seeking the perverse delight of making those who love her unhappy. She has been with me two hours and an half this morning and has been very good and industrious—but sometimes we have terrible Battles—and long confinements. I hope that perseverance may conquer her, and that the sense will in time come that it is wiser not to make herself miserable. Poor Kate had no ill humours! God bless you for ever. I happened to be at Penrith 2 hrs after Tom had passed through—I hope we may see him here. Oh my dear friend do come next year. My kindest love to your Husband, Father and Sister.

Yours Evermore

D. W.

256. D. W. to R. W.

Address: Richard Wordsworth Esq[re], Staple Inn, London.
Postmark: Two Py Post Lombard St. Unpaid. *Stamp*: Keswick Aug. 1 1812. *Endorsed*: 31 July 1821.
MS. WL. MY ii. 454, p. 515.

Grasmere 31st July [1812]

My dear Brother,

I write to inform you that William will have to draw upon you in the course of a few days for 50£ at one Month. I was at Watermillock and Eusemere last week and called twice at Sockbridge—I wish you had been there; but if you can receive me when you come again I will spend a few days with you. Pray write and let me know

[1] i.e. Richard Sharp, M.P. See *EY*, 214, p. 468, n. 2.

[2] W. celebrated this flute-playing with a sonnet—'The fairest, brightest hues of ether fade,' *Oxf. W.*, p. 252. See *PW* iii, p. 420, for W.'s note.

when it will be convenient to you. I suppose you will be there soon —I was very sorry to hear you had been poorly—I hope you are better.

William and Mary join me in Love—Yours affectionately

D Wordsworth

I wish very much that you would look into our accounts before you come, and bring a Statement along with you.

257. D. W. to CATHERINE CLARKSON

Address: Mrs. Clarkson, Bury, by favor of Mr. Bloomfield.
Endorsed: 10th Augt, before we left Bury.
MS. British Museum.
MY ii, 456, p. 518.

Grasmere, Monday 10th August [1812]

My dearest Friend,

Mr Bloomfield[1] must not leave us without bearing away some token for you that he has been with us therefore I must write a few hurried lines. We are very sorry to part with both him and his Friend, but I assure you Tillbrook is the favorite with us all; his blunt plainness is a sure earnest of his sincerity. I never saw a man who bore more openly upon his front the strong impression of honesty and disdain of all disguise—besides he has a very tender heart. Do not think I would detract from Bloomfield, we admire and like him very much; but without having genius or perhaps as much cleverness as B there is something in T's manners which has the same *sort* of effect upon one as originality and genius have—he touches one with surprize every now and then by his droll way of telling things for or against himself, or what he has heard or seen. He is quite the favourite with Sara and Mary M.[2]—B's views of everything he sees are contracted by his love of the picturesque—his amiable disposition and his sensibility will I have little doubt in time overcome this—and after a few visits to the North he will find that there is a wider range of enjoyment here than he at present conceives. They have been very pleasant amongst us, are fond of children and we have been quite at home with them. For particulars I refer you to them. To-day we are going to eat a parting dinner with Till. at Mr de Q's old cottage.[3] I believe Mr B is too busy to

[1] i.e. the Revd. C. J. Blomfield. See L. 254, above.

[2] i.e. Mary Monkhouse.

[3] i.e. with Tillbrooke, at the Wordsworths' old home at Town End (Dove Cottage), which De Quincey now rented. The Wordsworths frequently made use of it when De Quincey was away.

go. Yesterday was a very hot day—almost the first *very* hot day we have had this summer—yet now and then the weather has been very pleasant. We all attended church last Sunday and heard an exceedingly pleasing and interesting sermon from B. of his own composing at Grasmere—on fillial piety. T. read prayers. It was quite a treat for us for we seldom hear the duty so well performed.—Mary and William and J and D and myself went to Keswick on Saturday with Dr Bell. We left D. and brought Herbert Southey[1] back who is a delightful child—Tom and he are great friends. D is to stay a week, and happy she is, almost wild with joy in the company of Sara and Edith. I think the journey was of use to Mary; her spirits have been better these two days—but she is still very dejected. William is with Sharpe and Rogers[2] at Low wood and is to attend a wrestling match at Ambleside. Only think what a house-full they have at Keswick—Miss Fricker and Miss Barker[3] are there and they are seldom without other company—but these things are far easier than they used to be when Mrs Coleridge was mistress. I am sure Mr Clarkson will tell Blomfield that he has seen nothing 'as he did not see Eusemere and Pooley Bridge'—and we all say that he has seen very little and must come again. Do write my dearest Friend. May God bless you for ever. We all unite in best Love. Mr Bloomfield must tell you how much we have talked with him about our wish to see you again next summer and he must join his entreaties with ours and help to lay plans. My kindest love to Mr Clarkson your Father Sister and Tom

Yours evermore
D. Wordsworth.

I hope you will write as soon as you have seen and talked with Mr Bloomfield.

[1] Southey's eldest son, b. 1806. He died in 1816, to his father's lasting grief.

[2] Richard Sharp (1759–1835) and Samuel Rogers (1765–1855) had previously visited the Lakes together in 1801, and had called on W. W. at Grasmere and on Coleridge at Keswick. Griggs, ii, p. 737.

[3] Miss Fricker was an unmarried sister of Mrs. Coleridge and Mrs. Southey. Miss Mary Barker (1774–*c.* 1853), who, D. W. tells us, 'came into this country solely on Southey's account', was then living next door to Greta Hall. She was an amateur artist, and subsequently became quite intimate with D. W. See L. 311, 319, below. Together they climbed Scafell Pike in 1818. *DWJ* i, p. 425. In 1819 she left the Lake District and lived for a time at Boulogne, where she welcomed the Wordsworths on their way home from their continental holiday in 1820. *DWJ* ii, p. 331. For her poem on Byron, partly written by W. W., see L. 336 below. In 1830 she married a Mr. Slade; after that there are no further references to her in the Wordsworth or Southey correspondence, but in earlier years she corresponded frequently with Southey. See Warter, *passim*. Southey dedicated *The Doctor* to her.

10 August 1812

I have sent you a morsel of your dear God-daughter's hair—all that you have ever seen of her—and she was four years old when she died—this is a melancholy thought for us the survivors. The hair was cut off after her Death.

258. W. W. to R. W.

MS. WL.
MY ii. 457, p. 519.

August 12, 1812.

Dear Brother,

I write to beg that you would give up to Montagu every security except the Annuity Bond and Policy of Insurance.[1]

Do not fail to let us know when you come down into the Country, as Dorothy is anxious to go over to Sockbridge to see you, and I shall probably accompany her. I was concerned to learn through Captain Wordsworth that you had not been well when you left Sockbridge last, but Christopher writes that you look well, so we hope you are restored to health. We all here are well, except that Mary has been much enfeebled by sorrow for the loss of her daughter Catharine, and her spirits continue to be very bad.—I am with love from Dorothy and Mary your affectionate Brother

W. Wordsworth.

259. D. W. to CATHERINE CLARKSON

Address: Mrs. Clarkson, Bury St. Edmonds, Suffolk.[2]
Stamp: Kendal Penny Post.
MS. Cornell.
MY ii. 458 p. 520 (—).

16 August 1812

My dear Friend,

The evening before Sara and Mary M. set off to Appleby to spend a fortnight with Miss Weir,[3] your letter arrived. Sara said

[1] In 1813 Montagu repaid to W. W. the principal and outstanding interest of the loan of £300 made by W. W. to him in 1796, for which the Annuity Bond secured interest at the rate of £37. 10*s*. p.a. For the insurance policy see L. 300, below, and Moorman, ii, p. 241 and n.

[2] Franked and addressed by Richard Sharp, M.P., who was staying at Grasmere.

[3] See L. 87, pt. i, p. 170, n. 4.

she was incompetent to discharge the office you had imposed upon her, and referred it to William. W^m^ said he would do it; but when he came to think of it, he was not Master of the subject—and thus a post has been lost. So much depends upon the manner of travelling —time etc.,—that Mr Sharpe cannot make out a *route*[;] he has, however, hastily set down the principal things that *must* be seen,— if you would talk of having made the Tour of Wales—and a Welsh Itinerary and one or two of the Tours must be purchased—to study the Roads by—Give my kind love to your Sister. I wish her every blessing that this world can give —and I do rejoice in her prospects. She has the best reason to expect happiness, a perfect knowledge of the Man she has chosen,—and a like knowledge of her on his part. [Till]brook's account of Mr Corsbie's Character exactly corresponds with yours—Your Sister will make an excellent Wife— therefore if they have health and a reasonable share of worldly prosperity they cannot but be happy. I only grieve that they will not live in the same town with your Father—and I greatly grieve at that; though he is too disinterested not to have within himself a full recompense for his loss. Oh! that you were within a hundred miles of us! I would take the coach and spend a Month with you—for I see that you want a Friend—and I want to see you. Much as I always regret leaving home—and many as are the difficulties—and though the death of Catharine seems to bind me more to home than ever— I would not hesitate a moment. But Sara will be with you in the Autumn if she possibly can—and spend the winter—but mark the condition—you Must come back with her. She thinks she may ride up with Tom Monkhouse, who will be here at the Wedding[1]— and that will be after the Penrith Races. Say you will come—and I am sure you may rely on seeing her. Dear Mary Monkhouse is a *perfect Woman*, the only one I ever knew—except Mrs Rawson. I *know* not one fault she has—she would have been a treasure in your Family and as the Hutchinsons have already a possession in her— one would have wished another virtuous family to have had a share. Yet I feel confident that she will be a happy Woman. When I speak of Mary M's perfection do not think I would detract from others. Others whom I know have higher endowments—some in one way some in another—but I know none except herself without faults. We have been very sorry to part with them, for their horses are in the stable and the weather is so fine that they might have made good

[1] The wedding of Tom Hutchinson (M. W.'s brother) and Mary Monkhouse, her first cousin, which took place at Grasmere on 1 Nov. 1812. See W. W.'s sonnet, *Composed on the Eve of the Marriage of a Friend*, *Oxf. W.*, p. 256.

use of them and it is a pity to be confined at Appleby. There is one thing to reconcile us to their absence, Mary consents to ride and William goes with her, and her spirits are much improved—yet her dejection is miserable at times—I would give the world that she had been at home[1]—for I am convinced that she would have felt very differently. Tender regrets and a tender image of that innocent child will go with me to my grave. Yet the more I think about it the more do I feel that it is a sorrow in which comfort is found. She did not live long enough for us to know the extent of the injury she received from that first dreadful attack—but this was plain that she was never the same child—before she was the quickest creature I ever saw—the liveliest in catching ideas. It was not so afterwards yet she was merry, affectionate and of a surpassing sweetness of temper. These perfections are an inheritance that remain with us. I was led to this subject by thinking of her Mother's despondency, and you will hardly perhaps see the connection in my ideas—it is what we must talk of. If she had been here I think that she would have had more power to exercise her reason in looking at her loss.

We have had more company than usual and it has been well for Mary—Tillbrook and Bloomfield[2] were succeeded in their lodgings by Dr Bell[3]—Sharpe and Rogers[4] have been with us often. Mary walked to Brathay on Sunday and when she came home she found us at tea—Sharpe and R. and Sir James and Lady Mackintosh[5] and Miss Knott of Ambleside. Yesterday she rode with William to Low wood and drank tea there and was much delighted by a glorious sunset—but she saddened on her return to our own Valley. This morning Sharpe has breakfasted with us. I hope we shall now be quiet a little, but I am busy all day, for I am helping Dr Bell arrange and correct his various publications in one work—and this employs me constantly—and I suppose will do so for a fortnight longer. This must account for the hurry in which I write. We shall be much disappointed if we do not see Tom. Only think of my being at Penrith 3 hours after he was there! I was sadly vexed that I did not know. Before this reaches you you will have seen Mr Bloomfield.

[1] i.e. when Catharine died.

[2] See above, L. 254, p. 37 n.

[3] Dr. Andrew Bell who had stayed at Grasmere in the previous autumn, 1811. See L. 230, pt. i, p. 515, and *SH*, pp. 30–1.

[4] See L. 257, p. 42, n. 2 above.

[5] Sir James Mackintosh (1765–1832), barrister, law-reformer, and ethical philosopher. His first wife was Catherine Stuart, sister of Daniel Stuart, editor of the *Morning Post* and *Courier*. His second, whom he married in 1798, was Catherine Allen, of Crescelly, Pembrokeshire, whose two sisters married respectively Josiah Wedgwood and Sismondi, the Swiss historian, author of the *History of the Italian Republics*.

Give my very kind remembrances to him and tell him we shall look for him amongst us next year. William left my copy of the Narrative of the Greens[1] with Christ^r for you—I hope you have received it. Do write immediately. I wish you all—all the happiness that you can have, Georgiana Gower included. May God bless you my dearest Friend. I never since I parted from you so much wished to be with you again as now, when you are losing your Sister.

Yours evermore. D. W.

260. W. W. to LORD LONSDALE

MS. Lonsdale MSS., Record Office, The Castle, Carlisle.
Hitherto unpublished.

Grasmere 14th September 1812

My Lord,

On my return home after an absence of a few days I found a Letter from my Friend Sir George Beaumont communicating most kind intentions of your Lordship towards me.[2] I take the liberty to write this brief note to express my heartfelt thanks; and to say that I have written to Sir George explaining at length my sentiments upon an occasion so interesting to me and on which I feel myself so highly honoured; requesting him to transmit my Letter to your Lordship.

I purpose shortly to wait upon your Lordship at Lowther Castle to express my thanks personally for your most kind and thoughtful remembrance of me. In the meanwhile I have the honor to be

my Lord
your Lordship's
most obliged and obedt Servt
Wm Wordsworth

[1] D. W.'s account of the deaths of George and Sarah Green on the fells in 1808 and the measures taken to assist their children. See L. 101 pt. i, p. 204.

[2] W. here refers to his need for some remunerative employment, which would enable him to educate his children and at the same time would not impede his literary work. See L. 236 above. Lord Lonsdale's first efforts to assist him were not successful (see below, L. 269, p. 54), but ultimately, in the spring of 1813, he was able to obtain for W. the Distributorship of Stamps for Westmorland and part of Cumberland, a post which W. held until 1842. See further Letters 269, 271, etc., below.

261. D. W. to R. ADDISON[1]

Address: Messrs Wordsworth and Addison, Staple Inn, London.
Postmark: E 13 Oct 1812, *and* Penrith Oct 17 1812. *Endorsed*: 12 Oct 1812 From Miss D. W.
MS. WL.
MY ii. 459, p. 521.

Grasmere October 12th 1812

To Mr Addison
My dear Sir,

My Brother being absent from Town I take the Liberty of writing to you to inform you that I have drawn upon my Brother this day for Thirty Pounds, in favour of Miss Sara Hutchinson. The draft is to be paid at one Month after date.

Mr and Miss Monkhouse[2] and Mr Hutchinson and his two Sisters[3] left us on Saturday—all but Mr Monkhouse are gone to Wigton, Mr M. is at Penrith where they all intend to stay till after the Races, when we shall hope to see them again at Grasmere. They are in good health and spirits.

With kind Remembrances to your Mother, Miss Hindson and the rest of their Family—believe me, Sir,

Yours respectfully
Dorothy Wordsworth

262. W. W. to DANIEL STUART

Address: D. Stuart Esqre, Brompton Row, London.
Postmark: 10 o'clock Oc 20, 1812. *Stamp*: Kendal Penny Post.
MS. British Museum.
S.K (—). MY ii. 460, p. 522.

Grasmere, October 13th 1812.

My dear Sir,

I ought to have thanked you long since for the trouble you took, at my request, concerning the French Prisoners.[4] In consequence

[1] See L. 173, pt. i, p. 366, n. 1.
[2] Either John or Tom M., and their sister Mary.
[3] i.e. Tom H., Sara, and Joanna.
[4] Among these French prisoners, captured in Spain, was probably Eustace Baudouin, for whom see L. 243, p. 18, n. 2 above.

of your representation I declined interfering any further in the business. I wish now to trouble you about a matter concerning myself, presuming upon the kindness which you have always shewn me.—

Our powerful neighbour Lord Lonsdale has lately shown a particular wish to serve me;[1] having most kindly given me an assurance that he will use his interest to procure for me any situation which falls within the range of his patronage, the salary of which would be an object to me and the duties not so heavy as to engross too much of my time. His Lordship was so good as to express a regret that some time might elapse before such a place might become vacant, and he added that if I knew of anything, though not within the circle of his immediate influence, he would be happy to exert himself in my behalf if he were persuaded there were any chance of success.

Now you know I live chiefly in a retired corner of the world, and therefore there is no chance that I should hear of anything suitable, likely to become vacant, except through the superior information of my Friends. Nor is there anyone to whom I can apply with greater probability of receiving the requisite knowledge than to yourself.—Will you then be so kind as to point out to me anything which is likely to answer my purpose that may come to your knowledge.—Of course all this is *between ourselves*. I have no objection, I must add, to quit this part of the Country, provided the salary be adequate, and the duty what I am equal to, without being under the necessity of withdrawing myself wholly from Literature, which I find an unprofitable concern. Do you hear or see anything of Coleridge? Lamb writes to Lloyd that C.'s play[2] is accepted, heaven grant it success; if you see him, say we are well—Believe me, my dear Sir with great regard your's

W. Wordsworth.

[1] See L. 258, above.

[2] *Remorse*, a revision of *Osorio*. It was put into rehearsal towards the end of Dec. and produced at Drury Lane on the following 23 Jan. The play had considerable success, and C.'s share of the profits amounted to £400. (Note by de Selincourt.)

263. D. W. to R. ADDISON

Address: Richard Addison Esq[re], Staple Inn, London.
Endorsed: 26 Oct. 1812. From Miss D. W.
MS. WL.
MY ii. 461, p. 523.

Grasmere October 26th [1812]

Dear Sir,

I wrote a little while ago to inform you that I had drawn upon my Br for 30£ in favour of Miss Hutchinson; I trouble you with this, to apprize you that I have drawn upon you for the same sum in favour of Mr James Grave—at one Month. The last mentioned Bill was drawn on Wednesday. I am Dear Sir

yours truly D Wordsworth

Turn over—I believe my Brother will have to draw upon you for about 60£—; but if he does of course, he will write to inform you—

264. D. W. to R. ADDISON

Address: Messrs Wordsworth and Addison, Attornies at Law, Staple Inn, *London.*
Postmark: 2 Nov. 1812. *Stamp*: Kendal Penny Post. *Endorsed*: 29 Oct. 1812. From Miss D. W.
MS. WL.
MY ii. 461, p. 523.

Grasmere 29th October [1812]

Dear Sir,

I trouble you with this to inform you that my Br William has this day drawn upon Richard for 60£—in favour of Mr Edward Partridge, at one month after date.

By Mr Monkhouse you will receive a letter from me apprising you that I have drawn for 30£ in favour of Mr James Grave besides 30£ a little while ago in favor of Miss Hutchinson,

I am, dear Sir
Your obliged Serv[t]
Dorothy Wordsworth

265. W. W. to BASIL MONTAGU

Address: Basil Montagu Esqre, Lincon's Inn, London.
Postmark: 7 Dec. *Endorsed*: Account of the death of poor little Thomas.—
MS. Harvard University Library.
MY ii. 463, p. 524.

December 1st Grasmere [1812]

My dear Montagu,

I write to you two or three words only—but words of the heaviest sorrow. My sweet little Thomas is no more—he was carried off by an inflamation in chest;[1] he was seized with symptoms of the measles last Thursday went on most favorably till Tuesday at eleven, when the inflamation commenced and in spite of all that could be done he was a corse before 6 o'clock in the afternoon. Mary supports this second stroke with resignation and fortitude—I bear it as well as I can. His aunts tranquilize themselves after the Mother's example, who indeed supports us all. Heaven bless you; Mrs Montagu will be sore troubled at this our loss. But we must submit. farewell. farewell yours fai[thfully]

Your affectionate and sincere friend
Wm Wordsworth.

It would be a great satisfaction to Mrs Ross[2] to know immediately if Algernon has had the measles. I have received your last Letter in which you send your love to the Departed Spirit. You will sorrow for him, I know.

266. W. W. to THOMAS DE QUINCEY

Address: Thomas de Quincey Esqre, Mr. Merrith's, Stationer, Liverpool.
Stamp: Kendal Penny Post.
MS. Miss Maud Craig.
Japp. *K. MY i. 464, p. 524.*

Tuesday evening [1 Dec. 1812]

My very dear Friend

We have had the measles in the House, and I write under great affliction. Thomas was seized a few days ago, i.e., last Thursday he was held most favourably till eleven this morning, when a change

[1] Thomas W. (b. 1806) died evidently of pneumonia suddenly following measles. See W.'s epitaph, written several years later, in *Oxf. W.*, p. 576.

[2] The person with whom Algernon Montagu lodged while at school at Ambleside.

suddenly took place, and,[1] with sorrow of heart I write, he died sweet Innocent; about six this afternoon. His sufferings were short, and I think not severe. Pray come to us as soon as you can. My sister is not at home; Mrs. W. bears her loss with striking fortitude. and Miss Hutchinson is as well as can be expected. My Sister will be here to-morrow—

Most tenderly, and truly, with heavy sorrow for you my dear friend

I remain, yours,
W. Wordsworth.

267. W. W. to ROBERT SOUTHEY

Address: R. Southey Esq[re].
MS. Copy by Susan Wordsworth, WL.
Hitherto unpublished.

Wednesday Evening
[2 Dec. 1812]

My dear Friend,

Symptoms of the measles appeared upon my Son Thomas last Thursday; he was most favorable [*sic*] held till tuesday, between ten and eleven at that hour was particularly lightsome and comfortable; without any assignable cause a sudden change took place, an inflammation had commenced on the lungs which it was impossible to check and the sweet Innocent yielded up his soul to God before six in the evening.[2] He did not appear to suffer much in body, but I fear something in mind as he was of an age to have thought much upon death a subject to which his mind was daily led by the grave of his Sister. My Wife bears the loss of her Child with striking fortitude. My Sister was not at home but is returned to day, I met her at Threlkeld.[3] Miss Hutchinson also supports her sorrow as ought to be done. For myself dear Southey I dare not say in what state of mind I am; I loved the Boy with the utmost love of which my soul is capable, and he is taken from me—yet in the agony of my spirit in surrendering such a treasure I feel a thousand times richer than if I had never possessed it. God comfort and save you and all our friends and us all from a repetition of such trials—O Southey feel for me! If you are not afraid of the complaint, I ought to have said if

[1] A word erased here seems to be 'horiffied' [*sic*].
[2] i.e. 1 Dec.
[3] See L. 277 below.

you have had it come over to us! Best love from everybody—you will impart this sad news to your Wife and Mrs Coleridge and Mrs Lovel and to Miss Barker and Mrs Wilson.[1] Poor woman! she was most good to him—Heaven reward her.

Heaven bless you
Your sincere Friend
W. Wordsworth

Will Mrs Coleridge please to walk up to the Calverts[2] and mention these afflictive news with the particulars. I should have written but my sorrow over-powers me.

268. W. W. to LORD LONSDALE

MS. Lonsdale MSS., Record Office, The Castle, Carlisle.
Hitherto unpublished.

Ambleside
December 17th 1812

My Lord,

Your Lordship's Letter of the 12th Inst communicating to me the result of your most friendly applications to Mr Long and Lord Liverpool in my behalf[3] has reached me at a time of domestic distress which renders my heart more liable to be touched by the kindness of those who are so good as to exert themselves for my benefit and support in any manner. Ten days ago I buried a son, (six years and a half old) distinguished for sweetness of disposition, and for every quality of mind and body which could endear a Child to a Parent. His Complaint was the Measles; the medical attendant saw him between ten and eleven in the forenoon, and assured us that no Child could be more favourably held. And within an hour of that time his case was hopeless; an inflamation of the lungs having commenced which carried him off before five in the afternoon. The suddenness of this blow has overwhelmed me, falling so close upon another as sudden which deprived me of a Daughter[4] last midsummer. Of my three remaining children the youngest is now at the

[1] Mrs. Lovell was sister of Mrs. Southey and Mrs. Coleridge. Mrs. Wilson is 'Wilsy', for whom see L. 67, pt. i, p. 137, n. 1.

[2] i.e. William Calvert of Greta Bank and his wife. He was the brother of W. W.'s friend Raisley who d. 1794.

[3] See next letter in which Lord Lonsdale's exertions in London are described.

[4] i.e. Catharine W., who had died on 4 June 1812. See L. 248 above.

height of the fever attendant upon the measles, and the other two are recovering, one of whom has been severely held. So that you will easily conceive, my Lord, that I can scarcely trust I am in a state of mind that will allow me to decide upon the proposition laid before me in your Lordship's Letter.[1] Were I to trust to my present feelings I should indeed have no difficulty, but oppressed with sorrow and distracted with anxiety as I am, I fear that in a calmer state of mind I might hereafter disapprove of a determination formed at once under such circumstances. I must therefore beg leave to request that a few days may be allowed me to consider the subject before I give a final answer to your Lordship's Letter. In the meantime I am comforted by the present opportunity offered me of expressing my grateful sense of your Lordship's exertions to serve me, and of your generous disposition to remove those anxieties which might interfere with my pursuits. This will never be effaced from my mind, nor the affectionate regard with which I have the honor to be

my Lord
your Lordship's most obednt
and faithful Servant
W Wordsworth

269. W. W. to DANIEL STUART

Address: D. Stuart Esq[re], Courier Office, London.
To be forwarded immediately.
Postmark: 25 Dec 1812. *Stamp*: Kendal Penny Post.
MS. British Museum.
S (—). *MY ii. 465, p. 525.*

Grasmere, December 22 [1812]

My dear Sir,

I am afraid you will think that I have been insensible of your kindness in taking so much pains on my account,[2] as you have neither seen me, nor yet heard from me. In fact, I have felt myself very much obliged to you for your most judicious Letter, and only deferred returning my thanks till I should be enabled to impart to you something decisive concerning the result. Lord L—, happening

[1] Lord Lonsdale had asked W. to accept personally from him an annual gift of £100 until such time as a post under Government, or a pension, could be secured for him. See Letters 271 and 274 below.

[2] Stuart had also been endeavouring to assist W. in his search for a post. See L. 262 above.

to be in the country at the time I received your's and another Letter from another friend[1] on the same subject, I resolved to ride over, and lay the contents of both before his Lordship. This accordingly I did and found him in the best dispositions to exert himself. He gave me however no encouragement to go to London to make inquiries agreeable to your exhortation, but said that he should write to Mr. Long of the Treasury immediately upon the subject. Two or three days ago, I had a letter from Lord L—,[2] in which he tells me that he has had an interview with Mr. Long and with Lord Liverpool; but that they neither of them gave any encouragement to an expectation of anything being procured within a reasonable time, that would answer my purpose, that is, an office which would allow such a portion of leisure as would be requisite for a literary man to continue his pursuits. Lord L— is so obliging as to say that Lord Liverpool expressed himself favourably of me, and thought my acquirements deserving of a pension; but that this at first could not be considerable as the fund was limited. So that you see the business may be said to have fallen through, which is not a very different conclusion from what I expected as I did not even *wish* and certainly had not the least right to expect that Lord Lonsdale should make a *point* with the first Lord of the Treasury of demanding a place of value for me; and unless he had made a point of it, there was not much likelihood of anything coming of it in the present embarrassments under which administration labours. There is a place in the Stamp office for Westmorland[3] now holden by a man of upwards of 70 who is helpless from a paralytic stroke; it is worth 400 £ a year I believe at least, and this Lord L— has promised to procure me if it might be within his patronage (i.e. if it fall in in his life-time) at the time that it falls vacant; and it was only upon a supposition that a considerable time might elapse before that vacancy took place that I could have felt justified in putting Lord L— to any trouble to serve me in any other department. He is a man who does not often demand things out of the regular circle of his local patronage and told me that when he did, he found the utmost difficulty in procuring anything; as he condescendingly instanced in the case of a person who had been engaged in the education of his two Sons. 400 £ per ann. in Westmorland would be to me more desirable than 800 in London, and I must rest content with that expectation; for

[1] Sir G. Beaumont. See L. 258 above. 'Lord L—' throughout is Lord Lonsdale.

[2] i.e. the letter referred to in L. 266 above.

[3] This was the post which W. finally obtained about three months later. See L. 282 below. The present holder was Mr. Wilkin.

as to the pension, I do not see how I can accept it—but I have written to one or two friends to consult them and I should like to have your opinion if this letter reaches you duly, as I shall write again to Lord L— in a short time to give my final answer. Do not speak to any body of the contents of this letter.

You will be grieved to hear that my family are in great affliction, the measles having just torn from us, after an alarm of a few hours, a heavenly-tempered Boy, six years and a half old, who had the hope, delight, and pride, of us all, and the admiration of all who knew him.—I am, my dear Sir, with many thanks, most faithfully yours,

W. Wordsworth.

270. W. W. to BASIL MONTAGU

Address: Basil Montagu Esqre, Lincoln's Inn, London.
Stamp: Kendal Penny Post.
MS. Pforzheimer Library, New York.
K (—). MY ii, 467, p. 528 (—).

Ambleside
Sunday night
December 27th [1812]

My dear Montagu,

I have not been able to reply to your affectionate note. I have been so miserably anxious with respect to little Wm's health—it is now a fortnight since the eruption of the measles appeared upon him —in due time they disappeared no Child could be more favorably held, and we congratulated ourselves upon his escape from danger. But last Sunday night a change took place, which though not threatening immediate danger, disturbed us greatly, and he still remains in a state that [can]not be thought of without apprehension.

The only chance of saving Thomas would have been by bleeding him on the first symptoms of the inflammation; but the first indications of this are not intelligible but to those who have had experience, and our distance from Ambleside deprived us of Mr Scambler's assistance till too late. You will not therefore doubt but that as my three remaining children had not then had the complaint, I felt it my duty to guard against the worst, and to place them where in case of necessity there might be the best likelihood of obtaining medical assistance in the least time. Accordingly I knew that I might presume upon your friendship so far as to remove

Algernon from the Rosses, particularly as it is distinctly understood there, that you said he had had the measles, though Mrs Ross wished to have this assurance repeated, we placed him with Mrs Steele, and Robert is with him; last Tuesday we should have returned to Grasmere had not William's recovery been so suddenly retarded on Sunday. It was a most blessed resolution for us that we came to Ambleside, as I am certain that Mrs W's health would have otherwise sunk under the manifold anxieties which we have had on John's account and during this last week upon little William's.—His complaint is of the nature of spasms.—last night he had the best and most quiet sleep which he has known since his relapse. Mr Scambler gives us every encouragement, and seems to have little doubt that the child finally will do well. The measles have not been spread by us, and are no where in the Town, but they are on every side of it, have been at Keswick and are now prevailing at Kendal, so that from the connection with that place it seems impossible that Ambleside can escape. John and Dorothy returned to Grasmere several days since, and I hope that W^m may be conveyed back in a very short time. Many thanks for your tender remembrance of us we have suffered as much anguish as it is possible to undergo in a like case, for he was a Child of heavenly disposition, meek, simple, innocent unoffending affectionate tender-hearted, passionately fond of knowledge, and ardent in the discharge of his duty, but in every thing else mild and peacefull. I trust that almighty God has received him among the number of blessed and glorified Spirits. Dorothy and Sara are gone to Grasmere with the older children. Mary joins me in best love to you and your wife: God preserve [you] and all yours, and leave me what I now possess though I feel by a slender hold,

affectionately yours
W. Wordsworth

271. W. W. to LORD LONSDALE

MS. Lonsdale MSS, Record Office, The Castle, Carlisle.
K (—). *MY ii. 466, p. 527* (—).

Grasmere December 27th 1812.

My Lord,

I am happy that I took the liberty of requesting a short interval in order that I might put the first suggestions of my mind to the test of deliberation when circumstances might allow me to decide with more calmness than I could command at the time your Lordship's letter[1] found me.—After mature consideration, I have resolved to trust to the first feelings excited by that letter; these were, rather to owe any addition to my income, required by my present occasions, to your Lordship's friendship than to the Government, or to any other quarter where it was not in my power to return what in the common sentiments of men would be deemed an equivalent.—Asking permission therefore to retract my former determination, which I am encouraged to do by the personal intercourse and marks of regard with which your Lordship has since distinguished me, and by the irresistible delicacy of your last letter, I feel no scruple in saying that I shall with pride and pleasure accept annually the sum offered by your Lordship until the office becomes vacant, or any other change takes place in my circumstances which might render it unnecessary.—I cannot forbear to add, that I feel more satisfaction from this decision, because my opinions would not lead me to decline accepting a pension from Government, on the ground that literary men make some sacrifice of Independence by such acceptance and are consequently degraded. The Constitution gives to the Crown this power of rewarding acknowledged ability, and it is not possible to imagine a more worthy employment of a certain portion of the Revenue. But it seems to me that the provisions made by our Government for the support of Literature are far too scanty, and in this respect our practice is much inferior to that of the Continent, where, (I am now, my Lord, treating the subject generally) talents of importance to mankind and to posterity, but which from that very cause can bring little emolument to the possessor of them and which demand all the thoughts of all his life, are undoubtedly (where they are understood) fostered and honoured, even as a point of pride. This is the case in Germany and in France—whereas in England—but your Lordship knows well how the matter stands here. Now as to the general question it may be laid down as undeniable, that if to bestow be a *duty* and an *honourable* duty, to accept cannot be otherwise than *honourable*. As I cannot but be pleased with Lord Liverpool's good opinion, and as I have a high respect for his Lordship's character, would it be trespassing on your kindness, my Lord, to request that if an opportunity should offer, you would express to Lord Liverpool my grateful sense of his wish to distinguish and serve me.—

Having already mentioned my recent domestic affliction I cannot help feeling that you will have a wish to learn that my anxieties

[1] i.e. the letter referred to in L. 268 above.

are [? not] at an end. I hoped it would have been so by this time, but the complaint is apt to leave bad effects behind it; and I am sorry to say that my youngest child is in a state of health that calls for constant watchfulness, and occasions no little apprehension.—

May I beg that your Lordship will add a word in your next letter concerning the health of Lady Elizabeth and Lady Mary.—[1]

With sincere thanks for the trouble which your Lordship has taken on my account, and with other feelings which I will not attempt to express, I have the honor to be

my Lord
your Lordship's
obedient and humble servant
Wm Wordsworth

272. D. W. to MRS. COOKSON

Address: Mrs. Cookson, Kendal.
MS. Miss Helen Read.
MY ii. 468, p. 528.

Grasmere Thursday afternoon [31 Dec. 1812]

It is very long, my dear Friend, since I wrote to you, and lately I have been unable to summon courage to take up the pen, though I have often wished to write to you, till having a favour to ask I feel myself obliged to write. My Brother and Sister Sara and the children (John and Dorothy) join me in earnestly requesting that you will permit Strickland[2] and James to come to Grasmere for a few days. We find that their stay at Ambleside is limited to next Saturday, therefore if we hear nothing to the contrary we shall desire them to come hither on Saturday, and we will not encroach upon your goodness, but will send them home at whatever time, and by whatever means you shall appoint.

Sara and I left Ambleside with J and D this day week. Willy has been very poorly, having had a relapse, and is still at Ambleside[3] with his Father and Mother, but he has been so much better these two days that we hope they will all be able to return tomorrow. We are determined upon quitting Grasmere, for reasons which you will feel at once without my dwelling upon them. I trust that William and Mary and all of us are resigned to the will of Providence insomuch as not to *repine* at our heavy loss; but the poor Mother and

[1] Lord Lonsdale's daughters.
[2] i.e. Strickland Cookson, later W. W.'s solicitor and executor.
[3] This statement helps to date the letter. See L. 270 above.

some of us are too weak to be able to look upon those familiar objects now for ever before us without melancholy and pain. Oh my dear Friend wherever we look we are reminded of some pretty action of those innocent Children—especially Thomas whose life latterly has been connected with the church-yard in the most affecting manner—there he played daily amongst his schoolfellows, and daily tripped through it to school, a place which was his pride and delight—but enough of this—my heart fills to the brim when I think of it, and there is no comfort but in the firm belief that what God wills is best for all of us—though we are too blind to see in what way it is best. I dread my Sister's return and for her sake alone, independent of my feelings and those of others. I would not have us stay here if it were possible to do otherwise, for though she bears up with the greatest fortitude, I am sure that from the weakness of her body she would sink under depression of spirits, and her constitution would be slowly undermined. . . .[1]

Sara bids me ask if Mr Cookson is going to Hindwell this year. We were very sorry to hear that poor Henry[2] had been so ill—I hope he is now completely out of danger. Pray write and let us know, and how the little Hannah goes on. God Grant that the lives of both of them may be spared to you! Strickland says that Mr Harrison gave Henry a powder which relieved him. Do you know what the powder was? and pray tell us how Henry was held, and do write as soon as you can.

Sara joins with me in kindest love to you and your Husband, to Elizabeth[3] and all your little Flock. Believe me ever, my dear Friend,

affectionately yours
D. Wordsworth.

273. D. W. to CATHERINE CLARKSON

Endorsed: Relative to little Tom
MS. British Museum.
MY ii. 469, p. 530.

Tuesday 5th January [1813]

We received your letter yesterday, and I cannot delay a moment to tell you that the three remaining Children are recovered from

[1] Passage cut out of letter here.
[2] i.e. Henry Cookson, later Master of Peterhouse, Cambridge.
[3] i.e. Elizabeth Cookson, eldest daughter of Mr. and Mrs. Cookson of Kendal.

the measles. *What* I told in my last, or *when* that letter was written I know not—I know not whether I related the particulars of our darling's death. I will endeavour to retrace the history of the last five weeks—a time of anguish—sorrow—anxiety—hope—and sadness, for though we have returned to our home with thankful hearts that God has spared to us the rest of the little Flock, there is a heavy sadness remaining. I believe it was from Ambleside I wrote to you, whither we repaired one week after the death of Thomas, for the sake of being near Mr Scambler. John suffered extremely and we were in great anxiety for him. Dorothy was more mildly held—and William also; but after the fever had entirely left him and the measles gone back, he had a relapse and the cough increased, with feverish symptoms and a tendency to the spasmodic croup, therefore William and Mary stayed with him at Ambleside a week after Sara John Dorothy and I had returned to Grasmere. We left them for the sake of change of air for the children. Wm, M, and the little one returned on Saturday. It was a dismal coming home for all of us; but Sara and I had exerted ourselves to the utmost; yet in spite of all we could do, the very air of the place—the stillness—the occasional sounds, and above all the view of that school, our darling's daily pride and joy—that church-yard his playground—all oppressed us and do continue to oppress us with unutterable sadness—and his poor Mother seems almost to give herself up to it. She is as thin as it is possible to be except when the body is worn out by slow disease, and the dejection of her countenance is afflicting; insomuch that though we force ourselves into seeming chearfulness whenever we can, I feel that it knits about the heart strings and will wear her away if there is not a turn in her feelings. When I came home (I surely must have told you that I was away from home when the child died) she received me with the calmness of an Angel—she comforted me,—and in truth I was ashamed of my own weakness; and bitterly reproached myself that I could not bear the sorrow as she did. After *this* came on the anxiety for the other children. *This* I believe supported her, but that is now over—and the day through she is dejected—weeps bitterly—at times and at night and morning sheds floods of tears. All this I could bear to see in another—I should trust to time, and to the power of that resignation to the will of God which at length would become a habit of the mind, but now too well I see is only a revolution of feeling—I should trust to time and would gladly sympathize in the sorrow to its full extent—but in her case it must be struggled against or it will destroy her. When

Catharine died she was terribly shaken; for her body was not strong enough to bear up against the shock of the mind, and that corroding sorrow which followed. She was beginning to recover when this second shock came; and now she seems more feeble than ever. We are determined to quit Grasmere, and have every reason to expect that we shall get that house called Rydale Mount now occupied by Mr North (you recollect Mrs North in the history of the Greens);[1] he has sold the place to Lady Fleming.[2] William is in great favour at Rydale hall, and has applied to the Ladies Fleming and has received for answer that they will send Mr Jackson to him in a day or two to settle the business, therefore we may consider it as good as promised. I am sure you must remember the house—it is most delightfully situated—the very place which in happier days we longed for. There is no objection to it but that from the garden we shall view the Grasmere hills; yet on the other hand we should wish to be within a walk of Grasmere—and should wish to keep up that bond betwixt the living and the dead by going weekly to the parish Church beside which their bodies are laid; and I do not think there will be any thing unkindly in the sadness produced by the sight of those dear hills except in Mary's mind—and I am not sure that it will be so in hers. I would fain hope not and that her chearfulness may return when those familiar objects connected with the daily goings-on of the children are no longer before her eyes—objects which are to all of us perpetual sources of melancholy and of frequent anguish. Thomas was the darling of the house, and of every-one who looked at him—he was innocent as a new-born Babe—with a heavenly light on his countenance—peaceable, affectionate, yet lively and ardent in the pursuit of knowledge in the most extraordinary degree. This spirit was kindled in him a year ago—till that time he hardly knew his letters—he was absent in Wales three months which stopped his progress—and we were some weeks without a school Master—but no sooner did the new Master begin to teach after Dr Bell's plan than Thomas was distinguished among his school-fellows for his peculiar attention not only to his books but to his duty in every point. In truth he seemed to walk in the light of conscience, duty and order—but it was the spirit of pure innocence and an ardent soul that guided him. Oh my dear friend! he is an unutterable loss to all of us—and to his Sister and Brothers—he was the friend of each and all of them. They quarrelled with each

[1] D. W.'s *A Narrative concerning George and Sarah Green*, written in 1808, had been circulated among her friends. See L. 113, pt. i, pp. 235–6.

[2] See L. 33, pt. i, p. 61, n. 2.

other—they have wayward humours but they never quarrelled with Thomas. Dorothy feels this, and often with tears talks to me of Thomas's goodness. Yes, our loss is unutterable; and as you rightly say, it is a selfish grief when we pine after the pure spirit of a child returned to the Heaven from which it came—pure and unspotted as when it first came from the presence of its Maker. Yet this child seemed so particularly fitted to give and receive happiness—to calm the hearts of those who looked upon him, and to enjoy the best things of this life from the virtuous ardour which he possessed; that it is most hard to think upon his grave without the anguish of regret; which nothing can ever wholly repress save a Christian's faith in another world and in the Mercy of God which works always for our good though we are too blind to see *how* this is accomplished. I trust the time will come when his dear Mother will so be comforted; if not I am sure she will sink away, her constitution will be gradually undermined. It has been a cruel stroke for William—he loved Thomas with such a peculiar tenderness, from the meekness of his temper, which was such that I believe he never vexed anybody in the whole course of the six years and a half that he was lent unto us, and from that weakness at his chest, which, though it seemed not to threaten Death or even suffering gave gentle warnings that we were insecure in the possession of him.—But I said I would retrace the last 5 weeks—a painful task for both of us, me to write and you to read; but I would fain have you know all that you can ever now know about this darling Child. I had been at Watermillock a fortnight and on the evening preceding my departure I received a letter from Sara, telling me that all were well except Thomas, who had been confined to the house since Thursday and had a cough, and that they were looking out for the Measles. I read this letter among a company of chearful friends; and an unconquerable sadness overcame me, and poor Innocent I shed tears for him, little thinking that at that very time he was lying a senseless corse;—my Friends chid me; and in vain I strove to get up my spirits.—I answered them 'if I were sure it were the Measles I should have no fears; but I dread that cough which he had two years ago, and we always believed that he had had the Measles'. The next morning, with the morning light my fears vanished. I went in Mr Marshall's carriage to Penruddock and proceeded towards Keswick on the outside of the Penrith coach, intending, if I had good news from home, to stay a few days at Mr Calvert's[1] —but at Threlkeld I met my Brother—

[1] i.e. Mr. William Calvert of Keswick. See L. 267, p. 52 n. 2 above.

After I had come a little to myself, I was told that a Grasmere cart was going home, and I might either be conveyed in it, or send for a chaise. I chose the cart, and there I lay upon some straw—William beside me a part of the way—and part of the way he walked. It was dark when I reached home and I was rouzed by the sight of Candles at the door, from a kind of stupor. I have told you how I found Mary—and you may guess the rest. The morning before he had been quite chearful—the fever seemed to be gone—and he had talked of what he would do when he was well—how he would wait upon his sister and brothers—and he said to his Mother 'I hope I shall be as I am this morning as long as I lie in bed'—'Why how is that' said his Mother, and he answered 'Not so hot as I was yesterday'. He had not complained the day before and had been perfectly still and quiet. Poor thing! he looked at your profile and Mr Clarkson's which hung over the Chimney-piece and said (This was but about an hour before he was seized) and said 'Mother, they have been bad picture makers they have made no legs.' His Mother explained the reason of this, and satisfied with her explanation he said 'Ho!' as he always used to do. At 12 o'clock a coughing fit and sickness seized him—(Not an hour before Mr Scambler had seen him and said he was going on as well as possible) and William had walked out with Mr Scambler. He returned, found the child worse—went for Mr Scambler—though without much alarm, and when he returned dear Sara met him at the door and told him there was no hope—and he died at 5 o'clock. He did not suffer much pain except for the first hour and a half or two hours—he was relieved by bleeding, and the last words he said were 'I am getting better'.—Yet he had had the fear of death for a few moments during the coughing fit—and he said to his Mother 'I shall die, I shall die'—and he trembled very much—but agony though it must have been, it could only be the shapeless dread of a moment.—Yet it was heart-rending to hear it! We all, except Sara, followed him to the Grave. Poor thing! she has suffered and still suffers greatly; and it brought on the pain in her side; but it has now gone. These have been hard trials for her; but inexpressible is the comfort which she has been to me in both cases—and to all of us, but to me especially. I know not how I could have borne up if I had not had her when Catharine died—and I could never have kept up without her against Mary's depression of mind, God bless her poor thing! Mary is better this morning than when I began this letter, and my dear Friend do not afflict yourself—I hope when I write again that I shall have more hopeful tidings. Mr North is to leave his house in

February and we mean to request through Mrs Lloyd or some other acquaintance of the Norths, to go in immediately; but they have a right to the house till May-day, and they are such rancorous people that they will not only do nothing to accommodate Lady Fleming but everything that is in their power to injure her, and their dispositions towards us are not very friendly. We intend however to try; and if our pleadings for an afflicted Mother do not avail I shall give them up as reprobate spirits. William says that this [is] a hard expression so cut it out.[1] William has begun to look into his poem the Recluse[2] within the two last days and I hope he will be the better for it—he looks better and his stomach has been less deranged. It would have pitied the hardest heart to witness what he has gone through—he went for Mr Scambler to the child without fear of danger, he returned and found him dying—That miserable night—they went to bed; but slept not—and early the next morning he set out to meet me—and what a task had he then to perform!—but enough my dearest Friend I did not mean to distress you. I began for that little darling's sake to tell you what he suffered—but Oh! how vain the task to tell you what he *was*—The guileless creature—he was the very emblem of innocence and purity and infantine sweetness with an ardour of soul that would have beseemed one of riper years capable of understanding the full worth of knowledge and virtue, engaged in the noblest of causes, the pursuit of those precious endowments.

I have written this letter at three sittings. I am now returned from Ambleside whither I went with Dorothy to get 2 teeth drawn which thwarted the growth of those she had before cast. She behaved like a little heroine. I have left her at Ambleside for fear of cold. She has many faults; but is a sweet creature and I trust will make a valuable woman if we live to see it. She has great sensibility with liveliness in the extreme which is attended with its frequently accompanying fault, restlessness; and at times unquietness of manners. John and she are opposites —Thomas was between them—he had not the faults of either. Willy is a very quick and spirited child—I wish he —I wish any one of them was more like Thomas. Yet if it were so perhaps they would not be so fit for this world—*his* were heavenly

[1] This sentence is written above the line.

[2] i.e. *The Excursion*, to which W. now added the passage in Book III (ll. 584–679) describing the death of the Solitary's two children. The original drafts of this passage contain many lines which he cut out before the publication of *The Excursion* in 1814; some of these were afterwards published in another poem called *Maternal Grief*. See *PW* v, pp. 94–99, app. crit; and notes, pp. 418–19.

graces—and Catharine's temper was as sweet as his—in *her* temper too there was no seed of evil.

We have heard lately from Wales. As you may judge they were all greatly distressed by the death of their little darling. Mary Monkhouse (so I still call her[1]) had been poorly; but was better. She had had one of her bad colds. I am glad to think that you will see Coleridge. Poor soul! I only think of him now with my wonted affection, and with tender feelings of compassion for his infirmities. We have had several letters from him. Our sorrow has sunk into him, and he loved the darling the best of all our little ones. He talks of coming down as soon [as] possible, if his play succeeds.[2] I hope it will, and then I am confident he will come. Mrs C. is just the same as ever, full of troubles—one wiping away the other—full of bustle—and full of complaints—yet not against him. There is one comfort that nothing hurts her; otherwise it would be very painful to think of her, for cause enough she has had for complaint. Our kindest love attends you—do write for your letters do Mary good and all of us—then write my dearest Friend—what a comfort it would be to see you! God bless you for ever

Your affectionate
D. Wordsworth.

William who has just looked over this letter sends his tenderest love to you.

We have just heard of the death of my brother Christopher's [having lost his youngest][3] child even more suddenly than our two were taken from us. It was about 9 weeks old a 'noble—strong and beautiful Boy'—was well at 4 o'clock in the morning, and was found dead or nearly so by the nurse at six—lying thus upon her arm. I am thankful it is not one of the elder children, but at any age such strokes are hard to bear. He was to have been called William after my dearest Brother. I shall send this in two letters for fear of being too heavy and also a letter to Tom Monkhouse, which pray request Mr Smith[4] to frank for me.—God bless you again and again.—Do write soon—and as long a letter as you can. On thinking a third time about the letters I send the whole of mine to you by this post,

[1] She was now Mrs. Thomas Hutchinson. See L. 259, p. 44 n. above.

[2] See Griggs, iii, p. 423, S. T. C. to W. W., 7 Dec. 1812. In this letter Coleridge with many expressions of affection spoke of 'leaving Town after Christmas and living among you as long as I live'. But he did not come to Grasmere, in fact never returned to the North again. See L. 287 below, and Griggs, iii. 888, p. 437, where all his former complaints against W. are repeated without any mention of Thomas.

[3] So manuscript.

[4] Mr. William Smith, M.P.

and I enclose a few lines addressed to Mr Tom Monkhouse, which pray keep till you receive another cover from me which will contain a letter for France[1] to be enclosed in that addressed to Mr Monkhouse.

274. W. W. to LORD LONSDALE[2]

MS. Lonsdale MSS., Record Office, The Castle, Carlisle.
MY ii. 470, p. 537.

Grasmere Jan^ry^ 8 1813

My Lord,

The last Post brought me your Lordship's Letter enclosing a draft for £100;[3] for which I beg leave to offer my faithful acknowledgements. It is your generous desire that this act of kindness should be retrospective; but if an assurance on my part that, in the spirit of your Lordship's wishes I will 'call upon you whenever I have occasion to do so;' if this may reconcile you to my declining further assistance at present, I have no difficulty in giving such assurance.—But as a decisive backwardness to meet your most liberal suggestion would be unworthy of me and would not accord with the delicacy of your conduct towards me, I submit in this point to what may be most satisfactory to your Lordship's mind.

I cannot forbear, my Lord, to add that you have been the means of relieving my mind, in a manner that, I am sure, will be gratifying to your Heart.—The House which I have for some time occupied is the Parsonage of Grasmere. It stands close by the Churchyard; and I have found it absolutely necessary that we should quit a Place, which, by recalling to our minds at every moment the losses we have sustained in the course of the last year, would grievously retard our progress towards that tranquillity of mind which it is our duty to aim at. By your Lordship's goodness we shall be enabled to remove, without uneasiness from some additional Expense of Rent, to a most desirable Residence soon to be vacant at Rydale.[4] I shall be further assisted in my present depression of mind (indeed I have already been so) by feeling myself at liberty to recur to that species

[1] No doubt to Annette, with whom correspondence had been reopened probably through Eustace Baudoluin, whose brother married Caroline in 1816. See L. 262, p. 47 above.

[2] A draft of this letter exists in the Wordsworth Library from which De Selincourt took his copy.

[3] See L. 268, p. 53, n. 1 above.

[4] i.e. Rydal Mount. For Lord Lonsdale's 'goodness', see Letters 268 and 271 above.

of intellectual exertion which only I find sufficiently powerful to rouze me, and which for some time I could not have yielded to, on account of a task undertaken for profit.[1] This I can now defer without imprudence till I can proceed with it more heartily than at present would be possible. I have troubled your Lordship with this detail, being conscious that this is the best way of expressing my thanks to a mind like yours.

Your sympathy and that of your family in our distress much affects me and mine. I have a heartfelt Pleasure in saying that my Little-one is quite recovered.

I have the honour to be

with affectionate respect
my Lord
your Lordship's obliged &
faithful serv[t]
Wm Wordsworth

275. D. W. to R. W.

Address: Richard Wordsworth Esq[re], Staple Inn, London.
MS. WL.
MY ii. 471, p. 538.

Grasmere 11th January 1813.

My dear Brother,

William has intended writing to you for some time past; but the Task was so painful to him that he has put it off from day to day, and I have therefore taken it upon myself, being unwilling that any event which has had so material an effect upon our happiness should longer remain unknown to you. On the 1st of last month William's second Son, Thomas, died of an inflammation on the lungs, while the eruption of the measles was upon him. He had been carried on as favorably as possible; and but half an hour before the inflammation began, the Apothecary had seen him and pronounced him in a fair way of speedy recovery. In fact there had never been a moment's apprehension about him till the change took place, at once—and he was dead in five hours afterwards. This shock has been a dreadful one, coming so soon after the other which was equally sudden; and to add to the former affliction both the Father and Mother were absent, and could not be summoned to the Funeral. I was at

[1] See L. 276 below. We do not know exactly what this proposed 'task' was, but it was probably an anthology of some kind.

Watermillock when Thomas died, but I had the comfort of following him to his grave. He was the darling of the whole house and beloved by every body who knew him. His dispositions were affectionate and good—he was fond of his Book and was in all respects as promising a Child as ever breathed. God's will must be submitted to, and I hope his poor Mother and all of us will be enabled to submit as we ought; but it has been a hard stroke for her; and has shattered her very much. The Boy was six years and a half old. There are now but three left—John—Dorothy, and William—aged 9—8—and two and a half years. Our present Residence, which is close to the Church-yard and the school which was our darling's Daily pride and pleasure is become so melancholy that we have resolved to remove from it, and Wm has taken a house at Rydale which is very pleasantly situated; thither we shall remove at May-day, or before, if the present Tenant quits it before that time, which is expected. I hope you will come to see us as soon as possible after your return to Sockbridge—I was much disappointed that I did not see you when I was in that neighbourhood, and I do not think I can have the heart to make the same journey next summer—therefore I hope you will come to us.

We are much obliged to you for the account of the money that we have drawn for; but pray be so kind as to send an exact account of what we possess on the other side. I hope that there was enough remaining of the Remnant of my Father's property with what we had from my Uncle William to cover the debt to my Aunt Wordsworth;[1] but how this is pray let us know—and whether you have made any settlement with the Executors of my Uncle Crackenthorpe. Do be so good as let this statement be sent to us without delay. We wish to shape our expences accordingly.

William will draw upon you in the course of a week for 19£ in favour of Mr Edward Partridge at one month after date.

Again I entreat you to come and see us. Human life is short—year passes on after year and we do not meet, and I wish you to see

[1] Mrs. Richard W. (d. 1809), widow of W.'s uncle Richard of Whitehaven (d. 1794). Money which had been advanced by her husband for W.'s education in his Cambridge days was still owing to her estate. See *EY* 44, p. 130. 'My Uncle William' is Canon William Cookson of Binfield, who must at some time have given the Wordsworth's some money. 'My Uncle Crackenthorpe' (in the next sentence) was Christopher Crackanthorpe Cookson, d. 1799, of Newbiggin Hall on the Eden. He had been one of the guardians of the Wordsworths in their youth, and the reference in this letter is to the estate of their father which was administered by him and Richard W. of Whitehaven on behalf of the orphans. Some of this estate, evidently, was still owing to them. He had, on inheriting Newbiggin Hall in 1792 from his mother (*née* Crackanthorpe), dropped the name of Cookson. See *EY* 19, p. 65.

and know your Nephews and Niece. The late warnings make us feel daily, the uncertainty of their life, and ours—May God bless you, my dear Brother

Believe me your ever affectionate Sister
D Wordsworth

William and Mary send their kindest Love. I shall expect a letter from you very soon.

276. W. W. to SAMUEL ROGERS

Address: Samuel Rogers Esqre, St. James's Place, London.
MS. untraced.
MY ii. 472, p. 540.

Grasmere January 12th, 1813

My dear Sir,

I am gratified by your readiness to serve me in the affair of my intended Publication,[1] but I am obliged to defer it, and by a cause which you will be most sorry to hear, viz., the recent death of my dear and amiable Son, Thomas. He died this day six weeks past of the measles; he was seen by the medical attendant about twelve at noon, pronounced to be as favourably held as child could be, and his dissolution took place in less than 5 Hours from that time. An inflammation in the lungs carried him off thus suddenly. You must remember him well; he was our second Son (6 years and a half old), and I recollect well made one of the Party that fine afternoon when we all drank tea together with Dr. Bell in his garden. This sudden blow, coming when we were just beginning to recover from one equally sudden, has overwhelmed us. Last summer we lost a sweet little Girl, 4 years old, and Brother and Sister now rest side [by side] in Grasmere Churchyard where we hope that our dust will one day mingle with theirs. If at some future time I can force my mind to the occupation which was thus lamentably interrupted, as I trust I shall be able to do, then I will again have recourse to your kindness in this Concern. We find it absolutely necessary to quit a Residence which forces upon us at every moment so many memorials of the happy but short lives of our departed Innocents, and we have taken the House called Rydale Mount, lately the Property of Mr. North and occupied [by] him, but now belonging to Lady Le Fleming. We shall be pleased to see you there; you know that the House is favourably situated.

[1] See L. 274, p. 67 above.

It gives me much satisfaction to learn that your time has passed so agreeably in Scotland; may sorrow that is perpetually travelling about the world be long in finding you! I am glad that Sharp is in expectation of returning to Parliament; if you see him, remember me affectionately to him, and be so good as to communicate to him our loss. I am obliged to Miss Rogers for her remembrance of me; pray present my regards to her in return. Mrs. W., my Sister, and Miss Hutchinson join in kind remembrances to you,

And believe me, my dear sir, faithfully yours,

W. Wordsworth

P.S. You make no mention of the Volume of your Poems which you promised. I am disappointed at this. What you say of W. Scott reminds me of an Epigram something like the following—

Tom writes his Verses with huge speed,
  Faster than Printer's Boy can set 'en,
Faster far than we can read,
  And only not so fast as we forget 'en.

Mrs. W., poor Woman! who sits by me, says, with a kind of sorrowful smile—this is spite, for you know that Mr. Scott's verses are the delight of the Times, and that thousands can repeat scores of pages.

277. D. W. to ELIZABETH THRELKELD and JANE MARSHALL

Address: Miss Threlkeld, Saville Row, Halifax, Yorkshire.
Endorsed: Account of the death of Thomas, 2nd Son of W. Wordsworth, 1813.
MS. WL.
K (—). *MY ii. 473, p. 541.*

Grasmere Jan[y] 19th 1813

My dear Elizabeth,

No doubt you have heard the sad particulars of our last affliction, the Death of our Darling Thomas, within six months after the equally sudden Death of his Sister. You remember him a lovely Baby[1] with a heavenly sweetness in his countenance which he preserved to the last, an innocence as pure as at the day of his Birth. He took the measles when I was at Watermillock, and suffered as

[1] Elizabeth T. had seen Thomas when the Wordsworths paid a visit to Halifax after leaving Coleorton in the summer of 1807. Thomas was then a year old.

little in the disorder as any child could do, and at eleven o'clock on the morning of the day upon which he died the medical attendant saw him, and pronounced him going on perfectly well. Half an hour afterwards he was seized with an Inflammation upon the Lungs which carried him off in five hours. Oh my dear Friends, judge of the agony of my grief when I met my Brother at Threlkeld the following morning in my way home, and he told me that that most beloved child was taken from us for ever. It had been my intention to go to Keswick for a few days; but of course the Coach went on without me, and when I was able to think about going home we were on the point of sending for a Chaise when we were told that a Grasmere Man was going immediately to Grasmere with a Cart; so in that Cart I laid myself down and was conveyed to the house of mourning. My dear Sister received me with fortitude and composure. She was indeed a comforter; but I am sorry to say—*that first effort* being passed, and the anxiety over for the three remaining Children who have since had the measles, her spirits are very weak and she is so miserably thin—worn down, as I may say, that it is quite melancholy to look upon her. Yet I trust she does not repine at the decrees of Providence. I trust we all are submitted to them, but it has been a hard trial—for Thomas was of all the Children that one who caused us the least of pain, and who gave us the purest of delights. He was affectionate, sweet-tempered, ardent in the pursuit of learning, invariably doing his duty without effort or interference on the part of others—and above all had a simplicity which was his own, an infantine innocence, which I now believe marked him as not of this world; but chosen by God himself—to augment the number of blessed Spirits. Could we but have opened our eyes to receive that warning we might while he was lent unto us have better profited from the light of his happy Countenance, and his most innocent simplicity. But Oh! dear Child, never never shall I forget thee, and I hope I shall hereafter find healing and comfort in the Remembrance. I did not intend to distress you; I did not mean to dwell upon our unutterable loss; and I will not speak of it again. He is happier than we can make him, and though I cannot yet bear to visit his grave, as I used to do his little Sister's even from the first week of her Interment, I trust I may yet find comfort there, being admonished by the Text of Scripture which is engraven upon her Tomb-stone—'Suffer the little Children to come unto me and forbid them not; for of such is the Kingdom of God'.

I requested Miss Pollard[1] to inform my Aunt of our Loss, and I

[1] Sister of Jane Marshall. 'My Aunt' is Mrs. Rawson.

wrote to my Aunt myself about a week after directing to the Post-office Bath. I think she must have received my letter, therefore I am uneasy that I have not heard from her, fearing that she is unable to write on account of Mr. Rawson's having had a relapse. Pray, when you write to her, if she be not returned to Halifax, tell her that I have been very uneasy at not hearing from her; and in the mean time, my dear Elizabeth, pray write to me and tell me how Mr. Rawson's health goes on, and all other Particulars respecting Mrs. R., your Mother, the Fergusons, and all my Halifax Friends.

I ought to write to Mrs. Marshall; but I do not feel myself in spirits to write a long letter, and a short one would be of little value, therefore I must beg that you and she will let this letter serve for both of you; and I am sure you will have the goodness to re-direct it, and send it to New Grange.—John Dorothy and William have all had the measles—they did not sicken till a week after their Brother's death. John and William were both very ill—John had the disorder worse a hundred times, to all appearance than Thomas—and William after the measles were gone, caught cold and had an attack of spasmodic croup. Thank God they are all well now.

You will be glad to hear that we are going to remove from the Parsonage House, a place which is so very melancholy to us now that we resolved immediately to look out for another house, and we have got the promise of the pleasantest residence in this neighbourhood. The house is in perfect repair, comfortable and convenient, and is in the very situation which in the happiest of our days we chose as the most delightful in the country. We have some hopes of entering upon it before May-day (the regular term) as the present occupant talks of removing in March. — —

I have had a most kind letter from Miss Pollard, which brought me a very agreeable account of the two dear Children left at Watermillock, I hope they will escape the measles, for I should have many fears for Ellen. Yet the Race is not to the Swift nor the Battle to the strong. *She* perhaps might get over it better than a stronger Child. She is the same age as our Thomas; and for that reason when at Watermillock I looked at her with a more tender interest, little thinking that the Child whom she reminded me of was so soon to be taken from us for ever. She is a very sweet Girl.—I spent a happy time at Watermillock; but it is a time which I cannot now look back upon without sadness. — —

It gives m[e] the greatest pleasure to hear of your Mother's hea[lth] and strength, blessings which, at her time of life, cannot be sufficiently prized. I wish I may hear that my fears for our good Friend Mr. Rawson are unfounded.

Give my kind Love to all my Cousins. I congratuate Mrs. Sutcliffe upon the Birth of her Daughter. They will, I am sure sympathize with us in our affliction. Have you heard from America lately, and what sort of Tidings? In short; tell me every thing; and forgive this melancholy letter. Perhaps when I write again I may be able to speak of other matters. God bless you my dear Friend, may you and your Mother yet enjoy many years of peace and happiness together. My Brother and Sister beg their kind Love, and Miss Hutchinson—who has been a sharer with us in the sorrows of the last year. Believe me your affect^e^

D. Wordsworth

I will say one word to Mrs. Marshall on the other side.

My dear Jane,

I do not ask your forgiveness for sending you a letter not addressed to yourself. I have not the spirits to take up the pen again at this time—but write to me and I promise you shall hear from me again very soon, and do not be uneasy about me. I walk daily and strive against sadness, but I cannot conceal from you that this is a hard trial—the hardest I have ever had except when my Brother John died—but God himself knows that he hath worse in store for us. Give my love to your Husband, and the children big, and little—I love them all, though I mention the names of none. I shall write to your Sister in a few days. God bless you. Believe me ever your affect^n^,

D. W.

278. W. W. to BASIL MONTAGU[1]

Address: Basil Montagu, Esqre, Lincoln's Inn, London .
Postmark: [Jan] 22 [181]3. *Stamp*: Kendal Penny Post.
MS. Cornell.
Hitherto unpublished.

[about 19 Jan. 1813]

My dear Montagu,

The Person who has the Money to advance is a Miss Weir of Appleby[2]—a particular friend of our's. She has for some time taught

[1] The letter is in the handwriting of M. W. until the account of Thomas, when W. takes over.

[2] See L. 87, pt. i, p. 170, n. 4.

a Boarding-School and has saved £500 which with a little addition which she hopes to make in a few years, is to be the support of her declining life—so that while the smallness of the sum renders annuity interest more desirable for her than the common rate of 5 per cent, it is evident that security is not only desireable, but indispensible. Now if it were an affair of my own I should not scruple to act upon an assurance from you in general terms that the proposed security was unobjectionable but in the present case I cannot take upon me [to] act without the power of laying before Miss W. materials upon which she may exercise her own judgment—therefore I must thank you to let me know 1st What sum she will annually receive by way of interest for this £200? [*sic*] 2dly What is the situation of the Borrower, and what is the Nature of the Security offered?—By the bye in one of your former Letters you stated that 'you would by no means entrust Money to a Person in Trade.' When you have answered these questions will [you] be so good as give your opinion as a friend and a Lawyer whether it is desireable for one in Miss Weir's situation to employ her Money in this manner—that is, whether the risks, and impediments in the way of regular payments do not too frequently occur to render such things eligible etc. [An] answer to this question as far as relates to the £200 is indeed involved in your last letter now before me—for you say 'I may rely upon its being safe.'

Algernon[1] is now staying with us along with Miss Jameson[2]—he looks and is well and behaves very well. It is impossible that Mrs Ross[3] can think any slight put upon her by your removal of Algernon with such views—but I think you had better communicate your intentions yourself—it would be more kind and respectful to do so. I shall with great pleasure explain your motives at length after you have broken the matter to her.

You say you should like to *assist* in sending Robert to College—Now Mrs Ross has no resources either at present or in expectancy to serve as a ground work for any thing of this kind.[4] There are Scholarships and Exhibitions to be procured by interest, which if one of these could be obtained would perhaps render it possible to do so great a service to a most deserving Young Man—But your knowledge of College arrangements and of meeting and reducing the expense of a College education is much superior to mine and to that I refer you for determining how far such a plan is feasible.

[1] See L. 190, pt. i, p. 402 n.
[2] For the Jamesons, see L. 156, pt. i, p. 331, n. 1.
[3] See L. 265 above.
[4] About a dozen words erased after 'kind'.

I have a slight favour to ask of you. Algernon is in possession of a translation of Don Quixote[1] which professes in the Title Page to be printed Verbatim from the Translation of 1616. I wish you would request him to turn this over to me in exchange for one more recent—which I would procure for him. The Old Trans. would be prized by me and one more recently executed would at Algernon's time of life be full as eligible for him.

We continue to be oppressed with sorrow which we endeavour to lighten as much as we can—The Boy whom we have lost was the pride and darling of the House—as sweet and faultless a child as ever breathed. Mary and Dorothy and Sara all look poorly; but I cannot say, thank heaven, that they have any illness. We shall quit this House for Rydale Mount; we have too many distressful Memorials here to be justified in remaining when we have the liberty of moving. I hope we shall be something less sad when we get away from the heavyness of this Dwelling in which we have been so pitiably smitten by the hand of providence. I cannot think of quitting home. I hope we shall see you and Mrs Montague at Rydale Mount. God bless you both—affectionate love from all here.

Your faithful friend
W Wordsworth.

279. D. W. to JANE MARSHALL

Address: Mrs. Marshall, New Grange, Leeds.
Endorsed: 1813, 24 Jan. After the death of Thomas Wordsworth 2 months before going to Rydal Mount.
MS. WL.
K (—). *MY* 474, *p.* 545.

Sunday 24th Jan. [1813]

My dear Friend,

I received your letter about two hours ago along with one from our dear Friend Mrs. Rawson, and I hasten to thank you for your kindness in writing to me, and in thinking so much about us. I hope you will have received, before this reaches you, a letter which I addressed to Elizabeth Threlkeld a few days ago; and which I desired her to forward to you, for I felt myself unequal to the task of writing a second long letter, and a short one *to you* would neither have satisfied you nor myself. Forgive me, my dear Friend, for having been so long silent. My spirits have at times been weak and

[1] See further L. 294 below.

I shrank from the thoughts of writing, persuading myself that to-morrow or the next day I should be more fit for it. But do not be uneasy about me, I am very well in my health, and I go on as usual with my daily pursuits; and I trust I do not *repine* at the loss of that beloved Child, who is returned to that Heaven from whence he so lately came, as pure a Spirit as ever was received into those holy regions.

Untainted he remained in this world—and is now happy—and gone but a few years before us—so I feel—so I think of him; yet my tears will flow—I cannot help it. The image of him, his very self, is so vivid in my mind—it is with me like a perpetual presence; and at certain moments the anguish of those tender recollections is more than I can bear—followed by that one thought—'I shall never see him more'! You know how I loved him when he was alive—how fondly I prized his promising virtues. But my dear Friend, I want not to distress you; yet I write as if I did—no it is not so—my heart is full of the sweet image of him whom I shall see no more; and it is yet too soon for me to think of what he was in this world without *anguish*. At times, when I muse on a future life and on his blessedness in another world, I lose those thoughts of anguish; the child becomes spiritualized to my mind. I wish I could have such musings more frequently—and longer; but alas! the image of the Boy disturbs me—and I weep again. Time, I know, will soften this, but as long as I have breath and life, thy Grave beloved Child! will be remembered by me with pensive sadness. — —

I have been weeping a torrent of tears my dear Jane, and I am better—forgive me—and do not try to reason me out of this indulgence of grief—it does me good—for it must have its course—and when I write to you, the tender Mother of ten Children, and the Companion of my youth, the sorrow comes fresh upon me. To another I should have written calmly, and shall be able to do so to you again.—My poor Sister I have spoken of at large in my letter to Elizabeth. I think she has looked rather better these two days.—My Brother is grown very thin, and at times I think he looks ten years older since the death of Thomas — — I hope we shall not remain more than two months or 10 weeks longer in this house, and you must come and see us when we get to the other. It is a place that ten years ago I should have almost danced with Joy if I could have dreamed it would ever be ours.

My dear Jane you tell me you have been ill and do not say what has been your disorder. Pray take care of yourself. I am much hurt to hear of it. — — It is a great pleasure to me that all the Children are so well—and that they are so comfortable at Watermillock. I often think of sweet Ellen, and innocent Julia.

Give our kind love to Mr. Marshall with many thanks for his kindness to us. I am called off and must conclude directly or I shall lose a post.

God bless you—do write soon again, and tell me more about yourself.

Yours evermore
D. W.

Remember me to Miss Brown. You can hardly imagine how useful your apples have been to us.

I walk every day—work—read etc. etc.

280. D. W. to MARY HUTCHINSON (*née* MONKHOUSE)

Address: Mrs. Hutchinson, Hindwell, near New Radnor.
Stamp: Kendal Penny Post.
MS. WL.
MY ii. 475, p. 547.

Febry 1st 1813.

My dear Mary.

Little did I think when I parted from you all that it would be such a hard task to resolve to write to you. Very soon after you left us, William, Mary and Dorothy went to Keswick, and the morning after their return I set off on my long-promised visit to Watermillock—and never more did I see that blessed Darling alive. He slept that night with Willy and me by his own particular desire—and Oh! how well I recollect feeling him in my arms after Willy had left us, and how sweetly he asked me if he might get up; and came to me to be dressed. The last view I had of him was in the Church-yard on his way to school. His Father met me at Threlkeld and there he told me the sad event—I came home in a cart—It was on the Wednesday, and on the Saturday we followed him to his grave—Oh Mary! why do I repeat this dismal story? Because you loved his innocent spirit—Because you can measure my affliction, and it fills my heart when I talk to you, and I cannot write till I have disburthened myself of what was a heavy load when I took the pen in my hand. The ways of Providence are inscrutable. That child was taken from us who never disturbed our minds with one wayward inclination—Right forward did he tread the path of duty—and we looked at him with the fondest hopes, that in after years he would be our pride and comfort as he was then a source of tender delight. But he was destined for a better world; that divine sweetness in his countenance marked him out as a chosen Spirit, and if we could but have seen it we might have known that he was not intended for *us*. Therefore let us rather thank God for having so long lent to us this Blessing, than repine that he is taken away; for the gain is his—he is happier than we could have made him, and it is but for ourselves that we grieve.—I have been obliged to stop; for alas! I am very weak at times though I trust I am resigned to this affliction, and am sensible that far heavier might have fallen upon us, and that it is [rather] our duty to be thankful for what is left than to shed unavailing tears for the Departed; and I will distress you no longer; I am lighter hearted now myself, and I bless God for his Goodness in having showered so many gracious Gifts upon that child whom we once possessed, and whose sweet image only Death, which will again join us to him can remove from us. His poor Mother supported herself and all of us at first like a guardian Angel: but her spirits sank very low when the anxiety was over and she returned to this melancholy place; and lately she has been very poorly; but Mr. Scambler has given her some tonic medicines which (with wine which she now drinks) we hope will be of use to her. The medicines agree with her, and she has twice ridden out upon Sara's pony. Mr. Scambler wishes her to be in the open air as much as possible; but lately the weather has been too stormy except on a chance day now and then. She is thinner than ever, and has that same black complexion which is so dismal with her thin cheeks. Dear Sara has been poorly but she is better now. It will however be better for her and for all of us when we are removed to another house, though I agree with you that the distance to which we are going is not perhaps enough for Mary; yet I am by no means sure of this. It is having those objects continually present in which the Children used to delight—above all the school and the Church-yard which is the greatest evil. At Rydale we shall be removed from these, while at the same time many new and pleasing objects will be constantly before us. It is true that when she comes to Church, on a Sunday, it will be like coming to the home of the dead Children; but on the other hand to be entirely removed from them would be a source of lingering regret, and we all wish that our Bodies may lie beside theirs. Do not imagine from this, my dear Mary, that, if my brother and sister would have been likely to consent to it, I should have opposed our removing into your neighbourhood. The motives to such removal are very strong, and if I thought it would conduce to Mary's benefit (which I am sure it would if she would consent to it) I should be the last person to utter an objection, whatever might be my pangs at leaving this country, where I have spent so many happy days. The Norths do not intend to go to Ambleside till the end of April, therefore we shall not enter the house till May-Day. I hope you have written to your Brother Tom about the carpet, as we should like to have it when we go to Rydale, that we may get ourselves settled and all upholstery work done at once. We expect that Miss Green will get the new house at Rydale, as there is no demur except a trifling one on the score of Rent which I have no doubt will be settled by the Landlord's yielding to her terms. I am glad on Mary's account, as I think a little of Miss Green's company now and then will be of use to her. Poor Mrs. King[1] departed on Sunday Fortnight. Mr. King and *Mr. Wilcock* accompanied her to Kendal, and the next day got down together—I suppose in triumph. She writes to us that her journey was as pleasant as could be expected under such circumstances; and says that she hopes to be happier than she has been when she is used to the change. Mr. King is removed to Patterdale, and *the plate and linen* are gone thither. If I had been in Mrs. King's place my pride would never have suffered this—I would have taken those Badges of Consequence with me, and have let them provide for themselves. Mr. Astley is in treaty for the house, and Mr. Crump's new house is thrown upon his hands; for Mr. Humphrey and he have disagreed upon the Terms and Mr. H. is going to quit Grasmere, so there will be three houses to let, the parsonage, the Taylor's Cottage, and the Wyke Cottage. I think we have no other news except that Peggy Ashburner has lost a fat pig ready for the knife—choked with paste and poor Aggy's mismanagement is the cause. Peggy is as usual—very ill one day—and the next as lively as if she had taken up a new lease of life. We like Mr. Poolley[3] exceedingly—he seems to be very conscientious both in the discharge of his office as minister and Schoolmaster. He is grown quite fond of teaching; and the progress that was made before our little Darling's death was very great; and I have no doubt has made no stop since, from what I gather from Mr. Poolley's conversation; but I have not had the

[1] For the unhappy married life of the Kings of the Hollens, Grasmere, see De Quincey's account, Masson, ii, pp. 425–31.

[2] A local land-agent and auctioneer.

[3] The schoolmaster and curate at Grasmere who had succeeded Mr. Bamford. See L. 237, p. 7, n. 5 above.

courage to enter the school again. John is not to go to Mr. Dawes till we have removed—and I think that his improvement has been greater under Mr. Poolley; but with his shy disposition it is desirable he should associate with Boys his equal in Rank. He now goes to Mr. de Quincey for a *nominal hour* every day to learn Latin upon a plan of Mr. de Quincey's own 'by which a Boy of the most moderate abilities may be made a good latin scholar in six weeks!!!' This said nominal hour now generally is included in the space of twenty minutes; either the scholar learns with such uncommon rapidity that more time is unnecessary, or the Master tires. Which of these conjectures is the more probable I leave you to guess. At present Sara teaches Dorothy Latin and if she were steady she would get on rapidly, for she is as quick as lightning. She goes to Mr. Poolley to learn to write. Willy is a sweet creature—the greatest Gossip—for he knows all people and all the news, and the greatest chatterer you ever saw—Sweet he is—but Oh! how different from Tom! I used, when Tom was alive to see a likeness in their faces, but now I never see it (and this often distresses me for I can see no likeness in any of them to Him)—I suppose the reason of it is this, that the *Sentiment* of Thomas's face continually abides in my recollections, and that same sentiment (whatever resemblance there may be in the features) does not exist in any of their countenances.—Willy is now beside me—'What must I say to your Godmother?' 'Bring me some Bide cake Tell her!' He has taken up a book, and there he reads fragments of a hundred little songs—about Cock-Robin, pussy cat and all sorts of things. He is very entertaining; but one half of the heart is sad while the other laughs at his strange fancies.—I suppose Joanna will have left you before this letter reaches you, but when you write to her pray tell her that we have had a letter from Mr Johnson, who is in good health and quite satisfied with his situation, and I suppose his *prospects*. The Bishop of Hereford[1] has done him the honour to call upon him and sit an hour, and has given him the privilege of having his letters sent under cover to him. I think it would be a nice thing for Joanna and him[2] if the Bishop would give him a good Herefordshire living; but he is in favour with all the Bishops, and no matter if he should be fixed in another Diocese. I hope he will have the courage to call upon her—I have told him where she is to be found

[1] John Luxmoore (1756–1830) was Bishop of Hereford from 1808 to 1815, when he became Bishop of St. Asaph.

[2] This sounds as though it was expected that Mr. Johnson and Joanna might marry.

in London. We were very sorry to hear of the Death of little Henry's Brother; and we trust that Joanna did not venture to go to Mr. Robinson's unless you heard that the disease was stopped in their family.—I think I have nothing more to tell you about our own concerns except that we are going to keep a Lad and one Maid at Rydale, for the sake of the garden; instead of two maids, and Fanny will continue with us. Molly is probably going to be Mrs Southey's nurse. Mary Dawson talks in private to us of leaving Mr. de Quincey—What a prize she would be to your brother John as housekeeper! She is tired of Mr de Q's meanness and greediness.—My dear Mary with what pleasure did I once think of setting forward to see you in May! but you know that I cannot now turn my mind from home—indeed I feel at present as if it were impossible—I feel as if I should be for ever haunted by the fear of something dismal happening, if I were at a distance—I only walked over the mountains—fifteen miles—and what a change awaited me at my return—and poor Mary. Only three days before Catharine's death I had written such an account of her, as was calculated to make her more fearless and secure than she had been for years before. Give my kindest love to Tom—tell him that I used to talk of Powys Castle and all the places that we were to see by the Road and to think of the joy I should have at meeting him and seeing you all at Hindwell. It often grieves me to think I have never been there; but I cannot cannot yet bring my mind to look forward to a time for going. God bless you all my dear good Friends—Long may you be happy together and long may it be before you are visited with afflictions like that which we have been suffering under! Give my love to your Aunt and to John. Dorothy often asks about her Godmother. Do accept this melancholy letter in good part—I thought I had had more to tell you or I think I should hardly have taken the office from Sara, who has many more subjects to write upon in connexion with Wales than I have; but my heart has long yearned to tell you, my dear Mary that I love you tenderly and shall ever think of the days that Mary *Monkhouse* spent here—*Thomas's* God-mother. May God bless all your doings, and may you be as happy in this world as you deserve to be.—Much however as I wished to utter my affectionate sentiments towards you, I should not now have taken the pen if I had not fancied myself better provided with ordinary matters to talk about. Believe me ever your affectionate Friend D Wordsworth.

We had a letter from Mrs. Clarkson last night. She was in London—but going back to Bury in a week or two—her health and spirits variable—Her Sister well—Coleridge's play[1] has been completely successful—Mrs Coleridge is much elated as you may guess—Again God bless you.

I fear you cannot read this scrawl.

Do not think that I require an answer addressed to *me*, though at all times I should be glad to hear from you but it is the same thing when you write to Sara.

281. D. W. to R. W.

Address: Richard Wordsworth Esqr, Staple Inn, London.
Endorsed: 16 Feb. 1813. *Postmark*: Feb 19 1813. *Stamp*: Kendal Penny Post.
MS. WL.
MY ii. 476, p. 552.

16 Febry 1813.

My dear Brother,

I thank you for your kind Letter, which I was very glad to receive. I hope you have seen Wm Crackanthorp[2] and are likely to bring matters to a conclusion with him, and I trust you will be able to come over Kirkstone to see us in the Spring, and do not fail to bring our accounts with you for we wish very much for an accurate Statement of what we are entitled to.

I drew upon you yesterday for £50 in favour of Mr Henry Thompson, at one Month—and today I have sent an Order (I do not know that it is quite regular) to Messrs. Twining for 16£–3s–6d, which we owe them. They will present the Paper to you; and be so good as to pay that Sum to them.

We have desired them hence-forward to take their account to you. We have just ordered a fresh supply of Tea, and the Bill for that Tea will probably be presented to you about this time next year; I will however, the first time I write after we have received the Tea, inform you of the amount of the Debt, to prevent any mistake or delay when it is demanded.

Mary continues to be but poorly, and I think nothing will have power to overcome her melancholy while we remain here.

[1] *Remorse*, a recast of *Osorio*, see L. 262, p. 48, n. 2 above The early version, *Osorio*, had been written at Nether Stowey in 1797 and rejected for theatrical production at that time.

[2] William Crackanthorpe (1790–1888) was the son of the Wordsworths' uncle, Christopher Crackanthorpe (*née* Cookson) (1745–99), who had been the guardian of the Wordsworths after their father's death, 1783. See L. 275 above.

I am very glad, my dear Brother, that your health is so much improved. You must not relax in your care of yourself; yet I would fain hope that a journey over Kirkstone w[oul]d not hurt you.

William and Mary send their kind love—Believe me ever your affecte Sister

Dorothy Wordsworth

282. W. W. to LORD LONSDALE

MS. Lonsdale MSS., Record Office, The Castle, Carlisle.
Hitherto unpublished.

Grasmere
Saturday March 6th 1813

My Lord,

Your Lordship's most obliging letter of the 28th Febry (enclosing Mr Wilkin's, which I have the honor to return) did not reach me, I am sorry to say, till this morning. I shall be happy, through your Lordship's patronage, to become successor to Mr Wilkin in his present office,[1] under such engagement for his benefit as your Lordship shall think proper. I need hardly say, my Lord, that I have been little accustomed to the management of Accounts; the assistance of one with more practice in that way will therefore be necessary to me;[2] but my own superintendance shall be carefully given.

I am much obliged to your Lordship for your kind enquiries after the state of my family, and my own health and spirits. I cannot say that we are ill, nor can I conceal from myself that we are a good deal shattered (Mrs Wordsworth especially) by our afflictions.

With the warmest gratitude to your Lordship for the manifold marks of regard with which you have distinguished me; and for this last in particular, I have the honor to be

my Lord,
your Lordship's
most faithful servnt
W. Wordsworth

P.S. I have this moment learn'd upon enquiry at Ambleside, that my not receiving your Lordship's letter duly is owing to the neglect of

[1] i.e. the Distributorship of Stamps for Westmorland and the Penrith district of Cumberland.

[2] Wordsworth appointed John Carter as his clerk, who remained in the service of the family until his death in 1856.

the Person to whom the Postmaster entrusted it. I very much regret this.

283. D. W. to ROBERT FOSTER[1]

Address: Mr Robert Foster, Hebblethwaite Hall, near Sedbergh (*readdressed to* Newcastle on Tyne).
MS. Mrs. Spence Clepham.
Hitherto unpublished.

Grasmere, March 11th [1813]

My dear Sir,

I know that I need not beg you to excuse me for troubling you with a letter of inquiries, therefore I will come to the point at once.

A Friend of ours,[2] who has a Son, sixteen years of age, whom he wishes to place under the care of a competent Instructor, for the sake of learning Mathematics, etc., has requested me to inquire whether Mr Peacock[3] continues to take pupils, what number of pupils he has, and whether they are boarded in his own house. At the same time may I be allowed to ask of you as a Friend, whether you think from what you know of Mr Peacock's habits and character and mode of instruction, that the situation would be an eligible one? The Boy is likely to have a considerable Fortune; but, though he is the eldest son, as there is a large Family, he will probably he brought up to one of the professions, and though mathematical studies are the main object at present, his Father would wish him to go on with the Classics, etc.

It is very long since we have had the pleasure of seeing you, therefore I am afraid you have given up your accustomed visits to this country.

Since you were here we have had two heavy afflictions. In the month of June, when my Brother and Sister were at a great distance from home, their youngest Daughter died suddenly in convulsions,

[1] The Wordsworths first met Robert Forster (or Foster) in 1804. See *EY* 235, p. 515. See also L. 112, pt. i, p. 232, and the description of him given by Southey to Richard Duppa, 23 Feb. 1806: '. . . Oh! W. sent me a man the other day, who was worth seeing; he looked loke a 1st assassin in Macbeth as to his costume—but he was a rare man. He had been a lieutenant in the Navy; was scholar enough to quote Virgil aptly; had turned Quaker or semi-Quaker, and was now a dealer in wool somewhere about 20 miles off. He has seen much, and thought much; his head was well stored, and his heart in the right place . . .'

[2] Perhaps Mr. John Marshall of Leeds.

[3] Daniel Mitford Peacock, Fellow of Trinity, Cambridge, a Senior Wrangler, from 1798 to 1840 Vicar of Sedbergh.

and on the first of December their Second Son, as hopeful a Boy as ever blessed a house, died as suddenly of an inflamation on the lungs, which seized him after he was supposed to have passed the height of the Fever of the Measles. Three days after that poor Darling was buried, the three remaining Children sickened, and the eldest and youngest were very severely held in the measles, but thank God! their lives were spared, and they are now in perfect health.

My poor Sister has been greatly shattered by these afflictions and she is but in delicate health. We are going to leave the Parsonage at May-day and my Brother has taken a house at Rydale, called Rydale Mount where you must seek us out, and take your bed with us the next time you come into this part of the country, and I wish it may be soon, for it always gives us all great satisfaction to see you.

My brother and Sister and Miss Hutchinson beg their kind Remembrances,

I am, dear Sir,
Your sincere Friend
Dorothy Wordsworth

I shall be much obliged to you if you will favour me with an answer as soon as convenient.

Is Mr Peacock the Master of the *Grammar* School at Sedbergh?

284. D. W. to R. W.

Address: Richard Wordsworth Esqre, Staple Inn, London.
Postmark: 12 o'clock MR 15 1813. *Endorsed*: 'Rec' the 15 March 1813. *Stamp*: Two Py Post unpaid Lombard Street.
MY ii. 477, p. 553.

[about 12 March 1813]

My dear Brother,

Enclosed is a letter which I beg you will send to Messrs. Twining. It is an Order for Tea for a Friend of ours, Mr Cookson, of Kendal, who has begged me to discharge the enclosed account for [him]. I have therefore sent an order upon you for 14£–12s–6– which be so good as to answer when Messrs Twining send it to you, and I enclose the Bill for which pray procure a Receipt, and bring it with you when you come into the North.

I am your affect^e^ Sister
D Wordsworth.

285. W. W. to LORD LONSDALE

MS. Lonsdale MSS., Record Office, The Castle, Carlisle.
Hitherto unpublished.

Grasmere
March 14th 1813

My Lord,

I have just received the letter of the 10 Inst, with which your Lordship has honoured me; and I beg you will accept my sincere thanks for the communications therein contained. Whatever terms of allowance might have been proposed, under the sanction of your Lordship's approbation, for the benefit of Mr Wilkin,[1] it would have been clearly my duty and my pleasure to have acceded to; but I may be permitted to say that, the circumstances considered, the sum of £100 per Ann: specified by Mr Wilkin appears to me to be very moderate.

Upon the confirmation of the appointment to which I have the honour of being recommended by your Lordship, I shall be ready to take such steps as may be necessary to fit me for the discharge of the Office. In the meantime I have the honour to be,

with the most grateful sense of the kindness conferred upon me
my Lord
your Lordship's
most faithful servant
Wm Wordsworth

P.S. I have the honour to return Mr Wilkin's letter to your Lordship.

286. D. W. to JOSIAH WEDGWOOD

Endorsed: Miss Wordsworth, 30 March 1813.
MS. Wedgwood Museum, Barlaston.
Hitherto unpublished.

Grasmere, 30th March–1813

Dear Sir,

Not knowing the Firm of the House of Wedgwood I take the liberty of addressing you to request that you will have the goodness to desire that the articles which I shall set down on the other side of

[1] See L. 282 above. There being no pensions system, Wordsworth was obliged to pay Mr. Wilkin a proportion of the income for the rest of the latter's life.

the paper may be forwarded as speedily as possible to[1] Kendal. You will know best, by what mode of conveyance the Package should be sent.

I cannot close my letter without saying a word or two of the state of our Family. We have within the last nine months suffered great affliction, in the sudden death of two of my Brother's Children. He has now only three remaining. My Brother is in good health, and begs to be respectfully remembered to you. He has taken a house at Rydale, two miles distant from our present Residence, whither we are going to remove.

With best wishes to yourself and Family, I am, dear Sir,

Yours sincerely
Dorothy Wordsworth

On second thoughts we determine that it is better to have the Hamper directed to a Friend at Kendal, who will forward it to my Brother.

287. D. W. to CATHERINE CLARKSON

Address: to Mrs. Clarkson, Bury St. Edmonds, Suffolk.
Stamp: Kendal Penny Post. *Endorsed*: April 6, 1813.
MS. British Museum.
K (—). *MY ii.* 178.

Thursday April 6th [1813]

Your letter, my dearest Friend, reached us last night, I am grateful for an unexpected pleasure, and my grateful feelings impel me to write immediately. You have been better than you are wont in writing again so soon. Do not think that under this praise is implied a censure, I too well know how many cheerless bodily feelings you have to struggle with to wonder, or to lament selfishly that your letters are sometimes slow in coming. On the whole you give a good account of your health, and there is comfort in the hope, though distant, of seeing you next year; and though with all hopes fear is linked in my mind in a way unknown before, I shall often turn to the idea of our meeting. God grant that *you* may live many years and that *we* may be able to enjoy as we ought to do the Blessings which Providence yet allows us to possess—and Oh! may we all if further afflictions are speedily to visit us—may we all be

[1] D. W. here wrote first: 'Rydale Mount near', and then erased it.

enabled to see in them the hand of mercy, and to trust that our sufferings in this world are given to us in order that we may be perfected in a better world! Truly, as you feelingly speak in your last letter, all other consolations are unstable and weak. But this leads me to the green graves in the corner of our Church-Yard and let that ground be peaceful! I feel now that my heart is going to struggle with unbefitting sorrow—while I talk of resignation—but I trust the time will come when all the tears I shed shall be tears of hope, and quiet tenderness.—Yet if you had known Thomas—if you had seen him—if you had felt the hopes which his innocent intelligent and eager—yet *most* innocent and heavenly countenance raised in our hearts many a time when we silently looked upon him—you would wonder that we have been able to bear the loss of him as well as we have borne it; but with an humbled spirit I must confess we have not been submitted as we ought to have been.

I have laid down the pen for some minutes, and I can write upon other matters less deeply interesting. Yet once more—blessings be on his grave—that turf upon which his pure feet so often have trod—Oh![1]

William left us this morning to go to Appleby to receive instruction from his predecessor in the Stamp Office, having received the confirmation of his appointment. Never man set off upon such an errand with less of the importance of office upon him—his grand consolation was, that he should find Sara there, and that they would be companions on the journey home. She had thought herself obliged to go to Appleby to assist Miss Weir in nursing one of her Brother John's daughters (the eldest of the second Brood). She had recovered from the Measles, caught cold, which took the shape of an Influenza then going about, and she was in imminent danger. Miss Weir never left her Bed-side for 8 days or nights. The account reached Sara when she was at Kendal assisting Miss Green to purchase some furniture for a house she has taken at Rydale, and Sara though the child was recovering, with her accustomed humanity offered to go to Miss Weir. If she had been at home we should not have suffered it, for though Sara's health is much better on the whole, she is ill able to struggle with sorrow or the fatigues of watching, and of sorrow she has had her share at home. William's going will however be a relief to her. The Income of the place is better than 400£ per annum. From this deduct the expense of a clerk who is to serve the double purposes of Clerk and Gardener. This morning Mary and I walked by William's side (who rode on

[1] The manuscript is here blotted with a tear stain.

Sara's pony) as far as Rydale, and on the way we met Miss Knott,[1] from whom we learnt a curious circumstance, namely that the same office of Distributor of Stamps for the County of Westmoreland was held forty years ago by her Grandfather in that very house whither we are going. Mr. Knott was succeeded by our relation[2] Mr Wilkin who has resigned on account of inability to conduct the business. This resignation would not have been necessary; but he had unfortunately entrusted the business to the management of a drunken man who neglected it. Old Mr Knott held the office many years after he was incapable of performing the duties himself; and, as Miss Knott informs us they were performed by his Servant, who waited at table &c &c &c—. It is impossible for me, unless you saw Lord Lonsdale's letters, to give you an idea of the delicacy of his conduct towards my Brother. We are all very thankful for the prospect of an entire release from care about spending money for any little luxuries that we may desire or providing against future wants for the children; but at first we hardly seemed to be glad—glad we were not—we hardly *thought* about the change.—I was with Mrs Lloyd and while I was talking with her it came into my mind that I had something to tell her; but what it was I could not recollect—and about half an hour after it came into my mind that it was about the place. You will rejoice to hear that dearest Mary is much better —she was very poorly after I wrote to you—her complaint was of the most weakening kind—for seven weeks! We began to think she might be with child; however tonic medicines and riding on horseback, whatever was the case, were likely to prove equally useful, and she grew better, and it has since been proved that she is not with child; and she is grown considerably stronger, and by the help of a quiet and resigned mind her spirits are better, much better than I expected they would have been by this time. Some have wished that she might have another Child; but I cannot join in this wish; for her anxiety would be so great in case of illness or weakness of the child, and of its death her sorrow so overwhelming that I think it is more to be desired, as far as we can foresee anything that it should not be so. After I wrote to you last I was vexed with myself for having spoken so ill-naturedly of the Norths; for we had occasion to have some communications with them respecting the house and they were very civil; but I do not now repent me of my malice; for I believe that their civility was only forced from them

[1] See L. 217, pt. i, p. 464, and n.

[2] De Selincourt suggests that 'our' should be 'her'. No relationship between the Wordsworths and Mr. Wilkin is known.

because they had no plea to behave in any other manner, and wanted the courage to be uncivil; for a few days after the Family was removed from the house; and when we had been informed by a person to whom Mr North had said it, that he had nothing left in the house but a few bottles, William wrote a note requesting Mr N's permission to enter upon the house; and giving his reasons in a very delicate manner, *hinting* plainly at the most important one, and we received an answer, couched in civil terms, to the following effect: that Mr N. would be happy to accommodate Mr W. as soon as he had got preparations made for the reception of at least nine cart-loads of goods which were yet in the house. Now these goods are the wine in his cellars, and he has bins to make for his wine at Ambleside. Would not anyone but himself have requested permission to keep the wine locked up in the cellars, and have given the free use of the house which he no longer wanted himself? It is three weeks or more since the house was empty, and we hear nothing further, so we shall not remove till May day. We are beginning to prepare—making curtains quilting bed-quilts (old fashioned work!) etc etc.

My dear friend, as to Coleridge[1] you have done all that can be done, and we are grieved that you have had so much uneasiness, and taken so much trouble about him. He will not let himself be served by others. Oh, that the day may ever come when he will serve himself! Then will his eyes be opened, and he will see clearly that we have loved him always, do still [love] him, and have ever loved—not measuring his deserts. I do not now wish him to come into the North; that is, I do not wish him to do it for the sake of any wish to gratify us. But if he should do it of himself I should be glad as the best sign that he was endeavouring to perform his duties. His conduct to you has been selfish and unfeeling in the extreme, which makes me hope no good of him at present, especially as I hear from all quarters so much of his confident announcement of plans for this Musical Drama, that comedy, the other essay. Let him doubt, and his powers will revive. Till then they must sleep. God bless him. He little knows with what tenderness we have lately thought of him, nor how entirely we are softened to all sense of injury. We have had no thoughts of him but such as ought to have made him lean upon us with confidential love, and fear not to confess his weaknesses. The boys come to us almost every week. Hartley is as odd as ever, and in the weak points of his character resembles his Father very much; but he is not prone to sensual indulgence—quite the contrary—and has not one expensive habit. Derwent is to

[1] See L. 273, p. 65, n. 2.

me a much more interesting Boy. He is very clever. I should wish him to be put in the way of some profession in which *scientific* knowledge would be useful; for his mind takes that turn. He is uncommonly acute and accurate. William will now be enabled to assist in sending Hartley to college;[1] but of course this must not be mentioned; for the best thing that can happen to his Father will be that he should suppose that the whole care of putting Hartley forward must fall upon himself. You have been long absent from your dear Tom. I hope you will think he has made good use of his time—God grant that he may be a blessing to you. Give my tenderest love to him and your Husband and Father. Remember me to Mrs. Kitchener. Do write soon, as soon as you are able. This is a beautiful day. You set forward on your journey to-morrow.

Yours evermore
D. W.

Do forgive my scrawling—You have Willy's pencil writing on the outside of my letter. It is well Mr Clarkson will not have the reading of this letter—he would make a pretty story out of it.

288. W. W. to LORD LONSDALE

MS. Lonsdale MSS., Record Office, The Castle, Carlisle.
Hitherto unpublished.

Grasmere April 7 1813

My Lord,

I have the honour to acknowledge the Receipt of the letter kindly transmitted to me by your Lordship, from which I learn that directions have been given for my appointment to the Office of Distributor of Stamps for the County of Westmoreland.

I beg permission to repeat in one word that I am truly grateful to your Lordship for placing me in a situation from which I trust that by the blessing of Providence I shall receive the most important benefits during the remainder of my life.

I have the honour to be

my Lord
your Lordship's
most obliged and faithful servnt
Wm Wordsworth

[1] See L. 320 below. Wordsworth was not ultimately obliged to contribute towards Hartley's support at Oxford, funds having been secured—largely through Wordsworth's means—elsewhere.

288a. W. W. to R. W.

Address: Richard Wordsworth Esqr, Sockbridge, Penrith.
Stamp: Keswick 298. *Endorsed*: April 1813.
MS. WL.
Hitherto unpublished.

Keswick Tuesday
Morng. [April 1813]

My dear Richard

Herewith I transmit to you a Copy of a Letter which I received by Sunday Nights Post, from the Stamp Off.—It relates to the Procurement of securities for the due execution of the Employment. Had you been at Sockbridge I should have come over immediately to consult you upon the subject; and did in fact yesterday proceed thus far on my way to Wigton[1] for the purpose, but as I could not have reached Wigton till this day, and then perhaps might have missed you I resolved to act without the benefit of your advice—Accordingly, determined by the urgent manner in which Lord L. has repeatedly request[ed] that I would resort to him for any assistance I might require I have applied to his Lordship on this occasion to become one of my sureties;[2] stating at the same time that if for general rules or particular reasons he should deem it inadvisable to do me this honour, that I doubted not but that among my Relations and Friends of my own Part I could procure the requested security. I have also applied to Sir G. Beaumont to become the other. And now wait their answers which I have begged may be addressed to me at Penrith, as I purpose to be at Sockbridge by Sunday at the latest. Should they decline I must look to your brotherly kindness, and to the goodwill of some other friend, and upon that point shall consult you—I return to Grasmere to-day; and remain

Your affectionate Brother
Wm Wordsworth

All pretty well at Home—I reached Dobson's at a quarter before nine and home by half past nine on the Tuesday morning. I must entreat that you would not leave Sockbridge about the time I mentioned except on the most urgent necessity; as I shall want your advice about many points relating to this business.

[1] A small town, about 12 miles west of Carlisle, whither R. W. had presumably gone on business.
[2] See L. 289 below.

[*The letter of W. Kapper, Secretary to the Stamp Office, asking W. W. to propose two sureties* 'who are to join with you in a Bond for the surety of £8,000 . . . and you are also required to execute a separate Bond in the Penalty of £15,000,' *is copied onto the bottom of the sheet.*]

289. W. W. to LORD LONSDALE

MS. Lonsdale MSS., Record Office, The Castle, Carlisle.
Hitherto unpublished.

Penrith
April 19th 1813

My Lord,

I beg leave to return my most sincere thanks for the high honour done me by your Lordship's compliance with the wish I presumed to express that you would become one of my Sureties for the due execution of the trust reposed in me as Distributor of Stamps for Westmoreland, etc.: By this day's Post, I have also received a letter from Sir George Beaumont signifying that with great pleasure he will join with your Lordship in the Bond required;[1] and I shall take the Liberty of mentioning your Lordship's name and that of Sir George Beaumont to the Commissioners of Stamps.

Owing the benefit of this appointment to your Lordship's most friendly patronage, I feel highly grateful in standing in it by the joint support of your Lordship and Sir George Beaumont.

I have the honour to be

with great respect
my Lord
your Lordship's
most obliged and most faithful servant
Wm Wordsworth

[1] The 'Distributer's [*sic*] Bond', with that of the sureties, Lord Lonsdale and Sir G. Beaumont, is among the papers at the Wordsworth Library, Grasmere. In it W. is appointed to be 'Head Distributer [*sic*] of Stamped Vellum, Parchment and Paper within and for the County of Westmorland and Part of the County of Cumberland.'

290. D. W. to RICHARD ADDISON

Address: Richard Addison Esq[re], Staple Inn, London.
Postmark: 3 May 1813. *Stamp*: Kendal Penny Post. *Endorsed*: 27 April 1813. 3 May 1813 Ans[d] R A.
MS. WL.
MY. ii. 479, p. 558.

Grasmere 27th April [1813]

Dear Sir,

Some time ago Miss Hutchinson sent a Box to her Sister Joanna in London, which contained (among other things which we have been informed were duly received) a letter addressed to my Brother Richard in which was enclosed a letter to Messrs Twining which I desired him to send to them, and I desired my Brother to pay to them the Sum of 14£–12s–6d[1] on account of Mrs Cookson of Kendal, upon their demand. My letter to the Twinings contained an Order for 40lb of Souchong Tea at 7/- 1 lb Pekoe Tea—and 1 lb of the best black tea to be sent to Mr Cookson; which Tea has never been received, therefore I conclude that my Brother has forgotten to forward the letter to Messrs Twining.

I shall be much obliged to you if the money has not been paid, (namely 14£–12s–6d) if you will have the goodness to send immediately to Devereux Court to pay it for *Mr. Cookson*, and pray place it to my account, and at the same time I wish you would order the tea which I have set down on the other side of the paper to be sent immediately by the Kendal Waggon to Mr Cookson, in case it is not already sent; and whether the money is paid or not be so good as to cause inquiries to be made respecting the Tea.[2]

When you see Mr Thomas Monkhouse be so good as to tell him that we hope soon to hear that he has purchased carpets for us. We shall remove to Rydale about the 12th of May.

Pray make my kind Remembrances to your Mother and Miss Hindson

I am, dear Sir
Yours respectfully
D. Wordsworth

[1] D. W. first wrote and then erased 'some odd shillings'. See L. 284 above.

[2] A note on the outside of the letter says, 'per waggon 12 Ap'—indicating that the tea had been dispatched that day.

291. W. W. to RICHARD ADDISON

Address: Rich[d] Addison Esq[re], Staple Inn, London.
Postmark: C My 4 1813. *Stamp*: Kendal Penny Post. *Endorsed*: 1 May 1813.
MS. WL.
MY ii. 480, p. 558.

Grasmere May 1st [1813]

Dear Sir,

I have this day drawn upon my Brother for £7—7 in favour of John Hanson Esq[re] (at sight) which draft you will have the goodness to honour.

I am Sir with best respects from my family to yourself and your friends respect[ly] yours

W. Wordsworth—

It may interest you to hear that I am appointed to the Office of Distributor of Stamps for Westmorl[d] etc.

292. D. W. to JANE MARSHALL

Address: Mrs Marshall, Watermillock, near Penrith.
Endorsed: 1813. Arrival at Rydal Mount.
MS. WL.
K (—). MY ii. 48, p. 559.

Rydale Mount, Thursday morning [2 May 1813].

My dear Friend,

When I tell you that we removed yesterday, you will not wonder that I write a short note. We are all well, though some of us, especially my Sister, jaded with our fatigues. The weather is delightful, and the place a paradise; but my inner thoughts *will* go back to Grasmere. I was the last person who left the House yesterday evening. It seemed as quiet as the grave; and the very church-yard where our darlings lie, when I gave a last look upon it [seemed] to chear my thoughts. There I could think of life and immortality—the house only reminded me of desolation, gloom, emptiness, and chearless silence—but why do I now turn to these thoughts? the morning is bright and I am more chearful today.

I write now merely to request that you will send Miss Watson's Novel as soon as you have done with it—directed to Mrs. Coleridge to be left at Miss Crosthwaites' Keswick; and if you have to read it pray read it immediately, for I promised Lloyd long since to procure it immediately after your return. I have been disappointed at not hearing from you before now. God bless you all.

D. Wordsworth

The Novel may be sent by the coach from Penrith.

293. D. W. to ELIZABETH COOKSON

Address: Mrs Cookson, Kendal.
Stamp: Kendal Penny Post.
MS. Jonathan Wordsworth.
Hitherto unpublished.

Ambleside Monday Night
[17 May 1813.]

My dear Friend,

When we were setting out upon a walk to Brathay we met the post with your letter, which I hastily read, and gave it to Mary, who was going home, to carry it to Sara. I have since seen the Coleridges, who are delighted with your kind Invitation, and it is agreed that they and John shall go all the way to Kendal in Mr Longmyer's[1] cart which is going on that day empty. From my recollection of your letter, I think you will expect them on Tuesday therefore I write this. Poor John will be in raptures, but I have not seen him since we got your letter.

We are all well, and we have good cause to be thankful that we are placed in such a delightful situation, though it was a bitter pang when the parting hour came and we left Grasmere vale. We have lately suffered great anxiety from the unconnected account which came of the Loss of the Peacock Frigate. It was commanded by the Husband of our Cousin who has been staying with us, and her Brother was in the Vessel.[2] William went to the neighbourhood of Cockermouth to see her and her wretched Family. He found her in utter despair without a glimpse of hope that the news might be false—the rest of the family had *some* hope—but that is now over, for the dreadful catastrophe is confirmed—only there is [hope] remaining that John Wordsworth, a noble youth of 15 may be saved. Oh my dear Friend these sorrows are dreadful indeed—The poor Widow is overwhelmed and incapable at present of receiving

[1] The Rydal maltster.

[2] See *SH* 16, p. 53. The cousin was Mary, d. of the Wordsworths' first cousin Richard W. of Woodhouse, Whitehaven; her husband was Captain Peake. Her brother was Joseph W., mentioned in the same letter.

the least consolation. You will call to mind the loss of the Abergavenny and of *our* John Wordsworth—Joseph Wordsworth, Mrs Peake's Brother was saved, and is now disabled by a paralytic stroke[1]—God bless you my dear Friend

Yours ever D Wordsworth

We hope that the Bed will come soon as we want to have our work done.

William goes to Appleby tomorrow.

294. W. W. to BASIL MONTAGU

Address: Basil Montagu Esqre, Lincoln's Inn, London.
MS. untraced.
MY ii. 483.

Rydale Mount, May 30th 1813

My dear Montagu

I have been dancing about the Country for these last 6 Weeks arranging things for the conduct of my new business; this has prevented me from acknowledging the receipt of your several Letters. I have not however neglected their Contents; I spoke to Richard upon the subject of the sum you are about to pay,[2] I beg'd him to write to Mr Addison, to give up whatever may be in his hands. This I doubt not Rch^d^ has done. As to the Money, I have just made a purchase in the Vale of Keswick[3] and I shall want it to pay for the same.

We were happy to hear that Mrs Montagu got so well through her time, and as you say nothing to the Contrary we conclude that both the Mother and child are doing well. Upon the parcel which I received from Algernon was written *with two books*, but I only received one, which in our present unsettling and putting up of the Books I cannot turn to at this moment; so know not which Volume it is, but I will tell you at some future time.

[1] According to S. H.'s letter (*SH* 16, p. 53 and n.) Joseph W. was on board another ship, the *Lowther Castle*.

[2] i.e. the repayment of the loan of £300 made to Montagu by Wordsworth in 1796. See Moorman, i, p. 296.

[3] In 1803 W. had been presented by Sir George Beaumont with the small property of Applethwaite, close to Keswick, and this he retained to the end of his life. No other property in the Vale of Keswick is known to have belonged to him. Possibly he was merely adding some fields to the Applethwaite property.

The Bill which I drew for 20£ at two months will be due on the 7th of June.

I congratulate you on your professional success which you deserve.

Our new residence is a charming one And I hope it will not be lo[n]g before you and Mrs M— pronounce its eulogy upon the spot. The Season is now in its glory——The Title Page to the Don Quixote is as follows.

The History of the Valorous and Witty Knight Errant
Don Quixote of the Mancha
Written in Spanish by Michael Cervantes
Translated in to English
By Thomas Shelton
And now printed *Verbatim* from the 4to
Edit: of 1620
With a curious set of new Cuts, from
the French of Coypel
London, printed for D. Midwinter &c.
M.DCCXL

With affectionate Love Yours
W Wordsworth

295. W. W. to ROBERT BLAKENEY[1]

Address: Robert Blakeney Esqre, Whitehaven.
MS. Cornell University Library.
Hitherto unpublished.

Rydale Mount
Monday Evening
June 12th 1813

Dear Sir,

I did not receive your most obliging Letter till yesterday, on my return from Penrith and Appleby where I had been detained some days by private business and by settling with the new Subdistributors whom it has been necessary to appoint in those places. I need scarcely repeat how sorry I was to miss your society on my last visit to Whitehaven and how much I sympathized with your vexation in being hurried away upon such a provoking occasion. Every

[1] He matriculated at Magdalen, Oxford, 1785, and was a member of Lincoln's Inn, 1787. As subsequent letters show, Mr. Blakeney was not popular with the Wordsworth ladies, although W. W. seems to have liked him well enough. He was Secretary and Treasurer to the Whitehaven Harbour Trustees. (Hughes, *North Country Life*, ii, p. 372). He died in 1822. See *LY* i, 691, p. 95.

amends was made to me that could be by Mr White,[1] and the kind care which your Housekeeper and Servants took of me and my Helper. I look foreward with much pleasure to the thought of seeing you in Whitehaven, upon your most friendly invitation, and I probably shall come accompanied with Mrs Wordsworth; and at some future time I know that Mr Southey would esteem himself happy in being shewn the interesting things about Whitehaven under your guidance. At present he is on the point of going to London.—I must add also that a few weeks must elapse before Mrs W. and myself can have the honour of visiting you as I am forced to go again to Penrith, where I shall be detained in settling some family accounts with my Brother; and also it is my wish to pay my respects to my noble Patron the Earl of Lonsdale as soon as he comes into the Country, which will probably be about the beginning of next month; but perhaps you will know to a certainty.—After this is done, should it suit you I should be happy to wait upon you.

How mortifying that Liverpool[2] errand! As you say nothing about the result, I hope it has been settled with as little unpleasantness to you as the case would admit. I need not say that we regretted much that you could not call on your return, and that we shall be at all times happy to see you.

I thank you for your Care of my interests at Kendal with Mr Fell.[3] Mr White pleased me much, pray make my best Comp^ts^ to him and say that such is my confidence in him that he shall want nothing that I can supply.—I received a Letter by last night's Post announcing that a large Parcel of Stamps had been sent (by Coach) according to my desire; so that if they have not unluckily been detained upon the Road, they will be here by tomorrow's Coach and Mr White shall have his Order completed the next day. My Brother will draw out the Bonds for me immediately; when the securities to be given by the several Subdistributors will be completed.

Mrs Bullfield, cannot I think, but have been satisfied with the new arrangement.

Mrs Wordsworth and my Sisters join me in respectful compliments, and believe me my dear Sir

with much regard
Your obedient humble Serv^nt^
W. Wordsworth

[1] Mr. White was the Sub-distributor at Whitehaven.
[2] W. W. writes 'Leverpool'.
[3] Mr. Fell was an attorney at Kendal.

296. W. W. to GEORGE THOMPSON[1]

Address: Mr George Thompson, Appleby.
Postmark: Penrith. Ju 30 1813 and Penrith 29 Ju 1813.
MS. Henry Huntington Library.
MY ii. 484, p. 561.

Penrith June 28th [1813]

Dear Sir,

On the 22nd of May last I received an acknowledgement from Mr Robison of Penrith for stamped Papers and parchments received from me to the amount of two thousand two hundred and forty six pounds, having at the same time given an acknowledgement that he had transferred this amount of Stamps to me, he acting for Mr Wilkin.—Soon after Mr Robison informs me that he had in his possession six skins at 3/6, Duty £2. amounting to £13. 1s 'which came in his last parcel from Mr Wilkin and which were packed up to return but neglected to be given to the Carrier'; They had therefore, writes he, 'be added to the amount of stock taken from himself.'[2] Accordingly this was done; and I gave Mr Wilkin credit for these stamps, and took them into the account sent to Government of stamps received by me.

On the 9th of June I took Mr Robison's stock again at which period it amounted to 2157. 6. 2—he paid me in Cash £87. 14, 4, which sum with the Poundage £1. 2. 2½ made an amount of 2246, 2. 8, the stock as taken on the 22nd of May.—At this time the 6 skins which I had given Mr Wilkin credit for at his desire slipped my memory,—so that I now by my own acknowledgement stand debtor through Mr Wilkin to Government for £13. 1. 0 more than I have received.—

I represented this to Mr Robison to day; having called upon him for the money or the stamps—and he refers me to you for the money he having accounted to Mr Wilkin for it. —— I will thank you to inform me if Mr Wilkin be agreeable that I should charge him with that sum viz.—13. 1. in account.—

An early answer will oblige me. I was very much mortified at missing you, another time I hope you will contrive by all means to call.

Yours sincerely
Wm Wordsworth

[1] The principal banker at Appleby. Mr. Robison, mentioned in this letter, was the Sub-distributor of Stamps at Penrith. For Mr. Wilkin, see Letters 282, 285 above.

[2] So manuscript.

297. W. W. to MR WHITE[1]

Address: Mr White, Stamp Office, Whitehaven.
MS. Tullie House, Carlisle. Stamp: Kendal Penny Post.
Hitherto unpublished.

[late June 1813]

Sir,

I have just received your letter of the 24th enclosing a Bill of Exchange for £442 13s and 11d, and your account shall be credited according to your Desire, with the Amount.

I have forwarded your Legacy Receipts to the Board; there was a slight error in the calculation of the Duties of one of them which I mention, in order that when opportunity offers, you may beg of the several Attornies to make them accurate even to farthings, as the board notice the most trivial errors.

On consulting my Instructions in regard to the Legacy Business I find that I am required to forward the Receipts on the first Tuesday in every Month. You will therefore be so good as in future to send them so as that they may reach me a few days before that Period in order that I may have time to examine them carefully (as my Instructions prescribe) before they are sent up.

I should be happy to accept of Mr Blakeney's invitation; But as it is so uncertain how long Lord Lonsdale will stay at Whitehaven, Mrs Wordsworth and I think it better to defer our visit, till I *am sure* of an opportunity of seeing Lord L.—either at Whitehaven or at Lowther.[2] Through your means may I beg of Mr Blakeney to let me know if his Lordship is sure to stay some time at Whitehaven.

Yours truly
Wm Wordsworth.

[1] The Sub-distributor of Stamps at Whitehaven.
[2] D. W. writing to R. W. on 3 Aug. 1813 says, 'William and Mary are at Whitehaven. Lord Lonsdale is there.' See L. 299 below. The date of this letter must therefore be before August, and is probably June.

298. W. W. to GEORGE THOMPSON[1]

MS. New York Public Library.
Hitherto unpublished.

[about July 1813]

My dear Sir,

I fear that I must continue to be troublesome to you from time to time as new Circumstances arise. Will you be so kind as to answer for me the following questions.—

I have received an affidavit from Mr Branthwaite of Kendall, in which a person employed by him makes Oath that a certain number (which is specified) of the last Westmorland Advertiser is printed on unstamped [ ] for[2] accordingly. Pray [ ] the Revd Mr Shaw[3] when you happen to see him; also pray take the trouble of reading it, and if you can throw any light upon the subject of it I will thank you to do so.

I hope Mr Wilkin is satisfied in regard to the six skins—and I wish to know from you how that matter is to be settled? I understand from your Letter that I am to consider Mr Wilkin as Debtor to that amount—£13–1s if I remember right; but I am writing this Letter at Ambleside where I have not the Papers before me.[4]

298a. W. W. to R. W.

Address: Richard Wordsworth Esqr, Staple Inn, London.
Postmark: 5 Aug. 1813. *Stamp*: Whitehaven, 2 Aug 1813. *Endorsed*: 2d August 1813.
MS. WL.
Hitherto unpublished.

Whitehaven. August 2nd
1813.

My dear Richard

I am here, having come over to pay my respects to Lord Lonsdale—I write this merely to say that Mr. Burrow of the neighbourhood of Ravenglass has represented to my friend Mr. Blakeney[5]

[1] The name of the addressee is missing but the mention of Mr. Wilkin and the 'six skins' seems to indicate that it is to the same correspondent as L. 296 above, and later in date.

[2] The paper is here cut away. The missing words after 'unstamped' were probably 'paper, and was not paid'. A line is also cut away after 'Pray—'.

[3] The *Westmorland Advertiser* (also called the *Kendal Chronicle*) was edited by a Nonconformist minister, Mr. Shaw. The missing words might be 'show him the affidavit'.

[4] Rest of letter cut off.

[5] See L. 295 above.

that your Land at Ravenglass[1] is at present without a Tenant, and I understand, as the [? phrase] is lying to the 'crown of heaven' without any Body to look after it. Ashburner the late tenant says, that he wrote to you and not having an answer, he has not taken possession, of the farm. Probably by this time you are acquainted with these circumstances, but I thought it best to let you know how things had been reported to me.—I wish much also that you would procure a Copy of the Bond required of me by government, letting me know when you send it upon what stamp I ought to [? have] my securities. We have had Wm Crackenthorp[2] and his sisters at Rydal Mount and like them much; pray send the Papers relating to the accounts with them as soon as possible, as I am anxious to have the matter settled before Mr. Crackenthorp goes abroad. We are all pretty well. Your very affectionate Brother,

Wm Wordsworth

299. D. W. to R. W.

Address: Richard Wordsworth Esq[re], Staple Inn, London.
Stamp: Kendal Penny Post. *Endorsed*: 3 Aug[t] 1813.
MS. WL.
MY ii, 485.

Rydale Mount August 3rd [1813]

My dear Brother,

I write to entreat you that you will not delay to send down the Accounts to be presented to Mr Crackanthorp. Pray do it immediately—I should think it would be as well to send them at once to Mr Grave, only we should like to hear from you when they *are* sent. Mr Crackanthorpe and his Sisters have been here and we spent some very pleasant days with them. He is a very pleasing young Man, and I like what I saw of him exceedingly—and also of his Sisters.

He intends going abroad very soon, and he told William that he was extremely anxious to get the accounts settled before his Departure.

I hope that we shall hear from you that you are pretty well—and I trust I shall have the pleasure of visiting you at Sockbridge

[1] A small fishing village on the Cumberland coast. In ancient times it was the terminus of the Roman road from Ambleside to the sea.

[2] See L. 281, p. 82, n. 2 above.

again this Autumn—but you must [come] first to see us. Willi[am and] Mary are now at Whitehaven. Lord Lonsdale is there. Before William went to W. he desired I would write, to press you to send the Accounts.

I remain, dear Richard
Your ever affect^e Sister
D. Wordsworth

Pray send us the statement which you promised, that we may know exactly what we are worth.

300. W. W. to R. W.

Address: Richard Wordsworth Esqre, Staple Inn, London.
Postmark: C. 24 Aug 1813. *Endorsed*: 19 Augt 1813 Relating to Mr. T. Monkhouse's payment for carpets.
MS. WL.
MY ii. 487, p. 566.

Rydale Mount August 19th [1813]

My dear Richard,

I reply to your letter by return of Post. When Montagu expressed by letter his wish to pay off the Annuity[1] I begged in my answer to know what I had best do with the Policy, not doubting that it belonged to me; but not knowing at that time, nor indeed till I received your letter that any benefit might arise from it except the contingent one from continuing the Insurance till the event of Montagu's death. He replied that, as he had paid the Insurance, it ought to be considered as belonging to him, and to the best of my remembrance I returned no answer to this, so that, as far as *silence implied consent*, I certainly did *agree* that any advantage arising from it should be his, in the full conviction that he would make no proposition but what was right and honourable, and being not much interested in it on account of the misconception before stated.[2] The question for consideration is this; though the Money was actually paid to the Insurance Office by me through your hands ought it not to be considered as primarily paid by Montagu to me? I received 37£–10*s* per annum for 300£: and though it was *at my option* whether to insure or not, yet I have reason to believe, though I am

[1] For Basil Montagu's debt to Wordsworth, see *EY* 66, pp. 182–4, and Moorman, i, pp. 296–7.
[2] This last clause was added afterwards.

not certain of the fact, that Montagu was induced to pay so large an Interest as this seems to be, that I might be enabled to insure his Life. Therefore it appears to me that in Equity he is entitled to the benefit of the Policy. I mean if he has allowed me larger Interest than in the common course of Annuity dealings, not raised on landed property or otherwise, I had a right to expect, induced thereto by a wish that I might be enabled to insure his life. If what he has allowed be *not* more than in similar circumstances is usually granted it seems reasonable *then* that the benefit of the Policy should be mine. Having stated these facts and opinions I leave it to you to settle the matter with him.

It was in the Autumn of the year 1788 that our Grandfather[1] died —either in the month of September, October, or November. We are exceedingly glad to hear that the accounts are in a state of forwardness, wishing much that every thing should be settled as soon as may be. Mr Hutton[2] can learn from the Register at Penrith the precise time of our Grandfather's death.

I am very anxious to have my Sureties[3] complete, and wish to have the Form, with all directions as soon as possible, in order that I may have the Bonds executed when I take my quarterly rounds, which will be shortly.

There was a sum of Money which I desired Mr Thomas Monkhouse[4] to apply for at Staple Inn some time ago, which Mr Addison declined paying in your absence. If it is not already done pray let the money be paid immediately as he has already been too long without his money. The sum, I believe, was 53 £ odd—but he has since that time paid something more therefore you will answer his demand, whatever it may be.

Mary and Dorothy beg their kind love and hope to see you here this year. By means of Mr Hutton you may have a copy of the Register of my Grandfather's death.

We shall hope to hear from you again as soon as you have made out the Accounts.

I remain your affectionate Brother

Wm Wordsworth.

[1] i.e. Mr. William Cookson of Penrith, the Wordsworths' maternal grandfather.

[2] Solicitor at Penrith. See L. 415 below.

[3] i.e. for his appointment as Distributor of Stamps.

[4] See endorsement. The carpets were for Rydal Mount. See L. 415 below.

301. W. W. to ROBERT BLAKENEY

Address: Robert Blakeney Esqr, Whitehaven.
Stamp: Kendal Penny Post.
MS. Cornell.
Hitherto unpublished.

Rydale Mount Aug^st 20th 1813

My dear Sir,

I have had an Interview with Mr Jackson[1] and read him the Copy of your Letter to Mr. H.[2]—The result I will give.—The Sale commenced on Monday as advertized, but the Bidders were disgusted by an Interference of Mr H. to push it, so that little was sold, H. not being satisfied with the offers, and the thing was abruptly terminated. We are of opinion however that you should write to H. forbidding the Removal of any part of what has been sold, as should you permit it, it would seem that he had your consent for that proceeding. Now it is of great consequence that this should not be; for unless you had given your consent that the crops should be carried off he has already broken the agreement existing between you; and without any consideration of its legal invalidity on account of the stamp, it is annulled by this unauthorized act of his. It is also annulled upon another ground. The custom of the country here is that no man should plough more land than he can sufficiently manure; now Mr Jackson says that he has already ploughed three times that quantity; therefore on both these considerations the preliminary agreement has been violated, unless it contained express stipulations to this effect: you are therefore at perfect Liberty to get rid of him if you chuse. Which Mr. J— advises you by all means to do, as from this specimen of his conduct he has shown what you must expect: not to speak of the probable failure in payment of Rent. But observe, the time of discharge is the 12th of August; and the sale took place on the 13th, H— thus artfully deferring it, till he was secure of the Farm for another year. So that all that you can do at present is to prevent his ploughing an undue proportion next year, and to give him his discharge in due time, if you resolve to get quit of him. Which as a Friend I cannot but advise you to do,—. There can be no occasion for your coming over on this disagreeable business, at least I should suppose so, but you will hear what he says in answer.

We shall be most happy to see you here whenever it suits you.

[1] The Revd. Thomas Jackson, Vicar of Grasmere and agent to Lady Fleming of Rydal Hall. See L. 193, pt. i, p. 408, n.

[2] Mr. Humphrey. See L. 315, p. 136 below.

Mrs Wordsworth I think is in better health than when at Whitehaven, and She My Sister and Miss Hutchinson, all unite most truly in their best regards.

I am my dear Sir
with much respect
your obliged
W Wordsworth

I have paid Clark and Hartley[1] £12. 8s. and have their receipt.

The uncouth appearance of this Letter was owing to an Inadvertence. [? Pray] excuse it

302. W. W. to R. W.

Address: Rich[d] Wordsworth Esq[re], Staple Inn, London.
Postmark: C. 31 Aug 1813. *Stamp*: Kendal. *Endorsed*: 27 Aug[t] 1813.
MS. WL.
MY ii. 300.

Rydale August 27th [1813]

My dear Brother,

I have received the Parcel containing the Accounts etc, and have written to Mr Crackanthorpe,[2] from whom I expect an answer daily, to appoint a time for our meeting; when I hope this Business will be finally settled.

I shall be glad to receive the proper Form for my Subdistributors Bonds as soon as convenient and will thank you to advance whatever sum may be justly demanded on my account from the Treasury.

We are all well and join in Love to you. I am dear Brother
yours affec[ly]
Wm Wordsworth

[1] Bankers at Whitehaven.
[2] See L. 281 above.

303. W. W. to FRANCIS WRANGHAM

Address: Revd Francis Wrangham, Hunmanby, Bridlington.
MS. Henry Huntington Library.
Grosart (—). K. MY ii. 489, p. 568.

Rydal Mount near Ambleside
August 28th 1813

My dear Wrangham,

Your letter arrived when I was upon the point of going from home, *on business*, I took it with me intending to answer it upon the road, but I had not courage to undertake the office on account of the inquiries it contains concerning my family. I will be brief on this melancholy subject. In the course of the last year I have lost two sweet children, a girl and a Boy, at the ages of 4 and six and a half. These Innocents were the delight of our hearts, and beloved by every Body that knew them. They were cut off in a few hours—one by the measles—and the other by convulsions; dying one, half a year after, the other. — — I quit this sorrowful subject secure of your sympathy as a Father, and as my Friend.

I have transmitted the request in your Letter to my Brother, so that no doubt you will hear from him; but this act of Duty I have only discharged today, from want of fortitude. — —

My employment I find salutary to me, and of consequence in a pecuniary point of view, as my *Literary* employments bring me no emolument, nor promise any. As to what you say about the Ministry—I very much prefer the course of their Policy to that of the Opposition, especially on two points most near my heart,—resistance of Buonaparte by force of arms, and their adherence to the principles of the British constitution in withholding Political Power from the Roman Catholics. My most determined hostility shall always be directed against those statesmen who, like Whitbread, Grenville and others, would crouch to a sanguinary Tyrant; and I cannot act with those who see no danger to the constitution in introducing Papists into Parliament. There are other points of policy on which I deem the Opposition grievously mistaken, and therefore, I am at present, and long have been by principle a supporter of [the] Ministry, as far as my little influence extends.

With affectionate wishes for your welfare and that of your family, and with best regards to Mrs Wrangham

I am my dear friend
faithfully yours
Wm Wordsworth.

304. D. W. to SARA HUTCHINSON

Address: Miss Sara Hutchinson, at T. Hutchinson's Esqre, Stockton-upon-Tees.
Stamp: Kendal Penny Post.
MS. WL.
MY ii. 491, p. 574.

[11 Sept. 1813]

My dearest Sara,

Though my letter cannot go off till tomorrow night, being in an unsettled way I think I had best try to recollect what has passed since you left us; but I am in a stupid humour (though I *have* a pinch of snuff) and perhaps it would have been better for you if I had waited till tomorrow. You left us on Tuesday, and we all went to the Sale, where there were few bidders but they staunch ones and things went very dear, yet we got one good Bargain, 6 buff chairs, with cushions and cane Bottoms for the Study—at 9/-. William's cushions therefore are not wanted and we have asked Mrs Cookson to see if Holland will take them again and William made a purchase of which he is very proud but it is dear enough—the drawing room curtains with a grand cornice the length of the Room—admirable if we were going to join the Company of Mr and Mrs Dean. He would fain persuade us that his curtains—and with a stripe above ¼ broad—are handsomer than our own—and if we were to leave this house (which God forbid) and got another with 3 sitting rooms they would do very well; but I think they will come to be cut up for sofa covers—lined with green stuff—4 curtains—1 £–13^s—William bid hard for two sofas but Mr. Harden[1] outfaced him—and Mrs Green (the Paintress!)—We thought her rather extravagant in giving 6 £ 15s for a sofa—but times have been better and her heart is up. Miss Green bought a curtain. We had a charming afternoon, and really it is worth while to go to a Sale, when there is so much to see from the windows. The next day came Peggy Ashburner, Mary, Jane, and their 3 Bairns[2]—and Mrs Fleming, Mrs Green, and Jenny Mackereth[3] to tea (By the Bye Ellen was married on Sunday). It was

[1] John Harden of Brathay Hall, amateur artist and friend of Constable. Exhibitions of his charming pencil sketches of his family, etc., were held at Bristol (1951) and at Kendal (1965).

[2] The Ashburners had lived opposite the Wordsworths in their early days at Town End. D. W. always remained on affectionate terms with Peggy and her family and this letter shows her holding a tea-party at Rydal Mount for several old Grasmere neighbours. Mary Ashburner, here mentioned, married James Fleming of Knott Houses, Grasmere, and her house in after years was, we are told, 'like a second home' to Wordsworth. See *DWJ* i, p. 433 (Appendix I) and *passim*.

[3] The Mackereths also lived at Knott Houses, near the Swan at Grasmere. Her husband George M. was parish clerk of Grasmere.

a charming Day and all were delighted with their visit—but when I was busy making cakes and pies they arrived, and as all our Bustles come at once a Miss Malcolm[1] and her Nephew, and Mrs. Richardson of Kendal came. We had had a letter from Mrs. Lloyd apprizing us of their Intention. Mrs R. was coming from Allonby to meet the Judge and was to return on Monday and Miss M. had taken the opportunity of coming along with her to see a little of the Lakes. Miss M. is the Sister of my Br. Christr.'s most intimate Friend, and of Sir John Malcolm and Wm. said we must ask her to stay at our house. Luckily she was going on to Elleray that day, where she stayed all night, and when Wm went to the Bishop's[2] to dine he met her at Ambleside and she and her nephew came and stayed till Monday. She is a pleasant *Scotch* woman—Scotch in her accent, and Scotch in her manners, with the frankness which you often see in her country-women, quiet activity, and I dare say, industry—and is a pleasant companion having many anecdotes, and a large acquaintance. Friday was rainy—Saturday morning rainy; but at 10 it cleared up and we went to Grasmere to dinner. D. carried our basket crossed over the stepping Stones at the head of Rydale and we all walked round the Lake and to Butterlip How—We had a pleasant quiet day—and on Sunday by invitation Mr Richard Watson[3] and Mr. Wilson[4] came to dinner. Mrs. Wilson expected but the Farriers arrived so she did not come. We had Miss Green. The day went off very well—Richard Watson is a very gentleman-like canny man who tempts one to forget his naughty ways. The morning was wet, so we had prayers at home after our cooking preparations were over. Monday we were alone all day—and I went with Wm. in the evening to Ambleside and we called at Mrs Green's—for this has been on our consciences long. She was very gracious; though we gave her no Invitation. Mrs Royds and her Niece and Miss Barlow were there and William was chatty, so the visit told. Came home after 9 o'clock, in a heavy rain—but I ought to have told you that William took off to the 2nd day's sale at Dove

[1] There were four Miss Malcolms; see L. 250, p. 27, n. 1 above, and *SH* 21, p. 73. Their brothers were all distinguished in various fields—Sir John as a soldier in India, Sir Pulteney and Sir Charles as naval officers. For Gilbert M. see L. 250, p. 27 and n.

[2] i.e. To Calgarth, on Windermere, the home of Dr. Richard Watson, Bishop of Llandaff and sometime Professor of Chemistry at Cambridge. Long before, in 1793, Wordsworth had written, but did not publish, a tract strongly attacking the Bishop for his views on political matters. See Grosart, i. The Bishop died in 1816.

[3] A son of the Bishop of Llandaff; he became a prebendary of Llandaff and also of Wells.

[4] John Wilson of Elleray.

Nest,[1] and bought a Meat Safe and another writing Desk. Tuesday morning (Grasmere Fair day) was very rainy—heavy showers with scarcely a pause between—but we thought it was all in our favour and resolved to go; and Miss Green came up in one of her fair fits and to our great surprise *she* would go too—, we were very sorry and advised against it being sure that she would be ill; but she resolved not to be ill, and accordingly though it rained heavily most of the way she was no worse. Luckily Mr Harden was not there and there were store of cheap pennyworths of which we got our share and two or three *dear* ones. The Sale was in the Barn and we entered into the spirit of it, Wm and Mary and Miss Green took up lodgings at the Black Bull. I walked home in pouring rain and arrived at ½ past 9. I stayed at home all day and Fanny[2] went to see Tamar who was ill and came home by Hacket. Sara getting better—but I fear the worst, though Fanny, it is plain suspects nothing. She brought the orders to return with her in the morning with a cart—a glorious morning and clear sunshine till night. The day before had been showery. The dining room Tables were bought in. They bid them to 14£ and William offered 14guin. They are very beautiful, but I am not sorry he did not get them. We stayed the sale out to the very last and the beds were sold by candle-light and all walked home in the bright moonshine, I with a water decanter and Glass in my hand and William and Mary with a large looking glass—oval with a gilt frame—to be hung in the best lodging room—very cheap—1£ 13s. Fanny went home with a fully loaded cart and John[2] is gone today with one which will be half loaded. Miss Green is below [*seal*] and never weary with talking of her cheap purchases—Tea China—Desert China—2 Lustres for her chimney. She put them up at a guinea and nobody bid against her—a Bed for her Maid—and the German clock. We bought a Bed, Tubs and chairs for Fanny—and many things for ourselves. Amongst the rest your cupboard table which is a very nice thing. We have got a stock of Decanters—some glasses—a dozen knives—2 pillows—Baskets—a p^r of stocks for D—Enough of *these* sales. Mr Humphries has gone off—Wilcock has taken possession of his furniture and it will be sold; but we must take care of ourselves and not buy. I had

[1] Probably the house of that name near Low Wood above Windermere, but they seem also to have gone to a sale (as appears below) at Coniston. 'Grasmere Fair Day', the first Tuesday in September, was this year on 7 Sept. D.'s letter was not completed till the following Saturday, 11 Sept.

[2] Fanny, one of the W.s' servants: John, i.e. John Carter whom W. had engaged to assist him in the clerical duties connected with his office of Stamp Distributor, and to act as gardener and general handyman. See L. 282 above.

forgotten that William had bought a sort of sofa for his Room—at about 1£ 5s—very nice and it will answer his purpose. Mary is no worse for her fatigues—and Miss Green snorts and nods—and chatters—Chatter oh me! till I am weary. She is dining with us, Sally being gone to Conistone with John Carter. D is in the next room at her Latin and I hear the Ladies below—no doubt from the china to the Lustres—from the Lustres to the Clock—with now and then a transition to our more humble wares. Mrs Calvert cannot come at present which I am not sorry for. William went to Penrith this morning. I walked with him to the Swan. He will be 8 or 9 days absent for he goes to Lowther and Kirkby Steven—He means to dismiss Mr. Winter[1] I believe. Nothing done in the garden but John has little work in the office at present and is to go out tomorrow. Mary has been in good spirits, the sales were the very thing for her. Sally Green is working for us—She is very neat and industrious but miserably slow. It rains now fast enough to hinder work in the harvest field; but the day is pleasant enough for walking. I leave the rest of my paper till tomorrow—I often wish you were back again. William bitterly regretted you were not here to talk over the humours of the Sales—Indeed if I had written the day after Mr Pedder's I should have told you some funny stories. Sally has almost finished the Bed but we want more Bed lace. We hear nothing of Miss Fletcher.—I think D has been rather steadier; but I fear we shall have no school for her, and every hour I see faults in her that at school would be cured at once without trouble. *Saturday morning*. Last night a letter came from Eliz^th^ Wordsworth[2] that she, and Mrs Peake and D.^t^ would be here today; they to stay a week and proceed to Chester, and D. to remain with us. They have been a week at Eusemere, I wish they had stayed there another week, but I guess that the Captn and his Lady find it irksome to remain long without gayer company. We wanted to get our sofas and carpets arranged. The London carpetting came yesterday, but no Bill of parcels. Tom Monkhouse in a letter which came last week said that he would note down the particulars at the Bottom; but he did not. Therefore write to him and ask him to send the Bill because

[1] Presumably the Sub-distibutor of stamps at Kirkby Stephen.

[2] Elizabeth, wife of Richard W. (1752–1816), first cousin of W. W. and D. W., the son of Richard W. of Whitehaven (d. 1794), D. W.'s and W. W.'s uncle and guardian. 'D.' = Dorothy, youngest daughter of Eliz. and Richard W. (See L. 305 below.) Dorothy Wordsworth, or 'middle Dorothy' as she was called, lived at Rydal Mount for about a year, sharing lessons with Dora. She married Benson Harrison, an ironmaster, and they settled at Ambleside, at Green Bank, now the Charlotte Mason College. Mrs. Peake was Dorothy's sister. Her husband had been killed at sea in the spring of this year. See L. 293 above.

we want to present it to the carriers, and desire him to draw on Staple Inn[1] for the money. What a pity we cut up the Buff sofa cover. Try at Mrs Dixon's if you can get enough for 2 sofa covers and pillows. You will have only a small cover to work. We are quite bewildered amongst our furniture. This comes of [? buying] pennyworths—We have far more chairs than [? we know] what to do with, and the dining room will not be [? at all] nice with the sofa. We had three Black ch[airs in] the middle of the Room but they cannot s[tay if] we keep all the worked Bottomed ones: I caught a cold with standing upon the grass plot at Coniston to bid—but Miss Green who went in opposition to advice ails nothing—I believe her *cheap* dusters and *cheap* Desert china kept away all uneasiness. Only think, she could not find in her heart to buy a Bed or Mattress for her Maid's Bedstock—and laid out so much money for what she does not want, Bargains which Dorothy is charmed with and wonders at the cheapness of them. Miss Green asked to borrow our chaff Bed yesterday but we cannot spare it.

My kindest love to Henry.[2] The horse is paid for.

Get me some fur for my pellisse. What was the price of our Decanters? No news from Ann Hutton. William desires me to tell you that if he had been with you, you would not have got to Barnard Castle when you meant to go to Richmond. Dear Sara write soon and often. I wish you were back again. They have been at work these ten minutes, trying to move the great sofa, and I do believe it cannot be done. Remember to get my money from Hindwell. Mary looks much better. All the Bairns well—poor things! Willy in ecstacies with the purchases.

305. D. W. to CATHERINE CLARKSON

Address: Mrs Clarkson, Bury St. Edmonds, Suffolk.
Stamp: Kendal Penny Post. *Endorsed*: First Letter from Rydale.
MS. British Museum.
MY ii. 490, p. 569.

[about 14 Sept. 1813][3]

My dearest Friend,

I take a large sheet of paper because I do not like to begin with my scrawling hand as if I *intended* to write you a short Letter, though as I am determined to save the post, and as I do not know when the Man goes to Ambleside or what interruptions I may have,

[1] i.e. on R. W.

[2] i.e. Henry Hutchinson, M. W.'s brother.

[3] In L. 304 above, D. says, 'William went to Penrith this morning. . . . He will be 8 or 9 days absent.' At the end of this letter she says that 'William is at Penrith on Stamp business', consequently the date must be a few days after L. 304 above.

I do not know whether the letter will turn out long or short; but I have this satisfaction that to you it will be twice over worth the postage when I tell you that there has been no unpleasant cause for my long silence. Many employments and a little bustle that perhaps we have sometimes impatiently wished to be over have been no evil to any one of us, and I hope the minds of all by these means, and by the intervention of pious thoughts (which must needs bring on Resignation to all the sorrows of this world, especially when so many blessings are left) have been strengthened and that we shall be able to enjoy the pleasures of leisure when leisure comes. Oh that you were here! or that you were coming in a fortnight for then we shall have our carpets laid down and shall be all complete. I talk lightly but you cannot think (for you have never been at this beautiful place) you cannot think with what earnestness I utter the wish. The carpets popped in after the wish was uttered and with a smile and a tear I set down the foolish thought—but now I must tell you of our grandeur. We are going to have a *Turkey*!!! carpet—in the dining-room, and a Brussels in William's study. You stare, and the simplicity of the dear Town End Cottage comes before your eyes, and you are tempted to say, 'are they changed, are they setting up for fine Folks? for making parties—giving Dinners etc etc?' No no, you do not make such a guess; but you want an explanation and I must give it to you. The Turkey carpet (it is a large Room) will cost 22 guineas, and a Scotch carpet would cost 9 or 10. The Turkey will last 4 Scotch, therefore will be the cheapest, and will never be shabby, and from this consideration we were all of one mind that the dining Room carpet should be a Turkey one; but Mary and I were rather ashamed of the thought of a Brussels, and inclined to the Scotch as looking less ambitious and less like setting up ourselves upon the model of our neighbours—the Ambleside gentry, who all intend calling upon us, though happily most of them considered it would be inconvenient at present, and I assure you we take their apologies very quietly and say as few civil things in return as possible. Our Master was all for the Brussels and to him we yielded—a humour took him to make his Room smart, and as we think that in the end, even that will be cheaper than a Scotch carpet we did not oppose his wish. Tom Monkhouse has been the purchaser of these sumptuous wares, and has got them at the cheapest hand. The Study is furnished with a large book-case, some chairs that we had at Allan Bank painted black, and Sir George Beaumont's pictures—and looks very neat. We have got window curtains for it, and a nice writing-table—and a new bed for Sara and stair carpets and oil cloth for the passage—and these are all the new things we wanted and the house is very neat and comfortable—and most convenient—though far from being as good a house as we expected. We had never seen the inside of it till we came to live in it. We have three kitchens one of which is called the *Deep* kitchen. The grate is decked out by the Kitchen Maid with flourishing green Boughs, which are only displaced in the washing week, when this same kitchen is used as a laundry. At other times the clock lives there in perfect solitude, except that it has the company of two nice white tables and other appropriate furniture.

You cannot imagine what a deal of work removing from one house to another causes—there is so much unripping of curtains etc—and so much carpenter's work—but before the end of next week all will be over and would have been long since if we had not had to *wait* for what we wanted. We are all gardeners, especially Sara, who is mistress and superintendent of that concern. I am contented to work under her—and Mary does her share, and sometimes we work very hard, and this is a great amusement to us though sad thoughts often come between. Thomas was a darling in a garden—our best helper—steady to his work—always pleased. God bless his memory! I see him wherever I turn—beautiful innocent that he was—he had a slow heavenly up-turning of his large blue eyes that is never to be forgotten. Would that you had seen him! But my dear friend why have I turned to this subject? Because I write to you what comes uppermost the pen following the heart—but no more. You must indeed you must come next year. I never talk of *next year's* plans, but I think of Death. Come however you must if you live whether we are *all* alive or not. It is the place of all others for you—so dry that you need never have a wet foot after the heaviest shower; and the prospect so various and beautiful that an Invalid or a weakly person might be accused of discontentedness of disposition who should wish for anything else, or repine at not being able to go further than round our garden.

John Gough[1] takes Boys to prepare them in Mathematics for the University, and it has struck Sara and me as a likely plan for you to adopt to place Tom under his care for a while, and then there could be no possible objection to your coming into the North for a while—and in our house you might have every accommodation. It is large enough for both you and your Maid—and Tom occasionally, and Mr Clarkson as long as he could stay. Do come—and say in your

[1] The blind mathematician and naturalist of Kendal. See *Excursion*, vii, 482–515.

next that you will. Often do we talk of it and have wished that you were here even in the midst of our worst bustles. You may judge how busy we have been when I tell you that we knew nothing about the Curate Bill[1] and William was not at home to explain it to us. We have had no time to read Newspapers but have been obliged to content ourselves with William's Report even of the late most important battles in Germany and all other proceedings. Murders we do read and were horror struck with that of Mr and Mrs Brown and the confession of the murderer—Good God! If the thought of murder is to come in that way into the head of a person apparently not insane, nobody seems to be safe; but it seems to us that all these murders have been committed by people of no education, and are strong arguments in favour of the early and universal instruction of the Children of the Poor. Blessed be your Father and all good people who labour in this holy work! Pray tell us anything further that you know, which is not in the papers, respecting Mr and Mrs Brown their family and the Murderer. What you have told us, affected us very much. William is decidedly against the Catholics, and I think he would convince you if you had an hour's talk with him and you *shall*, and you *must* have it next summer. We have such a Terrace for you to walk upon and such a nice seat at the end of it. Oh my dearest Friend that you were here.—We have not received Mr Clarkson's Book[2] which vexes us much. Pray how is it sent that we may inquire after it. I do not think that a copy has reached this neighbourhood, or we should have heard of it. I long to see it; most of it must be new to *me* at least and the subject is a very interesting one. Of course I need not ask you to inquire the reason why the Book has not reached us if by so doing you can forward it to us. I am glad that your Brother Robert is going on so well—why does not he fix upon a wife to grace his pretty dwelling?—Sam is my favourite of all your brothers and I should much rejoice to hear that he had his Farm on good terms—nicely fitted up and had a good Wife to make him as happy as he deserves to be. Remember me to them all and to your dear Father whom I hope before I die to see again. We have had a letter from Luff[3] dated January. They were only just arrived at the Mauritius. You may judge what a tedious passage they had had, for a Friend of Miss Dowling's[4] who sailed

[1] A Bill to make £80 the minimum salary for a Curate. The Bill was attacked as hard on Incumbents, and defended as likely to discourage absenteeism. At this period the average salary for Curates was £20. (Note by De Selincourt.)

[2] *Memoirs of the Private and Public Life of William Penn*, by Thomas Clarkson, M.A., in two volumes, 1813.

[3] See L. 6, pt. i, p. 11, n. 4.

[4] See L. 237, p. 6, n. 3 above.

4 months after them had arrived before them. They give a wretched account of the place, overrun with insects continually biting—provisions and everything else enormously dear—and the country without fertility or Beauty. They hoped to be removed to Java—or possibly to Lisbon which would be far better, but what a voyage! Poor Mrs Luff! I pity her the most for she must have the Pangs of Remorse. He went chiefly to satisfy her, and the Remembrance of his Motives may bear him up. Luff mentioned you and all his friends but his letter was very short. Mrs L. has written to others in the same style of regret. Mary is well in health, though weak and miserably thin, yet it is amazing what exertions she can go through. Sara has been poorly but is better. We expect Miss Barker to morrow, Sara has been with her at Keswick.[1] William is at Penrith on Stamp business. Till the end of this Month he will be entirely engaged with it. He has done nothing else for weeks and been from home 2 thirds of his time. Afterwards all will be easy, little for him to do. He has got a clerk who promises well. He is to work in the garden also.—Do write very soon, tell us about the Book. This is a reason for your writing immediately and pray do—May God bless you my dear Friend. ever yours

D. W.

My kindest love to [Mr. C.] and to Tom.

No news of Coleridge! Charles Lloyd is pretty well at present, but poor soul he is often *dreadfully* ill.

305a. W. W. to MESSRS WORDSWORTH AND ADDISON

Address: Messrs. Wordsworth and Addison, Staple Inn, London.
Postmark: C 27 Sep [18]13. *Stamp*: Kendal 261. *Endorsed*: 24 Sept. 1813.
Hitherto unpublished.

Kendal Sept^{br} 24th
1813

Dear Sir

I shall esteem it a favour if you will call upon Mr. Kapper Sec^{ry} to the Commissioners of Stamps and pay to him £24. 4s on my account.

[1] Sara had gone to Stockton-on-Tees on 31 Aug., probably staying with Miss Barker on the way. See her letter to Tom Monkhouse, 27 Aug. 1813, *SH* 19, p. 62, and also L. 304 above, where D. W. says to her, 'you left us on Tuesday', i.e. 31 Aug.

I mentioned to my Brother whom I left well at Sockbridge last Monday that I should trouble you with a Letter to this effect.

I am dear Sir
Your obedient Servant
Wm Wordsworth

Pray do this *immediately* as Mr. Kapper's Letter has been waiting during my absence.—

[*On the back of the letter is the following note*:]

27th Sept[r] 1813 Paid Mr. Kapper twenty-four pounds four Shillings on Mr. Wm. Wordsworth's Acco[t]—Step[n] Lambert.

306. W. W. and M. W. to SARA HUTCHINSON

Address: Miss Hutchinson, Grassy Nook, Stockton-upon-Tees.
MS. WL.
Hitherto unpublished.

October 4th. 1813

(*W. W. writes*)
My dearest Sarah,

Dorothy you know is at Kendale; but Mary and I received your letter last night which was forwarded to her, by today's Post—We long for your return which I shall be most happy to facilitate. The Bolton scheme[1] need not stand in the way; I have resolved to defer it to another year; for many reasons which I need not trouble you with. Your B[r] John will take care of the farm at Stoc[k]ton for us;[2] and you will believe me when I say, that I would rather ride over as far as Stockton for half an hour's conversation with you or any friend whom I loved, than I would take that trouble for the sight of 300 Acres of land of my own, which had no beauty to recommend it, and which I knew (owing to the kindness of friends resident of the Spot) did not stand in need of my superintendence. Therefore as I know you are not indisposed to meet me I must decline your Brother's invitation to Stockton; particularly as we have been so much engaged with company at home, and long solitary journies on horseback are things which I have no relish for. Endure then the slow travel of Bessy[3] as far as Appleby or Penrith and I will meet you

[1] To meet at Bolton Abbey; see *SH* 20, p. 69.

[2] John Hutchinson, M. W.'s eldest brother, farmed at Stockton-on-Tees. From this sentence it appears that W. W. had purchased a farm at Stockton-on-Tees. Nothing further is known of it.

[3] Bessy Hutchinson, eldest daughter of John H. by his first wife.

there; (if John does not think it worth his while to come forward with you) or, if that be possible, let Henry[1] borrow a horse to set you as far as Hawes, and thither will I come with readiness and pleasure to accompany you home at any time you like; only let me add the sooner the better. Write immediately and tell us which plan you prefer; or if H. cannot procure a Horse exact a promise from Jack to go to Penrith, or if that promise cannot be gained and depended upon tell me, and I will come as far even as Stockton to conduct you home again—But what I myself should like best would be to meet you at Hawes, and what I should like infinitely the worst would be that you should prolong your stay, and deprive us of your presence and company for I love you most tenderly. This is the anniversary of my Wedding Day, and every year whether fraught with joy or sorrow has brought with it additional cause why I should thank God for my connection with your family. Mary joins with me in blessing you, as we have blessed each other. We look for Dorothy home on Wednesday by the opportunity of Mr Blaken[e]y's carriage, which I hope she will not miss. Tomorrow I expect a les agreeable arrival, that of an Inspector of Stamps; he will not however be unwelcome, as I wish for information which he will be enabled to give me. D. no doubt has told you the dreadful news of Watson murdering his aged Mother; he gave her 25 wounds including two fractures; the Coroner's inquest brought in a verdict of wilful murder. Our neighbours of Rydale Hall are returned; Lady D.[2] all alive and regenerated, Lady F.[3] pale and wan and feeble—She wants that moral stimulus, which you speak of as not abounding in other places and her youth is passing away without hope aim or interest, a deplorable condition in which she resembles tens of thousands. Lady D. has brought a little present for Willy who is the sweetest of little [?][4] what it is she has not told us; nor have we hinted at anything of the kind to him; but he is very anxious to call there; expecting gratification from her little Dogs, her Peacocks, or perhaps from the sight of her perennially blooming and brilliant cheeks!—It is now dusk and I hear him running along the passage to his Mother, having just come in from School, which is a happy place of confinement for him. I will leave the rest of this sheet for Mary. Farewell, and believe me, wishing ardently to have you here again, your most affectionate friend and Brother

Wm. Wordsworth.

[1] Henry Hutchinson, M. W.'s sailor brother.

[2] Lady Diana Fleming.

[3] Lady Fleming, daughter of Lady Diana: married to her cousin Sir Michael Fleming, but living apart from him.

[4] Seal obliterates manuscript.

(*M. W. writes*)
Dearest Sarah, William has mentioned our *agreeable* visitors. Think of having Mr Blaken[e]y glue'd to us from morning to night! I am glad you and D. are spared this punishment.[1] Yet I could have liked that you should have seen what a mountain of vanity he is that you might have been in sympathy with me. W. bears him with patience —Nay I think he likes him for they never cease talking, and they agree in all things—we pay dearly for this new acquaintance however! We had a letter last night from Joanna—She wants me to write —But O Sarah if you knew what I feel at the thought of turning my pen to them you would wish me to avoid it. I wish you would write for me. Tell Joanna that after I may have seen any of them again I shall be able to express what may be passing round me to them— but at present I sicken at the thought—this is great weakness I grant—but I know I should be more weak were I not thus to resist. She talks of Mr Jackson's farm for Geo. Tell her it is let—and say all kind things for me to them—if I loved them less I could write to them myself. Ask my aunt[1] what became of the Picture of the Countess of Pembroke, the two fading Flowers and the Venus which were in my Grandfather's[2] house. W. would like to see them. Miss F.[3] is not come yet nor have I heard anything further. I suppose D. to have told you that she was coming. Miss [? Hutton] is however begun at Edinburgh so she is lost for one 6 months. Mrs White means to engage *one* for 6 months by way of trial. This is the great encouragement she is to look for after all!—What a sad accident Mary H's might have been—blessed be God it was not so! I scarcely read your letter this [morning] before it was sent to the Post for D. so if I do not seem to have read it you know the reason. Miss G.[4] is terrible! Her Sofa is come, a most ugly thing, but I do not say so. I want you my most dear Sister painfully—Give my love to all who remember us with kindliness—I dropped the thought of a servant from you as soon as I had sent my letter off for it occurred to me that a Dartmoor or Yorkshire lass would not do in our cow-house—we have not got one nor heard of any. Bring me something to make caps or what would be better make 2 or 3. I like them best (spite of what D. says) that go under the chin for they spare trouble

[1] Miss Elizabeth Monkhouse (1750–1828), maternal aunt of M. W. She lived later with Thomas and Mary Hutchinson at Radnor and Brinsop.

[2] Mr. John Monkhouse, the postmaster at Penrith, d. 1796.

[3] i.e. Miss Fletcher, a governess who had been engaged by the Wordsworths, Hardens, Lloyds, and others to set up a school in Ambleside. See *SH* 18, p. 58

[4] Miss Green. See *MY* 491, pp. 574 and 578; *SH*, p. 59.

and save ribbons which I always *mislay*—I am rejoiced at what you say of Mrs Elstob and Betsy.[1]

Old Mrs Knott has just sent me a letter she has had from her niece written at Carlisle on her return from the Highlands and Edin: with Miss Lloyd and Miss Stanley. She is in high spirits and they were going to stay on this week at [?]. Never was seen such fine weather —Yesterday was a wet day the only one for ages—today is beautiful again but we cannot expect a continuance of such unexampled season as it has been—the leaves are only just beginning to fade, and the corn is more beautiful than ever I remember it.

Tuesday—We have not been a moment alone since D. went. We had H. Lowther[2] and his Bride i.e., they dined here and we dined with them at A. and then the day they went this Blossom[3] arrived. The Lloyds are not come home. C.[4] has been very ill. Mrs Harden[5] says he hates Brathay and is going to quit it immediately. Joanna said G. was come off to Brough Hill[6] and would be here if he was not obliged to drive what he might purchase himself.

307. D. W. to CATHERINE CLARKSON

Address: Mrs Clarkson, Bury, Suffolk.
Endorsed: 'Without date probably Jany 1814'.
MS. British Museum.
K (—). *MY i. 492, p. 578.*

4th October [1813]

My dearest Friend,

I am utterly inexcusable for having been so long in writing to you though I have had a thousand reasons for it. First and foremost (and in that are involved all the rest) I was resolved not to write until I had read your Husband's Book,[7] of which literally I have not even now read ten pages, from want of time to read anything. My whole summer's reading has been a part of two volumes of Mrs Grant's American Lady[8], which Southey lent to be speedily re-

[1] Elizabeth Hutchinson, M. W.'s sister who was in the care of Mrs. Elstob. See *SH*, 20, p. 67.

[2] The Revd. Henry Lowther, Rector of Distington, Cumberland. He married Eleanor Younger of Whitehaven on 14 Sept. 1813.

[3] i.e. Mr. Blakeney.

[4] Charles Lloyd.

[5] Wife of John Harden of Brathay Hall. See L. 304 above.

[6] Brough Hill was the scene of the annual horse fair which George Hutchinson had been attending.

[7] See L. 305, p. 116, n. 2, above.

[8] *Memoirs of an American Lady*, by Mrs. Anne Grant of Laggan, 1808, author of the popular *Letters from the Mountains* (1806). (Note by de Selincourt.)

turned, and a dip or two in Southey's Nelson[1]—with snatches at the Newspaper and Sunday's readings with the Bairns. I look forward to long evenings and winter's quiet; and I hope they will not be succeeded by such a bustling summer as the last, though of that we have had no reason to complain, for it has not been of a very fatiguing nature nor such as *exclude* the intervention of serious thought, and harshly banish reflections which *will* have their course at one time or another, and which must be indulged [at times] or tranquillity can never come; and it has been much better for all of us, especially Mary than perfect stillness would have been. Yet in looking back upon it I feel that much of the knowledge which I had formerly gained from Books has slipped from me, and it is grievous to think that hardly one new idea has come in by that means. This in itself would be no great evil, but the sorrows of this life weaken the memory so much that I find reading of far less use than it used to be to me, and if it were not that my feelings were as much alive as ever there would be a growing tendency for the mind to barrenness. But how I have wandered from my point. We shall have more leisure in Winter, and we never *can* have such a summer, for consider the work of removal—and we have had so many visitors, [who had not been with us][2] who had not been to see us for a long time before, and who came to see the new place almost as much as to see *us*. Our domestic occupations are now comparatively few. We have fitted up the house completely—Willy goes to school—and there is no likelihood of more children to nurse; and though, if we could nurse them with the same chearful confidence as before I should be glad that Mary were likely to have another Child, I do not now wish it. I should so dread the anxieties attending the common diseases of Infancy—but there is no prospect of it—and a Lady[3] is going to begin a school at Ambleside, which will release us of 4 hours in the day employed except when other engagements absolutely prevented it in attending to Dorothy. I earnestly wish that the school may answer. First because if it does, D will make ten times the progress with far less trouble to herself, and because it is a painful reflection that we are thus employed in what another could perform better, and at the same time doing a service to herself, while to us it is quite the contrary. Of all the Girls in the world Dorothy most requires the discipline of a school. She is as quick as lightning but thoughtless and unsteady. From the

[1] Southey's *Life of Nelson*, an expansion of his article in the fifth number of the *Quarterly Review* was published in 1813. (Note by de Selincourt.)

[2] Erased.

[3] Miss Fletcher. See L. 306, p. 120, n. 3 above.

restlessness of her disposition continually needing the silent influence of example to keep her, if it were only from shuffling in her chair. For the last three weeks her name-sake Dorothy W[1]—a fine girl three years older but very backward at her Books has been with us, and I taught them regularly, and it is inconceivable with how much more ease than with Dorothy alone. This little Girl who is like an elder Sister of the Family, resembling both J and D in Features, is to stay till Midsummer and go to school. They are delighted with the idea of taking their dinners and the walk will do them good—it is not quite a mile and a half. John goes to Mr Dawes' school so they will be a nice party. Poor Mrs Peake[2] has been with us a fortnight. She is a sweet gentle Creature beloved by every one [she] has known either in prosperity or adversity. She had more enjoyment while she was with us than I could have thought possible; for the loss of such a Husband is a heart-breaking sorrow. I came with her and her Sister and Brother as far as Kendal last Tuesday—she is on her way to her Husband's Friends in London. That Brother, a lad of 15, was wounded by the same cannon Ball which killed her Husband, was taken up insensible and covered with Captain Peake's Blood. The poor Widow seems to feed on his discourse taking in every circumstance, and making a hundred thousand inquiries which cannot be answered. We had the Mother[3] also for several days, a mild sweet-tempered woman, who could not have lived till this day if she had not been gifted with a surpassing patience. She has an indolent Husband, who has long been helpless from corpulency; and is subject to the most frantic passions—her eldest son is skaken in body and mind by a paralytic stroke. She lost one son by the yellow fever, a Daughter by the hydrophobia—and to crown all—and worst of all; another Daughter, who was the housekeeper of the family, a remarkably steady and sensible young Woman to all appearance, has lately connected herself with a young lad—their servant—an idle Blackguard—was with child by him, and that, disgraceful as it was, would have been comparatively a small affliction, if she had not stolen away to be married. The Father is frantic with rage—and as the Man is worthless nothing can be looked forward for them but poverty and wretchedness. We hope that Mrs Peake will have a pension from Government and her Husband's Friends are very good and respectable people, so she in worldly matters will not be ill off; but the needs of her family and the claims of a selfish Father I fear will press upon her kind nature—but she must not live

[1] See L. 304, p. 112, n. 2 above.
[2] See L. 293, p. 96, n. above.
[3] i.e. Mrs. Richard W.

near them. You have heard no doubt of our Friend Tillbrook's sad accident. I met him in Ambleside streets, and I cannot express how much I was shocked when I recognized him after looking steadily at him some time. He was going on Crutches and naturally I feared something even worse than the truth—at the same time remembrances of changes at home rushed upon me and I was much affected. He was 3 times at Rydale—and very chearful—and I hope that Mr Grosvenor will soon set him right—he recovered daily while he was at Ambleside. I like Tillbrook well—he is a kind honest creature and always seems at home with us. When you see him he will tell you all about us and Rydale, and I hope will get your husband into such a genial mood that you will at once plan your journey into the North. You took no notice of my hint about John Gough for Tom.[1] I do think from what I see it would be as nice a [? situation] for him. There are two very nice lads with him now, one is the son of Mr Marshall of Watermillock. He seems to be very happy and his mind is awakened to great activity by the society and instructions of Mr Gough. I have been at Kendal since Tuesday and shall stay there till the end of the week. Luckily for me I have escaped a visitor at home, a Mr Blakeney[2] from Whitehaven, a kind creature but ridiculously vain. He has been at Rydale ever since I came to K. I shall stay till Friday or Saturday. I could tell you some droll stories of this said Mr B with whom William and Mary spent a few days at Whitehaven lately. Southey is in London—Perhaps that accident may bring Coleridge down. He *ought* to come to see after Hartley, who wants removing to another school before he goes to College; for his oddities increase daily, and he wants other Discipline. But because he ought to come, I fear he will not; and how is H. to be sent to College? These perplexities no doubt glance across his mind like dreams—but nothing ever will rouze the Father to his duty *as Duty*. Tillbrook told us of the Edinburgh review and of Mr. Graham's Rage.[3] They are a vicious set and as such have now begun to be hated by all good people, and as judges of literature the Few who know anything have long despised them; but the misfortune is that they are but a *Few*. This Book cannot be so interesting we know as the History of the Abolition, but whenever Mr Clarkson is deeply interested he writes well and *must write* well—he cannot help it—and in the flatter parts of all [his] works there is always a pleasing

[1] i.e. Tom Clarkson. For Gough, see L. 305, p. 115 n.

[2] See L. 295 above.

[3] The *Edinburgh* reviewed Mr. Clarkson's *Life of William Penn* in which Mr. Graham is apparently Mr. Graham of Glasgow. See L. 29, pt. i, p. 50, n. 3.

simplicity and good sense which the Edinburgh Reviewers can neither understand nor value.—I cannot feel as you do respecting the Laureateship.[1] It seems to me there is no disgrace attending to the Office itself, and it may be filled without sacrificing to servility or flattery. Surely we cannot be so disgraced but this great nation may perform acts worthy of praise, and even if personal comp^ts^ to the Monarch are necessary surely there will be something to praise without falsehood or bad indeed must he be. I have written this letter under all sorts of interruptions and a meagre letter it is for I have told you nothing; and my Brains are never very clear when I am from home for a short visit. Mary is much better than she was—all else well. We expect Sara from Stockton about the 20th. She has been there nearly a month. Henry has been at Rydale and rode to S. with her. William has been at Lowther where he met the Duchess of Richmond,[2] and *heaps* of fine folks. Do write immediately. Oh do say you will come next summer—Now do not put off writing and I assure you I will [not]. Love to Mr Tom your Father and Mrs Kitchener. I must not forget *her*. Tillbrook gives a charming account of your Tom. God bless you my beloved Friend and do write. I will not do the same again, I will write very soon and I will write a long answer when I can have a whole quiet evening—a great relief you escaped as you did when your horse played that trick. Kendal 4th October. Wm and M's Wedding day—

308. D. W. to SARA HUTCHINSON

Address: Miss Sara Hutchinson, at John Hutchinson's Esqre, Stockton-upon-Tees.
MS. WL.
MY ii. 486.

Kendal Saturday 10th October [1813]
[D. W. writes 'August'.]

My dearest Sara,

You will be surprized to find me still at Kendal. The Marshalls wrote that they could not come till the middle of the month, so as Mrs Cookson very much wished me to stay, and as I wished to pay her a visit that was worth something I consented; and indeed I have

[1] Southey had just been appointed Poet Laureate, on Scott's declining the office.

[2] Lady Charlotte Gordon, d. of the 4th Duke of Gordon and wife of the 4th Duke of Richmond, hostess of the famous ball in Brussels on 14 June 1815, which was interrupted by the beginning of the Waterloo campaign. See Byron, *Childe Harold*, Canto IV.

been in great luck for they have had Mr Blakeney[1] and crowds of other company. I was truly glad to escape him; but I think if I had known how very much they [were] going to be bustled with company and going out I should have gone home for the sake of regular attendance on the children. After all we hear no more of Miss Fletcher,[2] and I cannot but fear she will not come—and from whim and lack of spirit I fear if she does they will never make it answer for her. They dined on Wednesday at Mr de Q's, met the Wilsons,[3] and took Dr Parry the Inspector of the Stamp Office,[4] who has stayed at Rydal M.—a pleasant Man, and he and the Distributor are great friends; but it does appear that nothing can be gained by Interest, and there is no allowance for extra expenses excep[t] 1.s in the 20.s for carriage; so our place is prettily docked. Wilkin or his Friends must have acted a roguish part in the representation for the sake of getting a larger allowance. I verily believe that Wm, deducting expenses and clerk will not make above 100£ this year, but the sale of stamps next half year will be much more. Mary says that Miss Green has been poorly since the Lowthers were here—and adds 'thereby hangs a tale'. She had never been up at the Mount—I guess she had been offended at not being invited,—what a foolish Body that she could ever think Rydale could suit her! Nothing but poverty keeps her there this winter, and what has made her poor but furnishing that house so expensively? Mary desires you will get Miss Green some Remnants of dark-coloured calico to make out her patch work, for window curtains, and she adds that you are to get her some beautiful pale blue calico to line them with; but she say nothing of the quantity. Here is a letter for you from Miss Dolbie. It contains nothing particular, except that Miss King will not believe that Luff did not know what use was to be made of the house when he lett it. I have one from Miss King also which confirms this. Mary tells me that poor little D. continues to look very ill. She was overstimulated when her cousin John[5] came and looked wretchedly when I left home. This is very grievous, for she was particularly well, and looked so before that time. Her eyes are very weak. Miss Knott writes to her Aunt in great spirits. She and Mrs Ll. had been at L. Lomond, Katterine, Inverness etc. etc—Lloyd met them at Carlise, and they returned to Allonby for a week.

[1] See L. 295 above.
[2] See L. 306, p. 120, n. 3.
[3] i.e. John Wilson of Elleray and his wife, formerly Jane Penny.
[4] Dr. Henry Parry. See L. 434 below.
[5] i.e. John W., eldest son of C. W. and his wife Priscilla, sister of Charles Lloyd.

Wonders cease not. It is inconceivable to me how Mrs Ll. could have a moment's comfort. I think that Mary will hire Mary Allison so trouble yourself no further. As to your return, though Mary when she desires me to answer your letter, says nothing about it, I think I may positively assure you that William is not likely to fetch you. He has had so many engagements that I believe he will wish to be quiet. I am very sorry for this, as I foresee a troublesome and disagreeable journey for you, if you come with John—and delays upon the Road. It would be far better if H.[1] could come with you and stay a while, but that would cause delay also; for he could not leave home during John's absence. Mrs Cookson desires me to tell you that we have plenty of snuff here as well as you: and have greatly the advantage over you in point of liveliness for we are merry till 12 o'clock at night. This liveliness I can assure you does not extend to the town in general. We have visited very often in a *free* way, and that I thought dull enough; but yesterday we were at a party at John [Bunyon]'s and that for dullness surpassed all my conceptions—only Mr B in a private room introduced me to the old Woman, and she was exquisitely amusing. The Cooksons are the kindest people in the world and it is impossible not to be comfortable with them, if we could but keep aloof from visiting. I shall return to Rydale on Monday—and then no more going from home for me!—But what do you think? (and this shall prevent my promised visit to Miss Barker[2] at Keswick) What do you think? Coleridge and the Morgans are coming down immediately, in such a hurry that they cannot wait for Southey.[3] The M.s intend to settle at K for cheapness. Mary says 'I suppose you know that the Morgans have *smashed*'. Now this I did not know, but I had heard that they were poor, and had had losses I believe. Mary says that she doubts not Coleridge had given them to understand there was room enough for them at G. Hall; but Mrs C has taken lodgings for them. Where will the poet's home be now? Dear Sara, It is altogether a melancholy business—com[ing] with them and would not come to see his children! No plans laid for H.![4] I foresee nothing but jealousies and discomforts. Happy we in being 15 miles off! I have bought Willy a Doll—so you much chuse something else for him. I can think of no more commissions but you must refer to my last letter, and remember the fur for the collar and bands of my pellisse. Dear Sara,

[1] i.e. John and Henry Hutchinson, S. H.'s brothers with whom she had been staying.

[2] See L. 257, p. 42, n. 3 above.

[3] This projected visit of Coleridge never took place.

[4] i.e. Hartley Coleridge.

this is a sad hurried stupid letter—I have only seen Parson Harrison[1] once. Mr C seems to think that he follows low company and he complains of poverty and Alicia trails about the streets. Truly sorry I am for these things and certainly his never coming to see me looks badly. Ma'am I had the pleasure of meeting Miss Yates Maa'm at Mr Rawson's Ma'am, and she was very well Ma'am and made many inquiries about Rydale Mount Ma'am and the Ladies at the Hall Ma'am! She has a good countenance and I found her one of the pleasantest people of the party. I like the [?]s, the Thompsons and Miss Holme, but all people are better when they keep away from parties—and their fine clothes.

I expect every moment to be called to dinner and after dinner we are going to call at John Gough's.[2] I long for dear Rydale again—and to see them all and you there my dear Sara. Keep at home all winter—and if D goes to school we may have time for quiet Reading. I brought the measure of the Darling's tombstone, and William was to have written out the two texts and sent them to me, but it is not done. This hangs on my spirits—but when I go home I will perform the task myself—Dear Sara, I am little fit for it, for, do what I can the thought of him rends my heart at times and hard work have I had since I came t[o Ken]dal to bear up often and often. If you can get any cheap and good Towelling pray do—I wanted to get 12 at Mrs. Tallon's like those you got but could not. Mrs. Cookson enquires about some sheep skins that were to be sent to [? from] Hindwell. Before a fortnight I hope you will be with us.

[*unsigned*]

309. W. W. to the COMMISSIONERS OF STAMPS

Address: To the Honourable Commissioners, Stamp Office, London.
MS. Public Record Office.
Hitherto unpublished.

22 Nov. 1813.

Honourable Sirs,

In answer to the Complaint that upon application to my Subdistributor at Appleby, no printed forms of Legacy Receipts could be procured of him, I beg leave to mention that the late Subdistributor at Appleby having declined the employment, I was obliged to appoint another, who being new to the business could not previously be aware how soon his Stock of Forms might be exhausted. Upon

[1] A Dissenting Minister, the Revd. John Harrison. See L. 472 below.

[2] See L. 305, p. 115 and n. above.

application to me he was immediately furnished with what he desired. And all my subdistributors have received directions not to suffer their Stocks to be consumed before they write for a fresh supply. In regard to the like Complaint from [? Mr.] Elsham I beg leave to state that there is a mistake in this. There is no Subdistributor belonging to this District residing in that place, nor to my knowledge ever has been.

I shall do all in my power to prevent future disappointments in this respect.

I have the honour to be
Honourable Sirs,
Your most obedient humble Servant
Wm. Wordsworth.

310. W. W. to BASIL MONTAGU

Address: Basil Montagu Esq[re], Lincoln's Inn, London.
MS. Houghton Library, Harvard University.
MY ii. 492a, p. 583.

Rydale Mount
Thursday 20th Jan[ry] [1814]

My dear Montagu,

My sister went over to Keswick yesterday to see Basil[1] and to assist Miss Barker. She found him easier, and he had had a better night. But since I wrote you he had been considerably worse having had several copious discharges of blood, which led Mr Edmundson to apprehend the worst.—When D. wrote yesterday he had been 24 hours without a renewal of the discharge, but he is deplorably reduced.

He begs me to thank you for your kind offers and intentions and will let you know when he wants anything.—This is from himself. For my own part I think it would be well that you should send a supply of money immediately. Not that I know that he is at present without, but he is scrupulous about putting you to expence; and your sending his money before it may be wanted might spare him inconvenience and pain. Mrs Lloyd went over with my Sister to see

[1] The eldest son of Basil Montagu; he had been cared for by the Wordsworths as a small boy at Racedown and Alfoxden. See *EY* 50, p. 147. He was now both mentally and physically in a very bad way, and his father had sent him to Ambleside, hoping that the company of the Wordsworths would do him good. D. W. stayed for three months with Miss Barker, to help nurse him when he fell ill. For Miss Barker, see L. 257, p. 42, n. 3, above.

him, Mrs Lloyd returned last night in the Chaise, but late and through a violent storm of snow—so that we did not see her on her return. I understand that Basil is in good [? spirits] but tranquillity is indispensable to him, he [? appears] to be agitated when he [?] receives Letters concerning his health. Therefore what you have to say, had better not be addressed to him directly, but to Miss Barker. —With much concern for the situation of poor Basil who has much interested all who have known him in this country, I remain dear Montagu,

Your very affectionate Friend
Wm Wordsworth

If he recovers I should most strenuously recom[mend] Horse exercise to him. He [has] walked too much.

311. D. W. to R. W.

Address: Richard Wordsworth Esq[re] Staple Inn, London.
MS. WL.
MY ii, 493, p. 584.

Keswick 23rd Janry 1814

My dear Brother,

William has desired me to write to inform you that he drew upon you on the 20th of this month for 40£–15s–8d in favor of Mr Isaac Dickinson, at one Month after date.

I came to Keswick on Wednesday to assist Miss Barker, a Friend of ours, in nursing poor Basil Montagu, (M's eldest Son) who came to Ambleside to spend the winter, and chancing to be at Miss Barker's upon a Visit he was seized with a most violent spitting of Blood, and is brought to great weakness. He is only moved out of bed every other day to have his bed made. If the severity of the weather should abate he will probably get out again; but I fear there is little chance of his final recovery. We apprehend that a Consumption will come on.

I hope you bear this cold weather better than you did the *heat* of summer. We are all well. William and his Son John skating on Rydale Water every day.

Believe me, dear Richard
your affect[e] Sister
D Wordsworth

Dorothy Wordsworth (Rd W's youngest Daughter)[1] is at Rydale.

[1] See L. 304, p. 112, n. 2, above.

She has been there four months and is to stay till the midsummer Holidays. She is a very good Girl, and we are all exceedingly fond of her.

312. D. W. to R. W.

Address: Richard Wordsworth Esq[re], Staple Inn, London.
MS. WL.
MY ii. 494, p. 584.

Keswick Feb[ry] 2nd [1814]

My dear Brother,

I am sorry to have occasion to trouble you again so soon with a letter, for if I had known of the occasion which I have had today to draw upon you I might, when I apprized you of William's draft, also have informed you of mine.

I drew upon you this day in favour of Miss Mary Crosthwaite for 50£, at two Months. I am going today to write to Messrs Twining with an order for Tea, and I must desire them to draw upon you for the amount of their last year's Bill against William. I believe the Sum is £[*seal*] or upwards.—I am still [at] Keswick—Basil Montagu continues in a state of great weakness; but the discharge of Blood has ceased, and we hope he will be enabled to move from this place in the course of a few weeks, if the Frost should go away; but this extreme cold is much against him. I hope you are pretty well, and that we shall see you n[ext] Spring. I am, dear [Richard]

Your affect[e] [Sister]
D Word[sworth]

313. W. W. to RICHARD SHARP

Address: Richard Sharp Esq[re], Mark Lane, London.
MS. untraced.
MY ii. 496, p. 585.

Rydal Mount 21st Feb[y] [1814]

My dear Sir,

Having an inflammation in my eye I am obliged to employ an amanuensis, which will be a gain to you as you will be sure of legible writing.

21 February 1814

About the time when I received your last, enclosing the £10 for charitable uses, Miss Hutchinson (whose pen I now employ) had a melancholy Letter from a connection of her's the contents of which being communicated to me at that time, made me think that your benevolence and ability might perhaps furnish some relief for the distress there described. The particulars are as follows. Mrs Monkhouse[1] the person who writes the Letter, is by marriage an Aunt of Mrs W. and Miss H. She has been a few years a widow having nothing but an annuity to live upon which expires with her. This Annuity she shares with her Niece, a widow likewise, who is principally supported, along with her two Children, by that allowance—they all living together—Mrs M., the Aunt, is advanced in years; and has some reason to dread a Cancer; and under this apprehension expresses herself under great anxiety for the fate of her Niece and the two Children after her death—and adds that her mind would be relieved from a heavy load if she could see the Boy in a way of being educated without being burthensome to his Mother. With this view she has made application to some of her Friends to procure him admission into Christ's Hospital but without success. Now the purport of this Letter is—not to avail myself of your general benevolence, or particular kindness to me, so far as to tax you with obligations or disagreeable exertions for the relief of this afflicted Woman; but merely to communicate the facts to you in the full confidence that the case is one which will excite your sympathy, and that if you have an influence, direct or indirect, over the Trustees of that Institution you will be likely of your own accord to exert it, unless there should be weighty reasons to the contrary. If nothing can be done in this Institution could you point out any other from which a Person so situated might be benefitted?

I have the pleasure to say that we have made four or five worthy families happy in this Country out of your donation—and Mrs. W., your Almoner, will furnish you in writing with an account of the Disbursements when we have the pleasure of seeing you next summer, which we confidently hope for—unless a Peace wafts you over to Paris.

I take the Pen to subscribe myself
most truly and respectfully yours
Wm Wordsworth

[1] Mrs. William Monkhouse, whose husband d. 1809, was Ann Cowper, whose sister Dorothy married the Wordsworths' uncle Dr. William Cookson. William M. was the eldest son of John M. of Sebergham and Penrith, M. W.'s maternal grandfather.

314. D. W. to JOSIAH WADE

Address: To Mr. Josiah Wade, Bristol.
Stamp: Keswick 298.
MS. Cornell.
Hitherto unpublished.

Keswick 27th March 1814
Miss Wordsworth[1]

My dear Sir,

I am sure that you will at once recognise the name of an old Friend though the hand-writing will appear to you like that of a Stranger, so many years have elapsed since we have seen each other or heard any tidings except through the medium of mutual acquaintances.

I write at the request of Mrs Coleridge, who is in an anxious and unhappy state of mind, not having had letters from Coleridge or any direct intelligence concerning him for a long time, and as he is at Bristol she and I hope that through your means her wishes may be communicated to him. She wrote to him many weeks ago to remind him of the Insurance upon his Life which ought to be paid about this time, and she would take it very kindly if you would ask him if it has been paid. Her letter touched upon several other important points, especially the completion of Hartley's education, she being now most anxious (for he is now 17 years old) that some plan should be settled and the means pointed out for the execution of it. I hope you may be able to learn from his Father what his views are respecting Hartley, and I should be exceedingly happy and most grateful to you if you could communicate to me any thing satisfactory on this head: but, at all events, I beg you will not fail, without delay, to put the question to him respecting the Insurance; and all other information which you can give us concerning Coleridge will be very acceptable. Many Months ago he gave Mrs Coleridge and his Friends reason to expect that he would be coming into the North;[2] and I hope that the Spring or Summer may tempt him down, provided he can go on with such labours as he may have planned, which I should think might be better done in the Country than in London, Bristol, or any large town.—. I have been staying nine weeks at Keswick with a Miss Barker, Mr Southey's next door

[1] D. W. writes this at the head of her letter to acquaint Wade at once with the identity of the writer. For Wade, see L. 45, pt, i. p. 80.

[2] D. W. must be here referring to S. T. C.'s promise to visit them early in 1813, after the death of Thomas Wordworth in Dec. 1812. See L. 273 above, and Morley, i. 30, p. 71.

Neighbour, at whose house, Basil Montagu, whom you were so kind to at Bristol, was taken dangerously ill three months since. I came hither to assist her in attending upon him. His disorder was a violent Haemorrage, which brought him to the last state of weakness; but he is now recovering, though I fear that his Life will not be long. There is great cause to apprehend a Consumption. I hope to be able to return home in about three weeks. We now live at Rydale, fifteen miles from Keswick. Coleridge's Boys are at School within two miles of us, & we frequently see them. They are fine Lads—both good and clever—favorites with their School-master, and approved of by every Body else who knows them. Sara Coleridge is also very clever, & a good Girl; but poor thing! her health is not strong; & she has at present unfortunately sprained her ancle which hinders her from using as much exercise as is desirable. Mrs Coleridge is well in health, and desires to be kindly remembered to you.

My Brother and his Wife and Children are well. He has now only three Children, having suddenly lost two in the course of one short half a year, an interesting Girl almost four years old, and a lovely and most promising Boy of six years and a half. These were heavy afflictions. — —

I have now only to beg that you will favor me with a letter as soon as possible—directing to me at Miss Barker's Keswick. I am aware that on a first interview with Coleridge you may probably not be able to touch upon some of the subjects of inquiry which I have proposed to you: but I beg that you will not fail in the first instance, and *immediately*, to ask him concerning the Insurance; and for Mrs Coleridge's satisfaction pray write as soon as you can give an answer on that head; and any further information hereafter will much oblige me.

I beg you will inform me of the state of your own health, and any other particulars respecting your own prospects or way of life will be very acceptable. If my Brother were here he would join with me in kind Remembrances and good wishes.

I am dear Sir with lively recollections of kindnesses received from you long ago. Yours sincerely

Dorothy Wordsworth

[*written at foot of last sheet*]

ans^d^. Ap^l^. 1. J. W.

315. W. W. to ROBERT BLAKENEY

Address: Robt. Blakeney Esqre, Cross Street, Whitehaven.
MS. Cornell.
Hitherto unpublished.

Rydale Mount 1st April 1814

My dear Sir,

I cannot forbear writing to you on the Subject of your House at Fox Gill.[1] I was there yesterday with the Ladies of my Family and we are unanimously of opinion, that neither yourself nor any of your Friends could have satisfaction in the sitting rooms with Windows of the present dimensions.—They are all too short; they cannot be set lower in the wall, and therefore it is impossible to remedy the defect but by new ones. At present when you enter the Rooms, and place yourself on a chair by the fire you seem *almost* to be in a well or dungeon. This is a strong expression, but I mean to say the Country is excluded, the windows being so high. This is particularly the case with regard to those that look up the beautiful stream towards Rydale. The Chamber Windows need not be altered. If, then, there is any prospect of your having the House for your own use, I should most strenuously recommend four new Windows of a different construction, the present being taken in part of payment on the best terms you can procure. I speak this with the utmost confidence that if they be suffered to remain as at present, and you come to live at the place, you will be obliged to alter them at three times the expense.—The Windows I should recommend for a House of this kind, are *french* windows opening in the middle like folding doors, and with very small panes, according to the model in Mr Wilson's Cottage (not his large House)[2] at Elleray.—But this is *comparatively* insignificant but certainly they ought to be much of a length exceeding the present by one pane at *the very least*. An alteration also is indispensible in the door of the smaller front Room, which door-way was made for a Pantry, and is large enough for that purpose but contemptibly narrow for a drawing or dining Room. The Main entrance door into the House being at first intended for a back door, is also too small; but as there is to be a glass door for the front Parlour this perhaps may be tolerated.—I

[1] Fox Ghyll, one of the houses 'under Loughrigg', successively inhabited by Mr. Blakeney, De Quincey, who took it (in addition to the cottage at Grasmere) from 1820 to 1824, and ultimately (1825) by Mrs. Luff, who bought it. See *LY* i. 735, p. 187.

[2] On the slope of Orrest Head, Windermere, occupied intermittently by John Wilson, 1808–15.

heard from the Workmen that Humphrey has paid all arrears and had sent to know when the House would be ready, being I suppose impatient to come. This vexed me much.—I have scarcely left myself room to congratulate you on your success in the matrimonial pursuit. I heartily wish you the happiness you deserve.—

Mr Stanly of Ponsonby[1] has been at Rydal Hall lately; he stayed upwards of a fortnight—I saw much of him and liked him much better than I had done before, though he is no Conjuror.
With best regards from the Ladies I remain

Most truly yours
W Wordsworth

(Turn over)

We were very sorry to hear of the Death of your worthy Housekeeper! I don't think I ever saw a person in that rank of life who interested me so much.—Excuse this miserable scrawl. — —.

316. W. W. to R. W.

Address: Richd Wordsworth, Esq., Sockbridge, near Penrith, to be forwarded.
MS. WL.
MY ii. 497, p. 587.

Rydale Mount 1st April 1814

My dear Richard,

In my last Letter I am afraid I forgot to request you to call yourself if in London, and receive from Basil Montagu two hundred pounds on my account, delivering up at the same time the securities relating to the annuity.[2] I have already received one hundred, and Montagu, when the two hundred shall be paid which is now, he assures me, ready, will owe me nothing but about a year's interest of three hundred pounds, and what may be due to me on account of the policy which will be settled as soon as he and I meet.

If you are not in Town yourself pray write *immediately* to Mr Addison, to receive the money for me and to give up the writings.—I shall want the money to pay for the small purchase I made near Keswick, and shall draw upon you for 250£ in a short time.

Most affectionately yours
Wm Wordsworth

[1] Ponsonby Hall, Cumberland, near Calder Bridge, between Gosforth and Egremont.

[2] This letter refers to the final settlement of Montagu's debt to Wordsworth of £300, secured on annuity, which was first contracted in 1796. See Moorman, i, pp. 269, 296–7.

317. D. W. to RICHARD ADDISON

MS. Messrs. Bleaymire & Shepherd, Penrith.
Hitherto unpublished.

Keswick 16 April [1814]

Dear Sir,

I write to inform you that I yesterday signed a draft for the sum of £250 in favour of Mr John Fleming,[1] payable at one month after date to be placed to my Br. William's account. Most likely you will hear from Richard upon this subject as Mr Montagu has £200 ready to pay into your hands for my Brother William's use;[2] and I believe the trouble of receiving this sum will fall upon you. I thought it proper to write to you respecting the draft, the sum being so considerable. [My Br.] thinks it probable that you may not have heard from my Br. Richard and about the affair with Mr Montagu and that his letter apprising you of the Draft may be delayed on account of his distance from the Post Town.

I am Dear Sir
yours respectfully
Dorothy Wordsworth

I shall draw upon my Brother Richard in a day or two for £10 on my own account in favour of Miss Barker.

318. D. W. to CATHERINE CLARKSON

Address: Mrs Clarkson, Bury St Edmonds, Suffolk.
Stamp: Keswick 298.
MS. British Museum.
K. MY ii. 498, p. 587.

Keswick Sunday April 24th [1814]

You will be surprised at the date of this letter 'still at Keswick'. True it is that I am still here but I should have been at home to day if all-day rain yesterday had not kept me here—and to-day there is such a storm of wind and rain and snow upon the mountain-tops that I cannot stir. I hope the elements will have satisfied their rage

[1] Probably W. W.'s early friend of Hawkshead days, now curate of Bowness. If this sum was in repayment of a loan, it may have been in connexion with the pension he was obliged to pay to his predecessor in the Stamp Distributorship, Mr. Wilkin. See L. 282 above.

[2] This sum must represent the repayment of what remained of the £300 loan which W. W. had made to Montagu from Raisley Calvert's legacy as long ago as 1796. See L. 316 above.

before to-morrow morning when I would willingly depart on foot with Hartley Coleridge who is returning to school; but if otherwise I must submit to the Coach, for I am now restlessly impatient to be at home again. It is a month today since I returned to Keswick after a visit to Rydale of a week; for though I was no longer wanted as a Nurse, Miss Barker had, perhaps, more need than ever for me as a companion.[1] Basil was then and has been ever since able to sit in the Drawing-room; and as Miss Barker's dining-room is his Bedroom she had but one place to sit in and nothing could have been more irksome or melancholy than to be all day long confined with him, without the intervention of any other society; for I am sorry to tell you that almost at the very first [day] of my coming hither she had a dispute with the Females of the other house,[2] which unfortunately, and I think very injudiciously Southey took up—and though he comes to this house to sit with Montagu, he takes care that Miss Barker should know that his visits are not to *her*, yet they talk to each other as pleasantly as can be, and each has a high esteem for the other—But the Ladies 'cannot possibly enter Miss B's house', and there is no free intercourse except with the children whom Miss Barker loves very much and has always been excessively kind to; and they run in and out at their pleasure. *I* go to the other house as usual, and I assure you the part I have had to play has not been over agreeable; for between my zeal for Miss Barker, and the hotness of their tempers, with the utter impossibility of making them look coolly either upon her supposed faults, or her virtues, I have had much ado to prevent quarrels with *me* also. These however, I determined to avoid, and when irritation of mind bubbled over I was obliged to desire that the subject might be dropped. To act as a Mediator is impossible; for Miss B would speak her opinions so plainly if any discussions were to take place between them; and *they* would be in such an outrageous passion that the Breach would only be widened. I trust to their being *forced* together in the Summer, or jumbling upon one another in the Garden—for their gardens join—without any partition but a low railing, and the Road to each house is the same. Should this happen both parties may be hereafter more comfortable than before this estrangement; for there was formerly far too much familiarity between them, considering the total difference in their characters and the perfect incapacity of all of the

[1] D. W. had been at Keswick since Jan. 1814, helping Miss Barker to nurse Basil Montagu junior. See Ls. 311 and 312 above.

[2] i.e. Mrs. Southey and her sisters Mrs. Coleridge and Mrs. Lovell at Greta Hall.

Fricker name[1] from forming a conception of the merits of Miss Barker. How should they assimilate with Generosity, Frankness, Sincerity and perfect disinterestedness; above all when the person possessing these qualities is of a warm temper and disdains to conceal her opinions on any point, and is in the habit of expressing a worthy indignation at all trick and meanness. We have long foreseen that a rupture would take place; or at least that each party would be exposed to so many petty irritations that there would be much less of pleasure than of discomfort in their intercourse. They never can again be on exactly the same terms and keeping (if ever a reconciliation does take place) at a greater distance they will be much better Friends. Miss B came into this country solely on Southey's account and it is a hard case for her that Southey should so yield to the influence of his wife and her sisters as to make him blind to the solitude and uncomfortableness of Miss B's situation if deprived of *his* society—for though she is of a very independent mind, and has numerous resources within herself, yet she has a high enjoyment of society—has been accustomed to it all her life, and is of a very social nature. But I am using half my paper and you are looking for something about Rydale—myself and our own Family. I was led into this long story to show you *how* it could possibly be that I should feel myself bound to stay more than three months from home. Miss Barker is to follow me in a fortnight to Rydale, where after her long confinement and anxiety she will spend a few weeks very pleasantly. I am to take Lodgings at Ambleside for Basil M, who, I am sorry to say, has shewn very little delicacy, being loth to remove from good quarters where he lives *Scot Free*. This I much suspect to be the case, or some expression of uneasiness would long since have broken from him, from the reflection that he had for four months kept Miss Barker and her house and servants constantly devoted to him, and he would have proposed to move as soon as there was any possibility of it. He rides out daily and is now to all appearance nearly as well as before he had the first attack of haemorrhage; but he must spend the next winter in a warmer Climate. If it had not been for this unlucky quarrel I should have been at home many weeks since but as things stand I could not find it in my heart to leave Miss Barker, and the thought of being of so much importance to her, and the pleasure of her society have reconciled me in great measure to my absence from my Family, though I have had many an hour of homesickness. Besides *now* above all other time I should have wished to be at home, for William is actually printing 9 books

[1] The maiden name of Mrs. Southey and her sisters.

of his long poem.[1] It has been copied in my absence, and great alterations have been made some of which indeed I had an opportunity of seeing during my week's visit. But the printing has since been going on briskly, and not one proof-sheet has yet met my eyes. We are all most thankful that William has brought his mind to consent to printing so much of this work; for the MSS. were in such a state that, if it had pleased Heaven to take him from this world, they would have been almost useless. I do not think the book will be *published* before next winter; but, at the same time, will come out a new edition of his poems in two Volumes Octavo, and shortly after—Peter Bell, The White Doe, and Benjamin the Waggoner[2]. This is resolved upon, and I think you may depend upon not being disappointed. Both Wm and Mary looked very ill when I saw them, Mary thinner than ever and evidently weak, though enabled by the power of her spirits to go through more exertion than many a strong and healthy woman would think herself fit for. The worst of it is that she has a bad appetite, and the habit which she has always had of disregarding herself makes her unwilling that any little things not going in the Family should be provided for her—and we always observe that when we happen to have anything nicer than common she always eats of it heartily. Unfortunately we happen for the last ½ year to have had the worst cook in England—but Mary Dawson is coming to live with us at Whitsuntide (whom you remember our servant at the Town End) and Sara and I intend to give *her* an unlimited commission to cook all sorts of nice things for Mary, to which Mary will not object; for (strange it is) Mary in these little things would be far more easily ruled by a servant than by us. Thus extremes meet. The more she loves people the less attentive she is to their happiness in trifles which make up so much of human life—but her own health is not a trifle yet that same disposition of self-sacrifice which has characterized her through life prevents her from taking any care of herself, though she sees and knows how uneasy it makes us. We cannot persuade her to drink wine which both Sara and I are sure is of great service to her. She will never take a glass except when we have company, and we always find that she looks better and is stronger when she has been

[1] *The Excursion*, published in July 1814. It was considered by him to be 'a portion of *The Recluse*'.

[2] The new edition of the shorter poems, with the title *Poems, including Lyrical Ballads*, appeared in 1815, and *The White Doe* in the same year. But *Peter Bell* and *The Waggoner* were not published until 1819, perhaps because of Wordsworth's disappointment over the reception of *The Excursion* and *The White Doe*.

obliged to drink wine for a week or a fortnight together. William was sadly pulled down by the Influenza in the winter, and his hard work since has prevented him from gaining flesh; but he is well and goes on with great vigour and chearfulness in his labours. Sara too was poorly in the winter—she is pretty well now though she is grown thinner. *I* am in excellent health and all persons both in the neighbourhood of Rydale and at Keswick say thay have not seen me look so well for many years. I am really growing fat. The children have all had dreadful coughs—but they are now quite well. Dorothy goes to school and goes on with her Books as well as you can expect any child to do, who does not willingly make it her business and her pleasure, and I hope the time will come when this blessed change will take place, without giving myself much uneasiness at present, as her mind is active and she is by no means backward with any part of learning. As to dear John—as far as scholarship goes he is certainly the greatest Dunce in England; yet I am confident that if the difficulty of learning were once got over he would have great pleasure in Books. He has an excellent memory and his attention never sleeps when any one is reading to him.—

He is gone; the darling who loved his books, and whom his father used to contemplate as the future companion of his studies. Why do I turn to these sad thoughts! Oh! my dearest friend, the pangs which the recollection of that heavenly child causes me it is hard to stifle; and many a struggle have I in all situations, in company and alone, and when in converse as now with you,—but I trust there is no wickedness in this, which is unavoidable. I am reconciled, and resigned, and chearful, except when the struggle is upon me. His poor mother was shaken bitterly by Catharine's Death and I fear she never will be the same chearful creature as heretofore. When left to herself she is dejected—and often weeps bitterly—but I must turn to other subjects. Willy is a dear child—exceptionally lively and very clever—but utterly averse from books. This I think is entirely owing to his having been so much indulged, and I hope that like Thomas, he will at once awaken, and when he begins to learn as with Thomas, there will be no difficulty. I truly sympathised with you when you expressed regret that none of our children loved Books. Herbert Southey[1] is the perfection of a child loving Books and learning, he is all a *Child* at play, and has all the simplicity of a child in all his attainments. The Coleridges are all scholars; but there is not one of them wholly free from affectation—the rest of the

[1] Southey's elder son, who died in Apr. 1816 at the age of ten, to Southey's lasting sorrow.

Southeys are excellent learners and though there is nothing as yet to be seen of extraordinary in any but Herbert they are so ready and industrious that it is nothing but a pleasure to teach them. I trust in the goodness of your Son's heart and understanding for a final relief to all your anxieties. You are over anxious as all Mothers are and all who dearly love children and are intimately connected with their education who are *not Mothers*. So I feel in my own case; but I think I am amending in this way; seeing how little we are capable of governing the effects of others upon our best, and to ourselves seemingly, our wisest endeavours. Pray give my kindest love to Tom and tell him when I next come to Bury I shall expect to find quite the polite well ordered young Gentleman and that he will no longer plague me with noises. To the last page I am come, and not a word of the Emperor Alexander, the King of France or the fallen Monarch! Surely it might seem that to us, encircled by these mountains, our own little concerns outweigh the mighty joys and sorrows of nations; or I could not have been so long silent. It is not so—every heart has exulted—we have danced for joy! But how strange! it is like a dream—peace peace—all in a moment—prisoners let loose—Englishmen and Frenchmen brothers at once!—no treaties—no stipulations. I am however vexed beyond my strength that Buonaparte should have been thus treated—the power was in the hands of the Allies. If he would have stood out with a few of his Miscreants they should have fought him to the Death, and, yielding himself a prisoner he should have been tried for the murders of the Duc d'Enghien, of Pichegru, of Captain Wright—of Palm—of one or all,[1] and what a pension they have granted him! This is folly rather than liberality; for of what use can a large income be in an island without luxuries, and without company. He can have no *wants* beyond a bare maintenance. Therefore if the Superflux be used it must be for the purposes of intrigue or the support of bad people. In short he ought not to be suffered to live, except utterly deprived of power, and while he has so much money he will certainly contrive to convert it into power. Your last letter is not [?] but there were many parts of it which I intended to reply to but I have left myself no room. Do write as soon as possible, tell us everything and if possible gives us hopes by mentioning the *time*, that you will come to see us. My love to your Husband, your dear Father and to

[1] In this month (Apr. 1814) an armistice was signed between the French and the Allies, and Napoleon abdicated and retired to Elba. The Duc d'Enghien and Pichegru had been executed by him in 1804, Capt. John Wesley Wright in 1805, and Johann Philip Palm in 1806. (Note by de Selincourt.)

your Sister when you write. Remember me to Henry Robinson when you see him.

Coleridge is at Bristol doing nothing—and how living I cannot tell. He is at the house of an old Friend, Mr Wade, and has no money. The Morgans are near Bath and had not heard from him for many months. He has talked of coming down to Keswick but all is hopeless. My Brother Richard has married his servant—a young woman about two and twenty!!![1] God bless you my dearest Friend yours evermore

D. Wordsworth.

I should like to see Mrs Kitchener among her Bacons. My love to her. If you should see the Beachings at Bury do not speak of the quarrel between Miss Barker and the next house.

319. W. W. to FRANCIS WRANGHAM

Address: The Rev[d] Francis Wrangham, Hunmanby, Bridlington, Yorkshire.
MS. Henry Huntington Library.
K (—). *MY ii. 499, p. 593.*

Rydal Mount Ap. 26 [1814]
N[r] Kendal

My dear Wrangham,

I trouble you with this in behalf of a very deserving young Clergyman of the name of Jameson,[2] who is just gone from this neighbourhood to a Curacy at Shirborne in the neighbourhood of Ferry Bridge. He has a Mother and a younger Brother dependant upon his exertions; and it is his wish to take pupils in order to encrease his income, which, as a Curate, you know cannot but be small.—He is an excellent young Man, a good Scholar, and likely to become much

[1] Her name was Jane Westmorland. The marriage, although socially somewhat unacceptable to the Wordsworths, was not unhappy. Richard died in May 1816, leaving a son, John, to whom W. W. and C. W. were guardians. He entered the Army as a surgeon, contracted tuberculosis in the Ionian Islands, and returned to England in 1843. He died at Ambleside, tenderly nursed and loved by the Rydal Mount family, in 1846.

[2] Thomas Jameson of Ambleside, younger brother of Robert Jameson, whose wife Anna Brownell was a writer on European art. His youngest brother Joseph, here mentioned, was ordained in 1817 and in 1821 became a minor canon of Ripon Minster, where he remained until his death in 1875. There is a large stained-glass window in the Minster to his memory. For the Jamesons, see L. 156, pt. i, p. 331, n. 1. See also L. 351, p. 209 below.

better, for he is extremely industrious. Among his talents, I must mention that for drawing; in which he is a proficient having at one time designed himself for that profession.—Now my wish is, that if it fall in your way you would voutchsafe him your patronage, and notice.—You come to York upon occasions and if you could drop him a Line at such times he would reckon nothing of going over to wait upon you, were he at liberty.—He thinks of taking pupils at £50 per Ann. and if you could recommend any body to him, relying upon my judgement, I should take it as a great kindness done to my self: as I [am] much interested in his welfare and that of his Family. —Mr J—could have abundant favorable reports from references as to character competence &c, in this part of the Country. But he fears they would not turn to as much account, as a good Word from any distinguished Yorkshire Scholar; and in particular from yourself, who perhaps don't know how famous you are throughout the wide Region of your native County—not to allude to your Celebrity else-where. Of course you cannot speak for him directly till you have seen him; but might he be permitted to refer to you, you would have no objection to say, that you were as yet ignorant of his merits, as to your own knowledge; but that your *esteemed* friend Mr Wordsworth, that *popular* Poet, Stamp-Collector for Westmorland &c, had recommended him strenuously to you, as in all things deserving.—

I am busy with the Printers' Devils. A Portion of a long Poem[1] from me will see the light ere long. I hope it will give you pleasure. It is serious, and has been written with great labour.—Are you likely to be in these parts, during the Summer. I hope so, but should be very sorry that you come dur[ing] my absence, which will be of some weeks. [I] mean to make a tour in Scotland with Mrs W. and her sister Miss Hutchinson. I congratulate you on the overthrow of the execrable Despot:[2] and the complete triumph of the *War-faction* of which noble body I had the honour to be as active a Member as my abilities and industry would allow. Best remembrances to yourself and to Mrs Wrangham, and believe me,

Affectionately yours
W Wordsworth

[1] i.e. *The Excursion, being a Portion of The Recluse, A Poem.*

[2] Napoleon's defeat at Leipzig in 1813 was followed by his abdication and exile to Elba.

320. W. W. to THOMAS POOLE

Address: Thos Poole Esqre, Nether Stowey, Somersetshire.
Endorsed: fr. Wordsworth 28th April 1814 on Hartley Coleridge, Himself, Poems.
MS. British Museum.
TP.
K. MY ii. 500, p. 595.

Rydale Mount near Ambleside
April 28th 1814.

My dear Poole,

I have long thought of writing to you upon the situation of Hartley Coleridge, and have only been prevented by considerations of delicacy towards his Father, whose exertions on behalf of this child I hoped would have rendered any interference of the Friends of the Family unnecessary. But I cannot learn that poor C has mustered courage to look this matter fairly in the face; it is therefore incumbent on his Friends to do their best to prevent the father's weaknesses being ruinous to the Son. H is now 17 years and a half old; and therefore no time is to be lost in determining upon his future course of life.—Knowing your attachment to C and to his family, and that C is now residing at no great distance from you,[1] I beg that you would contrive to see and converse with him upon this subject. I do not expect that C will be able to do anything himself, but his consent will be indispensable before any of his Friends can openly stir in exertions for H.—It is a subject on every side attended with difficulties; for in the first place it is not easy to determine what the youth is fit for. His Talents appear to be very considerable, but not of that kind which may be *confidently* relied upon as securities for an independence in any usual course of exertion. His attainments also though in some departments far exceeding the common measure of those of his age are extremely irregular; and he is deficient in much valuable knowledge both of books and things that might have been gained at a Public School. But could he be *immediately* sent for one year to a school of this kind, I should be emboldened to hope somewhat confidently that such a preparation would enable him to go successfully through either of the Universities.—But it avails little to think or write much about this, till a fund has been secured for his maintenance, till he can support himself, in whatever course of life may be determined upon. Now, I know of nobody who has declared intentions to contribute to this,

[1] Coleridge was at present living in Bristol, with his friend Josiah Wade, giving (in the intervals of illness) a course of lectures on English literature. See E. K. Chambers, *Coleridge*, pp. 258–62.

but Lady Beaumont, who has most kindly offered to advance thirty pounds a year towards maintaining H at the University. Southey has a little world dependent upon his industry; and my own means are not more than my family requires; but something I would willingly contribute, and if it were convenient to you to assist him in this way or any other, it would encourage one to make applications elsewhere. But in all this I defer to you, and wish to know what you advise, and most happy shall I be, to join in anything you recommend.

Having said all that appears necessary on this subject, I cannot but add to an old Friend two or three words about myself; though you probably will have heard from others how I am going on. I live at present in a most delightful situation; and have a public employment which is a comfortable addition to my income, but I pay £100 per annum out of it to my predecessor, and it falls nearly another 100 below the value at which my noble Patron, Lord Lonsdale, had been led to estimate it. My marriage has been as happy as man's could be, saving that we have lost two sweet children (out of five), a boy and girl of the several ages of six and a half and four years. This was a heavy affliction to us, as they were as amiable and promising creatures as a House could be blest with. My poetical Labours have often suffered long interruptions; but I have at last resolved to send to the Press a portion of a Poem[1] which, if I live to finish it, I hope future times will 'not willingly let die'. These you know are the words of my great Predecessor,[2] and the depth of my feelings upon some subjects seems to justify me in the act of applying them to myself, while speaking to a Friend, who I know has always been partial to me.

When you write, speak of yourself and your family. I hear wonders of a niece of yours.[3] May we not hope to see you here? Let it not be during my absence. I shall be from home at least for six weeks during the ensuing summer, meaning to take a tour in Scotland with my wife and her sister. My sister joins in affectionate remembrances to you; and I shall say for my wife that she will be most happy to see you in this place, with which I venture to promise that you will be much pleased. Believe me, my dear Poole,

Most faithfully yours,

W. Wordsworth.

Excuse my wretched penmanship.

[1] i.e. *The Excursion*, 'a portion' of *The Recluse*.

[2] i.e. Milton. The words are from the Preface to *Reason of Church Government*.

[3] Elizabeth Poole, b. 1799, an accomplished classical scholar and musician. In 1823 she married Archdeacon John Sandford.

321. W. W. to SAMUEL ROGERS

Address: Samuel Rogers Esq., S. James Place, S. James St., London.
Postmark: C 9 My 1814. *Stamp*: Kendal Penny Post.
MS. Harvard University Library.
Rogers and his Contemporaries, ed. P. W. Clayden, 1889.
K (—). MY ii. 501, p. 597.

Rydale Mount May 5th 1814

My dear Sir,

Some little time since, in consequence of a distressful representation made to me of the condition of some Persons connected nearly by marriage with Mrs. Wordsworth, I applied to our common Friend, Mr. Sharp,[1] to know if he had any means of procuring an admittance into Christ's Hospital, for a Child of one of the Parties. His reply was such as I feared it would be notwithstanding my firm reliance on his kindness; and as he could do nothing himself, he referred me to you as a Governor of a charitable institution in the City, equally eligible.—He said, he would speak to you on the subject, and inform you of the particulars of the Case which I laid before him, and need not repeat.—If you cannot assist me, pray, point out any means of relief that you are acquainted with, as the Parties are very deserving and the Case a melancholy One.—I should have written sooner, but as I knew that applications were making elsewhere I had hopes that their success would have rendered it unnecessary for me to trouble you.—

I have to thank you for a Present of your Volume of Poems, received some time since, through the hands of Southey. I have read it with great pleasure. The Columbus[2] is what you intended, it has many bright and striking passages, and Poems, upon this plan, please better on a second Perusal than the first. The *Gaps* at first disappoint and vex you.

There is a pretty piece in which you have done me the honour of imitating me—towards the conclusion particularly, where you must have remembered the High-land Girl.[3]—I like the Poem much; but the first Paragraph is hurt by two apostrophes, to objects of different character,[4] one to Luss, and one to your Sister; and the

[1] See L. 313 above.
[2] *The Voyage of Columbus* was published in 1810, and the *Poems* in 1812 and 1814.
[3] W. refers to Rogers's lines 'written in the Highlands'. His own poem, *To a Highland Girl*, had been published in the *Poems in Two Volumes*, 1807.
[4] Here follows a sentence in brackets, afterwards erased: it appears to be '(This is a figure which less than any other would bear abuse)'.

Apostrophe is not a figure, that like Janus, carries two faces with a good grace.—

I am about to print—(do not start!) eight thousand lines, which is but a small portion of what I shall oppress the world with, if strength and life do not fail me.[1] I shall be content if the Publication pays its expenses, for Mr. Scott and your friend Lord B.[2] flourishing at the rate they do, how can an honest *Poet* hope to thrive?

I expect to hear of your taking flight to P[aris,] unless the convocation of Emperors [? Kings] and other Personages by which London is to be honoured, detain you to assist at the festivities. For me, I should like dearly to see old Blucher, but as the fates will not allow, I mean to recompense myself, by an excursion with Mrs. W. to Scotland, where I hope to fall in occasionally, with a Ptarmigan, a Roe, or an Eagle; and the living Bird I certainly should prefer to its Image on the Pannel of a dishonoured Emperor's Coach.

Farewell—I shall be happy to see you here at all times, for your Company is a treat.

Most truly yours.
W. Wordsworth.

322. W. W. to LORD LONSDALE

MS. Lonsdale MSS., Record Office, The Castle, Carlisle.
Hitherto unpublished.

June 4th 1814
Rydale Mount
near Ambleside

My Lord,

I have now in the press and almost ready for publication a Portion of a Work in verse, which I ask permission to inscribe to your Lordship;[3] as the best testimony I can give of my respect for your Lordship's character, and in gratitude for particular marks of favour shown to myself. My Labour is yet very far from being brought to a conclusion; but if this specimen receive your Lordship's approbation, I shall cherish a hope of being enabled, at some future period, to request the same honour for the finished Poem.[4]

[1] W. refers to *The Excursion*, which was published in July 1814.

[2] i.e. Lord Byron. W. W. on more than one occasion expressed his opinion that Scott could scarcely be classed as a poet. Byron had published the first two cantos of *Childe Harold* in 1812; it reached its eighth edition in 1814.

[3] *The Excursion* was dedicated to the Earl of Lonsdale.

[4] i.e. *The Recluse*, of which *The Excursion* formed 'a portion'. But W. W. never completed *The Recluse*.

At present it affords me high satisfaction to know, and to declare, that your Lordship's kindness has removed from my mind many anxieties which interfered with the prosecution of the Work.

I have the honour to be

my Lord
with great respect
your Lordship's most obliged and faithfully
affectionate servant
Wm Wordsworth

323. W. W. to R. W.

Address: Richard Wordsworth Esq[re], Sockbridge.
Endorsed: Delivered 7 Month called July either 1814 or 1815. Thomas Wilkinson.[1]
MS. WL.

[July 1814]

My dear Brother—

I have been long expecting to receive from you the account of our affairs. For heavens sake do expedite this business, and let it be brought to a conclusion—We wish to know what we have, and are most uneasy that we do not know; and it is just and reasonable that we should have command of our money.

The Stocks have already had a great depression, and may suffer a still greater—Again let me beg of you to do justice in this case—We are all well—with best regards to Mrs. W.

Affectionately yours—
W. Wordsworth

324. W. W. to FRANCIS WRANGHAM

Address: The Rev[d] Francis Wrangham, Hunmanby, Bridlington, Yorkshire.
MS. Henry Huntington Library.
K. MY ii. 562, p. 598.

Rydale Mount near Ambleside.
July 16th 1814

My dear Wrangham,

I depart for a Tour in Scotland to morrow, and sit down with this most wretched pen merely to let you know, that I have ordered

[1] M. W. and W. W. were away till mid July in 1815, and in 1814 started for Scotland, 18 July. The probable year is 1814, from the reference to the state of the stock-market, for S. H. writing to her cousin Mrs. Tom Hutchinson in June 1815, says, 'Stocks are up again'. *SH*, 23, p. 81. See also L. 330a below.

a Copy of my Poem[1] to be forwarded as soon as out, to your Publisher; who he is Longman will, I trust, know. I have unfortunately mislaid your last and could not recall to mind the directions you gave me. I thought of desiring Longman to hand the Book to Montagu's to be by him forwarded to you; but when I reflected what a gulph (that word looks queer so spelt) the house in Newman street[2] is, I deemed it best to give the above direction to Longman; if you apprehend that the Poem will not reach you in this way, pray write to Longman stating how you would have it sent: it will be out I hope in ten days from this time at the latest.

I should have been glad to meet you in the late scene of festivities, in London. But having this Tour in view, I could not spare cash for Both, nor indeed should have liked to be so long from home as the two absences would have required. Scotland might have indeed been deferred till another year, but I was anxious that Mrs W— should have the benefit which I hope she will derive from this Excursion, both as to health and spirits.

Excuse this wretched Scrawl which is written in extreme haste. Miss Hutchinson has just opened the door. I asked her if she had any commands. 'Nothing', was the answer—'but He (scilicet Mr W—) may give my Love to Brompton Spire.'[3] Mind, therefore, you do not forget to comply with the Lady's request; I know you are duly sensible of the importance of such messages, being a man of sentiment, and gallant withal without being a m[an] of gallantry: Which Mrs W— and [your] cloth forbid! This is unaccountable, and, I fear, inexcusable levity, farewell; I shall wish myself (for you) a good journey, and a happy return. May all that's good attend you and yours. very affectionately your sincere friend

W. Wordsworth

[1] i.e. *The Excursion*, which was published during July 1814.

[2] The Montagus lived in Frith Street, Soho, until Dec. 1814, when they moved to Bedford Square. W. W. appears to have used the name 'Newman Street' by mistake.

[3] Brompton Church, near Scarborough, had been the scene of Wrangham's wedding to Dorothy Cayley in 1801, and of W. W.'s to M. W. in Oct. 1802.

325. W. W. to LORD LONSDALE

MS. Lonsdale MSS., Record Office, The Castle, Carlisle.
Hitherto unpublished.

Rydale Mount Ambleside.
July 18 1814

My Lord,

I take the Liberty of mentioning to your Lordship that I have given directions to my Publisher, Mr Longman, to send to your Lordship's House in Town a Copy of my Poem, previous to its publication, which I hope will take place in the course of a fortnight. If you should have left London before the work is ready for publication I have begged Mr Longman to forward it. I am upon the point of setting out this day, for a Tour of Scotland with Mrs Wordsworth. We shall be absent at least six weeks; on my return I hope to have the honour of waiting upon your Lordship at Lowther.

With due sense of the mark of favour conferred upon me by the permission to dedicate my work so agreeably to my earnest wishes,[1]

I have the honour to be

with the highest respect
your Lordship's
most obliged and humble servant
Wm Wordsworth

326. W. W. to DR. ROBERT ANDERSON[2]

Address: Dr Anderson, Edinburgh, favored by Mr. Hogg.
MS. National Library of Scotland.
Hitherto unpublished.

Rydale Mount near
Ambleside
September 17th 1814

Dear Sir,

Literature is much indebted to you for the, at that time, unexampled comprehensiveness of the Edition of English Poetry of

[1] *The Excursion* was dedicated to the Earl of Lonsdale with a sonnet—'Oft, through thy fair domains, illustrious Peer! / In youth I roamed, on youthful pleasures bent.' It is dated 'Rydal Mount, July 29th 1814'. Wordsworth then was in Scotland, and either 'July' must be a mistake for 'June', or he instructed Longman's to date it on the day the poem was published.

[2] Robert Anderson, M.D. (1750–1830), the editor of *A Complete Edition of the Poets of Great Britain* (1792–5), which was given to W. by his brother John during the latter's long visit to Grasmere in 1800. W. depended on it to a large

which you were the Editor. I have no doubt that if your wishes had been complied with, this Collection would have included many valuable works of our elder Poets which have no place there. Chalmers' Edition,[1] which would probably never have existed without the Example of yours, is also very incomplete. The Public therefore is still unprovided with an entire Body of English Poetry; which might be furnished at a reasonable rate, if a few volumes were added to your Collection, with such Biographical Notes and Critical Notices as your Researches and your taste would furnish. I have long wished this to be done; and have talked with several of my Friends Messieurs Coleridge and Southey in particular upon the subject who both participate my desire to see your Edition adequately enlarged; tho regretting however at the same time that so valuable a work should have been printed so incorrectly. A few days ago I had a conversation with Mr Southey on this subject, and we both agreed that it would be a fortunate thing for the interests of Literature; if the Proprietors of your Edition would encourage you to supply what is yet wanting to make the work complete, by furnishing a few additional volumes.—We drew out a list of the following authors, and works, which I take the liberty of submitting to your consideration; only observing, that if the scheme be judged feasible, the fewer of the following that are excluded the better.—1st all that are in Chalmers and not in yours, adding to the works of Skelton[2] many pieces which have lately come to light which C. has not included. Mr Heber[3] has most or all of them. And to the works of Turberville[4] may be added what Chalmers has omitted, His letters from Russia which are in Hackluyt.

extent for his knowledge of Chaucer and the earlier English writers, and his own modernized versions of Chaucer's *The Prioress' Tale*, *The Cuckoo and the Nightingale*, and *Troilus and Cressida* were based upon Anderson's incorrect text. W. had just met Anderson during his tour in Scotland in July and August. See Hogg's *Reminiscences of Wordsworth*, in *Poetical Works of the Ettrick Shepherd* (1855), v, pp. cvi–cix.

[1] Alexander Chalmers (1759–1834), a voluminous writer and compiler, whose most celebrated work was *The General Biographical Dictionary*, in thirty-two volumes (1812–17). In 1810 he published an enlarged edition of Dr. Johnson's *Collection of the English Poets*, in twenty-one volumes. This is the work to which W. here refers.

[2] John Skelton (d. 1529), Rector of Diss, Norfolk, poet and satirist, author of *Colyn Cloute*, etc.

[3] Richard Heber (1773–1833), book collector, brother of Reginald Heber (1783–1826), the first Bishop of Calcutta. In a letter to Alexander Dyce, 21 July 1832 (*LY* ii. 1027, p. 630), W. says that Southey had told him that 'in Mr. Heber's Library were certain printed poems of Skelton's not to be found in any collection of his works'. Heber kept eight houses—four of them on the Continent—full of nothing but books.

[4] George Turberville (?1540–1610), author of *Poems on Russia*, 1568.

17 September 1814

Occleve[1]	Watson[6]	Chalkhill[12]	Quarles[18]
Minot[2]	Willoby[7]	A. Fraunce[13]	May[19]
Hawes[3]	Southwell[8]	Sir P. Sydney[14]	Herbert[20]
—	B. Googe[9]	Lord Brooke[15]	Herrick[21]
Churchyard[4]	N. Breton[10]	Sylvester[16]	Lovelace[22]
Constable[5]	Chapman[11]	Best parts of Wither[17]	Henry More[23]

[1] Thomas Hoccleve (*c.* 1370–1450), a clerk of the Privy Seal, author of *La Male Regle de T.H.*

[2] Laurence Minot (*c.* 1300–55), author of poems about war—*Bannockburn, Sluys*, etc., first printed by Ritson in 1795.

[3] Stephen Hawes, *temp.* Henry VII and Henry VIII. His *History of Grande Amour*, printed by Wynkyn de Worde, was reprinted by Southey in his *Select Works of the British Poets with Biographical Sketches, 1831*, and some stanzas from it are in Percy's *Reliques*.

[4] Thomas Churchyard (*c.* 1520–1604), author of *The Legend of Shore's Wife*, 1563, which was reprinted in Percy's *Reliques*.

[5] Henry Constable (1562–1613), a Catholic, author of *Diana*, 1592.

[6] Thomas Watson (*c.* 1557–92), translator of the *Antigone* and of Italian madrigals; author of *Hecatompathia*, 1582.

[7] Henry Willoughby (*c.* 1574–96), author of *Willobie's Avisa*, 1594, in which there is a reference to 'W. S.'—who may be Shakespeare.

[8] Robert Southwell (1561–95), Jesuit priest, executed at Tyburn. Author of some remarkable religious poems, especially *The Burning Babe*.

[9] Barnaby Googe (1540–94), *Eglogs, Epytaphes, and Sonettes*, translated from Montemayor, 1563.

[10] Nicholas Breton (1542–1626), a voluminous writer of lyrics.

[11] George Chapman (?1559–1634), translator of Homer and the inspirer of Keats's first great sonnet, *On first looking into Chapman's Homer*.

[12] John Chalkhill (*fl.* 1600), a friend of Spenser—Isaac Walton edited his *Thealma and Cleachus* in 1683.

[13] Abraham Fraunce (*c.* 1587–1633), a protégé of Sidney and of his sister Lady Pembroke, to whom he dedicated translations of Tasso's *Aminta* and Watson's *Amyntas* in 1591, with the title *The Countess of Pembroke's Ivychurch*.

[14] It is strange that Sidney should have been omitted from both Chalmers's and Anderson's collections.

[15] Fulke Greville, Lord Brooke (1554–1628), friend and biographer of Sidney, author of *Coelica* (Sonnets) *Mustapha* (1609), *Alaham*, etc.

[16] Joshua Sylvester (1563–1618), chiefly known for his poetical translations of the Gascon poet Du Bartas, much read by Milton in his youth.

[17] George Wither (1588–1667). His early poems include the song 'Shall I, wasting in despair'; he later wrote *Hymns and Songs of the Church*. His poems though neglected by Chalmers were reprinted by Sir Egerton Brydges.

[18] Francis Quarles (1592–1644), *Emblems*, his most famous work, was published in 1635.

[19] Thomas May (1595–1650), for a time a court poet to Charles I, but he fought on the side of the Parliament. Dramatist, translator, historian, and author of *The Reign of King Henry II*, etc.

[20] George Herbert (1592–1634), Rector of Bemerton, Wiltshire, author of the most famous book of spiritual lyrics ever written, *The Temple*, published 1633.

[21] Robert Herrick (1592–1674), was Rector of Dean Prior; author of *Hesperides* (1648), and as famous for profane, as Herbert for sacred, poems.

[22] Richard Lovelace (1618–1658), royalist soldier and poet, renowned for two or three lyrics—one being 'Tell me not, sweet, I am unkind.'

[23] Henry More (1614–87), theologian and voluminous prose writer, but he wrote *The Song of the Soul*, published 1647 with other *Philosophical Poems*.

Chamberlain[1] Cleveland[2] Randolph[3] Marvel

including in the works of Marvel the Poems which the Quarto Edition of his Prose Works contains[4]—

Norris of Bemerton[5]
Lady Winchelsea[6]
A selection from Tom D'Urfey[7]
A volume of Ballads and state Poems
A volume of Metrical Romances
P. Ploughman's Vision and Creed and [*seal*]
Miscellanies of the age of Tudor.

Of old Translations the following are desireable,
Chapman's Homer
Fairfax's Tasso[8]
Goulding's Ovid[9]
Phaer's Virgil[10]
May's Lucan[11]

And as a curiosity the few books of Stanyhurst's Virgil[12]— —

Now Sir I should be much obliged to you if you could prevail

[1] William Chamberlayne (1619–89), author of *Pharonnida, an Heroick Poem,* which was a favourite of Southey's. It was reprinted in 1820.

[2] John Cleveland (1613–58), a royalist political writer, published *Poems* in 1651.

[3] Thomas Randolph (1605–35), author of some dramas—*The Muses' Looking-Glass* and *The Jealous Lovers*: his poems include an amusing address *To Ben Johnson,* whom he calls his 'father' in poetry.

[4] Andrew Marvell, *Works, Poetical, Controversial and Political etc with a new Life by Capt. Edward Thompson* was published in three volumes 4to, in 1776.

[5] John Norris (1657–1711)—another Rector of Bemerton and high churchman, chiefly known for his theological writings.

[6] Ann, Lady Winchelsea (1660–1720), Wordsworth's favourite female poet, mentioned by him in his *Essay Supplementary to the Preface* to his *Poems,* 1815. In his anthology of extracts from English poets made for Lord Lonsdale's daughter, Lady Mary Lowther, in 1819, seventeen out of the fifty poems in it were by her. Her *Miscellany Poems* were published in 1713.

[7] Thomas D'Urfey (1653–1723), dramatist and song-writer, who survived the dangers of four reigns full of plots, revolutions, and political upheavals without incurring the enmity of either side.

[8] *Godfrey of Boulogne or the Recoverie of Jerusalem, done into English heroical verse,* by Edward Fairfax, gent., 1600.

[9] Arthur Goulding, *The XV Books of Ovidius Naso entitled Metamorphoses,* translated by A. G., 1584.

[10] *The Seven First Books of the Eneides of Virgill, converted into English metre,* by T. Phaer Esquire, London, 1558.

[11] *Pharsalia, A Continuation of Lucan's historical poem till the death of Julius Caesar,* by T. M., 1630.

[12] Richard Stanyhurst (1547–1618). *The first Foure Books of Virgil his Aeneid translated into English heroicall Verse,* Leyden, 1582. He also wrote *De Rebus in Hibernia Festis,* Antwerp, 1584.

upon the Proprietors of your Edition, to enlarge so as to include as many of the above as possible. The present possessors of your Collection, I think, would almost all become purchasers. Many also who have bought Chalmers would be glad to complete its deficiencies by your Volumes. And if the work were correctly printed I have little doubt that it would answer; I am certain that it would meet with patronage amongst my literary Friends. Hoping that you will excuse this Liberty, I beg leave to subscribe myself

With gratitude
Your obliged and humble servant
W. Wordsworth

327. D. W. to RICHARD ADDISON

Address: Messrs Wordsworth and Addison, Staple Inn, London.
Postmark: C 27 Sep 1814. *Stamp*: Shrewsbury, Se 25 1814.
MS. WL.
MY ii. 503, p. 599.

Shrewsbury, Sept[r] 25, 1814

To Mr Addison.
Dear Sir,

I write to inform you that I drew upon my Brother on the 21st Inst (in favor of J G Crump Esq[re]) from Liverpool, at one Month for thirty Pounds. Miss Hutchinson and I are now at Shrewsbury in our way to Hindwell, and are waiting in expectation of Mr Thomas Hutchinson, who is coming to meet us—

I am, Sir Yours truly
D Wordsworth

328. W. W. to LORD LONSDALE

MS. Lonsdale MSS., Record Office, The Castle, Carlisle.
Hitherto unpublished.

Rydale Mount October 1st.
[1814]

My Lord,

The enclosed Paper contains an extract from a Letter of my Friend Mrs Clarkson, just returned from Paris, where she has been residing with her Husband a month. It relates to the disposition of the French Government and some of the leading persons in France in respect to the slave Trade; and if your Lordship has not received information to the same effect from higher authority the perusal of it will, I think, interest you.

I look forward with pleasure to the thought of another visit to your hospitable Mansion at Lowther, with respectful remembrances to Lady Lonsdale, and the young Ladies of your Lordship's family, I have the honour to be

my Lord
your Lordship's
obliged and faithful servant
Wm Wordsworth

(*Enclosure*)

The very day before we left England Mr Wilberforce entreated Mr C. not to see any of his old friends and to be very cautious of writing or printing anything in his own name. The first interview with the Duke of Wellington took off this interdict which I felt to be very heavy indeed. The Duke said that in an interview which he had had with the King of France the night before, the King had said that there was a party in France who believed the Slave Trade essential to their interests; that these persons, if any attempt were made to alter the Law as it now stood, might become clamorous; and the people of France being entirely ignorant of the subject, might join in the clamour; and he added emphatically 'I can no more abolish the trade against the will of the people of France than the King of England can continue it against the will of the people of England.' But Lord Wellington understood from the King that he would be glad to find a current of popular feeling excited in the country strong enough to enable him to abolish the trade immediately. Accordingly Lord Wellington directed Mr C. to go to work in our good old English fashion. He reprinted the short address to the potentates and summary of the evidence and distributed it to all the persons in power at Paris, accompanied by a letter signed with his own name. We found also in Paris a copy of a translation of his own Impolicy which by this time is reprinted and in the hands of every member of the legislature of France. When this work was presented to the censor he returned it in twelve hours (they usually keep a work of this size three days). Not a word was altered and the censor desired that Mr C. should be informed privately that he wished to see the work in circulation in every town in France. During the last week persons (entire strangers) were coming in daily to offer their assistance; and these persons every way respectable, some of very high rank. I am persuaded from what I saw, that it would be as easy to establish a Committee for the Abolition in Paris, as in any town in England.

Talleyrand is in favour of immediate abolition and our Government will certainly do their utmost at the Congress.

329. W. W. to LORD LONSDALE

MS. Lonsdale MSS., Record Office, The Castle, Carlisle.
Hitherto unpublished.

Rydale Mount
October 8 [1814]

My Lord,

I entirely concur with your Lordship in questioning the propriety of the mode of proceeding in Mr C's[1] case. He has been returned from France some time, having stayed a month.

I was induced to send the transcript from recollection of a conversation with your Lordship on the subject of the slave trade; and because the facts mentioned came from a quarter that entitled them to regard. Towards the beginning of next month I hope to revisit Lowther Castle; in the meantime I have the honour to be

my Lord
most faithfully yours
Wm Wordsworth

330. D. W. to CATHERINE CLARKSON

Address: Mrs Clarkson, at John Clarkson's Esq, Purfleet, near London.
MS. British Museum.
K (—). MY i. 504, p. 600.

Hindwell Sunday night 9th October [1814]
near Radnor

The date of this letter will surprise you, but before I enter into an explanation of it I must speak of what is at this time most interesting to me, you and your travels. During the solitude at Rydale Mount,[2] I for a long while anxiously expected a letter from you from Paris by every post; but at last I gave it up, divining the

[1] i.e. Thomas Clarkson. See L. 328 above.
[2] While W. W., M. W., and S. H. were in Scotland.

true reason, and I cannot help very much regretting that you forgot to tell me where to address you while you were there, as I should have been exceedingly glad that you had seen the young woman[1] whom I mentioned to you, the more so as a treaty of marriage is now on foot between her and the Brother of the Officer Beaudouin[2] whom I mentioned to you as having been at Rydale, and she and her Mother are extremely anxious that I should be present at the wedding, and for that purpose pressed me very much to go in October. This, unless such good fortune had attended us as being taken under your and your Husband's protection, we could not think of at this season, and therefore I wish that the marriage should be deferred till next spring or summer, because I desire exceedingly to see the poor Girl before she takes another protector than her Mother, under whom I believe she has been bred up in perfect purity and innocence, and to whom she is life and light and perpetual pleasure; though from the over-generous dispositions of the Mother they have had to struggle through many difficulties. Well, I began to say that I particularly wished that you could have seen them at this time as through you I should have been able to enter into some explanations, which, imperfectly as I express myself in French, are difficult, and as you would have been able to confirm or contradict the reports which we receive from Caroline's Mother and Mr Beaudouin of her interesting and amiable qualities. They both say that she resembles her father[3] most strikingly, and her letters give a picture of a feeling and ingenuous mind. Yet there must be something I think very unfavourable to true delicacy in French manners. Both C and her Mother urge my going in October on the account, that after a young person is engaged to be married, it is desirable that the delay afterwards should be as short as possible, as she is subject to perpetual scrutiny and unpleasant remarks, and one of the reasons which they urge for marriage in general, is that a single Woman in France unless she have a fortune is not treated with any '*consideration*'. But now I have wandered from the point where I intended to begin! and that was you yourself. My dear Friend, I congratulate you first and foremost upon your health and strength. The blessing of strength I hardly ever dared even to wish that you might enjoy in a degree equal to your present powers. I now do not despair of climbing some of our own mountain heights with you before we die—and how little could this have been expected when you used to enter our Cottage pale and worn out after a slow walk from Robert Newton's. We are delighted to hear that you are so

[1] i.e. Caroline Vallon. [2] See L. 243, p. 18, n. 2 above. [3] i.e. W. W.

much pleased with Paris and the French people—and now we venture in our little way to expect pleasure and amusement. All the accounts we have received from other quarters have been unfavourable—that neither provisions nor anything else was much cheaper than in England, which, allowing for the loss in exchange we thought would make things dearer—and the people rude and brutal in their manners. Now I guess there must have been some fault in the manners of the Reporters, yet we cannot help thinking at the same time that your judgement is formed from the best of the people, to whose society your pretensions and the Recommendations which you carried with you naturally introduced you. There are many things which we want to know, yet when I set myself about asking the questions I can hardly recollect anything, and as a help to my bad memory all the Hutchinsons are chattering by the fireside. With respect to the *mode* of travelling—we of course, must go as cheaply as possible consistent with tolerable comfort—and in an open carriage because Sara cannot ride in a close one. Are any of the diligences so constructed?—and, supposing we can meet with no eligible companions from England do you think we might venture to go alone? *I* think I should have no fears; but Sara would fain have a gentleman, and we can, at all events, desire Mr Beaudouin to come from Paris to meet us at Calais; the expense however makes this last plan somewhat objectionable. Oh! that Henry Robinson were going again! You know I like him well as a companion. And still a thousand times better—Oh! That you were going! We should wish to convey presents of English manufacture. Can this be done without much risk or disagreeable trouble? When William and I were at Calais our Trunk was simply opened—we paid half a crown or three shillings—and the Trunk was closed again. In returning also we should like to bring back some things of french manufacture; under what sort of management is this practicable? Of course it would be easy enough to hide lace and such small articles, but can silks be brought unmade up—or if made up is there any danger of their being seized?—I am sure I had many other matters to enquire about; but really I cannot call any thing else to mind, therefore I will sum up all by desiring you to send us whatever information you may think likely to be useful to us.—I wish you had but sent your address, I should have liked to have introduced our friend Beaudouin to you, and should have very much wished that it had been possible for you to see his Brother. You say that you have told us very little—so it may seem to you, and we should have liked to have heard from you ten times as much; but I do assure you your letter was most interesting to us. You must indeed have a great deal to tell us having seen so many remarkable personages. I wish you had but visited La Fayette in his retirement, it was, however, a high gratification to see him anywhere. You do not say when you intend to leave London or Purfleet; but I suppose not very soon as you say Mr C has gone to Bury and you must wait for his return before you see the Book. Hazlitt's review appeared in the *Examiner*.[1] It is not half so good a review as I should have thought he would have written; for, with all his disagreeable qualities, he is a very clever fellow. He says that the narrative parts of the poem are a dead weight upon it; but speaks in raptures of the philosophical. Now that the narrative will be liked the best by most Readers we have no doubt; therefore we are always most glad to hear that the religious and philosophical parts are relished. Of their merits I cannot entertain the faintest shadow of a doubt; yet I am afraid that for a time an outcry will be raised by many Readers and many Reviewers, which may injure the Sale. It is now time to lead you to Hindwell and back again to Rydale. Here Sara and I arrived last Tuesday but one after a very delightful journey. The Travellers[2] arrived at home the Friday preceding our departure and three days before we set off I had not a thought of coming here till next Spring —and I had great difficulty in resolving to leave William and Mary so soon after their long absence—but Mr Crump was coming as far as Liverpool—Sara who had promised to spend some time with her Friends here now resolved to come along with him or with Mr Cookson of Kendal who was coming on horseback the week following. I thought I never could have so good an opportunity for coming—the weather was delightful. I was loth to part with Sara and unwilling to let her come alone, so last Friday fortnight on a lovely afternoon we set off to Kendal in the Irish car. It seemed to us that we never had seen the vale of Windermere and the mountains of Langdale look so glorious, but we were determined to be merry, and Sara, with all the bustle of our sudden resolution was almost spared the pang of parting. We had a party of gentlemen to dinner on that very day, who walked with us to the bottom of the hill at Rydale to see us seated in our Car, amongst them were Mr Wilson and Mr Hogg the Etrick shepherd.[3] We stayed Saturday at Kendal and on Sunday

[1] Hazlitt reviewed *The Excursion* in the *Examiner* of 21 and 28 Aug.; a third article appeared on 9 Oct. which D. cannot yet have seen.

[2] i.e. W. W., M. W., and S. H.—returning from their tour in Scotland.

[3] Hogg visited the Wordsworths at Rydal Mount immediately after the return of W. W. and M. W. from Scotland. See *Poetical Works of the Ettrick Shepherd* (1855), v, pp. civ–cix.

morning at 5 o'clock mounted the top of the coach with Mr Crump. The morning was charming and we were lucky enough to have a delightful companion as far as Preston, an American of the name of Warner. He was about 40 years of age, very well informed upon all subjects, evidently had had the education of a scholar, expressed himself always with propriety, often with eloquence, and there was a sweet benevolence in his countenance, and in all the sentiments which he expressed—in short we were half in love with him and very sorry his destination was to Manchester instead of Liverpool. He had just returned from Scotland and like Sara had been travelling in the Highlands, which was a strong bond of connection between us; and besides Sara mentioned that she had been particularly impressed by an American Preacher whom they had heard at Perth, the most eloquent and apostolic preacher beyond all comparison that any of them had ever heard or seen. They could not learn his name and I was quite vexed with William that he had not introduced himself to him. It was a most agreeable surprise to us to hear that he was an intimate friend of Mr Warner, had come over in the same ship; his name Dr Romayne.[1] Do you or does Mr Clarkson know anything about him? We reached Liverpool at 7 o'clock on Monday evening not at all tired, stayed there with Mr Crump (the Ladies are at Grasmere) till Thursday, remained at Chester till Saturday with our cousin formerly Nancy Wordsworth[2] now Mrs Ireland—proceeded on the outside of the coach to Shrewsbury where we stayed till Monday morning. T. H. met us there with a Gig, on Monday we came to Ludlow and on Tuesday to Hindwell where we shall have been a fortnight to-morrow. We were much entertained and interested with Chester and delighted with Shrewsbury and Ludlow—all Friends are well at H. Mrs Hutchinson is one of the sweetest creatures in the world and her Husband is as good and kind as it is possible, and I believe one of the most contented of Men. Joanna is very well—she was poorly all the spring and summer, Mary and she have just returned from Swansea where they both received great benefit. This is a very pretty place and the country around is mostly beautiful. We have walked a great deal. Sara is very strong—she can walk 6 miles at a stretch. Her Scotch journey agreed with her wonderfully, and Mary was always in good spirits and everybody said her looks were much improved when she returned; but I am sorry to tell you that I fear it will have no

[1] Jeremiah Romayne, Calvinist divine.

[2] Youngest daughter of Richard W. of Whitehaven. The Revd. G. Ireland was her second husband.

permanent effect upon her spirits for she fell very low again after her return. She will however now be kept busy and that is the best thing for her. She writes that they have crowds of company. The Southeys and children were with them last week. Sara and I are going upon a little Tour up the Wye with T. H. He is very kind and thinks nothing a trouble by which he can contribute to our comfort. Mary[1] is now busy with her little scholars, whom she teaches on Dr Bell's plan, and she is so happy amongst them and so well fitted for the duty of instruction by Books, and all other cares belonging to children that it grieves us very much that there is no prospect of a family at present. Pray write immediately and send us Tillbrooke's address—he wrote to me and I have left the letter at home and forgotten the address—

You could hardly believe it possible for anything but a Lake to be so beautiful as the pool before this house. It is perfectly clear and inhabited by multitudes of geese and Ducks, and two fair swans keep their silent and solitary state apart from all the flutter and gabble of the inferior birds.[2]

John Monkhouse lives at the distance of 12 miles, before we return from our Tour we shall pay him a visit, so if you write before or on next Sunday direct at Stow near the Hay, Brecon. The farm is a partnership concern. John M lives a very lonely life yet he is chearful and happy. Fortunately he is very fond of reading.

Sara sends her very best love. She longs with me to hear from you again, so pray write immediately and believe me ever-more your affectionate Friend

D. W.

Mary H. desires to be particularly remembered to you. Adieu again. God bless you my dearest Friend—Your letter was forwarded to us from Rydale. I fear that the French *people* will never stir themselves in the African cause.[3]

[1] i.e. Mary, *née* Monkhouse, wife of T. Hutchinson.

[2] The 'pool' at Hindwell is still as D. W. describes it and still inhabited by duck and a pair of swans (1966).

[3] i.e. the anti-slavery cause.

330a. W. W. to R. W.

Address: Richard Wordsworth [Esq.], Sockbridge, near Penrith.
MS. WL.
Hitherto unpublished.

Rydal Mount
October 13th 1814.

My dear Richard,

I was over at Lowther some little time since, and called at Sockbridge, but you were then at Allonby.—

It hurts me very much, and surprizes me not a little, that I never hear from you on the subject of our affairs. There is something apparently very unbrotherly in this silence, which neither Dorothy or I seem to have the power to induce you to break—

Have you ever done us the justice to ask yourself what situation our affairs would be in if you should happen to die? If you have provided for the accident pray let us know immediately, and in what manner; if you have not, for heaven's sake, do [not] omit any longer to do what is right. I have told you what is our wish—to have the money[1] at our command.—At present I suppose it is holden in your name, and we have no power over it independent of you.

I shall probably be at Sockbridge in the course of the next month, towards the beginning of it—Let me entreat of you to be prepared to satisfy me on these points, by that time.

I am dear Brother most faithfully yours
Wm Wordsworth

331. W. W. to THOMAS DE QUINCEY

MS. untraced.
MY ii. 514, p. 628.

Sat: Morn. [late Oct. 1814[2]]

My dear Sir,

Many thanks for your obliging Note. I have the pleasure to say that after a persevering search we have found a Copy of the Descriptive Sketches this morning: so that you need not persist in the

[1] i.e. the money owed by the late Earl of Lonsdale to the Wordsworths' father, and repaid by his successor to the family in 1803.

[2] The date of this letter is settled by the reference to finding a copy of *Descriptive Sketches*. M. W. in a letter to D. W. dated 22 Oct. 1814 says they had found 'Sarah's copy' and had sent extracts from it to the printer for inclusion in *Poems including Lyrical Ballads*, which appeared in the following spring. *MW* 9, p. 18.

kind search which you were prepared to undertake. This Discovery enables me to proceed with the printing, under the superintendance of my Sister,[1] without delay.

ever most sincerely yours
Wm Wordsworth

332. D. W. to CATHERINE CLARKSON

Address: Mrs. Clarkson, Bury, Suffolk.
Postmark: G 15 Nov 1814. *Stamp*: Kington 162.
MS. British Museum.
MY ii. 505, p. 605.

November 11th [1814]

My conscience has long been busy prompting me to write to you, and if I could have done so unknown to Sara I would have written; but as she had determined to write tho' she put it off from day to day, I was unwilling to take the pen, being well assured that she would so satisfy her mind saying 'There is no need for me to write as you have written'. I rode over to the Stowe[2] yesterday with Joanna Hutchinson, and while she and John Monkhouse are walking through the fields I think I cannot do better than thank you for your last most satisfactory letter, briefly tell you that we are all well, and transcribe a poem which we have received from William—you will have an opportunity of reading it very soon in the Octavo Edition of his poems, which is now printing and speedily will be published; but I think you will not say my time is mis-spent in giving you a pleasure beforehand which would only have been half a pleasure when at the same time you should have seen many other poems that are new to you; for he is printing considerable additions to the old stock. He wrote to me from Lowther Castle on the 4th and intended to return to Rydale on the 7th. He was unlucky in not arriving at L. a few days earlier as the Duke of Devonshire[3] had been there and expressed a great desire to see him. He had just returned from Ireland, where he had made 'the Excursion' the Companion of his tour

[1] D. W. with S. H. had gone to Hindwell, Radnor, at the end of Sept. 1814. See Letters 327 and 330 above. While there, she supervised the preparation of the *Poems* for the press.

[2] See L. 330, p. 162 above.

[3] William George Spencer Cavendish, 6th Duke (1790–1858), succeeded to the dukedom in 1811. He was a man of literary tastes who built up the great library at Chatsworth.

and had been greatly pleased with it. I say he was unfortunate because his enemies will be busy enough in the Reviews and elsewhere, and it is really of no little importance to us that the Work should sell—and for another reason. He intends publishing the 'White Doe' in the spring, and the scene of that Poem is Bolton Abbey, the favorite and much admired by him property of the Duke of Devonshire. Perhaps you may not guess for I have but half explained myself why I am sorry that William did not see the Duke on account of the sale of the Excursion. I think the more Friends he has either of Rank or Talents or notoriety the better, that they may *talk* against the Writers, for the more that is said of the work the better; none deny that he has talents and poetic Genius. I saw two sections of Hazlitt's Review[1] at Rydale, and did not think them nearly so well written as I should have expected from him—though he praised *more* than I should have expected. His opinion that all the Characters are but one character, I cannot but think utterly false—there seems to me to be an astonishing difference considering that the primary elements are the same—fine Talents and strong imagination. He says that the narratives[2] are a Clog upon the poem. I was not sorry to hear that for I am sure with common Readers those parts of the poem will be by far the most interesting. Mary tells me that they have seen the last part of Hazlitt's Review which is more a Criticism upon Country Life and its effects than upon the poem, and amongst other evils he has the audacity to complain that there are no Courtesans to be found in the country. He makes another bold assertion that all people living in retirement hate each other. Mary tells me that William has a plan for going up to London with me when we go to France in April. Sara will remain here and I shall go home before the December moon is at the full—probably about the 18th. I wish you may be in London either when we go to France or return; but if we have not that good fortune I would fain return by Bury. This if all goes well we certainly shall do; but I have a depressing timidity when I speak of plans for any distant time. Thank God! all goes well at home. I left home on the 16th September so I shall have been more than three months absent when I return. I have been very happy at Hindwell. The country is beautiful, and we have been so fortunate in weather as not to have been confined to the house a single day. By little and little I have become a tolerable horse-woman. I have no fears and that is a great point—but I cannot attain the power of managing my horse; I can however ride for four or five hours with-

[1] See L. 330, p. 160 above.

[2] i.e. the life-stories of villagers in Books VI and VII of *The Excursion*.

out fatigue, at a pace which was torture to me when I first began. To-morrow I am going to Hereford with John Monkhouse, a distance of 16 miles and we shall return in the evening. I often think of your rides when I used to walk by your side. They were very pleasant but would have been still more pleasant if we could have ridden side by side, and if I had been mistress of my present skill I should certainly have endeavoured to procure a horse. We shall return to Hindwell on Sunday or Monday. We came unexpectedly upon John Monkhouse, to his great joy; for he leads a solitary life; but his temper is so happy and his mind so busy that he is never dull. He is a thoroughly amiable man; of such kindly affections, and so happy in communicating his sentiments on Books (he is a great Reader) and everything else that I cannot but more than ever regret that his wife was taken from him, or that he has not been fortunate enough to fix his affections upon another amiable woman to supply her place. His sister is very happy, and a sweet creature, and her husband is most truly sensible of her worth. I only regret that she should live where her merits are hardly seen or felt except by her own family. They are however those of the most importance and she is very contented and expresses her benevolent and charitable disposition towards her poor neighbours—but I am going on and shall not have Room for the poem. I shall put my letter into the Post Office at Hereford, and shall not tell Sara that I have written that I may not prevent her fulfilling her intentions.—Now for the poem it is printed after 'Yarrow unvisited'—

[*Here follows* Yarrow Visited, 1814, *as* Oxf. W., *p.* 301, *but ll.* 2, 3.

Of which so long I cherished
A fancy dear to waking thought

l. 6 words *for* notes
l. 13. And, with her own St Mary's Lake
ll. 62–4. It promises protection
To studious ease and generous cares,
And every chaste affection]

Alas! I am as bad as Sara. I have not yet written to Tillbrook, but I hope I shall very soon. In the meantime give my kind love to him if you see him. Your anecdote of Tom that he sate up all night reading William's poem gave me as much pleasure as anything I have heard of the effect produced by it. I must say I think it speaks highly in favour of Tom's feeling and enthusiasm that he was so wrought upon. Do write as soon as you can. I believe Sara's letter will reach you ere long; but do not wait for it I pray you. I feel cheared now while I write to you because I seem to see before me a little way. If we are all alive I am almost confident that we shall meet somewhere before the end of next summer—at Bury—in London, or in Westmorland.

I have had one of the worst pens that ever was used—John Monkhouse cannot find his knife to mend it for me. I should not mind this if it were not for the poem; but I am afraid you will not find it easy to make it out and that will spoil the first effect of it.

Joanna Hutchinson and John M. beg their best remembrances. They are busy putting up Books and they want me to help them. We have been making ourselves merry with their unscientific way of putting them up—all by the backs.

My love to Mr Clarkson and Tom. God Bless you my dearest Friend

Yours evermore
D. W.

333. W. W. to ROBERT PEARCE GILLIES[1]

MS. untraced.
Gillies.
K (—). MY ii. 506, p. 609.

Rydal Mount Nov. 12. 1814

You are a most indulgent and good-natured critic, or I think you would hardly have been so much pleased with *Yarrow Visited*; we think it heavier than my things generally are, and nothing but a wish to show to Mr Hogg[2] that my inclination towards him, and his proposed work were favourable, could have induced me to part with it in that state. I have composed three new stanzas in place of

[1] R. P. Gillies (1788–1858), poet and miscellaneous writer, had met W. in Edinburgh in the previous summer. He had just lost much of his fortune in a rash speculation: in 1825 he lost the rest of his money, and went to London in 1827 to edit the *Foreign Quarterly*; in 1847 he was in prison for debt, and W. helped him in his financial embarrassment. He had a great admiration for W., of whom he spoke as his 'unalterable friend'. His chief works were *Childe Alarique, a poet's reverie with other poems* (1813), *Rinaldo, a desultory poem*, and *Illustrations of the Poetical Character in Six Tales* (1816); a novel, *Confessions of Sir Henry Longueville* (1814), and *Memoirs of a Literary Veteran*, 1851.

[2] James Hogg (1770–1835), the 'Ettrick Shepherd'. His *Queen's Wake* referred to in the next letter, was published in 1813.

the three first, and another to be inserted before the two last, and have made some alterations in other parts; therefore, when you see Mr. Hogg, beg from me that he will not print the poem till he has read the copy which I have added to Miss E. Wilson's MSS,[1] as I scarcely doubt, notwithstanding the bias of first impressions, that he will prefer it.

In the same MSS. you will find a sonnet addresed to yourself,[2] which I should have mentioned before, but for a reason of the same kind as kept you silent on the subject of yours. I am not a little concerned that you continue to suffer from morbid feelings, and still more that you regard them as incurable. This is a most delicate subject, and which, perhaps, I ought not to touch at all, considering the slender knowledge which circumstances have yet allowed me of the characteristics of your malady. But this I can confidently say, that poetry and the poetic spirit will either help you, or harm you, as you use them. If you find in yourself more of the latter effect than of the former, forswear the Muses, and apply tooth and nail to law, to mathematics, to mechanics, to anything, only escape from your insidious foe. But if you are benefited by your intercourse with the lyre, then give yourself up to it with the enthusiasm which I am sure is natural to you. I should like to be remembered to Mr. Lappenberg,[3] to Mr. Hogg, and our friends in Queen Street,[4] of course. Mr. Sharpe,[5] I hope, does not forget me. Adieu, most faithfully, and with great respect. Yours,

William Wordsworth.

[1] Elizabeth Wilson was the sister of John Wilson ('Christopher North' of *Blackwood's*), who had formerly lived at Elleray on Windermere and was now in Edinburgh. He soon afterwards became a chief contributor to *Blackwood's*. The original manuscript of *Yarrow Visited* sent to Hogg is not extant. Hogg had requested his literary friends to supply him with material for a collection of poems, but instead he produced a book of parodies of modern poets (including Wordsworth) called *The Poetic Mirror* (1816). *Yarrow Visited* was published by Wordsworth in *Poems, including Lyrical Ballads* in 1815, the only poem arising out of his tour in Scotland in 1814 to be included in them.

[2] 'From the dark chambers of dejection freed'. See *Oxf. W.*, p. 260.

[3] Translator of several of W.'s poems into German.

[4] i.e. John Wilson, his wife, mother, and sister.

[5] Charles Kirkpatrick Sharpe (1781–1851), antiquary, artist, and friend of Scott, lived in Edinburgh.

334. W. W. to R. P. GILLIES

MS. untraced.
Gillies.
K (—). *MY* ii. 507, *p.* 610.

Rydal Mount, Nov. 23, 1814.

My dear Sir,

You must have feared that notwithstanding your care, the parcel has not reached its destination; I have, however, the gratification of saying that it arrived punctually at Kendal. I have to thank you, also, for *Egbert*,[1] which is pleasingly and vigorously written, and proves that with a due sacrifice of exertion, you will be capable of performing things that will have a strong claim on the regards of posterity. But keep, I pray you, to the great models; there is in some parts of this tale, particularly page fourth, too much of a bad writer —Lord Byron; and I will observe that towards the conclusion, the intervention of the peasant is not only unnecessary, but injurious to the tale, inasmuch as it takes away from that species of credibility on which it rests. I have peeped into the *Ruminator*,[2] and turned to your first letter, which is well executed, and seizes the attention very agreeably. Your longer poem[3] I have barely looked into, but I promise myself no inconsiderable pleasure in the perusal of this.

I thank you for the *Queen's Wake*; since I saw you in Edinburgh I have read it. It does Mr. Hogg great credit. Of the tales, I liked best, much the best, the *Witch of Fife*, the former part of *Kilmenie*, and the *Abbot Mackinnon*. Mr. Hogg himself, I remember, seemed most partial to *Mary Scott*, though he thought it too long. For my own part, though I always deem the opinion of an able writer upon his own works entitled to consideration, I cannot agree with Mr.

[1] *Egbert, or, The Suicide*, a poem first published in *Illustrations*, etc., 1815. See p. 167, n.1 above.

[2] A series of essays by R. P. Gillies and Sir Egerton Brydges, published in 1813. Brydges (1762–1832) was a bibliographer, antiquary, essayist, and novelist of great industry, but without enough talent to acquire lasting fame. He printed his own works on a private press, at his home, Lee Priory, Kent, where in 1828 W. W. visited him. (See M. K. Woodworth, *The Literary Career of Sir Samuel Egerton Brydges*, Oxford, 1935.) His daughter Jemima married Edward Quillinan and died at Rydal in 1822. See *LY* i. 68, p. 79. Many years later, in 1841, Quillinan married Dora Wordsworth. In the Preface to *The Ruminator*, Brydges states that 'the major part of these Essays, as far as No. LXXIII, were first printed in the *Censura Literaria*'—a collection of extracts from various writers made by Brydges between 1805 and 1810—but that 'the rest are principally by the author's friend, R. P. Gillies Esq, the author of *Childe Alarique*'. The 'first letter', or essay, referred to by W. W., is an effusion on the delights of solitude.

[3] *Childe Alarique*, etc., 1813. See p. 167, n. 1 above.

Hogg in this preference. The story of *Mary Scott* appears to me extremely improbable, and not skilfully conducted; besides, the style of the piece is often vicious. The intermediate parts of the *Queen's Wake* are done with much spirit, but the style here, also, is often disfigured with false finery, and in too many places it recalls Mr. Scott to one's mind. Mr. Hogg has too much genius to require that support, however respectable in itself. As to style, if I had an opportunity I should like to converse with you thereupon. Such is your sensibility, and your power of mind, that I am sure I could induce you to abandon many favourite modes of speech; for example, why should you write, 'Where the lake gleams beneath the *autumn* sun,' instead of 'autumnal', which is surely more natural and harmonious? We say 'summer sun', because we have no adjective termination for that season, but 'vernal' and 'autumnal' are both unexceptionable words. Miss Seward[1] uses 'hybernal', and I think it is to be regretted that the word is not familiar. But these discussions render a letter extremely dull.

I sent the alterations of *Yarrow Visited* to Miss Hutchinson and my sister, in Wales, who think them great improvements, and are delighted with the poem as it now stands. Second parts, if much inferior to the first, are always disgusting, and as I had succeeded in *Yarrow Unvisited*, I was anxious that there should be no falling off; but that was unavoidable, perhaps, from the subject, as imagination almost always transcends reality. I remain, hoping that you will excuse this most hasty scrawl, with great regard and respect, yours most truly,

William Wordsworth.

335. W. W. to C. W.

Address: The Very Revd the Dean of Bocking, Essex.
Postmark: 29 Nov 1814
MS. WL.
MY ii. 508, p. 612.

Nov. 26th [1814]

My dear Brother,

Not hearing from you I had some apprehensions (as the Booksellers are not the most attentive persons in the world to directions given them) that my intentions in sending you *The Excursion* might

[1] Anna Seward, of Lichfield (1747–1809), friend of Erasmus Darwin and later of Scott, whose poems, of very indifferent quality, were edited by Scott in three volumes, with a memoir, in 1810. In 1811 the Edinburgh publisher, Constable, with Scott's help, published her *Letters* in six volumes.

not have been fulfilled. But a few days before the receipt of yours I learned from Mrs. Lloyd that the Work had reached you. I should have been sorry had you not been pleased with it; sorry both as a Poet and an Englishman. I hear from many quarters high commendations and not a few from the members of your Profession. Yesterday I had a letter from Sir George Beaumont in which he says the Bishop of London is enchanted with the Excursion, and indeed I hear but one opinion on the subject! The Printers have just begun the 2nd Volume of my Poems, so that I hope they will be ready for Publication about the beginning of Janry.[1] Many delays have taken place, for none of which I was accountable, or they might have been before the public ere this time. I have not yet heard anything of the Sale of the Excursion; which I should have done had it been such as was likely to lead the way to the steady demand of a second Edition which many Persons are waiting for; and I should be sorry if their disappointment be of long continuance, as must be the case if the work does not go off in reasonable time.—I see that you have some sermons ready for Publication; Why did not you mention this to me? I remember that I am in your debt for a bound set of your Ecclesiastical History[2] which was presented to Mr. Johnson; and which you shall be paid for the first convenient opportunity; therefore pray let me know the amount.— Dorothy is in S. Wales with Mr. Hutchinson's family; we expect her home by the next moon: She is well. I saw Richard and his Bride[3] at Sockbridge; he was pretty well and she is a very decent and comely person, but he has done a foolish thing in marrying one so young; not to speak of the disgrace of forming such a connection with a servant, and that, one of his own. Mrs Lloyd is but poorly, and Charles has not been well lately; though when we saw him a few days ago he was unusually so. He has printed his Alfieri, and composed a novel recently with his usual rapidity.[4] I have not seen it.—Mary is well and so are the children except that Wm has a bad cold; which always somewhat alarms us, as his colds never fail to be accompanied with considerable difficulty in breathing, and a croupy sound in the throat which is most painful to hear. He is a stout lively and healthy child, of great promise. His sister is quick and clever. She is very careless and inattentive, but

[1] W.'s *Poems including Lyrical Ballads*, containing, besides the earlier *Lyrical Ballads*, almost all the poems written since 1807, appeared in Mar. 1815.

[2] *Ecclesiastical Biography, or Lives of Eminent Men connected with the History of Religion in England*, by C. W., was published early in 1810.

[3] See L. 318, p. 143, n. 1 above.

[4] Lloyd's translation of Alfieri (*The Tragedies of Vittorio Alfieri*, three volumes, 1815) was dedicated to Southey. The novel, *Isabel*, was privately printed at Ulverston in 1820.

capable of learning rapidly would she give her mind to it. John is for book-attainments the slowest Child almost I ever knew. He has an excellent judgment and well regulated affections; but I am much disappointed in my expectations of retracing the Latin and Greek classics with him. Incredible pains has been taken with him, but he is to this day a deplorably bad reader of *English* even. You do not mention your farming. How does it answer, verily and truly?

With best love from Mary to yourself and our sister Priscilla I remain my dear Christopher most faithfully yours

W. Wordsworth

Our neighbour the Bishop[1] is declining gradually but more in mind than in body. Pray tell how your expectations stand as to succeeding him.[2] Do not forget this.

335a. W. W. to D. W.

Address: Miss Wordsworth, Mr Hutchinson's, Hindwell, Radnor.
Stamp: Kendal Penny Post.
MS. WL.
Hitherto unpublished.

[probably 4 Dec. 1814]
Sunday night

My dearest Sister,

At the sight of this short Letter do not be alarmed—these are my first words; for I trust there is no reason why you should. My present[3] writing is occasioned by the cold of Wm[4] which I mentioned in my last. When the Southeys were here not above a month ago he had such another attack. This has been longer and more tedious—the barking cough—a good deal of fever—with the latter part of the night restless and something of a croupy sound but not at all worse than he has often had. There is also a thick respiration—By Mr. Scambler's advice we tried a Blister, and it began to act like a charm—but the pain of it made him cry so much that we thought that distressed him more than the blister relieved him—so that we have just taken it off before it could work its full effect.—But as you will suppose dearest Mary has been a good deal exhausted with waiting upon him and amusing him the day through—and I cannot but wish that instead of waiting till next moon you would come home, and for

[1] Richard Watson, Bishop of Llandaff. See L. 101, pt. i, p. 206, n. 1.
[2] i.e. as Professor of Divinity at Cambridge.
[3] Erased.
[4] i.e. Willy W. aged four and a half.

my own feelings the sooner the better. Mary will not consent that I should write, till we can say that the Child is quite well; nor indeed would I have written now if tuesday had been a post day. Tell dearest Sara and every body not to be alarmed—it is solely to relieve Mary from fatigue—who at the best you know is not very strong. Wishing to see you and hoping with much confidence, that you will find the Darling quite well on your arrival and will hear that he is well at Kendal—

I remain dearest Dorothea
Your most affectionate Br
W. Wordsworth

I repeat that I have no motive for writing but an earnest wish you were at home on Dear Mary's account, and that when I have had any anxiety I always wish for you—

336. W. W. to SARA HUTCHINSON

Address: Miss Hutchinson, Hindwell, Radnor.
MS. WL.
Hitherto unpublished.

Tuesday two o'clock.
[probably 6 Dec. 1814][1]

All well.
My dearest Sara

In consequence of my last,[2] Dorothy will probably have left Hindwell. Soon after my return from taking that letter to the office Mr Scambler pronounced Wm's a dangerous case of inflammatory croup; the spasms were frequent and severe and the difficulty of breathing great—a wheasiness that alarmed him much. He attempted to bleed him in the arm but luckily, as it has proved no blood flowed, about nine or ten next morning an abatement showed itself though he was extremely heavy—We had Mr Scambler yesterday evening and all last night, which was comparatively easy, the breathing much better and the spasms less frequent—It is now two o'clock Tuesday; and I shall keep this letter open to the last moment; the danger is over, if he has no relapse; the barking is nothing compared with what it was; the respiration free; he is in excellent spirits and not at all weak as you would suppose; considering how low he has

[1] The date of this letter is clearly Dec. 1814, the date of Willy's severe illness. See L. 335a above.
[2] i.e. L. 335a above.

been kept, and the quantity of calomel he has taken which is most exhausting. But oh dearest Sara what an anxious, and for some hours, what a wretched time have we passed. The time since Thursday night has appeared to me as long as half a century. If he goes on well he must not quit his room till Saturday; nor the house for several days. That was that sudden fit of snow with cold rainy weather, that gave him the complaint—and I am determined that he shall be most carefully watched till next summer; and not suffered to go about starving himself[1] with Joe and the other cottage children. What a transition from our warm rooms to the cold and wet grass where he often sits.

Mary is looking ill as you will suppose; for she has had little or no sleep since last Thursday night; nor indeed have I—so that I am glad Dorothy is coming home, as W. will require so much looking after; and it wearies her spirits to have him *constantly* with her. I ought not to forget Mrs. Lloyd's kindness; we were in extreme anxiety all yesterday, she came as soon as she had learned of his illness; and encouraged us much; pronouncing decisively that he was mending in all the symptoms, then favorable. We attribute (under God) his cure first to the Blister, and then to the calomel. [*Seal*] present I am most thankful he was not bled; he must now [? remain] in bed from mere weakness.

[*unsigned*]

All going well at 4 o'clock.

337. W. W. to SARA HUTCHINSON

Address: Miss Hutchinson, Hindwell, Radnor.
MS. WL.
Hitherto unpublished.

Saturday Noon
[probably 10 Dec. 1814]

My dearest Sara,

Mother will be obliged to you if you will write a few lines to Hindwell, is the message I have this moment received from Dorothy. —I am happy to say that little W. has never looked back since the turn of his complaint; but we are advised by Mr Scambler to keep him in his bedroom for two or three days longer; his little pipe of a voice is slender and he coughs still occasionally; today he is to begin with strengthening medicine. Dorothy[2] also has had a very

[1] In the North 'starve' means to be cold. [2] i.e. Dora.

bad cold, which has reduced her much; but her fever is abated; and she is doing excellently; but she is as white almost as a flower.

Last night we received Dear D's[1] Letter; the same day perhaps as you would receive my first melancholy one. Hers was dated Sunday, yet we did not get it till Friday.—Mary was quite melancholy on hearing of her Brother's purchase; for my own part I have a firmer mind upon the occasion; the North of England is a bad country to purchase Land in, it sells so very high and surely Tom's fortune was not large enough to suffer mere inclination (provided he had wished to look forward to coming northward) to interfere with a prudential purchase. Say to him that he has my congratulations; and above all my sincere and earnest wishes that he may prosper in this and every other concern. I also salute him with due respect upon his honours, as lord of the Manor of *Nash Splash*, *Nill*, *Nell* or whatever odd half-welsh half-english name his seignory may be known by. Mary has just come downstairs; she says she never can have any pleasure in thinking of it; she is sure it must be a low, damp, miry, unwholesome place. What sad work Lord Ox— it ought to be Lord Ass-ford[2] has made of it—dissipating so noble an inheritance. Mary begs me to say that she does not believe in her own mind notwithstanding Mr Scambler's unqualified assertions, and the exact coincidence of Wm's symptoms with the description of the disease in Dr Hamilton's book, that Wm Ever had the *inflammatory* Croup. For my own part I know not what to say; alarmingly ill he certainly was: and heaven defend us from the recurrence of such horror and anxiety. When I wrote first I had not the least impression that it was the inflammatory croup; it was only on my return Mr S. declared that it was that complaint carried to a Dangerous height—and *then* I bitterly regretted that I had written before the crisis was over.—Miss B. is a cunning jade as to her verses[3]—from old Helvellyns brow sublime to genuine English

[1] D. W.'s. Dorothy was staying at Hindwell.

[2] Edward Harley, 5th Earl of Oxford (1773–1848), succeeded his uncle in 1790. His father John H. was Bishop of Hereford. The family seat was at Brampton near Hereford.

[3] A poem by Miss Barker: *Lines addressed to A Noble Lord; (His Lordship will know why) by one of the Small Fry of the Lakes*, London: printed for W. L. Pople, 76 Chancery Lane, 1815. This poem is addressed to Byron, who had recently referred, in a letter to James Hogg, to the poets of the Lakes as 'running about their ponds'. It exhorted him to leave his evil ways and visit the happy Lake District. A manuscript of the poem, differing in several respects from the printed version and preceding it, and signed 'M. Barker', but apparently in the hand of Mrs. Coleridge, is in an album belonging to Mr. Jonathan Wordsworth. This letter reveals what passages were contributed to the poem by Wordsworth—five stanzas out of sixteen, except for the lines ('verses') which he

Nature is all written by your humble servant: except one couplet about lords and squires and the pass[age] about attending and blending: in these I put in the words 'Little children and music'—Except also six verses or eight beginning 'Ever in the obscure delights' and ending reverence thy betters; which to gratify her I transplanted from her first Paragraph as first composed, but in fact these lines had better be out. I concluded the Poem, with 'genuine English Nature'; and I think what she has added very much weakens it;[1] and the concluding invitation is wholly inconsistent with the Introduction; it is given in such serious earnest as to imply, what is truth, that the fair Authoress would be very happy to see his crack-brained, skull-bearing[2] Lordship at Greta Hall [none] the less. Do not mention even among your friends at H.[3] that I had anything to do with this [? Retort] as I should be sorry Lord B. should think I honoured him so far. It will be suspected that I and Southey, too, had some hand in it. Mr Wilson was sure that I had written the first stanza—sure also that I had written part at least of the description of the rural feast.[4]

Mrs Mogg[5] departs today in sorry plight by the Roof of the Coach—she cannot ride inside. She takes with her none of the money from the sale of her goods. She wrote a note—asking to be paid the half-crown she had advanced for your steel Pin. This was right and I respect her for doing so—ten shillings in the Pound have been paid with promise of more if ever in their power: but that fortune never

specifies. For Miss Barker of Keswick, see L. 257, p. 42, n. 3. For the letter to Hogg (which seems not extant) see *HCR* i, pp. 167, 199; and Prothero, *Byron's Letters and Journals*, vi, p. 398.

[1] The stanza which he considered inferior was omitted from the printed poem which concludes as he wishes, the last stanza running as follows:

Come! and listen to a measure
Framed by Hope for lasting pleasure;
Listen, till thy heart be sure
That nothing monstrous can endure.
To unlearn thyself, repair
Hither, or grow wise elsewhere;
Striving to become the creature
Of a genuine English nature!

[2] In the second stanza Byron is described as:

Holding forth (that spirits dull
May be cheer'd) a goblet skull,
Whence thy morbid soul hath quaffed
Many a foul Avernian draught.

[3] i.e. Hindwell.

[4] See L. 348 below. 'Mr. Wilson' is probably John W., 'Christopher North'.

[5] The Moggs are mentioned by M. W. as having a sale of their '£100 worth of furniture' in Oct. 1814; *MW* 9, p. 16.

will be, I think. Miss Alne[1] has been here all night with little Priscilla[2] of whom Willy is surprizingly fond. Poor innocent, heaven be thanked that he is doing well.

Farewell my dear friend and sister—best love

W. W.

All well. Mary Bell[3] comes today or tomorrow—I am glad. Ellen is terribly stupid. Fail not to write often and long letters—very long —largest sheets and closest hand. The Printers have failed. We have had no sheets this week which vexes me—. the last was the 82nd page of the 2nd Vol. Tintern Abbey.[4]

338. W. W. to R. W.

Address: Richd Wordsworth Esqr, Sockbridge—Penrith.
MS. WL.
Hitherto unpublished.

Rydale Mount
December 15th 1814

My dear Rich^d^,

I write to beg that you would request Mr. Addison to pay into the Stamp Office on my account £325 on, or before the 31st Inst. without fail.

Dorothy is just returned from Wales quite well:—She was hurried home a fortnight before her appointed time by rather an alarming Illness, the croup, of my youngest Son.

We are sorry that we have not yet heard from you on the subject of the settlement of our affairs. P[lease] dispatch this business.

The weather has been dreadful here; and our Invalids, for my daughter also has had a severe Cold, recover more slowly than I hope would otherwise have been the case.

With best regards to Mrs. W.
I remain
Your affectionate Br
Wm Wordsworth

[1] A friend of the Lloyds.
[2] One of the Lloyds' children.
[3] A valued maid. See *MW* 9, pp. 18–20.
[4] In the *Poems including Lyrical Ballads*, as printed in 1815, 'Tintern Abbey' begins on p. 73 and ends on p. 80. This sentence gives some indication of the date of this letter. In L. 335 above, to C. W., dated 26 Nov., W. W. says, 'The Printers have just begun the 2nd Volume of my Poems'. The present letter must therefore be somewhat later.

N.B. I returned your Great Coat the same day by the Carrier from Patterdale—

Pray do not omit to answer this Letter.

339. W. W. to R. P. GILLIES

MS. untraced.
Gillies.
K (—). *MY ii. 509, p. 613.*

Rydal Mount, Dec. 22, 1814

My dear Sir,

Your account of yourself distresses me. Flee from your present abode. If you resolve on going to London, let me beg of you to take Westmoreland in your way. You can make a trial here, and should it not answer, you are only so far on your way to town. We shall be glad to see you, though I know that my house is too small, and my family far too noisy, for a person whose nerves are out of tune. But there are lodgings in the neighbourhood which might possibly suit you, though their accommodations are not very luxurious. But you remember Horace's invitation to Maecenas:—[1]

> 'Plerumque gratae divitibus vices,
> Mundaeque parvo sub lare pauperum
> Cœnae, sine auleis et ostro,
> *Solicitam explicuere frontem.*'

Your first position, that every idea which passes through a Poet's mind may be made passionate, and therefore poetical, I am not sure that I understand. If you mean through a poet's mind while in a poetical mood, the words are nothing but an identical proposition. But a Poet must be subject to a thousand thoughts in common with other Men, and many of them must, I suppose, be as unsusceptible of alliance with poetic passion as the thoughts that interest ordinary men. But the range of poetic feeling is far wider than is ordinarily supposed, and the furnishing new proofs of this fact is the only *incontestible* demonstration of genuine poetic genius. 2dly, 'The moment a clear idea of any kind is conceived, it ought to be brought out directly and rapidly as possible, without any view to any particular style of language.' I am not sure that I comprehend your meaning here. Is it that a man's thoughts should be noted down in prose, or that he should express them in any kind

[1] Horace, *Carm.* iii. xxix. 13–16.

of verse that they most easily fall into? I think it well to make brief memoranda of our most interesting thoughts in prose; but to write fragments of verse is an embarrassing practice. A similar course answers well in painting, under the name of studies; but in Poetry it is apt to betray a writer into awkwardness, and to turn him out of his course for the purpose of lugging on these ready-made pieces by the head and shoulders. Or do you simply mean, that such thoughts as arise in the progress of composition should be expressed in the first words that offer themselves, as being likely to be most energetic and natural? If so, this is not a rule to be followed without cautious exceptions. My first expressions I often find detestable; and it is frequently true of second words as of second thoughts, that they are the best. I entirely accord with you in your third observation, that we should be cautious not to waste our lives in dreams of imaginary excellence, for a thousand reasons, and not the least for this, that these notions of excellence may perhaps be *erroneous*, and then our inability to catch a phantom of no value may prevent us from attempting to seize a precious substance within our reach.

When your Letter arrived I was in the act of reading to Mrs. W[ordsworth] your *Exile*,[1] which pleased me more, I think, than anything that I have read of yours. There is, indeed, something of 'mystification' about it, which does not enhance its value with me; but it is, I think, in many passages delightfully conceived and expressed. I was particularly charmed with the seventeenth stanza, first part. This is a passage which I shall often repeat to myself; and I assure you that, with the exception of Burns and Cowper, there is very little of recent verse, however much it may interest me, that sticks to my memory (I mean which I get by heart). The recommendation of your Volume is, that it is elegant, sensitive, and harmonious, —a rare merit in these days; its defect, that it deals too much in pleasurable and melancholy generalities. But if you preserve your health of body, I am confident that you will produce something in verse that will last.

I have read the *Ruminator*,[2] and I fear that I do not like it quite as much as you would wish. It wants depth and strength, yet it is pleasingly and elegantly written, and contains everywhere the sentiments of a liberal spirit. Mr. Hogg's *Badlew*[3] (I suppose it to be his) I could not get through. There are two pretty passages; the flight of the deer, and the falling of the child from the rock of

[1] In *Childe Alarique*, etc.
[2] See L. 334, p. 169, n. 2 above.
[3] *The Hunting of Badlewe, a Dramatic Tale*, by J. H., Edinburgh, 1814.

Stirling, though both are a little *outré*. But the story is coarsely conceived, and, in my judgment, as coarsely executed; the style barbarous, and the versification harsh and uncouth. Mr. H. is too illiterate to write in any measure or style that does not savour of balladism. This is much to be regretted; for he is possessed of no ordinary power. I am delighted to learn that your Edinburgh Aristarch[1] has declared against the *Excursion*, as he will have the mortification of seeing a book enjoy a high reputation, to which he has not contributed. Do not imagine that my principles lead me to condemn Scott's method of pleasing the public, or that I have not a very high respect for his various talents and extensive attainments. I sent him the *Excursion*, and am rather surprised that I have had no letter from him to acknowledge the receipt of it. Pray, present my regards to him when you see him. I have seen a book advertised under your name, which I suppose to be a novel.[2] How comes it that you do not mention it? I am afraid that my indolence will prevent me from prefixing any prose remarks to my poems. The old preface will be reprinted as an appendix. I have not ventured to place your name *before* the sonnet addressed to you, but I have assigned it a place in the volume.[3]

With great respect, I remain yours,

William Wordsworth.

340. D. W. to R. W.

Address: Richard Wordsworth Esqre, Sockbridge, near Penrith.
MS. WL.
MY ii. 510, p. 616.

December 27th [1814]

My dear Brother,

William is engaged with company therefore he has desired me to say that he has filled up the Draft which you sent him for 325 £ and transmitted it to the Kendal Bankers who will duly accept it, and remit to the Stamp office Bills due at the end of this month. There will be no other inconvenience arising from your not being able to advance Cash at present, than that Wm will have to pay so much per Cent for its passing through the Bank, and, of course, the discount.

[1] i.e. Francis Jeffrey, editor of the *Edinburgh Review*, whose severe review of *The Excursion* had appeared in Nov. 1814.

[2] *Confessions of Sir Henry Longueville*, 1814.

[3] See L. 333, p. 168, n. 2 above.

I am happy to inform you that my Nephew William is now restored to perfect health, after a most dangerous illness. All the rest of the Family are well and join with me in kind Love.

I spent ten weeks very agreeably with Mr Thomas Hutchinson and his Family in Radnorshire. Miss H. went with me to Hindwell, and I have left her there.

I am sorry to hear that your Wife is so poorly—with best Respects to her, and, wishing you both a happy new year, I remain, dear Richard

Your affectionate Sister
D Wordsworth

341. W. W. and D. W. to CATHERINE CLARKSON

Address: Mrs Clarkson, Bury St Edmonds, Suffolk.
Stamp: Kendal Penny Post.
MS. British Museum.
K (—). *MY ii. 512, p. 621.*

New Year's Eve [1814]

[*W. W. writes*:]

My dear Friend,

It is very selfish of me to write to you only upon my own concerns. But I am encouraged by finding so much of your letter devoted to the Excursion. I am glad that it has interested you; I expected no less, and I wish from my Soul that it had been a thousand times more deserving of your regard. In respect to its final destiny I have neither care nor anxiety being assured that if it be of God—it must stand; and that if the spirit of truth, 'The Vision and the Faculty divine' be not in it, and so do not pervade it, it must perish. So let the wisest and best of the present generation and of Posterity decide the question. Thoroughly indifferent as I am on this point, I will acknowledge that I have a wish for the *sale* of the present Edition, partly to repay the Expense of our Scotch Tour, and still more to place the book within reach of those who can neither purchase nor procure it in its present expensive shape. I therefore beg of you or Mr Clarkson or both of you [that you] will immediately set to work and give it what help you can in the Philanthropist or any well circulated Periodical publication to which you may have easy access. I mentioned the Philanthropist because it circulates a good deal among Quakers, who are wealthy and fond of *instructive* Books. Besides, though I am a professed admirer of the Church of England, I hope that my religious sentiments will not be offensive to *them.* I smiled at your notion of Coleridge reviewing the Ex. in the Ed. I much doubt whether he has read three pages of the poem, and Jeff. has already printed off a Review; beginning with these elegant and decisive words: 'This will not do'.[1] The sage Critic then proceeding to show cause why. This precious piece is what the Coxcomb's Idolaters call a *crushing* Review. Therefore you see as the evil Spirits are rouzed it becomes the good ones to stir, or what is to become of the poor Poet and his Labours? I will now tell you by way of chit chat the little that I have heard of the receipt of the poem. Dr. Parr[2] (who you recollect gave a proof of his critical acumen in the affair of Ireland's MSS which he pronounced to be genuine Shakespear) has declared that it is 'all *but* Milton'; Dr Johnson a leading man of Birmingham that there has been nothing equal to it since Milton's day. Mr Sergeant Rough[3] had spoken to the same effect. The Bishop of London[4] is in raptures—the Duke of Devonshire made it his companion in a late jaunt to Ireland and was so much delighted that he frequently expressed his sorrow that he missed me in his late visit to Lowther where I was expected about the same time. All the best endowed readers even of Edinburgh are enchanted with it; this I had from a respected acquaintance who himself purchased three copies. A gentleman of Derby unknown to me pronounces it an *admirably fine poem.* A Lady of Liverpool, a Quaker, breaks through all forms of ceremony to express her gratitude by letter, which she does in most enthusiastic terms. Charles Lamb (I cannot overlook him) calls it the best of Books; and lastly your son Tom sate up all night reading it! If this won't satisfy you I could give you a deal more by rummaging my memory. By way of per Contra, I ought to tell you that the renowned Poet and critic Antony Harrison of facetious memory, and the whole family of Addison (certain proof that the blood is adulterated, though the name continues to be spelt as formerly) found the Excursion not un peu but tres pesant.[5] It was

[1] The opening words of Jeffrey's review in the *Edinburgh* were in fact, 'This will never do'.

[2] Samuel Parr (1747–1825), was one of many 'literati' deceived by W. H. Ireland (1777–1835), and his forgeries of Shakespeare in 1795.

[3] William Rough (1772–1838), lawyer and poet, became a judge in Ceylon (1830) and Chief Justice of its Supreme Court (1836). He was an intimate friend of Christopher W. at Cambridge, and later of Crabb Robinson.

[4] William Howley (1766–1848), in 1828 appointed Archbishop of Canterbury.

[5] In a letter to D. W. dated Christmas Day (British Museum Add. MS. 36997), C. C. had told her that Mr. Smith, M.P. for Norwich, had brought from London the report that *The Excursion* was 'very fine but un peu pesant'.

too low in the subjects for their high-flying fancies. Perhaps you may not remember that A. H. selected as a topic for his Muse, the Bark-house Beck; so called from its collecting into its bosom all the sweets of Jack Hindson's tan-yard.—Do not fail to thank Tillbrook[1] for his exertions. I have a great respect and regard for that man; and do earnestly wish that those inconsiderate people the Moggs, whom he thinks highly of, and who are now in great want, may not beguile him of some part of his money. Could he by any means be cautioned against an appeal to his heart in this case if it be not too late. I should fear his consenting to be surety for them or something of that kind; it would be very injudicious and might be ruinous to him and could not possibly render any substantial service to such thoughtless people. Poor Mary Lamb, you perhaps may have heard is again under confinement. I have this night received a letter from Charles written in great depression of spirits. Our own anxieties have been dreadful, and I seem to possess all my children in trembling, the youngest in particular after so narrow an escape. The ordinary health of them all is excellent, but they are all subject occasionally as all my Father's family were to bad Catarrhs. Wm is a charming Boy; beautiful and animated; I wish you could see him, he is the delight of my eyes; pray heaven that I may not have to say with Ben Jonson, 'My sin was too much hope of thee loved Boy'.[2] John is of good dispositions but marvellously slow in the acquisition of book-learning. Dorothy is quick generous and affectionate, but she has great faults which probably you may have heard of from her Aunt. I will now conclude with my blessing, every good wish for yourself, your husband, son and all about you. Most affectionately and faithfully yours

Wm Wordsworth.

I believe the poem *has* received a powerful band of fresh admirers, but not powerful as to the *Sale*.

[*D. W. writes*:]

Your letter came by last night's post and after Miss Weir of Appleby and her teacher Miss Jameson, who are staying with us, were gone to bed, William sate up till twelve o'clock to write to you. If my voice were likely to add anything to the power of his I should join earnestly in entreating that you will not let this occasion slip of serving a good cause in opposition to the impudent malice of an ignorant Pretender to literary skill. I think with William that

[1] C. C. had told D. W. in the same letter that T. had disposed of five copies.
[2] Ben Jonson, 'On his First Sonne', *Epigrammes*, 1616.

something might be done among the Quakers, there is no one of their own Body who has as much influence over them as your Husband; and there is no one better fitted for the task imposed than you, in case Mr Clarkson is not inclined to it or has not sufficiently studied the Book to perform it himself. I could be half angry with you for leaving the Excursion with William Smith. Who *is* to buy two guinea Books if not people with such fortunes as his? William gave Charles Lloyd a copy with this charge, that he should lend it to no one who could afford to buy it, and accordingly upon the application of our summer neighbour Mrs Green (a widow with 1500£ per annum of whom you must have heard us speak—a blue-stocking Dame) he refused, giving his reasons. She had before exclaimed with horror 'Two guineas! and for a *part* of a work!' and she then pettishly told him that she must wait till her return to York when she could have it from a circulating Library; for she never bought books unread! This Lady has stayed under our Roof and has been extremely anxious to number William in the Train of her Friends. By the Bye I think that so small an Edition *must* sell, though I see clearly that the effect of the publication has not been such as I expected. I thought that a powerful Band of fresh admirers would have been immediately formed, though I did not expect that it would escape ridicule or severe censure. All I care about—the sale or anything else is here bounded—I should wish the present Edition to go off, and quickly that it may be printed in a cheaper form: and that we may have some small pecuniary advantage from it. As to the permanent fate of that poem or of my Brother's collected Works I have not the shadow of a doubt. I know that the good and pure and noble-minded will in [*seal*] days and when we sleep in the grave be elevated delighted and bettered by what he has performed in solitude for the delight of his own Soul independent of lofty hopes of being of service to his fellow-creatures.—I congratulate you on your return to your own home and one year passed without any harsh or distressing changes. Yet the gradual change in your Father's looks cannot but lead to melancholy thoughts. Such are forced upon us and we cannot quiet them, and though I hope some part of the change may, as you say, have been owing to the cold; yet one must expect after a longer absence than usual from a dear Friend at his period of life, to note something that reminds us of what was different in former times. I am rejoiced more than I can express that you have reason to be so well satisfied with your son. I doubt not he will make a noble character—he always had—that I saw clearly—a good foundation and how almost could it be otherwise with such a Father and Mother!

but there seemed cause to fear that his wayward and provoking freaks might take root and become habits. They are now over—at least in their former childish shape, and I trust and believe that whatever freaks of *youth* you may now have to contend with, his love of study and his good sense will get the bettter of—and may God grant his parents many years of life to enjoy the comfort of possessing a good and dutiful son. Your anecdote of Tom's sitting up all night with the Excursion, and of his dread to hear the contents of my letter shew that he has very strong sensibility. Give my kind love to him and tell him I long to renew our old acquaintance, and begin a new one with him. You do not say a word of coming northwards next Summer. Sara is determined to visit you at Bury before her return to Rydale; but it is not possible for her to make any precise arrangements till our French journey[1] is either set aside, or the time fixed.—April is the month proposed, and if the weather be tolerable we might as well go then as at any other time; but I find the King is to be anointed in June—all France will be gathered together, and I fear there may be disturbances; for though all is quiet at present it is evident enough that the party of discontented and turbulent spirits is very strong. On this account (as we cannot think of staying less than 9 or 10 weeks) I should wish our journey to be *after* June—if to be at all. But I never-never-so much dreaded to leave home as now, so deeply am I impressed with the image of what William and Mary have lately suffered in my absence, and with the uncertainty of all things. Besides, the journey will be very expensive which we can ill afford, and the money could be better spent in augmenting my Niece's wedding portion. To this effect I have written to her. She would not consent to marry without my presence; which was the reason that April was fixed. A few weeks will decide the point, whether we go to France or not—and Sara will then be able to form her plans. At all events I think it would be her wisest way to take the first opportunity of going to Bury; yet that can hardly be before April, and then the other journey will most likely be forced upon us! I will if possible contrive, if I go, to see you on my way back, though for a short time, and will trust that you will soon be coming to Rydale.—This is a plaguy business that I have teased you about. If it were not for my fears for what may happen at home I could think of it with satisfaction—nay with delight, for that dear young woman's sake,[2] whom I believe to be

[1] i.e. to Paris for Caroline's wedding. See L. 330, p. 158.
[2] i.e. Caroline Wordsworth-Vallon.

thoroughly amiable. Oh! that you were going again to France.[1] Do you know of anybody going? William waits for me to walk. It is 5 o'clock—a sweet Evening. We have had a two days thaw. The weather very severe the last fortnight. William and I have walked daily—sometimes Mary with us—and sometimes little Dorothy who is a sweet companion in walking—so lively—so animated—so open to impressions of delight in natural objects, with a most discriminating tact. She gets knowledge quickly through her feelings and her fancy; but sadly wants steadiness and has fits of waywardness and ill-humour with unquietness of manners frequently. Mary is very well and her spirits much amended. Yet she is excessively thin, and her eyes have sadly failed—she can see to do nothing by candle-light except reading large print. Do write again very soon. Did you receive my last letter from Stow? I was vexed when I found that Sara had also sent you the poem. My love to your Father, Sister, and all Friends, not forgetting Mrs Kitchener.

D. W.

New Year's Eve.

342. W. W. to ROBERT SOUTHEY

Address: Robt Southey Esqre, Keswick.
MS. Copy by Susan Wordsworth, WL.
Hitherto unpublished.

[Jan. 1815]

Dear Southey,

The Enclosed is from Lamb pray return it by a speedy opportunity. I should be infinitely obliged to you if you could procure from Gifford, from the Printer, or from anybody his original MS which has been so cruelly garbled and disfigured.[2] I am so vexed on his account and for the apprehended loss of the original Composition, that I have not the slightest feeling for any injury done to myself, by Gifford's treatment of it. I cannot say how happy I should be if a piece of prose that so exquisite a Writer as Lamb thinks the prettiest he ever wrote could be recovered. I know that you will sympathize with me; and I am confident you will do all that can be done.

[1] The Clarksons had been to Paris in Sept. 1814. See L. 328, p. 155 above.

[2] See *Lamb*, ii. 257, p. 139, and 263, p. 149. The October *Quarterly* for some reason was not published until December. Lamb had written review of *The Excursion* for the *Quarterly*, but the editor Gifford, altered it drastically.

As to the Excursion I have ceased to have any interest about it, since I read Lamb's Letter, let this benighted age continue to love its own darkness and to cherish it. I shall continue to write with I trust the light of Heaven upon me.

I am obliged to Scott for his book, and I love Scott much, and greatly admire his various Tales etc; but it would be superfluous to say to *you* what I must think of the Lord of the Isles as a *Poem*.

Very affectionately yours

W W

Did I thank you for Roderic,[1] I hope so, it was very acceptable.

343. W. W. to CATHERINE CLARKSON

Address: Mrs Clarkson, Bury St Edmonds, Suffolk.
MS. Cornell.
K (—). *MY ii. 511, p. 617* (—). *Broughton, 46, p. 56.*
Morley, i, pp. 78–82.

[Jan. 1815]

(Transcribed by Mary and Dorothy, on account of the vile penmanship) (*Note by W. W.*)

[*Mary begins the copy*]

My dear Friend,

I don't know that it is quite *fair* to sit down to answer a letter of friendship the moment it is received; but allow me to do so in this case.—Unitarian hymns must by their dispassionate monotony have deprived your Friend's ear of all compass, which implies of all discrimination. To you I will whisper, that the Excursion has one merit if it has no other, a versification to which for *variety* of musical effect no Poem in the language furnishes a parallel. Tell Patty Smith[2] this (the name is a secret with me and make her stare); and exhort her to study with her fingers till she has learned to confess it to herself. Miss S's notion of poetical imagery is probably taken from the Pleasures of Hope or Gertrude of Wyoming[3] see for instance stanza first of said poem. There is very little imagery of that kind; but, I am far from subscribing to your concession that there is little imagery in the Poem; either collateral in the way of metaphor

[1] *Roderick, the Last of the Goths*, by Robert Southey, published 1814. It was the last of his epics.

[2] Daughter of William Smith, M.P. for Norwich. See L. 48, pt. i, p. 87.

[3] Both by Thomas Campbell (1777–1844). *The Pleasures of Hope* was published in 1799, *Gertrude of Wyoming* in 1809.

coloring the style; illustrative in the way of simile; or directly under the shape of description or incident: there is a great deal; though not quite so much as will be found in the other parts of the Poem where the subjects are more lyrically treated and where there is less narration; or description turning upon manners, and those repeated actions which constitute habits, or a course of life.—Poetic Passion (Dennis[1] has well observed) is of two kinds imaginative and enthusiastic; and merely human and ordinary; of the former it is only to be feared that there is too great a proportion. But all this must inevitably be lost upon Miss P. S.—

The Soul, dear Mrs C. may be re-given when it had been taken away, my own Solitary is an instance of this; but a Soul that has been dwarfed by a course of bad culture cannot after a certain age, be expanded into on[e] of even ordinary proportion.—Mere error of opinion, mere apprehension of ill consequences from supposed mistaken views on my part, could never have rendered your correspondent blind to the innumerable analogies and types of infinity, insensible to the countless awakenings to noble aspiration, which I have transfused into that Poem from the Bible of the Universe as it speaks to the ear of the intelligent, as it lies open to the eyes of the humble-minded. I have alluded to the Ladys errors of opinion—she talks of my being a worshipper of Nature—a passionate expression uttered incautiously in the Poem upon the Wye has led her into this mistake, she reading in cold-heartedness and substituting the letter for the spirit. Unless I am greatly mistaken, there is nothing of this kind in the Excursion. There is indeed a passage towards the end of the 4th. Book where the Wanderer introduces the simile of the Boy and the Shell, and what follows, that has something, ordinarily but absurdly called *Spinosistic*. But the intelligent reader will easily see the *dramatic* propriety of the Passage. The Wanderer in the beginning of the book [*Dorothy takes the pen*] had given vent to his own devotional feelings and announced in some degree his own creed; he is here preparing the way for more distinct conceptions of the Deity by reminding the Solitary of such religious feelings as cannot but exist in the minds of those who affect atheism. She condemns me for not distinguishing between nature as the work of God and God himself. But where does she find this doctrine inculcated? Where does she gather that the Author of the Excursion looks upon nature and God as the same? He does not indeed con-

[1] John Dennis (1657–1734), a remarkably able literary critic whose work was much admired by Southey. *The Advancement and Reformation of Modern Poetry* (1701) and *Three Letters on the Genius and Writings of Shakespeare* (1711) are his most valuable works.

sider the Supreme Being as bearing the same relation to the universe as a watch-maker bears to a watch.[1] In fact, there is nothing in the course of religious education adopted in this country and in the use made by us of the holy scriptures that appears to me so injurious as the perpetually talking about *making* by God—Oh! that your Correspondent had heard a conversation which I had in bed with my sweet little Boy,[2] four and a half years old, upon this subject the other morning. 'How did God make me? Where is God? How does he speak? He never spoke to *me*.' I told him that God was a spirit, that he was not like his flesh which he could touch; but more like his thoughts in his mind which he could *not* touch.—The wind was tossing the fir trees, and the sky and light were dancing about in their dark branches, as seen through the window—Noting these fluctuations he exclaimed eagerly—'There's a bit of him I see it there!' This is not meant entirely for Father's prattle; but, for Heaven's sake, in your religious talk with children say as little as possible about *making*. One of the main objects of the Recluse is, to reduce the calculating understanding to its proper level among the human faculties—Therefore my Book must be disliked by the Unitarians, as their religion rests entirely on that basis; and therefore is, in fact, no religion at all—but—I won't say what. I have done little or nothing towards your request of furnishing you with arguments to cope with my antagonist. Read the Book if it pleases you; the construction of the language is uniformly perspicuous; at least I have taken every possible pains to make it so, therefore you will have no difficulty here. The impediment you may meet with will be of two kinds, such as exist in the ode which concludes my 2^d^ volume of poems.[3] This poem rests entirely upon two recollections of childhood, one that of a splendour in the objects of sense which is passed away, and the other an indisposition to bend to the law of death as applying to our own particular case. A Reader who has not a vivid recollection of these feelings having existed in his mind in childhood cannot understand that poem. So also with regard to some of those elements of the human soul whose importance is insisted upon in the Ex^n^. And some of those images of sense which are dwelt upon as holding that relation to immortality and infinity which I have before alluded to; if a person has not been in the way of

[1] This analogy was used by William Paley (1743–1805) in *Natural Theology: Evidence of the Existence and Attributes of the Deity*, 1802. It was illustrated with diagrams.

[2] i.e. Willy Wordsworth, b. 1810.

[3] i.e. *Ode: Intimations of Immortality*, first published 1807 in *Poems in Two Volumes*.

receiving these images, it is not likely that he can form such an adequate conception of them as will bring him into lively sympathy with the Poet. For instance one who has never heard the echoes of the flying Raven's voice in a mountainous Country, as described at the close of the 4th Book will not perhaps be able to relish that illustration; yet every one must have been in the way of perceiving similar effects from different causes;—but I have tired myself, and must have tired you—

One word upon ordinary or popular passion. Could your correspondent read the description of Robert, and the fluctuations of hope and fear in Margaret's mind,[1] and the gradual decay of herself and her dwelling without a bedimmed eye then I pity her. Could she read the distress of the Solitary after the loss of his Family and the picture of his quarrel with his own conscience (though this tends more to meditative passion) without some agitation then I envy not her tranquillity. Could the anger of Ellen[2] before she sate down to weep over her babe, though she were but a poor serving-maid, be found in a book, and that book be said to be without passion, then, thank Heaven! that the person so speaking is neither my wife nor my Sister, nor one whom (unless I could work in her a great alteration) I am forced to daily converse with. What thinks she of those Relatives about the little Infant, who was unexpectedly given, and suddenly taken away? But too much of this—Farewell. I wish I could have written you a more satisfactory letter. Lamb is justifiably enraged at the spurious Review which his Friends expect to be his.[3] No Newmarket jockey, no horse-stealer was ever able to play a hundredth part of the tricks upon the person of an unhappy beast that the Bavius of the Quarterly Review has done for that sweet composition. So I will not scruple to style it, though I never saw it. And worst of all, L[amb kept no copy] and the original M S [we] fear, destroyed.—As [to the Ed Review] I hold the Author [of it in entire] contempt, and therefore shall not pollute my fingers [with the touch] of it.[4] There is one sentence in the Ex^{n}. ending in 'sublime att[ractions] of the grave'[5] which,—if the poem had contained nothing else that [I valued,] would have made it almost a matter of religion with me to [keep out] of the way of the best stuff which so mean a mind as Mr [Jeffrey's] could produce in connection

[1] *The Excursion*, i. ll. 566–91, 730–915.

[2] Ibid., ll. 970–82.

[3] See L. 342, n. 2 above.

[4] Francis Jeffrey's review of *The Excursion* in the *Edinburgh* appeared in Nov. 1814.

[5] *Excursion*, iv, ll. 237–8.

with it. His impertinences, to us[e the] mildest te[rm,] if once they had a place in my memory, would, for a [time] at least, [sti]ck there. You cannot scower a spot of this kind ou[t of] your mind as you may a stain out of your clothes. If the m[ind] were under the power of the will I should read Mr J^{y} merely to expose his stupidity to his still more stupid admirers. This not being the case, as I said before, I shall not pollute my fingers with touching his book. Give my affectionate regards to Henry Robinson, and the sa[me] to Mr Clarkson. Remember me also kindly to your Father.—I am sure you are competent to write the Review as well as I could wish to have it done. I am very sorry for the indisposition under which your last was written. Headaches are plaguey things, I hope you are better—

[*Wordsworth ends the remainder in his own hand*]—Sunday Morning—I have just read over this Letter; it is a sad jumble of stuff and as ill expressed.—I should not send it but in compliance with the wish of Mary and Dorothy. The reason of the thing being so bad is that your Friends remarks were so monstrous. To talk of the offense of writing the Ex^{n} and the difficulty of forgiving the Author is carrying audacity and presumption to a heigth of which I did not think any *Woman* was capable. Had my Poem been much coloured by Books, as many parts of what I have to write must be, I should have been accused as Milton has been of pedantry, and of having a mind which could not support itself but by other mens labours.—Do not you perceive that my conversations almost all take place out of Doors, and all with grand objects of nature surrounding the speakers for the express purpose of their being alluded to in illustration of the subjects treated of. *Much* imagery from books would have been an impertinence and an incumbrance: where it was required it is found. As to passion; it is never to be lost sight of, that the Excursion is *part* of a work; that in its plan it is conversational; and that if I had introduced stories exciting curiosity, and filled with violent conflicts of passion and a rapid interchange of striking incidents, these things could have never harmonized with the rest of the work and all further discourse, comment, or reflections must have been put a stop to.—This I write for you and not for your friend; with whom if you would take my advice, you will neither converse by letter nor *viva voce* upon a subject which she is [in every] respect disqualified to treat. farewell.

[?Your most] affectionate friend W. W.

You had sent a promise that Mr C would give me an account of the impression my Book made on him.

[*In M. W.'s hand*] Six o'clock Monday morning—Wm and I are going to Bowness to take the Quarterly bath—a fine day—

344. W. W. to SIR GEORGE BEAUMONT[1]

MS. untraced.
MY ii. 513, p. 627.

Rydal Mount, February 1, 1815.

My dear Sir George,

Accept my thanks for the permission given me to dedicate these poems to you. In addition to a lively pleasure derived from general considerations, I feel a particular satisfaction; for, by inscribing them with your name, I seem to myself in some degree to repay, by an appropriate honour, the great obligation which I owe to one part of the collection—as having been the means of first making us personally known to each other.[2] Upon much of the remainder, also, you have a peculiar claim,—for some of the best pieces were composed under the shade of your own groves, upon the classic ground of Coleorton; where I was animated by the recollection of those illustrious poets of your name and family, who were born in that neighbourhood;[3] and, we may be assured, did not wander with indifference by the dashing stream of Grace Dieu, and among the rocks that diversify the forest of Charnwood. Nor is there any one to whom such parts of this collection as have been inspired or coloured by the beautiful country from which I now address you, could be presented with more propriety than to yourself—who have composed so many admirable pictures from the suggestions of the same scenery. Early in life the sublimity and beauty of this region excited your admiration; and I know that you are bound to it in mind by a still strengthening attachment.

Wishing and hoping that this work may survive as a lasting memorial of a friendship, which I reckon among the blessings of my life, I have the honour to be, my dear Sir George,

Yours most affectionately and faithfully,
William Wordsworth.

[1] This letter forms the Dedication of W.'s *Poems, including Lyrical Ballads*, 1815, the first collected edition of his poems. It was in two volumes and did not include *The Excursion*.

[2] W. here refers to *Lyrical Ballads*, 1800, which Sir G. Beaumont first admired at Keswick in 1803, when he presented to W., through Coleridge, the little estate of Applethwaite, under Skiddaw. See *EY* 193, p. 406.

[3] Francis Beaumont (1584–1616), and Sir John B. (1583–1627). See Letters 37 and 230, pt. i, pp. 70 and 514 n.

345. W. W. to DR. ANDERSON

Address: Dr. Anderson, 11 Windmill Street, Edinburgh.
Postmark: 1815 25 Feb. *Endorsed*: (To Robert Anderson, M.D.) William Wordsworth the Poet to Dr. Anderson.
MS. National Library of Scotland.
Hitherto unpublished.

Rydal Mount Jan^{ry} 4th 1815

[*but see postmark; probably a mistake for Feb^{ry}*]

My dear Sir,

Accept my thanks for your obliging Letter, brought by Mr Knox whom I was not lucky enough to see, being then from Home.—I communicated its interesting contents to Mr Southey: we both are afraid that nothing can at present be done towards accomplishing our wish;[1] and are duly sensible of your very liberal offer.

I was happy to hear that you and Miss Anderson had received pleasure from the 'Excursion'. Miss Hutchinson is now in Wales but Mrs Wordsworth joins me in best regards to yourself and your Daughter; we both often talk of the pleasure we enjoyed in your society at Traquair and in Yarrow. When you see your friends at the Manse fail not to remind the Pastor of his promise to visit us next summer; and give to him and his Lady our kind remembrances, and also to our friends at Traquair Know.[2]—

I remain my dear Sir
Most truly your
obliged Servant
W. Wordsworth

[1] See L. 323 above. The wish was for an enlarged edition of Anderson's *Poets of Great Britain*.

[2] S. H.'s notes of the Scottish tour of 1814 are in the Wordsworth Library and show that on Tuesday (30 Aug.) they 'slept at Mr. —— Traquhair'. Thursday's entry begins: 'Traquhair Hall', and describes how they met Dr. Anderson and his daughter at dinner at the Manse, and next day accompanied them up the Yarrow to 'Hogg's Father's Cottage', 'he being a Shepherd in Yarrow'. Hogg is James Hogg, the poet, known as 'the Ettrick Shepherd'. See L. 330, p. 160 above. Traquhair Hall or House, near Innerleithen, was the home of Charles Stuart, Earl of Traquhair (s. 1779, d. 1827): the family was of strong Jacobite tradition. 'Traquhair Know' was evidently not the Hall, for Sara says 'they slept at Mr. ——, Traquhair.' They evidently visited the Hall as sight-seers.

346. W. W. to THOMAS DE QUINCEY

Address: Thomas Dequincey Esqr, to be left with the Treasurer of the Middle Temple, London, or if not there at the Inner Temple.
Postmark: 8 Fe[b] 1815. *Stamp*: Kendal Penny Post.
MS. Miss Maud Craig.
K (—). *MY ii. 515, p. 629.*

[about 5 Feb. 1815]

'When in his character of philosophical Poet, having thought of Morality as of implying in its essence voluntary obedience, and producing the effect of order, he transfers in the transport of imagination, the law of moral to physical natures, and, having contemplated, through the medium of that order, all modes of existence as subservient to one spirit, concludes his address to the power of Duty in the following words:

To humbler functions awful Power'[1]

The above is the Quotation.—

Mrs Lloyd will be obliged to you to bring her a bottle of Compound Volatile Camphor Lineament, from Godfrey's Southampton St. Covent Garden

My dear Sir,

I have sent to the Printer another Stanza to be inserted in Laodamia after,

'While tears were thy best pastime, day and night:' (not a full Stop as [before])

And while my youthful peers, before my eyes,
(Each Hero following his peculiar bent)
Prepared themselves for glorious enterprize
By martial sports,—or, seated in the tent,
Chieftains and Kings in council were detained;
What time the Fleet at Aulis lay enchained,
The wish'd for wind was given:—I then revolved
Our future course,' etc, so I fear it must be altered from The oracle, lest these words should seem to allude to the other answer of the oracle which commanded the sacrifice of Iphigenia.[2]—

[1] The quotation, for which De Quincey must have asked, is from W.'s *Letter to Mathetes*, published in Coleridge's short-lived periodical *The Friend* on 14 Dec. 1809 and 4 Jan. 1810, and explains the much-criticized penultimate verse of the *Ode to duty*:

Stern Lawgiver! yet thou dost wear
The Godhead's most benignant grace, etc.

[2] W. had evidently originally written 'I then revolved the Oracle'; but in 1820 he altered 'Our future course' back to 'The Oracle' which remained so in all subsequent editions. See *PW* ii, p. 270 *app. crit.*

I wished you had mentioned *why* you desired the *rough* Copies of the Preface to be kept, as your request has led me to apprehend that something therein might have appeared to you as better or more clearly expressed—than in the after draught; and I should have been glad to reinstate accordingly.[1] Pray write to us. We are all well,

I remain affectionately and faithfully yours
Wm Wordsworth

347. W. W. to LEIGH HUNT[2]

Address: To the Editor of the Examiner, (to be sent with a copy of Mr W.'s poems).
MS. Harvard University Library.
MY ii. 516a, p. 630.

Rydal Mount, Feb. 12th 1815

Mr Wordsworth presents his Compliments to Mr Hunt and begs his Acceptance of the accompanying Volume Mr W. being induced to take this liberty by a conversation which he had last summer, with Mr Brougham, on which occasion Mr W. heard with pleasure, that his writings were valued by Mr Hunt.

348. W. W. to R. P. GILLIES

Address: R. P. Gillies Esqre, 9 King Street, Edinburgh. (*Re-addressed*: Berrington House by Berwick). *Endorsed*: Feb 14, Feb 17th.
Postmark: Feb 17 1815.
MS. Wellesley College, Mass.
K (—). *MY ii. 517, p. 631.*

Feb. 14. 1815.

My dear Sir,

Your very acceptable Lr of the 17th Jan^{ry} was well entitled to a speedier answer; and the Poem of Albert,[3] which I received about

[1] It appears from this letter that De Quincey was once more correcting proofs for W., as he had in 1809 for the *Cintra* pamphlet. The *Poems* of 1815 comprising the *Lyrical Ballads*, the *Poems in Two Volumes* 1807, and some poems written since, including *Laodamia*, appeared in Mar. 1815. De Quincey, however, allowed one serious error in punctuation to creep into *Laodamia*—a full stop, instead of a comma, after 'enchained', which was never corrected until de Selincourt's edition of the *PW* (1944).

[2] This note is pasted in the front of a copy of Vol. I of W.'s *Poems*, etc., published in two volumes in 1815. For the meeting with Brougham, see L. 393 below. B. had inherited Brougham Hall, near Penrith, in 1810.

[3] Published in *Illustrations of a Poetical Character*, 1816. See L. 333, p. 167, n. 1 above.

the same time to earlier notice. But I have been pestered for some weeks past with a number of trifles which did not leave me at sufficient leisure to take up the Pen with that complacency which I should wish to feel upon such an occasion. Nevertheless if I had not thought that a holyday would have come sooner I should not have remained silent so long. One of my engagements has been the writing of an additional preface and a supplementary Essay, to my Poems.[1] I have ordered Longman to send the book to you as soon as printed, which I hope will be in a fortnight at the latest; and I cannot but flatter myself that you will read it with pleasure. You will find a few hits at certain celebrated names of Scotland, I[2] do not mean persons now living, which will give great offence; yet not much, I think to you- -But let me turn from my own to your productions; and first to the Poem. The lines which I liked best, I think, were (2nd and 3d pages) from 'I prayed for madness', to 'and even that Image faded on my mind', and page 12. Blam'st thou &c to 'human voice' inclusive- -I fear that towards the conclusion you attribute more influence to Nature and to Poetry than they can justly claim. The style of Albert is spirited; but the Poem has the same defect as the other; in turning so much upon internal feelings, and those of a peculiar kind, without a sufficiency of incident or imagery to substantiate them.—We now understand each other with respect to the positions of your former letter, and there remains I think no difference of opinion between us upon the subject. —But I confess if there is to be an Error in style, I much prefer the *Classical* model of Dr Beattie[3] to the insupportable slovenliness and neglect of syntax and *grammar*, by which Hogg's writings are disfigured. It is excusable in him from his education, but Walter Scott knows, and ought to do, better. They neither of them write a

[1] The full title of the *Poems*, which were published in Mar. 1815, was: *Poems by William Wordsworth including Lyrical Ballads, and the Miscellaneous Pieces of the Author, with Additional Poems, a New Preface, and a Supplementary Essay, in two Volumes*. The old Preface to the *Lyrical Ballads*, 1800, was placed at the end of the second volume. The writing of a new Preface was a new idea, not formed before Jan. 1815. See L. 346 above. It delayed publication for two months, for W. had originally spoken of the appearance of the volumes at the beginning of January. See L. 335, p. 171 above. For Gillies, see L. 333, p. 167, n. 1 above.

[2] Particularly James Macpherson, spurious 'translator' of *Ossian*, a work for which W. entertained a strong contempt and which he castigated in the *Essay*.

[3] James Beattie (1735–1803), Professor of Moral Philosophy at Aberdeen, author of *The Minstrel*, one of the seminal poems of the early romantic movement, and one which deeply influenced the youthful Wordsworth. See Moorman, i, pp. 60–1.

language which has any pretension to be called English; and their versification—who can endure it when he comes fresh from the Minstrel?—Impute it to any thing but a wish to say agreeable things for the sake of saying them, when I tell you that the harmony of your verses in the *Varia*[1] in particular, does in my estimation entitle you to no mean praise; especially when it is considered what a hobbling pace the Scottish Pegasus seems to have adopted in these days.—You advert in your notes to certain stores of highland Character incident and manners, which have been but slightly touched upon. Would not it be well to collect these as materials for some poetic story, which if you would set yourself to work in good earnest, I am confident you could execute with effect. Let me recommend this to you or to compose a Romance, founded on some one of the many works of this kind that exist, as Wieland has done in his Oberon: not that I should advise such a subject as he has chosen. You have an ear, and you have a command of diction, a fluency of style: and I wish, as your friend, that you would engage in some literary labour that would carry you out of yourself, and be the means of delighting the well-judging part of the world.—In what I said upon the setting down thoughts in prose, I only meant, briefly, as memorandums, to prevent their being *lost*. It is unaccountable to me how men could ever proceed as Racine (and Alfieri I believe) used to do, first, writing their plays in Prose, and then, turning them into Verse. It may answer with so slavish a language and so enslaved a Taste as the french have; but with us, it is not to be thought of.

Mr Wilson has probably reached Edin: by this time; for ourselves, we have not seen him for many months, except once when Mrs W. and I called at his House. To use a College phrase, he appears to have *cut* us.—Let me know if you continue in the mind of trying the effect of Westmorland air upon your spirits. Mr Wilson has a charming little Cottage at Elleray which perhaps he is not likely to make use of—but this you would find very lonely; and it is nearly [?] miles from us. I fear there would be some difficulty [in finding] lodgings that would suit you but the trial shall be made. The country is at present charming, [the] first spring flowers peeping forth in the gardens abundantly—

I hope that you continue to like the Excursion. I hear good news of it from many quarters. But its progress to general notice *must* be slow. Your opinion of Jeffrey is just—he is a depraved Coxcomb; the greatest Dunce, I believe, in this Island, and assuredly the Man

[1] A section of Gillies's *Child Alarique* is so named.

who takes most pains to prove himself so. Have you read Lucien B's Epic?[1] I attempted it, but gave in at the 6th Canto, being pressed for time. I shall however resume the Labor if an opportunity offers. But the three first Stanzas *convinced* me that L. B. was no *poet*. Farewell Miss Hutchinson is still in Wales. Mrs W. begs her best regards.

Faithfully yours W. Wordsworth.

349. W. W. to DANIEL STUART

Address: D. Stuart Esqre, Courier Office, London. To be forwarded.
MS. British Museum.
S. MY ii. 516, p. 629.

Rydale Mount near Ambleside. [Jan. or Feb. 1815]

My dear Sir,

I take the liberty of writing this at the wish of Mr. De Quincey. He is a friend of mine whom you will recollect, with no very pleasant feelings, perhaps as having caused you some trouble while my Tract occasioned by the Convention of Cintra was printing.[2] He is preparing a short series of Letters, to be addressed to the Editor of some periodical Publication, say of *The Courier*; upon the subject of the stupidities, the ignorance, and the dishonesties of the Edinburgh Review; and principally as relates to myself, whom, perhaps you know, the Editor has long honored with his abuse.[3] My works have been a stumbling block to him from the commencement of his Career. What I have to request is that, if it consist with your plan, you would give these Letters a place in your Columns, which I see have lately given more space to Literature than heretofore: and very properly I think, for nothing can be more flat and uninteresting than the present course of Public News.[4] Mr. De Quincey will call upon you, and I hope this letter will serve to remove any little prejudice which you may have against him.—I thank you for the

[1] Lucien Bonaparte (1755–1840), brother of Napoleon, published in 1814, *Charlemagne, ou L'Église Sauvée, poème épique en 24 chants*. It was translated into English in 1815. W. mentions it with disparagement in the *Essay, Supplementary to the Preface* of his *Poems*, 1815.

[2] For the printing of *Cintra*, see L. 140, ff. pt. i.

[3] These letters of De Quincey's were in fact never published, though parts of them are probably incorporated into his articles on W. W. in later years. See Jordan, p. 216. The editor of the *Edinburgh* was of course Francis Jeffrey.

[4] This remark helps us to date the letter to the beginning of 1815. On 1 Mar. 1815 Napoleon escaped from Elba, after which no one could have called 'the course of public news' 'flat and uninteresting'.

notice of the Excursion in *The Courier*. It will serve the Book, though I owe the Editor a bit of a grudge for having *appeared* to join in, at least to countenance, the vulgar clamour against me; but I forgive him.—We hope that you and Mrs. Stuart are well; and Mrs. W. and my Sister join me in kindest remembrances to her and to yourself. I am my dear Sir with great truth your obliged servant

W. Wordsworth.

You need not doubt but that the Letters will be a credit to any Publication, for Mr. D. Q. is a *remarkably* able man.

350. D. W. to SARA HUTCHINSON (with postscript by W. W.)

Address: Miss Hutchinson, Hindwell, Radnor. By Worcester.
Stamp: Keswick.
MS. WL.
MY ii. 519, p. 634.

Sunday night. 18th February [1815]

How the months depart! February more than half gone—March is next—and then comes April; and if we do go to France, the end of April being the time talked of we cannot be later than the middle of May—but I fervently wish it may be given up for this year. If however we find that we shall have no peace or rest without it I must try to imitate your good example and make a pleasure of it. A fortnight or little more must settle the point. William talks at times as if he wished to go to London and if he does, of course it will be in the spring, and we shall travel together if we go to France, and meet you there—but Oh! far rather would I have him conduct you to Mrs. Clarkson's and after his visit to London bring you hither. In my own mind however I do not think he will go at all. The reasons for staying at home are very strong, and he really seems to have no strong one for going except the meeting you. You entreat with so much earnestness that we would write often, and I know so well the value of letters to you that I am determined, having an opportunity of sending to the Keswick post office tomorrow not to let this day pass by. I was engaged all the afternoon writing letters of duty to Mrs Rawson and Miss Pollard and I could not save the post for you. We have gone on very quietly since my last was sent off which I hope you would receive on the Monday or Tuesday after you wrote.

William has had one of his weeks of rest and we now begin to wish that he was at work again, but as he intends completely to plan the first part of the Recluse before he begins the composition, he must read many Books before he will fairly set to labour again. The correcting of the proofs will, however, keep us doing in a little way. I feel sure that you will like the preface and essay,[1] and will approve of the lofty tone which he has taken up. It is vexatious that the printers are so slow. We have only had one sheet of the preface, and there is nothing tonight but stamp office letters.—It has been a wet day and we had prayers at home; but William and I walked round the Lake, and viewed Grasmere from Loughrigg. The vale was wrapped up in that soft misty veil which so well becomes its sober dignity—a veil concealing nothing from the view except the tops of the highest mountains. We stopped a long time looking to the opposite shore of Rydal to admire the exquisite beauty of the colouring near the water-side—The oak bushes have all the brightness of Autumn and being intermingled with hollies, green turf, and silvery rocks, the combination of colouring was so various that we exclaimed how much more beautiful is that little spot than in summer. We have had no visitors except the Bests whom for his sake we are always glad to see—He has lost his property at Newmarket and by being bound for a Brother, and lives now upon an allowance of 500£ per annum from his Uncle. He has a horror of the Turf and gambling, and I hope will never return to it. Poor fellow, like Luff he has been ruined by a bad education and early indulgence with the prospect of an independent and large fortune. He tells many pleasant stories of former times. We often think of Luff when he is with us. He is not however nearly so clever a man, but his manners are free from those defects which make Luff so unpleasing at first—but how strangely I have wandered from the point whence I set out—I might however as well go on with matters at a distance from home and return thither when I have finished.—Poor Mrs Harden[2] was delivered of a dead child a fortnight ago. It was a most dangerous labour and she has been very ill; but they hope that with extreme care and good nursing she will recover. On Thursday William and Mary walked to Brathay—Mary saw her she looked very delicate and interesting—poor woman! She had never been out of bed since the child was born; nor has yet probably,

[1] In the *Essay Supplementary to the Preface* he turned on Jeffrey and his other critics in vigorous self-defence.

[2] Wife of John Harden the artist, of Brathay Hall.

for we have heard of her being worse again. Lloyd was in his better way; yet he is exceptionally nervous at this time. The publishing of Alfieri has done him no good[1]; and I fear that it will not sell; Mrs Lloyd is grown much stronger—She walked hither one day with Miss Alne, and though much tired was no worse for it. She brought home a story which frightened us very much, but we have long since been quite at ease concluding it not true, though we wonder we have not heard again from Mrs Clarkson. The story was this that Tom Clarkson had died at William Smith's of a fever[2]—the scarlet or some other fever. The tidings had come to her not in the shape of a report, but as direct communication by the schoolmaster at whose school William Smith's Boys are educated; therefore we were very very unhappy at first, though inclined very much to believe that her tale was untrue. Every post confirmed our hope by bringing us no tidings. We anxiously examined the newspapers, and their silence too, strengthened by degrees our hopes with a firm conviction that it was all false. Yet as I said we wonder that we have not heard again from Mrs Clarkson, and are rather uneasy on her account, especially as she was not well when she last wrote, and the letter was evidently not written in good spirits. I wish very much if we have not a letter soon that you may have one. Hartley is to go to Oxford in the next month.[3] I have written to Lady Beaumont at Mrs C'.s request, for the 30£. His Mother has no money, of course, even to fit him out — she took my comments very kindly upon her report that he had slackened in his studies and tells me that he is now again very industrious. She says he will not have time to spare to come and see us before his departure, which I am very sorry for—Derwent left us last Monday, and Mary saw him when she went to Lloyd's and said he was very comfortable at Mrs Robinson's. The Crumps are gone[4]—George stays at Mr Pigot's and rides to school, and John is removed to business, therefore I think, as quietness is what he wants he will on the whole be better off at Mrs Robinson's than anywhere else. Mary asked him to come to Rydale on Saturday; but we have not seen him. This looks as if he were contented with his quarters. Christopher and Priscilla[5] have been at the Beaumont's, they stayed a few days and were much interested with Sir George

[1] See L. 353, p. 214, n. 2 below.

[2] The rumour was untrue: Tom Clarkson d. 1837.

[3] Hartley Coleridge in fact went to Oxford (Merton) in May 1815. See L. 321 above.

[4] i.e. from Mrs. Robinson's lodgings. The Crumps were the owners of Allan Bank. D. W. refers to the two boys, George and John.

[5] i.e. C. W. and his wife who was the sister of Charles Lloyd.

Priscilla says that Lady B. is the most enthusiastic admirer of the Excursion—I am afraid her zeal will outrun her discretion, and prevent her from aiding the sale of the work as were she more moderate in her expressions she might do. Christopher called at Dunmow 10 days ago and Sir G. put the White Doe into his hands which they were to convey to London last week—Priscilla tells Charles that when he is nervous he ought to take a journey—risk fresh scenes—as she does! Thus she cures herself of, I suppose, her *periodical* maladies—I believe the best cure would be a less indulgent husband. Christopher is sending us his sermons—but we have not yet received them. Longman has been desired to send two Copies of the poems bound in Russia to Tom Monkhouse. Of course you will give him directions about them, and pray present one copy to John Monkhouse with my best Regards. I wish you had them. You would almost feel as if you were nearer to us, especially the preface and the essay will have this effect. From all hands we hear the same story that Jeffrey has played the fool,[1] has suffered his malignity to cheat him into producing passages as fit matter for ridicule, which are so beautiful that even the eyes of his worshippers must be opened. Old Mrs Lloyd is enraptured with the Book—It expresses what she habitually feels; in a manner that she had never either the power to express or conceive—and that passage where he says the 'raving begins'[2] is one that she should have selected as among the finest that ever were composed. Mr. de Quincey writes—but I will give you his own brief words. 'Miss J Hutchinson[3] must have been amongst people who read nothing but novels, because I find far more persons acquainted with the Excursion than I thought likely: among others I could not help smiling to find two fervent admirers, Unitarians, from whom you anticipated nothing but hostility!' This letter is merely about some business with the printer—Not a word of his letters in the Courier.[4] He is going to see his mother for '*two days*'. Longman informs us that exclusive of those Copies of the Excursion sent by William's order, 'they appear to have sold 269 copies'. This is not so bad. We have had above 30—so the 4th hundred is begun with and I think the influx of fine folks this spring, with the help of Jeffrey's benevolence will carry off the rest—yet I cannot but regret that it was published in Quarto—William and Mary and little Willy paid a visit to old Mrs Knott

[1] i.e. in his review of *The Excursion* in the *Edinburgh Review* for Oct. 1814.

[2] Jeffrey had quoted fourteen lines from the first book, describing the Pedlar's feelings in youth (ll. 148–62), and then continued: 'But this is but the beginning of the raving fit.'

[3] i.e. Joanna, youngest sister of M. W. and S. H.

[4] See L. 349 above.

yesterday with the Ex^{n} in hand, William intending to read to the old Lady the history of the Grasmere Knight.[1] She could not hear his loud voice; but understood the story very well when her Niece read it, and was greatly delighted. Today they have returned the Book and poor Miss K has written a complimentary but alas! unintelligible note—unintelligible but by courtesy. She must have been in a strange ruffled state of mind, she concludes however by saying in plain words that she had written to Kendal to order the Book. She says she had been told by Mrs Green and others that it was above their capacity, and of course above *hers*, but what she had read had given her infinite delight. I tell William that the family made a trading voyage of it. Certainly the Book would never have been bought by Miss K. if Willy and his Father and Mother had stayed quietly at home. The Eclectic Review was written by Montgomery.[2] He is very religious therefore your conjecture respecting the sincerity of the opening of the Review must have been unfounded.—Mary is deep in the 2nd volume of the 'Recluse of Norway' by Miss Porter[3]—there is a wonderful cleverness in this book, and notwithstanding the badness of the style the 1st vol is very interesting. I began the 2nd last night but could do no more than skim it. There is a good deal of Miss Watson[4] in the colouring of the Ladies; and when love begins almost all novels grow tiresome. The first volume has not a word of it. With respect to Waverley[5] the author has completely failed in one point—you care not a farthing for the hero, Waverley, and as you observe the Scotch Characters are so outrageously masked by peculiarities that there is no pleasure in contemplating them—indeed in the delineation of character he greatly fails throughout—and as usual the love is sickening. The highland manners and costume are the most interesting feature in the work.—We had a letter from your Brother John about 3 weeks ago—he sent us some excellent haddocks. He said that he expected George and that most likely he would be coming to see us; but I am afraid he had no better authority for this than his own suppositions. We have got one piece of Diaper. I hope Joanna is quite reconciled to giving up the Farm unless times mend, and that she will make up her mind to come to Rydale as soon as possible.

[1] *The Excursion*, vii. ll. 923–1057.

[2] James Montgomery (1771–1854), evangelical poet and hymn-writer, author of *The World before the Flood* (1812). Some of his hymns are still popular—e.g. 'Hail to the Lord's Anointed!', 'For ever with the Lord!', etc.

[3] Anna Maria Porter, romantic novelist, published *The Recluse of Norway* in 1814.

[4] Perhaps another contemporary novelist whose works now seem wholly forgotten.

[5] The first of Walter Scott's novels, published in July 1814.

I am delighted that she is grown so youthful at Bath and I hope that if your Aunt is well enough, she will take her thither every year as long as she lives. Poor woman! I am very sorry for her and all of you that she is so ill—it is however a happiness that the air of Bath can produce such amazing effects. Notwithstanding the disorder is so easily wrought upon by company and change, I do believe that her sufferings are great, and that she cannot live long. You do not mention Mary's[1] looks or her health—I trust she is well—God bless her! I often think of her sweetness and goodness,—and of all the dear Family and fancy how you are sitting by the fireside. I only wish that Charles[2] was away, yet when I assemble the figures in the picture strange it is, I generally forget him as I often used to do when he was occupying his Chair and before my eyes at Hindwell. You do not say whether Tom intends to sell his Estate—I cannot express how earnestly I wish he may—What a comfort would it be to have them at the distance of 50 miles. When I was at Hindwell I fancied the journey to Rydale was nothing; but Willy's illness has made it take a different shape, it looks like a frightful distance. We were very glad that the pony was so well—The journey must have been of great use to it for its cough was very bad at Rydale. Mary says I must tell you that its native air agrees with it. I hope you have had some pleasant rides upon his Back. We have had some very fine weather. It was kept at Mrs Cookson's old servant Jane's publick house 1/3 per day very cheap I think. It is 11 oclock William has been reading the Fairy Queen—he has laid aside his Book and Mary has set about putting her nightcap. The Children all well and fast-asleep—Willy says now that Father's preface is done he must write a letter to his Godmother. He talks so familiarly of his Father's works it would divert you to hear him. Give my kindest love to Tom and everybody and tell him I entreat that he would think about [? buying] an estate near T. Monkhouse's. The reading of this letter will be at least as hard a work as your two last.

Another long letter from Miss Barker today—The poem[3] is corrected and William tired himself with three hours labour at the first stanza and at last did not do it to our mind. It is 12 o'clock and before I go to bed I must write to Miss B.—Those two lines 'Fixed yet soaring' are William's—This she did not mention to us; I recollect your mentioning the rural feast as probably the beautiful minute picture which had passed through my mind, but I thought

[1] i.e. Mary Monkhouse, now the wife of Tom Hutchinson.

[2] Probably Charles Francis Hutchinson, 1796–1866, a cousin of M. W.

[3] See for the title and for W.'s part in the poem, L. 337, p. 175, n. 3 above.

she could not have spoken so slightly of it as it was so considerable a part of the poem, and that therefore it must be the first stanza she meant.

God bless you dearest Sara Ever more, yours tenderly D. W.

(*W. W. adds*)

Dearest S. I am astonished that you can find no better use for your money than spending it on those silly Reviews. You have none too much of it. Miss Younghusband of [? Troutbeck] has addressed to me a copy of verses occasioned by my Yarrow visited. Mary Ann and Letitia Hawkins have also written me panegyrical letters on the Excursion. So thanks [to] those ladies [the ladies] here are becoming quite jealous. Adieu. I send you love and a kiss, two or three if you like that prove the better for being liberal.

Most affectionately yours W. W.

351. D. W. to PRISCILLA (MRS. CHRISTOPHER) WORDSWORTH

Address: [*erased and redirected.*] For Mr Wordsworth at Abel Chapman's Esqr, or, Thomas' Hospital, Borough.
Postmark:
MS. WL.
MY ii. 520, p. 640.

[27 Feb. 1815]

My dear Sister

Your letter from Hampstead arrived last night. In reply to it there is no need to enter into particulars as the situation offered would not, I am sure, suit Mr. Jackson[1] under his present circumstances, nor do I think that *he* would altogether suit the situation, his religious opinions being, though orthodox, moderate, and not what are now styled (surely with no great propriety!) evangelical. Mr. Jackson's employments at College are at present so lucrative, and his prospects so good that I do not think it likely the curacy at Bocking would be a temptation to him, therefore my Brother had better be on the lookout, not at all considering Mr. Jackson; and when he is determined on having a curate it will then be time enough to propose the matter to Mr. J's consideration, provided my Brother has not met with one entirely to his satisfaction. The ground

[1] The Revd. William Jackson, son of the Revd. Thomas Jackson, Rector of Grasmere. He was intimate with the Wordsworths, and was later Rector of Lowther; in 1846 he became Chancellor of the diocese of Carlisle. For W'.s opinion of him, see L. 394 below. He became a Fellow of Queen's College, Oxford in 1816.

upon which I conclude that Mrs Hoare's proposal would not suit Mr. J. is this, that the situation of schoolmaster or Tutor to a set of Children is not what he wishes to undertake.

The day before yesterday Miss Alne dined with us, and from her we learned that Chris's sermons were just arrived at Brathay, so William walked to B. with Miss A. and borrowed one volume—It is the second. William and Mary have read several of the sermons and are very much delighted with them—I have not yet had leisure when the book has been at liberty and have only snatched a look at the subjects and the mode of treating them which appear to me to be very interesting. Pleased I was to greet that discourse upon Paul and Festus[1] which I heard my Brother preach at Binfield, a pleasure which I shall never forget; and often do I lament that you are so far distant from us that I am not likely *often* to enjoy the same pleasure. I may say to you that I never heard a preacher so exactly to my mind, and I flatter myself that my admiration of my Brother's discourse and of the manner in which it was delivered was thoroughly impartial; for my opinion was supported by that of many others, who could not be supposed to have any likings predisposing them to a partial judgment. I have not read any part of the sermon on Paul and Festus; but on looking it over it seems to me as if it had been shortened. Is it so? The only sermon of which I can say that I have *read* any part is that upon National Education and an excellent discourse it appears to be. What can be the reason that the Copy destined for us is not arrived? Your Brother's and ours might just as well have come together by the Coach. The expense would have been no more of two sets than of one. If our copy is sent off pray let us know how, and when, that we may inquire after it; and if it be not sent let Christopher order it to go to Longman's to be forwarded to Rydale with the copies of the two volumes of poems which are nearly through the press and which we hope will be ready to send off in less than a fortnight. William had desired that the poems may be sent you—pray read the new preface and the supplementary Essay with particular attention. You will find that he speaks in a lofty tone which will no doubt surprize the blind adorers of that ignorant Coxcomb Jeffrey. We have seen none of the Reviews. The Eclectic, we are told, is highly encomiastic, and probably it may be of use towards promoting the sale of the Excursion amongst the serious and religious part of the reading public; but I am convinced, notwithstanding the zeal of a whole Body of the admirers of the

[1] So written by D. W., but corrected throughout in pencil to 'Felix'.

Edinburgh Review that [? that] Review will do less harm than the feeble praise of the Quarterly. An injudicious and malignant enemy often serves the cause he means to injure; but a feeble friend never attains that end. By the bye the history of that same criticism in the Quarterly is very provoking. It was originally drawn up by Charles Lamb at the request of Southey; but so deformed by the lopping-knife of Gifford, and by the substitution of his own flat phrases that not even the skeleton of Lamb's production remains; which Lamb says was pronounced by his sister to be in his best style—'the best piece of prose that he ever wrote.'[1] From this we have learned one lesson, which I hope Christopher also will profit by, never to employ a friend to review a Book unless he has the full command of the Review; so that the master critic can neither add to nor diminish. Last night's post brought two sheets of the White Doe. William will do all he can to hurry it through the press that it may come out in the busy time of London gaieties. I have no anxiety about the fate of either the Excursion or the White Doe beyond the sale of the first Edition—and *that* I *do* earnestly wish for. There are few persons who can afford to buy a two guinea Book, merely for admiration of the Book. The edition has no chance of being sold except to the wealthy; and they buy books much more for fashion's sake than any-thing else—and alas we are not yet in the fashion. I guess you are not going to Binfield[2] before your return home, as you speak of being at Bocking in the first week of next month. It is three or four months since we heard any thing about my Uncle's family and at that time my Aunt was in bad spirits having just lost her sister. I wish you had been likely to see them. I should like very much to know from you whether Mary[3] has quite got the better of her dis-appointment. I wish, poor Girl! she had never seen Mr. Sandys; but having been so unfortunate it is a great blessing that she has escaped a closer connection with him. All who know him [? say] that he is a weak young Man; his Mother is odious and his Father, I believe, little better. Add to this that probably they would have been in narrow circumstances for the best part of their lives. Your account of your son John is delightful. I wish I could send you a similar one from this quarter; but we do not produce scholars. John

[1] See *Lamb*, ii. 263, p. 149, to W. W., Jan. 1815. The review appeared in the *Quarterly* for Oct. 1814.

[2] Canon William Cookson's parish near Windsor. See L. 208, pt. i.

[3] Mary Cookson ultimately married Archdeacon Fisher, son of John Fisher, Bishop of Salisbury, the friend of John Constable the painter; she became the mother of Emmeline, the child poet much admired by W. W. in later years. See *LY* iii, Letters 1075, 1081, etc.

is without exception, unfortunately the slowest Boy at his books that ever I was acquainted with; yet he has a good understanding, and as just a sense of right and wrong as the best philosopher. He is tall, strong, and well-looking, a good player and well liked among his schoolfellows for his sweetness of temper and his plain honesty; Dorothy is quick enough—but *she* wants steadiness—and that is all she wants. She likes reading for her own amusement; but is so fond of many other things that the love of reading is not yet a passion with her as it used to be with her Godfather (your husband) when he was her age. She learns latin and her quickness helps her forward very tolerably, notwithstanding the sad drawback of unsteadiness. William is a very clever child—No doubt you have heard of his dangerous illness, the Croup. I was in Wales at the time, and was hurried home on his account. He is mostly confined to the house, the weather having been very unfavourable this winter; but as he is quite well, we hope he will grow vigorous and blooming when he can be trusted freely to the open air. It is a sad pity that your children should be so far separated from their numerous cousins in this part of the world. The Lloyds are all very fine children. Your Brother is pretty well, and Mrs Lloyd's health much improved by her journey to Birmingham. We were very pleased with Mary Hawkin's letter—It is written with an appearence of much earnestness and sincerity. William has of course answered it. Oh! I had forgotten that he had sent the answer to Christopher to be forwarded by him—I should think that Mr. Jameson[1] was not unlikely to suit the Hoares as a Tutor—He is very religious and is a good Teacher, but he has not had a College Education.

If you or they should be inclined to write to him his address is

The Revd Thos. Jameson
Sherburne, near Ferry Bridge, Yorkshire.

The Bishop[2] is pretty well, he has not been worse lately.

(*P.S. by W. W.*)

My dear Brother. I cannot speak of your sermons comparatively with other *modern* ones, for I read none; but in themselves I can say that they are admirable, both for the matter and the manner. W. Wordsworth.

[1] See L. 156, pt. i.

[2] Richard Watson, Bishop of Llandaff. He died at Calgarth, Windermere in 1816. See Letters 416 and 417 below.

352. W. W. to THOMAS POOLE

Address: Thomas Poole Esqre, Nether Stowey, Somersetshire.
Endorsed: fr. Wordsworth, March 1815, on Derwent[1] Coleridge.
MS. British Museum.
K. MY ii. 521, p. 644.

Rydal Mount Ambleside
March 13 1815.

My dear Poole,

A few days ago I was at Keswick, where I learned that Hartley was to go to Oxford about Easter. Mrs. Coleridge wished me to write to you and mention this, and also that if it were not inconvenient to you, that the ten pounds which you were so kind as to offer, would be convenient at this time;—as she has not the means of fitting him out, and she does not like to apply to his Uncles in the first instance. He is to go to Merton College, where his Cousins or Uncles (I am not sure which) have procured him an office, the title of it, Postmaster, which is to bring him in £50 per annum, which with his Uncle's £40, Lady B.'s £30, and your ten, it is hoped will maintain him. Cottle also allows £5 per annum; if more be wanted, Southey and I must contrive to advance it. I have done all in my power to impress upon H.'s mind the necessity of not trusting vaguely to his talents, and to an irregular sort of knowledge, however considerable it may be, in some particulars; and of applying himself zealously and perseveringly to those studies which the University points out to him. His prime object ought to be to gain an independence; and I have striven to place this truth before his understanding in the clearest point of view; and I took the opportunity of speaking to him on the subject in the presence of his uncle Southey, who confirmed and enforced all that I said. So that if good advice have any virtue in it, he has not been left unfurnished with it.—Southey means to look out for a place in some public office for Derwent; he hopes to succeed in the Exchequer where the situations are very good. Sara has made great progress in Italian under her mother; and is learning French and Latin. She is also instructed in music by Miss Barker, a friend of Southey's, who is their near neighbour; so that should it be *necessary* she will be well fitted to become a Governess in a nobleman's or gentleman's family, in course of time; she is remarkably clever; and her musical Teacher

[1] A mistake for Hartley.

says that her progress is truly astonishing. Her health unfortunately is but delicate.

It was my intention to write to you if Mrs. C. had not requested it, and I am happy to give this account of our Friend's children, who are all very promising. Nevertheless, I have some fears for Hartley, as he is too much inclined to the eccentric. But it is our *duty* to hope for the best. Coleridge, we have learnt, is still with the Morgans, but removed from the neighbourhood of Bath to Colne or Caln in Wiltshire.[1] His friends in this Country hear nothing from him directly. A sister of my Wife's,[2] who was staying at Bath, walked over to call upon him, but found the family removed. His late Landlady was very communicative, and said that Mr. C. used to talk with her of his children, and mentioned that his Eldest was going to college. So that you see he expects the thing to take place, though he wished to put it off when you conversed with him on the subject. I rejoice to hear of your thriving School. I have not yet seen your Relation's pamphlet which you recommend; I have heard it praised by others, and shall procure it.—If you have read my Poem, the 'Excursion', you will there see what importance I attach to the Madras System.[3] Next to the art of Printing it is the noblest invention for the improvement of the human species. Our population in this neighbourhood is not sufficient to apply it on a large scale; but great benefit has been derived from it even upon a small one.—If you *have* read my Poem, I should like to have a record of your feelings during the perusal, and your opinion afterwards; if it has not deeply interested you, I should fear that I have missed my aim in some important particulars.—I had the hope of pleasing you in my mind during the composition in many parts, especially those in which I have alluded to the influence of the manufacturing spirit; and in the pictures, in the last book but one, which I have given of Boys in different situations in life: the manufacturer, the boy of the yeomanry, and the Clergyman's or Gentleman's son.[4] If you can conscientiously recommend this expensive work to any of your wealthier friends, I will thank you, as I wish to have it printed in a cheaper form, for those who cannot afford to buy it in its present

[1] Coleridge lived at Calne from Dec. 1814 to Apr. 1816 and wrote there most of his *Biographia Literaria* and prepared his poems—*Sibylline Leaves*—for the press. Neither was published until 1817.

[2] i.e. Joanna Hutchinson.

[3] For W.'s obsession with this method of teaching children, see Moorman, ii, p. 178. *The Excursion*, ix, 293–415, contains W.'s plea for National Education. The writing of it followed the visit to Grasmere, in the Autumn of 1811, of Dr. Andrew Bell, the founder of the 'Madras System'.

[4] *The Excursion*, viii, 302–433, 556–81.

shape. And, as it is in some places a little abstruse, and in all, serious, without any of the modern attractions of glittering style, or incident to provoke curiosity, it cannot be expected to make its way without difficulty, and it is therefore especially incumbent on those who value it to exert themselves in its behalf. My opinion as to the execution of the minor parts of my works is not in the *least altered.* My Poems are upon the point of being republished, in two vols octavo, with a new preface, and several additions, though not any pieces of length. I should like to present you with a copy as a testimony of my regard, if you would let me know where you wish to have it sent; or if you could call, or desire anybody to call, for it at Longmans. Pray give me your notions upon the Corn Laws; what restricted price you think high enough: some one seems indispensable.

Most faithfully yours,
W. Wordsworth.

353. D. W. to CATHERINE CLARKSON

Address: Mrs Clarkson, Bury, Suffolk.
Endorsed: Mar 1815.
MS. British Museum.
MY ii. 523, p. 653.

16th March [1815]

My dear Friend,

I cannot help writing to inquire after you; not that I am afraid that you are seriously ill; for in that case you would have informed us; but that you are poorly and in bad spirits as you evidently were when you last wrote (and that is a long time ago). We had flattered ourselves that you would answer William's letter speedily (that is Mary and I) for he did not think that a letter from him would have so much power as we were willing to suppose; you have however been silent much longer than usual, and we cannot help being uneasy. Every post day when the letters are brought in some one says 'Is there one from Mrs Clarkson?' and the answer disappoints and often saddens us. Enough of this, I know you will write immediately if it be but a few lines to let us know how you are; however if you *can*, let it be a long letter. We heard from Sara last night in answer to a proposal of mine that we should set off for France in the first week of May, this determination was made a few days before the news of Buonaparte's entrance into that unhappy country had reached us; and of course our plans are for the present put a stop to. Whatever be the result of his projects it is not likely that it would be prudent for us to go as soon as we had intended; and a very little time will shew whether we can go at all or not. Though the manner of his entry appears to be as rash, and his followers as insignificant as possible, it is scarcely believable that even *he* would have acted with such folly as to enter the Kingdom without some assurance of a powerful Body of adherents; but if, happily, he have done so, he must speedily endeavour to make his escape, or be caught and punished as he ought to have been when the Allies had him in their power; and I hope his rash spirit will hurry him forward to this end. His aim (in case he attempts to return) will be to go to Italy and there he will probably find strong upholders. The Italians have been shamefully used, and Murat may persuade them that with going with him to oppose Austria he serves only their interests while he enters into a league of ambition with Buonaparte. We are very anxious, as I am sure you are, for every day's news, and it is one comfort that the suspense respecting the probabilities for and against France will soon be at an end. I do not, at present, carry my cares much further. For the sake of our Friends I am truly distressed. The lady whom I mentioned to you[1] from the first was a zealous Royalist has often risked her life in defence of adherents to that cause, and she despised and detested Buonaparte. Poor Creature! in the last letter which we had from her she spoke only of hope and comfort; said that the king's government was daily gaining strength and Buonaparte's friends were daily coming over in their hearts to the other side. A few days after the [?] tidings reached her she would receive my letter containing the plan of our journey. Sara tells me that you had kindly proposed, in case we could not go to Bury, to meet William and me in London. It is now idle to talk of any plans in connection with a journey to Paris; but at any rate William has given up the idea of going to London this spring.[2] I trust, however, that if Sara does not go to Bury this spring or summer, we shall see you either there or in London on our return from France provided it be safe to venture thither this year; and provided that you do not come into the North, which I would gladly hope you will, though your late letters have said nothing about it. Mr de Quincey is just returned from London, where he saw Henry Robinson frequently;[3] from him we learn that Tom is flourishing at Cambridge, where I

[1] i.e. Annette Vallon.
[2] He went, however, with M. W. in the first week of May. See L. 362 below.
[3] See *HCR* i, pp. 160–2, entries for 4 and 15 Feb.

hope he will do credit to himself and satisfy your most anxious wishes. If we go to Paris I shall apply to Henry Robinson for full instructions, both with respect to the journey and what is to be seen at Paris and in the neighbourhood. Mary Lamb was better, and was to leave her place of confinement the day after Mr de Quincey's departure from London—but that, by the bye, was three weeks ago; for he has since been in Somersetshire. There he saw Hannah More[1] (the particular Friend of his Mother), holy Hannah as he calls her; and he tells us that William has made a conquest even of *her*, though she does think that the Edinburgh Reviewers have right on their side when they condemn the choice of a person in the rank of a Pedlar as a principal personage; but it is curious enough that Hannah has never seen the poem, and has seen no Review of it except the Edinburgh. Yet she is determined to buy it, and is only waiting for the Octavo Edition. I wish somebody would but puff the Book amongst the fashionable and wealthy—This once done the Edition would soon go off, and that is all I am anxious about. When it is to be had at a reasonable price then let it fight its own way. There are not quite 200 copies remaining of 500. This is a poor sale and I fear even that small remaining number will not go off for a long time without the help of some fortunate turn, either in the whims or the understandings of a portion of the fashionable and wealthy. William had an interesting letter last night from the 'ingenuous poet' of Derby whom he quotes in the *Essay on Epitaphs*.[2] I will give you an extract from his Letter. He says: 'I could not comply with your injunction not to purchase *The Excursion*, etc., etc. I would not now be without the book for twice its value.' He goes on to say that he had had a letter from his friend Montgomery, the poet,[3] from which he quotes as follows: 'The poem in my opinion, an opinion confirmed by repeated perusals of it, is incomparably the greatest and the most beautiful work of the present age of poetry; and sets Mr. W. beyond controversy above all the living, and almost all the dead, of his fraternity. I assure you that the spirit of that book, which I read first at Scarborough in September, so possessed me that I have scarcely yet recovered my relish for any other modern verse. The peculiar harmony of rhythm, felicity of language, and splendour of thought for a while made all poor or feeble in comparison. I am gradually returning to sober feelings, and though the transcendent powers of Wordsworth, etc etc'

[1] See p. 225, n. 3 below. [2] i.e. John Edwards. See L. 219, pt. i, p. 470.
[3] See L. 350, p. 203, n. 2 above.

This passage I think will interest you. Montgomery was the author of The Eclectic Review,[1] but though he there speaks with profound respect and admiration, and though he shews (which nobody else in the way of criticism has done) that he is deeply sensible of the *labour* and *skill* with which the poem has been wrought up, he does not speak with the same *feeling* as in this private letter, probably because in the *Review* he wrote under another *head*. He there says nothing of the versification which I wonder at as in that point he could not be influenced by the opinions of the Managers of the Review. We have had a very changeable season—never two fine days together—and lately we have had torrents of rain, with snow and high winds. This weather has been very unfortunate to Willy's strengthening, and besides he has had another bad cold. Dorothy too has been ill in the same way. She has never been so strong as formerly since she had the measles, that frightful disorder which carried her dear Brother Thomas away from us. To-day the sun shines and they both, being recovered from their colds, have been enjoying the pleasure (which for a fortnight Willy has been deprived of) of running about in the open air. The young Lloyds are all very healthy—eight of them. Mrs Lloyd has been in a bad state of health but she is now remarkably well. Charles is in his better way though always very nervous. Have you seen his translation of the plays of Alfièr?[2] I wish you would recommend it amongst your Friends; for it is of considerable importance that the Book should sell. What does Mr Clarkson say to the Corn Laws? For William's opinion I refer you to Mr Wilberforce's speech which is exactly in substance what William has before said to us by the fire-side.[3] William and Mary join in kindest love to you and in entreating that you will write to us immediately.—This is a sad scrawling letter but I trust to your friendship for not grumbling, and to your quickness for decyphering the characters, and making out my meaning.

God bless you my dearest Friend Believe me ever your affectionate D W.

Give my kind love to Mr Clarkson, your Father, Mrs Kitchener and remember me to any one else who may inquire after me. Your Brother Sam, you know, was always a particular favourite of mine.

[1] i.e. of the review of *The Excursion* in the *Eclectic Review*.

[2] *The Tragedies of Vittorio Alfieri, translated*, 3 vols. 1815.

[3] See L. 357, p. 220 below, for W.'s views on the Corn Laws.

354. W. W. to MISS M. MALCOLM[1]

Address: Miss M. Malcolm, Burnfoot, near Langholm.
MS. Cornell.
Hitherto unpublished.

[mid-March 1815]

My dear Madam,

It would give me the greatest pleasure to see Colonel Paisley under my roof.[2] Coleridge is in Wiltshire; but I know that Southey would be very happy to see him. He resides in Keswick—and Colonel Paisley's name would be a sufficient introduction. The best approach to Keswick is from Carlisle through Wigton and Ireby; but no coach goes that road. From Penrith a coach starts for Keswick, at eight o'clock in the morning, every Monday, Wednesday and Friday, which falls in at Keswick with a daily coach that passes under our house. If Colonel Paisley should decline going to Keswick—it is 26 miles from Penrith to Ambleside, by Ulswater side and up Patterdale, a glorious ride, but no Coach this way; from Kendal to Ambleside a Coach runs every day—but the distance from Penrith to Kendal is 27 miles of dreary road. Had it been later in the season I should have proposed that Colonel Paisley should put himself into a chaise at Carlisle with two of the Ladies of your House, and escorted you hither by way of Keswick. Mrs Wordsworth received a kind Letter from you a week or two ago; to which she will reply as soon as any thing occurs to give interest to her Letter. At present she joins with me and my Sister in saying that we look forward with great delight to the time when we see Miss Malcolm, and any part of your family; which we trust will be in the course of the ensuing summer. My sisters had made up their minds to go to France; but the unaccountable and frightful aspect which things now wear has banished every thought of the kind, for the present. If Bonaparte should reinstate himself as Emperor of France, it will be the most disheartening event, and the most discreditable to human

[1] Wordsworth, with M. W., S. H., and Johnny W., on their tour in Scotland in 1814, had stayed with the Miss Malcolms at their farm at Burnfoot in Eskdale. See *SH* 21, p. 73.

[2] See L. 356. We learn from D. W.'s letter to S. H., 1 Apr. 1815 (see L. 359 below), that Col. Pasley did visit R. M. at the end of Mar. 1815. For W.W.'s letter to him, 28 Mar. 1811, on political and military affairs, see L. 221, pt. i. This mention of him, and the reference later in the letter to 'Bonaparte's' escape from Elba, helps us date this letter the middle of Mar. 1815. Col. Pasley's daughter Magdalene married in 1808 Miss Malcolm's brother, Charles M., a distinguished naval officer.

Nature, that History has yet had to record. With best remembrance to all beneath your roof. I remain dear Madam,

Your faithful friend
Wm Wordsworth.

We rejoice in the honour of your family.[1]

355. W. W. to ROBERT SOUTHEY

MS. untraced.
LY iii, 523a, p. 1362.

Friday evening. [March 1815]

Dear S——

Mary Bell the Bearer of this returns to Rydal Mount on Thursday next, and on Wednesday evening will call at the Hall. Would you be so kind as to send me by her Humbold's (is that his name) books upon South America and Montgomery's World before the Flood[2] — — — All the world here is in dejection—for my part I shall think that B——[3] will not succeed even should he get possession of Paris, provided the Legislature retire with the King towards the Frontiers, or perhaps even to any of the great Cities of France. I am further of opinion that if [he] be reinstated in his imperial seat he will not long continue to hold it—But what a wretched foppery of magnanimity and generosity &c &c has been exhibited towards him!——

We shall here have no more news till Sunday evening, it seems long to wait at such a moment——

Affectionately yours
W. W.

[1] Sir John Malcolm (1769–1833), Indian administrator, diplomat, and author of the *History of Persia*, and other works, was one of several distinguished brothers of the Miss Malcolm of Burnfoot to whom this letter is addressed. He was made K.C.B. in Apr. 1815.

[2] See L. 350, p. 203, n. 2 above.

[3] i.e. Bonaparte. Napoleon had escaped from Elba and arrived in France, 1 Mar. 1815. He entered Paris on Mar. 20.

356. W. W. to COLONEL PASLEY

MS. Cornell. Hitherto unpublished.

[mid-March 1815]

To Colonel Paisley
My dear Sir,

Gratify me with a visit if you possibly can. I would give a great deal for the opportunity of conversing with you.

Your sincere friend
Wm Wordsworth

357. D. W. and W. W. to SARA HUTCHINSON

Address: Miss Hutchinson, Hindwell, Radnor, by Worcester.
Stamp: Kendal.
MS. WL.
MY ii. 522, p. 647.

Thursday 16th March [1815]

(*D. W. writes*)
My dearest Sara,

Your letter reached me last night—it was written on Sunday—and on Monday, probably the tidings of the Buonapartite's entrance into France would reach you. As Dorothy said 'Why did they not kill him when they *had* him'. So you would say, with many an indignant reflection upon the childish folly of the Allies. I wrote to poor Annette on the Thursday; and on Monday morning Mr Scambler brought us the news. He had not read the papers, so William posted off to Ambleside, for we felt that seeing only was believing—At first I considered our French journey as entirely put a stop to; but if no great Body of adherents rise up he *may* be crushed at once, hanged and gibbeted—In which case the government would be stronger than ever. The Report was that Toulon had surrendered to him; but that appears to be false; but one could hardly suppose that he would be so mad, notwithstanding the ludicrous and ragamuffin way in which he has proceeded to venture unless he had had some encouragement from France. If that encouragement be not very powerful he will attempt to fall back to Italy, and there William thinks Murat[1] and he may be very troublesome; but God grant that his insane mind may push him on till he is surrounded and captive! At all events at present we have nothing to do but be

[1] Joachim Murat, one of Napoleon's generals, whom he had made King of Naples. Murat married N.'s sister Caroline.

thankful that we are not already in France; and it is very unlikely that it will be prudent for us to think of going so soon as we had intended; therefore you will not be forced to leave Hindwell till Mary's[1] troubles will be at end, and she I hope a happy Mother of a healthy Child. I am exceedingly distressed for poor Annette and Caroline, especially Annette—Caroline is young, fresh hopes will spring up for her—but her Mother! so near happiness and again to lose it! This is a very hard case and hard to be endured—Only in her last letter she spoke (like one who had been worn out with anxiety and exertion during the reign of the tyrant) of present happiness and peace for all France, and said that even those who had been warm admirers of Buonaparte were satisfied and perceived the wickedness and misery he had caused. I hope we shall have letters from her very soon. I am *sure* she will write as soon as she can perceive anything like comfort. It is very fortunate that I wrote to say that we were going. She will at least have the satisfaction of being assured that we were prepared to fulfill our promise, and it will serve as an earnest that we shall take the first opportunity of so doing. Miss Alne left us on Friday. She wrote from Keswick, where she stayed till Monday—and while she had the pen in hand the news from France reached them—She begins by saying that Miss B.[2] is in high spirits, determined not only to go with us but to be under the same roof—The marriage has done away all her scruples which were only founded on a fear that we should be too *melancholy* for her—She shewed Miss A. all her gold muslins etc, was determined to win a French Marquis—would accompany Miss Alne to Tours—and with a very little encouragement would have planned the Tour of Europe. Miss Alne's observations upon the news are simply that it probably may not be prudent to go so soon. I rather suspect that the Keswick politicians consider the affair as of less importance than it will prove in the end. It seems foolish at present to talk of any plans in connection with our going; but I will just observe that I told Annette that Miss A, you and I would lodge with her—and to Eustace B. I mentioned that Miss B's going was uncertain; but that if she did she would not lodge with us. Now I think it very probable that A. will already have taken lodgings and that Miss B cannot be accommodated; and, at all events, it would be far better for us if we could persuade her to be in other lodgings in the same street or very near us. A maid of her own she *must have*. The Riots appear to be stopped, and as we cannot think of the two

[1] i.e. Mary, wife of Tom Hutchinson of Hindwell.
[2] Miss Barker. See L. 257 above.

things at once, being English people, Buonaparte seems quite to have put the Corn Laws out of our heads. William has however carefully read all that has been said about them, and his opinion is this—that 80 is too high a price for the standard—76 he thinks would be very well; some restrictions being absolutely necessary. He approved very much of Mr Wilberforce's Speech, and said that Baring and others[1] talked a great deal of pernicious nonsense—William also thinks that rents should be lowered. Altogether I am very sorry that Tom has purchased his Estate. His living there for many years is quite out of the question (and I hope with Mary that he will *never* live there) and how much more might he not have made of his money elsewhere! and if the present rents are high it will be even worse. We should be very sorry that Mary has been so poorly if it were not that

(*W. W. writes*)

Dearest Sara—I will repeat in other words what D has said of the Corn Laws. The opinion that importation should [? not] be restricted is monstrous; I wish you could see Mr Wilberforce's speech, it is almost word for word what I had said by our fireside before—I have not sufficient knowledge of facts to fix upon the best restrictive price; but it is clear that rents have had an unnatural rise; and if they keep at their present pitch by aid of the present price of 80 shillings, I have no hesitation in saying that the price is too high—and I could have wished that a sum below 80 shillings had been tried; though with 80 shillings corn I should expect would not be saleable at that price for any length of time together; because it must fall from the moment that importation is likely to take place—so that it is possible that the price may answer for the good of the community. Nothing can be more deplorable than the errors of the mob; who seem never to have had a thought, that without a restriction upon importation no corn could be grown in this country, and consequently that it would become insupportably dear; and perhaps could not be got at all—The advocates for the Corn Laws are in fact the friends of the poor; though as I have said they may be mistaken as to the best price to fix upon. If Buonaparte were a man of genuine talents, such is the present state of Italy I am persuaded he might yet atchieve a noble work, which would almost redeem him in

[1] Alexander Baring (1774–1848), later Baron Ashburton, financier and advocate of free trade.

my estimation; I mean the making and consolidating the several states of that divided Kingdom into one;[1] and if this were done the independence [of] that people would be established—one of the most desirable political events that could possibly take place. The Italians have been abominably used, in being transferred to Austria, to the King of Sardinia and the rest of those vile Tyrants. B.'s is a strange adventure, he must doubtless have very many adherents in France, but I must be in deplorable ignorance of facts, if it be possible that such an Enterprize should succeed. I quit the pen to walk with Mary very affectionately yours W. W.

(*D. W. writes*) When Wm took the pen I was going on that we hope she will be warned and take care of herself. But indeed Sara you must rally her out of her bad spirits. Don't be so much afraid of talking to her about all that Joanna is disposed in general to treat as matter of so much fun. The prospect, however, of your stay at Hindwell, at least till after July will no doubt chear her spirits at present (I cannot say that it has cheared mine.)—The French people are not worth grieving for if they do not rise en Masse to destroy the Tyrant, and my griefs are only for our friends and other good quiet people who have fancied themselves at once released from their misery. Mary desires that you will tell Mary H. that she must come to Rydale if you are to go away and *she* will not only laugh away her fears but nurse [her] up to good purpose. Her husband may come to her, she says, in July, and fetch her and the Baby at the six week's end. No living thing travels nicer than a young Baby. I am very sorry I so often forgot to mention the tea urn and fender to you—but Mary has done it. Mrs Lloyd says if you get one of the common urns you may make a brass one of it when the outside is worn off—and we all think brass ones are very [*seal*]. It was the urn I said we objected to, not the Fender—so I suppose I must have expressed myself ill, or had not written the words plain.—I had before made up my mind that it would be foolish to take places further than Dover; for the reasons you have stated.—The fare in the Packets is 10/6—but it is time enough to talk of that. I only mentioned that you were to fix the place of meeting thinking it might not be possible to manage matters so that one or other of us should not be obliged to wait in London at least one day. I should infinitely prefer seeing nobody till we come back again; and if

[1] W.'s enthusiasm for a united Italy had already been expressed in the *Cintra* pamphlet in 1808. See also his sonnets, *At Rome*, and *After leaving Italy*, *Oxf. W*. pp. 359, 366–7.

matters brighten we might arrange with Mrs Clarkson either to meet us in London or might return to Bury; but I do not like to think of any delay in the homeward course; and certainly after so long an absence could not, at this distance of time calculate upon more than a week or fortnight—but perhaps, as our journey at all events is *delayed* you might now venture to go to Bury first, and either meet me in London from B, or return to Hindwell till Octr. I am afraid Mrs C is not well, and shall write to her to-day. Tom is flourishing at Cambridge—Willy has had another bad cold; owing I think to the searching cold winds—The weather has been dreadful; but to-day it is very fine—he is gone out with his Father, Mother and D. Both the last have also had bad colds, and I am sorry to tell you that Mary has not been so well of late—Her appetite has been bad, and she is weaker. Happily her cold has not lasted long. D goes on pretty well with her Latin. If she were steady she would improve rapidly; there is not however much reason for complaint; and in everything her improvement is satisfactory compared with what it was at school; but the revolution in Miss F's[1] school is wonderful. The Teacher seems to be quite a treasure and all the scholars are improved greatly in reading, spelling, working and writing, and they like her too, very much, though they say she is exceedingly strict. Young Simpson teaches some of them latin and he is a very good master, so that if it were necessary to send D again to school she might do very well, and even in some respects better than at home, which it is comfortable to think of. Miss F has 17 scholars—The Music goes on well, and every body is satisfied. I am very glad for Miss F's sake; for she is a generous good soul.—We have had no letter from Robert Jameson.[2] This looks very ill—I lent him £3 which he was to have repaid at Xmas and he owes 3 to Miss Crosthwaite for shirts. The Bill is come in and we have had it to pay—We told Mary and desired her to write to him, and did not conceal from her what we thought of his conduct. I fear he will do no good. Mr. de Quincey arrived on Monday from West Hay. William has made a conquest of holy Hannah,[3] though

[1] Miss Fletcher. See L. 307, above, and *SH* 18, p. 58.

[2] Robert Jameson, one of the Jamesons of Ambleside, eventually became a judge in the West Indies, and Attorney-General of Toronto. He married in 1825 the talented Irish lady Anna Brownell Murphy (1794–1860), who in 1826 published anonymously *The Diary of an Ennuyée*, which W. W. read (see *LY* i. 778, p. 251), and subsequently several other works. His character was not such as to make a happy marriage and they lived apart, she supporting herself mainly by her varied and attractive writings on literature, art, and social life.

[3] i.e. Hannah More (1745–1833), the famous evangelical lady who lived at Cowslip Green in Somerset, author of *Coelebs in Search of a Wife* and pioneer of philanthropic work among the poor.

she had not seen the Book, had seen nothing but the extracts in the Edinbrough Review. She intends to buy it; but is waiting for a cheaper Edition. As usual Peter[1] is very entertaining, now that he is fresh. We have seen him almost every day. The proof of his letters to the Courier is actually in the hands of the Editor. His youngest brother must be insane and so Q. pronounces him. He has spent all his property and is now at West Hay with his passion for moving from place to place unabated. Wm had a very interesting letter from Edwards[2] of Derby last night—I will quote a part of it he begins 'I could not comply with your instructions not to purchase the Exn' and goes on—'I would not be without the Book for twice its value' etc, he then gives an extract from a letter he has received from Montgomery. M. says 'The poem in my opinion, an opinion confirmed by repeated perusal of it, is incomparably the greatest and the most beautiful work of the present age of poetry, and sets Mr W. beyond controversy above all the living and almost all the dead of his fraternity. I assure you that the spirit of that Book, which I first read at Scarborough in Septr, so possessed me that I have scarcely yet recovered my relish for any other modern verse. The peculiar harmony of Rhythm, felicity of language, and splendour of thought for a while made all beside poor or feeble in comparison. I am gradually returning to sober feelings, and though the transcendant powers of W. are not at all diminished in my estimation, those of others of his contemporaries' etc etc He adds 'you have got a passport to posterity signed by Wordsworth.' It is the great price of the work that keeps it on hand there is no doubt: for many who cannot spare 2 guineas are waiting—and unfortunately the fashionable will not buy till Wm becomes one of their fraternity—or till with one voice the Nation proclaims his merit—and when will that be?—Alas alas—but this I care not for,—I only want the Edition to be sold. Montgomery says nothing of the versification in the Review, which surprized us. This Extract from his letter is written with much feeling. Give my tenderest love, and best wishes to Mary. Love to Tom, Joanna, your Aunt, George and John Monkhouse—You are now I suppose at Kington[3] unless yesterday was as stormy with you as here.

This is a sad illegible letter. The poems are endless and we have got no more than 3 sheets of White Doe—it is printed at Edinburgh.

[*Unsigned*]

[1] Evidently a nickname for De Quincey.

[2] See L. 219, pt. i, p. 470.

[3] Where George Hutchinson lived, a few miles from Hindwell.

358. D. W. to RICHARD ADDISON

Address: Richard Addison Esq[re], Staple Inn, London.
MS. WL.
MY ii. 524, p. 657.

April 1st 1815

Dear Sir,

I have this day written to Messrs Twining Devereux Court and have given them an order upon my Brother for 26 £–10s. which I beg you will be so kind as to pay to them when they demand it—I suppose my Brother is still in the Country—

I remain, dear Sir,
Yours respectfully
D Wordsworth

359. D. W. to SARA HUTCHINSON

Address: Miss Hutchinson, Hindwell, Radnor. By Worcester.
Stamp: Kendal Penny Post.
MS. WL.
MY ii. 525, p. 657.

Saturday April 8th ½ past 12. Forenoon [1815].

I am alone in the house, and have given orders to say I am not at home, if any one calls—This fine morning is likely enough to tempt Lady Fleming, and I am determined not to miss another post. I hope you have been kept so busy and amused with the goings-on of the spring that you have not had time to grumble, and complain of our long silence—Indeed Sara, ever since the arrival of your last letter I have been more uneasy than I would willingly believe you have been; and every day I intended to write but I have put it off and I hardly know how. You must forgive me—I will never I promise you (for my own sake) do the like. It is so long since I wrote that I hardly know what I have to tell you. Thank God we are all well, and that is the best news. William and Mary set off at 2 o'clock on Monday towards Kendal, intending to be taken up by the coach. The morning had been very wet, but it was a fine afternoon—not too hot, and at 6 they found themselves at Staveley not much fatigued. There they got tea, and (I think rather imprudently) set off after tea on foot and reached Kendal at 8. They write that Mary was not at all fatigued. This is very extraordinary; for she has seldom walked to Church lately without being heavy and exhausted all the afternoon; and she has neither looked so well nor been half so strong for the last five or six weeks as for a long time after I came home, and her appetite has lately been very bad. They intended coming home yesterday, and I expect them today. Mrs Cookson has been very ill with influenza and still has a troublesome cough. William dined with Dr. Harrison on Thursday and yesterday Mary writes that he had not fallen asleep till six o'clock—Wine and company the first cause, the second his verses and he was very poorly. W's business at Kendal was to appoint a new Sub. in the place of poor old Mr. Pennington who died suddenly about a fortnight ago. Dawson has applied—and Wm. intended to give the place to him provided no relations of Mr. P. should succeed him. You will be sorry to hear of Mr. P's death. All the Cooksons except Henry go to school with Parson Harrison. If they bring a good report of the progress made by Mr. C's boys I should almost wish that John should be boarded at Kendal and go to Mr. H. In short I wish most earnestly for a change; John never, unless there is complete inwrought mental revolution will improve here. He is inveterately lazy and there is no industry in Mr D's[1] school, no discipline, therefore the change cannot here come from without—Oh! that the Malcolms[2] would take him! William sometimes talks of sending him to Dr Wilkinson's school at Halifax, where Miss Alne's nephew is. Dr W. was usher at Hipperholme school and his wife Teacher of the Girls; and is a most excellent-tempered motherly and sensible woman as I know by experience and the Rawsons would be a great comfort—but it is such a long way off! Much time however must not be lost—something must be done. His understanding is I am sure very good, as far as he *does* understand; but he is naturally slow; that however I am convinced, does not stand half so much in his way as his shyness and laziness. Mr. Best is exceedingly fond of John, and when they are alone together he is surprised at his observations. Yesterday all the children drank tea with me at Mr. Best's and I could not but admire John whenever he spoke or was spoken to. With Mr. Best he casts off his shyness, and nothing more than an ingenuous modesty, and his honest simplicity of sentiment appears. Do not think I despair about him—Far from it—Only this I am confident of, that the change must be wrought by himself alone if he changes here and that is too much to expect. After D's lessons Willie and

[1] i.e. The Revd. John Dawes, schoolmaster at Ambleside. See Letters 135, p. 282 n. and 190, p. 402, pt. i above.

[2] John had had lessons for a short time with the tutor of the Malcolm nephews during the tour in Scotland in 1814. See *SH* 21, p. 3.

she set off very proud for Brathay Hall to keep Jane Harden's Birthday, and John dines with the Lloyds—At four o'clock I must fetch Willie home and leave my letters at the post office. Mrs Harden has been very ill a premature labour on the 1st January. Yesterday she called in the car. She looks most delicate. The weather has been very bad for invalids. We had 3 beautiful days last week; but since the beginning of February—indeed all winter the weather has been perpetually changing—and in February and March we had torrents of rain. Thursday was very fine—Friday raining in the morning—today beautiful, yet the spring is unusually backward—the shrubs before the house are not yet in full leaf; but they are thickening fast and the vallies are becoming green. It is really quite mortifying to hear from all quarters how dry and warm the spring has been; when we have but had a warm day now and then, as if only to prepare the delicate to catch cold the next day by the horrible transitions. Willie has caused us to notice all transitions, and to rejoice doubly in every fine day. Oh! Sara it is ten thousand pities he should be so spoiled—If he were under discipline he would learn to read write spell—without the smallest difficulty; for he is one of the quickest children I ever saw and has an admirable memory—I often wish that Mary[1] had him beside little Sally. As it is, however, he cannot but learn and I have no doubt, that at 8 years old Mr. Dawes will be proud of him. It is impossible unless you have seen it, to have an idea of the Father's folly respecting this child—We strive against it as much as possible but it is all in vain. I should ask you to say something when you write if it would do any good; but as it will not you had better take no notice.

Miss Barker wrote on Monday with the joyful news of Mr. Littleton having told her that she was to have her money—In fact she sent us his letter, which was very handsomely and respectfully expressed. This has been a great relief to my mind, for I could not help having fears, from what I had heard from various quarters. This reminds me of Basil Montagu,[2] who wrote to Lloyd thanking him for Alfieri—but no letter for us! This looks as if he were willing to be a complete Slave, for he certainly in answer to mine might have written a note just to tell us about his health. Miss B said she would write to you the next day concerning Mr. Gretton's school. Strange that we should never have thought of that school! I have

[1] i.e. Mary Hutchinson of Hindwell where S. H. was staying. Sally was her eldest daughter.

[2] i.e. Basil junior, who had been nursed for several months by Miss Barker at Keswick during his serious illness the previous year. See L. 311 above.

no doubt it will answer, at present at least, infinitely better than Green Row—but that school I detest. Dinah Black is dead—Poor thing! she suffered much at last. Dorothy and Mary Bell were at her funeral on Wednesday. There was a dinner at the publick house, but D and M did not go there—they only went to Blintern Gill.[1] Mr. Powley tells me that it was by her own desire that they had the dinner—no doubt from her savings. This the ruling passion strong in death. She had a proud spirit and no doubt she thought the family would be honoured by a genteel funeral. The poems are printed: but it is not for me to say when they will be published. Never more would I have a Book printed in London—Ballantyne goes on like Buonaparte in his march to Paris, and the White Doe will, if they do not make haste in London, beat the Poems.[2] There was a long and most provoking delay after the first 4 sheets for want of paper; but now we have nothing to complain of. Colonel Pasley[3] came last Monday but one and stayed till Wednesday evening. Unfortunately Mary and I had him to ourselves for 3 hours when he first arrived (William was at the funeral of Mrs Robinson's husband, the Overseer of the Quarries) and you may imagine how grave and formal we were—It always seemed as if we were not wise enough for him he gave such short answers to our observations or questions; but we liked him very much before he left us—He was very fond of the Children, and his reserve wore away with us. Like many other shy and grave men he has a talent for humour, and told us many pleasant things in a very pleasant way. I suppose you know his wife died in the summer or autumn of a consumption. The War will not carry him out of England. His Station will still be at Chatham. Dear love, I sympathized from the bottom of my heart in your distress for want of newspapers—Never was I in such a fever of anxiety as till we heard that the wretch had reached Paris.[4] Then I was in despair —Now again my hopes revive. It is plain that if the Allies are resolved to repair the follies they committed last year and if they do not quarrel among themselves they must conquer and speedily. The Mob of France and the Armies are B's friends. The Mass of respectable people is with Louis in heart. The Mob will side with the strongest, which the Allies must be if the respectable side with

[1] Blintern or Blentarn Gill was the small farmstead in Easedale where the Green family had lived during the Wordsworths' early years in Grasmere. For the disaster which overtook George and Sarah Green in 1808 see L. 100, pt. i.

[2] *The White Doe of Rylstone* and Wordsworth's first Collected Edition of his poems—*Poems, including Lyrical Ballads*—were both in the press at this time. Ballantyne, the Edinburgh printers, were printing *The White Doe.*

[3] See L. 354, p. 215, n. 2 above.

[4] Napoleon entered Paris on 20 Mar. 1815.

them, which I have no doubt they will. Buonaparte's conduct, in direct contradiction to former practice and profession proves his weakness—Did you not smile with scorn when you read his decree of Abolition of the slave trade and Liberty of the press?—Then his fine professions of renouncing Conquest after his first declaration that he was come to avenge the Cause of France stripped of her Conquests!—Those villainous Sunday newspapers are my abhorrence—I read in one the other day the following sentiment 'Surely it would be wise that the Allies should at length give Buonaparte time to show whether he is sincere or not!' In other words give him time to be quite prepared to fence himself in in his wickedness. Then that impudent assertion follows so often repeated that *we* shall be the aggressors if we meddle with the internal government of France. I see by last night's paper (we take the evening Mail) that Murat stands against Buon. I expect we shall go to France never[theless] and this I am determined upon, that nothing shall stop me again, from seizing the first possible opportunity. We had a long letter from A and C.[1] written on the 19th and 20th.—A concludes at 12 o'clock at night—hears troops which she conjectures to be the Avantgarde of Buonaparte—She concludes 'Good God what is to become of us?' Caroline's letter was written first and not without hope of seeing us this summer. She said the people were astounded; but Paris in good heart. The next day the king gone. She gives a very pretty account of the Lodgings they have taken for us—an eating Room—another sitting room—and bedrooms—all apart from the rest of the house. They have a servant who would do anything for us, C. says, which she cannot do. Her mother took the young warrior she having to be so much out of doors on the business of sollicitation.—Alas! all this is to no purpose, and we have written to state that William only consented to the marriage on supposition that they would obtain an increase of income; and urging that they wait for a change. Their servant serves them for love more than profit they tell us. We had another letter written the day after in great depression of spirits—C. was ill in bed—all was quiet at Paris—Oh! with what bitter anguish must Annette have lighted her candles for the illumination.—In her first letter she told us that Eustace B.[2] had been with them the day before (the 18th) when they received my letter. He was to take leave and was going into Camp near Paris—He parted from them with tears: but said he hoped yet to be our 'Chevalier'—She says 'he is honorable—he has high

[1] i.e. Annette Vallon and Caroline.

[2] i.e. Eustace Baudouin. See L. 243, p. 18, n. 2 above.

duties to perform, and *will* perform them'—but in the next letter not daring to speak out she gives us to understand that he is returned to Paris by saying with a stroke under the word, '*Messieurs* B. send their regards'. I cannot be angry with him knowing that the virtue of an Abdiel was more than could be expected especially from one, who no doubt is still dazzled by his youthful recollections, whatever change his year's service of Louis may have brought about in his opinions—Miss Barker urges me so vehemently to go and see her, that I am determined to refuse no longer, as we shall certainly not go to Paris *before* the end of summer. William promises to accompany me and I think we shall go towards the latter end of the week after next. I do not mean to stay *more* than a week, but most likely I shall be at home in 4 or 5 days. I have just ate my solitary dinner and visited the mount the garden and the Terrace—the spring flowers are very pretty; but though John[1] is much improved as a gardener, and really seems almost fond of the work, we are much behind-hand owing to the bad weather—besides we cannot get hold of Lonsborough. Most part of the Thrift is transplanted—We have plenty of greens—the Colliflower Broccoli is delightful. Dear Sara I hope you will be back again before October, unless indeed Buona should be conquered in a couple of months, in which case we must journey to Paris in September. Joanna says nothing of coming to us this spring—Do persuade her if you can—she will be fast bound when she gets to Radnor. Did I ever tell you that the Excursion is gone to Luff? I am ashamed and grieved to say we have never written. If William does not write next week *I* will. I wish you could see Roderick,[2] though I am sorry to tell you (which I would not like to say to any-body else but our own family) that I never was so much disappointed in a Book in my Life, in spite of its very great merit—My reasons I cannot now give you. I longed for your arm when I was sauntering in the garden—and remembered old times when you and I were alone. My best love to all. I often think of every one. Do write often—your last had been long expected. Compliments to Sammy B.

Kind love to John Monkhouse

[*Unsigned*]

[1] John Carter, Wordsworth's clerk.

[2] Southey's epic poem, *Roderick, the Last of the Goths*, recently published.

360. D. W. to CATHERINE CLARKSON

MS. British Museum.
MY ii. 526, p. 663.

Tuesday April 11th [1815]

My dear Friend,

In common with you our minds have been occupied continually by the tremendous changes in France. Till we heard of the arrival of B. in Paris I never slept without dreaming of troubles connected with his fiendish ambition; and every night I was kept awake for hours. After he had entered the City, having passed through France without opposition, I was at first in despair—but this lasted for a very short time: and now I feel confident that we shall be more secure than ever; provided the Allies act promptly and with unanimity. There seems to be no doubt that the middle Ranks of Society are almost universally against Buona, and when they have a military force to aid them they will act with voice and hand. Our military must be much stronger than B's and the mob will side with the strongest. The infatuation of the Governments in not being warned by the information given of the conspiracy; and of the French Government in particular argues an inconceivable weakness. If they had exercised half the understanding and zeal which the wicked have shewn in conducting their plots, things could never have been in this state. Refer to the 4th Book of the Excursion[1] and you will find an admirable comment upon the conduct of the Allies from beginning to end. God grant that if they have once again the Sword and the Victory in their hands no puny relentings of mercy may stop the slaughter till the Tyrant is taken and his wicked followers completely subdued. To this result I look forward with hope —Nay I may almost say with confidence—but let them begin quickly—there is no time for pondering. The people of England in general are eager to begin. At Kendal this spirit is almost universal. We had given over taking a Newspaper (except the Courier which came from Keswick) but we could not exist without one sent directly to us; and every post-day, though till the war-fare actually begins we can expect nothing of much importance, we are full of anxiety and catch at every favourable omen. The attempts at insurrection in different parts of France, and the timidity evinced by the tenor of B's conduct throughout are very favourable signs. In short day by day hope springs in us. We laughed with scorn at his abolition

[1] *The Excursion*, iv, ll. 295–319.

of the Slave Trade—his liberty of the Press!!! Pray let me have all the private information that you receive. Everybody here is anxious, but none a hundredth part so much as we are. We had a long letter from France written on the 19th or 20th. The letter was concluded at Midnight and my Friend[1] says 'I hear Troops entering the City. I think it is the avant-garde of Buonaparte. Good God what is to become of us!' We have had another letter written the next day in miserable dejection; but she says no more of public affairs than that 'all is quiet'. Lodgings were taken for us in the Hôtel du Jardin Turc Boulevard du Temple, a pleasant part of Paris as they describe it. Poor creatures they say they are shipwrecked when just entering into port—indeed it is a distressing situation but I trust that we shall see them in Paris before the end of another twelve-month. The White Doe is printing and will I hope be out in two or three weeks. William will order a copy to be sent to you; but perhaps you could devise somebody to call for it at Longmans. The two volumes of poems are published, and he is sorry he cannot also spare you a Copy of them; but he has only a certain number to dispose of. If you cannot afford to buy them, by applying to Henry Robinson, to whom William sends a copy, you can see them. I want you to read the new poems. Your Receipt for a Criticism in the Philanthropist[2] is excellent and we pray you earnestly to do the work yourself; for there is no-body here who *can* do it. It would be too impudent in us to set about it; and Mr de Quincey, notwithstanding his learning and his talents, can do nothing; he is eaten up by the spirit of procrastination; but if once in two or three years he actually does make an effort, he is so slow a labourer that no one who knows him would wish to appoint him to it, if it might not as well be 3 months in hand as three hours; though in itself but the work of one sitting for another person. If it is not very irksome to you I entreat you that you will resolve to write, and not be over nice yourself. You cannot but satisfy others, and will do the sale of the Excursion service. That is all we care about. If this edition were once sold I should not have a moment's anxiety afterwards. To turn to your last letters—you speak of domestic troubles in the first of them, but with hope that they would terminate happily.

[1] i.e. Annette Vallon.

[2] *The Philanthropist or Repository for Hints and Suggestions calculated to promote the Happiness and Comfort of Men*, 1811–19, produced by William Allen. In vol. v (1815), pp. 342–63, is a review of *The Excursion*, with a note 'To be continued', but there does not seem to have been a sequel. Allen (1770–1843) was a friend of Clarkson and Wilberfore, and, after the end of the war, of the Czar Alexander. He was a keen educationist in the non-Anglican or 'Lancastrian' interest, and for some years was partner with Robert Owen in the Lanark Mills.

Such I trust has been the case. You do not mention Tom, no doubt he is not at Cambridge; for I find that the fever is still rife there. Give my kind love to him and tell him I hope to see his name in the papers before his Term at Cambridge is out, as being the successful candidate for some medal or other prize. It is not, I think, to be expected that he will distinguish himself in Mathematics; but if he pays a reasonable attention to that study and is zealous in other studies it is all that you can desire. I cannot but wish that you may not get that farm near Ipswich. What is the use of farming for you beyond what is just sufficient to keep Mr Clarkson employed? and twenty acres would serve that purpose as well as 300. This is at best a bad time for farming, and a large farm does but increase your anxieties; besides you cannot chuse your own country if a farm is necessary to fix you. No—I should wish you to have your two years to look about, and gladly would I say, take lodgings or a house near us for one of them, if I were not afraid of the climate for a whole year. I am obliged now reluctantly to confess that the transitions here are more sudden and frequent than elsewhere, and that we have much more rain. From all quarters we have heard of a fine season and dry weather, while till within this fortnight from the beginning of December we have never had three fine days together, and the spring has been unusually backward. As to rainy weather; for myself I do not mind it and there are few days when I cannot walk, because our roads are good, between the showers; but

[*rest of letter and address missing*]

361. W. W. to R. P. GILLIES

MS. untraced.
Gillies. K. MY. ii. 527, p. 666.

Rydal Mount, April 25, 1815

My dear Sir,

I think of starting for London in a few days with Mrs. Wordsworth,[1] and as I wish to leave home with as clear a conscience as I can, I sit down to atone for one of my offences in not having replied sooner to your kind letter. Your health, I hope, is better, and if it be much improved, what should prevent you from taking a trip as far south as we think of going, and meeting us in town? We shall be

[1] The Wordsworths (W. W. and M. W.) arrived in London on Saturday, 6 May (*MW* 14, p. 30). See L. 362 below.

in lodgings somewhere at the west-end, and may easily be heard of, by inquiries at Sir George Beaumont's, corner of North Audley Street, Grosvenor Square.

You ought to have received my two volumes of poems long before this, if Longman has done his duty. I ordered a copy likewise to be sent to Walter Scott. I cannot but flatter myself that this publication will interest you. The pains which I have bestowed on the composition can never be known but to myself, and I am very sorry to find, on reviewing the work, that the labour has been able to do so little for it. You mentioned *Guy Mannering*[1] in your last. I have read it. I cannot say that I was disappointed, for there is very considerable talent displayed in the performance, and much of that sort of knowledge with which the author's mind is so richly stored. But the adventures I think not well chosen or invented, and they are still worse put together; and the characters, with the exception of Meg Merrilies, excite little interest. In the management of this lady the author has shown very considerable ability, but with that want of taste, which is universal among modern novels of the Radcliffe school, which, as far as they are concerned, this is. I allude to the laborious manner in which everything is placed before your eyes for the production of picturesque effect. The reader, in good narration, feels that pictures rise up before his sight, and pass away from it unostentatiously, succeeding each other. But when they are fixed upon an easel for the express purpose of being admired, the judicious are apt to take offence, and even to turn sulky at the exhibitor's officiousness. But these novels are likely to be much overrated on their first appearance, and will afterwards be as much undervalued. *Waverley* heightened my opinion of Scott's talents very considerably, and if *Mannering* has not added much, it has not taken much away. Infinitely the best part of *Waverley* is the pictures of Highland manners at Mac Ivor's castle, and the delineation of his character, which are done with great spirit. The Scotch baron, and all the circumstances in which he is exhibited, are too peculiar and *outré*. Such caricatures require a higher condiment of humour to give them a relish than the author of *Waverley* possesses. But too much of this gossip. I heard casually the other day that Mr Mackenzie[2] might take up his residence in our neighbourhood during some part of the

[1] W.'s criticism of *Guy Mannering* and *Waverley* in this letter well illustrates his qualified admiration for Scott as a writer, and his definition of what should constitute 'good narration' is an interesting revelation of his own taste in fiction.

[2] Probably Henry Mackenzie (1755–1831), author of *The Man of Feeling*, described by Gillies in his *Memoirs*, ii, pp. 180–4.

approaching summer. I am sorry for the occasion, which I am told is the delicate health of one of his daughters. Houses and lodgings might be had hereabouts if applied for early in the season, otherwise are difficult to find. I mention this in order that if you happen to see Mr Mackenzie, you may repeat it to him, and add that I should be happy to be of service to him on this occasion. My sister will continue at Rydale Mount during Mrs Wordsworth's and my absence; and if Mr Mackenzie has no friend to whom he can apply, she would be happy to transmit to him any information that she thought likely to be useful.

Excuse this Dull and hasty letter, and believe me

Most sincerely yours
William Wordsworth

362. M. W., W. W., and D. W. to SARA HUTCHINSON

Address: Miss Hutchinson, Hindwell, Radnor.
Stamp: Kendal Penny Post.
MS. WL.
Hitherto unpublished.

Tuesday Morning May 2nd [1815]

(*M. W. writes*)

My dearest Sarah,

I have no doubt but you will join us in London[1] but I much wish that it may be immediately as assuredly we shall wish you to *see everything* and if we either have to wait for your coming, or have to go over the same things again that will cause our absence from home to be prolonged which you may well believe I do not wish to be the case—so do not wait to hear of our being settled but set off. T. M.[2] shall know our address immediately, so make your way to him—greatly should I rejoice to meet Tom[3] at the same time—but I shall say no more—We set off today, shall drop Hartley[4] at Oxford and

[1] W. W. and M. W. went to London mainly so that W. W. could explain to Lord Lonsdale why he had decided to refuse the offer of the Collectorship of Customs at Whitehaven. See L. 363 above. The visit, which lasted till mid June, saw the first meeting between W. W. and Haydon the painter and also between W. W. and Leigh Hunt. See Moorman, ii, pp. 253, 280–2, and *MW* 14, p. 30 (where M. W.'s letter to T. Monkhouse is wrongly dated 1816.)

[2] i.e. Thomas Monkhouse.

[3] i.e. M. W.'s brother, Thomas Hutchinson of Hindwell.

[4] The Wordsworths escorted Hartley Coleridge to Oxford where he entered Merton College. See Griggs, *Letters of Hartley Coleridge*, pp. 11–14.

hope to contrive to reach London before Sunday, as it will be very disagreeable to enter without lodgings on that day—God bless you all. M. W.

(*W. W. writes*)

Dearest Sarah.

This letter must not depart without my expressing an earnest wish that you would comply with Mary's request in setting off as soon as possible for the reasons she assigns. Could Tom join you it would prodigiously enhance our pleasure. Tell him so from me.

Henry[1] seems well, but a good deal more inert in his appearance and perhaps in his habits than when last here. A slight deafness which he has, may be in part the cause of this—He talks of lodging and boarding somewhere, but hasn't yet fixed in what place—

very affectionately yours

W. W.

(*D. W. writes*)

Dearest Sarah, I must say a word to entreat that dear Tom will accompany you to London and that you will make no unnecessary delay—I wrote to you on Sunday in such confusion and hurry that I scarcely know what I said; but I hope you would make out what I wished you to understand —— They are going off by Coach—and I now wish them fairly off—We have wandered about all day—upstairs and down—and in the garden—hot and tired. God grant—that all may go on well! Willy is wonderfully improved of late—does not cry at all—I cannot say he is over obedient; but much of that does not appear he is so much out of doors and that makes him independent. He is a darling creature—You must write *very* often. I write to Mrs Clarkson by this Post—God bless you dearest Sara—Love to all.

(*M. W. writes*)

All well do not let a short letter frighten you. M. W.

[1] M. W.'s brother Henry Hutchinson.

363. W. W. to LORD LONSDALE

Address: The Earl of Lonsdale, 12, Charles Street.
MS. Lonsdale MSS., Record Office, The Castle, Carlisle.
Hitherto unpublished.

24, Edward St.,
Cavendish Square.
Saturday evening May 6th. [1815]

My Lord,

I take the liberty of informing your Lordship that in consequence of your letter of the 28th Inst I have thought it right to communicate to you my sentiments in person upon this signal mark of your Lordship's consideration.[1]

If I do not hear from your Lordship that you are otherwise engaged, I purpose doing myself the honour of calling in Charles Street tomorrow morning at ten o'clock.

I have the honor to remain

my Lord
your Lordship's
most obliged and faithful servant
Wm Wordsworth

364. W. W. to JOHN TAYLOR COLERIDGE[2]

Address: John Coleridge Esq., 24 Edward Street, Cavendish Sq.
MS. Bodleian Library.
Hitherto unpublished.

Tuesday 9th [May 1815]

Mr Wordsworth has the pleasure of informing Mr J[ohn Taylor] Coleridge that he accompanied his Cousin Mr Hartley Coleridge to Oxford where he left him under the protection of Mr W[illiam Hart] Coleridge last Saturday.[3] Mrs Coleridge of Keswick and her

[1] Lord Lonsdale had offered W. the Collectorship of Customs at Whitehaven, a more lucrative post than the Distributorship. Wordsworth declined it, apparently because he and his family had become so deeply attached to Rydal Mount and its neighbourhood. See *Mem.* ii, p. 4.

[2] 1790–1876, nephew of S. T. C., son of his brother James C. of Heath's Court, Ottery St. Mary, and at Oxford a friend of John Keble, Thomas Arnold (of Rugby), and other distinguished scholars and divines, to whom in their undergraduate days he introduced the poems of Wordsworth, given to him by his uncle S. T. C. See his *Life of Keble*, i, p. 17. He became a judge.

[3] For the journey to Oxford in 1815 see L. 359 above. William Hart Coleridge (1789–1849), afterwards Bishop of Barbados, was also a nephew of S. T. C., son of his brother Luke.

son and daughter were quite well when he left Keswick. Mr Wordsworth is to dine with Sir George Beaumont to-morrow at six, who, if Mr Coleridge will excuse this sudden invitation, without a previous introduction, will be most happy to have the honour of seeing Mr Coleridge at dinner; He would not have taken this liberty had not he thought it would have been an inducement to meet Mr Wordsworth but Sir Geo would be glad to know as soon as possible. Sir Geo lives at 29 South Audley St. Grosvenor Square.

365. W. W. to MESSRS. LONGMAN & CO.

Address: Messrs Longman and Co, Paternoster Row, London.
Postmark: 4 o'clock 10 May 1815 Ev. Py Post Marchmont St. Unpaid.
MS. Bodleian Library.
MY ii. 528, p. 667.

24 Edward Street
Cavendish Sqre
[10 May 1815]

Dear Sirs,

Being called suddenly to Town I left the Correction of the Press, of the prose part of the White Doe (the poetry had been printed off) to Mr Ballantyne; and I hope that you will hear shortly that the work is finished—

I have brought with me the first Vol: of three Sets of my poems[1] to have the error rectified in putting the work into Boards. I wish you to be so kind as to send me three first Volumes in a correct state, and these shall be returned by the Bearer.

The Letter forwarded to me by you was to inquire whether I purposed to print an Octvo Edition of the Excursion.[2] Many applications to the same effect have been made to me from different Quarters; and I wish to know whether the Sale goes in such a way as to afford a hope that the wishes of these persons may be gratified—

I shall do myself the pleasure of calling upon you as soon as my numerous engagements in this quarter of the Town will allow

I am dear Sirs
Your obedient servant
W. Wordsworth

[1] i.e. *Poems, including Lyrical Ballads*, etc., two vols., 1815.
[2] This did not appear until 1820.

I should be glad to learn that the deplorable mistake in putting the work into Boards has been rectified.—

366. W. W. to JOHN SCOTT[1]

Address: John Scott Esqre., 3 Maida Place, Edgeware Road.
Postmark: 7 o'clock 15 May 1815 Nt. Five Py Post Unpaid
MS. New York Public Library, Berg Collection.
K (—). *MY ii. 529, p. 668* (—).

Monday May 14th 1815
24 Edward Street,
Cavendish Sq^{re}

Sir,

Amid the hurry consequent upon a recent arrival, with a view to a short Residence in London—I have found leisure to peruse the volume[2] which you have presented to me, and for which I return you my sincere thanks — —

During the earlier days of the french revolution I resided upwards of twelve months in France,[3] and have since had some opportunities of studying the character of that people; and the impressions then made upon my mind place it out of my power to doubt whether the unfavourable picture which you draw of what they have now become, be unfaithful.

Thanking you for the pleasure and Instruction which I have received from your 'Visit to Paris', I remain

With great respect
faithfully yours
Wm Wordsworth

[1] John Scott (1783–1821), editor of the *Champion* and of the *London Magazine*, published in 1815 *A Visit to Paris in 1814*, followed in 1816 by *Paris revisited in 1815 by way of Brussels*. Scott was killed in a duel in 1821, following a dispute with J. G. Lockhart.

[2] i.e. *A Visit to Paris*.

[3] Wordsworth's stay in France was from Nov. 1791 to Dec. 1792.

367. W. W. to S. T. COLERIDGE

Address: S. T. Coleridge Esq[re]., Calne, Wilts.
MS. Clifton College, Bristol.
MY ii. 529a, p. 669.

24 Edward Street
Cavendish Sq[re]
Monday Morn: 22nd May 1815

My dear Coleridge,

Let me beg out of kindness to me that you would relinquish the intention of publishing the Poem addressed to me after hearing *mine* to you.[1] The commendation would be injurious to us both, and my work when it appears, would labour under a great disadvantage in consequence of such a precursorship of Praise.

I shall be thankful for your remarks on the Poems, and also upon the Excursion, only begging that whenever it is possible references may be made to some passages which have given rise to the opinion whether favourable or otherwise; in consequence of this not having been done (when indeed it would have been out of Place) in your Letter to Lady B—[2] I have rather been perplexed than enlightened by your *comparative* censure. One of my principal aims in the Ex[n]: has been to put the commonplace truths, of the human affections especially, in an interesting point of view; and rather to remind men of their knowledge, as it lurks inoperative and unvalued in their own minds, than to attempt to convey recondite or refined truths. Pray point out to me the most striking instances where I have failed, in producing poetic effect by an overfondness for this practice, or through inability to realize my wishes.

I am happy to hear that you are going to press.[3]

And believe me my dear Coleridge in spite of your silence
Most affectionately yours
W. Wordsworth

I hope to send you the White Doe in a few days. Some prefatory Lines have found their way into the Courier, much to my regret,

[1] W. refers to S. T. C.'s lines *To William Wordsworth*, written at Coleorton in Dec. 1806 after hearing W. W. read aloud the 'poem on his own life'. See *Poetical Works of S. T. Coleridge*, Oxford, 1912, i, p. 403.

[2] For Coleridge's letter to Lady Beaumont, and his answer to W.'s letter, see Griggs, iv. 964, p. 564, and 969, p. 570.

[3] Coleridge had intended to publish *Biographia Literaria* and his poems (*Sibylline Leaves*) in two volumes in 1815. But owing to difficulties with the printers, they did not appear until July 1817. See *Biographia Literaria*, edited by George Watson (Dent, 1956), introduction.

and printed with vile incorrectness. I remain in Town nearly three weeks longer.

368. W. W. to SIR WALTER SCOTT

Address: Walter Scott Esqe, Corner of White Horse Street, Piccadilly.
Postmark: 24 My.
MS. Bodleian Library.
The Heber Letters: 1783–1832, ed. R. H. Cholmondeley, 1950, p. 269.

[probably 23 May 1815]

Dear Scott,

I begin to fear that we are destined not to meet.—I mentioned to Mr Heber[1] an original picture of Milton recently rescued from a Broker's shop. The sight of this Portrait *I am sure* would delight you. Mr Heber expressed a wish to see it—Sir George and Lady Beaumont feel the same desire; and I now write to beg that, if you should be at leisure on Friday morning next, or any morning next week after Tuesday, you would arrange it with Mr Heber that we might all meet at Sir George Beaumont's at half past nine for Breakfast, and proceed to the Picture. This appointment is suggested as the most convenient for accomplishing an object which I *know* would be interesting to Mr. Heber; and on this account Sir George and Lady B. hope that Mr. H. will dispense with the formality of a note; and in fact at this moment, I have not Mr. Heber's address by me. Will you then have the kindness to communicate this proposal to him; and direct your answer to Sir George Beaumont Grosvenor Sqre. I remain my dear Scott

Very faithfully yours
W. Wordsworth

N.B. Sir George's carriage can contain us all.

369. D. W. to CATHERINE CLARKSON

Address: Mrs Clarkson, Bury, Suffolk.
Stamp: Kendal Penny Post.
MS. British Museum.
K. MY ii. 530, p. 670.

28th June, Wednesday [1815]

My dear Friend,

My heart is sad feeling for you the sadness after parting with our dear Friends.[2] This is the day on which I am sure they would leave

[1] See L. 326, p. 153, n. 3 above.
[2] i.e. W. W. and M. W., who had gone on to stay with the Clarksons after their visit to London.

you; for unwillingly would they give one day to Bocking[1] which might have been given to you and Mary told me that you expected the John Clarksons tomorrow, therefore they *could* only stay till Wednesday. If I had written to them by last night's post my letter might have arrived before their departure from Bocking. They only talked of staying there till Saturday—and after that I know not where to direct to them—but they *may* stay longer at Bocking and this you will know, at all events you must know their address and I wish you would write to tell them by the post of that day when you receive this that you have heard from me, and that we are all well; for I daresay they would expect a letter at Bocking and it was quite impossible for me to write. What comfort have I had in thinking of my Friends while they were with you! In London I never could guess what they were about—but at Bury I could fancy I was among you. Yet ever since they left me I have had the satisfaction of knowing that they had great enjoyment—and this has reconciled me to all. But indeed my dearest Friend I have had an anxious time of which they know nothing. It has been the sickliest season in the North that was ever known—and none of my Flock were spared, but as there was no danger (at least if there *was* any it was over in one day) I thought it much the wisest way to spare my Brother and Sister all anxiety. This in *any* case; but in theirs particularly; for if I had told what was to my mind the truth it would not have been the truth to theirs—They would have magnified the evil a hundred fold and would either have come home immediately or have spent an anxious and miserable time of absence.—I will not enter into particulars. They had violent coughs—fever, hoarseness &c &c—. Mr Scambler ordered a blister immediately for Willy; which removed all alarming symptoms—D had the same applied twice. Thank God Willy is now quite well and D except the cough in the mornings—but they both look very ill—yet Willy's looks mend daily. D is very thin. The weather kept me fluctuating between hope and fear—a damp day always came to throw us back again—and though I was not very fearful for the present evil, because I had the power of watching them continually and guarding against every attack—yet all *tranquillity* of mind and power of *free* enjoyment was destroyed. In short I had a most anxious time, yet I had far less *unhappiness* than if William and Mary had been at home. In the first place I was glad that they were spared the anxiety, and in the second I always suffer a thousand times more from my Brother's unconquerable agitation and fears when Willy ails anything than from any other

[1] Where C. W. was Dean (i.e. incumbent).

cause. But enough of this, we are now doing all as well as possible, and the weather is glorious and likely to keep us well. Only this I am determined upon, to urge Mary to take D and Willy to the sea-side, which I hope will so far strengthen them that they shall not be so liable to catch cold. You have heard of *my* illness—it has left me quite unable to use much exercise, but in other respects I am very well, and I expect soon to regain my strength. I have not mentioned the sea-side to Mary, nor shall I till their return, for even that would alarm them, though they talked of it before they went away. Dorothy is gone with Sophia Crump[1] upon her Asses to inquire of Mr Harden whether his cottage is engaged—I think it would exactly suit Mr Tillbrook but I know of no other that would. Yesterday D. and Miss Grisdale, Willie and I went in a Boat up Rydale Lake. We parted at the Head, D took Willy to Mr de Quinceys and Miss G and I made a three hours walk of it to the Tailor's cottage (now Fanny's, an old servant of ours) where we dined. I called at Mr Newton's who enquired anxiously if Mr Tillbrook was likely to come to Grasmere again—so at all events he might have his old lodgings and a servant could be provided for him; but I told them I thought he would like to be nearer Ambleside and Rydale. I rejoice far more than words can tell you that a time is now appointed for your coming to see us—yet I wish they could have brought you now. If you *are* to settle far from us I am glad that you are going to the neighbourhood of Ipswich[2] for I know that the country is delightful. My Sister gives me chearing accounts of you all. She speaks highly of Tom and says that you are in a comfortable state of health. I hope they have not over fatigued you with walking. Lately I have contented myself with strolls—and creeps—a slow walk to Brathay or Ambleside was quite as much as I could do—and I am now well convinced by experience that fatigue from walking is the worst thing possible for people who have any sort of weakness at the chest or elsewhere internally. My sweet little Willy would delight your very heart he is so full of enjoyment, now that the weather is fine and he is quite well—nothing escapes his observation—I have now no other care for him than to keep him in the shade during the heat of the day—and sitting out of doors is my delight—so we agree very well together; he plays about while I am at work in the shade. Dorothy was a great comfort to me while I was poorly myself—but poor thing! we were both ill together.—

[1] A daughter of Mr. Crump of Allan Bank. See L. 14, pt. i, p. 23, n. 1.

[2] The Clarksons settled at Playford Hall, near Ipswich, in Dec. 1815. See L. 274.

I should not have written you all these stories of illness and anxiety if William and Mary had been with you.—But strange it is that I can talk so long of private concerns when I have so much cause to be anxious for the arrival of this night's post which is to bring tidings of the fate of Nations. Upon the Ambleside coach this morning was affixed a paper 'Great News. *Abdication of Buonaparte*,' but no particulars. Now I do not like the word abdication. What right has he to abdicate, or to have a word to say in the business? I am only afraid that the armies have stopped too soon, as they did before. A few hours will explain all, but I confess I dare not hope that matters will not be again mismanaged. The particulars of the battle of the 18th are dreadful. The joy of victory is indeed an awful thing, and I had no patience with the tinkling of our Ambleside bells upon the occasion; nor with the Prince Regent's *message*, the passage dictated as he says by 'serious consideration,' recommending that further proofs of the munificence of the people should be shewn to the Duke of Wellington. It is perfectly childish to be in such a bustle while even his own family ought to have been *at least* paying the tribute of respectful tears to the memory of the gallant Duke of Brunswick.[1]

11 o'clock. Before I go to bed I must tell you that, saving grief for the lamentable loss of so many brave men, I have read the newspapers of to-night with unmingled triumph; and now I wait anxiously for Friday's post, to know how our armies will proceed. So the abdication was made to his own people! That is as it should be; and I hope he is now a safe prisoner, somewhere—My little messengers brought me a note from Mr Harden saying that he was very sorry Mr Tillbrook could not be his Tenant this year. His cottage is lett for the whole year. Lodgings he might certainly have in abundance, but I know not which way to turn for a house. Mr Jackson, our parson would be glad to take him as a Boarder, and he might make his own terms. His Son from Oxford is here, a very worthy and pleasant good-tempered young man—and the house is very nicely fitted—all very neat—and he has two extremely tidy maidens. Pray tell this to Tillbrook with my kind love and hearty wishes to see his chearful face among us. Give my affectionate Regards to your Father and Sister—believe me I am not a little proud of being remembered by your excellent Father with such lively affection—I trust I shall one day see him again at Bury. France will soon be at peace and open to us and then events will carry me thither this year

[1] Frederick William, killed at Quatre-Bras. See Byron's *Childe Harold*, Canto iii, stanza 23: 'He rushed into the field, and foremost fighting, fell'. 'The battle of the 18th' is of course the battle of Waterloo.

or next, but most likely *not* this year. This has been a most tranquil beautiful evening and I feel myself perfectly well—strong and well, which in truth I have not done for I believe these six weeks the day through till to-day, though I have often said to Mary that I was well. So I was; for I had nothing to complain of but indescribable uncomfortableness. Poor Mrs Lloyd has been ever [so] much worse than I in the same complaint—so has Charles. They are gone to Allonby[1] with their 4 girls, one boy and 3 maids. I trust the change of air will entirely cure Mrs Lloyd. She was much better before she left home. Do write to me immediately—a 'short letter' is all I ask for you must have very little spare time. I hope Mary told Mrs Kitchener that I remembered her and sometimes talk of her. I must go to bed to keep myself well—My little ones are all sleeping sweetly, yet I ought not to include John among the little—and very soon they will all be big. It seems but the other day since Tom Clarkson was in petticoats. God bless you for ever my dearest Friend. Do not fail to write to Mary the day you receive this, telling her we are all quite well. I do not reckon upon seeing them before the 15th. They will be loth to leave Coleorton[2] and I do not wish them to hurry—a few days or a week will make little difference to us, and the longer they stay the better we shall look when we greet them. Adieu adieu —what a scrawl! Longman has sent 'the Champion' with a long criticism on William's poems.[3]

The White Doe has arrived at last—I long to know what you think of it.

I have seen the British Critic which contains a Review by a Friend of the Coleridges' which between ourselves I think a very feeble composition. It was highly praised to me.

Thomas Wilkinson has sent a poem on the death of his [?Mother] Hannah which made Dorothy[4] and me weep bitterly. It is no great thing as a poem, but very affecting, and in parts very sweet in simple expressions.

Thursday morning—another beautiful day—We are all well and all alive with the bleating of sheep. Clipping day at our neighbours'.

[1] A small seaside resort on the coast of Cumberland.

[2] Sir George Beaumont's home in Leicestershire, where the Wordsworths had spent the winter of 1806/7.

[3] John Scott was editor of the *Champion*. See L. 366 above.

[4] i.e. Dora.

370. D. W. to CATHERINE CLARKSON

Address: Mrs Clarkson, Bury, Suffolk.
Stamp: Kendal Penny Post. *Endorsed*: Septr 1815.
MS. British Museum.
K (—). *MY ii. 531, p. 674.*

Tuesday 15th August [1815]

My dear Friend,

Mr Tillbrook arrived this day week with his little pony and little carriage, all in fresh plight, and he himself well satisfied with the pleasures of his journey of which he gave us a humourous account. We cannot, however, pretty as the pony is, look at it without regretting that a pair of asses were not substituted by his Master, who might just as well have gone back in the coach which would have saved time, and this is the more to be lamented as he declares he cannot give us more than a fortnight on his brother's account. I always liked Tillbrooke very much; and his character rises in my esteem seeing the day through with what uncomplaining chearfulness he submits to all privations. He who was so active and vigorous, and who so much delighted in exercise, and is equally chearful now that he is compelled to measure his distances before he ventures to set out upon a walk however tempting, and to watch the clouds in the sky lest he should increase his lameness by being exposed to a shower. He is an affectionate, honest, upright man, detesting vice and scorning flattery; and in these days when French impudence and French vices seem to have dazzled the judgements and vitiated the feelings of one half of the nation such a man should be doubly praised by honest English hearts. Oh I am sick of the adulation, the folly, the idle Curiosity which was gathered together round the ship[1] that held the dastardly spirit that has so long been the scourge of all whom he *could* injure. *He* kill himself! No, he is too much of a coward, and we can be so dull of perception—so insensible to the distinctions between vice and virtue, as to bend—to bow—to take off our hats to him—and call him great—his looks!—fancy them filled with magnanimity—but he is not worth talking about—and how I got on so far I do not know. As to the French Government and the French people they too would not be worth a thought, if it were not that, left to themselves they would soon plague us and the rest of the world. Would that all the English had Prussian hearts

[1] i.e. the *Bellerophon*, on which Napoleon was held prisoner in Plymouth Harbour until his departure for St. Helena. Sightseers paid to be rowed out to the ship on the chance of a glimpse of 'Bony'.

and that our Generals and Councillors had the will of Blucher. Then we should not have seen the Jacobins lift up their audacious heads—there would have been no fear—no affected magnanimity in our councils. It is impossible for me to think of going to Paris this year. We have had letters from our Friends written just after the return of the king. They were in great joy at that event, and urged me and my companions to go, all being safe and quiet—at the same time they awaited our determination respecting Caroline's coming over.[1] We could only answer that the time of meeting my Br and Sr was gone by, and that we could not appoint any particular place, knowing of nobody about to return from Paris, and having no Friends in London to whom we could with propriety entrust her; but we proposed that the Mother should look out for some person or persons coming to London, to whose care she might be consigned till we could hear from her of her arrival there. This I trust may not be difficult as Madame Vallon has a numerous acquaintance—I wish you had been in London—in lodgings—the great difficulty will be there; for people who might be relied upon for the journey must be constantly coming from Paris. We hope to see Sara before the end of next month with John Monkhouse; our house will then be full to overflowing; for the Beaumonts will be here again. They are now in very small lodgings at Keswick, after having spent 9 delightful summer days at Rydale—wandering all the mornings in the park, which is as good as our own. We spent one day on Windermere and one at Grasmere with them. They were enchanted with our home and everything around us. Oh my dearest Friend why have *you* not been here? I will give over writing to you I declare if you do not come next summer. There is no pleasure in talking to you in this way of things and places that you have never seen. You owe us all—each and every one a visit now—for we have all been to see you and this I am glad to think of. Tillbrooke will tell you about each of our young ones, their dispositions and ways, their faults and virtues. He is very fond of Willy and perceives with us, though his attainments by Books are yet very small, that he is likely if God grant him life and health to take delight in learning. He has a strong memory and a lively fancy.—A fortnight ago it was determined that I should go with him and D to the sea-side. *I* was deputed to go on account of my bad looks, want of strength and appetite, but all at once I took to eating like a ploughman, and am now quite well; and as Mr

[1] There had evidently been a plan for Caroline to come to England and meet William and Mary in London. As a London meeting was no longer possible, and yet Caroline's coming is still being discussed, it is probable that D. W. would have gone to meet her.

Scambler seemed to think that washing all over in cold water would be just as likely as the sea to harden Wm against the winter we have given up the scheme. Dorothy is also washed every morning in the same way. We had one terrible struggle with her; but she now likes it and I hope we shall have no more difficulty about the matter with her or Willy, and that an ugly cold may not come in the way to stop us. Dorothy's temper is very obstinate by fits, and at such times nothing but rigourous confinement can subdue her. She is not to be moved by the feelings, and the misfortune is that the more indulgence or pleasure she has, the more unmanageable she is. Yet she is affectionate in the extreme and patient and docile whenever she is called upon to perform the duty of attending upon the sick or helping to nurse—or to do anything that is of importance. Her faculties are very quick and if she were *steady* she would learn anything—industrious enough she is at times and indeed she never goes about anything lazily;—but she is wandering—unthinking—unsteady. If a perfect school could be found that would be the place for her. She now goes to Miss Fletcher[1] and learns Latin at home. We find we cannot keep her regular at home now that we have so much company. Miss Fletcher's teacher, under whose care Dorothy is chiefly, is very well pleased with her. John is to be boarded with Mr. Dawes.[2] Some change we find absolutely necessary to give him a chance of being rouzed to activity and exertion. We have no other fault to find with him but extreme laziness. His faculties certainly are slow, but he has a sound understanding and a noble nature. He is beloved by the little Boys at school—and *respected* by the great ones, for his probity and honourable spirit. John may always be trusted—He would not betray a secret for all the world. But I tire you telling old things over again, however, you who have so anxiously watched the dispositions of your own son, will bear with me. Pray give my kind love to Mrs Kitchener, and tell her that I was [?gra] tified by the account given me by my Sister of her [? daughter] by the pretty specimen of my young Friend's geographical labours which she sent to John. In her medical capacity, I must call upon her for her judgement concerning the place in Willy's head which had alarmed his Mother. Before your answer came we had applied mustard plaisters; but *for my part* I could not fancy that it ailed anything and my sister hopes that it is really nothing; but consult Mrs Kitchener. The place has no roughness—It is a small triangular spot—without hair and rather of a whiter colour than the rest of the head. That is all which can be

[1] See *SH* 18, p. 58. She had opened a school for girls in Ambleside.

[2] The Revd. John Dawes, vicar and schoolmaster at Ambleside.

seen. Give my love to your good Father and to your Sister. You will guess that I was very sorry to find that the domestic troubles which you hinted at in one of your letters to me some time ago, had an especial connection with your sister and her husband, I was however much pleased when with this information I was at the same time assured that she bore the change with chearfulness; and that her future happiness was not likely to be materially affected by it. Yet I do not like the notion of Mr Corsby's becoming a farmer—Farming is a bad trade and a very anxious one at this time—Sara gives us a sad account of George Hutchison's prospects—his farm is small and Tom is sure that it will not do more than pay his rent and labourers—or something to that effect as Sara reported. At all events it will not half maintain his house. They at Hindwell are growing poorer every year—and this, though they have happy contented minds, is a serious evil now that there is a prospect of an increasing Family. I wish that Tom had not bought that Estate in Wales—it binds them in banishment from this part of England as long as they possess it; locks up their money at present and pays poor interest. As to us *we* shall never grow rich; for I now perceive clearly that till my dear Brother is laid in his grave his writings will not produce any profit. This I now care no more about and *shall* never *more* trouble my head concerning the sale of them. I once thought *The White Doe* might have helped off the other,[1] but I now perceive it can hardly help itself. It is a pity it was published in so expensive a form because some are thereby deprived of the pleasure of reading it; but however cheap his poems might be I am sure it will be very long before they have an extensive sale—nay it will not be while he is alive to know it. God be thanked he has no *mortification* on this head and I may safely say that those who are most nearly connected with him have not an atom of that species of disappointment. We have too [? rooted] a confidence in the purity of his intentions, and the power with which they are executed. His writings will live—will comfort the afflicted and animate the happy to purer happiness when we and our little cares are all forgotten.

I trust my dear Friend that your hopes in your son will be fulfilled, that he will pass through the University with Credit, and become a good and useful member of society—I am very glad that he is to study Mathematics in the North: for that seems to secure you to us for next summer. Tell dear Mr Clarkson I shall never forgive him if he does not bring you. I want to see both him and Tom very much—Cannot Tom bring us the curricle? He used to glory in a

[1] i.e. *Poems, including Lyrical Ballads*, 1815.

'Dicky Cart', but perhaps he has now a nobler ambition, to curb the fiery steed. Yet I think he would condescend as an act of friendship to us and of mercy to our limbs for age does tell upon their strength in spite of us. I am sure it would be of great use to Mary to have a little carriage to drive about in and to church. As for me I am in general as well able to walk as ever I was—yet at times I feel a difference—a little illness tells [more] than formerly—and I could not take a long [walk] (for instance from Eusemere to Grasmere) with so little fatigue as 15 years ago.

A sad sad scrawl.

I hope Mr John Clarkson's prospects with the Whitheads are better.

Tillbrooke's best regards—He begs you will let his Mother know he is well. Write I pray you and soon and believe [me] ever your true and affectionate D W.

371. W. W. to BENJAMIN ROBERT HAYDON[1]

Address: B. R. Haydon Esq, 41 Gt Marlbro' St, London.
MS. untraced.
Haydon (—) MY ii. 532, p. 679.

Lowther Castle, Sept 12—1815.

My dear Sir,

Agreeable to your request, (for which I am much obliged to you, and to your friend for his offer of undertaking the Bust)[2] I forwarded to you from Rydale Mount a few days ago the dimensions of my pericranium, taken by the hand of Sir George Beaumont—He is entitled to our common thanks for he exerted himself not a little upon the occasion; and I hope the performance will answer your purpose. Sir George begged me say that the hair on that part of the skull where the crown is, is thin; so that a little of the skull appears bald; and Sir George thinks that a similar baldness there might have

[1] Benjamin Robert Haydon (1786–1846), painter and art critic, friend of Leigh Hunt and Keats, had made a life-mask of W. W. in June 1815. See Haydon's *Diary*, ed. W. B. Pope (1960), i, p. 450.

[2] It appears that Haydon had asked Leigh Hunt's brother John to make a bust from a 'profile' or cut-out silhouette made by Sir George Beaumont. (See L. 372.) It was made in clay (Haydon to W. W. [1816], MS. *WL.*), but was probably not considered successful, for no caste is known and the first bust of W. W. was made by Sir Francis Chantrey in 1820. See Blanshard, *Portraits of Wordsworth*, pp. 50–1, 145.

a good effect in the bust. I should have sent the drawing immediately on Receipt of your Letter, but I had nobody near who would execute it.—

I hope Christ's Entry into Jerusalem[1] goes on to your satisfaction: I cannot doubt but that Picture will do you huge credit; and raise the Reputation of Art in this Country.—I was much pleased to hear that Mr Scott is gone again to the Continent; as his Tour will undoubtedly prove both entertaining and instructive in the perusal.—

I have not forgotten your Request to have a few verses of my Composition in my own handwriting; and the first short Piece that I compose, if it be not totally destitute of merit, shall be sent you.[2] I hope also that you bear in mind the promise you threw out of letting me have some production of your pencil; for my gratification would be high in possessing a memorial of you to place by the side of those I have received from Sir George.

I am writing in a crowded room of this splendid Castle at a Sofa Table, where two other Gentlemen are engaged in the same occupation; and one of the company has turned all eyes on us by [decl]aring that we look like three boys at a writing School.—This may plead my excuse for this incoher[ent] Letter; which I shall conclude with assuring you that Mrs Wordsworth and I often remember with pleasure the agreeable hours which we passed in your Company, and that we cherish the hope, that in the course of next Summer we may see you at Rydale Mount.—Sir George and Lady B. are now here—they have taken a small House at Keswick for the summer months of the three ensuing years.—

Farewell; and believe [me] my dear Sir,
with sincere respect
faithfully yours
Wm Wordsworth

[1] An immense picture by Haydon into which he introduced the faces of Wordsworth and Keats. See Blanshard, op. cit., Plates *6a, 6b*. The painting is now in Mount St. Mary's Seminary, Norwood, Ohio.

[2] See L. 377 below.

372. W. W. to B. R. HAYDON

Address: B. R. Haydon Esqre, Great Marlbro' St., London.
MS. untraced
MY ii. 533, p. 681.

Rydale Mount Oct^{br} 8th
1815

My dear Sir,

This Letter will be presented to you by Mr Monkhouse,[1] a respected Friend of mine, and a near Relation of Mrs Wordsworth, whom I have begged to charge himself with the delivery of it that the enclosed Pencil-case may safely reach your Hands.—The one which you kindly received from me in return for that I possess from you, was so small as not [to] be likely to be any use [to] you nor had it been so long in my possession nor of so much service to me as the present, which I hope that you will preserve for my sake.

Many thanks for your obliging letter; the one for Sir George I forwarded to him at Mulgrave Castle, where he has, no doubt received it, some time since. I am glad that you liked the Profile;[2] Sir George and Lady B— Mrs W— and my Sister thought that it resembled me much: but Mrs W— is sure that the upper part of the forehead does not project as much as mine.

I was greatly concerned to hear that your eyes had failed you— To a Painter this is more lamentable than to any one else. It would give me much pleasure to hear that you are better.

Mr Monkhouse would be much gratified by a sight of your great Picture, or anything that you [*rest of letter missing*].

373. W. W. to C. W.

Address: Rev^{d} Dr. Wordsworth, Deanery, Bocking, Essex.
Postmark: 16 Oct 1815. *Stamp*: Kendal.
MS. Jonathan Wordsworth.
TLS, 12 June 1959.

Friday Night, Kendal
[13 October 1815]

My dear Brother,

I am just returned home, after accompanying Charles and Sophia to Manchester, where we arrived last night. I saw them into the Birmingham Mail; Mrs Lloyd will no Doubt give you an account

[1] Tom Monkhouse, M. W.'s first cousin. He was present at the Christmas party at Haydon's on 28 Dec. 1817 at which Keats, Lamb, and W. W. were all present.

[2] See L. 371 above.

LIFE-MASK OF WORDSWORTH
by B. R. Haydon, 1815, in the National Portrait Gallery

of [the] journey [and] the state of her Husband's health—after his arrival at Birmingham whither it was absolutely necessary that he should go.

Your Letter my dear Brother affected us all deeply; we received it on Wednesday night; and I have not since had time to sit down and write to you, as I could wish; scarcely have I had ten minutes that I could call my own—Dorothy is at Brathay with the Children,[1] but I left her most anxious to contribute to your present support. Let us hear from you immediately; and who you have with you; some female friend I trust. If you wish that Dorothy should come to Bocking she will do so, as soon as you desire—Heaven preserve you, and what remains to you on earth of yours: for her who is gone[2] she is among the blessed—farewell, our prayers shall not be wanting on your behalf—for myself as a Husband I feel for you to the utmost—I would write more could I suggest any consolation; I only can assure you, of what you well know, our heart-felt sympathy and our wish to relieve you, in any way you can point out—

Your ever affectionate Brother—
Wm Wordsworth

374. D. W. to JANE MARSHALL

Address: Mrs. Marshall, Hallsteads, Ulswater, Penrith.
Stamp: Kendal Penny Post. *Endorsed*: Death of Mrs. P. Wordsworth. Mr. Lloyd's insanity.
MS. WL.
MY ii. 534, p. 681.

Sunday 13th October[3] [1815.]

My dear Friend,

A melancholy event has taken place since I received your letter. My Brother Christopher's Wife[4] is dead. About a fortnight ago she was safely delivered of a still-born girl after 'tremendous sufferings' during four and twenty hours; but when my Brother informed us of this she was going on perfectly well, though much afflicted at the loss of her Child, she having set her heart upon a Daughter. She had had 5 Sons; two of whom died of convulsions in infancy. She continued perfectly well till last thursday but one, when she had some

[1] The Lloyds had at this time eight children, whom D. W. had gone to look after at Low Brathay, when their father Charles Lloyd was taken to Birmingham suffering from insanity. See L. 374 below.

[2] i.e. Priscilla W., sister of Charles Lloyd. She died after the birth of her fourth child. See L. 374 below.

[3] Sunday was in fact Oct. 15.

[4] See L. 373 above.

flying spasms, but in no respect alarming until within three hours of her death, which took place yesterday week (Saturday). My Brother wrote to us immediately after the event, saying that he then felt that he had the power to perform a task, which he should probably soon be unable to perform. Only conceive the shock to him! Four hours before he took the pen in hand to tell us of his Wife's death he had not had the faintest idea that her life was in danger. This is a sad history yet I have another even more dismal (though not immediately connected with our own family) to communicate. Mr. Lloyd, Priscilla's Brother and our neighbour, has been in a state of mental derangement during eleven weeks, with no other companion but his Wife, no attendant but a man-servant occasionally called in when coercion was necessary. Poor dear Mrs. Lloyd (she has a family of eight Children!) was nearly worn out with sorrow and watching, in which nobody could relieve her till latterly, namely within about three weeks, during which time I have been almost daily here, I or my Sister being the only persons whom Mr. Lloyd could bear to see or to have sitting near him. To me he has never objected—he liked me when he was well, and the same liking has continued during his woeful depression, though for a long time he was confined to his bed-room and could not even see me. It has been a great comfort to me that I have been able in the slightest degree to relieve Mrs. Lloyd. There was a time when he would not lose sight of her even for a ¼ of an hour in the course of the day—and she got little or no sleep at nights. The end of all has been a determination on Mrs. Lloyd's part to go with her Husband to Birmingham, where there are medical men devoted to the management of insane persons; and either under his Father's Roof, or in a house of their own as shall be judged best, she will place him under such superintendence. They left Brathay on Thursday morning and my Brother accompanied them as far as Manchester, and arrived at home yesterday morning, bringing on the whole a better account of their journey than we could have expected. Mrs. Lloyd's intention, when she left Brathay, was to return in *a fortnight* to settle her Boys with Mr Dawes at school, and to take her 4 girls with her to Birmingham; but as Mr. Lloyd's Father is now gone to Bocking to my Brother Christopher I think it probable that she may not return hither so soon, as she can make no final arrangements without a personal consultation with old Mr. Lloyd. In the meantime I am stationed at Brathay with the care of the Children. I shall be mostly here through the day, and always at nights to gather the stragglers together and keep them to their business round a warm fire-side. Poor things! they are happy, chearful, tractable Children, and I find a melancholy consolation in being of some little use to their dear Mother. Perhaps, too, after her return she may wish me to stay and I cannot leave the house as long as I can do any good here. Thus, my dear Friend, you see how sad reverses may interrupt our pleasant scheme of spending a little time with you this Autumn. At present it is utterly impossible to say whether we may be able to cross the Mountains at all or not; for it is possible that my Brother Christopher may summon me to Bocking. No other female Friend can stay with him any length of time, Priscilla having no unmarried Sisters. William has told Christopher that if he wishes it I will go to him for a time. Of course you will conclude that I have no thoughts of residing with him. I could not give up my present home for any other, but perhaps he will find comfort in me in his present desolation; and I am glad that it is in my power to offer him my feeble support.—My first impulses would have led me to go immediately; but I concluded, as it has proved, that old Mr. Lloyd would make no delay, and if one or two friends be near him it is enough, especially as I think that a Miss Chapman who was like a Sister to Priscilla and was half her time with them, will probably also have gone to him. She cannot stay long should she actually be with him now; but upon mature consideration I thought it best to wait for a summons, as in the very first agonies of such a loss nobody can be of any service in the way of society or of withdrawing the mind from its affliction—grief will have its way. I will write to you again as soon as we hear from Christopher, for I am sure you will share my anxiety concerning him. The news of Priscilla's death came on the evening preceding Mr. and Mrs. Lloyd's departure—she durst not communicate it to her husband, so, poor Soul! she travelled with that secret in her breast. I was here at the time and saw them go off at 7 o'clock on Thursday morning.

My dear Jane I am sorry to distress you with this woful history. Death is nothing to the misery of living as poor Charles Lloyd lives now in the wofullest agonies of utter depression; and his Wife's sufferings are a hundred-fold more difficult to support than the final separation by Death. I hope, however, that the burthen will be lightened, that it may possibly be removed, as Mr. Lloyd has never before been put under proper management, and as he has recovered from other slighter fits of insanity without such management.

I am going to write to Mrs. Rawson; but I have not spirits to relate a second time the distresses of this house. I shall only tell her of poor Priscilla's Death, therefore keep this letter, and when you have an opportunity send it to her, or, when you meet, read it to her.

Give my kind love to your Sisters and all your Family. I wish I may be able to see them.

All were well at Rydal yesterday. Dorothy and John are here, and are gone to Church with six of the Lloyds. They are to dine with us today, and D will stay all night and go to school in the morning with Sophia Lloyd.

We are over head and ears in debt to you—there is Miss Hutchinson's grey gown besides the yarn cloth, and perhaps some other etceteras. If unfortunately we should not meet this year you must send us the bill, but I would fain hope that we may meet at Hallsteads.

[*Unsigned.*]

375. W. W. to ROBERT LUMB[1]

Address: To Robt Lumb Esqre, Lowther, nr Penrith.
Stamp: Kendal Penny Post.
Endorsed: Oct 14. 1815 W. Wordsworth Esqre.
MS. Lonsdale MSS., Record Office, The Castle, Carlisle.
Hitherto unpublished.

Rydal Mount, Ambleside, 14th Oct, 1815

Sir,

I beg leave to acquaint you that your Bill on Goslings and Sharpe by Lord Lonsdale, for Five Hundred pounds—came safe to the Office.

I am Sir,
For Willm Wordsworth Esqre
Your obedient Servant,
John Carter.
signed,
Wm Wordsworth

(Turn over)

Dear Sir,

Agreeable to your request I have inquired into what has been done at Elterwater.—I went to the Spot accompanied by the Revd Thos Jackson Agent for the Rydale Hall Family.[2]—It appears that the object of the Work, is to make a readier passage for the Water in time of Flood: this has been in some degree accomplished by a cut in the rock, for some little space, of between two or three feet deep; but to be of any material benefit it must be considerably

[1] One of Lord Lonsdale's agents. The baptisms of his children are recorded in the parish registers of Penrith from 1804 onwards, the family being 'of Lowther'. This letter is an example of W. W.'s keen interest in the details of local events and of the trouble he was willing to take in investigating them.

[2] See L. 193, pt. i, p. 408, n. 1.

widened as well as deepened; and should the Earl of Lonsdale, Sir Daniel and Lady le Fleming, and the tenants give their consent, I do not even then think that the work can proceed for want of Subscribers; for nobody seems to take much interest in it except Mr. Harden[1] who first began it, without considering that he had no right to make any attempt of the sort till he had previously procured the assent of Lord Lonsdale, of the Rydale Hall Family, and of all the tenants, who have Lands lying below the place where the Cut has been made.—Of this Mr Harden is now convinced, and regrets much that he should have infringed the rules of law, in this case, through precipitation.—*The work is to be suspended*, while the consent of the Lord is procured and that of the tenants.— — The Earl of Lonsdale is in no way likely either to be benefited or injured by the measure—His Lordship has no Lands in the course of the stream or adjoining the Lake; nor is the fishing of the Lake worth a Farthing. But Mr Jackson tells me that the Family of Rydale Hall pay to the Earl of Lonsdale as paramount Lord a small sum (five shillings and fourpence I believe) for the right of fishing in Elterwater and some other small waters and rivers in the neighbourhood —If the tenants give their consent to going forward with the work I do not see a shadow of Reason why his Lordship should withhold his—The utmost that it is possible to be done is merely to let the Water run off more speedily in floods; for as to *draining* the Lake it is quite out of the question or even lowering it so as to affect it more than a few inches. I told Mr Harden that, this being evidently the case, I was [surprised] that he should ever have alluded to the intention of draining for the acquisition of soil. Upon which he acknowledged that it was quite a mistaken notion of his, and he seemed sorry that it had been mentioned in the Paper entitled Thoughts etc. sent to you — — Could the Lake be drained the beauty of the country would be rather improved; so that on this account Lord Lonsdale would have no reason to refuse his assent.— Would it not then be advisable that in answer to Mr Harden's Letter you should simply express a regret that the work had been so hastily begun; but that if a memorial were sent to the Earl of Lonsdale, signed by the Tenantry, and the other persons interested, there is little reason to believe that his Lordship would withhold his consent for the work going forward.

I am dear Sir
your obedient Servant
Wm Wordsworth

[1] Of Brathay Hall. See L. 304 above.

376. W. W. to CATHERINE CLARKSON

Address: Mrs Clarkson, Bury St. Edmunds, Suffolk.
Stamp: Kendal Penny Post. *Endorsed*: Nov 1815 W. Wordsworth.
MS. Cornell.
K (—). *MY 535, p. 684* (—).

Rydale Mount Nov^{br} 25th 1815

My dear Friend

We were wholly ignorant of the death of our dear and lamented Friend,[1] till your Letter informed us of it. Sarah is on a visit to Kendal, but Mary and Dorothy were sitting by me when I opened your Letter, which seeing how short it was, I was sure, conveyed some bad news—We are truely afflicted by the event; as he was much valued by us all; and we looked forward to their resettling themselves in our neighbourhood as one of the pleasantest hopes that this Family entertained. Many, many times has he been present to my mind;—in the course of last week, particularly; for my Sister has just made a little scarlet Spenser for Willy out of a uniform Jacket which dear Luff left for the use of any of the Children; it has been worn every day with great pride by the little Boy, and to the no small pleasure of my heart, in seeing the memorial of my absent Friend, employed in a way that he would have delighted to witness. ——I am happy to learn that he has left enough behind him to make his Widow independent. I hope and trust that she will draw towards her Husband's Friends, both from the inclinations of her own mind; and from a desire to fulfill his wishes. We shall all be most happy to render her any support in our power, both for her own and her departed Husband's sake.—This news has made me more dejected and melancholy than I can express; Luff's death is truly a loss to me; as it has cut a pure and innocent hope out of my life; a hope founded upon long-lived remembrances. And at the age of forty-six which is almost mine, there is little reason to give the future credit for new acquisitions of this kind of possession, to supply in some sort what is taken from us of the old.—

We thank you for having communicated this Intelligence. I know my dear Friend that you will have felt upon this occasion much as we have done—and that your mind will not have overlooked the consolation which we all feel in being assured, that, though it was [not] allowed to him to realize the pleasant dreams which he had formed of returning to these hills, and passing here the remainder of his days, he lived long enough to place his Widow in a state of

[1] Captain Luff. For the Luffs' emigration to Mauritius, see Letters 234, pt. i, p. 526 and 303 above.

independence by his virtues; and to prove to his Friends, as well as to be satisfied within his own mind, that he had conquered the rebellious part of his nature, and was capable of persevering in a rational course.— —

I am sorry that dear Sarah is not here; as she will be much distressed, and will stand in need of the company of those who can best sympathize with her.—

Luff was a genuine lover of his Country, and a true and enlightened Friend of Mankind. On this account I think it right that his surviving Friends should not suffer him to pass out of the world, without a notice or record of his worth, which may stand a chance of being generally perused. The main difficulty lies in finding out a channel for things of this kind. A notice in a newspaper must be short; and those in the obituaries of magazines, are, I fear little read; there being no magazine existing which appears to be in general circulation.—What is your opinion of the best way of doing this?—With affectionate remembrances to yourself and Mr Clarkson

I remain your faithful Friend
W Wordsworth

377. W. W. to B. R. HAYDON

Address: B. R. Haydon Esq[r], Great Marlborough Street, London.
MS. untraced.
Haydon (—). *K* (—). *MY ii. 536, p. 685.*

Rydale Mount near Ambleside
Dec[br] 21st 1815.

My dear Sir,

I sit down to perform my promise of sending you the first little Poem I might compose on my arrival at home. I am grieved to think what a time has elapsed since I last paid my devoirs to the Muses, and not less so to know that now in the depth of Winter when I hoped to resume my Labours, I continue to be called from them by unavoidable engagements. Tomorrow I quit Rydale Mount[1] and shall be absent a considerable time. But no more of this. I was much hurt to learn that you continue to suffer from weakness of sight and to be impeded in your Labours by the same cause. Why did not you tell me what progress you had made in your grand Picture?—and how far you are satisfied with your performance.— I am not surprized that Canova expressed himself so highly pleased with the Elgin Marbles. A Man must be senseless as a clod, or

[1] He did not actually leave until Christmas Day. See L. 379 below. The visit was to R. W. at Sockbridge. See L. 378, p. 261 below.

perverse as a Fiend, not to be enraptured with them—Have you read the works of the Abbé Winkelman[1] on the study of the Antique, in Painting and Sculpture. He enjoys a high reputation among the most judicious of the German Criticks—His Works are unknown to me, except a short treatise entitled Reflections concerning the imitation of the Grecian Artists in Painting and Sculpture, in a series of Letters. A translation of this is all I have read having met with it the other day upon a Stal[l] at Penrith—It appears to me but a slight thing; at the best superficial, and in some points, particularly what respects allegorical Painters, in the last Letter, very erroneous. This Book of mine was printed at Glasgow 1766.—Probably the Author has composed other works upon the same subject, better digested; and to these his high reputation may be owing.—Now for the Poems, which are Sonnets; one composed the evening I received your last Letter the other next day, and the third the day following, I shall not transcribe them in the order in which they [were] written, but inversely. The last you will find was occasioned, I might say inspired if there be any inspiration in it, by your Letter. The second records a feeling excited in me by the object which it describes, in the month of October last; and the first notices a still earlier sensation which the revolution of the seasons impressed me with last Autumn—

[*Here follow the three Sonnets*:

I

While not a leaf seems faded, *etc. as* Oxf. W., *p.* **263**, *but*
l. 2 harvests *for* harvest;
ll. 9–10 For me, a lone enthusiast not untrue
To service long endeared,
l. 11 Through the green leaves,
ll. 13–14 Mid frost and snow, poetic ecstasy
Joys nobler far than, etc.

II

How clear, how keen, *etc. as* Oxf. W., *p.* **263**, *but*
l. 3 as smooth as Heaven *for* smooth as the sky
l. 13 vicissitude *for* vicissitudes *and l.* 14 Have *for* Has

III

High is our calling, Friend! etc. *as* Oxf. W., *p.* **260**.
but l. 12 Soul]

[1] Johann Joachim W. (1717–68), pioneer archaeologist, author of *Geschichte der Kunst des Altertums*, 1764.

I wish the things had been better worthy of your acceptance, and of the careful preservation with which you will be inclined to honour this little offering of my regard.

With high respect
I remain my dear Sir
Most faithfully yours
Wm Wordsworth

Mrs W— desires her kindest remembrances: Miss H— is absent.

378. D. W. to CATHERINE CLARKSON

Address: Mrs Clarkson, Playford Hall, near Ipswich, Suffolk. *Erased and re-addressed*: To Mrs Clarkson, Bury St. Edmunds, Suffolk.
Postmark: 27 Dec 1815. Ipswich. *Stamp*: Kendal Penny Post.
MS. British Museum.
K. MY ii. 537, p. 687.

23rd December [1815]

My dear Friend,

I have not the heart to congratulate you upon your arrival at your new habitation. At this bitter season you cannot but miss many accustomed comforts, and it is not the time for the attractions of a country residence to shew themselves. I only venture to hope that your health does not suffer from the change, and if so I trust your spirits will bear you up against what is disagreeable, hoping for new pleasures and comforts in the milder season. In weather precisely of this kind, except that the snow did not then lie *thick* upon the ground, on the shortest day of the year, sixteen years ago, did William and I at 5 o'clock in the evening enter our cottage at Grasmere.[1] We found no preparation except beds, without curtains, in the rooms upstairs, and a dying spark in the grate of the gloomy parlour. Your entrance upon your new house is not like this, but we were young and healthy and had attained an object long desired, we had returned to our native mountains, there to live; so we cared not for any annoyances that a little exertion on our parts would speedily remove.—The melancholy changes of last year may at times render you less fit to struggle with little difficulties around you from the depression of spirit that they may cause, yet on the other hand they will tend to make such difficulties appear trivial. Last night we received *one* frank containing a very interesting letter from a Frenchman in the Isle of Bourbon to poor Luff, and a sheet of his journal which we suppose is the unfinished conclusion; but

[1] i.e. on Friday, 20 Dec. 1799. See Mark Reed, *Wordsworth, The Chronology of the Early Years* (Harvard, 1967), pp. 283–4 and n. *EY* 126, p. 273.

another frank certainly ought to have come; for there are two sheets wanting between. We should have been very uneasy about this if the like had not happened before, the missent frank arriving by the next post. We trust it will arrive to-morrow night—and that there will be a few lines from you, explanatory of the how and the why and the *when* the Frenchman's interesting letter came into your hands, and what further than the letter tells you may know concerning him—also we hope there will be a word or two about yourselves and Playford Hall. We have now nine sheets of the journal—I do not intend to *read* it until we have the whole, yet I have looked at and been detained by many parts and carried away, until the lively recollection of our dear Friend whom we never more shall see,[1] became so painful that I stopped and was glad to renew my resolution of reading no more until I could read the whole. It will be a great pity if he has not written an account of the Mauritius. The present journal is invaluable to his Friends as a record of his mind; and most interesting to all it must be for the manner in which it is done. I need not ask you if you should hear of anything concerning Mrs Luff, or any further particulars concerning her Husband, to write immediately; we anxiously wish to know all that can be known.—I know not what to say respecting the wide-spreading distresses of the Corsbies—You have rested upon the grand consolation in cases such as these, and your Sister you say bears her losses with magnanimity; but indeed, my dearest Friend, I was very much distressed by the contents of your last letter and more especially for your Father, and for the possibility of dear Mr Clarkson being involved in anxieties which may disturb your quiet and his. The Corsbies are young and may begin life afresh, yet I do not like the idea of their burying themselves upon a farm—Why cannot he enter again into business? Farming with a large Capital is no profitable concern and with a very small one it is a continual care—besides that the pair must be exclusively confined to each other—shut up by their own fire-side; and there is a danger that their thoughts and affections will gradually be wholly centred there and in the few fields which with anxiety they will cultivate. Pray give my kindest love to your Sister and to your dear Father.—We had a letter from Tillbrooke very lately—he appears to be more desirous than ever to procure a little hold in this country; and we are now not without hopes of getting the very spot of his choice, the Ivy cottage at the foot of the Rydal hill.[2] You remember it I am sure—

[1] i.e. Captain Luff. See L. 376 above.

[2] Now incorporated into the Glen Rothay Hotel.

It is the very place for him, to see all strangers passing and to greet all familiar faces, and catch every opportunity of friendly chat which is his delight—and much more so since his lameness. Sara has been a month at Kendal—thence she went to Penrith, and was to stay there a few days and to go to Miss Barker at Keswick on Monday, but on that day the snow began, and on Wednesday the road was completely closed up. It was the most dreadful day we have had these sixteen years—so we have had no communication with Keswick this week, though the day before yesterday the coach did come over the Rays with six horses; and some few travellers have passed since. Last winter but one we had not half so much snow. The coach was never stopped during the whole winter except for twelve hours. Friday was the day fixed for William and Mary to go with Mrs Lloyd and a Miss Alne in a chaise to Keswick—thence William and M were to have gone to Lowther the next day, and to Sockbridge and Appleby. A thaw is now beginning, and if it holds, or if we have no more snow, in case the frost does not continue they may get off the day after Christmas day; but at present they could not travel without four horses, which would not agree with the purses of the parties concerned. William's object is to settle accounts with my Brother Richard, and to visit Dr Satterthwaite; Mary's to visit the Doctor; and Miss Weir at Appleby. They will be absent at least a fortnight. Yesterday fortnight William and I set forward upon a like journey, to make the preparations necessary for a final settlement with Richard. The weather was frosty without snow, and I never in my youngest days, in the summer season, had a more delightful excursion; except for the intervention of melancholy recollections of persons gone, never to return. We set off at one o'clock, walked over Kirkstone, and reached Patterdale by daylight; slept there, and rose early the next morning, determined to walk to Hallsteads (Mr. Marshall's new house, built upon Skelly Nab) before breakfast —the lake was calm as a mirror, the rising sun tinged with pink light the snow-topped mountains, and we agreed that all we saw in the grander parts of the scene was more beautiful even than in summer. At Hallsteads we breakfasted, rested till twelve o'clock. I parted from William at Red Hills and he went to Sockbridge, and I proceeded to Penrith, where at a little before three o'clock I arrived without the least fatigue, found Mrs Peake, Captain Wordsworth's Niece (whose husband was killed in the Peacock) staying with him. The next day Richard and his wife came to see us—our first meeting William was at Lowther. On Monday Richard and his wife and their son, and William also came to dinner and on

Tuesday William and I walked to Lowther and stayed all night, viewed the Castle, and walked to Sockbridge to dinner on Wednesday. On Thursday left Sockbridge—slept at Hallsteads; were conveyed to Brothers-Water in a Car, and reached home at 5 o'clock. I was just as fresh as on that day week when we began our journey. My dear Friend have I not reason to be thankful that my strength is thus continued to me and that my pleasure in walking remains as keen as ever? You will be glad to hear that I like my Brother R[d]'s wife very well—the circumstances of her education—her rank in Society—her youth etc being got over. She is a very respectable woman and kind and attentive to her Husband. She is not vulgar, though she has nothing of the natural gentlewoman about her. Her face is very comely and her countenance excellent. But now for the little Boy—he is indeed a sweet creature, very pretty and most intelligent and engaging. This in an extraordinary degree, for he forces every one to admire him. Our Cousin William Crackenthorpe who returned from the Continent ten weeks ago, heard by accident that we were at Sockbridge, and hastened to see us. He is a very worthy man, much superior in the cast of his mind to the generality of the gentry of the country; but there is a most unfortunate appearance of affectation in his manners. Our business with Richard is of a serious nature—his disposition to procrastination has prevented him from making any settlement with us; in spite of our earnest entreaties especially since his marriage. This we cared little about while he was unmarried; but if he should die before it is done we must wait till his son's coming of age before we could get anything settled, and the trouble we might have could not be calculated. I trust, however, as all due preparations have been made that the business will be completely done next week, and that we shall either have our money or security for it. Richard was, as usual, very kind and affectionate, and will I dare say be as glad as we when the settlement is made. At present we have neither accounts nor security of any kind whatever; through a most blameable carelessness respecting such concerns on our parts. William begs that if you have old Mr Luff's address you will send it him. He wishes very much to draw up a memorial of the Life of our Friend; but without dates, and other circumstances connected with his youthful days this cannot be properly done. You will be glad to hear that Mary is growing fatter, and looks very well though she has been confined to her chair for a week by a boil on her thigh. John is boarded with Mr Dawes, and is now come home for the holidays. He is much improved since he went to Mr D. and we hope he will be a scholar in time. Dorothy has been kept at Mrs Lloyds two days by the weather—they go to Brathay 3 times in the week to learn to dance. Mrs Lloyd is preparing to depart after the holidays. The accounts from Birmingham of poor Charles are not very favourable. —My brother Christopher bears his affliction with true Christian fortitude. He does not wish to see me at present, and as he must look to *himself* for support, it is well he is able to rest upon the hope of finding it in himself by the discharge of the duties of his vocation. He is much comforted with his children. Perhaps he may wish to see me next summer. If so you and I will meet at Playford Hall should you not first come hither. Willy is quite well. God Bless you my dearest Friend Ever yours D. W.

My love to Mr Clarkson and Tom.

I ought to have written to you long ago and have blamed myself very much for my idleness, but Luff's death made me shrink from writing. My hands are stiff with cold—I am ashamed of this letter as I almost always am—Can you read it?

379. D. W. to CATHERINE CLARKSON

Address: Mrs Clarkson, at William Buck's Esq, Bury, Suffolk, *to be forwarded*.
Stamp: Kendal Penny Post. *Endorsed*: the last day of 1815.
MS. British Museum.
K. MY ii. 538, p. 692.

Sunday the last day of the old year [1815]

My dearest Friend,

Tillbrooke led us into an error. We had a letter from him lately wherein he said 'Our Friends the Clarksons are gone to Playford Hall;' and thither I sent a letter to you a few days before Christmas day. I am so desirous that your wish to hear from us should be satisfied that I will risque sending this to Bury, though if you keep your intentions you will have left that place before its arrival. We have been the slaves of wind and weather lately, and so may you be this week, and I think you will do well not to relinquish the comforts of your Father's house to enter upon the bustle and annoyances of a new establishement until the weather is more chearing. In my head I have such a chronicle of snow, thaw, frost, rain and wind as never before. I think I told you that William and Mary were waiting for the opening of the roads to go to Keswick. There was a thaw on Christmas Eve and on Christmas day a keen frost, and on Christmas day they set off. I was very uneasy till I heard of their safe arrival at Keswick for the roads in most parts were covered with one sheet of solid ice. A very deep snow, with fierce wind, fell in the night. I concluded they would be detained at Keswick; but there the snow was not so heavy and they went to Penrith the next day. Mrs Lloyd, however, who went with them to Keswick was detained there until Wednesday, when with great difficulty she prevailed upon the driver of a returned chaise and four to bring her. *She* (because less snow had fallen at Keswick) could not believe the man had reason in his scruples, but she found the contrary. They travelled with great labour through a 'sea of snow', the horses could hardly drag the chaise though Mrs Lloyd was alone in it, and without luggage. At 9 o'clock at night she knocked at our door and stayed all night, we had six of her children who came with her on Christmas-day in the morning, and with Sophia Crump[1] and our own three—and now and then another hardy Boy or two who waded through the snow to visit us, the six remained until Thursday noon—a merry Christmas they had. I have not seen Mrs Lloyd since; but I hear she was no worse for her walk to Brathay through the snow. The girls went in a cart. Sara has been weather-bound at Penrith and is still there; but we have now a complete thaw, and I think she will probably get to Keswick to-morrow, where she may perhaps stay a week; and will then come home to be my companion until Wm and Mary return which I think will not be sooner than the middle of January. William's business with my Brother Richard is no less than settling all our Family accounts, and obtaining security for all our property, for which we have not now a single bit of paper to show; and if he should die before the settlement is made we might be involved again in suits at Law, and *must* remain till old age without any settlement at all; for, as a Man of the law tells us, nothing could be done until Rd's son's coming of age. Richard is as well disposed to do what is good and right as his procrastinating Disposition will let him be. I have heard from Sara that Wm and Mary arrived safe at Penrith on Tuesday, after a troublesome journey, and proceeded to Lowther the same evening. They are now, I suppose, at Appleby, where William will leave Mary in the beginning of this week. She is paying a long promised visit to her Friend Miss Weir. Sara tells me that my Brother Richard has been confined to his bed a fortnight. I trust his disorder is not alarming; but it may detain William, who is determined not to stir from the spot till all is settled. I am sorry to tell you that my Brother Richard's health is very unsteady—He is subject to violent bilious attacks. He was just recovered from one of them when William and I were at Sockbridge. I have given you the history of *our* journey in my letter to Playford. We were favoured

[1] See L. 369, p. 242, n.

in weather for a whole week, and performed the entire journey except about 6 miles on foot, to our infinite satisfaction, pacing side by side along the shores of Ullswater, as we did years ago, when hospitable dwelling was the bourne to which we tended. Oh my good Friend how much have we to be thankful for in spite of sorrowful change!—I cannot relish the thoughts of Playford Hall. To that spot you will be bound—I am sure you will—all this year—first by business next by the necessary expenses attending upon it—and we shall not see you here! Thus year passes on after year and we become unable or unwilling to travel. If my Brother Christopher should wish to see me in the summer I shall certainly go to Bocking —and then we shall meet, but his occupations are so many and his mind is so bent on the performance of his duty; and he is so strong in Christian fortitude; that he does not seem to want any one to lean upon even for a time. He is going to Birmingham for a fortnight with his sons and Mr Crackenthorpe tells us that he hears from Binfield[1] that he intends to halt there. This I am very glad of; for though his spirits may be comforted in the way in which he is going on at Bocking, I fear that his health may be undermined; and I hope that the Society of sympathising friends of his own Family may be of use to him. Poor old Mr and Mrs Lloyd have a weight of care and sorrow—an orphan Family of Grand-children have fallen to their care, as perhaps you know, Priscilla and Charles were their darlings—the one is dead—the other at present worse than dead—and Plumstead their Son has been insolvent and caused to his Father the loss of many thousand pounds—and this without any alleviating circumstances,—imprudence and folly and unfeeling extravagance being the cause of all. Mrs. Charles Lloyd is a most extraordinary woman. Her fortitude and presence of mind can never be sufficiently admired, but happily for her she does by nature delight in activity; and it is that disposition which keeps her from sinking in despondency. She feels deeply the awful situation of her husband and the weight of her own duties; and when she pauses from employment and is left alone, or when she wakes in the morning the oppression of her mind is dreadful. She is engaged in preparing for their final removal which will be after the Christmas holidays. The Boys are to remain with Mr Dawes as Boarders. You cannot think how desolate old Brathay now looks. All the Books are

[1] The parish near Windsor where the Wordsworths' uncle, Canon William Cookson, lived. See L. 10, pt. i, p. 18. 'Mr. Crackenthorpe' is William, son of the Wordsworths' Uncle Christopher Crackanthorpe Cookson, and himself a nephew of Canon Cookson.

packed, the pictures taken down—the dining-room converted into a nursery—in short nothing as it used to be. The letters from Birmingham vary very little—the medical men hold out strong hopes; but the best is but a melancholy prospect; for there is, I think, not even a chance that the disorder will not return hereafter even in its present dismal excess; and it is my belief and that of most of poor Lloyd's friends that he has never been in what might justly be called a sane state of mind these 15 years past—and probably much longer. It is a great comfort to the survivors that Priscilla was spared the sorrow of knowing her Brother's miserable state; and in my sympathy for my Br Christ[r]'s loss I cannot but say to you that I see much cause of consolation, if not for him for his Friends, dimly as we discover good and evil in this world; for there was evidently a strong tendency in Priscilla's mind, if not to insanity, to that excess of nervous irritability which puts our feelings and actions almost as much out of our own power as if we were actually what is called insane—and who knows what this might at length have become? Mrs Charles Lloyd reporting what was told her by the old Housekeeper at Bingley[1] says that my Brother's tenderness and patience were almost beyond belief—night after night did he sit by her bedside when they were at Birmingham 2 or 3 years ago, she labouring with indescribable sensations, he comforting her and waiting for the moment when he would lie down beside her. No doubt all this endeared her to him, he being strong to walk in what seemed to him the path of duty—but to many this would have been very difficult—and perhaps Priscilla might have suffered less if she had had a less indulgent Husband. God bless her memory. I believe she was as sweet tempered a woman as ever lived, and thoroughly conscientious and good of heart.

In reading the 3rd Book of the Excursion last night what a pang did I feel for our poor widowed Friend Mrs Luff when I came to these lines

> Oh never let the Wretched, if a choice
> Be left him, trust the freight of his distress
> To a long voyage on the silent deep! . . .

and going on I was reminded of pangs she had spoken of, pangs of self-reproach at the outset of their voyage for having been the cause

[1] Bingley House, near Birmingham, the home of Charles Lloyd senior, the banker, father of Charles Lloyd of Brathay and of Priscilla W.

of an undertaking at first attended with so much disappointment—vexation, and I may say sorrow.

> For like a plague, will Memory break out
> And, in the blank and solitude of things,
> Upon his spirit with a fever's strength
> Will conscience prey.[1]

But I trust that now such vain regrets will not return to her. Such awful dispensations of Providence as these are, tend (when we have erred without evil intention) to wean the mind from a disposition to self-reproach; and we become habitually possessed with a sense of our own weakness and inability of ourselves to do anything that is good, and thus calmly look upon ourselves as having been the agents by which the Almighty power has wrought for us our afflictions for his own wise and good ends. I incline to think that there is little chance that Mrs Luff will remain at the Mauritius until [? Mr] Dent's arrival—I should fear if she were prevailed upon to stay so long, it would be through weakness of Body and unconquerable melancholy. I trust we shall have letters either from her or from some of her Friends by the first opportunity if she does not arrive in England.—My Brother sent the Excursion to Luff; but I fear he never received it. The period was very short between the date of his last letter and the day of his death.—It was a great relief to me when I read that you suspected you had missed sending two sheets of the Journal—This you certainly have done; for we have not received them. In my last I told you this; but as one frank was before mis-sent we thought the same had happened again. Hartley Coleridge is arrived—not at all altered in manners or appearance. I have no doubt he applies industriously to his studies. I am very glad to hear so good an account of Tom. Give my kind love to him and Mr Clarkson and your dear Father—and Mrs Corsbie—for whose disappointment and anxieties I am deeply grieved. With you I admire her fortitude; but it does not surprize me for (I may be presumptuous) but I think I could act and feel in the same way in case of loss of property. But Mrs Lloyd's fortitude in her afflictions does indeed surprize me. I should be utterly incapable of doing as *she* does and bearing what *she* bears. I refer you to the Playford letter for what I have missed. Excuse this letter if confused or dull—The children and a playfellow have been beside me all the time.

You told us about Capel Loft's[2] Lock of hair. I should pity his

[1] *The Excursion*, iii, ll. 844–50.

[2] Capell Lofft (1751–1824), lawyer and philanthropist, patron of Robert Bloomfield, author of *The Farmer's Boy*.

wife if it were not her own fault that she married him knowing what he was. My kind love to Mrs Kitchener—I am very sorry for her anxiety about her son. Believe me ever with true anxiety for your happiness next year and all your life—

D. W.

380. W. W. to ROBERT SOUTHEY

MS. untraced.
K. MY ii. 518, p. 633.

[1815][1]

Dear Southey,

. . . My opinion in respect to epic poetry is much the same as that of the critic whom Lucien Bonaparte has quoted in his preface. Epic poetry, of the highest class, requires in the first place an action eminently influential, an action with a grand or sublime train of consequences; it next requires the intervention and guidance of beings superior to man, what the critics, I believe, call machinery; and lastly, I think with Dennis[2] that no subject but a religious one can answer the demand of the soul in the highest class of this species of poetry. Now Tasso's is a religious subject, and in my opinion a most happy one; but I am confidently of opinion that the movement of Tasso's poem[3] rarely corresponds with the essential character of the subject; nor do I think it possible that, written in stanzas, it should. The celestial movement cannot, I think, be kept up, if the sense is to be broken in that despotic manner at the close of every eight lines. Spenser's stanza is infinitely finer than the *ottava rima*, but even Spenser's will not allow the epic movement as exhibited by Homer, Virgil, and Milton. How noble is the first paragraph of the *Aeneid* in point of sound, compared with the first stanza of the *Jerusalem Delivered*! The one winds with the majesty of the Conscript Fathers entering the Senate House in solemn procession; and the other has the pace of a set of recruits shuffling on the drill-ground, and receiving from the adjutant or drill-serjeant the command to halt at every ten or twenty steps. Farewell.

Affectionately yours,
W. Wordsworth.

[1] The date of this letter is probably 1815, owing to the reference to Lucien Bonaparte's epic. See L. 349 above.
[2] See L. 343, p. 188, n. 1 above.
[3] *Gerusalemme Liberata*, written about 1573.

381. W. W. to BERNARD BARTON[1]

Address: Bernard Barton Esq., Woodbridge, Suffolk.
MS. Cornell.
K. MY ii. 540, p. 699.

Rydal Mount, near Ambleside,
Jan. 12, 1816.

Dear Sir,

Though my sister, during my absence, has returned thanks in my name for the verses which you have done me the honour of addressing to me, and for the obliging letter which accompanies them, I feel it incumbent on me, on my return home, to write a few words to the same purpose with my own hand.

It is always a satisfaction to me to learn that I have given pleasure upon *rational* grounds; and I have nothing to object to your poetical panegyric but the occasion which called it forth. An admirer of my works, zealous as you have declared yourself to be, condescends too much when he gives way to an impulse proceeding from the —,[2] or indeed from any other Review. The writers in these publications, while they prosecute their inglorious employment, cannot be supposed to be in a state of mind very favourable for being affected by the finer influences of a thing so pure as genuine poetry; and as to the instance which has incited you to offer me this tribute of your gratitude, though I have not seen it, I doubt not but that it is a splenctic effusion of the Conductor of that Review who has taken a perpetual Retainer from his own incapacity to plead against my claims to public approbation.

I differ from you in thinking that the only poetical lines in your address are 'stolen from myself'. The best Verse, perhaps, is the following:

Awfully mighty in his impotence,

which, by way of repayment, I may be tempted to steal from you on some future occasion.

It pleases, though it does not surprize me, to learn that, having been affected early in life by my verses, you have returned again to your old Loves after some little infidelities, which you were shamed into by commerce with the scribbling and chattering part of the World. I have heard of many who, upon their first acquaintance

[1] Bernard Barton (1784–1849), Quaker, a bank clerk at Woodbridge, Suffolk, published *Metrical Effusions* (1812), *The Convict's Appeal* (1818), *Poems by an Amateur* (1818), and *Poems* (1820). His daughter married Edward Fitzgerald, but the marriage was wholly unsuitable and they separated.

[2] i.e. the *Edinburgh.*

with my poetry, have had much to get over before they could thoroughly relish it; but never of one who, having once learned to enjoy it, had ceased to value it or survived his admiration. This is as good an external assurance as I can desire that my inspiration is from a pure source, and that my principles of composition are trustworthy.

With many thanks for your good wishes, and begging leave to offer mine in return, I remain, dear sir,

Respectfully yours,
Wm. Wordsworth.

382. W. W. to C. W.
(with postscript by D. W.)

Address: To the Rev^{d} Dr Wordsworth, at Charles Lloyd's Esqre, Birmingham.
MS. WL.
MY ii. 539, p. 697.

Rydale Mount 12th Jan^{y} [1816]

My dear Brother,

Understanding that through God's mercy you have been enabled to bestow the requisite attention upon your various duties I have ventured to break in upon you with a request that you would employ a small portion of your time in taking into consideration a matter which though not immediately concerning you, is of great importance to a most worthy individual, Mr Johnson of the Central School.[1] He has just been with us, induced to come principally by a desire to consult me and my family upon his future conduct. He is determined to withdraw from the Central School; and wished to have my opinion how he ought to proceed, in regard to a Resolution entered in the journals of the School-Committee, in which, as appears through a Cabal of certain of the members he has been most unjustly censured. Distrusting my own judgement, and knowing your superior experience in these cases, I have encouraged him to call at Birmingham[2] in his way to London, and lay the particulars before you, with a view to benefit by your advice. For my own part I cannot reconcile myself to the notion of so meritorious a Teacher quitting his situation, with this stigma so unjustly attached to him; and which any of his enemies, (for enemies his deserts have raised

[1] For William Johnson, formerly schoolmaster at Grasmere, see L. 223, pt. i, p. 487, n. 1. He was still at the Central School in 1820.

[2] C. W. was visiting the Lloyds, parents of his wife Priscilla, who had died in the previous October (see L. 374 above), and of Charles Lloyd of Brathay.

against him) might turn to his prejudice through the whole course of his future life. With your permission he will lay the papers before you, and probably repeat the sentiments which I expressed upon them.—The Central School will suffer I fear greatly for the want of his services. But he says that it is insupportable to him to continue, in a situation where he finds the person who introduced him there and whom he long regarded as his best Friend and firmest Supporter, converted into a jealous opponent.[1] Besides, the four years which have been given already to this employment, though eminently useful he hopes to others, have been utterly lost as to his own improvement in every thing but the management of the School.

It is not unreasonable also that he should look by this time to an independent situation, which his own industry and talents will support if Friends would enable him to attain in a reasonable time. But on this point also, he will be happy to profit by your counsel.—I have just returned from Sockbridge where Richard and I have been employed in adjusting the accounts. He has given us security for a certain sum, subject to a deduction if upon balancing the accounts, it [? appear to] exceed what is due. On one point you are interested, and it has been arranged only upon condition that you approve. In December 1812 Richd paid £412 to the Heirs of our late Uncle Richard Wordsworth being due to them on balancing the account between his Estate and ours.[2] Of this debt the most considerable part had been incurred by the expenses of my education at College. About two years ago we received from William Crackenthorp some thing more than £300 due from his father to us.[3] I thought it but reasonable that this sum should be appropriated as far as it would go in liquidation of the claim of my Uncle W's heirs; and expressed an opinion that you would not object to it. This I was induced to do by the consideration, that it would be troublesome to ascertain what portion of this debt had accrued exactly from the expenses of each; and above all that it would be unjust, that I should have to pay from my own individual fortune, for an expensive education when you had received yours from an Uncle who though generous to you had been *unjust* to every one of us else.[4] I allude more particularly to his having permitted his Mother in her feeble state of Health to

[1] i.e. Dr. Andrew Bell, for whom see L. 126, pt. i, p. 269, n. 1.

[2] See L. 275 above.

[3] William Crackenthorpe (or Crackanthorpe) was the only son of the Wordsworths' maternal uncle, Christopher Crackanthorpe Cookson (d. 1799), who on succeeding to his mother's property of Newbiggin Hall had dropped the name of Cookson. See further L. 386 below, from which it appears that C. W. had raised objections to W. W.'s proposal.

[4] i.e. Christopher Crackanthorpe Cookson.

make a present to his Wife of £500,[1] when he had the certainty of succeeding to the estate at her Death.—We wish for your answer upon this head, as the Account cannot be settled without it. We are all well, and earnestly praying, that you may gradually recover your peace of mind, and as far as is possible be reconciled to your loss. I remain my dear Brother most faithfully yours

W Wordsworth

We have not seen Mrs Lloyd for some days.

[*D. W. adds*]

My dear Brother, [I wish] it had been possible for you to have [?come] thus far with your Boys. I hope [to see] Mrs Lloyd today or tomor[row] when I trust I shall hear of [you]. God bless you. Your aff[ectionate] D. W.

383. W. W. to BENJAMIN ROBERT HAYDON

Address: B. R. Haydon Esqr, Great Marlborough Street, London.
MS. untraced.
Haydon (—). MY ii. 541, p. 700.

Rydale Mount Jan^ry 13 [1816.]
near Ambleside

My dear Sir,

On my return home my Sister delivered to me your Letter, which on many accounts gave me great pleasure. Mrs W— and I had been absent some time; and indeed I have been much unsettled by business during the best part of this winter. It gratifies me much that the Sonnets,[2] especially the one addressed to yourself, find favor in your eyes, and those of your friends.—As to your request for permission to publish them I cannot refuse to comply with it. In regard to that addressed to yourself, you deserve a much higher Compliment; but from the nature of the subject it may be found pretty generally interesting. The two others, particularly the Snow-crested Mountain, full surely are morsels only for the few. But if Mr Scott desires it, he is at liberty to give them a place in his Journal when and how he likes.[3] At the same time my own feelings

[1] Mrs. Christopher Crackanthorpe had been Miss Charlotte Cust of Penrith, whom and her sisters D. W., in one of her early letters to Jane Pollard, had described as 'a mixture of ignorance, pride, affectation, self-conceit, and affected notability [i.e. skill in household crafts] . . . so ill-natured too'. *EY* 3, p. 10. See also D. W.'s letter to her, 21 Apr. 1794, *EY* 39, p. 116.

[2] See L. 377 above.

[3] 'High is our calling, Friend' was published by Scott in the *Champion* of

urge me to state in sincerity, that I naturally shrink from solicitation of public notice. I never publish any thing without great violence to my own disposition which is to shun, rather than court, regard. In this respect we Poets are much more happily situated than our Brother Labourers of the Pencil; who cannot, unless they be born to a Fortune, proceed in their employments without public countenance.

I thank you for the Number of the Champion; after being found worthy of such eulogy as is there bestowed upon you, the next enviable thing is the ability to praise merit in so eloquent a style.—There is also an excellent political essay of Scott at the head of the same number.—Pray give my regards to him; and I will take this occasion of stating, that it may be agreeable to Mr Hunt to learn that his Mask[1] has been read with great pleasure by my Wife and her Sisters under this peaceful Roof. They commend the style in strong terms; and though it would not become *me* to say that their taste is correct, I have often witnessed with pleasure and an entire sympathy, the disgust with which in this particular they are affected by the main part of contemporary productions.

I am glad to learn that your Picture[2] advances.—It is as grand a subject as could be selected. The feelings to be excited are adoration and exultation, and subordinate to them, astonished suspension of mind.[3] In all the Evangelists it is written, that our blessed Lord was accompanied with hosannas. These a silent Picture cannot express, and but imperfectly indicate; but Garments may be spread, and boughs may be carried in triumph, and prostrate forms exhibited, as you have done. From the manner in which I have dwelt upon these images you will infer that I think you have done well in rejecting the character of the supercilious Prude.—I cannot but think such a person discordant with the piece. One of the Evangelists says that the Pharisees called on Jesus to rebuke his disciples, and this is the only feeling mentioned that does not fall directly in with the general triumph and exultation. For there is nothing discordant with these in the Question, who is this? immediately succeeded by the answer, 'The King of Jerusalem;' in fact in no stronger manner could the overwhelming presence of Jesus Christ be expressed. The request of the Pharisees has *indirectly* the same tendency, they wished that

4 Feb. and by Hunt in the *Examiner* of 31 Mar.; the other two in the *Examiner* of 28 Jan. and 11 Feb.—'How clear how keen, how marvellously bright' (the 'Snow-crested Mountain') and 'While not a leaf seems faded, while the fields'.

[1] *The Descent of Liberty.*

[2] i.e. 'Christ's Entry into Jerusalem'.

[3] The manuscript has 'astonished and suspension mind'.

the Disciples should be rebuked; and why? because their pride was wounded and their indignation raised by the homage which the multitude paid with such fervor to Jesus on his approach to Jerusalem.—A character like that of the haughty prude belongs rather to the higher kinds of Comedy, such as the works of Hogarth, than to a subject of this nature, which to use Milton's expression is 'more than heroic'.——I coincide with you in opinion as to Raphael's characters, but depend upon it he has erred upon the safer side. Dramatic diversities aid discrimination, [and] should never be produced upon sublime subjects by the sacrifice of sublime effect. And it is better that expression should give way to beauty than beauty be banished by expression. Happy is he who can hit the exact point, where grandeur is not lowered but heightened by detail, and beauty not impaired, but rendered more touching and exquisite by Passion. —This has been done by the great artists of antiquity, but not frequently in modern times; yet much as I admire those productions I would on no account discourage your efforts to introduce more of the diversities of actual humanity into the management of sublime and pathetic subjects. Much of what Garrick is reported to have done for the stage, may by your Genius be effected for the Picture Gallery.—But in aiming at this object, proceed with reflection, and if you are in *doubt*—decide in favour of the course which Raphael pursued.

Before I conclude, I have one word to say of the mode of publishing the Sonnet addressed to you. I could wish that it should appear, that the thing was not first addressed to you through the medium of a Public journal, but was a private communication of Friendship. Don't you think that the Sonnet on the sight of a beautiful Picture,[1] the second I believe, it stands in my large edition, would come with effect if paired with the one addressed to yourself.—It is a favorite of mine, and I think not unworthy of the subject, which was a picture painted by our Friend Sir George Beaumont; though this is not mentioned in the title of the Piece.—The Editor might add in a foot note, that the Landscape which had suggested the verses, was he understood from the pencil of Sir George.—My poems are not so extensively known but that a Reprint of this piece would be new to a great majority of the Readers of the Champion.

[1] i.e. 'Praised be the Art', *Oxf. W.*, p. 252. In the Fenwick note to the sonnet (*PW*, iii, p. 420) Wordsworth says that the 'features of the picture are Bredon Hill and Cloud Hill near Coleorton'. It was composed in Aug. 1811 and sent in a letter to Sir George Beaumont. See L. 227, pt. i. It was not, however, reprinted, as W. here suggests, in the *Champion*, along with 'High is our calling, Friend'.

You do not speak of your eyes; I trust, therefore, they are much better.—

My Wife and Miss Hutchinson send their kindest regards; and join with me in best wishes for your health happiness and success. This last word reminds me of your desire that my merits as a Poet might be acknowledged during my life-time. I am quite satisfied on this head—with me it must be a work of time; but I frequently receive acknowledgements of gratitude from persons unknown, in all quarters of the Island.

faithfully yours
W Wordsworth

Remember that the frame of the Study you so kindly promised me is to be at my expense, but I wish you to procure it because you will know what sort of one will best suit the picture, and also though this is an occasion on which I am not scrupulous about economy, because the dealer will let you have it cheaper. What is the price of one of my busts?

384. W. W. to FRANCIS WRANGHAM

MS. Henry Huntington Library.
K. MY ii. 542, p. 704.

Thanksgiving Day,[1] Jan^ry^, 1816.
Rydal Mount.

My dear Wrangham,

You have given an additional mark of that friendly disposition, and those affectionate feelings which I have long known you to possess, by writing to me after my long and unjustifiable silence. But as I have told you, though I don't remember in these words, I was not born with a pen in my mouth, nor in my hands or toes.—I am painfully conscious how poor a genius I possess for epistolary communications; and if I had any native flow of this kind, my miserable penmanship would at once check it. How can such matters, and in such a garb, be worth any body's acceptance? This is the interrogation which now and always stares me in the face when I would converse with my friends by means of paper and ink.—'*Heaven* first taught letters for some wretch's aid,'[2] but presumptuous indeed

[1] i.e. 18 Jan., the day appointed for a national thanksgiving for the final overthrow of Napoleon.

[2] Pope, *Eloisa to Abelard*, l. 51.

should I be if I were not assured that such *Letters* as my pen makes are excepted. Neither Cupid nor Minerva, nor Phœbus nor Mercury, nor any of the Pagan Gods who presided over liberal and kindly inventions, deign to shed their influence over my endeavours in this field.—But may the Goddess of Patience support you, while you attempt in friendship to read, what I am now preparing for the perplexity of your understanding and the annoyance of your eyesight.

Unluckily I have neither seen nor heard of your translation from Virgil. You have done well to amuse yourself in this way; but the employment must have been somewhat too difficult for mere pastime. The Ecglogues of Virgil appear to me, in that in which he was most excellent, polish of style and harmony of numbers, the most happily finished of all his performances.—I know that I shall be much gratified by your Translation when it finds its way to me, which I hope it will do, soon.—

Of the White Doe I have little to say, but that I hope it will be acceptable to the intelligent, for whom alone it is written.—It starts from a high point of imagination, and comes round through various wanderings of that faculty to a still higher; nothing less than the Apotheosis of the Animal, who gives the first of the two titles to the Poem. And as the Poem thus begins and ends, with pure and lofty Imagination, every motive and impulse that actuates the persons introduced is from the same source, a kindred spirit pervades, and is intended to harmonize, the whole. Throughout, objects (the Banner, for instance) derive their influence not from properties inherent in them, not from what they are actually in themselves, but from such as are bestowed upon them by the minds of those who are conversant with or affected by those objects. Thus the Poetry, if there be any in the work, proceeds whence it ought to do from the soul of Man, communicating its creative energies to the images of the external world.

But too much of this. I am happy to hear that your family prospers, and that your Children are to your mind. In my own I find much to regret, and something to complain of; faults most of which have probably been created by my own mismanagement. I am, however, truly and deeply thankful to God for what he has left me. Do not imagine, dear Wrangham, that though I am a bad correspondent, I therefore forget either you or my other early friends. Farewell. I am always glad to hear of you.

Most faithfully yours
W. Wordsworth

385. W. W. to JOHN SCOTT

MS. Harvard University Library.
MY ii. 543, p. 705 (—).

Rydale Mount
near Ambleside Jan^ry^ 29th 1816

My dear Sir,

I know not that the three following Sonnets,[1] occasioned by the Battle of Waterloo will do any credit to your journal; but perhaps the subject may make up with your Readers (if it does not tell the contrary way) for the deficiencies of the execution.—If you think them deserving of publication, they may follow those three which I understand from Haydon you expressed a wish to publish in the Champion.—On recurring to Haydon's letter, I find that I have been mistaken, and that the wish is on *his* part only. It matters not; if you have thought it worth while to print the two Descriptive Sonnets[2] sent to Haydon, these I think will be acceptable to you; though they are composed rather to decline the subject than to grapple with it.

A Friend of mine, in this neighbourhood has just ordered your journal, but forgot to specify that it was to commence with the year. In consequence of this oversight the first Number is dated Jan^ry^ 22nd. Would you be so kind as to order the preceding ones of the year to be sent addressed to

Mr Nicholson
Post Office
Ambleside

I am dear Sir
with great respect
faithfully yours
W. Wordsworth

P.S.
I ordered my publication to be sent to Haydon.—Pray correct on your Copy an error which entirely destroys the effect of one movement of the first Ode—[3]

'Sully the limpid stream of thankfulness.
—What robe can gratitude employ

[1] The sonnets enclosed are 'Intrepid Sons of Albion' (*Oxf. W.*, p. 325), 'The Bard—whose soul is meek' (*Oxf. W.*, p. 326), and 'Oh, for a kindling touch' (*Oxf. W.*, p. 326). Scott printed the first and third in the *Champion* of 14 Feb.

[2] i.e. 'While not a leaf seems faded' and 'How clear, how keen, how marvellously bright' (*Oxf. W.*, p. 263), sent in the letter to Haydon of 21 Dec. 1815. See L. 377 above.

[3] *Thanksgiving Ode,* published 1816 (*Oxf. W.*, p. 329).

So it ought to stand; but the stupid Printer, (why I cannot conceive) has broken the paragraph into two. Let me know (at your leisure) if you agree with me on the subject of Bards.[1]

386. W. W. to C. W.

Address: To the Rev[d] Dr Wordsworth, Deanry, Bocking.
Postmark: C 5 Fe 1816. *Stamp*: Kendal Penny Post.
MS. WL.
MY ii. 544, p. 706.

Jan[ry] 31st [1816] Rydal Mount

My dear Brother,

I am much obliged to you for your kind dispositions to serve Mr Johnson,[2] and for having taken so much trouble on his account.—I am quite of your opinion that Mr Johnson is bound to keep the question of the injuries that may have been done him in his Capacity of Teacher, quite separate in his own mind from any hope or expectation of benefit to accrue to himself from a change of situation.—And I do not scruple to add that I believe him to be more influenced by hope and expectations of this kind than he is himself aware of.

Mr Johnson would probably tell you that we have lately seen Dr Bell,[3] and how we conducted ourselves towards him in respect to this business.—Mr J— will be much missed at the school if he quits it; nor am I sure that Dr B— however he may be indisposed to him, would wish him to withdraw yet awhile; though I do not doubt that if the Dr and his adherents found they could dispense with Mr J—, they would contrive to render his situation more uncomfortable than it has been. And on this account as a Friend of Mr J— I should be less inclined to press his continuance; lest it might happen that in course of time he might be dismissed by their intrigues.——

I fear that I must have expressed myself very imperfectly respecting the sum of money due to my father's Estate from our Uncle Crackenthorp.[4] Two or three years ago, by very great and most disagreeable exertions, I contrived to get the Account with my Uncle C drawn out, and it then appeared that he was indebted to our Father's Estate about £300—about the same time Richd settled the account with our Uncle Wordsworth's[5] Estate, paying

[1] i.e. in 'The Bard—whose soul is meek as dawning day'.

[2] See L. 223, pt. i, p. 487, n. 1.

[3] See L. 126, pt. i, p. 269, n. 1.

[4] See L. 382, p. 271, n. 3.

[5] i.e. Richard W of Whitehaven, d. 1794. He, with their mother's brother C. C. Cookson, had been guardian to the Wordsworth children after the death of their father in 1783.

400, the sum which my Father's Estate stood indebted to his Heirs. What could be more obvious than the reasonableness of applying the overplus in the hands of the heirs of Mr Crackenthorp, to make up the deficiency due to the Heirs of our Uncle Wordsworth—as far as it would go.—It seemed to me a case on which there could not be a moment's hesitation; nevertheless, as I was sensible that this debt to our Uncle Wordsworth was incurred chiefly on account of the expenses of *my* education, I thought myself bound in delicacy to notice the fact to you, though, as I was a Minor at the time of these expenses, I never considered that my Brothers and Sister would think themselves justified in bringing a separate Bill against me for this any more than for any other part of my education; it is a principle that never could have been thought of amongst us. And I mentioned the circumstance of Mr Crackenthorp's kind conduct towards [you as] an a fortiori argument, in my consideration, why such [a] principle, would not, I conceived be introduced by you.—I am still of opinion that you will see the thing in the same light in which I do; and must request a positive answer from you one way or the other, as I cannot admit any more cause or occasion of delay into the settlement of my account with my Br Richd. This is the *only* point in which you are concerned in the account between us.—If you could conceive a hundredth part of the obstacles, which I have had to get over from my Brother's procrastinating habits, and knew the time which I have sacrificed in this business, which I really never would have done on my own account merely, I am sure that you would acknowledge the reasonableness of this determination. Not less than five weeks of this winter has been by me sacrificed to this subject; besides what it cost me in the summer, and has cost me for the last two or three years.—

It avails little, I believe nothing, to write to Richd, but I will write to him as you desire. But it would be much the best to write yourself, though if your accounts be intricate I cannot, from my own experience, hold out a hope that they can be settled without a personal interview.—

Mrs Lloyd's sales are now going on; she herself is gone to York to determine by inspection what can be done there for her poor Husband.[1] She is quite worn out—her situation moves the compassion of every one who knows her.—Love from every body here

most faithfully and affectionately your Brother and friend

W. W.

[1] i.e. Charles Lloyd of Brathay. See Letters 374 above and 394 below.

387. W. W. to JOHN SCOTT

MS. untraced.
K. MY ii. 545, p. 708.

Rydal Mount, near Ambleside,
February 22, 1816.

My dear Sir,

Your *Paris Revisited* has been in constant use since I received it—a very welcome sight it was. . . .[1] Nothing in your works has charmed us more than the lively manner in which the painting of everything that passes before your eyes is executed. Every one of your words *tells*; and this is an art which few travellers, at least of our days, are masters of. Your estimate of Buonaparte's character is, I think, perfectly just. . . . I wish that I could think as favourably as you do of the Duke of Wellington.[2] Since his first début in Portugal I have watched his course as carefully as my opportunities allowed me to do; and notwithstanding the splendour of those actions at the head of which he has been placed, I am convinced that there is no magnanimity in his nature. You have laudably availed yourself of the temptation to contrast his mode of proceeding with Buonaparte's; and undoubtedly he appears to great advantage opposed to that audacious charlatan and remorseless desperado. But depend upon it, the constitution of his mind is not generous, nor will he pass with posterity for a hero. One would desire that in all cases the personal dignity of the prime agents should correspond with that of important actions; but this rarely happens in human affairs either military or civil; and I have found nothing more mortifying in the course of my life than those peeps behind the curtain, that have shown me how low in point of moral elevation stand some of those men who have been the most efficient instruments and machines for public benefit that our age has produced. We live in inquisitive times, and there is but too little reserve in gratifying public curiosity. Happy will it be for this distinguished leader, and I will add for his country, if his name be a gainer from the communications which his character and actions will give birth to! I fear that upon the whole it will be otherwise; and I express this fear to you, who from the best motives have so ably defended and panegyrized him, with strong regret, but sincerity requires it. . . .

This personal question is the only material point in your books in which I differ from you. I approve of all that you have said upon

[1] Dots presumably denote omissions made by K.

[2] W. W.'s dislike of the Duke of Wellington had arisen at the time of the Convention of Cintra in 1809. See Letters 155, 156, etc., pt. i.

the subject of the removal of the works of art from Paris. The Emperor of Russia[1] was the main cause of their being left in French possession by the first peace. His is a Frenchified intellect—to that degree that it was not without much difficulty he gave his consent, on the first occupation of Paris, to the King of Prussia removing his own cannon which he found there. The calamities of these times, as far as they were occasioned by the domination of the French, have been mainly owing to this, that they . . . never ventured upon an entire reliance on those rules of justice which were alone competent to save them. Had they been capable of this elevation of mind, a moment's reflection would have shown them that they had no right to confirm to the French the possession of these articles without the free unbiased consent of the original owners; that they were not lawful conquests but infamous plunder; and the allies by taking upon themselves to concede these things to the robbers, acted not less unjustly, whatever were their motives, than the original despoiler. . . . It is the duty of an English Opposition to be rigorously hostile to the Ministry, but never let their endeavours to accomplish the downfall of their political antagonists excite in them a favourable aspiration for the enemies of their country. The Opposition party were unable to discern that a time of war and a time of peace required very different modes of proceeding on their part; that a style of hostility, which would have been laudable in the one, became detestable in the other. Through the whole course of the late war the party out of power blushed not to behave as if they had been retained by Buonaparte for his advocates. This was unsupportably revolting to all true-hearted Englishmen, who were not actively engaged in the contest, and could therefore see clearly and feel naturally. . . . I will only add a word on Spanish affairs. The Cortes were what Lord Castlereay describes them, and worse. They thirsted after the independence of their country, and many of them nobly laboured to effect it; but, as to civil liberty and religious institutions, their notions were as wild as the most headstrong Jacobins of France. Their plan was to erect an Iberian Republic—and they were pushing matters desperately to that extremity. Think of a Republic in Spain—what horror to go through before such a thing could be brought about; and what worse than horrors would have attended its rapid destruction! Farewell.

Most faithfully and respectfully yours,

W. Wordsworth.

[1] Alexander I (1801–25).

388. W. W. to JOHN SCOTT

Address: John Scott Esq[re], No 1, Catherine Street, Strand, London.
MS. British Museum.
K (—). *MY ii. 546, p. 710.*

Rydal Mount Feb 25th [1816]

My dear Sir,

Most readily would I undertake the office which you propose to me, but for a reason which I am sure you will think sufficient for my declining it for a short while at least.—I am myself engaged with an attempt to express in Verse some feelings connected with these very subjects, and till that engagement is over neither in justice to you nor to myself can I introduce into my own mind such a stream as I have no doubt your Poem will be felt to be.[1] I am truly glad to hear that you are determined to try your strength in this way as I am convinced that you have the eye, the heart, and the voice of a Poet.—My short Essays, for there are two pieces,[2] cannot possibly interfere with your work, as they stand at a distance from the Body of the subject—which I do not doubt will be ably embraced by others.—Southey is a Fellow labourer.[3] I have seen but little of his performance, but that little gave me great pleasure.—I repeat that my wishes to serve you in the way you desire are as strong as they well can be; and that as soon as I am set [at] liberty, if you have not satisfied yourself by reference to some other friend, I shall be most happy to give my judgement to your work.

I sent you the other day a long ill-penn'd and ill-digested letter; and containing opinions upon men and things, which I should not have entrusted in that crude state to any one whom I did not greatly respect. Do not suppose from what I have there confidentially said that I think ill of mankind, and feel dejectedly concerning human nature. I am glad that you have lately read my tract occasioned by the Convention of Cintra. You must have seen therein what my views were—and are—for in nothing are my *principles* changed. In verse I celebrated the King of Sweden[4]—he proved I believe a Mad-

[1] Scott had evidently asked W. W. to act as critic to his intended poem on national affairs. It was never completed. See L. 389 below.

[2] W. refers to his *Ode: the Morning of the Day appointed for a General Thanksgiving, January 18, 1816*, and its companion piece, called on its first publication, *Ode composed in January 1816*, and subsequently, *Ode, 1814. Oxf. W.*, pp. 329, 323.

[3] Southey published in 1816 *The Poet's Pilgrimage to Waterloo,* written after a tour of Belgium and a visit to the battlefield.

[4] Wordsworth wrote two sonnets on Gustavus IV, King of Sweden, who abdicated in 1809. The first, *The King of Sweden*, was written in 1804 and published in *Poems in Two Volumes,* 1807. The second, 'Call not the royal Swede

man—what matters that—he stood forth at that time as the only Royal Advocate of the only truths by which, if judiciously applied, Europe could be delivered from Bondage. I seized on him as an outstanding object in which to embody certain principles of action which human nature has thousands of times proved herself capable of being governed by. I boldly announced in prose[1] the benefit which Spain would derive from a Cortes—but I was under a considerable mistake as to the degree in which the men who might compose it, would be liable to french delusions.—But a representative legislation is still in my opinion the best of political blessings when a Country has materials fit to compose it. Such had Spain for the purpose of atchieving her national Independence; and I hope may have, ere long, to establish for herself a frame of civil Liberty. The later Cortes were not equal to that task.

As to the Duke of Wellington, I am almost sorry that I touched upon the subject; especially since I have heard of your design. Poetically treated he may pass for a Hero; and on that account I less regret what I wrote to you. But to the searching eye of the Historian, and still more of the Biographer, he will, I apprehend, appear as a man below the circumstances in which he moved.

I hear what you say of the Champion with regret. Pity that your other labours cannot proceed without injury to that periodical writing which has, I know, been very beneficial. Could not you procure assistance, relinquishing profit accordingly?—Thank you for the verses—I have the satisfaction of not infrequently receiving tributes of the same kind. What numbers must find their way to your namesake! and to the 'bold bad Bard Baron B.'[2]

I have said in my last what will have been an answer to your kind offer of sending the Champion. I have only to repeat my thanks.—Excuse this infamous penmanship; I am not able to do much better at any time, but at present it is very late at night and my pen execrable

farewell with much regard and increasing respect I

remain [?]

W. W.

unfortunate', was written after his abdication in 1809, and published in *Poems*, 1815. See *Oxf. W.*, pp. 305, 317.

[1] i.e. in his pamphlet *Concerning the Convention of Cintra*, 1809.

[2] i.e. Byron.

389. W. W. to JOHN SCOTT

Address: John Scott Esq[re], Champion office, 1 Catherine Street, Strand, London.
Postmark: C. 15 Mar 1816. *Stamp*. Kendal Penny Post.
MS. Harvard University Library.
K (—).*MY ii. 547, p. 712.*

Rydal Mount, March 11th 1816

My dear Sir,

I wrote to you some little time since[1] giving my reasons why I felt myself obliged to decline the undertaking which you did me the honour of proposing to me. Those reasons no longer exist; and I now write to let you know that having finished all that at present I have any intention of executing in connection with the great events of our time, I shall be happy to comply with your request, if you continue in the same mind.

When I wrote the Sonnets inserted in the Champion I had no design of doing anything more. But I could not resist the Temptation of giving vent to my feelings as collected in force upon the morning of the day appointed for a general Thanksgiving. Accordingly, I threw off a sort of irregular Ode upon this subject, which spread to nearly 350 lines;[2] the longest thing of the Lyrical Kind, I believe except Spenser's Epithalamion, in our language. Out of this have sprung several smaller pieces, Effusions rather than Compositions, though in justice to myself I must say that upon the correction of the Style I have bestowed, as I always do, great Labour. I hope that my pains in this particular have not been thrown away, and that in their several degrees the things will not be found deficient in spirit. But I do not like to appear as giving encouragement to a lax species of writing except where the occasion is so great as to justify an aspiration after a state of freedom beyond what a succession of regular Stanzas will allow. But as I before hinted these smaller pieces are but offsets of the larger; and their defects in this point may be charged upon their parent; though I shall not call upon the public to be so indulgent.—From my Country I solicit no mercy; I have laboured intensely to merit its approbation, and in some smaller degree to secure, in future times at least, its gratitude; and for the present I am well contented with my portion of distinction.—If I wish for more I can honestly affirm, it is mainly from a belief that it would be an indication that a better taste was

[1] See L. 388 above.

[2] i.e. *Ode. The Morning of the Day appointed for a General Thanksgiving, January 18, 1816*, published in Mar. 1816 in a volume containing the 'smaller pieces, Effusions rather than Compositions', mentioned below.

spreading, and high and pure feelings becoming more general.—In regard to your own announced adventure upon the sea of Poetry I may truly say that I was most glad to hear of it; because your Prose has convinced me that you have a mind fitted to ensure your success.—Nevertheless my pleasure was not absolutely pure;—for if you have not practised metre in youth, I should apprehend that your thoughts would not easily accommodate themselves to those chains, so as to give you a consciousness that you were moving under them and with them, gracefully and with spirit. I question not that you have written with rapidity; nothing is more easy; but in nothing is it more true than in composing verse that the nearest way home is the longest way about.—In short I dreaded the labour which you were preparing for yourself.—You are a Master of Prose; and your powers may be so flexible and fertile as to be equal to both exercises—so much the better!—I mean equal to them without injury to your health. But should it appear to me that the Specimens you send of your Poem require additional care and exertion, I shall not scruple to tell you so; and with the less reluctance because I am confident that you may attain eminence in English prose which few of late have reached. That field is at present almost uncultivated; we have adroit living prose writers in abundance; but impassioned, eloquent, and powerful ones not any, at least that I am acquainted with. Our Prose taking it altogether, is a disgrace to the country—I ought to apologize for putting your patience to the test, by these wretched scrawls. But take me as I am; in this way I treat all my friends, and happy should I be to rank you among the number. — —The Champion still arrives, the superfluous one I mean; pray, order it to be discontinued. The two numbers, or three? (I believe three) which I begged might be sent to Mr. Nicholson the Post Master of Ambleside have never reached him. I was very sorry for this; of course I have not seen your notice of my political tract on Spanish affairs, nor what I more regret the Essay or whatever it might be which led you to recommend it.—Would you object to see my Thanksgiving Ode, etc., before Publication, if not, they will be sent you, and I should be grateful for your remarks.

P.S.—I fear what I have said on Prose as now produced, may be misunderstood. Charles Lamb, my friend, writes prose exquisitely; Coleridge also has produced noble passages, so has Southey. But I mean that there is no body, of philosophical, impassioned, eloquent, finished prose now produced.

Your publisher must have been negligent, for a second copy of your Paris revisited has reached me. — — [*Unsigned.*]

390. W. W. to C. W.

Address: The Rev[d] Dr Wordsworth, Deanry, Bocking.
Postmark: C 18 Mar 1816. *Stamp*: Kendal Penny Post.
MS. WL.
MY ii. 548, p. 715.

March 12th 1816
Rydale Mount

My dear Brother,

We thank you for your Consecration Sermon,[1] which we received free of expense. We have read it with much pleasure, and unite in thinking it excellently adapted to the occasion. For my own part, I liked it still better upon the second than the first reading.—At first I felt it somewhat disproportioned (and perhaps it actually is so) the base seeming too widely spread, (and too deeply laid in some respects) for the superstructure.—Afterwards I was less sensible of this defect (if it really exist) and could feel the strength of the thoughts and dignity of the sentiments, without discomposure. Your style is grave and authentic; and wants neither grace nor harmony.—It appears to me that it would be a reasonable practice, if Bishops of authority in the Church were to preach frequently upon these occasions; they might then with propriety bring their discourses more closely to the point; by setting forth and insisting upon the episcopal duties, as imposed by the Church of England.—This could not be done by a clergyman of inferior rank, and therefore it came not within your province. In regard to the Person who requested you to undertake this office on his account I will mention to you a little Anecdote, which perhaps you may have heard from another quarter as I related it to Mr Johnson, concealing only my authority. Lord L[2]— said to me, that the Prince Regent, speaking of Dr R— used these irreverent words—'By G— it shall be some time before they catch me making such another Bishop'. So you may be assured he is no favorite in that quarter. I recounted this to Mr Johnson, knowing his former leaning to methodistical heresies—I should on no account wish this to be repeated in any connection with the name of Lord L.—

I would gladly be instrumental in drawing the attention of the Public to your valuable Sermons, if I knew how—but I have not

[1] *A sermon preached in the Chapel of Lambeth at the Consecration of the Hon. and Right Rev. Henry Ryder, Lord Bishop of Gloucester, 1815.* Ryder was the first 'evangelical' to become a Bishop. Hence his sympathy with Methodism, noted with disapproval by Wordsworth.

[2] i.e. Lord Lonsdale. 'Lonsdale' has been erased, and 'L.' substituted.

access to any periodical Publications. Besides if I had it would be little avail; for unless a Person makes himself the humble Servt of the Editors, it is quite impossible that the dew of their regards should fall upon him.—I never mean to take any steps to ensure for my own Publications a favorable introduction.—Critiques upon my Poems have I know been sent to some of the Reviews, the Quarterly in particular, by admirers of mine, who were Strangers to my Person; but refused admittance; and if one of them had been admitted, it would have been so garbled and sophisticated by the stupidity of the Editor, as scarcely to have been recognizable by the author. This was actually done in Lamb's review of the Excursion. So that I know not how to be of service in your case; I will however write to Wrangham, who has a considerable connection with this sort of Literature.

My reason for not writing to you sooner was, that I hoped to repay you for your Sermon, by sending you in MSS an Ode supposed to be composed on the morning of the day appointed for a General Thanksgiving. It has been finished some time; extending to nearly 350 Lines—out of it have grown several smaller pieces; and I propose to send them all to the Press, immediately.

I have not much scruple in referring you to the Printed copy, which I hope will soon appear; as Poetry reads so much better in Print than in MSS—this Publication will contain 700 verses, and I mean to print in the same size as the two Vols of Poems,[1] in order that it may be bound up along with them.—At the same time, though not in the same Publication, you will see from me a Letter in prose,[2] addressed to an Acquaintance of Robert Burns the Scotch Poet, on the intended republication of Dr Currie's Life, and Burns' Letters—this Letter is about the length of a middle sized sermon. My son Wm aksed me a little while since 'whom are you writing to, Father?'—'to your Uncle Christopher'; 'do give my love to him'. We are all pretty well; though Dorothy not quite so, but her indisposition, I hope, is of no consequence. We hope you continue to make progress in subduing your distress and that your health and that of your Children is better. Richd and his wife are I hope in town by this time. He has been very unwell. Now is the time to press the settlement of your affairs.

[1] i.e. *Poems, including Lyrical Ballads*, published in 1815.

[2] *A Letter to a Friend of Robert Burns: Occasioned by an Intended Republication of The Account of the Life of Burns, by Dr. Currie; And of the Selections made by him from the Letters*. By William Wordsworth: London, 1816. The letter is addressed to James Gray, Esq., Edinburgh, and dated Rydal Mount, Jan. 1816. See Moorman, ii, pp. 295–301.

With best love from Mary and D— I remain
my dear Brother
Your faithful friend
W. Wordsworth

I should with great pleasure order a copy of my Thanksgiving Ode etc to be sent you—did I not know what Blunderers the Publishers are—they would send it Per Coach, and the Carriage would cost more than the Pamphlet. But if you can order a copy to be called f[or] do; I also wish that you would present [one in] my name to the Archbishop; that might be done [*seal*] by yourself, or if this were improper through Mr [*seal*].

391. D. W. to R. W.

Address: Richard Wordwsorth Esq[re], Staple Inn, London.
MS. WL.
MY ii. 550, p. 719.

March 15th [1816]

My dear Richard,

We were very sorry to hear that you had been so ill, and that your disorder had been attended by so distressing an effect as dimness of sight. I trust that as your bilious symptoms depart, that will also entirely leave you; but pray consult some physician in London on whose judgment you can rely. We should be very glad if you would contrive to let us know how you are, and how you both supported the journey. Where have you left little John?[1] I conjecture with his Grandmother or his Aunt.—My Brother Christopher is, I believe in London or in the neighbourhood, so I hope you will meet. If Captain Wordsworth is in London, pray tell us how he is.

Montagu intends to talk with you about the disputed 30£. He *might* [have] draw[n] upon you for 30£ with the intention of sending it to us in Scotland in 1803; but 5£ was all that we received from him at that time. We *did* receive 5£ at Edinburgh, which he said was all that he could spare, and, as it happened, we wanted no more. That 5£ no doubt stands in his Books against William.

[1] John Wordsworth, R. W.'s only child, b. 1815, d. 1846, became the ward of his uncles W. W. and C. W., on R. W.'s death two months after this letter was written. For R. W.'s marriage, see L. 319 above.

My Sister and I would have been very glad if John could have been with us during your absence, and his Cousins would have been delighted. I trust you will receive good accounts of him; otherwise his poor Mother will have an anxious time while she is in London. Pray give my kind Love to her, and believe me, dear Richard

Your affectionate Sister
D Wordsworth

392. W. W. to JOHN BRITTON[1]

MS. Folger Library.
Broughton 47, p. 61.

Rydal Mount—March 18th 1816

Sir,

I am much pleased to hear of the intention of commemorating the birth of Shakespear, on the day, and in the manner, you mention; and I thank you for the honor done me by requesting my assistance, upon the occasion.

I regret that I have nothing by me suitable for a purpose so interesting; nor do I feel it to be in my power to produce any thing worthy of your acceptance, at this time. My verses have all risen up of their own accord; I was once requested to write an inscription for a monument, which a Friend purposed to erect in his garden;[2] and a year elapsed before I could accomplish it. Besides, I should have before me the tender exclamation of Milton,

> Dear Son of Memory, great Heir of Fame,
> What need'st Thou such *weak* witness of thy Name.

Wishing that the Festival may proceed in a manner that shall honour the Parties who celebrate it, for its object is above all local or occasional honour, I remain, Sir

respectfully yours
Wm Wordsworth

[1] John Britton (1771–1857), antiquary and topographer, author of *Auto-Biography* (1850), attempted to organize a festival in 1816 in honour of the bicenteneary of Shakespeare's death. He asked Southey and Wordsworth to contribute poems; they both declined. See also L. 422 below.

[2] i.e. at Coleorton. See L. 230, pt. i.

393. W. W. to JOHN SCOTT

MS. Cornell.
K. MY ii. 551, p. 719.

Rydal Mount, March 21, [1816.]

My dear Sir,

I had packed up my little pieces of Verse,[1] intending to send them to you; but on second thoughts, I have forwarded them direct to Longman, knowing that you are so much engaged; and apprehending, that you might not possibly be at home; which would have occasioned a delay. I was also desirous that the effect of my verses upon you, should not be interfered with, by a blotted and blurred MSS and by uncouth characters, irresistibly distracting attention. I shall be not the less anxious for the benefit of your Remarks after Publication—I have not yet received any MSS. from you—

In the same Parcel I have sent for Publication a Letter in Prose, to a Friend of Burns, the Poet, which I hope you will read with some satisfaction.—

No doubt you are personally [acquainted with] Brougham; I have some knowledge of him likewise. Our last interview was terminated among the majestic woods of Lowther, near his own beautiful residence. Thither I would gladly remit him, 'inter sylvas academi quaerere *verum*'.[2] Mr. B. is not content with scribbling in the Edinburgh review to the praise and Glory of the Corsican, but he must insult the People of England by expressing in their House of Legislature, and that of the three kingdoms, His hope that that *great* man may be *kindly* treated in his insular Prison. What is there in the conduct of this government that justifies an apprehension that the claims of *humanity* will not be attended to by it in this case; though if there ever existed one in which those claims might be set aside it is the present. Be persuaded, my dear sir, that men who in that assembly or indeed anywhere else, can talk in this manner have no tact, and whatever may be their cleverness, no intellectual sanity. I congratulate you on having expressed in your last Champion, a decided opinion on this subject—Haydon has done himself credit by his essay on the Elgin Marbles.[3]—

[*signature cut off*]

[1] i.e. the *Thanksgiving Ode* and other related poems, published May 1816.
[2] Horace, *Epodes*, II. ii. 45. See L. 347 above.
[3] *The Judgment of Connoisseurs upon Works of Art compared with that of Professional Men, in reference more particularly to the Elgin Marbles*, 1816, first published in the *Examiner* and *Champion*.

394. W. W. to C. W.

Address: The Rev^d Dr Wordsworth, Deanry, Bocking.
Postmark: 29 Mar 1816. *Stamp*: Kendal Penny Post.
MS. WL.
MY ii. 552, p. 720.

Rydale Mount
March 25th 1816

My dear Christr.

Your Letter has given us all much satisfaction; the situation in question appears admirably suited to you; and cannot but stand in need of services such as you will be capable and ready to perform.—This is not merely a Letter of congratulation,[1] though I should have been strongly disposed to write from that impulse; but I wish to mention to you, that our present Curate, Mr Wm Jackson (Son of our Rector)[2] now upon the point of succeeding to a Fellowship at Queens Oxford, is desirous of removing Southward; and might suit you if you should stand in need of a Curate at Sundridge.—I know no objection to him whatsoever, but that his health is somewhat delicate; in every other respect, he is without exception one of the most admirable Clergymen for his years that I have known. He is very clever, very zealous, an excellent Scholar, has no discernible northern dialect or pronuntiation [*sic*], for he went very young to Oxford, and in my opinion reads the Liturgy most impressively. His sermons likewise, which are of his own composition, are exceedingly good.—I therefore think it my duty to point him out to you as a man in every respect deserving of regard; so that if you have no occasion for such an Assistant you may bear him in mind, as one who might be an important acquisition to some of your Friends.—His health, I am sorry to repeat is delicate, and on this account I could not conscientiously recommend him to a situation, in which the weight of occasional duty is very great.——

The Publication will contain the Sonnets you allude to; I am glad to learn that my Uncle was pleased with them.[3] I shall give directions to Longman to furnish you with *two* Copies both of the Poem and prose,[4] when you call or send—not that I mean you to

[1] C. W. had just been appointed by Manners-Sutton, Archbishop of Canterbury, to the Rectory of St. Mary's, Lambeth, and also to that of Sundridge in Kent.

[2] The Revd. Thomas Jackson, Rector of Grasmere. See L. 193, pt. i, p. 408, n. 1.

[3] W. alludes to the publication of his *Thanksgiving Ode* with a number of sonnets not included in the *Poems* of 1815. 'My Uncle' is Dr. William Cookson, Canon of Windsor and Rector of Binfield.

[4] i.e. *A Letter to a Friend of Burns.*

present the prose to the Archbishop; it is a little too profane for his Grace's acceptance. The state of the public Mind is at present little adapted to relish any part of my poetical effusion on this occasion.—There is too much derangement in the taxation of the Country; too much real distress, and above all too much imaginary depression and downright party fury. But all this I disregard as I write chiefly for Posterity.——

You do not allude to the emolument of your future living which we may be permitted to advert to—nor do you mention the state of your health and that of your boys; but we augur well from your silence on all these important particulars.—I fear Richard has not been much benefited by his Journey as you saw him look so ill—His health is deplorably delicate.——

We are sorry to learn that Dr Satterthwaite was not well; pray remember us all very affectionately to him. Poor Charles Lloyd is at length lodged in the Retreat at York, which ought to have been done long ago. We understand that he has lately been considerably worse.—His boys here are all well; one or two of them dine with us, every Sunday. We are all pretty well,—though at the moment I am suffering from a very severe headache.—With best love from Dorothy and Mary, I remain

affectionately and faithfully
your friend and Br
Wm Wordsworth

The Bishop of Gloucester has ordained a Son of Mr Carus Wilson rejected by the Bishop of Chester on account of heterodox opinions.[1] I am for my own part much hurt at this proceeding of Dr Ryder, as it is notorious that the person in question is a rank Methodist—one traitorous Mind may thus inundate the whole church with its most dangerous enemies. Mr. W— preached the other day in Kendal, in a chapel which under the management of a person whom I will not name has long been a scandal to the Establishment.

[1] William Carus Wilson, b. 1791, became Vicar of Tunstall near Kirkby Lonsdale in April 1816 and founded the Clergy Daughters' School at Cowan Bridge, to which in 1824 Maria, Elizabeth, Charlotte, and Emily Brontë were sent as pupils, with consequences so momentous for English literature, for the school was the 'Low Wood' afterwards described by Charlotte in *Jane Eyre*. The rejection of Mr. Wilson, for 'inclining towards Calvinism', was mentioned in a letter from Charles Simeon to the Revd. T. Thomason, on 25 Nov. 1815. 'It has made a great noise', he said. *Memoirs of the Life of the Rev. C. Simeon*, by the Revd. William Carus, 1847, pp. 417–18. Mr. Carus Wilson senior lived at Casterton, Westmorland, and was M.P. for Cockermouth.

395. D. W. to CATHERINE CLARKSON

Address: Mrs Clarkson, Playford Hall, near Ipswich.
Stamp: Kendal Penny Post.
MS. British Museum.
K. MY ii. 553, p. 722.

4th April [1816]

My dear Friend

Believe me it is a heartfelt satisfaction for us to hear that you are so chearful and so well pleased with your new situation. That you are not oppressed by the fatigues and bustle of workmen and domestic arrangements and up-turnings is a sure proof that your health is radically amended, and that is the best news you could tell us—therefore why should I interpose my regrets that you are settled so far from us and with fresh tyes to bind you to the soil? Because I cannot help it—they mingle with all my thoughts concerning you; for I had looked forward to your release from the house at Bury, though not as the means of establishing you near us, yet as bringing a time of liberty and free choice. It is however of no *use* to talk of this and as much as I can I discourage these painful feelings, and will endeavour to hope with you that being enabled to move with less difficulty and hazard will in part counteract the tendencies of your present situation to bind you down. Sara has, I believe written to you from Keswick, she said she would do so, or I should not have been so long silent. She is still there with Dorothy and though we hope their visit is almost at an end it is not possible to say when they will come home. It will be two months on Monday since they left us and they were only to stay one month at the most. But poor Sara was confined nearly that time to the house by illness, and it was impossible to leave Miss Barker's[1] hospitable roof immediately after her recovery, and last week Dorothy had one of her coughs, which, as the weather is so dismally cold may keep them for some time longer, though she is now quite well. With the above reasons for staying so long (which could hardly be got over) a reconciling reason has combined. Dorothy has been learning from Miss Barker the notes on the Harpsichord, with a view to her going on under Miss Fletcher provided she has the inclination (which at present is strong in her) but this we are not much set upon, only it would be a pleasant thing if she could attain skill enough to amuse herself, and such friends as like a little tolerable music by the fireside. She has had a Latin master to attend her, and we hope that he

[1] See L. 257 above.

has been of service in causing her to apply with more attention than she has ever done at home, and besides her Aunt Sara, having the whole of the mornings to herself has been enabled to attend to her more steadily than it is possible to do here. We hope some good effect may have been produced; and if she goes to school after her return she may have a master to teach her Latin—or if she does *not* go to school (for that point is not yet decided) perhaps the master might attend her from Ambleside. It is very mortifying that hitherto she should have had so little steadiness in learning; and my belief is that if we had been less anxious about her and had taken less pains she would have done much more for herself. It grieves me to think how the childhood of these dear children passes away and you see nothing of them. Dorothy is now in her twelfth year, and John will be thirteen years old in June. She is lively, affectionate, and quick in faculties; but is often wayward and has fits of obstinacy with pride. Vanity she has little or none, and is utterly free from envy. She is a fine-looking girl; but at times her face is very plain, at other times it is even beautiful. She is rather stout and tall—but neither in the extreme—holds her head up well—has a broad chest, and good shoulders—but walks and runs most awkwardly.

John is much improved since he went to Mr. Dawes as a boarder, and his father hopes he will be a decent scholar in time. He is a noble, ingenuous-looking boy, and is thoroughly sweet-tempered—beloved by all his schoolfellows—and respected by them for his integrity. Little Willy (I am glad to give him that title, for it makes me sad sometimes when I think how we are losing the others as children) is a very sweet and interesting child; a happy mixture of tenderness and infantine simplicity, with liveliness, ardent curiosity and great quickness. He is backward at his Books, for he has only just begun to learn at all; but he is now under a new Master, his Father's clerk,[1] and his progress is very rapid. All at once under him he became steady, whereas his mother, his aunt Sara, and I, have all by turns undertaken him, and we could make nothing out. The lesson was the signal for yawning, and for perpetual motion in one part of the body or another. He has been perfectly well during the whole of this severe winter till Saturday, when he had the old symptoms; but we applied to medicine and a Blister immediately, and he is now quite recovered. Surely this is the longest winter or the most tardy spring that has ever been since we came into this country. It is the 4th of April and there is not beyond the fences of our gardens the faintest symptom of vegetation. The larches shew

[1] i.e. John Carter. See L. 282, p. 83, n. 2.

not a gleam of greenness and the fields are perfectly yellow—the gooseberry bushes are not in leaf, so that we have nothing but a few bunches of flowers to tell us that winter *should* be gone or going. The winds are dry and cold, and it is very pleasant weather for exercise for those who are in perfect health but very bad for invalids, old people and children. All the children at Keswick have had bad colds, and Herbert[1] has been very ill, but thank God, he is better. His Father has been in a state of miserable anxiety. William has sent to the press an ode and some sonnets and a few other poems called forth by our late victories. We hope they will be out in a few weeks. The printing might be done in a fortnight; but printers are so provokingly slow. We would gladly have had these poems out before Easter; but that is impossible. Cannot you get some friend to call at Longman's for a copy when you see that they are published? There will also be a letter (a separate publication) addressed to a Friend of Burns on the character of Burns and the misrepresentations that have been made concerning him. My brother Richard and his wife are in London. You will be sorry to hear that he is very ill. His bilious disorder has been unrelenting for some time and has produced a dimness of sight almost amounting to blindness. I trust that warm weather and a journey to Bath may restore him. The medical men say that the complaint in his eyes will go off. Christopher is going to accept the Rectories of Lambeth and Sundridge[2] in Kent. This I am very glad of for the charge at Bocking must have been dismally melancholy to him. Sundridge is a beautiful place, with a sweet parsonage house. He says that without the comfort of that spot to retire to he could not have brought himself to consent to undertake the cares of Lambeth. You ask me if I mean to go to France this spring or Summer. I wish it very much, but William and Mary are unwilling that I should venture so soon. For my part I believe that there is nothing to fear for an obscure individual like me and I believe William would consent provided I could hear of proper companions for the journey. I wish therefore that if you hear of anybody going who would be likely not to object to let me be of their party for the journey you would lose no time in letting me know. I do not like to put off year after year—another war would make it impossible and if I do not go when I can I think it may be out of my power to go at all, and my motives for the journey are very

[1] Herbert Southey, who died a fortnight after this letter was written. See L. 399 below.

[2] S. H. describes Sundridge Rectory as 'a nice old-fashioned crinkum-crankum house.' *SH* 35, p. 112. Sundridge is near Sevenoaks.

strong. The young person[1] is married to Mr. Beaudouin's Brother. We have just had a letter from them both written a month after their marriage. I believe him to be a noble minded excellent man and she seems to have well grounded hopes of happiness provided poverty can be kept out of doors; but though their present income is very well for two persons it is not enough for a family—Mr B. has a place under Government and will have, they assure us, a certain increase of income in a short time; besides C's Mother has the promise of a place for herself or one of her family in recompense for services performed by her for the royal cause; but I fear she may wait long for this, as the poor King has not the wherewithal to reward all who deserve it. In case of Mr B's death, his widow will have half the amount of his present income as a pension. Mr Eustace Baudouin is still one of the Gardes du Corps. He is much attached to his sister-in-law and has given us a very pleasing account of her. Her Mother's details of the wedding festivities would have amused you. *She* was to give the fête, she who perhaps for half a year to come will feel the effects of it at every dinner she cooks! Thirty persons were present to dinner, ball and supper. The deputies of the department and many other respectable people were there—the Bride was dressed in white Sarsenet with a white veil.—'was the admiration of all who beheld her but her modesty was her best ornament.' She kept her veil on the whole of the day—how truly French this is! Sara's desire to go to France is much abated since the removal of the pictures[2] etc, and indeed I know not how we can afford the expense of both going this year and I should be very unwilling if I could hear of companions to put off either for the sake of better times or for the insecure promise of the company of any friends, great as would be the comfort of having an English friend with me at Paris. Should I go to France this summer, I should also have the happiness of seeing you, for I could not be so near you without it; but unless this should be I cannot look forward to visiting you *this year*. We have got the Ivy cottage[3] for Tillbrooke and he talks of being there in June. It is the very place for him with his social dispositions, and it will be very pleasant to have him so near us in the summer months. Your sister will probably be with you when you receive this. Give my kind love to her. I hope the affairs of the nation are not in quite so bad a case as most people seem to fear. Nothing but

[1] Caroline Wordsworth-Vallon, W. W.'s daughter. She was married to Jean-Baptiste Baudouin on 28 Feb. 1816.

[2] i.e. the pictures brought to Paris by Napoleon from the occupied countries, now restored to their former homes.

[3] The cottage at the foot of the lane leading to Rydal Mount.

Ruin was talked of after the American war—As to a change of Ministry, that I am sure would do nothing for us. These Ministers are more likely to act honestly than the prating Opposition and I hope they will be frightened into more efforts towards economy; but what an immense Royal Family have we to maintain and the Princess of Wales spending her money abroad![1] but Buonaparte is most galling of all. The very names of humanity and magnanimity make one sick. The Relief given to the farmers we hope will be felt to be very great. The Malt tax thrown off is a great gain.

My dearest Friend do write to us soon again, we are always delighted with the sight of a letter from you when it brings good news, and deeply interested whatever be its contents. I wonder why I could rest without having written to you long ago. William's Ode is entitled a Thanksgiving ode composed on the morning of the gen'l Thanksgiving. You will see in the advertisement and post-script to William's poems part of what he has to say on the present state of affairs.[2] Mary is well but has a bad appetite and is thin. I am very strong and well. I walked to Keswick a month ago without the least fatigue.

Believe me evermore
Your affect:
D W——

396. W. W. to R. P. GILLIES

Address: R. P. Gillies Esq, King Street, Edinburgh.
Postmark: Apr. 9 1816. *Stamp*: Kendal Penny Post.
MS. Henry Huntington Library.
Gillies (—). *K.* (—). *MY ii. 554, p. 727.*

Rydale Mount

My dear Sir,

Your obliging Present reached me yesterday, several Hours before the Post brought me your Letter. I read the volume through immediately; and paid particular attention to the parts that were new to me. I need not say that I found much that gave me considerable pleasure; nevertheless, as your Preface encourages me to

[1] George III and Queen Charlotte had fifteen children, of whom twelve reached maturity. 'The Princess of Wales' is Caroline of Brunswick, the wife of the Regent, afterwards George IV; their prolonged matrimonial disagreements culminated at length in her famous 'trial' before the House of Lords in 1820, when she was successfully defended by Henry Brougham, and the 'bill of pains and penalties' brought by the Government against her was abandoned.

[2] See *PW* iii, pp. 462–4, for the 'advertisement'.

speak with sincerity, I should act unjustly both to you and myself, if I do not frankly state to you; that these Compositions, while they possess the same beauties as those which I have formerly seen of yours, labour also under the same defects, in full as great a degree. —Your mind does not look sufficiently out of itself; and it is impossible that you should do justice to your Genius till you have acquired more command over the current of your somewhat morbid sensibilities.—I trust, that you will not be hurt at my speaking thus without reserve; what would it avail to be insincere? Besides, you seem thoroughly aware of your own infirmity, and what I say if objectionable, must mainly be so, on account of being superfluous. Your Friends will value this little Volume;[1] I assure you that I value it much; and should prize it still more, were I assured that it would not be given to the Public to be trampled under foot by every bestial hoof that it may happen to encounter; I mean to express a wish that its circulation should be confined to those who being capable of feeling its merits will also understand the true quality of its imperfections. As I have before said, the constitutional disease of your Poems is want of variety. I find therefore some difficulty in pointing out which has most pleased, or displeased me. Of the Tales, I shall not repeat what I wrote heretofore; the same praise and censure apply to the new, which I presumed to give to the old. The sonnets are more or less agreeable separately considered; but they stand in each other's way from not being sufficiently diversified. I think I was most pleased with the 27th, but I could easily point out many that I liked. Nevertheless, as a friend and a Critic, I recommend that the work should not be published; though I shall not be in the slightest degree hurt on my own account, as to the point of self-love, if yourself and your other friends should think otherwise.

I am glad to hear so good an account of Mr. Wilson's Poem;[2] it has not yet found its way to us; nor have I heard of it, except from a Lady, a neighbour of ours, now in Edinburgh, who wrote to her Husband that she has been delighted with it. But Mr. W knows that Ladies for the most part are very sorry Critics, and the person in question, is perhaps not an exception, though I have no doubt that in this case she is in the right, knowing Mr. Wilson's genius; and hearing from you that he has done so well. Mr. De Quincey has taken a fit of Solitude; I have scarcely seen him since Mr. Wilson

[1] *Illustrations of a Poetical Character, in Six Tales, with other Poems*, 1816. The volume had been sent to W. before publication.

[2] *The City of the Plague, a dramatic piece in three Acts*, by John Wilson ('Christopher North'), formerly of Elleray, Windermere, now living mainly in Edinburgh, where he soon afterwards founded *Blackwood's Magazine*.

left us.—You are very obliging in having taken so much trouble about so slight a thing as the Sonnet[1] of mine you sent me.—It is not worth while to tell you, by what circuitous channel it found its way into the Examiner; a journal which I never see; though I have great respect for the *Talents* of its Editor.[2] In the Champion another weekly journal, have appeared not long since, five sonnets of mine,[3] all of them much superior to the one you have sent me.—They will form part of a Publication which I sent to the Press three weeks ago,[4] which you have been given to understand was a *long* work; but it is in fact *very short,* not more than 700 verses, altogether. The principal poem is 300 lines long, a Thanksgiving Ode, and the others refer almost exclusively to recent public events. The whole may be regarded as a *Sequel* to the Sonnets dedicated to Liberty; and accordingly I have given directions for its being printed uniform with my Poems, to admit of being bound up along with them.—I have also sent to press a Letter in Prose, occasioned by an intended Republication of Dr. Currie's Life of Burns. I ought to tell you that the Sonnet you have sent me is thus corrected.

For me *who under kindlier laws belong*
To *Nature's tuneful quire,* this rustling etc
Mid frost and snow *the instinctive* joys of song
And nobler cares etc.

When these little things will be permitted to see the light, I know not; as my Publisher has not even condescended to acknowledge the Receipt of the MSS, which were sent three weeks ago; from this you may judge of the value which the Goods of the author of the Excursion at present bear in the estimation of the Trader. N'importe, if we have done well we shall not miss our reward; farewell, yours faithfully

W. Wordsworth

I shall send you my little Publications as soon as they are out. Mrs. W.'s best regards. Miss H. is at present at Keswick. I have

[1] As appears later in this letter, the sonnet is *Miscellaneous Sonnets,* Part II. xiii, 'While not a leaf seems faded', *Oxf. W.*, p. 263.

[2] Leigh Hunt.

[3] Three sonnets had appeared in the *Champion* in 4 Feb. 1816; these were, 'High is our calling, Friend!' (addressed to B. R. Haydon); 'Intrepid sons of Albion, not by you'; and *Siege of Vienna raised by John Sobieski.* In the volume of 1816 to which he refers in the next sentence, were two others—'The Bard—whose soul is meek as dawning day' and 'Feelings of a French Royalist on the Disinterment of the Remains of the Duke D'Enghien'. They may have been omitted for want of space from the *Champion.*

[4] i.e. the *Thanksgiving Ode,* etc.

been for some time wholly unemployed, so that your kind scruples were needless.

397. W. W. to R. P. GILLIES

Address: R. P. Gillies Esqre, King Street, Edinburgh.
MS. untraced.
Gillies (—). *K* (—). *MY ii. 555, p. 730.*

Rydale Mount April 15th [1816]

My dear Sir,

You will excuse my acknowledging your kind attentions so early; but really I am afraid of my own habits of procrastination, and should I not write now, I might put off the act till having become disagreeable in thought by reminding me of my own infirmities, it might be performed so late as to rob it of every grace and all merit.—The last Post but one brought me your Letter; and this morning's coach the little tract containing Sir E. B's Essay.[1]—First let me correct a mistake Mr. Wilson has led you into; I never saw Sir E— *but once*; it was at dinner but in so large a Party that I had scarcely any conversation with him; and to the best of my recollection, he said little. He seemed a Person of very mild and pleasing manners, but with something of that feebleness in his tout ensemble which I cannot but think is diffused through such of his writings as I have seen. Nor does the present Essay constitute, to me an exception, though it becomes me, in some respects to approve of it, as no small portion of the sentiments it contains, have already been publicly expressed by me, in the preface to the L.B., and in the supplementary Essay to my last two Vols. It is plain that Sir E— cannot have read them, or he would not have so formally quoted a publication from Mr Leigh Hunt, of yesterday,[2] for a sentiment which I announced 15 years ago, and took some pains to enforce and illustrate, as being the fundamental principle of my own style. I should have no right to tax Sir E. with any blame on this account, if he had not more than once alluded to me, as one of whose writings he was not ignorant. Even in this Essay my name is *Mobbed* with the 'chief of the present day',

[1] As appears later in this letter, the work referred to is *Restituta, or Titles, Extracts and Characters of Old Books in English Literature, Revived,* 4 vols., 1814–16, by Sir Egerton Brydges.

[2] *The Feast of the Poets*, by Leigh Hunt, first published in 1811, and again in 1814. In 1815 a new edition appeared, with notes in which he apologized for having spoken with 'unqualified and therefore unbecoming distaste' of Wordsworth. In fact Hunt had read none of W's poems until 1814.

most of whom Posterity will know just as much about, as we do about the Restituta of your worthy Friend. The fault of the Essay in question is, not that the opinions are in general erroneous; but they are brought forward in a loose straggling manner; there is no necessary succession in the thoughts, no developement from a seminal principle.—Sir E. is quite correct in stating that no Poetry can be good without animation. But when he adds, 'that the position will almost exclude whatever is very highly and artificially laboured, for great artifice must destroy animation,' he thinks laxly, and uses words inconsiderately.—Substitute for the word 'artificially' the word, 'artfully', and you will at once see that nothing can be more erroneous than the assertion. The word, 'artificially' begs the question,* because that word is always employed in an unfavourable sense. Gray failed as a Poet, not because he took too much pains, and so extinguished his animation; but because he had little of that fiery quality to begin with; and his pains were of the wrong sort. He wrote English Verses, as he and other Eton school-Boys wrote Latin; filching a phrase now from one author, and now from another. I do not profess to be a person of very various reading; nevertheless if I were to pluck out of Grays tail all the feathers which, I know, belong to other Birds he would be left very bare indeed. Do not let any Body persuade you that any quantity of good verses can ever be produced by mere felicity; or that an immortal *style* can be the growth of mere Genius—Multa *tulit* fecitque, must be the motto of all those who are to last. There are Poems now existing which all the World ran after at their first appearance (and it will continue to run after their like) that do not deserve to be thought of as *literary* Works—every thing in them being skin deep merely, as to thought and [feeling,][1] the juncture or suture of the composition not [a jot] more cunning or more fitted for endurance than the first fastening together of fig-leaves in Paradise. But, I need not press upon you the necessity of Labour, as you have avowed your convictions on this subject. I assure you that if I had not had a very high opinion both of your heart and head, I should not have ventured to dissuade you from Publishing at a time when I was upon the point of committing the act myself. I felt that my situation would have been very awkward, had I acted in that manner towards a Person less deserving than yourself. I shall give you my opinion of

* There is the same fault in the use of the word 'apes' in what is said upon imitation. Studious imitators are not in general affected; but I have not room for my thoughts. [W. W.]

[1] Words torn off by seal, supplied from Gillies's *Memoirs of a Literary Veteran*. (Note by de Selincourt.)

your Mss. with the same freedom which I have hitherto used, if you should resolve upon sending it. Pray remember me to the Wilsons most kindly—When does Mr W. return to Westmorland? I have not yet seen his *City of the Plague*; the more the pity for I quarrel with the title, it not being English and being unintelligible. The English phrase is, the City *in* the Plague; if the subject be a City suffering under the Plague. Tell Mr W— this from me, and repeating to him the two following quotations;

But whate'er enjoyments dwell
In the *impenetrable* cell
Of the silent heart which Nature
Furnishes for *every* Creature.[1]

and this—

Cockadoodle doo
My dame has lost her Shoe
My master's lost his Fiddlestick
And knows not what to do!—

Mr W. will be able to solve these Ænigmas!

farewell with great regard and esteem
yours W. Wordsworth

P.S. I will take care to return your Restituta by the first opportunity, that will convey it free of expense.

398. W. W. to JOHN SCOTT

Address: John Scott Esqre, 14 Park Place, Upper Baker St., London.
MS. untraced.
K. MY ii. 556, p. 732.

Rydal Mount, Thursday, April 18th, 1816.

My dear Sir,

I deferred answering your last melancholy Letter in the hope that I might be able to announce the arrival of your Mss.[2] by this morning's Coach: but I am disappointed; some delay must either have occurred, or it has not suited you to send off the Parcel on Monday. The best conveyance is by the Manchester Mail, Swan

[1] From *The Kitten and the Falling Leaves*, see *Oxf. W.*, p. 171.

[2] i.e. the manuscript of Scott's long poem on 'the recent Victories of England'. See L. 389 above. Scott had, however, by now abandoned the idea of completing the poem. See his letter to W. W., 2 Apr. 1816, in the Wordsworth Library, Grasmere.

with two necks—but I am under no apprehension of your Packet being lost, even if it has been detained on the road. A few days ago I received a Parcel which was six days travelling hither; though two and a quarter is the regular time; a Parcel by the Manchester Mail, would have been at Kendal yesterday, and I should have received it this morning at Breakfast.

With very deep concern did I read your account of Mrs Scott's deplorable situation; and you may judge of my sympathy when I assure you that I should have been much, very much hurt, if it had come to my knowledge from other quarters that you had concealed from me these anxieties, and distresses, or even if you had restricted yourself to a bare mention of them. I know not in what situation this Letter may find you; but if your prospects have brightened, which I pray God they may have done, it will not be indifferent to you to be told that these lines are traced by the hand of one who will rejoice in your joy; and if sorrow is to be your portion, be assured that under this roof there is more than one heart that will feel for you in a degree which is rare, where personal intercourse unfortunately has been so inconsiderable. Being aware how much at all times you are engaged, I scarcely looked for a reply to any part of my Letters except the mere matters of fact. I shall value as a proof of your esteem what you purpose to write on your Opposition bias; but do not for a moment suppose that I regarded anything of that sort as necessary.

There is such a striking coincidence between your opinions and mine, as to all the fundamentals of politics, and morals, that I do not think it possible that there can really be much difference between us upon the point of the merits of the opposition. The Nation is interested in this question under two points of view. How are they likely to demean themselves while *out* of place; and what good would they do if *in*? For my own part, supposing the latter event to happen, which I do not think by any means to be desired, I own that my chief reliance would be, not upon their wisdom, but on the salutary restraint which a change of situation would impose upon their opinions, and in the favorable alteration which would be wrought in their passions by the kindly moulding of new circumstances. If one did not depend upon these influences; who could think without trembling of men like Sir Samuel Romilly[1] and Lord

[1] Sir Samuel Romilly (1757–1818), radical law-reformer, was at present M.P. for Arundel. He had voted in 1815, with Samuel Whitbread, for a motion deprecating the resumption of war against Napoleon, and continued to act with the advanced reformers.

Holland[1] having important offices in the Government of this Country? The partialities of these individuals, from different causes and in different ways are both *foreign*: the one would play the coxcomb with the laws, and what would become of the morals, the manners and the religious sentiments of the country if Lord H. and his compeers had the remodelling of them. Suppose the opposition as a body, or take them in classes, the Grenvilles, the Wellesleys, the Foxites, the Burdettites,[2] and let your imagination carry them in procession through Westminster Hall, and thence let them pass into the adjoining Abbey, and give them credit for feeling the utmost and best that they are capable of feeling in connection with these venerable and sacred places, and say frankly whether you would be at all satisfied with the result. Imagine them to be looking from a green hill over a rich landscape diversified with Spires and Church Towers and hamlets, and all the happy images of English landscape, would their sensations come much nearer to what one would desire; in a word have [they] becoming reverence of the English character, and do they value as they ought, and even as their opponents do, the constitution of the country, in *Church* and State. In fact, is there a man of the old opposition, I mean a man that puts himself forward, who is capable of looking at the subject of Religion with the eyes which an english Politician ought to possess? But I must stop. Let me only say one word upon Lord B.[3] The man is insane; and will probably end his career in a mad-house. I never thought him anything else since his first appearance in public. The verses on his private affairs[4] excite in me less indignation than pity. The latter copy is the Billingsgate of Bedlam.—Your Correspondent A. S. has written, begging his pardon, a very foolish Letter upon the Verses that appeared in the Chronicle—I have not seen them, but I have no doubt that what he praises so highly is contemptible as a work of Art, like the Ode to the Emperor Nap.—You yourself, appear to me to labour under some delusion as to the merits of Lord B's Poetry, and treat those wretched verses, The farewell, with far too much respect. They are disgusting in sentiment, and in execution contemptible. 'Though my many faults defaced me' etc. Can worse doggrel be written than such a stanza? One verse is

[1] Lord Holland (1773–1840) was the nephew of Charles Fox, and a leading Whig. His wife was the famous hostess of Holland House.

[2] i.e. followers of Sir Francis Burdett (1770–1844), the radical baronet, M.P. or Westminster.

[3] i.e. Byron.

[4] Byron's poems on the failure of his marriage, *A Farewell* and *A Sketch from Private Life*, had been published in the *Champion*, but not with Byron's knowledge.

commendable, 'All my madness none can know', 'Sine dementia nullus Phœbus'; but what a difference between the amabilis insania of inspiration, and the fiend-like exasperation of these wretched productions. It avails nothing to attempt to heap up indignation upon the heads of those whose talents are extolled in the same breath. The true way of dealing with these men is to shew that they want genuine power. That talents they have, but that these talents are of a *mean* order; and that their productions have no solid basis to rest upon. Allow them to be men of high genius, and they have gained their point and will go on triumphing in their iniquity; demonstrate them to be what in truth they are, in all essentials, Dunces, and I will not say that you will reform them; but by abating their pride you will strip their wickedness of the principal charm in their own eyes. I have read your late Champions with much pleasure. I cannot conclude without mentioning that my friend Southey yesterday lost his only son, a most promising child, nine years of age.[1] This is a great trouble to us all; the poor Father supporting himself with admirable fortitude. Mrs. W. is very thankful for your kind remembrance of her; and joins me in best wishes and prayers for the restoration of Mrs. Scott.

Affectionately yours,
W. Wordsworth.

399. W. W. to ROBERT SOUTHEY

Address: Robert Southey Esq[re].
MS. Copy by Susan Wordsworth, WL.
Hitherto unpublished.

[21 April 1816]

My dear S.

It would have done no good to break in upon you. I was therefore silent after I first heard so suddenly of your affliction.[2] Even now I can offer nothing but my sympathy and that of Mary and the rest of this family with you and the Mother of the departed. As soon as you feel, I will not say the least inclination, but no aversion to see me as a friend and one who has been a fellow sufferer, pray let me know and I will come over. Let this suffice for the present adding only my fervent prayer that God may enable you and your family to support

[1] Southey's son Herbert (at present his only son) died on 17 Apr. See L. 399 below.

[2] i.e. the death of Southey's son, Herbert. See L. 398 above.

this and every other affliction to which His will may subject them. Assured that your heart will echo this prayer for me and mine when it shall please the Almighty to exercise us with affliction, I remain my dear Southey

your very affectionate and faithful friend
Wm Wordsworth

Sunday Evening

400. W. W. to ROBERT SOUTHEY

MS. Harvard University Library.
K. MY ii. 557, p. 735.

Friday [26 April 1816]
Rydal Mount

My dear Friend,

Miss H.[1] informs us that both you and Mrs Southey support yourselves under your loss with admirable fortitude. I need not say what a consolation it is to me to learn this. You will indeed stand in need of resignation and patience and all the passive virtues; and these will not desert you because in your mind, they will be supported by faith and hope, without whose assistance I think it utterly impossible for a good man of tender heart to bear up under an affliction as heavy as your's.

Whether I look back or forward I sorrow for you; but I doubt not that in time your retrospective thoughts will be converted into sweet though sad pleasures; and as to your prospective regards in connection with this dear Child, as they will never stop short of another and a more stable world, before them your disappointments will melt away; but they[2] will make themselves felt as they ought to do, since it will be for a salutary purpose.

I will come over to see you, as soon as you desire it: or if you prefer that mode of meeting we should be thankful to see you here. An opportunity would offer when the Children return[3]—They are well and apparently happy.——

In the meantime accept the heartfelt condolence of my wife my Sister myself, and my little Boy, whose thoughts have often been painfully busy upon this sad occasion.

[1] It seems that S. H. had been staying at Keswick. She was devoted to the Southeys and in later years was often the counsellor and confidant of the girls.
[2] i.e. the disappointments.
[3] i.e. the Southey children who appear to have been staying at Rydal Mount.

Farewell—and the God of Mercy and love sustain you and your partner

Most faithfully and affectionately
Your friend and fellow sufferer
Wm Wordsworth.

401. W. W. to BASIL MONTAGU

Address: Basil Montagu Esq[r], Lincoln's Inn, London
MS. Harvard University Library.
MY ii. 557a, p. 736.

Rydal Mount, April 29th 1816

My dear Montagu,

Your account of the state of my Brother Richard's health has affected and distressed us much; we have, however, a heartfelt consolation in the knowledge, that he is in such good hands; and feel most grateful to yourself and Mrs. Montagu for the kind care you have taken of him; and for the opportunity which the accommodation of your aery house will have afforded him to rally if it should please God that he recover. Say to him, from his sister and my self, everything that is affectionate and tender; poor Fellow, he has had many a long and weary fit of sickness from which he has recovered so far as to enjoy a comfortable existence; and we would gladly encourage a hope that the like may recur; but your letter scarcely allows us to do so.—As to the state of his affairs, there is much reason to regret that he has not made a will, and appointed Guardians for his Child,[1]—especially considering the situation of life from which his wife was taken, and the great probability of her returning by a second marriage into that class. She is, I believe, a very good affectionate Creature, but neither she nor any of her Relations can be deemed proper Persons to superintend the education of his Boy. I am much concerned at this; and do think that if it be possible he should make arrangements for this particular, and for the management of his Property during the long minority of his son.

As to his sister's affairs and mine, in connexion with Rich[d] we have no security but a bond[2] for three thousand pound, which perhaps will be some hundred pounds less than the sum owing us.—But this is uncertain.

[1] Before his death on 19 May Richard was persuaded to remedy this omission and make a will appointing his brothers joint guardians of his son. See L. 402 below.

[2] See Letters 377, 399 above and 402, 403 below.

I leave it to Christopher and you, to do whatever shall seem best, under these melancholy circumstances.—If Christr had not been in town, I should have gone up immediately—as it is, there seems to be no necessity for it.

With most grateful acknowledgement I remain, my dear Montagu

faithfully yours
Wm. Wordsworth

Is Dr. Lawson in town, and what is he about?

402. W. W. to BASIL MONTAGU

MS. untraced.
K. MY ii. 558, p. 737.

Kendal, May 3d Friday morning [1816]

My dear Montagu,

You will be perplexed by receiving three letters from me. One was sent from Rydal yesterday, another in the shape of a parcel this morning from Kendal, under an expectation, which I find is erroneous, that it would be delivered to you on Sunday. Since that letter was written I have consulted an intelligent attorney here, and from him I learn that the bond[1] will be of no use to me for either principal or interest (without an expensive process in chancery), till Richard's son is of age, if Richard die without a will providing for the payment. I therefore beg you, as a friend and a man of business acting as my *representative*, to state to my brother that, under the present circumstances, it is my duty to enforce upon him the necessity of making and executing a will by which his estates shall be charged with the payment, within a year after his decease, of whatever sum shall be found due from him to his sister and myself, from the estate of our father, or otherwise. I sincerely beg of you to see that this is done immediately. My brother and I examined the accounts together, and agreed upon everything relating to this, according to the memorandum attached to this, so that there can be no difficulty on this part of the subject. I shall be most anxious till I hear from you that this is done; for do think of my poor sister's situation at present, forty-four years of age, and without the command of either principal or interest of her little property, in case Richard has not

[1] See L. 401 above, and also L. 403 below, to C. W. Wordsworth's urgent request to C. W. and Basil Montagu was fortunately effectual and Richard made the necessary provision in his will, as we learn from L. 404.

provided otherwise. I will now repeat my thanks for your goodness to Richard. You hint that a sale should have been made. It seems as if there was reason to apprehend that dilatoriness may still interfere. Surely Richard will be sensible of what he owes to his own family, and to his father's. Farewell,

Affectionately yours,
W. Wordsworth.

403. W. W. to C. W.

Address: To the Rev[d] Dr Wordsworth.
MS. WL.
MY ii. 559, p. 738.

Kendal Friday May 3[d]
1816

My dear Brother,

In consequence of the distressing accounts which I received from Montagu of the state of our Br Rd's health, I proceeded thus far on my way towards London; but I have been stopped by a Letter received this morning from M—[1] mentioning that Rd is considerably better; and that hopes are now entertained of his recovery which did not before exist. M— tells me also that he has made but not *executed* his will—on the subject of Rd's Will I wrote you some time ago, addressing as I am obliged now to do to Mr Manners Sutton;[2] and I am very much concerned that we have received no Letter from you, letting us know whether you have seen Richd, how he is, etc—

I am now going to beg of you to undertake a service for my Sister and myself, which when I have stated to you, I am sure, you will feel to be a sacred duty of Conscience to perform for us. I did not know till within this hour, that the bond for £3000 which Richd has given me for the debt due to us,[3] on account of my father's Estate and otherwise, would be of no use, for putting us in possession of either principal or interest, due thereon, till Richd's Son now a year old become of age; unless Richd make a will by which his

[1] i.e. Montagu.

[2] It seems that letters to C. W. were being sent under cover to the Archbishop's son, Charles Manners-Sutton, who was M.P. for Scarborough and became Speaker of the House of Commons in 1817. Letters addressed to any M.P. could be forwarded free of postal charge, being 'franked'.

[3] See Letters 401, 402 above. This letter illustrates the danger into which Wordsworth had allowed his financial affairs to fall by entrusting them so entirely to the dilatory Richard.

Estates are especially charged with the payment of this debt in particular, or all his just debts in general; and Trustees appointed with power to sell or mortgage for this purpose; or unless he leaves personal Property to cover this and all his other debts. Now as Rd has lately made large purchases in Land, I apprehend that he has not personal effects to cover his debts; and on this account I beg of you as a Brother and a[s] a Friend; and for your Sister's sake, every farthing of whose property is in Richard's hands, to urge Richd to excecute his will; he having taken care, therein, to charge his trustees to pay this debt if required, within a year after his demise; I mean, whatever may be found justly due to our Sister and myself. I have written to Montagu to the same effect; I beg most earnestly, my dear Brother, that you would confer with him on the subject, and together take such measures, as will place our minds at ease upon this most anxious and painful subject. It would little become me to doubt, but that the will made by Richd has provided for this and every other just demand; but this Will may not yet be executed, and it is reasonable that we should be tranquillized by an assurance from himself that justice has been done. I do not write to himself, because I would not abruptly break in upon him knowing how ill he has been and still may be.

So much have I this matter at heart, especially on Dorothy's account, that I should have proceeded to London, notwithstanding this favorable account; had I not had the fullest confidence, that yourself and Montagu will represent me, and act as earnestly and zealously as I could have done myself. To leave home would cost me much at present, for I am in much anxiety about my son Wm, who has been ill; and looks very poorly—our Sister Dorothy also has had a severe attack with cold and fever—and really the expense of travelling is what I can little afford. Besides, Richd might deem that it implied a suspicion of his disregarding his duty, if nothing less than a journey to London would satisfy me that he had done right.

In my former Letter I stated urgent reasons why Richd ought to make a will, drawn entirely from considerations respecting his own family; for at that time I supposed that this Bond would enable us to touch both principal and interest; in which opinion, it appears that I was lamentably mistaken.

I know not what is become of my little Publications.[1] I hear nothing of them; they ought to have been out many weeks ago—most affectionately your friend and Brother

W Wordsworth

[1] i.e. *A Letter to a Friend of Burns*, and the *Thanksgiving Ode*.

404. W. W. to BASIL MONTAGU

Address: Basil Montagu Esq., 10 Lincoln's Inn, London.
Postmark: C 14 May 1816. *Stamp*: Kendal Penny Post.
MS. Cornell.
Hitherto unpublished.

Saturday 11th May 1816

My dear M—

I am most happy to hear that Rd has executed his Will; and am much obliged to you for the trouble you have taken in this anxious business—It would have been a most shocking thing, for my Sister especially, to have been left in the decline of life, in the State in which that Bond would have left us; without the provision made by R's Will for the payment of what may be found due to us—We have now only to wish that it may please God that our dear Brother may be restored to health—

In regard to the Bond respective [to] R. Calvert;[1] if I recollect right, the purport of it was to prevent his friendly intentions towards myself being frustrated, in respect to my future life, by claims on the part of my Uncle Wordsworth, for money which he might possibly have advanced for my education.

If this be the purport of it, let it be given up—

If it please God that Rd should recover, I shall be most anxious not to lose a moment in settling our affairs—so much indeed have I suffered on this account that I would most readily undertake a journey to London tomorrow for that purpose; if it were fit and proper that my Brother should enter upon the business—

I also wish that you would conclude your little affairs with me; for I am heartily sick of all long-pending accounts, whether small or great—

With many and heartfelt thanks My dear Montague for your kindness to my Br and the services you have rendered him

I remain
faithfully yours
W Wordsworth

Algernon,[2] we think much improved.

[1] Raisley Calvert, W's early friend at Keswick, who d. Jan. 1795, leaving to W. a legacy of £900. For the story of the legacy and in particular of the bond here mentioned, undertaken by Richard to prevent the legacy being used for the purpose of repaying debts to Uncle Richard W., see Moorman, i, pp. 251–2, and *EY* 44, pp. 130–2.

[2] For Algernon, see L. 190, pt. i, p. 402, n. 1.

405. W. W. to JOHN SCOTT

MS. untraced.
K (—). *MY ii. 560, p. 740* (—).

May 14, [1816.]

My dear Sir,

. . . Some years ago I wrote at length upon the subject of the military and civil character to Colonel Pasley,[1] author of the *Essay on the Military Policy of this Island*. . . . *Scientific* military establishments, upon a scale proportioned to the necessary size of our army, are, I think, indispensable in the present state of Europe. To say nothing of the plea of humanity, nothing of national reputation for military efficiency, the state of the *finances* of the country will not allow us time, in a future war, if one should break out, to re-acquire the degree of military skill which can alone ensure success, if we should suffer our present knowledge to languish for want of due care in keeping it up. Poverty would compel us to give in long before we had accomplished anything important for the relief of the party whose interest we had espoused. Unquestionably, if the inevitable consequence of keeping up those institutions is to be the impairing of our civil energy, let them perish. But I cannot see that this need follow. . . .

406. D. W. to C. W.

Address: The Rev[d] Dr Wordsworth, Rectory, Lambeth, London.
Postmark: 10 o'clock M[a]y 17 1816. *Stamp*: Kendal Penny Post.
MS. Jonathan Wordsworth.
TLS 12 June 1959.

Tuesday 14th [May] 1816

My dear Brother,

Your letter which we received last night gave us great satisfaction. I trust that our poor Brother is actually recovering, which I had before hardly ventured to hope, though we had heard from Montagu from time to time that he was better. The swoln legs, difficulty of breathing, and excessive weakness made me apprehend an inward decay. We have great reason for thankfulness to Basil Montagu for having prevailed upon him to quit his lodgings in Warwick Court; and, as long as Mr Carlyle's[2] advice and prescrip-

[1] See L. 221, pt. i, p. 473.

[2] Anthony Carlisle, a physician who had attempted to cure Coleridge of opium-taking, when he came with the Montagus to London in 1810. See Griggs, iii. 809, p. 298 and n.

tions have benefited him we have reason to be satisfied with him also—I have always heard that he was a clever man, but apt to venture upon too bold experiments. Knowing how much you are engaged we cannot expect long or *very* frequent letters from you; but pray my dear Brother, until Richard's health is in a less delicate state, let us hear from you as often as you can; for we cannot help continuing to be very anxious while he remains so extremely weak.— We are very glad that he has settled his worldly affairs: this must be a great relief to his mind; and on our account we are perfectly satisfied with what has been done.—Give my kind love to Mrs Wordsworth[1] tell her that I have sincerely lamented over her sufferings—indeed we have all felt very much for her. I suppose her little boy is with his Grandmother, who no doubt will take good care of him—I trust he is well as we have heard nothing to the contrary. He is as fine and interesting a Child as ever I saw— William thought him like what your Charles was when he was a baby: and I, too, thought I could see a resemblance. I am happy in the knowledge, both for Richard's sake and his Wife's that they are under your roof; and it must be a great comfort to you that you can see him daily—Poor Fellow! he will be very anxious to get into the country again; and I fear he will not thoroughly regain his strength in London—and that is the worst of it; for, no doubt, it was *business*, and without strength he *can* transact no [?business]—It is a long time since we heard anything of my Uncle Cookson's Family. Pray tell us what you know of them. In my Aunt's last letter she informed us that Mary was likely to be married to a Nephew of the Bishop of Salisbury;[2] and I have been disappointed in not hearing before now, that she was actually married. William ordered a Copy of his Ode, and of 'the Letter'[3] to be sent to my Uncle. I hope he has received them; and that you also have got your copies—The letter I think is a beautiful composition. I hope you will be pleased with it, and that you will agree with me in admiring the Poems.

I shall be very glad when you have got settled in your new livings. It is a great comfort that you have so quiet and beautiful a place to retire to as Sundridge.[4] I look forward to a melancholy pleasure in visiting you there at some future time, if it please God to grant us health and strength. That these Blessings may be continued to you

[1] i.e. R. W.'s wife.

[2] See L. 351, p. 207, n. 3.

[3] W. W.'s *Thanksgiving Ode*, and the *Letter to a Friend of Burns*, both published in May 1816.

[4] C. W.'s living near Sevenoaks, Kent, which he held with the Rectory of Lambeth.

for many many years is my earnest prayer, and that your Boys may grow up a Blessing to their Father. We are all pretty well and unite in kind Love to you and the Children—Believe me, dear Christopher

your ever affectionate Sister
D Wordsworth

Do not fail, I pray you, from time to time [? to let] us hear how Richard goes on—Give our [? kindest] Love to Richard and his Wife. Should we direct under cover to Mr. Sutton?[1]

407. W. W. to C. W.

Address: The Rev^d Dr. Wordsworth, Rectory, Lambeth.
Postmark: 22 M[a]y 1816. *Stamp*: Kendal Penny Post.
MS. Jonathan Wordsworth.
TLS 12 June 1959.

Sunday Evening
May 19th 1816

My dear Brother,

We have just received two Letters from you, and one from Montagu—And this is intended merely as a Letter of thanks to you Both. These melancholy accounts have prepared us for the worst. Knowing how much illness Richard has had, which cannot but have impaired his constitution, we do not encourage an expectation that he will be able to struggle through so severe a trial.

—It is of no use to write to us either on *Tuesdays* or *Thursdays*; we have a Post only 4 days a week. Be so good as to remember this.

Pray send this Letter to Montagu by the 2penny Post; we are very sorry for Richard's Wife, whose sufferings and fatigues must both be great.

If it be proper to present to our dear Brother, our most affectionate love, do not fail to discharge this melancholy duty, and assure him, that if he should not recover, nothing will be wanting on our part to fulfill his wishes, to the best of our interpretation of them and the utmost of our power.

I remain your most affectionate
Br and friend
Wm Wordsworth

[1] .i.e Mr. Manners-Sutton. See L. 403 above.

408. W. W. to C. W.

Address: The Rev[d] Dr. Wordsworth, Rectory, Lambeth.
Postmark: 10 o'clock M[a]y 23 1816. *Stamp*: Kendal.
MS. Jonathan Wordsworth.
TLS, 12 June 1959.

Monday Evening
[20 May 1816]

My dear Brother,

You will have learned by a Letter despatched yesterday that we were prepared for an account as hopeless as that of yours Sat. last—We join in the prayer with which your's concludes—God Almighty have mercy upon us all for Jesus Christ's sake!

Using my utmost speed I could not reach London before Thursday; and everything respecting the funeral must have been determined probably before this time. Since we have had little hope of Richard's recovery I have congratulated myself on the thought of his being buried in a place with which you have so important a connection—As he did not express a wish to be carried down into the North, there surely cannot be a reason for incurring so heavy an expense; particularly since neither his father nor mother were buried at Barton Church;[1] which probably would have been the place of his choice if it had been convenient.—

I shall send this Letter by express to Kendal, as we have no post from Ambleside to night. I shall be able to hear from you on Wednesday and on Friday; an answer to this may be at Kendal on Saturday; but it will not reach me 'till Sunday Evening unless I send for it, express—

I regret very much that I did not proceed to London some time since; to divide with you and Mrs W. the cares, fatigues, and anxieties of your distressful duties. But the accounts were so favorable, as to seem to render it unnecessary—I have now only to say, that I will set off for Town immediately after I receive an answer to this, if you deem it adviseable—I much fear that in the capacity of Executors we shall have a great deal of anxiety and trouble, and that Richard's affairs will be found in a far worse state than he himself apprehended. Indeed I am by no means easy on the score of the debt due to Dorothy and me; though I do not feel this to be a time to dwell upon so painful a subject. If in the capcity of Executor, or as

[1] Between Pooley Bridge at the foot of Ullswater, and Eamont Bridge near Penrith. W. W.'s grandparents, Richard and Mary W., are buried there. It was the parish church of the Wordsworth property at Sockbridge. R. W. was buried in Lambeth parish church, of which C. W. was Rector.

a support to you, and Mrs Wordsworth, you think it well and right, that I should come to Town, be assured that my duty will in this instance, be performed with promptness and alacrity—

Our dear Sister is far from well: she caught a violent cold a few weeks ago which has left her extremely deaf in one ear; and her spirits have been much shattered by Richard's illness—

Give our best love to Mrs W. and assure her that every support which I can lend her and her orphan Son, will be afforded. My dear Brother farewell.

God in heaven bless you
W Wordsworth

409. W. W. to C. W.

Address: To The Rev^d^ Dr Wordsworth, Rectory, Lambeth.
Postmark: C 27 My 1816. 10 o'clock. *Stamp*: Kendal Penny Post.
MS. WL.
MY ii. 561, p. 741.

Thursday May 23^d^ 1816

My dear Brother,

My previous Letters would inform you that we were prepared for the Contents of yours of Monday. As there was no hope of recovery we derived satisfaction from learning that our poor Brother had not lingered long.[1]—We condole with you most affectionately on the loss which our Family has sustained; and join in your prayer that God may give us grace to profit by this awful event.—

Richard has acted judiciously in appointing yourself and me joint Guardians with his Widow, for his son—and I am pleased to hear that it is believed that the execution of the Trust will not be attended with much difficulty—For my own part, I cannot but apprehend that it may be attended with *unsatisfactory* circumstances; knowing how little our Brother has looked into his affairs for these several years past, and that he must have had long-pending accounts, both with Lord Abergavenny[2] and Mr Addison,[3] and perhaps with several

[1] R. W. died on 19 May.

[2] Henry Neville, 2nd Earl of Abergavenny (1755–1843), married Mary, only daughter of John Robinson, M.P. and Secretary to the Treasury, who was a cousin of W. W., being the nephew of W. W.'s grandmother, Mary Robinson of Appleby, wife of Richard W. of Sockbridge who d. 1750 and, with his wife, was buried in Barton Church, Westmorland. The East Indiaman of which W. W.'s beloved brother John was captain, and in the wreck of which he perished in Feb. 1805, was called *Earl of Abergavenny* after this nobleman.

[3] Richard Addison, R. W.'s partner.

others. I wish from my heart that the arrangements made by him may be found equal to the paying of all his debts—for I cannot but think that for some time past his estate must have been rapidly diminishing; owing to two acts of imprudence; the 1st, making such considerable purchases of Land, and the 2nd, his taking the management into his own hands—It is clear that his Lands cannot be reconverted into money without great Loss,[1] and not less clear, that his management cannot have been productive; but much the contrary—It is useless, however, to trouble you with these suggestions and conjectures, as an inspection of his affairs will, I hope, soon shew us the real state of the case——

We have much satisfaction in learning where our dear Brother is to be buried[2]——Say to Mrs Wordsworth, that unless I learn that it is proper I should come to London, I will meet her at Sockbridge as soon after her arrival there as she desires; and I will thank you to let me know her wishes upon this subject.—I shall write to Mr Hutton[3] to day; and if I learn from him that my presence will be useful at Sockbridge, I shall go thither immediately.

I cannot but think with you, that it is probable my presence will be of more service in the North than in London——

The Stamp office will require my presence from about the 15th till the 20th of July; till then, I should be at liberty to attend to any important business; if all continue well at home—

We have felt much for you my dear Brother on this melancholy occasion; and I have often regretted that I did not proceed to London, when I was at Kendal on my way thither. But the favourable accounts seemed to render it unnecessary; and I am so anxious when from home least[4] any evil should befall my family, that I do not like to face the notion of being long absent, except when necessary.

most faithfully yours with best love

W Wordsworth

Dorothy is pretty well.

Sir George and Lady Beaumont have expressed to us a hope that you will call on them. We shall inform them how, and how much you have been engaged.—

[1] In Sept. 1816 W. W., with Crabb Robinson, attended sales of R. W.'s properties in west Cumberland. Crabb Robinson notes in his diary on 15 Sept., 'Mr. Wordsworth was satisfied with his journey, having sold better than he expected the Ravenglass property and part of the property at Cockermouth.' *HCR* i, p. 192.

[2] i.e. Lambeth Parish Church. See L. 408, p. 315, n. 1 above.

[3] See L. 415, p. 328, n. 1 below.

[4] i.e. 'lest'.

It would be highly gratifying to me if you could find a moment to call on Lord Lonsdale—in Charles Street; he has been always so very kind to me.

410. D. W. to CATHERINE CLARKSON

Address: Mrs Clarkson, Playford Hall, near Ipswich.
Stamp: Kendal Penny Post.
MS. British Museum.
K. MY ii. 562, p. 742.

Sunday May 26. [1816]

My dear Friend,

Before this reaches you, you will have been informed by the newspapers of the death of our poor brother Richard, and for our sakes I am sure you have been affected by it though you did not know him personally. He left Sockbridge with his Wife in February, in a bad state of health, to transact business in London and at the same time to procure medical advice. We were not particularly apprehensive of danger as he had been so frequently ill for a great length of time though we heard that he did not cast off his malady;—but at the last Basil Montagu, seeing him grow worse and worse in confined lodgings, prevailed upon him to remove to his house—There he was very ill—and William set forward intending to go to London; but at Kendal he found a letter telling us that he was very much better; and for more than a week we had accounts of his convalescence. He was then with Christopher at Lambeth. Last Saturday but one again he worsened. On the Wednesday an abscess burst on the Liver; and from that time, poor Fellow! he struggled—not I trust in great pain—until Sunday morning the 19th when he expired, nature being quite exhausted. His sickness and the anxiety attending upon it latterly affected us very much, the contemplation of the death of a *Brother* was solemn and distressing—and when all was over we felt it deeply, though we were very thankful when God had taken him from his sufferings—and heartily do we join in Christopher's prayer that God may give us grace to profit by the awful event. We have seen very little of Richard for many years therefore as a companion his loss will not be great; but when we did meet he was always amiable and affectionate; and there has been in all our connections with him a perfect harmony. It is a great comfort to us that he died in the house of his Brother and that his body rests where Christopher may probably also spend his latter days. He was to be buried in the Church at Lambeth on Friday. He made his will about three weeks before his death, and has appointed William and Christopher joint guardians to his Son and executors with his Wife. There is also another Executor, Mr Thomas Hutton of Penrith. We have reason to believe that the Will is a just one. I must add, which will give you pleasure, that my poor Brother's wife has been a faithful and affectionate nurse to him. She is almost worn out, as Christopher says, with fatigue and watching. Poor thing! she means to return to Sockbridge as soon as possible. We are very much indebted to Montagu for his kind exertions.—Now my dear Friend I must turn to a subject which has been much upon our minds lately. Only I had not the heart to write to you while we were so anxious about Richard, and I am afraid you may have thought us careless or unkind. Sara promised me over and over again that she would write —and she much wished it—but you know she is idle—and I dare say persuaded herself every post day that we should hear from you, —as indeed I thought we should—respecting the Riots in Suffolk and the degree of apprehension you might entertain for the property of your Brothers and other Friends—that was the reason of our particular wish to hear from you. I trust that you, being out of the circuit of the Riots, are safe, and surely the Poor could not by any possible means take the fancy that Mr *Clarkson* was their enemy! but you cannot help having great anxiety and distress for others. Pray tell us how you feel—and what you fear or have feared—perhaps the newspapers exaggerate the mischief; but at best it must be very great. In this part of England we are happy—no public disasters seem to touch us. Labourers find the benefit of the cheapness of corn; and their wages are not much reduced; so that except from those who have property we have little or nothing of complaints—and they are only suffering under an evil which they can well bear, and which will certainly pass away. You sympathized in poor Southey's distress I am sure.[1] His loss is indeed irreparable; for it was impossible for any child more completely to satisfy the wishes of a Father. Herbert was in all pursuits likely to have grown up the Companion and friend of his Father—at nine years of age he had in study the eagerness of a fellow student, while he was as fond of play as an ordinary child—and his Father in his half-hours of relaxation made himself his playmate. Southey, you know, has uncommon self-command, and after the child was buried he addressed himself to his labours as before, and so has continued to do, but all agree that he

[1] i.e. the death in April of Herbert Southey. See Letters 398 and 399 above.

is an altered man—his buoyant spirits I fear will never return and it will be very long before he regains his chearfulness. Mrs Southey supported herself wonderfully at first but she is in great dejection, and I fear that it will long continue; she is not of that turn of mind which makes her, under less afflictions than this, struggle through and bear up. Therefore how can we hope that she will speedily overcome this heavy sorrow? Poor Sara had the melancholy lot of being at Keswick during the whole of Herbert's sickness—she could not bear to leave them till all was over. Dorothy was with her and on the day of the child's death she came home with Edith[1] and Sara Coleridge, who stayed a week. Sara H brought with her a cough, the remains of her illness, and for some time she looked very ill; but she is now much better, and she has got her pony from Wales which will I hope set her completely strong again. Sara Coleridge is much improved in health and strength and is much grown. She is a delightful scholar, having so much pleasure in learning. I know no greater pleasure than to instruct a girl who is so eager in the pursuit of knowledge as she is—often do we wish that Dorothy was like her in this respect—*half* like her would do very well, for with all Dorothy's idleness there are many parts of her character which are much more interesting than corresponding ones in Sara, therefore, as good and evil are always mixed up together, we should be very contented with a moderate share of industry, her talents being quite enough. But I am perhaps misleading you. I have no fault to find with Sara in anything—but yet there is a something which made me make the observation—a want of power to interest you,—not from anything positively amiss, but she wants the wild graces of nature. Edith is a delightful girl—scholar good enough, and to me very engaging. I hope you got my Brother's Odes, and the letter on Burns. All are gone to Church but me, and I expect them home every moment. William and Mary are well; but Mary has had a bad appetite and looks very thin. I hope we shall hear from you immediately. May God bless you, my dearest Friend, Believe me

Ever faithfully yours,
D Wordsworth.

Herbert Southey died of an inflammation on the heart. I wish we could hear of Mrs Luff. All join with me in kind love and in begging that you will write.

[1] Southey's eldest daughter, b. 1804. She married the Revd. J. W. Warter who many years later brought out an edition of Southey's letters—*Selections from the Letters of Robert Southey*, 4 vols., 1856. Sara Coleridge, the Coleridges' only daughter, was at this time thirteen years old.

411. W. W. to C. W.

Address: The Rev[d] Dr. Wordsworth, Rectory, Lambeth, London.
Postmark: Ju 4 1816. *Endorsed*: Br. Wm. No. 7. Request not to pay money as Trustee.
MS. Jonathan Wordsworth.
TLS, 12 June 1959.

Saturday Night
1st June [1816]
Mr Harrison's Penrith

My dear Brother,

You shall hear from me at length by next Post: I now write merely to beg that, in character of Trustee, you would pay no debts whatever owing by our late Brother—

Affectionately your's
W. Wordsworth

I left home yesterday. Mrs Wordsworth[1] arrived at Sockbridge a few hours before, as well as could be expected.—

The Caution above given arises from a considerable doubt whether the real Estate devized in aid of the Personal will suffice for the payment of the debts, which I apprehend will be found *much* larger than was calculated upon by my Brother, or Mr Addison.[2]

[*For 411a, W.W. to C.W., see Addenda.*]

412. W. W. to JOHN SCOTT

MS. untraced.
K (—). *MY ii. 563, p. 746* (—).

Rydal Mount, Tuesday, June 11, [1816.]

My dear Sir,

I am only just returned after more than a week's absence upon painful and anxious business, which has devolved upon me as trustee under the will of my eldest brother, recently deceased. He has left an only child, a boy sixteen months old, and a widow not twenty-seven years, and though his property is considerable, yet the affairs are in an intricate and perplexed situation, so that much of my time and more of my thoughts will in future be taken up by them; and I need scarcely say to you that I am wholly inexperienced in things of this kind. But to return to your situation and prospects. My best wishes will follow you to the Continent, and I shall be anxious to hear that your hopes keep their ground and strength

[1] i.e. R. W.'s widow. [2] R. W.'s partner at Staple Inn.

from the influence of a milder climate. I have no doubt that the world will be benefited by your observations abroad; yet in a public point of view I cannot but regret your departure from your own country. It would give me pleasure could I say that I have any acquaintances in the literary world, through whom I could hope to aid you in disposing of *The Champion*. It will be very difficult, I fear impossible, to place the work in such hands as would support its present reputation, after you have resigned the management of it; and therefore I cannot but think you judge well and prudently in being desirous to *sell* the property, rather than entrust it to an editor or partner during your absence. But I have not a single acquaintance except Southey, to whom it would be advisable even to make known your intentions; for there is a disadvantage, as well as an advantage, in publicity upon occasions of this sort. . . . The queries you put to me upon the connection between genius and irregularity of conduct may probably induce me to take up the subject again, and yet it scarcely seems necessary. No man can claim indulgence for his transgressions on the score of his sensibilities, but at the expense of his credit for intellectual powers. All men of *first* rate genius have been as distinguished for dignity, beauty, and propriety of moral conduct. But we often find the faculties and qualities of the mind not well balanced; something of prime importance is left short, and hence confusion and disorder. On the one hand it is well that dunces should not arrogate to themselves a pharisaical superiority, because they avoid the vices and faults which they see men of talent fall into. They should not be permitted to believe that they have more understanding merely on that account, but should be taught that they are preserved probably by having less feeling, and being consequently less liable to temptation. On the other hand, the man of genius ought to know that the cause of his vices is, in fact, his deficiencies, and not, as he fondly imagines, his superfluities and superiorities. All men ought to be judged with charity and forbearance after death has put it out of their power to explain the motives of their actions, and especially men of acute sensibility and lively passions. This was the scope of my letter to Mr. Gray.[1] Burns has been cruelly used, both dead and alive. The treatment which Butler and others have experienced has been renewed in him. He asked for bread—no, he did not *ask* it, he endured the want of it with silent fortitude—and ye gave him a stone.[2] It is

[1] i.e. *A Letter to a Friend of Robert Burns*, 1816.

[2] Samuel Butler (1612–80), author of *Hudibras*, was buried in St. Paul's, Covent Garden; the monument was erected in 1721. W. is referring to a poem,

worse than ridiculous to see the people of Dumfries coming forward with their pompous mausoleum, they who persecuted and reviled him with such low-minded malignity. Burns might have said to that town when he was dying, 'Ingrata—non possidebis ossa mea!'[1] On this and a thousand other accounts his monument ought to have been placed in or near to Edinburgh; 'stately Edinburgh throned on crags.'[2] How well would such an edifice have accorded with the pastoral imagery near St. Anthony's Well and under Arthur's Seat, while the metropolis of his native country,—to which his writings have done so great honour—with its murmuring sounds, was in distinct hearing! . . .

I must not conclude without a word upon politics. . . . I will not at present recur to our military disagreement, further than to repeat the expression of my own belief, that no danger to the civil liberties of the country—in the present state of public information, and with our present means of circulating truth—is to be apprehended from such scientific military establishments as appear to be eligible. And surely you will allow that martial qualities are the natural efflorescence of a healthy state of society. All great politicians seem to have been of this opinion; in modern times Machiavel, Lord Brooke, Sir Philip Sydney, Lord Bacon, Harrington, and lastly Milton, whose tractate of education never loses sight of the means of making man perfect, both for contemplation and action, for civil and military duties. But you are persuaded that if you take care of our civil privileges, they will generate all that can be needed of warlike excellence; and here only we differ. My opinion is that much of immediate fitness for warlike exploit may co-exist with a perfect security of our rights as citizens. Nay, I will go farther, and affirm that tendencies to degradation in our national chivalry may be counteracted by the existence of those capabilities for war in time of peace. But this point I do not wish to press. War we shall have, and I fear shortly—and alas! we are little fit to undertake it. At present there is nothing relating to politics, on which I should so

On the Setting up Mr. Butler's Monument in Westminster Abbey, by Samuel Wesley, eldest brother of John and Charles Wesley.

While *Butler*, needy Wretch! was yet alive,
No gen'rous Patron would a Dinner give:
See him, when starv'd to Death and turn'd to Dust,
Presented with a Monumental Bust!
The Poet's fate is here in emblem shown;
He ask'd for Bread, and he receiv'd a Stone.

[1] Scipio Africanus (234–183 B.C.) ordered these words to be carved on his tomb near Naples after his rejection from Rome.

[2] *The Excursion*, iv, l. 913.

much like to converse with you, as the conduct which it is desirable that the king of France should pursue. The French nation is less fitted than any other to be governed by moderation. Nothing but heat and passion will have any sway with them. Things must pass with them, as they did with us, in the first and second Charles's time, from one extreme to the other. Something to this effect is thrown out in a late number of *The Courier*; and I confess I have myself been long of that opinion. The reforming Royalists in Charles the First's time vanished before the Presbyterians, they before the Independents, they before the Army, and the Army before Cromwell; then things ran to the opposite extreme, with a force not to be resisted. Louis the Eighteenth stands as the successor of Cromwell, and not like our Revolution William. The throne of a James-the-Second Louis cannot I fear stand, but by the support of the passions of an active portion of his subjects; and how can such passions be generated but by deviation into what a moderate man would call ultra-royalist. Justice in the settlement of affairs has been cruelly disappointed, and this feeling it is which gives strength and a seeming reasonableness to these passions. The compromises *once* were intolerable. . . .

413. W. W. to ROBERT SOUTHEY

M.K. MY ii. 549, p. 717.

[Probably June 1816]

My dear Southey,

I am much of your mind in respect to my ode. Had it been a hymn, uttering the sentiments of a multitude, a stanza would have been indispensable. But though I have called it a *Thanksgiving Ode*, strictly speaking it is not so, but a poem composed or supposed to be composed on the morning of the thanksgiving, uttering the sentiments of an individual upon that occasion. It is a dramatised ejaculation; and this, if anything can, must excuse the irregular frame of the metre.[1] In respect to a stanza for a grand subject designed to be treated comprehensively, there are great objections. If the stanza be short, it will scarcely allow of fervour and impetuosity, unless so short that the sense is run perpetually from one stanza to another, as in Horace's alcaics; and if it be long, it will be as apt

[1] The *Thanksgiving Ode* was first divided into stanzas in the 1820 edition of W.'s poems.

to generate diffuseness as to check it. Of this we have innumerable instances in Spenser and the Italian poets. The sense required cannot be included in one given stanza, so that another whole stanza is added not unfrequently for the sake of matter which would naturally include itself in a very few lines.

If Gray's plan be adopted,[1] there is not time to become acquainted with the arrangement, and to recognize with pleasure the recurrence of the movement.

Be so good as to let me know where you found most difficulty in following me. The passage which I most suspect of being misunderstood is,

> And thus is missed the sole true glory;

and the passage where I doubt most about the reasonableness of expecting that the reader should follow me, in the luxuriance of the imagery and the language, is the one that describes—under so many metaphors—the spreading of the news of the Waterloo victory over the globe. Tell me if this displeased you.

Do you know who reviewed *The White Doe* in the *Quarterly*?[2] After having asserted that Mr. W. uses his words without any regard to their sense, the writer says that on no other principle can he explain that Emily is *always* called 'the consecrated Emily'. Now, the name Emily occurs just fifteen times in the poem; and out of these fifteen the epithet is attached to it *once*, and that for the express purpose of recalling the scene in which she had been consecrated by her brother's solemn adjuration that she would fulfil her destiny, and become

> A soul, by force of sorrows high,
> Uplifted to the purest sky
> Of undisturbed humanity! (Canto iii, 585–7).

The point upon which the whole moral interest of the piece hinges, when that speech is closed, occurs in this line,

> He kissed the consecrated maid;

and to bring this back to the reader I repeated the epithet.

The service I have lately rendered to Burns's genius[3] will one day be performed to mine. The quotations, also, are printed with

[1] i.e. Thomas Gray's plan of versification.
[2] The review of *The White Doe* in the *Quarterly* appeared in Oct. 1815.
[3] i.e. *A Letter to a Friend of Burns*, published May 1816.

the most culpable neglect of correctness; there are lines turned into nonsense. Too much of this. Farewell! Believe me,

Affectionately yours,
W. Wordsworth.

414. W. W. to ?R. ADDISON*

MS. WL.
Hitherto unpublished.

[probably June 1816]

My dear Sir,

Herewith I send you the Statement of my Brother's Account with my Sister and myself, as it was examined and agreed upon between him and me last Jan^{ry}.—The account would then have been finally settled but for the want of the memorandum of the price of Stocks at the time when[1] the money Richard rec^{d} for us from Ld Lonsdale was placed there. I have since January carefully examined all the Papers at Sockbridge, and those which were sent down from, and returned to London, but have discovered nothing that requires any change to be made respecting the Items as agreed upon between us. — — My Brother's Clerk, to whom I wish you to deliver these Papers, requesting him to make the calculations and settle the Balance, will find only two Items that were left undecided by my Brother and myself. The one relates to a sum which my Br received from Dr. Cookson,[2] and for which he was to give us credit; but neither the precise sum nor the exact time could be fixed between us, nor have I found any trace of this sum among my Brother's Papers. The occasion of its being received from Dr. C. by my Br. was this. When my Grandmother Cookson came into possession of the Crackenthorp Estate, she gave £500 to my Uncle Mr. Crackenthorp,[3] and soon after the same sum to her second Son, the Rev^{d}

* Draft of letter (incomplete) from W. W. probably to Richard Addison, R.W.'s partner, after the death of R. W. (In hand of W. W. with a few corrections by M. W.)

[1] Written over, in hand of M. W., is the erased line, 'Richard bought in with the money received from Lord Lonsdale'. James, Earl of Lonsdale, had died in 1802, and his successor the present Earl had repaid to the Wordsworths the debt owing originally to their father John W., about which a lawsuit had been indecisively fought from 1786 to 1791. See Moorman, i, pp. 167–9.

[2] i.e. the Revd. Dr. William Cookson, the Wordsworths' maternal uncle. See L. 10, pt. i p. 18 n.

[3] Mrs. Cookson, the Wordsworths' maternal grandmother, was born Dorothy Crackanthorpe, and through the death of her brothers became heiress to the family house and estates at Newbiggin near Appleby. Her eldest son, Christopher Crackanthorp Cookson, then assumed the name of Crackanthorp.

Wm Cookson; purposing to divide £500 amongst us the Children of her Daughter as a present; but she died before her intentions could be fully realized. Her death took place 25 years ago, and soon after Mr W. Cookson paid to my Brother a sum of money upon the principle of making up the deficiency which the death of Grandmother had caused, so that his share might be no larger than ours. 200£ had been received from her by us, and if Mr Cookson paid £150 that would produce the equality intended.[1] But Richard when he conversed upon this subject seemed pretty confident he had not received quite so much and set the sum down, as will be found in the memorandum at £136 I believe; and so let it stand, our share being one half and be taken into the account twelve months after our Grandmother's death. Mr. W. Cookson (now Dr. C) on being applied to could throw no light upon the affair as he did not at that time keep regular accounts.—Mr. Nicholson[2] will also find, another item which was reserved till our knowledge of the rate at which the interest of the Stock account was to be calculated would enable us to adjust the whole. It relates to the excess of the sum, paid to our Uncle Wordsworth's[3] Representatives £412 above what was received from those of Uncle Crackenthorp—318.9.2½—upon the final balance of the several accounts. Dr. Wordsworth will determine what part of this sum it is reasonable should be refunded to Richard's Estate. As the account, for above mentioned reason, could not be adjusted my Brother offered me a Bond for £4000 in the meanwhile; I contented myself with one for 3000 which I now hold. I am very anxious that Mr Nicholson who is so well acquainted with these matters would proceed immediately to balance the Account.—He will find from the Papers now sent, which were the sums received from Lord Lonsdale; and from the memoranda in my Brother's Pockett Books at what rate the Purchases of Stock were made. 27th of July 1803, 2500 three per cent consols at 52½ cost 1312–10^{s}. Commission £3–2–6, 1315–12–6. 10th July 1804, 3200 three per cent Consols reduced at 56¼ cost £1800.—These several sums do not amount to the sum of 3825, the amount of the money received from Lord L. on our account—But Richard had in his hands of his Sister's money and mine considerably more than the deficiency, and our instructions were that the whole sum received from Lord L. should be disposed of in that way if he thought it best.—Mr.

[1] i.e. The Wordsworths would then have received the £350, equal to what their uncle Dr. Cookson, after paying them £150, would have left of his mother's legacy.

[2] R. W.'s clerk.

[3] Richard W. of Whitehaven, d. 1794.

Nicholson, as agreed upon between my Brother and me, will calculate Lord L's money according to the several prices of the Stocks. —— Allowing for the other sums due to my Sister and me a rate of five per cent; and as soon as from the account it appears that Richd is overdrawn, and the principle reduced, the interest is to be reduced accordingly. The whole Balance of the account whatever it may be, is to be rated according to the price of Stocks at the settling of the account. This was agreed upon when my Brother gave me the Bond which I hold, and Mr. Nicholson will balance the account accordingly.

It appears from memoranda 1803 or 4 in my Brother's pocket book, that with respect to Lord Lonsdale's money he considered several sums drawn for as taken from that, and he represents himself in his Books as overdrawn; but in his statement he overlooks the sums then owing from him to my Sister and me on other accounts; so that the most equitable way of drawing out the account is to consider the whole money paid by Lord Lonsdale on our account as lodged in the Stocks.

415. D. W. to THOMAS HUTTON[1]

Address: Thomas Hutton Esqre Junr, Penrith.
Endorsed: 13 July 1816 From Miss Wordsworth. *Stamp*: Kendal Penny Post.
MS. W.L.
MY ii. 564, p. 749.

Rydal Mount Saturday
13th July, 1816.

Dear Sir,

In the absence of my Brother I opened your letter addressed to him, and shall transmit it to him, with the enclosed copies of Mr Addison's letter and your answer, by this day's post. I am very sorry that he did not happen to be at home when your letter arrived, but I trust that much inconvenience will not arise from this circumstance, as he will receive the letters on Monday.—If you should

[1] Thomas Hutton was a solicitor in Penrith whom R. W. had appointed co-trustee of his estate, with W. W. and C. W. He subsequently (see L. 427, below) declined the Trusteeship, but transacted the legal business involved in winding up R. W.'s estate. He was a figure of some importance in Penrith, contributing to the improvement of the streets in 1806 and again in 1813. He had been the Wordsworths' solicitor for many years, for in 1798 R. W. mentions him in his letters to William Calvert about the final release of Raisley Calvert's legacy to W. W. See *EY*, Appendix III, pp. 670–1.

have further occasion to write to my Brother William in the course of a few days pray direct to him at John Hutchinson's Esqre, Stockton upon Tees. I think he will not leave that place before the middle of next week.

I am, dear Sir,
Yours respectfully,
D. Wordsworth

416. D. W. to W. W.[1]

MS. WL. Hitherto unpublished.

[n.d. but must be 19 July 1816]

My dearest William,

The above[2] came last night. I wish you had gone by Sockbridge; but by writing to Mr. H. you can give him the necessary instructions etc. as the discharges for Tenants must first go to London to be signed by Dr. W. I see no need for your cutting short your Tour or (if you are inclined to go to Newcastle) to give up that journey.[3] With respect to Thos. Wilkinson, from what passed between you and him in my presence I do not think he will like to accept the trust under the present circumstances, nor does it seem necessary that he should. You will have all the benefit of his advice and help without his incurring the responsibility. Of course you will immediately write your opinion of this to Mr. H. and he must be referred to the Sockbridge papers and to Mrs. W.[4] for the names of the Tenants. With regard to the Sale of the Estates it seems that advertisements should be put out as soon as possible, and the management and arrangement of this I would entrust to Mr. Hutton.

We have sent the other advertisement to the agent for the papers at Penrith and to Whitehaven.

I wrote to-day to Mr. Hutton to tell him where you are,[5] and that I have transmitted his letter to you. I shall also write to Christopher, copying that part of Mr. H.'s letter which relates to Lord

[1] This letter is written at the end of a letter to Thomas Hutton from Richard Addison, 3 July 1816, which D. is forwarding to W. W. at Stockton-on-Tees. On the same sheet D. has copied a note from Hutton to W. W., dated 18 July.

[2] i.e. the note from Hutton.

[3] W. W. and M. W. were paying a visit to M. W.'s brother John at Stockton-on-Tees. They returned home in the last week of July. See L. 417.

[4] i.e. Mrs. Richard Wordsworth.

[5] i.e. at Stockton-on-Tees. See previous letter.

Abergavenny. I hope he may have already concluded to call, from Mr. Addison's representation of the case. Now for a word about ourselves. Willy and Dorothy are both perfectly well. We think that Willy looks much better than before his cold. D's looks are mending; but as she is so very thin I am afraid her Mother will not be satisfied with her looks when she comes home. She is however quite well. John went to Hallsteads on Wednesday, and last night we had a letter from Mrs. Marshall telling us that he had got well thither and was not tired.—The weather has been on the whole very pleasant once you left us, though, except Wednesday, showery, and cold in the evenings. Peggy Ashburner[1] is very ill—We were at Grasmere on Wednesday evening—and saw her and again on Thursday when we all drank tea with Mary Dawson.[2] I am afraid that poor Peggy is at last going to die—but I have thought so before.—The Bishop[3] is to be buried this afternoon and what a tricky thing it would be if the Calgarth and Rydal Hall[4] processions should meet on the Road! Mrs. Watson has sent you a scarf and Hat-band—very rich and handsome—as a Mark of her respect. The note says that the Bp always expressed a wish that his funeral should be as private as possible—and none but the clergy were to attend— —From Rydal Hall there came a note of invitation but no mourning. The funeral is to be on Monday. Miss Hay and Mrs. Pearson were expected at Grasmere on Thursday—we have not heard of their arrival. On Thursday we received a letter from Mrs. Lloyd, which we found had been sent by Hartley[5]—he had lingered many days I suppose at Birmingham,[6] and we imagined that he had gone through in the Coach and left the letter at Mrs. Fleming's; but what was our surprize when we found that he had been at Ambleside and at Brathay and had drunk tea with a party at Brathay. We hope for a letter from you on Sunday night—God bless you both my dearest Friends. My love to Henry.[7]

Ever yours affect[e]

D. W.

[1] Wife of Thomas Ashburner of Town End. She was one of the Wordsworths' earliest friends at Grasmere and is frequently mentioned in D. W.'s Journals.

[2] She was for a time De Quincey's housekeeper when he came to live in the cottage at Town End.

[3] i.e. Richard Watson (1737–1816), Bishop of Llandaff, who died at Calgarth on Windermere on 4 July and was buried at St. Martin's, Bowness.

[4] Lady Diana Fleming of Rydal Hall had also died.

[5] Hartley Coleridge was at present at Merton College, Oxford.

[6] Presumably to see Charles Lloyd who was under medical care there. See L. 373 above.

[7] Probably M. W.'s brother Henry Hutchinson.

417. W. W. to LORD LONSDALE

MS. Lonsdale MSS., Record Office, The Castle, Carlisle.
Hitherto unpublished.

Rydale Mount
Sunday 28th July 1816

My Lord,

Permit me to return thanks for the obliging accommodation of your Lordship's Horse which carried me pleasantly to Brotherswater; from which place an unfatiguing walk through Roads comparatively quite clean brought me home; where Mrs. W. and I had the satisfaction of finding our Family quite well.

A letter from Sir George Beaumont had been waiting for me some time: it is dated Coleorton 12 Ins^{nt} and informs me that they would set off for the North in little more than a fortnight.

The letter which I take the liberty to enclose is from Dr Wordsworth to his Sister; it assigns his reasons for declining to stand candidate for the Professorship;[1] and I could not resist the inclination to beg your Lordship would be so kind as to peruse it; and give it to Dr Satterthwaite,[2] whom from his friendship for the writer, I know it will interest. Dr S. need not take the trouble of returning it.

I find, as I mentioned to your Lordship, that Lady Fleming[3] returns southward shortly, to visit Lord Suffolk.[4] All her Friends here are glad of this, as it is felt that she stands in need of a protector and adviser.

The funeral of Lady Diana appears to have been conducted with a good deal of Pomp. At the head of the Attendants came, of course, the Master-undertaker; and he brought his Lady along with him all the way from London, not as an indispensable part of the ceremony but to show her the Lakes. There is something 'bizarre' in this mode of mixing the *utile* with the *dulce*.

[1] i.e. the Regius Professorship of Divinity at Cambridge, held since 1781 by Bishop Watson who had for the last thirty years appointed a deputy to discharge the duties of his Cambridge office. See Winstanley, *Unreformed Cambridge*, pp. 101–13; *SH* 27, p. 92; and L. 416 above.

[2] See L. 226, pt. i, p. 560. Satterthwaite was Rector of Lowther.

[3] Daughter of Lady Diana Fleming of Rydal Hall who had just died. See L. 273 above. Sara Hutchinson gives a touching account of the funeral as it affected the Wordsworth children: *SH* 27, p. 92.

[4] Lady Diana Fleming had been the only child and heiress of Thomas Howard, 14th Earl of Suffolk and Berkshire, who d. 1783. The present Earl was a distant relative, John, 15th Earl (1739–1820), who married Julia Gaskarth of Penrith.

I have not yet heard anything absolutely to be depended upon concerning the tenor of the Bishop's will; nor who is to be entrusted with the superintendence of the MSS which he has left for Publication. It was mentioned to me from respectable authority that Mrs Watson[1] was to reside at Calgarth if she chose, and that the Bishop had left his daughters £7000 each.

With respectful regards to Lady Lonsdale and Lady Mary Lowther[2] and Lady Ann,

I have the honor to be,
My Lord
Your Lordship's faithful and much obliged Servant
Wm Wordsworth

418. W. W. to H. C. R.

Address: To Henry Robinson, Esqre, 5 Essex Court, Temple, London.
Postmark: C. 7 Au 7, 1816. No. 2. *Endorsed*: Wordsworth, Aug. 2, 1816.
MS. Dr. Williams's Library.
K (—). *Morley, i. p. 85* (—).

Rydale Mount near Ambleside.
August 2nd 1816

My dear Sir,

It gave me much pleasure to see your Friend Mr Cargill;[3] though I am sorry to say that his looks and appearance were so much altered by delicate not to say bad health that I did not at first recollect him.—In fact he had found himself so far untuned on his arrival at Kendal as to deem it adviseable to halt there for two days: and in consequence of this consumption of his time he could only spare one day for this neighbourhood, being anxious to reach Edingh[4] as quickly as possible. I need not say that I found his

[1] She was Dorothy, d. of Edward Wilson of Dallam Tower, near Milnthorpe, Westmorland.

[2] She married in 1820 Lord Frederick Bentinck. In 1819 Wordsworth made for her a little album of extracts from his favourite poets, chiefly Ann, Lady Winchelsea, dedicating it with a sonnet, 'Lady, I rifled a Parnassian cave' (*Oxf. W.*, p. 264). The album was published in 1905 by J. Rogers Rees, with the title *Poems and Extracts chosen by William Wordsworth for an Album presented to Lady Mary Lowther, Christmas 1819,* with an introduction by H. Littledale.

[3] A native of Jamaica, and a pupil of John Thelwall who, after his acquittal on the charge of treason, had a school in Upper Bedford Place where he taught 'oratory'—especially to those who had 'defects arising from the malformation of the organs of speech'. Cargill studied law under Serjeant Rough, by H. C. R.'s advice, but afterwards became a clergyman. Sadler, I, p. 379.

[4] i.e. Edinburgh.

manners and conversation answer the promises of your introductory letter, and that I parted from him with regret, which was not a little encreased by an impression upon my mind that rest would have been a better thing for him than Eñborogh bustle, or a fatiguing and harassing journey among the bad and widely-parted Inns of the Highlands.

The hope of seeing you here is very grateful to me; and upon a supposition that you propose to take some pains in seeing the Country I will proceed to give you directions for doing it to the best advantage. London, Manchester, *Lancaster*, (the Castle is extremely well worth your notice): at this Town, instead of proceeding by the Coach to Kendal, enquire about the best mode of crossing the Sands to Ulverstone; a Coach used to go, but whether it runs now or not, I cannot say: of course you must take care to cross these sands at a proper time, or you will run a risk of being drowned, a catastrophe to which I would not willingly be instrumental. At Ulverstone you will be within 7 or 8 miles of the celebrated abbey of St Mary's, commonly called Furness Abbey. These Ruins are very striking, and in an appropriate situation; if you should think it worth while to go and see them, the best way would be for you and your Friend to hire a Chaise, as by so doing you would preserve your strength, and only need consume three hours in the Expedition. Should you not deem this sight [? to your] taste (for you would have to go and to come back by the same way), you will proceed straight from Ulverstone to Coniston Water, by Penny Bridge, where is a decent Inn; and at the head of Coniston Lake a very good one delightfully situated. If so inclined, you might pass a whole day very pleasantly there, the morning rowing upon the water, the afternoon walking up and through Eugh-dale into Tilberthwaite and taking care to return from Tilberthwaite, by a house called the Eugh-tree, and up a road which will lead you near another Farm-house called Tarn Hows, at a point in this Road you will suddenly come upon a fine prospect of Coniston Lake, looking down it. From Coniston to Hawkshead; At Hawkshead walk up into the Church-yard, and notice below you the School House, which has sent forth many northern lights, and among others your humble servant. From Hawkshead proceed to the Ferry-House upon Windermere, and less than a quarter of a mile before you reach it stop, and put yourself under the guidance of an old Woman, who will come out to meet you if you ring or call for her at a fantastic sort of gateway, an appurtenance to a *Pleasure-House* of that celebrated Patriot Mr Curwen, called the Station. The Ferry Inn is very respectable, and that at Bowness excellent. Cross at the Ferry, and proceed by Bowness up the lake towards Ambleside; you will pass Low-wood, an excellent Inn also, but here you would be within four miles of Rydale Mount, where I shall be most happy to see you and furnish you with a bed as long as you like; but I am sorry to say it will [not] be in my power to accommodate your Friend, who nevertheless shall be welcome for your sake. Here you will have further directions. I shall do everything in my power to be at home when you come, but many engagements have devolved upon me in consequence of the lamented death of my Brother, and some, I fear, are too likely to press upon me about the time of your intended Tour.

The Road I have chalked out is much the best for com[m]encing the Tour, but few take it. The usual way is to come on directly to Kendal, but I can assure you that this deviation from the common course will amply repay you.

I am glad that you were pleased with my Odes &c [?] They were poured out with much feeling, but from mismanagement of myself the labour of making some verbal corrections cost me more health and strength than anything of that sort ever did before. I have written nothing since—and as to Publishing I shall give it up, as no-body will buy what I send forth: nor can I expect it seeing what stuff the public appetite is set upon. As to your advice about *touring*, that subject we will talk of when we meet. My whole soul was with those who were resolved to fight it out with Bonaparte; and my heart of hearts set against those who had so little confidence in the power of justice or so small discernment concerning its nature, as to be ready at any moment to accept of such a truce, as under the name of peace he might condescend to bestow. For the personal character of the present ministry, with the exception of Lord Hawksbury[1] I cannot say to you that I entertain any high respect, but I do conscientiously believe that they have not been wanting in efforts to economise and that the blame of unnecessary expenditure, wherever that exists, rests with the Prince Regent. Adieu.

Faithfully yours,
W Wordsworth

The ladies under my roof join in best regards and remembrance—[D. W. adds:] My brother desires me to add that your halting at

[1] Robert Banks Jenkinson, Lord Hawkesbury (1770–1828), who had succeeded his father as 2nd Earl of Liverpool in 1808, first took office under Pitt in 1799. In 1812 he became prime minister after Spencer Perceval's assassination.

Coniston, and the deviations from the common track must depend upon the length of time which you have to spare. I shall be very glad to see you again. D. W.

419. W. W. to THE REVD. W. CARR

Address: The Rev[d] Wm Carr, Bolton Abbey.
Endorsed: Wordsworth. Autograph, Sep 23rd 1816.
MS. Dr. Williams's Library.
Morley, i. p. 88.

Rydale Mount
Sept[br] 23[d] 1816

My dear Sir,

I take the Liberty of requesting that you will be so kind, as to furnish the Bearer Mr. Robinson[1] of the Middle Temple, a particular Friend of mine, with directions to the favourite points of view about your delightful Place.

I remain Sir
with much respect
truly yours
W[m] Wordsworth

420. W. W. to B. R. HAYDON

Address: B. R. Haydon Esq[r], Great Marlborough Street, London.
MS. untraced.
Haydon. MY ii. 566, p. 751.

Rydale Mount, Oct[r] 5th 1816

My dear Sir,

Your spirited and interesting Letter deserved a much earlier answer: it also merited a much *better* answer than it will receive. As to the former point, it reached me at a most busy time, in the height of my summer engagements with friends and acquaintance flocking from all parts of the Island to see this beautiful Country, which one day I hope to have the pleasure of shewing to you; and as to the second, weightier consideration, the reply when it does come being worthy of your perusal I have nothing to plead but general inability, aggravated by some distaste for a subject of which one has had so much.—

[1] i.e. Henry Crabb Robinson, now on his way back to London after his visit to Rydal Mount.

I regret this inability the less, upon the present occasion, because yourself, who have proposed the case, have pronounced a decision upon it so judicious, as in my opinion to do away the necessity of applying to any other authority. As to the right of a people to chuse their own Governor being sacrificed by the fall of Bonaparte it is ridiculous to talk about it—Some part of the *people* of France did indeed vote for him, as they would have voted for the Devil, but he was no more the choice of the wisdom and virtue of the nation, nor of their folly, than he was of the wisdom, virtue, or folly of the Chinese. Besides, if he had been chosen by the french Nation the other nations of Europe were convinced that he would never cease from attempting to subjugate them, they had as much right to attempt and to accomplish his overthrow, as the French had to elect him to their Imperial throne and to endeavour to uphold him there. Overthrown he has been, and the Heir of the old monarchy put in his place, and many professing and supposing themselves friends of freedom lament over these events; because, forsooth a great principle has been violated—One thing however is certain that if it were true that a principle has been rejected it has not been wantonly done, but in preference of another principle on which Nations have been accustomed to rest their tranquillity, and to rely for protection of that portion of civil Liberty which their ignorance and vices permit them to enjoy. But be assured, my dear Sir, that concern for *principle* has little sway over the minds of your opponents—they admired Bonaparte and his adherents because they were dashing Dogs at the head of expectations flattering to the discontented, and they hate the Bourbons because through them a check has been given to the career of profligate personal ambition. What has humanity to apprehend from this restoration as far as it is a question between their principles; why, that the respect paid to hereditary succession, by confirming the possession of their thrones to Princes may induce them to behave more tyrannically than they could have done without the additional security which by the termination of this struggle has been given them. But do you imagine that Kings or Emperors care a twentieth part so much about their heirs, as about themselves. In this particular they differ little from other men; now the fate, the undeserved fate,[1] of Louis 16th, who lost his throne and his life, because his people erroneously thought that he deserved to lose

[1] W. W. in youth had not thought Louis's fate was 'undeserved'. In his *Letter to the Bishop of Llandaff*, written in 1793 but never published, he deplores 'the idle cry of modish lamentation which has resounded from the Court to the cottage' at his execution.

them, will like that of Charles the 1st operate beneficially as a warning, and be fully adequate as far as example goes, to counteract any encouragement to misconduct which might be derived from the restoration of the Crown to the same family in the person of Lewis the 18th. Is it to be dreaded that nations will be too passive under their oppressors? Surely if the events of our time are likely to render them more so in future, it will not be in consequence of the restoration of Louis and other acts of that kind in preference to retaining the Corsican and his upstart crew; but because the powers and distinction which successful villainy has obtained after the overthrow of ancient institutions, and the destruction of the persons in whom authority was vested, will be likely to make wise and good men afraid of trying experiments. They will rather bear the ills they have, till they become absolutely insupportable, than rush on others which they know not of. Now the retaining Murat, Bonaparte, and the rest of those wretches, would have greatly aggravated this evil; and the deference to the claim of legitimacy in the same proportion tends to diminish it. And whatever bad consequences are to be dreaded from an excess in this quarter, they are to the truly discerning much less formidable than those to which the opposite extreme would conduct us. Our English forefathers at the time of the Revolution set us an example how to act on similar lines; if we are plagued with a grievous Tyrant, rise and destroy him; but do not look to another family for his successor; there is no necessity for that step, therefore avoid it; take the next heir and bind him over by such conditions as preserve a better security for your liberties. But do not let lawless ambition loose[1] upon you, by leaving the throne open to the pretensions of every daring adventurer.

But I have already written far too much upon a question which by the dispassionate may so easily be determined. I beg to say a word about painting, and to urge you to bend your attention morning, noon, and night, that way—How are your eyes and what progress do you make?—For a subject, let me recommend to your consideration the 16th chapter of Numbers, from the 46 to the end of the 48th verse, 'and the plague was stayed'[2]—Yesterday I left at Keswick Sir George and Lady Beaumont, both well.—Where, and how is Scott;[3] and is his Wife better; if you write to him remember

[1] Written 'lose'.

[2] The story to which W. refers is that of Aaron running out of the 'tent of meeting' into the assembly of the Israelites who had been stricken with a plague, and vigorously censing them by way of 'atonement'. 'And he stood between the dead and the living; and the plague was stayed.' Haydon did not adopt W.'s suggestion.

[3] i.e. John Scott of the *Champion*.

me to him most kindly, and add that I should be happy to hear from him at his leisure.—Mrs W— and Miss H— present to you their best regards—let me hear from you at some leisure moment, and believe me with great respect and true affection,

Yours
Wm Wordsworth

421. W. W. to THOMAS HUTTON

Address: Thomas Hutton Esqre, Solicitor, Penrith.
Stamp: Kendal Penny Post. *Endorsed*: 6 Octr 1816. From Wm. Wordsworth Esqre.
MS. WL.
MY ii. 565, p. 749.

Rydale Mount Octr 5th 1816

My dear Sir,

I found that Colin Satterthwaite would give me more for the field than the sum he had offered to you. But as he offered to take it on a Lease for 7 years at the old Rent, £17, I hope my Sister will be no loser by the resolution which I made to purchase it for her, at the price offered by Mr Senhouse.[1]—It is therefore to be considered as sold to her at that price.—

Mr Smith[2] will issue handbills for the sale of Ponder How, by private Contract; proposals to be received for one month; every effort will be made, but I have no hope of getting more than £270 for it at *the utmost*—as things are it would be fairly sold at that price.

Let the share of the Raceground be advertized as you propose.—I have forwarded your last to my Brother; recommending in support of your opinion that the London affairs should be left exclusively to his management and that of Mr Addison; and coinciding with your judgement as to the Reversion and the Lambeth House.

We have heard from Mrs Wordsworth giving an account that her son is much reduced by a complaint in his Bowels, and that the Apothecary has advized that she should return home with him unless he improves in a day or two. You may therefore probably have seen her by this time; if so she will have expressed her desire that an

[1] Probably Mr. Humphry Senhouse of Nether Hall near Maryport. He was an intimate friend of Southey's, and in the autumn of 1808 had joined with him, W. W., S. T. C., and John Spedding of Mirehouse in endeavouring to call a county meeting to protest against the Convention of Cintra. See Moorman, ii, p. 137. For the price of the field, see Letters 429, 441 below.

[2] Matthew Smith, attorney at Cockermouth. See L. 580 below.

attempt should be made to buy up Mrs Nelson's bond. I have mentioned this to Dr Wordsworth as adviseable could it be accomplished on good terms; though I am aware that the condition of the affairs being what it is, the Trustees cannot have much discretionary power as to the mode of getting rid of the debts.—

Pray mention to Mrs Wordsworth that if her Son be not better, I should like to be written to; as I should not be easy unless some of my family saw him; my Wife has had a good deal of experience in the complaints of children.

I remain my dear Sir
truly yours
Wm. Wordsworth.

422. W. W. to J. BRITTON[1]

Address: Jn Britton Esq., 10 Tavistock Place, London.
Stamp: Kendal; Penny Post No 2c; *Postmark*: 15 Oc 15 1816.
MS. Boston Public Library.
Britton, Auto-Biography, ii. (—). *RES, Nov. 1964.*

Rydale Mount,
Octer 12th [1816]

Dear Sir,

I have received through the hands of Mr Southey, a Portrait of Shakespear for which Print and the accompanying observations I beg leave to return you my cordial thanks—

The print is extremely interesting; and agreeing with your judicious observations upon the authenticity of the Bust, I cannot but esteem this Resemblance of the illustrious original as more to be relied upon than any other—As far as depends upon the intrinsic evidence of the features, the mighty Genius of Shakespear would have placed any Record of his physiognomy under considerable disadvantages; for who could shape out to himself features and a countenance that would appear worthy of such a mind: What least pleases me in the present Portrait is the cheek and jowl, the former wants sentiment, and there is too much of the latter—

Repeating my thanks for this mark of your regard, I remain
dear Sir
respectfully yours,
Wm Wordsworth

[1] For Britton, see L. 389 above.

423. W. W. to THOMAS HUTTON

Address: Mr Hutton, Solicitor, Penrith.
Stamp: Whitehaven [? 1816]. *Franked*: J. Wallace.
MS. WL.
MY ii. 567, p. 753.

Octobr 19th 1816
Sat. Castle Whitehaven[1]

My dear Sir,

I propose to call on Mr Senhouse on my return through Cockermouth, or if I am unable to do so I shall write to him.

I have consulted two Gentlemen whom I have met here about the value of the Share of the Race Course. The answer of both was that if they possessed a share they would not *sell* it at £10, neither perhaps might they *buy* one at that price. I refer the matter entirely to your judgement—suggesting merely whether (as I suppose it does not come under the denomination of personal property) as we are not ordered by the will to sell it, we are under obligation to dispose of it at any rate, at this time, however disadvantageous. But be assured my dear Sir, whatever you determine I shall approve of.

Mrs Wordsworth wished to have the wine at Sockbridge valued —as I am in want of wine myself, I will take it at the valuation.

I remain, Dear Sir, truly yours
W Wordsworth.

P.S. I return to Rydale towards the middle of next week.

424. W. W. to THOMAS HUTTON

Address: Mr Hutton, Solicitor, Penrith.
Franked: Lonsdale. *Endorsed*: 21 Oct 1816. From Wm. Wordsworth Esq
Stamp: Whitehaven.
MS. WL.
MY ii. 568, p. 754.

Castle Whitehaven Tuesday
Octr 21st 1816

My dear Sir,

The enclosed has just been forwarded to me from home.

I cannot say to whom the Bond was offered for sale—all I know on the subject is what I heard from you; who, I think, mentioned that Godwyn had offered it to Mr Dover; and what I heard generally

[1] Lord Lonsdale's house at Whitehaven was known by this name. W. W. frequently stayed there with the Earl. It is now a hospital.

upon the subject from Mrs Wordsworth. Will you be so kind as to write to Mr Addison if you have any information to communicate on the point that would be of use.—

Be so good as to write your opinion to Mr Addison or my Brother, on the subject of proving the Will—it is a matter upon which I have no suggestions to offer, being utterly ignorant about the mode of doing these things.

Mr Wood[1] writes me that Mr Senhouse is willing to give £395 for the field, he shall have it.

most truly yours
W. Wordsworth

P.S. I return home to morrow or next day.

425. W. W. to MESSRS. LONGMAN & CO.

Address: Messrs Longman & Co. Paternoster Row, London.
Postmark: 4 Nov 1816. *Stamp*: [Kendal] Penny Post.
MS. Cornell. Hitherto unpublished.

By W Leatham
Rydale Mount
31st Ocbr 1816

Dear Sirs,

Your last was duly received; and I now write to say that in consequence of a communication from a Friend in Edinburgh I wish a 100 copies of the Letter to Mr Gray[2] (to which may be added 10 of the Thanksgiving Ode) to be sent to Mr Jamieson, Bookseller in that Town, the same person who has already applied to you for a certain number—

He is described to me as a respectable Person, and unless you know something to the contrary, I am prepared to run the risk of the books being entrusted to him, without requiring the security which you properly demand—

With regard to the 3 copies of the Gold Finch,[3] Mr Monkhouse tells me that they were indeed sent (by the Publisher I suppose) to his House at Hampstead, but he ordered the Bearer to take them

[1] A Cockermouth attorney. See L. 429.

[2] i.e. *A Letter to a Friend of Robert Burns*, published in May 1816. The 'Friend' was R. P. Gillies, as appears from the next letter.

[3] A Series of little books of words for popular songs was published under the title of *The Goldfinch* in many editions from 1748 to 1806. See *SH*, 28, p. 96 and note.

directly to Messrs. Longman who had been requested by me to pay for them and to forward them by one of Mr Southey's parcels to Rydale. They must therefore be lying in your Shop, for they would not have been paid for by you unless you knew them to have been received at one place or the other. I am dear Sirs, sincerely yours W. Wordsworth

P.S. By this day's post I have requested Mr Monkhouse to call on you in explanation of this matter.

426. W. W. to R. P. GILLIES

Gillies. K (—). MY ii. 569, p. 755.

Rydale Mount, Nov. 16, 1816.

My dear Sir,

I am much obliged for the trouble you have taken respecting Mr. Jameson's ineffectual application to Messrs. Longman for the letter to Mr. Gray.[1] I hope that Mr. Jameson will be supplied in a few days with one hundred copies, as I wrote some little time ago to the publisher requesting him to send that number. It is my wish that this letter should be circulated in Scotland, and I should deem myself under obligation to any friend who will exert himself in making it known. The novels of Sir Egerton Brydges[2] I have not yet found time to look into; but your poem[3] I have read with considerable attention. The 'Visionary' contains many good lines and well-written passages, for example, 'the never-dying leaves of ivy bright',—'Fly when pursued, and when obtained expire.' The latter half of page 53 is finely conceived and expressed. So are many other passages, as in page 30, 'Long was the way, and led o'er trackless heath'; but you are probably aware that the poem, as a whole, is objectionable—upon the same grounds as the other tales. It wants substance, and is rendered puzzling in the conduct by the succession of persons not sufficiently discriminated from each other in character or situation, and who engage in no course of action. So that upon the whole I cannot say that I think this piece superior to its predecessors, and in point of versification I think it inferior. Your rhyme has in general more harmony than your blank verse, which

[1] i.e. W. W.'s *A Letter to a Friend of Robert Burns.*
[2] See L. 334, p. 169, n. 2 above.
[3] i.e. *Rinaldo, a desultory Poem.*

latter might in many instances be improved with little trouble. For example, at the top of page 100 are three lines, each having its pause on the sixth syllable. Read the second line thus: 'renews his wonted carol; stillness reigns,' and the sound will be improved without injury to the sense. You frequently introduce pauses at the second syllable, which are always harsh, unless the sense justify them and require an especial emphasis; but in such cases as the following observe their bad effect, page 21, 'the race;—the game of dice'.

I am sorry you should have been rendered uneasy by charges of plagiarism brought against you by your friends. I cannot deny that I have been frequently reminded of what I have written by your verses, but never under any circumstances which led me to any reflection discreditable to your ingenuousness of mind. The resemblances are such as you probably are for the most part wholly unconscious of, and were it otherwise, I do not see that they can be reckoned otherwise than as an indirect compliment to the original author. I therefore entreat of you, so far as I am concerned, to dismiss the matter wholly from your thoughts. Your poems are sufficiently original, and tinctured enough, perhaps too exclusively, from your own mind. I cannot conclude without noticing the introductory poem to your tales. It is written with much liveliness, and, I think, furnishes good ground for expectation that you will succeed when you look out of yourself. Of most of the other poems you have heard my sentiments before. Both 'Lucia' and 'Montalban' contain agreeable stanzas, but as wholes they are too deficient in substance. My penmanship is so bad, that in mercy I ought to conclude. If you write more blank verse, pray pay particular attention to your versification, especially as to the pauses on the first, second, third, eighth, and ninth syllables. These pauses should never be introduced for convenience, and not often for the sake of variety merely, but for some especial effect of harmony or emphasis. Mrs. Wordsworth and Miss Hutchinson are both well, and join in kindest regards. I remain, with great respect,

Most truly yours.
William Wordsworth.

[1] i.e. *Illustrations of the Poetical Character in Six Tales* (1816).

427. W. W. to THOMAS HUTTON

Address: Thos. Hutton Esqre, Solicitor, Penrith.
Stamp: Kendal Penny Post. *Endorsed*: 25th Novr 1816. From Mr. Wordsworth.
MS. WL.
MY ii. 570, p. 756.

Rydale Mount 25th Nov^{br} 1816

My dear Sir,

I entirely approve of the Letter which you have written in answer to Mr Rowland; if the Parties be disposed to act reasonably it cannot but produce the desired effect.

From your Letter to me *I infer* that when three Trustees are nominated by a Testator, and one of them declines to act, the two others if they undertake the trust are *under obligation* jointly to appoint a substitute for the one who has declined.[1] If this be the case I most earnestly entreat of Thomas Wilkinson to undertake the Office; for I know no other Person to whom I should apply with any thing like an equal confidence that the affairs would be properly managed. Of Mr Jn. Nicholson I certainly have but very slender knowledge, far from sufficient to justify me in applying to him.—Indeed should I adopt this plan it must entirely be from my reliance on T. W.'s judgement: and surely should any thing occur that was not satisfactory T. W. would feel regret that I had proceeded upon his recommendation. I would write to him to urge him again to consider the subject with a hope that he may come to a resolution more consonant to my wishes and those of Dr Wordsworth, but I think it would answer better, if you would contrive to see him again, and shew him this Letter, making such observations to the same purport as your superior knowledge would enable you to do.—

I am afraid that I must have expressed myself inaccurately, for some time ago in answer to a Letter of yours I meant to give my opinion that the lands at Clifton and Yanwath should be sold in public sale as soon as they had been adequately advertized; I was therefore sorry and somewhat surprized to learn from Mrs Wordsworth that you were concerned this had not been done. Pray let it be done *forthwith*. The Sockbridge House and Lands ought to be advertized to be let as you propose.

I will take this opportunity of mentioning a few particulars in which Thos Wilkinson will I hope be so good as to assist Mrs W.

[1] In a letter to W. W. dated 28 May 1816 (MS. WL Thomas Hutton begs leave to decline the office of Trustee of R. W.'s estate (to which R. W. had appointed him along with W. W. and C. W.), by reason of 'a regard to the Discharge of my professional Duties'.

with his advice. —— She asks what is to be done with the Horses. The black Mare ought to be sold; and T. W. will advise with Mrs Wordsworth about the best way of getting rid of her; and as to the old horse or horses if there be two, they ought, I think, to be shot as soon as possible if no body will give a price for them.—

With many thanks
I remain dear Sir
Wm. Wordsworth.

428. W. W. to J. H. REYNOLDS[1]

Address: J. H. Reynolds [Esq.] 19 Lamb [? Court].
Postmark: C 2 DE 1816.
MS. WL.
Literary Bypaths, by H. C. Shelley. MY ii. 571, p. 758.

Rydale Mount,
28th Novbr 1816.

My dear Sir,

A few days ago I received a Parcel through the hands of Messrs. Longman containing your Poem the Naiad, etc. and a Letter, accompanying it, for both which marks of your attention you will accept my cordial thanks. Your Poem is composed with elegance and in a style that accords with the subject; but my opinion on this point might have been of more value if I had seen the Scottish Ballad on which your work is founded. You do me the honour of asking me to find fault in order that you may profit by my remarks. I remember when I was young in the practice of writing praise was prodigiously acceptable to me and censure most distasteful, nay, even painful. For the credit of my own nature I would fain persuade myself to this day, that the extreme labour and tardiness with which my compositions were brought forth had no inconsiderable influence for exciting both these sensations. Presuming, however, that you have more philosophy than I was master of at that time, I will not scruple to say that your Poem would have told more upon me, if it had been shorter. How unceremoniously not to say ungraciously do I strike

[1] John Hamilton Reynolds (1794–1852), the friend and correspondent of Keats. In 1814 he published *Safie, an Eastern Tale*; in 1816 *The Naiad: a Tale*; in 1819 *Peter Bell*, a burlesque of Wordsworth; in 1821 *The Garden of Florence*; in 1825 with Thomas Hood *Odes and Addresses to Great People*. He also wrote much for magazines and newspapers. (Note by de Selincourt.)

home! But I am justified to my own mind from a persuasion that it was better to put the objection in this abrupt way, than to introduce it by an accompanying compliment which, however well merited, would have stood in the way of the effect which I aim at—your Reformation. Your Fancy is too luxuriant, and riots too much upon its own creations. Can you endure to be told by one whom you are so kind as to say you respect that in his judgment your poem would be better without the first 57 lines (not condemned for their own sakes), and without the last 146, which nevertheless have much to recommend them. The Basis is too narrow for the super-structure; and to me it would have been more striking barely to have hinted at the deserted Fair One and to have left it to the Imagination of the Reader to dispose of her as he liked. Her fate dwelt upon at such length requires of the reader a sympathy which cannot be furnished without taking the Nymph from the unfathomable abyss of the cerulean waters and beginning afresh upon gross Terra Firma. I may be wrong but I speak as I felt, and the most profitable criticism is the record of sensations, provided the person affected be under no partial influence.

I am gratified by your favourable opinion of my labours. As a slight return for your obliging attentions will you accept of a Copy of my Thanksgiving Ode and Letter upon Burns which will be put into your hands if you will take the trouble of presenting the under-written order to Messrs Longman. When you call there, will you be so kind as to mention that I have received complaints from Edinburgh that the two Publications have not arrived there as was expected, agreeable to the directions which I had given.[1]

Pray beg of Messrs Longman that as many copies of each as I requested may be sent forthwith.

I am, dear Sir, with great respect,
Your obliged servant,
W. Wordsworth[2]

[1] See L. 425 above.

[2] The bottom part of the last sheet of this letter has been cut away.

429. W. W. to THOMAS HUTTON

Address: Thomas Hutton Esq, Solicitor, Penrith.
Stamp: Kendal Penny Post. *Endorsed*: 6 Decr 1816. From W. Wordsworth Esqre
MS. WL.
MY ii. 572, p. 759.

Decbr 6th 1816
Rydale Mount

My dear Sir,

The following is a Copy of a Letter from Mr Wood of the Globe Inn Cockermouth to me, received when I was at the Castle Wven.[1]

Dear Sir,

This morning Mr Senhouse[2] called upon me respecting the field adjoining the River Derwent; with your approbation the Sale is concluded at the price you fixed, £395, subject to your agreement with Mr. Satterthwaite, the deposit and time of payment the same as the prior Sale. I am etc.

Cockermouth Oct 2 1816 Wm Wood

I answered the above by return of Post agreeing to let Mr Senhouse have the field upon the terms specified in Mr Wood's Letter, which I had previously informed Mr Wood were the only conditions upon which the said field would or could be sold.—I wrote yesterday to Mr Satterthwaite, sending him a copy of Mr Wood's Letter. I am not a little surprized that any difficulty should have been started and hope to hear no more of it.—

I know no person so proper to be applied to to undertake the trust as my Relation Captn Wordsworth;[3] and if the nature of the duty which would devolve upon him were explained I think, considering how very little trouble it could possibly cause *him*, having your advice always at hand, that he would scarcely decline it. If he be now at Penrith, which I fear he may not, will you be so kind as to wait upon him, and explain the situation in which we stand, and ask him from me to supply the vacant place. I would write to him, but the business may be more effectually done by viva voce representation. If we cannot make out a Title to any thing valid without a third Trustee, he will scarcely leave us in this embarassment; especially as I hope that we shall little need to trouble him except upon such occasions.

[1] i.e. Castle Whitehaven. See L. 423 above.
[2] See L. 421, p. 339, n. 1 above.
[3] See L. 427 above.

If he declines, I approve of Mr Littledale's opinion being taken as you propose, which you will be so kind as to get done—

I shall be glad to attend the sales on the 19th.

I am my dear Sir
truly yours
Wm. Wordsworth.

430. W. W. to THOMAS HUTTON[1]

MS. WL. Hitherto unpublished.

[about 11 Dec. 1816]

My dear Sir,

I have written both to Dr. Wordsworth and Captn Wordsworth upon the subject of a third Trustee, requesting the former to procure *immediately* Mr. Littledale's opinion upon it; and the latter [i.e. Captain Wordsworth] to undertake the office if necessary; and I have stated the urgency of the case. I have received from Mr. Smith a draft for £19.18.6 deposit money for [?] now sold for 200 guineas, and I have sent it to Messrs. Crewdson etc. Kendal.[2] Mr. Smith writes: 'I should recommend you to send the title deeds to my care, and I will be answerable for them, and shew them to his Attorney, which will save you the expense of extracting the Title.' If *you* approve of this let it be done; the Deeds in question are probably in your possession. Mr. James[3] is too sensible a man not to be aware, if he will reflect a moment, that it is my bounden duty to deposit the money that comes into my hands, with those upon whom *from my own experience* I can place reliance. With Mr. James I have only a very slight acquaintance, with the House at Kendal I have done business for many years. Most sincerely yours

W. Wordsworth.

[1] This letter is written on the back of a letter from C. W. to W. W., dated Rectory House, Lambeth, 7 Dec. 1816, about R. W.'s debts to Lord Abergavenny. A note at the end of C. W.'s letter by W. W. reads: 'I shall go to town as soon as this [is] done'—i.e. as soon as the interest demanded by Lord Abergavenny is known. He did not, however, go to London until Nov. 1817.

[2] The Maude, Wilson, and Crewdson Bank opened in Kendal in 1788. Thomas Holme Maude, at this date one of the partners, had been at Hawkshead School with W. W. and also at St. John's, Cambridge. From 1826 to 1840 the bank became W. D. Crewdson & Son, and in 1840 amalgamated with the Wakefield Bank as the Kendal Bank.

[3] William James of Penrith, agent for one of the Carlisle banks.

431. W. W. to THOMAS HUTTON[1]

Address: [tear] Solicitor, Penrith.
Postmark: [tear] 1816.
MS. WL. Hitherto unpublished.

[probably Dec. 1816]

My dear Sir,

I found from Mrs. Wordsworth that my Brother paid *separately* for the Wood of the Field sold at the George.[2] It cost him £30 in addition to the 399. I therefore regret that we did not state that the Wood should be reserved to be sold by us or taken by the purchaser at a valuation. What strange [*tear*] T. Wilkinson tells [me] that [there were] three or four people [who] meant to [bid for] the fields separate who [never] opened their mouths at the first time going over; reserving themselves for the second time; which never came; and so they were disappointed, deservedly I should say were it not to our loss perhaps.—I got very well home, and had a not unpleasant ride. Farewell.

With many thanks for your kind attention

I remain
sincerely yours
W. Wordsworth

432. W. W. to THOMAS CLARKSON

MS. untraced.
MY ii. 574, p. 761.

[1816?][3]

My dear Friend

I was much concerned to hear that your Son talked of declining to sit for an honour. To what is this unworthy determination to be ascribed?[4] I think it was Mr Tillbrook who mentioned to me that

[1] This letter, which has been badly damaged, apparently by mice, is written on the back of a letter from C. W. to W. W. about R. W.'s estate.

[2] The reference is to a sale at the George Inn, Penrith, perhaps of the two fields Katehow and High Moor Quarry Field, at Yanwath, the value of which was calculated at £300.

[3] T. C. (junior) matriculated at Trinity Coll., Cambridge, in 1814, and transferred to Peterhouse in 1816, taking a pass degree in 1818. In 1816 he began to read law in London. Hence 1816 seems a probable date for the letter. (Note by de Selincourt.)

[4] This letter is amusing when W. W.'s own failure to enter for an honours degree at Cambridge in 1790 is recollected.

he had been mortified in not succeeding in his attempt to obtain some university prizes. I entertain too favorable an opinion of Tom's good sense to suppose that a disappointment of this kind could be the real cause of his starting out of the University Course. What Candidate however well qualified can be justified in encouraging confident hopes of success upon these occasions where the prizes are so few and the Competitors probably so numerous, the whole Body of Undergraduates being, I believe, at liberty to put forth their skill and try their fortune. Besides is Tom sure that he bestowed sufficient labour on his attempt to entitle him fairly to the desired reward? A few weeks ago I saw a young man who had lately gained the prize for Latin verse at Oxford. He seemed not at all elated by the distinction and rather regretted that he had contended for it, because the pains which he had taken with his Composition, he thought, might have been more profitably directed to other objects. Again, even if a man could be assured that his Composition was the best sent in, how unwise to be chagrined where it is so easy for the judges to be mistaken, unless they confine themselves in estimating the merit of these things (which in fact they ought to do) to the absence of faults, and the proofs which the several exercises contain of accurate knowledge of the languages they are written in, rather than to the indications which may be found in them of genius and extraordinary intellectual Power. University prizes and honours are not a test of these rare gifts, but are conferred as rewards of application, and that they may be [? regarded] as unquestionable symbols of attainments deemed useful; now ingenuousness of mind and modesty require that the disappointed Candidate should admit that others have surpassed him in the excellent quality of application, and are richer than he in the fruit which it naturally bears. What then ought to follow? not spleen and disgust and petted aversion to what was before an object of desire; but firm resolve to saddle the future with a double portion of exertion in order to make up for the deficiencies of the past.—But I am persuaded that this disappointment was not the *cause* of your Son's making known his discreditable intention; though I can easily conceive that an unpleasant mood of feeling consequent upon this failure, might give him hardihood to avow to himself and to others an abandonment of purpose which however inwardly inclined to it he would have been ashamed of till that fit of false courage came upon him. If I saw Tom, I should say to him, Know thyself, look into the goodly garden of thy own mind, and pluck up the weeds, for it is yet springtime, early spring with thee, before they have choked the fragrant flowers and the profitable

Herbs. Bestir thyself and be a Son worthy of thy never to be forgotten Father; and this is within thy power, for however great be the Parent the Child dishonours not his origin who makes the most of the opportunities which have been granted him and of the powers, with which by God and Nature he has been endowed. Whatever profession Tom chuses, or whatever path of life he may walk in, he will find that in complying with his father's wish that he should take his degree accompanied with a University honour, he has done well. In the first place and as of main importance, he would have given proof that he can command his thoughts and submit to laws imposed upon him from without. He could therefore be spoken of as one capable of application; and who will submit to restraint; for mathematical studies are known to go against the grain with most of those who have been educated at our public Schools. Proficiency in these pursuits is to be valued not from considerations relating to science merely but to morals and the general constitution of the intellect. Besides looking at the subject only in a prudential view, how can a person be recommended by his friends to any situation, unless under great disadvantages, if he has had opportunities of giving proof that he has not thrown away his time, and has not availed himself of them? Some Persons decline to sit for University honours from pride fed by erroneous notions respecting the construction put upon what is called a low honour. If they cannot obtain a high one they had rather have none, imagining that if they do not contend at all people will give them credit for ability to have succeeded, whereas if their names are found not high in the list, then it is to be presumed, from their having been there at all, that they have done their utmost, and may fairly be regarded as industrious and well-meaning dunces. Now both these notions are false, at least as far as concerns [those who have sufficient judgement to make their opinion of any consequence].[1] No man with them is thought the worse of for being ranked among the distinguished though he may be [far] from the foremost; nay though he may be only among the rear guard, he will be deemed a deserving soldier.—He has given proof that he has a mind strong enough to submit to discipline, and that to a certain point at least he may be depended upon. In the mean while it is known that these honours are the reward of mathematical attainments; and that a Person may be possessed of very extensive information in classics and miscellaneous knowledge, the possession of which will set him on equality in public estimation with those who

[1] These words are deleted in favour of others which are illegible. (Note by de Selincourt.)

stand far above him in the mathematical tripos.—I have written these loose thoughts, with a hope that you may find some opportunity of conveying the substance of them to my young friend,—if he would be happy respected or useful let him be diligent.

Farewell, and heaven bless you and yours

W. Wordsworth

433. D. W. to CATHERINE CLARKSON

Address: To Mrs. Clarkson, Playford Hall, near Ipswich, Suffolk.
Stamp: Halifax Jan 10 1817.
MS. British Museum.
K. MY ii. 576, p. 765.

Wm Rawson's Esqre, Halifax,[1] Friday Janry 10th 1817.

Call me selfish—ungrateful—or what you will, but my dearest Friend, I pray you write to me. I am utterly inexcusable for, of every day since you were so kind as to comply speedily with my last request, I have had at least two hours at my own command, and surely nothing but the perverseness of human nature—some remnant of original sin could have brought about my *seeming* neglect of you,—any day—or every day I could have written to you and yet it has not been done—and at any given time I am sure I would willingly sit down and write a letter to you—not for *your* sake but my own, for the Gratification (I will not call it the *selfish* one, nor will *you*, I think, be quite so severe upon me) of receiving a letter from you in return. Such are my feelings, yet left to myself the evil spirit conquered and I have gone on deferring the work of today till tomorrow. But I am now determined by the law of necessity which is irresistible. If I do not write now in the course of a few days I cannot have an answer from you while I remain at Halifax, and that is what I especially desire; for poor Mrs Threlkeld's[2] sake, who remembers you with the greatest affection, an affection almost like that of a Mother or a kind Aunt. She never in all her life saw any human being whom she admired or loved half so much in a short time as you. You cannot but recollect her and her Daughter staying with us at the Cottage. We all drank tea with you at R Newton's and Mrs T had you to herself for a long time, as she says before our

[1] D. W. had been staying with the Rawsons since Oct. 1816. For Mrs. Rawson (formerly Elizabeth Threlkeld), see L. 19, pt. i and *EY passim*.

[2] Sister-in-law of Mrs. Rawson, widow of her brother William. For her daughter Elizabeth T., mentioned in this letter, see Letters 19, 77, pt. i, etc.

arrival; and she really seems to have as vivid a remembrance of your conversation as if it were but yesterday. You know it was at a time when any tender heart was most likely to be interested for you—when a Stranger could not but fear that you were going to the grave; and now her eyes sparkle with joy when she hears of your renewed health and strength. This fact will prove to you that her faculties and sensibilities are in no degree diminished at the age of 75; and to me it is delightful to observe what a lasting impression you have made upon the mind of so good a woman. I read her your last letter adding a few words for you, which were not there, of remembrance of her and her Daughter and she was so pleased both with that remembrance and the whole letter that I resolved to write to you again immediately for *her* sake, more especially that I might recall her to your recollection and have some true message or words of kindness from your own self to her and her Daughter. I hope my little trick in reading your letter was at the least an innocent one, and I flatter myself that, in the spirit, though not in the letter what I made you say was just and true—indeed if I had not felt it to be so, I should have been wounded instead of pleased by the pleasure which the dear good old lady expressed in hearing that she was remembered by you. This is a long preamble, and I dare say you have not yet got the better of your wonder that I am still here. I could not have believed it possible that my Friends could have prevailed upon me, or that I could have possibly had a desire to stay so long from home. Month has indeed been added to Month, and that is the only thing they reproach me with at home—whereas if it had not been so, I must have gone long since. At each full moon I have put off my departure till the next—and the last putting off has with justice much disappointed my friends at home. They say if I had fixed no day or week they would have had nothing to blame me for, and the last time I was very precise in the fixing. Yet I could not resist the after entreaties of my excellent (alas! aged) friend Mrs Rawson. It is now determined that, weather permitting, I depart on Wednesday the 22nd. Mr. Rawson's carriage will take me to Kigheley[1] and some of my friends will kindly accompany me thither and I shall proceed the next day in the Coach. This decree is irrevocable. I am, as you may well believe, very desirous to be at home again and to see all my dear friends—but so I have long been, therefore that is no security for my not staying longer here. My security is that Mrs Rawson has promised that she will not say another word on the subject—she is happy that I have made so long

[1] i.e. Keighley.

a stay with her and will chearfully give me up at the time which I have now fixed—indeed it was upon her entreaties urged in this manner that I yielded, and broke my word at home.—She is a woman of a heavenly mind—a temper not to be ruffled—yet ardent and chearful. She looks with composure towards her departure from this life, which she expects will be sudden, and I have heard her say that she cannot join in that petition of the Litany against sudden death.[1] But I am sure if she were to be afflicted with a painful malady it would not overcome her chearfulness and pious resignation. Her death would be an example, as her life has been, of all Christian virtues. She broke her hipbone (a small bone) some years ago, but though she is lame she is exceedingly active and strong and seems really to have not one bodily ailment, nor do I think that if she had not been lame her powers of loco-motion would have been, at the age of 72, much diminished. Her Father died suddenly—so did both her Brothers, and for that reason she is inclined to think that her end is most likely to come unexpectedly. Her Father, Mother, and Brothers were extraordinary men—each with a genius of his own; but one common gift of a sweet temper and loving hearts—Mrs Rawson, herself, has a remarkably fine understanding. She brought up 5 orphan nephews and Nieces, her sister's children.[2] This sister was a good sort of a common Body. The Nephews and Nieces are all good—and clever too, and each has a distinct and marked character. As to my goings-on here I seem to have nothing to tell you. They are just much as you may imagine. We visit more than I like; but as males and females are mixed together in our parties they are more agreeable than parties in general in country towns. I always take my walk when the weather is not very bad, and whatever it is I go into Mrs Threlkeld every day. I read to Mrs. R. in an evening when we are alone, and through the day I enjoy a pleasant freedom in general in the disposal of my time. This house is very pleasant with a large flower garden and green lawn. The view from the windows makes me often think of your nice gardens at Bury, but the country here is much more varied and is really beautiful—if it were not for the odious cotton and worsted mills—and steam

[1] Mrs. Rawson did not in fact die until 1837. See D. W.'s touching letter written after her mental breakdown: 'My friend Mrs Rawson has ended her ninety and two years' pilgrimage—and I have fought and fretted and striven—and am here beside the fire.' *LY* ii. 1257, p. 930.

[2] The Fergusons; D. W. also spent her childhood in the same household, from 1778 to 1787. She corresponded with the two Ferguson brothers Edward (1764–1843) and Samuel (1769–1816) in after years. See *EY* 204, p. 442; *LY* ii. 1238, p. 900. See also *EY*, p. 42, n. 1, and *Dorothy Wordsworth*, by Ernest de Selincourt, pp. 5–8.

engines—which are really now no better than incumbrances on the ground, trade being so bad. The wealthy keep their mills going, chiefly for the value of employing workmen—and few get more than *half* work—great numbers none at all, so that really a great part of the population is reduced to pauperism—a dreadful evil. Things cannot go on in this way. For a time whole streets—men, women and children may be kept alive by public charity; but the consequence will be awful, if nothing can be manufactured in these places where such numbers of people have been gathered together. It never can be expected, or even *wished* I think, that the state of our manufactures should again be what it *has* been; but if there be not a revival of trade in a smaller way people and things cannot go on as they are.—Looking round now I see 'many rich sink down as in a dream among the poor'[1]—and I daily hear of families accustomed to a plentiful maintenance through labour, completely 'broken down'—that is their expression. It is a great comfort to me that my home is out of the way of these dismal sights and sounds. We see little of distress in our neighbourhood that we cannot in some degree diminish—either by sympathy or help, but if one lived here it would be far otherwise. I trust you are tolerably removed from the extremity of distress in your neighbourhood as you have no trade—and that you have found, as you hoped you should find, comfortable employment and amusement for the winter's evenings. If you could have your needles threaded for you, making clothes for poor people is a good thing—at least so I find it. Here but till lately the manufactories have kept the women ignorant of plain work. With you they probably can sew for themselves. I have not heard a word either of you or any of your Family since your last letter, the most important contents of which I communicated to my Friends at Rydal, and I find that William has written to you; but if you had written again I should have heard. I am very anxious to hear about Tom. It is too late to say much on this subject, but I pray you tell me what your hopes and feelings are. I trust he will do well and repay you for your anxieties. Give my kind Love to your dear Husband, and do, I pray you, write to me immediately. Do not put it off if you cannot write a long letter—a short one—a *very* short one will satisfy me. I want to know how you are and how you feel, and to give Mrs Threlkeld a very great pleasure. So I pray you write—but remember no time is to be lost—or I shall be gone—do, dearest Friend, do write directly. All well at home, but poor William is at Kirby Lonsdale on a most disagreeable business. He has been

[1] *The Excursion*, i, l. 544.

obliged to seize his Sub-D's goods, and will lose £100, he says, at least.[1] This is the first beginning of our sorrows in Trade. The perplexity respecting Richard's affairs has no end, and my dear Friend I shall not see you this year. I have stayed far too long here for that—and expenses have been heavy and times are so bad I cannot think of it. This is a sad dull letter. Pray tell me how your dear Father is—and give my love to your sister and to Tom. God grant that the next year may bring assured hope to you that he will be a comfort and blessing to himself and his parents.

Yours evermore———write and write, I pray you write.

[*Written upside down on top of first page.*] Here I place my name D. Wordsworth you can read anything or this would puzzle you.

434. W. W. to HENRY PARRY[2]

Address: Henry Parry, Esq [*in W's hand*], Hamden Street, Somers Town, London [*in a child's round hand*].
MS. Cornell.
LY. iii. 576a, p. 1364.

Rydale Mount Ambleside Jan^ry^ 17th 1817

My dear Sir,

I am almost ashamed to present myself before you after having suffered the favour of your last to remain so long unacknowledged. Your Letter and the Portrait of Bonaparte which it enclosed were both very acceptable; but being from home at the time when they arrived, I did not receive them till it was too late to give you a line of acknowledgement while you were on your Tour of Inspection: and this having been impossible I deferred writing with a hope that I might have something to say that would make my Letter worth Postage.—I have now occasion to write but on matter not very pleasant. Hall my Sub: at Kirby Lonsdale has been playing the Rogue; and has brought nearly £300 of money due from me to Government into Jeopardy. On the 4th Instant I was apprized that he had been arrested for a debt of upwards £100 and was on his way to Appleby Gaol. I met him at Kendal; I could not learn from him what he owed to Government; but I gathered that

[1] See Letters 434, 435, 437, 440, below. The last reference shows that D. W.'s fears were not realized.

[2] An Inspector of Stamps. See L. 308 above. This letter well illustrates the various problems W. encountered in connection with his office as Distributor of Stamps.

he had no property except Household furniture and Shop goods to cover the demand: and that his Furniture was advertized for Sale. Upon this, I was professionally advized to procure a Bill of sale from him—he granted me one with power to collect his debts—But for greater safety, as it was in the Power of one of Hall's Creditors to make him a bankrupt, I made an affidavit of Hall's debt at £300 and forwarded it to Mr Hanson Solicitor of the Stamp Office to ground the issuing of an extent, if there were a possibility of setting aside my Bill of sale, in case the Creditor who had it in his power to make him Bankrupt should think it adviseable to do so, in that case I prayed that an Extent might be issued immediately. I begged an answer to know what was proper to be done—This Letter was despatched Monday before last (it is now Thursday) and to my extreme surprize and vexation I have not yet heard from Mr Hanson, or the Board whom I begged him to consult, a syllable upon the subject. How is this to be explained? —I put the Letter with my own hands into the Post Off: at Kendal in the presence of Witnesses; and it is yet taken no notice of; and in the meanwhile I cannot but be under great uneasiness lest the Creditors knowing that an extent has not been issued should proceed to make Hall a Bankrupt, and the money which I have raised to cover the debt to me as Agent of the Crown, be recalled for the benefit of the Creditors; and all my pains and trouble (I was ten days about the business) be entirely thrown away. — — You will wonder how Hall could owe so much so soon after balancing the annual account: the fact is that he had withheld and secreted the Legacy Receipts to a large amount; and it was not till after a long search I found them in an obscure part of his House, in what is called in this Country a *Swill*[1]—I had no sureties for Hall—unluckily for me! And if the Board by neglect or other wise, suffer the money which I have raised to be lost, or if I have been ill advized in the mode of proceeding mine will be a very hard case. For the debt has arisen from a rascality on the part of Hall which no vigilance of mine could prevent; and after I discovered it I did every thing in my power to repair the loss, proceeding in all things by the best professional advice which I could procure.— —By the bye among Hall's effects were two or three old Books *with Heads*[2] which I have lain aside, meaning to bid for them when their turn came to be sold; I had designed the Heads for you—But while my back was turned they were handed to the Auctioneer; and unluckily I missed them.—

[1] A kind of basket made of strips of oak or willow. [2] i.e. engravings.

There is a point relating to the emoluments of my Office in which I wish for the benefit of your [*seal*] Two coaches run between Leeds and Kendal and one or two between Kendal and Liverpool, none of these are licensed at Kendal, but several of the Proprietors (to whom the matter is of course indifferent) are very willing that one half of their duties should be paid at Kendal. I am at a loss what method to pursue to have this effected—The proprietor at Leeds who pays the duty of one of them has been written to on the subject, and he spoke to the Distributor himself but was told that it was usual to pay the duties where the Coach was licensed. This may be usual, but that it was not the invariable practice I have an instance in my own district; for there is a Coach which runs between Wh^en[1] and Carlisle which pays half at one place and half at the other.—Now it has struck me that if you would furnish me with the address of the Inspector of Coach Duties with an introduction, or leave to mention your name, he would point out to me the best manner of proceeding to effect this just and reasonable purpose; which would be a considerable object to this poor District——

There is yet another point in which you might serve me—I am desirous of Knowing the value of the several Distributions in the Kingdom; this might easily be effected by procuring a Copy of a List which I saw in the Stamp Off: of the [? sums paid] by them on account of the income tax. Could you procure me a Copy of one of these Lists, or point out how I might acquire it? It is of consequence to facilitate my attaining the object which you know I have in view.[2] —I hope you and your Sisters continue well—It is not unlikely that I may be in Town early this Spring, if I am I shall certainly find you out— —You will perceive how much I rely upon your friendly disposition, when I trouble you with the above tedious account, and these requests. But I know you will be glad to serve me, and be assured if on my part I can make any return I shall be glad to do it. My sisters are from home. My Wife is well and begs her kindest regards and best to yourself and sisters. Most truly yours

Wm. Wordsworth

[1] i.e. Whitehaven.

[2] i.e. the acquisition of further Stamp Districts. See L. 462, n. 2 below.

435. W. W. to THOMAS HUTTON

Address: Thomas Hutton Esq, Solicitor, Penrith. *Stamp*: Kendal Penny Post.
MS. WL.
MY ii. 577, p. 769.

Rydale Mount
18th Jan^ry 1817

My dear Sir,

I think it quite proper that application should be made to the Lord Chancellor for authority to sell till the several Creditors be satisfied; and am decisively of opinion that the Lands which you point out (viz those of Tyrrel, High Moor and the adjoining lands) are what ought to be sold as least affecting the Body of the Estate. It must not be overlooked, however, that I have a contingent interest in these lands; but should the infant[1] die during his minority, I presume that there would be no difficulty in having my Brother and Sister's claims under the will reduced and settled pro rata. Will it be necessary that any legal process should take place, before the Lands in question are sold, to effect a distribution of the remainder after the debts are paid, in case the Infant should die, according to the proportions intended for his Brothers and Sister, by our late Brother's Will. It is only upon a supposition that the law would enjoin a settlement of this kind, that I could be justified in giving consent to the sale of these Lands in particular, while those devized to my Brother and Sister in case of the Infant's death, remain untouched.

I know not what to say in regard to the House of Cross Cannonby. If I am not mistaken it came into my Father's hands as a lapsed Mortgage; and a Person appeared at Cockermouth at the Sale pretending to have a right to the Property. Under these circumstances I do not think I should be justified as a Trustee in warranting the Title.

A very unpleasant circumstance has lately occurred in my District. John Hall my Sub^r.[2] at Kirby Lonsdale has been arrested for debt.—He owes me (with expenses) full £300; I procured a Bill of Sale and raised the money from his effects. It will be a fortnight on Monday since I forwarded a Letter to Hanson, Sol. of Stamp Off. informing him that I was proceeding to act under the Bill of Sale which Hall had granted me; but begging for further safety that an Extent might be issued, if Hall's creditors by making

[1] i.e. John Wordsworth, son of R. W., b. Jan. 1815.
[2] i.e. Sub-distributor of stamps.

him a Bankrupt, and one of them had the power to do so as he owed him upwards of £100, could set aside my Bill of Sale, and bring the money raised by it under a provisional assignment to be divided among the Creditors.

To my great astonishment no notice has yet been taken of that Letter and the affidavit enclosed in it.—The money due I have raised but I am quite uncertain whether I can keep it. Last Monday I wrote the Board informing them that I had written to Mr Hanson, and that I had enclosed to him an affidavit to grant an Extent if necessary. I hope to hear tomorrow at the latest. I shall then know whether I shall [? have] to refund the money. I have a joint Bond from himself, Willm Bliss and John Wane Grocer, both of Penrith, for £200. Are these Persons that can be deemed sufficient securities for £200? You will oblige me much by enquiring, and communicating to me the result. Should they prove insufficient, I must request others of Mr Garnett.—

[*The end of the page cut off.*]

436. W. W. to B. R. HAYDON[1]

MS. untraced.
LY iii. 577a, p. 1367.

Rydale Mount, Ambleside. Jan. 20th 1817.

My dear Sir,

Your last came when I was absent, on irksome business which detained me from home a considerable time. I am sensible of the honour done me by placing my head in such company and heartily congratulate you on the progress which you have made in your picture[2] adding my earnest wishes that neither weak health nor any other cause may prevent the completion of your noble work in due season. Be assured that I shall set as high a value on any present from your pencil as a man so imperfectly skilled in your glorious art as I am is capable of; and whatever deficiency may be found in me on this score will be made up by personal regard.—Your account of young Keats interests me not a little; and the sonnet[3] appears to be

[1] This letter is endorsed: 'Copy by Mrs Turner of a letter of Wordsworth, the original of which I gave to Mrs Turner—B. R. Haydon.'

[2] i.e. of Christ's entry into Jerusalem, in which Wordsworth appeared as an onlooker, with Keats, Voltaire, and others.

[3] 'Great Spirits now on earth are sojourning.' Haydon's letter containing the sonnet is in the Wordsworth Library.

of good promise, of course neither you nor I being so highly complimented in the composition can be deemed judges altogether impartial—but it is assuredly vigorously conceived and well expressed; Leigh Hunt's compliment is well deserved, and the sonnet is very agreeably concluded.— —Your account of Scott[1] causes me deep concern—I am sorry that he is about to publish upon so melancholy an occasion—His verses I fear will have too large an infusion of pain in them to be either generally pleasing or serviceable whatever degree of genius they may exhibit.—Thelwall[2] the Politician many years ago lost a Daughter about the age of Scott's child. I knew her she was a charming creature. Thelwall's were the agonies of an unbeliever, and he expressed them vigorously in several copies of harmonious blank verse, a metre which he wrote well for he has a good ear. These effusions of anguish were published, but though they have great merit, one cannot read them but with much more pain than pleasure.

You probably know how much I have suffered in this way myself; having lost within the short space of half a year two delightful creatures a girl and a boy of the several ages of four and six and a half. This was four years ago—but they are perpetually present to my eyes—I do not mourn for them; yet I am sometimes weak enough to wish that I had them again. They are laid side by side in Grasmere Churchyard. On the headstone of one is that beautiful text of Scripture 'Suffer the little children to come unto me and forbid them not, for of such is the Kingdom of Heaven.' And on that of the other are inscribed the following verses,

Six months to six years added, he remained
Upon this sinful earth, by sin unstain'd;
O blessed Lord, whose mercy then removed
A Child whom every eye that look'd on loved,
Support us—teach us calmly to resign
What we possess'd—and now is wholly Thine!

These verses I have transcribed because they are imbued with that sort of consolation which you say Scott is deprived of. It is the only support to be depended on, and happy are they to whom it is vouchsafed—Like you I am glad that Scott has got rid of his

[1] John Scott, editor of the *Champion*. See L. 366 above.

[2] John Thelwall (1764–1834) whom W. had met at Alfoxden in 1793, and visited at his farm at Liswyn in Wales in Aug. 1798. The lines on his daughter occur in *Poems written chiefly in Retirement*, Hereford, 1801.

Champion,[1] I hope he has sold it well—at any rate it was advisable to sell for it was impossible that it should go on to his satisfaction while he was at such a distance from the spot. Now that Scott has nothing more to do with it I have given it up; besides to tell you the truth the politics of the few last numbers have been what I cannot approve of. They fall in with the humour of the violent and unthinking and that may answer by procuring a fresh set of Readers and subscribers for the work, but I am certain that many of its old supporters, will like myself abandon it if it goes on in this outrageous strain—I should like much to come to Town this Spring; but I dread the expence. My family consists only of three Children but their education is becoming more costly every year; and my income is barely sufficient for my outgoings. I have no extraordinary supplies—for my writings bring me no profit; nor do I look for any from them. Under these circumstances I fear I must remain at home from prudential considerations—Southey will be in Town in March —and I will take care that you shall meet.—I have had two letters from Sir George B.[2] His pencil is not idle—but I am sorry to say that he has suffered in health from a severe cold. The younger Westall[3] he met with at Keswick last summer is at present with him.—

Bloomfield the Poet[4] has been and I believe is, in considerable distress, probably owing to the failure of his Bookseller, by whom he has lost several 100 pounds. A subscription was set on foot for his benefit. You know perhaps that he is a native of Euston the Duke of Grafton's parish, his Grace's principal Seat and Residence. This Spot, and its neighbourhood are the scene of the Farmer's Boy; from this bond of connection something was expected from the noble Duke,[5] nor was that expectation wholly fruitless—for he has given—five Pounds!!! This same illustrious person sold the Library which his Father had collected—God help the Literati of England if his Grace of Grafton be a fair specimen of the Patrons of the Day. But I know that he is not so.

[1] In 1818 Thelwall succeeded John Scott as editor of the *Champion*.

[2] i.e. Beaumont.

[3] William Westall (1781–1850), younger brother of the more famous Richard, visited the Lakes annually from 1811 to 1820, often staying at Rydal Mount. S. H. admired his work, and encouraged his friends to buy her engravings. See *SH* 55, p. 160, and L. 524 below.

[4] Robert Bloomfield (1766–1823), author of *The Farmer's Boy*.

[5] George Henry Fitzroy, 4th Duke of Grafton (1760–1844), for many years one of the members for Cambridge University and a close friend of Pitt. In his later years in the House of Commons he leaned much more towards the reformers and whigs.

O may the man who has the muses scorned,
Alive or dead be never of a muse adorned.[1]

Miss Hutchinson is not at home, but my wife joins me in very affectionate regards. Believe me my dear Sir with great respect and admiration

most truly yours
W. Wordsworth.

437. W. W. to THOMAS HUTTON

Address: Thomas Hutton Esq[re], Solicitor, Penrith.
Stamp: Kendal Penny Post.
MS. WL.
MY ii. 578, p. 770.

Rydale Mount
Friday 24th Jan[ry] 1817

My dear Sir,

I am satisfied with your representation respecting the contingent interest in the Lands designed for sale.—

After my Letter was sent off, I called to mind that I had omitted to mention the Lease. It struck me at the time of letting the Lands that probably the Trustees had no power to grant leases; and even if they had, in this case it would be highly inexpedient to exercise it. Therefore it must not be done, The Lands must be sold unburthened with a Lease.—

As to the Sale of the furniture and other effects at Sockbridge, this ought to be done, after consulting Mrs Wordsworth, as soon as it is deemed likely they can be sold without disadvantage from the season or any other cause.—

I have at last heard from the Sol. of the Stamp off. He says that he had written before on the 8th. I cannot but entertain some doubt of the truth of this assertion, as Letters rarely miscarry and his never reached me—I might have lost £300 by this mischance or neglect. Hall was a shopkeeper; and I have now only to hope that he may not be declared a Bankrupt, before the Extent which *in the first instance* I applied for, if the Stamp Office deemed it necessary, be carried into effect. He gave me a bill of Sale for £500—and under it I have sold to the amount of 300, reserving the rest of his effects, till the extent be carried into effect. It appeared to me a reasonable question

[1] Spenser, *The Ruines of Time*, but misquoted.

whether by this Bill of Sale I did not bar the operation of an extent in my own favor, but Messrs Fell & Johnson[1] assured me not.

Excuse my troubling you with this disagreeable business—

I remain dear Sir
faithfully yours
Wm. Wordsworth

I do not see what can be done with the House of Cross Cannonby beyond what you propose to write to Mr Heel.—

I have reperused your Letter. Hall's Bill of Sale comprized all his personal Estate as far as should be necessary to raise £500 if that sum were found owing—I heartily wish I were at the end of this troublesome concern—The extent will probably reach Mr Briggs of Appleby today.

438. W. W. to THOMAS HUTTON

Address: Mr Hutton, Solicitor, Penrith.
Stamp: Kendal Penny Post.
MS. WL.
MY ii. 579, p. 771.

Rydale Mount
2nd Febry 1817.

My dear Sir,

I can see no objection to Mr Bell's opinion being communicated to Mr Rowland—

The propriety of accepting the Composition offered by Rushworth must be determined in London by Dr Wordsworth and Mr Addison—

I have had no experience in the proving of Wills, though two or three Probates have passed through my Office. You beg me to inform you "when it may be convenient for me and you will send a Comm. from Carlisle to take the Probate at Penrith."—I infer from this that I shall have to go over to Penrith to execute this instrument; if so, I am at liberty at any time; and will appear at Penrith when things are ready.—Mr. Garnett[2] is not provided with Probate Stamps, nor am I, having a Call for so few. Pray let me know what will be the amount of the Stamp and I will send for it to London. If you see Mrs W. of Sockbridge be so good as to let her know that I have received the Parcel from Sockbridge.

I remain dear Sir
truly yours
W. Wordsworth.

[1] Attornies at Kendal.

[2] Postmaster of Penrith from 1818.

439. W. W. to THOMAS HUTTON

Address: Thomas Hutton Esqre, Solicitor, Penrith.
MS. WL.
MY ii. 580, p. 772.

Patterdale,
Tuesday 13th Feb^{ry} 1817

My dear Sir,

I received your Letter last night, having written on the subject of letting the Sockbridge House and Land, the day before. I do not think that Mr Sanderson ought to have liberty to underlet the Premises, unless subject to the approbation of the Trustees; for if the land be as I suppose, in any but bad times, worth three Pounds [an] acre, it cannot but be considered that the whole is let low. I shall be completely satisfied provided yourself, Thomas Wilkinson, and Mrs W. think the rent offered sufficient, and the Tenant unexceptionable—

In regard to attending at Keswick to receive the money, I should be perfectly satisfied in confiding that office to you, if your presence at Keswick be necessary as I suppose it will be; In which case I should hope that you would do me the favour of paying me and my family a visit at Rydale Mount where we should all be very glad to see you. Should this, however, be out of your power, and your presence at Keswick not be necessary, I would willingly meet the Parties at Keswick; only it seems scarcely necessary that we should *both* attend.

I am sorry that you have met with so many obstacles in respect to the Titles of the Cockermouth and Ravenglass lands.[1]

I am dear Sir
very truly yours
Wm. Wordsworth.

P.S. have enquiries been made as to what could be made of the Lands at Sockbridge separately from the house. This ought to be done before the bargain with Mr S— is concluded.

[1] John W., father of W. W. and D. W., who d. 1783, had owned small properties at Cockermouth and Ravenglass, besides the more considerable estate at Sockbridge. The former consisted of two 'closes' called Sand Air and St. Leonards by the river at Cockermouth, and at Ravenglass the 'Town End Tenement'. These were sold in Sept. 1816, W. W. going with Henry Crabb Robinson to attend the sale. See *HCR* i, pp. 191–2. The Cockermouth property was bought by John Spedding of Mirehouse.

440. W. W. to THOMAS HUTTON

Address: Thomas Hutton Esq, Solicitor, Penrith.
MS. WL.
MY ii. 581, p. 773.

Rydale Mount
Febry 17th 1817

My dear Sir,

I accede to the agreement made with Mr Sanderson for the House and Lands at Sockbridge provided a clause be inserted in the Lease that he is not to underlet the Premises except with the approbation of the Trustees and Mrs Wordsworth.

I am much concerned to say that I cannot find the copy of the agreement made with Mr Satterthwaite. I have informed Mr Rudd[1] that it has been mislaid, and have begged him to wait on Col. S.[2] with my compliments requesting from me that C. S. would allow him a Copy of it. I shall make further search to day and if I find it I will send a copy to Mr Rudd. The agreement was to this effect and no other, that Col. S. should have the field at the old rent £17 for a term of 7 years.

I purpose to attend the Sale at Sockbridge on the 3d of March; could it possibly be arranged that the Will might be proved at that time; or when I attend at Keswick for the money? I do not keep a Horse and it is some trouble to provide myself with one for so many journeys.

I shall lose nothing by the Subdistributor who has given me so much trouble. An Extent has been carried into effect against him, and his property is just sufficient to cover the debt and Expenses.

I am sorry that we are not likely to see you in my house, and much obliged by your hospitable invitation.

With sincere regards
I remain, dear Sir, your obedient Servant
Wm Wordsworth

[1] Attorney at Cockermouth.
[2] i.e. Colin Satterthwaite. See L. 421 above.

441. W. W. to THOMAS HUTTON

Address: Thomas Hutton Esq, Solicitor, Penrith.
MS. WL.
MY ii. 582, p. 774.

Rydale Mount
23rd Febry 1817

My dear Sir,

It will be convenient to me to attend at Keswick, on the 1st of March and I shall write to Mr Rudd to that effect immediately. Mr Rudd had informed me of Mr Satterthwaite's refusal to shew the agreement, and applied to me for a copy of it which I brought with me from Cockermouth, but I can nowhere find it; it was (as I informed Mr Rudd) to this effect and no other that Mr S. was to have the land at the old Rent for 7 years. Mr Senhouse refuses to complete the purchase without a sight of the words of the agreement; as I cannot furnish him with the precise words, nothing remained for me but to apply to Mr Satterthwaite for a Copy which I have done, and if he will not grant it, I have offered to indemnify Mr Senhouse for any conditions apprehended by possibility to exist in that agreement, beyond those specified. If Mr Senhouse refuses to complete the purchase the field must remain, as it was before, purchased by my Sister, for £370.[1]

Be so good as to let me know, if being confident as I am that the agreement between Mr S. and me was to no other effect, I have acted imprudently in offering to indemnify Mr Senhouse as above stated.

I remain my dear Sir,
faithfully yours
Wm Wordsworth

[1] See Letters 421 and 429 above.

442. W. W. to ROBERT LUMB[1]

Address: Rob[t] Lumb Esq[re], Lowther, Penrith.
Stamp: Kendal Penny Post. *Endorsed*: Feb[y] 24—1817—Mr. W. Wordsworth.
MS. Lonsdale MSS. Record Office, The Castle, Carlisle. Hitherto unpublished.

Rydale Mount
near Ambleside
Feb[ry] 24th 1817

Dear Sir,

I should take it as a great favor if you could meet me at Sockbridge on the 3[d] March respecting the Lands at Clifton—There is a sale on that day of my late Brother's effects; I shall attend, and purposed to call upon you, but I have this moment learned that some friends from Stockton upon Tees will be here on Monday and Tuesday, and I must see them—If it be inconvenient to you to come over to Sockbridge pray write to me, mentioning in what way you think the treaty respecting those Lands could be most satisfactorily managed for both Parties, provided the Earl of Lonsdale is not indisposed to purchase—

I am dear Sir
very truly yours
W[m] Wordsworth

443. W. W. to THOMAS HUTTON

Address: Mr Hutton, Solicitor, Penrith.
MS. WL.
MY ii. 583, p. 775.

Ambleside
Feb[ry] 24th 1817

My dear Sir,

I had apprized Mr Rudd that I was ready to meet him at Keswick on Saturday next as proposed. I feel somewhat at a loss at present in fixing a day; because I know not yet whether the Bargain respecting the field at Derwent Bridge End will be completed; and it would save much trouble, could that business be brought to a close at the same time with the rest. If Mr Satterthwaite will not grant me a Copy of the agreement and Mr Senhouse consequently persists in his objection to complete the purchase the treaty must fall to the

[1] See L. 375 above.

ground; unless he be satisfied with the proposal which I made (and mean to carry into effect provided you do not think it imprudent) to guarantee him from any claims under the Agreement, beyond those specified, viz. the letting the Field to Mr Satterthwaite for seven years at the old rent £17.

I mean to attend the Sale at Sockbridge on the 3d March; could we at that time together fix on the best day for the meeting at Keswick? If you think it ought to be settled immediately, I am sorry to say that I cannot name an earlier day than Friday the 7th March, having an Engagement with Mr and Mrs Hutchinson[1] and Colonel Sleigh, all of Stockton, for three days in that week.

I have this day written to Mr Lumb, requesting the favor that he would meet me at Sockbridge on Monday respecting the Clifton Lands; and if not convenient that he must communicate with me on the subject by Letter.

Could you assist Mrs Wordsworth in pointing out a proper person to value the wine, before the Sale?

I remain my dear Sir
Very truly yours
W. Wordsworth

P.S. I hope you will be able to give me an hour on the Sale day at Sockbridge. I must return home as speedily as possible.

I have not yet heard from Dr Wordsworth. Surely Mr Addison cannot have communicated to him the purport of Rowland's Letters, or I should have heard (ere this time) that he had taken steps to avert the mischief. I wrote immediately on receiving the Copies of those letters from you.

444. D. W. to CATHERINE CLARKSON

Address: Mrs Clarkson, Playford Hall, near Ipswich, Suffolk.
Stamp: Kendal Penny Post.
MS. British Museum.
K. MY ii. 584, p. 776.

Rydal Mount. March 2nd [1817]

With a thankful heart, thankful for the blessings of a chearful home, and the society of my own dear Family have I dated this letter, yet not without some self condemnation that I have not exactly complied with your wishes, that I should write immediately

[1] M. W.'s brother John Hutchinson and his wife Elizabeth Sleigh.

after my arrival,[1] the more so as you were so very good to me when I was separated from my Friends. It was a fortnight yesterday since my arrival; and I have had so many employments, and above all such a succession of happy, I may say joyous feelings, that the time seems to be twice as long, and I have more than once set myself to recollect dates, in order to be persuaded in my own mind that I had not been much longer at Rydal Mount. I never had this feeling before after my absence from home, and I attribute it to the contrast in all respects between my manner of spending my time here and at Halifax, and the perfect opposition, if I may so speak, in all domestic manners and arrangements. There I was in a large house with two old people,[2]—servants to perform the work as by magic—no child's voice—all perfect stillness. True it is that they are the most chearful and happy old people I was ever acquainted with; yet how different the chearfulness of their fireside from the chearfulness of ours—and how different the seriousness! I was very happy there, yet now that I am placed again in the perfect freedom of home, I rejoice many times in every day that I am here saying, 'how glad I am that I am among you once again'! Then notwithstanding this is but the *second* fine day we have had since my return I have had so much delight in the beauty of the country; I think the more from having come from a country in some points resembling this, abounding in vallies, streams, and gushing springs. When I was there I thought the hills and vallies beautiful—and so they are—and they reminded me of our mountain regions; but when I came *home* again I was even struck with *surprize* at the excessive loveliness of the objects before my eyes, the exquisite proportions, combinations of forms, and richness and harmony of colours. I stayed a whole fortnight at Kendal, having promised a visit to our good friend, Mrs Cookson last summer, which I never paid, and knowing how unwilling I should be to stir from home again after I had once got here. I was met at the door at 8 o'clock in the morning by Dorothy and Willy, who, thank God! are both now perfectly well; but they then looked very delicate, having only just recovered from very severe colds. Dorothy's was especially a serious indisposition, and I am very sorry to find that during the latter part of this winter she has been more than usually susceptible of cold. She is of a delicate constitution and her spirits lead her on to over-exertion and fatigue, then comes relaxation and she catches cold. Willy rides daily to school upon an ass, and this is of great use to him both body and

[1] i.e. from Halifax. See L. 433 above.
[2] i.e. Mr. and Mrs. Rawson.

mind, and will in time, I hope, make a Boy of him instead of a little Baby. After a five months absence I am astonished with his babyishness; and really his Father fondles over him and talks to him just as if he were but a year old; he has, however, so fine a temper from nature that I think it is utterly impossible to undo it, and by degrees he will be recovered from all leanings towards being treated as the little pet, 'the little darling'; for when he is amongst his schoolfellows none are more active, independent, and manly than he, and he disdains all notice from Father, or Mother or any of us at such times. John is greatly improved. He carries his ingenuousness up with him, but the way of learning is to him steep and difficult; and he flags, or turns aside; yet I trust he will be a respectable scholar in time. He has a sound understanding and a good memory; and an intuitive sense of the just and honourable. Dorothy began music in Autumn and she is now fond of it. At first she was very desirous to learn, and we thought, if she would persevere, that a moderate share of skill might furnish amusement for her and sometimes pleasure to us in after times, but the benefit we looked to was chiefly collateral—unsteadiness is her master fault, and we thought that should she go on it could not be without steadiness and diligence. For some time (when the first novelty was gone) setting at the Pianoforte was irksome and she was driven to it, with the assurance that if she did not choose to take pains it should be wholly given up. Her backwardness is now conquered and she is fond of it; and the judges say she makes a remarkable progress. She learns to draw from one of Mr Green's[1] daughters and offers very well. As to her Latin she makes a poor progress, for she has no pride in it; but in time she will, I hope, make a tolerable Latin scholar, and at all events she has a much better understanding of what she reads in English from the little she does already know of Latin. Sara returned from Keswick the week before my return. She looks remarkably well and is very strong, she can walk to Grasmere and back without fatigue. Today we have all been at Church, where the duty is now most admirably performed by Mr Jackson's son;[2] but, alas! we shall not have him long, and his father, the Rector, will take the office over himself. My sister's nephew, George Hutchinson,[3] is with him, a Boy of 14 years of age who has just had a fortune of 5000 per annum left him by his Mother's Uncle. Mr Wm Jackson

[1] Probably William Green of Ambleside. See L. 121, pt. i, p. 258.

[2] The Revd. William Jackson. See L. 351, p. 203, n. 1 above.

[3] George Hutchinson (1801–53), son of M. W.'s eldest brother John. He afterwards took the name of Sutton on inheriting this fortune. See *SH* 31, pp. 104–5.

(if his health permit, but he is very delicate) is to be George's private Tutor; and they are to go together to Oxford—Mr. J—n as College Chaplain; and George, of course, will have nothing to do with the University at present. The education of this Boy is a serious concern. He is of an amiable disposition, sweet tempered, quick and lively; but very giddy and unthinking, and I fear might be easily misled. Mr de Quincey is married;[1] and I fear I may add he is ruined. By degrees he withdrew himself from all society except that of the Sympsons of the *Nab* (that pretty house between Rydal and Grasmere). At the up-rouzing of the Bats and the Owls he regularly went thither—and the consequence was that Peggy Simpson, the eldest Daughter of the house presented him with a son ten weeks ago, and they were married on the day of my return to Rydal, and with their infant son are now spending their honeymoon in our cottage at Grasmere. This is in truth a melancholy story! He utter'd in raptures of the beauty, the good sense, the simplicity, the 'angelic sweetness' of Miss Sympson, who to all other judgments appeared to be a stupid, heavy girl, and was reckoned a Dunce at Grasmere School; and I predict that all these witcheries are ere this removed, and the fireside already dull. They have never been seen out of doors—except after the day was gone. As for him I am very sorry for him—he is utterly changed—in appearance, and takes largely of opium. My sister is very well; but miserably thin and eats very little. My Brother has had much vexation and anxiety respecting Richard's affairs and at this moment we are threatened with a Chancery Suit. If this cannot be put a stop to farewell to every farthing of the property I got from my Father (I have none else) and in the meantime we touch no Interest. Wm went this morning to attend the sale of furniture at Sockbridge. My dearest Friend, I have rambled on so long about ourselves that you will think I have forgotten the contents of your last most interesting letter, but not so I assure you. I was charmed with the account you give of your goings on at Playford Hall, and heartily congratulate you on the blessing of a bountiful harvest; and above all I was delighted to hear of your sister's happy prospects and heartily wish that it may please God to grant her all possible comfort as a mother. You will be glad to hear that Mary Hutchinson has got a Daughter. She and the Children both well. Farming concerns wretched—year by year they grow

[1] De Quincey's marriage to Margaret Sympson of the Nab farm by Rydal Lake took place on 15 Feb. 1817, in Grasmere Church. In spite of the unpromising beginning of the association, the marriage proved a stable and happy one and Margaret made De Quincey an excellent wife.

poorer. What do you say to the suspension of the Hab: Corp: Act?[1] If it *be* necessary I can only think that the feeble execution of the Laws which we have already is the cause of that necessity, and it is greatly to be lamented. Nothing can so much tend to irritate the minds of the people. I hope you will be able to give us a good account of Tom, to whom I beg my kind love and to your dear Husband, your Father and Sister, and remember me to Mrs Kitchener. The Kirkby Lonsdale business was with great trouble and fatigue settled without loss. I pray you write soon—Farewell, my dear Friend, yrs ever D.W.

Oh, that you would come and see us next Summer!

Have you seen Coleridge's 'Bible the Statesman's best Manual'.[2] I think it is ten times more obscure than the darkest parts of the Friend.

445. D. W. to THOMAS HUTTON

Address: Thomas Hutton Esq[re], Solicitor, Penrith.
MS. WL.
MY ii. 585, p. 780.

Rydal Mount 11th March 1817

Dear Sir,

A letter has arrived by this night's post from Dr Wordsworth, and, as it is possible that my Brother William may be detained at Penrith longer than he expected, so that this letter may reach you before his departure, I think it best to trouble you with a transcript of a part of Dr Wordsworth's letter, in order that, if you and my Brother Wm think it necessary to write to Mr Addison respecting the India Bonds, no time may be lost.

Extracts from Dr Wordsworth's letter dated March 8th.

'Immediately on the receipt of your Letter yesterday, I went in quest of Mr Addison, and have given him directions to proceed with all despatch in procuring the filing of the amicable Bill'. Dr W. then speaks of the state of accounts between Mr Addison and my late Brother; but with the probable state of these no doubt Mr Addison has made you acquainted, therefore I need not transcribe that part of the letter, and indeed the only matter of importance seems to be

[1] The Suspension of Habeas Corpus was a part of the repressive measures introduced into Parliament by Lord Sidmouth early in the year, as the result of the riots in the previous December.

[2] *The Statesman's Manual* was published in 1816.

the following. 'You are aware that there is a considerable Sum in hand in India Bonds. Of these Mr Addison has the custody; but will leave them with me before his setting out for the Lancaster Assizes, which will be in about ten days time. It strikes one however, on second thoughts, that perhaps the best way would be for you to turn them into money the instant the Will is proved, and to pay the Sum on your account into Masterman's hands. This would put a fresh Sum into your distribution, and perhaps you may think the same course advisable with respect to the Stock (550£) in the Funds.'

If my Brother is still at Penrith pray tell him that we think it not necessary to send the statement of Sale accounts as Mr Sleigh[1] or you must undoubtedly have a copy of it.

I ought to have prefaced this letter with an apology for the trouble I am giving you. I should have addressed it to my Brother if I had been certain that he would not have left Penrith before it arrives. I am, dear Sir,

Yours respectfully,
D. Wordsworth.

440. W. W. to DANIEL STUART

Address: Daniel Stewart Esq., Upper Harley Street, London.
Postmark: Ap. 11 1817. *Endorsed*: 1817 Wordsworth April 7.
MS. British Museum.
S. K. MY ii. 587, p. 783.

April 7, 1817, Rydale Mount.

My dear Sir,

It was only two days ago that I received an acknowledgement from France of the money having been received,[2] otherwise I should have thanked you before for your obliging Letter. You make mention only of £30; in fact I ordered £35 to be paid to you, and on application to the Bank of Kendal they tell me that Sum was paid, and I dare say you remitted to Mr Beaudouin to that amount, though his Letter does not specify the sum he received, but simply says 'la Rente'. I should like to know *at your leisure*, whether you actually received and remitted 30 or 35, for I do not like, for parti-

[1] Isaac Slee or Sleigh. See W. W.'s letter to him, L. 451 below.

[2] This was the annual sum which, after her marriage in 1816, W. W. caused to be paid to his daughter Caroline Baudouin. At this period Daniel Stuart was the intermediary, but in 1834 Crabb Robinson arranged the permanent settlement of £400 on her. See Batho, *The Later Wordsworth*, pp. 390–5, Morley, i. 152, p. 271, and *HCR* i. 452, ii. 454, etc.

cular reasons, to ask him what sum he received.—30 pounds was the sum you had sent on my account the year before, and probably that occasioned the mistake in your recollection.—

Many thanks for your communications on the subject of Politics. There has been a general outcry among sensible people in this neighbourhood against the remissness of Government in permitting the free circulation of injurious writings. It has been especially felt in regard to the blasphemous parodies upon the Liturgy; no one can comprehend why these things should not be suppressed and the Authors or publishers punished. The suspension of the Habeas Corpus Act is a measure approved by all the well disposed, who are a large majority of the influential part of the Country. In fact also the spirit among the labouring classes (with the exception of the populace of Carlisle) is incomparably better than it was in 1794 and 5. The agricultural population of Cumberland and Westmoreland is at present sound; but I would not engage that it will continue so, in case rebellion should get the upper hand in other parts of the Island. A Revolution will, I think, be staved off for the present,[1] nor do I even apprehend that the disposition to rebellion may not without difficulty be suppressed, notwithstanding the embarrassments and heavy distresses of the times. Nevertheless I am like you, an alarmist, and for this reason, I see clearly that the principal ties which kept the different classes of society in a vital and harmonious dependence upon each other have, within these 30 years either been greatly impaired or wholly dissolved. Everything has been put up to market and sold for the highest price it would bring. Farmers used formerly to be attached to their Landlords, and labourers to their Farmers who employed them. All that kind of feeling has vanished—in like manner, the connexion between the trading and landed interests of country towns undergoes no modification whatsoever from personal feeling, whereas within my memory it was almost wholly governed by it. A country squire, or substantial yeoman, used formerly to resort to the same shops which his father had frequented before him, and nothing but a serious injury real or supposed would have appeared to him a justification for breaking up a connexion which was attended with substantial

[1] Wordsworth's political feelings were now set in an 'alarmist' pattern which a year later caused him to take an active part in the Westmorland Election when Brougham challenged the Lowther interest there. See L. 462 ff. below. In this letter his diagnosis of some of the causes of the public discontents shows his correct understanding of what was happening—an understanding based on his personal knowledge of social conditions in his own countryside during the past forty years.

amity and interchanges of hospitality from generation to generation. All this moral cement is dissolved, habits and prejudices are broken and rooted up; nothing being substituted in their place but a quickened selfinterest, with more extensive views,—and wider dependencies,—but more lax in proportion as they are wider. The ministry will do well if they keep things quiet for the present, but if our present constitution in church and state is to last, it must rest as heretofore upon a moral basis; and they who govern the country must be something superior to mere financiers and political economists. Farewell do let me hear from you,

I remain very faithfully yours,
W. Wordsworth.

(turn over)

Southey is going to Town shortly on his way for a short trip on the Continent.[1] I saw him a few days ago quite well, and preparing a Rod for Mr Wm Smith.[2]

447. W. W. to BENJAMIN ROBERT HAYDON

Address: B. R. Haydon Esq, No 8, Great Marlborough Street, London.
MS. untraced.
Haydon (—). *MY ii. 586, p. 781.*

Rydale Mount, near Ambleside, April 7th 1817.

My dear Sir,

I have just received through the hands of Mr Southey the excellent Print from the Gypseys head.[3] The Glass was shivered, when it reached Mr S— into a thousand Pieces; but luckily the Print itself had sustained no damage. I have hung this memorial of you in my Study, and be assured that I prize it not a little. If I have any fault to find with the execution of the Engraving it is that some strokes appear wanting in the face and features to soften and qualify the expression of the eyes—

Mr Southey is going shortly to Town and will be happy to call upon you; I envy him this pleasure both in seeing the artist, and the Picture of Christ's Entry which I suppose is now far advanced towards a Conclusion. I have had a cast taken of one of my hands, with which, I hope, Southey will charge himself—You expressed a wish

[1] During this trip Southey, at Wordsworth's request, called on Annette Vallon and Caroline Baudouin in Paris. See K. Curry, 'Southey's Visit to Caroline Wordsworth Baudouin', *PMLA*, lix (1944), pp. 599–602, and Curry, ii, p. 159.
[2] See L. 448, p. 379, n. 2 below.
[3] A drawing by Haydon.

for an opportunity to paint them from the life—I hope this substitute may not be wholly useless to you—[1]

Your health continues good, I trust, so that your studies proceed —Where is Scott?[2] and is he well—His poem, I see, is published—I am afraid of looking into it on account of the subject[2]—If you write to him pray remember me most kindly and respectfully to him —I have ceased to be a reader of the Champion for several months, supposing that he had discontinued writing in it; and not approving the tone of its Politics. The miscreant Hazlitt continues, I have heard, his abuse of Southey Coleridge and myself, in the Examiner.[3] —I hope that you do not associate with the Fellow, he is not a proper person to be admitted into respectable society, being the most perverse and malevolent Creature that ill luck has ever thrown in my way. Avoid him—hic niger est—And this, I understand, is the general opinion wherever he is known, in London.

Faction runs high—The Friends of liberty and good order are alarmed at the corruption of opinion among the lower classes, and the Reformers and Revolutionists are irritated and provoked that their plans have for the present been defeated. For my own part I am full of fears, not for the present; the immediate danger will, I think be got over, but there is a malady in the social constitution which it will require the utmost skill to manage, and which if it is not met with firmness and knowledge will end in the dissolution of the body Politic. When I have the pleasure of seeing you, I will explain my views at length, and state to you the grounds of my apprehensions.—

Perhaps some of Southey's friends may think that his tranquillity is disturbed by the late and present attacks upon him—not a jot—Bating inward sorrow for the loss of his only son he is cheerful as a Lark, and happy as the day. Prosperous in his literary undertakings, admired by his friends, in good health, and honoured by a large portion of the Public, and as he thinks infinitely the wisest and best part of the Public, busily employed from morning to night, and capable from his talents of punishing those who act unjustly

[1] In 'Christ's Entry into Jerusalem', Wordsworth appears with one hand across his chest in an attitude of reverence. Presumably Haydon wanted 'to paint them from the life' for this purpose.

[2] i.e. John Scott, editor of the *Champion*. The poem, 'The House of Mourning', concerned the death of Scott's elder son, Paul, who died in Paris in 1816 while his parents were on their way to Italy. Hence W. W.'s dread of reading it.

[3] Hazlitt attacked Southey three times in the *Examiner* for this supposed apostasy from his early revolutionary views expressed in his poem *Wat Tyler*, written in 1794, which had been surreptitiously published in Feb. without Southey's knowledge. See Simmons, *Southey* (1945), pp. 158–62.

towards him, what cause has he to be disturbed. I left him the other day, preparing a rod for Mr Wm Smith.[1]—Pray let me hear from you, and believe [me,] my dear Sir, with great regard, and high respect

Most truly yours,
Wm Wordsworth

If you see Sir George and Lady B—give our kindest regards to them.

448. D. W. to CATHERINE CLARKSON

Address: Mrs Clarkson, Playford Hall, near Ipswich, *redirected to* William Buck's Esq, Bury St Edmunds.
MS. British Museum.
K. MY ii. 588, p. 784.

Sunday April 13th [1817]

My dear Friend,

We have long been expecting a letter from you, and I have said 'I will write again, for there is no knowing *when* we may hear from her now that she has put us off so long'; but perhaps if I had not had a sort of motive of business (in itself not worth the postage of a letter) I might yet have delayed many weeks. My business is simply this. Our Friend Mrs Cookson bought some Suffolk hemp many years ago which she liked better than any cloth she ever had in her life, and she thinks that as all other linen cloths are cheap that Suffolk hemp will be cheap also, therefore she desired me when I was at Kendal to ask you if you could purchase some for her. I said I would and forgot it, and to-day she has reminded me of my promise. She wishes to have two pieces proper for shifts for herself, and two of a finer quality for shirts. She would have it unbleached. If you can do this for her, I should be glad, and will inform you how it is to be sent; but do not disturb yourself if it be a very troublesome commission—and probably I think Suffolk Hemps have not fallen in proportion to other cloths of which there is a more extensive manufacture, but if they should be cheap enough to tempt you to buy for Mrs C. you may add two pieces for us of the *Shifting* kind.

You will be concerned to hear that our dear Sara has been very ill, in an inflammatory disorder, not an actual inflammation of the Bowels; but there was considerable inflammation in the parts

[1] William Smith, M.P. for Norwich. See p. 379, n. 2 below.

adjacent and she suffered violent pain. It is more than a month since she began, and her recovery was at first very slow; but she is now, I hope, approaching towards her usual state of health. She rides out daily and is now staying at Mrs Crump's at Allan Bank. We saw her at Church and I thought her looks a little improved since she left us on Friday; but she is very thin and I dare say it will be long before she regains the flesh she has lost. Notwithstanding a prevalence of inflammatory disorders all over the country the rest of the Family have escaped and Dorothy and Willy are strong and look uncommonly well. William has been sadly harassed by my poor brother Richard's affairs—delays of lawyers—difficulties in getting debts paid—threatenings of a Chancery Suit—perplexing letters—everything to disturb him, and all [? new]—and what is worse one can see no end of it; but I think he begins to take things more quietly, and, for the first time during more than a year and a half he has taken to his old employments. To-day he has composed a Sonnet,[1] and in our inner minds we sing 'Oh! be joyful!' It has indeed been most melancholy to see him bowed down by oppressive cares, which have fallen upon him through mismanagement, dilatoriness, or negligence. Alas! that is the truth. Nothing can exceed the apathy which our poor deceased Brother must have lived in, nor his irresolution and weakness. Southey is going upon the Continent and William has had a strong desire to go with him; but he has now given it up; for there are certain points in Rd's affairs pending which might remain longer unsettled if he were absent. I wish he could have gone for several reasons, and chiefly that he might have been out of the way of business for a while, for I think that when he returned to it he would have been able to carry it on with less labour and earnestness the vexatious chain would have been broken, and a fresh stream of thoughts admitted into his mind. I believe he will go next year, if we live and are well. What do you think of your Friend William Smith's attack upon Southey?[2] The publishing of the pamphlet[3] was an infamous thing; but neither that nor the triumphs of the malignant can do him harm. If I were in Southey's place, I sho[uld] be far more afraid of my injudicious defen[ders]

[1] Probably 'The Stars are mansions built by Nature's hand': *Oxf. W.*, p. 266.

[2] See L. 444 above. William Smith, M.P. for Norwich and father of Miss Patty Smith who had criticized *The Excursion* (see L. 339 above), attacked Southey's early radical play *Wat Tyler* in the House of Commons with some violence. Southey defended his change of opinions in the *Courier*, and Coleridge came to his aid in the same periodical in two articles on 18 and 19 Mar. These are referred to by D. W. in this letter. See Simmons, *Southey*, pp. 159–61, and L. 456 below.

[3] The play had been republished without Southey's knowledge.

than my open enemies. Coleridge, for instance, has taken up the Cudgels; and of injudicious defenders he is surely the Master Leader. If you do not see The Courier regularly, I hope you may be able to borrow those for the last 4 or 5 weeks, and you will see what Coleridge has written. He does nothing in simplicity—and his praise is to me quite disgusting,—his praise of the *'Man'* Southey in contradistinction to the *'Boy'* who wrote 'Wat Tyler.' I am very glad that Southey is going abroad. He works so hard, and looks so delicate, that one cannot see him without anxious thoughts; and, resolute as he is, he will for ever feel his bitter loss. It comes on him keenly at times and he has not the boyish glee he used to have. We have good accounts from Wales. Joanna will be here in a few weeks with her Br. Henry[1] who is going to live again at Hawkeshead—good I mean as to health of mind and body; but worldly concerns thrive not there. *We* are least touched by the misfortunes of the times, and there is a better spirit among the lower classes in this neighbourhood than in the former time of distress. I agree with you heartily in lamenting the licentiousness of the press, and I rejoice that Government seems now to be rouzed to vigilance; but it is our misfortune that we never act till our negligence has made it *necessary* that something should be done—also why suffer blasphemous and seditious works to come out weekly and in torrents as one may say? And why not have amended the Poor Laws when the poor were suffering less? Why not *then* have established Saving Banks? I had not time for a long letter and have scrawled over my paper without leaving room for any inquiries but pray tell me the concerns of yourself and all Friends. What is Tom doing? My kind love to him, to Mr Clarkson and to your Father and Sister. The spring is very backward here, weather cold and snowy—snow on the higher hills in patches—nothing *green*, larches green*ish*—the Shrubs just greening in the Gardens. Bless you my dearest friend.

Yrs Ever

D. W.

[1] Henry Hutchinson, M. W.'s sailor-brother, eventually settled with Joanna, the youngest of the Hutchinson sisters, in the Isle of Man.

449. W. W. to ROBERT SOUTHEY[1]

Address: To Robert Southey Esqre, No 1 [?] Queen Anne St, Cavendish Square, London.
Postmark: 28 AP 1817. *Stamp*: Kendal Penny Post.
MS. Massachusetts Historical Society.
NQ, Nov. 1965.

[about Apr. 25, 1817]

. . . farewell with best wishes for your happy return,
I remain my dear Southey,
faithfully yours,
W. Wordsworth.

I should be glad to hear from you at some leisure hour in the course of your tour, but do not let the suggestion encroach upon your freedom in any way. Best wishes to your Br and to your Fellow-Travellers.[2]

I have just received a letter from a Quaker of the name of Barton at Woodbridge—He addresses to me some complimentary verses on the Publication of my White Doe,[3] and now writes a very modest Letter, I do not speak ironica[lly,] to solicit my Subscription for a volume which he is about to publish[4]—you will probably hear from him to the same effect, though he does not mention to me that he has an intention to apply to you.

[*Endorsed in the hand of Edward Everett, American statesman:* Given to me by Mr. Southey, Keswick, June 30th, 1818.]

450. W. W. to SAMUEL ROGERS

MS. untraced.
K. MY ii. 589, p. 787.

Rydale Mount, May 13th 1817.

I presume you are in a state of earthly existence, as I have heard nothing to the contrary since we parted in a shower near the Turnpike Gate of Keswick: need I add that I hope and wish that you may

[1] The first part of this letter has been cut away, clearly because it referred to S.'s forthcoming visit to Paris, where he saw by arrangement Annette Vallon and Caroline Baudouin. See K. Curry, 'Southey's visit to Caroline Wordsworth Baudouin', *PMLA* lix (1944), pp. 599–602.

[2] i.e. Humphry Senhouse of Netherhall, Cumberland, and Edward Nash (1778–1821), portrait miniaturist. Nash made a drawing of W. W., probably in 1818. See Blanshard, *Portraits of Wordsworth*, pp. 60, 148–9.

[3] See L. 369 above.

[4] *Poems*, by 'An Amateur', 1818.

be well? In the former part of this sentence, you may have divined, there lurks a charitable reproach; for you left me with some reason to expect that I should hear of, from, or about you. Though this favour has not been granted, I am not discouraged from asking another, the exact amount of which I am unable to calculate. A Friend of mine, a near Relation of Mrs. Wordsworth, is smitten with a desire of seeing the Pictures brought together by the members of the British Institution, and exhibited in the Evening—I find I have expressed my meaning cumbrously and ill—he wishes to attend in the evening Assembly and has applied to me to procure him a Ticket, for one night, if I conveniently can. It is in your power to enable me to gratify this laudable ambition in a worthy Person? Having come to the point, I have only to add that his Address is, Thomas Monkhouse, Esq., 28 St. Anne's Street West; and could you enclose him a ticket, I shall be thankful.

Are we to see you among us this summer? I hope so—and also that Sharp[1] will not desert us. How is he in health—and what does he say of Switzerland and Italy, both in themselves, and as compared with the scenes in our neighbourhood, which he knows so well? Is George Philips[2] as great an orator as ever, and do you and Dante continue as intimate as heretofore? He used to avenge himself upon his enemies by placing them in H—ll, a thing bards seem very fond of attempting in this day,—witness the Laureate['s] mode of treating Mr. W. Smith.[3] You keep out of these scrapes, I suppose; why don't you hire somebody to abuse you? and the higher the place selected for the purpose the better. For myself, I begin to fear that I should soon be forgotten if it were not for my enemies. Yet now and then a humble admirer presents himself, in some cases following up his introduction with a petition. The other day I had a letter of this sort from a poetical, not a personal, Friend—a Quaker of the name of Barton,[4] living at Woodbridge in Suffolk. He has beguiled me of a Guinea, the promise of one at least, by way of subscription to a Quarto Vol: of poems, which he is anxious to print, partly for honour, and partly for profit. He solicits my interest to promote his views. I state the fact—I do not beg—I have not sufficient grounds to go upon—I leave the affair to the decision of your own mind, only do not contemn me for abusing

[*Rest of MS. missing.*]

[1] Richard Sharp (1759–1835), now M.P. for Portarlington in Ireland. See *EY* 214, p. 468, n. 2.

[2] Partner with Richard Sharp in business concerns. He had subscribed £5 to the fund for the Green children in 1808. (Note by de Selincourt.) See L. 104, pt. i, p. 210.

[3] See L. 448 above.

[4] See L. 381 above.

451. W. W. to ISAAC SLEE[1]

Address: To Mr Isaac Slee, Tirril, near Penrith.
Stamp: Kendal Penny Post.
MS. Cornell
MY ii. 575, p. 763.

[probably Spring 1817]

Dear Sir,

I thank you sincerely for your letter, to which I could not reply earlier having been from home.

Woodburn says that the Posts if they be nothing more than such as are here used (consisting principally of sap) would be extravagantly dear at 8d, half that sum being more than is given for such in this neighbourhood—If they were of heart of oak entirely, he says they would still be dear at 8d.—Under these circumstances I am at a loss what directions to give; it certainly is still my wish, as it was my determination when I saw you, to enclose the bank for planting, but I am disgusted with the notion of being imposed upon at this rate. I must therefore beg of you to make enquiries, if rail-posts cannot be procured in the neighbourhood at a cheaper rate—One could afford something more than a fair price from these being on the spot.

I approve of your proposal of distraining upon Jack[son] at the time you mention, and beg that you would instruct Mr Hutton to proceed against him as you propose.

In respect to Robinson he must be told that I expect the payment immediately of every farthing of Arrears. You know that affairs cannot go on unless what is owing be punctually paid.

Mr. Hutton writes me word that the Concerns of my late Brother are now brought into so narrow a compass that in his opinion you and I may manage them together without any interference on his part, but as a friendly adviser. I shall be happy if you think the same, which I am strongly encouraged to do from the satisfaction your last letter has afforded me. The first time I go over to Sockbridge, which will be shortly, you must be paid for the trouble you have had and an annual allowance for the future must be agreed upon.

With best regards to your Father and Mother and the rest of your family

I remain dear Sir
very truly yours
Wm Wordsworth

[1] A surveyor and land agent who was now looking after the estate at Sockbridge.

Be so good as to let Mrs Wordsworth know when she returns, or if you have occasion to write to her, that the demand of Jackson was a dishonest one—and he has proved to be £40 in debt to the Trust.

452. W. W. to R. P. GILLIES

Address: R. P. Gillies Esqre, King Street, Edinburgh.
Postmark: June 9 1817.
MS. Library of the Historical Society of Pennsylvania.
Gillies. K. MY ii. 590, p. 788.

My dear Sir,

I am unworthy of the many kind marks of attention which you bestow upon me. I knew nothing of the treatise of Wieland,[1] which you enquired after, or I should have written immediately on the Receipt of your Letter. But as I was absent when it arrived, and you must consequently have incurred some disappointment, without any fault of mine, I was foolish enough to press that circumstance into the service of my procrastinating habits. I have read your Poem.[2] I like it better than any of the preceding ones. There is a strong family resemblance, no doubt, in them all—but this as a whole is to me the most interesting. It is natural throughout, and contains many pleasing passages, though I think that in the merits of particular parts some of the others are equal and perhaps superior to it. But the general impression of this last is to my mind much more agreeable than any of the preceding ones. Oswald's feelings on learning that his first passion was hopeless, are given in an animated style—and his recovery.

Even in an hour of sun-illumined Rain

is very fine, but observe that here are eight lines together all rhyming in the Vowel *A*, which gives a heaviness to the movement of this paragraph which every Reader will feel, without being aware of the cause. Lady Clara's character and Residence are very well described, and one is pleased to meet such a couplet as this, it is a sort of beauty that seems natural to you.

All through the copse wood winding walks there were
That led to many a natural parterre

[1] Christopher Martin Wieland (1733–1813) was the first translator of Shakespeare's plays into German. He was also the author of the poetic romance *Oberon*, and of many essays, articles, and poems.

[2] *Oswald, A Metrical Tale*, published 1817.

But how could you write, 'at every step the scenery seemed improving'; this is a thorough bad verse; bad language even for prose —The apology for Oswald's second passion in the preceding Canto is well done. The 6 lines at the top of page 71—an excellent composition, the sentiment is natural to the character—Is there any thing like this in any of Lord Byron's Poems—the language is better than his for the most part appears to be—but the sentiment seems somewhat in his style. I could enumerate many couplets and passages that particularly pleased me, for example in the 36th stanza, 'Spring-tide came on', and the six succeeding lines, particularly 'and long sweet evenings were when mellow dyes Of Twilight lingered in the western skies'—Your essay is desultory enough—of the soundness of the opinion it does not become me to judge—The famous passage on Solitude which you quote from Lord B. does not deserve the notice that has been bestowed upon it. As *composition* it is bad— particularly the line (Minions of grandeur shrinking from distress)[1] which in defiance of all syntax is foisted in for the sake of the rhyme. But the sentiment by being expressed in an *antithetical* manner, is taken out of the Region of high and imaginative feeling, to be place[d] in that of point and epigram. To illustrate my meaning and for no other purpose I refer to my own Lines on the Wye,[2] where you will find the same sentiment not formally put as it is here, but ejaculated as it were [fortuit]ously in the musical succession [of preconceiv]ed[3] feeling. Compare the paragraph ending 'How often has my spirit turned to thee' and the one where occurs the lines

> And greetings where no kindness is and all
> The dreary intercourse of daily life,

with the lines of Lord B— and you will perceive the difference. *You* will give me credit for writing for the sake of truth, and not from so disgusting a motive as self commendation at the expense of a man of Genius. Indeed if I had not known you so well, I would rather have suppressed the truth, than incurred the risk of such an imputation.

Page 20—you say 'my Rustic lyre I cast away, unable to *pourtray*'. We do not pourtray with a Lyre but with a pencil. You frequent[ly] use *revive again* this is a Tautology.—

. . . You hold out a hope that you will visit this country—Do not disappoint us and if Mrs. Gillies come along with you so much the

[1] 'Minions of splendour', etc. *Childe Harold,* II. xxvi. 5.
[2] i.e. *Lines written a few Miles above Tintern Abbey.*
[3] Letters in brackets, torn away in MS., supplied from *Gillies.*

better. Farewell. best regards from Mrs. W. and Miss Hutchinson —and believe me my dear Sir with many thanks for your kind attention—

very faithfully yours
W. Wordsworth

453. W. W. to DANIEL STUART

Address: Daniel Stuart Esq, No 9 Upper Harley Street, London.
Postmark: C 27 Ju 1817. *Endorsed*: 1817. Wordsworth on Poor.
MS. British Museum.
K. MY ii. 592, p. 791.

Rydale Mount, June 22nd 1817.

My dear Sir,

I am sorry that Mrs. Stuart must be disappointed in her wish to procure honey from this neighbourhood. I cannot learn that there is any such thing in the country, last summer having been so extremely wet that the Bees were incapable of working, and most of them perished through hunger in the course of the Winter.—The ensuing season is likely to prove more favourable, and care shall be taken to procure for Mrs. S. a supply.

I congratulate you on your settlement in Oxfordshire;[1] what you have done is just what I should have recommended. I dreaded the notion of your throwing yourself far into the North, even in England—and as to Scotland, so long out of it as you have been, what permanent comfort or solid satisfaction could you have found there! Your lot is now cast in a fair land, and both yourself and your Posterity I trust will feel the benefit. Your purchase which is at a right distance from the Metropolis is both as to quantity and quality, I think, very judicious. In everything especially in land is it of consequence to have good stuff in little room. Buying a large tract of inferior soil, or waste, with a view to reclaim it, though flattering to the Fancy, is an expedient which within the few last years has ruined persons with more certainty than any other sort of speculation.—How are you as to Poor Rates?—If there be not a preparation for a *radical* reform in this branch of public economy, land hitherto

[1] In a letter to W. W., dated London, 29 May 1817, in the Wordsworth Library, Grasmere, Stuart says that he has purchased a farm near Banbury, 'where I intend concentrating and terminating my views on Landed Property'. After giving up the *Courier* (1822) he purchased Wykeham Park in Gloucestershire, but he retained his house in Harley Street whence he was still writing to Wordsworth twenty years later.

deemed the most stable species of property, will become the most insecure and treacherous. What an outcry in Parliament and elsewhere has been made against the absurdity of the Spencean system![1] Yet a reference to calculations will show that this *absurd theory* does at present regulate the *practice* of the country, as enjoined by law, in a degree truly formidable. The *Poor* are at this moment in actual possession of full one-fifth of the *real* estate of the Country.[2] They have it; and they are far stronger, a thousand times stronger, in the *admitted right*, than in the possession. There are scarcely any compulsory proceedings for the support of the Poor in Scotland, and it is said that many unhappy creatures die of hunger in consequence. I know not how far this shocking statement is true; but sure I am that the Poor Laws, as enacted and administered in this country, have degraded tens of thousands to that point that life is wretched to themselves, a plague to their neighbours and a burden to the Community.

There is not a single opinion stated in your Letter, in which I do not coincide. Coleridge you say viewed the matter in the same light some time ago; cogent reason for believing that our impressions as to facts are accurate, and our unwelcome inferences, just. Southey's last article in the *Q.R.*[3] I have not yet seen. We have repeatedly conversed upon the state of the country with little difference of opinion; except that in his vivid perception of the danger to be apprehended from the disaffected urging on the Rabble and the consequent necessity of government being empowered to keep them down, he does not seem sufficiently jealous of the Power whose protection we

[1] Thomas Spence (1750–1814), the author of a scheme of land nationalization by which the inhabitants of each parish were to form a corporation in which the land should be vested; parish officers were to collect the rents, and after payment of expenses divide the money among the parishioners. The Spencean system, promulgated in 1778, was revived in 1816, when the 'Society of Spencean Philanthropists' was formed. (Note by de Selincourt.)

[2] Stuart in the above-mentioned letter refers to the facility with which parish relief is given: 'the ideas the Poor have of a *right* to be maintained . . . their new notions of *right* to a share in the Land as well as the Government'. Wordsworth's statement is curious when compared with a very similar one made in 1793 by Richard Watson, Bishop of Llandaff, in his sermon, 'The Wisdom and Goodness of God in having made both Rich and Poor.' The bishop had ascribed one-ninth of the 'landed rental of the country' to the poor in the form of rates. Wordsworth, at the height of his republicanism, had written a vehement reply to the sermon, but did not publish it. (See A. B. Grosart, *Prose Works of William Wordsworth*, i.) The notion that the right of the poor to support by the rates constituted 'possession' of the land, is one that is not repeated in W.'s writings. In his Preface to *Yarrow Revisited* (1835) he upholds the principle of the right of the poor to maintenance.

[3] i.e. the *Quarterly Review* for Jan. 1817, in which S.'s article on 'The Rise and Progress of Popular Disaffection' appeared.

all feel to be necessary. There is a maxim laid down in my Tract on the Convention of Cintra, which ought never to be lost sight of. It is expressed I believe nearly in the following words. 'There is, in fact, an unconquerable tendency in all power save that of knowledge acting by and through knowledge, to *injure the mind* of him by whom that power is exercised.' I pressed this upon Southey's consideration with a wish that his excellent Letter to Mr. W. Smith,[1] in which he purposed to state his opinions, and to recommend measures, might contain some wholesome advice to Ministers grounded upon this law of our infirm nature.—

If I had access to a Cabinet Minister, I would put these questions. Do you think that the fear of the Law, and mere selfish or personal calculations as to profit or loss, in matter of property or condition, are sufficient to keep a numerous people in due subordination?—'No.'—What loss has the Country sustained within these last 20 or 30 years, of those habits, sentiments, and dispositions, which lend a collateral support, in the way of buttresses, of equal importance for the preservation of the edifice with the foundation itself? If the old props have been shaken or destroyed, have adequate new ones been substituted? A discerning answer to these queries would be the picture of danger, and nothing else can lead to a just consideration of the means by which it is to be lessened.—farewell do let me hear from you as it happens to suit.

By the bye, it was not till this morning that I read the case of Stuart versus Lovell.[2] What a miscreant—If I had been upon the Jury, and had found that the Man possessed property that would bear the damages I should have fixed upon £700 the precise sum which he accused you of embezzling.—Best regards to Mrs. Stuart, and believe me, faithfully yours,

W. Wordsworth.

A neighbour of mine says you may procure in London Majorca honey better than we get in this country.

[1] See L. 448 above.

[2] Lovell, editor of the *Statesman*, had charged Stuart with embezzling £7,000 belonging to the Reform Society, 'The Friends of the People'. W. writes £700, but must mean £7,000.

454. W. W. to JAMES IRVING[1]

MS. WL (draft). Hitherto unpublished.

Rydale Mount
22nd June 1817

Thank you for your civility in forwarding the Magazine containing the Article occasioned by my Letter to Mr Gray.[2] My Friends are at perfect Liberty to follow what course they approve under no restriction from me but one, which their own delicacy will suggest, that especial care be taken, if any reply be given, not to implicate Gilbert Burns. Cheerfully would I submit to any imputation, from such a Quarter, of vanity, impertinence, or presumption, rather than that he should be involved in the dispute. Mr Gray is acquainted with the facts—but he knows full well that a character which can support itself does not require that they should be publickly adverted to.

I have lost no time in answering your Letter; and as the best return which I can make for your attention, I venture to observe that your[3] infant publication must unavoidably fall into discredit if[4] it be made the vehicle of the malignant passions by which this anonymous article is disfigured. There are certain indecencies in writing which *no* merit can atone for. The Philosophy of Plato could not have been endured if it had been accompanied with the manners of Thersites. If this be true, what becomes of your correspondence?

I am, Sir,
your obedient Servnt
W. Wordsworth

[1] Information about this person has been sought in vain. He must have been in some way connected with *Blackwood's* but is not mentioned in the index to the Blackwood papers in the National Library of Scotland. Letters from him to W. W. are in the Wordsworth Library, Grasmere. In these his address is given as 33 East Richmond Street, Edinburgh, but he is not mentioned in contemporary directories.

[2] W. refers to the article in *Blackwood's Magazine*, June 1817, which violently attacked his *Letter to a Friend of Burns*. The article (anonymous) was by John Wilson, who in fact wrote three articles on W.'s pamphlet, two of them adulatory, and one (the subject of this letter) abusive.

[3] W. first wrote and then erased: 'I will take the liberty of observing, as a well-wisher to your' . . .

[4] W. afterwards wrote another draft for the remainder of this sentence: 'a better sounder judgement than the admission of the present Article evinces be not exercised in determining the quantity and quality of supposed general interest which may lawfully serve as a passport for quantity and quality of acknowledged personal abuse'.

[*In M. W.'s hand:*]

Sir

Though it seems unnecessary and indeed somewhat inconsistent to consult me on the point whether I am to be defended when I was not asked whether I chose to be attacked in a manner which you yourself deem obnoxious, nevertheless, etc.,

455. W. W. to [?] JOHN MAY

MS. New York Public Library, Berg Collection. Hitherto unpublished.

Rydale Mount
near Ambleside
June 24th 1817

My dear Sir,

I think it proper to inform you that the Sale of the property at Keswick[1] in which our Friend Mr Southey is interested will take place, according to advertisement, at Keswick on the 14th July—. If Mr Southey does not return to England before that time, I shall be much concerned, unless he has left instructions with you, what is to be done.—Pray be so good as to inform me how the matter stands;—Be assured that it will give me the utmost pleasure to contribute in any way to realize my Friend's wishes.

I remain dear Sir
with much respect
very truly yours
Wm Wordsworth

[?] 30th June 1817.

Endorsed 1817, Rydal Mount 24 June Wm Wordsworth recd 28th d ansd 30th d. as by copy annexed, C.B. fo 249

[1] The copy of the recipient's answer annexed to this letter shows that this property was Southey's home, Greta Hall, which he held on a lease of twenty-one years. He did not in fact purchase it, but remained tenant until his death. See J. Simmons, *Southey*, p. 109. In a letter to his brother Henry Herbert S., 'Easter Sunday' 1817, S. says that he has not yet made up his mind and 'if the ways and means are forthcoming [I must] leave Wordsworth to act for me'. To W. W. he wrote on 5 and 8 May 1817: 'I have determined upon purchasing the house etc., and John May will write to you about it, when all the previous arrangements are made.' Curry ii, pp. 152, 157. It is therefore most probable that May is the person to whom W. W. is writing. Southey had first met May in Portugal in 1796.

[The recipient's answer, copied onto W. W.'s letter:]

June 24th 1817

My dear Sir,

In the interval that elapsed between my first address, if you are on the subject of yr friend Robert Southey's wish to purchase the house which he occupies at Keswick, and the receipt of yr answer wherein you signify your willingness to co-operate towards the attainment of [?his] object, it pleased God to visit me with a severe domestic affliction by the unexpected death of a dearly beloved brother; and it was in the midst of this distress which I was suffering on that acct that yr first letter reached me. Upon its receipt I sent for H.S.[1] to whom jointly with yourself had been confided [?as I think] before his departure for France, the management of the affair, and I pressed him to proceed in it so that your friend's interest should suffer no detriment from my inability to do so at the moment. He undertook to do as I desired, but as I have not seen him or heard from him since I'm not certain that he has fulfilled the engagement. However as I go there tomorrow, I will ascertain the point and henceforward I will not confide to another what I can now do myself. I feel very much obliged to you for reminding me of the business in your 2nd letter of the 24th inst, as being directed to me, which only reached me on Saturday evening too late to be answered earlier than by this day's post.

456. W. W. to H. C. R.

Address: Henry Robinson, Esq., Temple, London.
Postmark: 2 o'Clock, 30. Ju. 1817 ANO. *Endorsed*: 24 June 1817, Wordsworth. On Southey's pamphlet on W: Smith's attack in the house of Commons.
MS. Dr. Williams's Library.
K (—). Morley, i. 91.

Rydale Mount
24th June 1817

My dear Sir,

Dr Chalmers,[2] (of whom notwithstanding his celebrity I had never heard which occasioned me to address him by the name of Dr Campbell a most unlucky blunder) delivered your Letter, and I gave

[1] Probably Henry Herbert Southey, Robert Southey's brother.

[2] Thomas Chalmers (1780–1847), presbyterian theologian and famous preacher, at this time minister of the Tron church, Glasgow. In his later years he led the movement which terminated in the great disruption within the Scottish Church, and the foundation of the Free Church, independent of the establishment.

him such directions for seeing the Country as best suited with the time at his disposal. His Friend mentioned by you was not with him.—I duly received your former Letter, I mean in due course of Post, for as to other *obligation*, if I may use so bold a word, it came like a bad debt unexpectedly recovered.—(A man of business is speaking to a Lawyer you will therefore excuse the Metaphor).—How came you to quarrel with Furness Abbey—Your old enemy bad weather must have persecuted you into bad humour, which powerful as your foe was, I think he would have some difficulty in effecting. Furness Abbey presents some grand points of view, which you must have missed—The Architecture never seems to have been so highly embellished as might have been expected from the princely power and revenues of the Community who erected it. This I allow, and it is dilapidated far beyond the point where entireness may advantageously be infringed upon, where the gratifications of the eye and the imagination meet each in their utmost perfection.—But after all why not be thankful for what has been done and yet remains?—How unlucky you were! we have had less rain during the last eleven or twelve weeks, than the average of as many hours taken for the time you were among us—It has been a cold spring but bright and beautiful, and we are now in a series of the old golden glorious summer days; the little corn that we have in the neighbourhood, and the grass growing as fast as in Russia or Finland—Yesterday Mrs Wordsworth and myself were on the top of Helvellyn, my second visit within these last three weeks. The former was with my Sister, we returned over its summit from Patterdale where we had been staying a few days. I describe nothing of these appearances in Prose—you will hear of them at some future time in Verse—In a fortnight or three weeks I visit Mr Stanley of Ponsonby, a mile from Calder Abbey[1] your favorite; I have invited Mr Hutton[2] to meet me at Ravenglass, and be assured the Place shall receive a few ill names from me on your behalf, if it does not make amends for past offences by putting on its best looks—

I hope you will see the Laureat[3] on his return also for news of which I am to look and indeed to long. He went away with a wish to

[1] Calder Abbey stands in the woods of Ponsonby, in west Cumberland.

[2] For Mr. Hutton, see L. 415 above. H. C. R. notes as 'a singular illustration of the maxim, "A prophet is not without honour save in his own country" ' that 'Mr Hutton, a very gentlemanly and seemingly intelligent man, asked me, "Is it true—as I have heard reported—that Mr Wordsworth ever wrote verses?" ' *Sadler*, ii, p. 26.

[3] Southey, who had been for three months on the Continent. In Paris he had called on Annette Valion and Caroline Baudouin, at Wordsworth's request.

purchase the house he occupies at Keswick it is advertised for sale on the tenth I believe of next month[1]—His Letter quoad Mr Wm Smith[2] is I think completely triumphant, but I am not satisfied with his statement of his own opinions, and his delineation of the course which he wishes to be pursued. It is too hastily executed and wants some passages of searching admonition to ministers both for their benefit, and to blunt the force of a charge which his enemies will bring against the author of being too obsequious to the throne the aristocracy, and to persons in office, or in plain terms of being a *Tool of Power*. A most false and foul accusation, for a more disinterested and honourable Man than Robert Southey does not breathe—Does Mr Smith expect that even his personal and party friends will in their consciences believe him whatever they [?may] profess, when he states, as he did in the Ho[use] that he did not censure a change of [?views] but the virulence with which they were now reproached who continued to think as their present Reviler himself had formerly done. How came he then to use the word Renegado? The practice to which he pretends his censure was confined is far from entering of necessity into the meaning of that word. The *act of change* is stigmatized by the word; which comes from a desertion of Christianity for Mohammedanism, which Christians cannot admit a possibility of, from other than a bad motive or a vitious impulse.—You remember the squabble I got into with young Roscoe[3]—a very shallow fellow! at Mrs Charles Aikin's.[4] He is suspected by a Scotch friend of mine to be the author of a vehement senseless and if I had not used the word before I should add virulent attack upon me in a publication now struggling into birth under the name of the Edinburgh Magazine.[5] This stupid diatribe is occasioned by my Letter on the subject of the new edition of Burns.—If it tends to make my Publication enquired after—I should be thankful to this *Young Gentleman*—such he was, and young in brain he must ever be—but as to the substantive in any

[1] See L. 455 above.

[2] *A Letter to W. Smith Esq., M.P., from R. Southey 1817* was published in the *Courier*. See L. 448 above.

[3] See *HCR* i, p. 83, for a description of this 'squabble' which took place on 13 May 1812. 'Young Roscoe' was the son of William Roscoe of Liverpool, author of a history of the Italian Renaissance. See L. 145, pt. i, p. 306, n. 2.

[4] The Aikins are frequently mentioned by H. C. R. in his Diary. Charles Aikin, a doctor, married Anne Wakefield. Arthur Aikin, his brother, edited the *Annual Review*, from 1803 to 1808, and Lucy Aikin, their sister, wrote history, reviews, and a memoir of her aunt, Mrs. Barbauld.

[5] i.e. *Blackwood's*. But the attack on W. was really by John Wilson. The 'Scotch friend' is probably R. P. Gillies. See L. 454, p. 389, n. 2.

creditable sense, nothing can be left but what he may owe to his Tailor—farewell.

Let me hear from you in reasonable time,. I have not seen Southey's article in the last Q.R. nor Mr Moore's ugly named Poem,[1] nor Lord Bys—Tragedy,[2] nor his last Canto of Child Harold where I am told he has been poaching on my Manor, nor any one new thing whatever—except abuse of myself and sometimes praise, that persons mostly unknown to me are officious enough to forward me these [?]

ever truly yours
W W

Miss H. is gone to the [? seaside] All well, with kindest regards. W. W.

457. D. W. to JANE MARSHALL

Address: Mrs Marshall, Hallsteads, near Penrith.
Stamp: Kendal Penny Post.
MS. WL.
K. MY ii. 593, p. 794.

Wednesday 25th June [1817]

My dear Friend,

When, on our way home, I viewed from the top of Helvellyn the fields of Skelly Nab and the dwellings of Hallsteads and Old Church I thought I would, the very next day write you an account of our journey; but, finding Miss Joanna Hutchinson ill in the rheumatism, I was unwilling to begin with a dolorous tale, and put off for a day or two, and thus, because I had begun with a delay I went on, and it is now more than a fortnight since I was at Hallsteads.——We had a most delightful prospect from the top of the mountain, and I did not find the ascent very toilsome; for we took plenty of time and reached home, I may almost say without fatigue, at about eight o'clock in the evening. We viewed the masses of snow with particular attention which Mary Anne[3] daily watches in their decay from the shores of Ulswater, and my Brother made a bold push to procure some of that very snow for our refreshment; but he could not accomplish it, so we were obliged to be satisfied with some a little further on, which her eyes had never gazed upon. When we

[1] *Lalla Rookh*, by Tom Moore.

[2] *Manfred*, by Byron.

[3] Mary Anne Marshall, eldest d. of John and Jane M. Many years later, in 1841, she married as his second wife Lord Monteagle, formerly Thomas Spring-Rice (1790–1866), the Irish whig politician.

were at Glen-riddin the Miss Askews[1] were eager in their hopes of ascending Helvellyn with Mary Anne, and, I think Miss Hazell;[2] but if they did not go to Mr. Askew's before the commencement of the very hot weather, I think it will not be thought prudent by the elders of the houses of Marshall and Askew that the young people should venture upon such a walk. The coolness of the air was very favorable to us; I never walked with more spirit in my life than on the lofty Terrace of Helvellyn, and the next day my limbs were not at all stiff, nor had I the least sensation of fatigue. Poor Joanna Hutchinson continued in great pain for several days; and as she neither regained her strength nor got rid of the rheumatic pains in the course of a fortnight she resolved to try a warm sea-bath, and she and Miss Hutchinson left us at six o'clock on Monday morning, intending to go either to Allonby or to Parton, a little village near Whitehaven. They would decide upon one of the two places on their arrival at Cockermouth, after consulting a person acquainted with both. I do not know how long they will be absent; but I should think certainly not less than three weeks if the sea air agrees with Joanna, though they will naturally be very impatient to return to this delightful place, which they have left in full beauty.—Dorothy is gone with them. We are in hopes that the sea-air will strengthen her. She has no particular ailment; but is excessively thin and pale—rather say black and yellow often times, and has had no appetite for some weeks.— —

I hope that Mr. Marshall arrived at Hallsteads at the promised time, and that he is now perfectly well; and that you all continue so. How do you like this very hot weather? It is of the right old-fashioned kind, and pleases me well; but certainly it is not the weather for stirring about or making journies either of business or pleasure; but we, at Rydal Mount, are well off, for when there is a breeze stirring we are sure to have our share of it in one part or another of the garden; and the evenings and mornings are most delightful. Are you not astonished with the progress of vegetation? I hope that if Mrs. Whitaker is not already with your Sisters, she will arrive before the very fine weather is gone, that she and all of you may enjoy the Luxury of floating upon still waters on long summer evenings. Nothing can exceed the glory of Ulswater at such a time. There is now a refreshing breeze, and if it continues we intend to stroll down the meadows to Winandermere, and shall take a Boat to Low Wood for the sake of the sunset on the Langdale

[1] Daughters of the Rev. Henry Askew, rector of Greystoke.
[2] For the Hasells of Dalemain, see below L. 542.

mountains, a spectacle I often have heard you speak of with delight. I have scrawled over my paper and hardly left Room to request that you will take the trouble to inform Mrs Askew if you should see her in the course of a week or two, that Miss Hutchinson does now always write to Mrs. Luff through the post-office. The *Inland* postage is to be paid. If you are not likely to see Mrs. A., pray be so good as to write a line to her to this effect. I would write to her, but my letter would not be worth the postage. Pray make my best Respects to Mrs. Askew and all the Family. With kind love to all at Hallsteads and Old Church,

I am, dear Jane
Your affectionate Friend
D. Wordsworth

what a glorious midsummer Ja[ne!]

458. W. W. to DANIEL STUART

Address: Daniel Stuart Esq, 9 Upper Harley Street, London.
Endorsed: 'is answered Wordsworth on Education. Vernon 1817.'
MS. British Museum.
K. MY ii. 594, p. 796.

Rydal Mount, Sat, Sept^br^ 7th, 1817.

Dear Sir,

The German scheme is out of the Question. C.[1] in recommending it, seems to have overlooked that, when he himself studied at Göttingen, he was 25 or 6 years of age, and before he went thither had resided several months in a Clergyman's house to acquire the language. A Public Office is wholly undesirable for those who have the means of doing better, that is, of a regular English Gentleman's Education.—I cannot understand what you report from the youth's Masters, that he will at Christmas have attained all that they in the usual way can teach him, if by this is meant that he cannot go further under their tuition. If he has done well where he is, why cannot he be continued there, reading such books in classics as he has not read, and continuing his exercises in prose and verse composition in the Latin and Greek languages? But as they have expressed this opinion it would seem that they would rather be without the Lad, than encounter this additional trouble on his account. It remains then to consider how he can make the best use of his time till he can enter

[1] i.e. Coleridge, who lived in a pastor's house at Ratzeburg, during the winter of 1798/9, while the Wordsworths were at Goslar.

at one of the Universities. You are perhaps aware that from Cambridge he must be excluded for the ensuing year, not having been entered previous to the Commencement, which is, I think about the beginning of July—and as he is so young, there is no reason to regret this. As you intend him for the Bar, I should by all means recommend a Public School for the ensuing twelve months, in preference to his being placed in the house of a Clergyman. I give due consideration to what you say on the subject of his overgrown stature, but I cannot accede to the truth of his own remark that, should he go to Winchester, Harrow, Rugby, or any other Public School of celebrity, he would have everything to go over again. Inconvenience no doubt would arise from his not having learnt perhaps the same Grammar, but if he be well grounded and respectably practised in the Latin and Greek languages, which he must be if what you say of his late Masters be just, then the obstacles from this cause would be easily surmounted. I am decisively of opinion that a Public School is the proper place of education for a *Lawyer*. I know several eminent English Lawyers distinguished for their knowledge of Law, as Chamber Counsel, who most probably would have been equally distinguished for their happy manner of displaying it in a court of justice, if they had fortunately been educated in public schools, but, not having had that discipline, they are obliged to keep their candle hidden under a Bushel. Shyness, reserve, awkwardness, want of self-possession, embarrassment, encumbered expression, hesitation in speaking, etc., etc., are sad impediments to an Advocate; and the best way of obviating all this is to place a Lad under the necessity of encountering the shock he will every moment meet with, in those Seminaries. As to private tuition it is such an irksome thing that scarcely any of those who undertake it, do their Duty. If they be Persons of known Competence, they mostly have several pupils of the same age, to qualify for the University. A certain plan of study is chalked out—the Scholars and Master begin with a resolution that everything shall be understood. This is stuck to for a *while*, but first one Lad falls off, and then another, and the course of Reading is persisted in when perhaps not one out of the three four five or six that the class is composed of, has any understanding of the subject. But they must go forward, else the master will not seem to have fulfilled his part of the engagement.—What then do I advise? That your Protégé should be immediately examined, in Latin and Greek, by some competent Person, who has been himself distinguished at one of the Universities, for his knowledge of classics, and educated at one of the public schools; and, if he find him well grounded and practised in construing and composition, and deems him so far advanced that he can be sent to one of our great public Schools with a prospect of benefiting in those studies, that is, without its being probable that he would be thrown back materially by the necessity of learning a new set of syntax rules, or other things of that sort, that then he should proceed forthwith to such school for the ensuing year, and be admitted at Trinity College, Cambridge, next commencement to reside in October following.— I advise Cambridge, in preference to Oxford, because at Cambridge he will have stronger incitements and inducements to apply to Mathematics; and, if he is able to fix his attention so far as to make a progress in those sciences, the assiduity and steady application of the thoughts requisite for success in Law will not be more than he will find himself already prepared for. I recommend Trinity College in preference to any other, because it is a more liberal foundation. I have now said all that strikes me upon the subject.—

The prospect for the ensuing harvest is very encouraging in the North of England and South of Scotland. The weather at present is more promising—I received a newspaper from you, some time ago, in which you had done me the honour of adopting a remark from one of my Letters. I have not seen Southey since his return.[1] I learn that he is looking uncommonly well, and has enjoyed himself much.— With best regards to Mrs. Stuart, I remain very truly yours,

Wm. Wordsworth.

P.S. Your [protégé] might go to College immediately and reside as a Non.-Ens., *i.e.*, without university rank. I have just learned that the masters of the great schools do not like to admit boys after the age of 15, unless from one great school to another; and it is certain that your protégé will be less likely to benefit in a general way, from his advanced age. So that, upon the whole, it is a puzzling case, and I wish you by all means to go by advice grounded upon his examination, as before recommended.

[1] i.e. from France, where he had gone in the Spring. See L. 449, p. 382 n.

459. W. W. to R. P. GILLIES

MS. Amherst Wordsworth Collection
Postmark: 23 Sept. 1817.
MY ii. 591, p. 791.

Friday [Sept.] 19th 1817[1]

My dear Sir,

Your letter of the 15th Instant, I have this moment received on my return from an Excursion of a few days.—I fear this note will arrive too late to be of use—but I write to mention that I quit home on the 22nd or 23d of this month. I shall be absent I fear at least a fortnight. I shall regret this much if it should deprive me of the pleasure of seeing you in this Country. My first visit is to Lord Lonsdale at Lowther, and afterwards I go to a Friend's House a Mr. Marshall who lives upon the Banks of Ulleswater; so that though absent for some time I shall not be far from home—

I have not read Mr. Coleridge's 'Biographia', having contented myself with skimming parts of it; so that you will not be surprized when I tell you that I shall never read a syllable of Mr. Jefferson[2] Critique. Indeed I am heartily sick of even the best criticism, of course cannot humor an inclination to turn to the worst—

I have no intention to print any of my little pieces in periodical works, a practice I never had recourse to, except in the case of poems which have a political bearing—Excuse this wretched scrawl written in extreme haste to catch the post— I shall be truly sorry if I hear of your arrival here after my departure.

Believe me most sincerely yours,
W. Wordsworth

[1] Although de Selincourt ascribed this letter to June, it cannot be earlier than July, when *Biographia Literaria* was published, and is most probably September as the June visit to the Marshalls was over before the 25th (see L. 457, p. 395), and on 16 Oct. D. W. wrote to Mrs. Clarkson that she and Mary had returned from Ullswater 'last Monday', i.e. 13 Oct., and that 'William was at Thomas Wilkinson's', probably after a visit to Lowther. See L. 460 below, and also n. 2.

[2] W. means 'Mr. Jeffrey's'. He refers to Hazlitt's review of *Biographia Literaria* in the *Edinburgh Review* for Sept. 1817, to which Jeffrey added a note, replying to Coleridge's strictures on him in *Biographia Literaria*. See *HCR*, i, p. 209.

460. D. W. to CATHERINE CLARKSON

Address: Mrs. Clarkson, Playford Hall, near Ipswich.
MS. British Museum.
K. MY ii. 595, p. 799.

Rydal Mount October 16th [1817]

My dear Friend

I will not enter on the subject which you have so sympathetically discussed, our long silence, except to suggest that, it becomes us both to profit from what has passed—we each know that however slow we may be in writing the other will neither be offended nor dream of the possibility of neglect and this assurance has often aided the suggestions of indolence and other motives for delay. I did not *expect* a letter from you for I had taken the whole blame to myself, therefore I was doubly pleased when Sara put yours into my hands on our return from Ulswater last Monday, and in answer to my inquiries, at the same time informed me that she had written to you. Your account of yourself, my dearest Friend, is certainly very satisfactory as regards your health, yet I cannot conceal from you that I felt a sadness at the close of your letter—entertaining as it was. You speak of that one day spent by the River-side as a thing to be repeated at the close of labours and expenses, and how *many* of such days have *we* passed this summer:—You talk of your Husband letting 'the farm sink too much into him'. This I know must be the case: but the confirmation from you was painful and strengthened me in the conviction that you have both taken upon yourselves care, anxiety, and even labour that you would have been better without. —Then follows that you cannot look to a time for visiting us—Why should you have been thus confined? Why have such a Bondage in a great farm that can never make you rich and if it could, by that time your wings would be clipped by age. You have both active minds and if Mr C had had two cows and a horse they would have furnished him with sufficient employment to withdraw him from fancies and cares that might sometimes oppress him in his study or by his fire-side. But what is the use of all this! You *have* the farm and must keep it for a time. I confess it is a selfish feeling that makes me thus lament to you,—I am grieved and it is some relief to me to tell you so.—It seems to me that you, with only one child, have no motive to imprison yourselves in this way, and involve yourselves in worldly cares, and I am half vexed that you should have done it. Do forgive me for having said what must be useless and may give you pain—and I will try to hope that in a year or two you will be more at liberty. I have spent six months out of the last twelve from home[1] and look forward to being stationary for a while with satisfaction, yet when an opportunity offers, I am determined to go to France. I am under promise to Caroline (she is married to Mr Baudouin's Brother and has a Daughter) and besides I have a great desire to see her and all the Family. At that time I shall certainly make my way to you, but as the how and the when are all uncertain it will not serve for either of us to fix our minds upon at present. I am very happy, much as we shall miss Sara, that she is likely to spend the winter with you—I cannot say when she will set off or how she will travel—therefore do not consider yourself as quite certain of seeing her; yet I am sure she will do her utmost.—Tom Monkhouse is at Penrith and will be here again after the Races; but she cannot accompany him; she has, however, some thoughts of going with John M who is also at Penrith and will stay perhaps 5 or 6 weeks in this country. We have a succession of company all this summer—one house-ful after another, but after the Monkhouses leave us we shall be settled to ourselves for the winter. The Autumn has been delightful, and your own Lake of Ullswater was enchanting while we were there. We spent two days at Eusemere with Captn. Wordsworth and his Bride,[2] and were exceedingly pleased with the hospitality and kindness of them both. He has made a most judicious choice. Eusemere is exactly as you made it excepting some alterations in the kitchens—every walk remains as made by your hands.—Often did Mary and I think of you, and often wish that you were walking by our side—The Lodging-rooms have the same papers on the walls and you would be surprized to see how little they are changed—They look as fresh and clean as if they had been put up this summer. William was at Thomas Wilkinson's—but we, M and I, did not see him—William says he is not altered in any respect but that he looks older—he labours just as hard as ever with the same contented chearfulness. I hope you will see Tillbrooke at Christmas. He will delight in talking with you of Rydal, and its inhabitants; we were very sorry when he was forced to go away; and he went with a heavy heart. You will be charmed with the Ivy Cottage whenever you see it. I would try to describe the beauty of the Orchard and garden, that are and that are to be, but you will hear all from himself and Sara.—Southey returned from the Continent in great spirits—quite himself when I saw him in Borrowdale which was just after

[1] D. W. had left Rydal for Halifax in Oct. 1816 and returned in Feb. 1817.
[2] Captain John Wordsworth, the Wordsworths' first cousin, of Penrith, married Elizabeth Littledale at Whitehaven on 16 Sept. 1816.

his return; but I am sorry to hear that home has already wrought sore change in him. How can it be other wise! A man cannot live with such a set of women and approve of them without being the worse for it. How can he be lively when his Wife is always dull and frown[s] at all his little gaieties? Southey saw Caroline and her Mother Husband and Daughter Dorothée[1] and was very much pleased with them—He says the Babe is a lovely Child, the Mother very interesting and the image of John Wordsworth—and something like Dorothy; and the Husband a fine man—sensible and animated and very fond of his wife and child. How sorry I am that you did not see these friends of ours when you were at Paris!—Derwent Coleridge is going to his Father in London—I can not see any good that can possibly arise from this, unless it forces his father to exert himself to put the Boy forward, or forces him to confess openly that he cannot do any thing—which will at least compel him to perceive that he or his Children have had, and have Friends, ill as he thinks he has been used in the world. I have hastily scrawled over my paper to save the post, and have hardly left Room to speak of ourselves or the Children in answer to your inquiries. William has sate for his picture,[2] written a few small poems, entertained company, enjoyed the country, and paid some visits and so his summer has been passed; he intends to work hard at the Recluse in Winter—The Children are healthy and well-looking, and only want stricter discipline to make them all we could desire—yet in respect of learning, John will never make a figure, though I hope he may pass very well through the University, which will be the best opening for him if his Uncle Chris[r] lives; or if his Father lives and preserves the Friends whom he has already made. Do you know of any good School for Girls that you can recommend? I have it much at heart that D. should go to school for a while if any unexceptionable school could be found—She is as fine a Girl as ever was; but there is too much pleasure and too little regularity at home.

Wm's picture is charming—What a sad scrawl—I am called to dress for a visit at Mr Gee's at the foot of the hill. Believe me ever my dearest Friend. Your affect[te]

D W

[1] For Southey's description of his visit to the Baudouins, see Curry, ii, pp. 160–1.

[2] By Richard Carruthers; see F. Blanshard, *Portraits of Wordsworth*, pp. 53–8.

461. W. W. to THOMAS MONKHOUSE

Address: Thomas Monkhouse, Esq., Budge Row, London.
Postmark: 21 Nov. 1817.
MS. WL.
LY iii, 595a, p. 1370.

Rydal Mount
Nov[br] 18th 1817

My dear Friend,

Your Letter was duly received for which and the kind and judicious exhortations it contains, I return you my best thanks—They fall in with my own determination, and I hope to act as you wish.—But I am now unsettled again.—My late Brother's[1] affairs are in such a state as seems to render it adviseable that I should repair to London to confer with my Brother[2] respecting them. Unless therefore I change my mind I shall be in Town about the middle of next week,[3] God willing—Mary and Sarah purpose coming along with me—We go to Lambeth, and from that place Sarah will proceed to Bury[4].—Sunday intervening, I do not think we shall be able to start before Monday, with comfort; our journal will then be—Kendal Monday—Leeds Tuesday—London, Thursday Noon—And as we have some reason to fear that Christopher may be at Sundridge[5] we will drive to your lodgings, to give you a call by the way.

Should this journey be dropped the Background will be sent along with some blank Legacy forms to be filled up according to the tenor of the Testator's will. You will observe that the Stamp Office does not require Legacy duties to be paid till a year after the Testator's decease, unless the will directed the Legacies to be paid within less than that time.—I mean to furnish you with the above mentioned Forms, because if procured at the Stamp office or elsewhere it would be expected that the money should be paid in there.—*When* you receive the Forms you will fill them up according to the directions of the will, procuring the requisite signatures from the several Legatees, and forward the forms to me, for my signature, and that I may transmit them to the Stamp Office, to be registered.[6]

[1] i.e. Richard W. who died in May 1816.

[2] i.e. Christopher W., at present Rector of Lambeth.

[3] This visit of W.'s to London, which lasted until 19 Jan. 1818, was an important one, as it saw his meetings with John Keats.

[4] i.e. to Mrs. Clarkson. But she now lived near Ipswich.

[5] See L. 394, n. 1.

[6] Tom Monkhouse as the executor of a will had been asked by W. to collect particulars from the legatees, so that the legacy duties could be paid through Wordsworth's hands as Distributor for the area concerned.

I am glad to hear so good an Account of Haydon. I could not help smiling at his friendly zeal in proposing to pay the expenses of my journey to Town, knowing as I do his circumstances. But he is a Despiser of money—too much so—I shall be very glad to see him.

I wrote to Mr Tilbrooke according to your wish, sometime since.

Whatever you decide upon, take care that your inclinations do not bias your Judgement—

Believe me very affectionately yours
Wm Wordsworth

462. W. W. to LORD LONSDALE

MS. Lonsdale MSS., Record Office, The Castle, Carlisle. Hitherto unpublished.

28 Queen Anne Street
Cavendish Square.
Dec^b 13th [1817]

My Lord,

Mr Parry[1] had not the least objection to grant me the permission I requested.

I shall have the honor of enclosing a Copy of my Letter to Mr Ramshay,[2] and his answer when I receive it.

This morning I heard of a piece of absurdity which your Lordship will permit me to mention. Mr George Troutbeck of Blencow, at present a student in one of the Inns of Court, dining with Mr Monkhouse yesterday, informed him, on the authority of a Gentleman who was present at the meeting,[3] that certain Persons had agreed to oppose your Lordship's interest for the County of Westmorland at the ensuing election. The honors of standing as Candi-

[1] See L. 308 and L. 434 above.

[2] Mr. Ramshay was the Distributor of Stamps for the Carlisle district of Cumberland. Wordsworth was hoping to take over his district, but for reasons connected with the Westmorland election he did not at this time do so. He had met him in July 1814 during the tour to Scotland with M. W. and S. H. See *SH* 21, p. 72.

[3] At the City of London Tavern on 10 Dec. It purported to be a meeting of 'freeholders and other gentlemen connected with Westmorland, resident in London', but was in fact very sparsely attended; and the self-styled 'London Committee', set up on this occasion, was subsequently ridiculed by the Lowthers. 'Mr. Monkhouse' is Tom M., M. W.'s first cousin.

date had been offered to Mr Brougham[1] but he declined it. Three thousand pounds were subscribed at the meeting for the purpose of the Election, and the Person to be brought forward is a Gentleman of £2000 per ann. landed estate in the neighbourhood of Temple Sowerby.[2] This is the history of this ridiculous business as reported by Mr Troutbeck. On my return to London I will try to learn who the parties were.

Your Lordship's Boots were of infinite service to me, as owing to the Mail's being full I was obliged to venture myself on the outside. I was no worse but better for exposure to the night air.

Yesterday London was covered with one of those thick fogs peculiar to it.

My best wishes attend your Lordship and every member of your family.

I have the honour to be
with the highest respect
my Lord
Your Lordship's
obedient and obliged Servant
Wm Wordsworth.

Please to turn over the page.

P.S. I am just setting off for Sundridge,[3] I shall return on Wednesday or Thursday next; my address as above.

[1] Henry (later Lord) Brougham (1778–1868). In 1818 he did in fact challenge Lord Lonsdale's practice of nominating the two county members for Westmorland. He was defeated after a four days' poll, and defeated subsequently in 1820 and 1826, but his candidature caused a great sensation from the vigorous manner in which he conducted it. Wordsworth's activities during the election on behalf of the Lowther brothers—sons of Lord Lonsdale—are described in detail in his letters to Lord Lonsdale and Lord Lowther from this date onwards. See also Moorman, ii, pp. 344–56.

[2] W. W.'s cousin William Crackanthorpe of Newbiggin Hall, who was in the opposite 'interest' politically to Lord Lonsdale, as his father, the Wordsworth's 'Uncle Kit', had been an agent of the Duke of Norfolk's in Cumberland. See L. 466 below.

[3] For a description of Sundridge, see *SH* 35, p. 112.

463. W. W. to LORD LONSDALE

MS. Lonsdale MSS., Record Office, The Castle, Carlisle. Hitherto unpublished.

my address
48 Mortimer Street
Cavendish Square.
Saturday, Dec^{br} 20th [1817][1]

My Lord,

I returned to Town on Thursday,[2] but could not procure the enclosed Paper[3] before this day, which I take the liberty of forwarding though I think it extremely unlikely that it has not reached your Lordship many days ago.

I need not say how happy I should be if I could be of any use in regard to the proceedings of these Persons[4]—your Lordship has only to point out the way in which you wish me to exert myself.

I have not yet heard from Mr Ramshay. Mrs Ellwood[5] has not yet been sounded upon the subject of your Lordship's kind offer. But Mrs Wordsworth's Sister, knowing Mrs Ellwood's determination to exert herself (the moment an opportunity can be found) for her own support, thinks that it is impossible that she can feel anything but gratitude for any benefit, which in her present situation your Lordship may be disposed to confer upon her.—But I need not add that her most anxious wish is to be employed, in any situation however humble, for her own maintenance. Her dispositions in this respect I know to be admirable.

I have the honor to be
My Lord
With the highest respect
Your Lordship's
most obliged and faithful Servant
Wm Wordsworth.

[1] W. W. wrote *1816* by mistake.

[2] From Sundridge.

[3] A London newspaper reporting the meeting mentioned in the previous letter.

[4] i.e. those who were promoting an 'independent' candidate to stand against the Lowthers at the General Election.

[5] The widow of the Penrith solicitor mentioned in L. 207, pt. i, p. 435, who was apparently seeking some kind of employment for herself. A member of the Wordsworth circle, she occasionally stayed at Rydal Mount, and her activities are often recorded in *MW* and *SH*; but the exact nature of Lord Lonsdale's offer here remains unexplained.

[*For 463a, see Addenda, p. 664.*]

464. W. W. to LORD LONSDALE

MS. Lonsdale MSS., Record Office, The Castle, Carlisle. Hitherto unpublished.

Janry 1st 1818

My Lord,

I am deeply sensible of Your Lordship's goodness in offering further aids to effect my negotiation with Mr Ramshay.[1] Should I propose to incur the responsibility and do the business giving Mr R. even the *whole* of the profits, it is scarcely possible he would refuse to resign; and this I purpose to do, in the last necessity, it is of so much consequence to secure the situation.

I shall carefully attend to all your Lordship wishes. This morning I have seen Colonel Lowther,[2] and I shall meet him again tomorrow.

Great pains will be taken to debauch the minds of the lower order of Freeholders. And if these be numerous considerable mischief may be done. It is clear that it is only upon Jacobinical principles, such as are propagated in Jollie's[3] and the Kendal paper,[4] and in the obnoxious Pamphlet which has just issued from the Press,[5] that this attempt can go forward. Nor is much to be apprehended from these Persons, unless others subscribed money to bring them to the Poll.

I have the honor to be
My Lord
Your Lordship's
faithful Servnt
Wm Wordsworth.

[1] See L. 462 above.

[2] Hon. Henry Cecil Lowther (1790–1867), Lord Lonsdale's second son. He served in the Peninsula under Sir John Moore and Wellington; was M.P. for Westmorland, 1812–67, and eventually 'Father' of the House of Commons. He was at this time canvassing the freeholders resident in London.

[3] *The Carlisle Journal*, founded by Francis Jollie in 1798 in the whig or liberal interest.

[4] *The Westmorland Advertiser and Kendal Chronicle*, founded in 1811. Although the editor was to protest his impartiality on 3 Jan., the paper was already turning against the Lowthers and airing radical views. For the role of the Cumberland and Westmorland Press in this election, see A. Aspinall, *Politics and the Press, c. 1780–1850*, 1949, pp. 354 ff.

[5] Probably the Yeoman's *Address*, for which see L. 497 below.

465. W. W. to LORD LONSDALE

MS. Lonsdale MSS., Record Office, The Castle, Carlisle. Hitherto unpublished.

48 Mortimer Street
Cavendish [Square]
4 Jan^{ry} 1818

My Lord,

The following is Mr Ramshay's answer[1] transmitted through his Friend Mr Maugham of the Bank—

'As the Idea rose with Mr Wordsworth I presumed he would have made some regular proposal, either by specific sum or annual payment for my life. But as for the present there seems little probability of an agreement taking place, I think it is as well for me to have no further trouble on the occasion which I will thank you to name to him.'—

The above answer your Lordship I think will agree with me is such as might have been wished for, inasmuch as it does not reject the principle of an annuity for Mr R's life—which accordingly I purpose to offer, and have written to him the following.

Copy

Dear Sir,

Mr Maugham shewed me your answer this morning. I shall with pleasure grant you an annuity for life; the amount it is out of my power to name, on account of my present ignorance of the profits. Will you be so kind as to state these for my guidance, and to mention the sum which would satisfy you.—You will pardon me for returning to the subject, as I have no doubt we can come to an agreement—

I am etc.,

I find Col. Lowther has left town. I have heard nothing more, worthy of being mentioned, on the subject of the Reformers. I have

the honor to be
with highest respect
My Lord
Your Lordship's
most faithful Ser^{nt}
Wm Wordsworth

We shall be at Coleorton from the beginning of next week.

[1] For the negotiations with Mr. Ramshay, see L. 462 above.

466. D. W. to THOMAS MONKHOUSE

Address: Thomas Monkhouse Esqre.
Endorsed: D. W. to T. M. Janry. 1818.
MS. WL.
MY ii. 597, p. 802.

[?5][1] Jan. 1818.
Monday night 10 o'clock

My dear Friend,

The pacquet from my Sister containing your kind note arrived about three hours ago. The pleasures of the Whist Table were suspended, and we were all in perfect stillness while Dorothy devoured *her* letter and I my two or three. Willy's was not published till we had gone through the others, nor did he suspect that there was one for him. I assure you the Letter was well bestowed; for it made him very happy—he has carried it up to his bed-room. Pray tell his cousin George this. Our Whist party consisted of Jonathan, Betty,[2] Miss Smith[3] and Dorothy—D. instructed Miss S for the first time in the rudiments of Whist during the ½ hour before we lighted candles, D. playing 3 hands, and directing Miss Smith at the same time. It was a very droll scene—D. was so clear-headed and so sharp, confounding neither the order of the Cards nor the laws of justice and strict honour, which I thought she had some temptation to do. After this one lesson, Miss S., with my overlooking her, performed her part to the satisfaction of Betty and Jonathan; and he, good Creature! after Cards were laid aside listened enraptured to the Duets which they played; hanging over the piano, and looking now and then up at his Wife in wonder and delight.—I have often wished I could be with you in an evening in Queen Anne St and back again to Rydal Mount; but as that is impossible, believe me I have had no painful regrets that I could not be of your joyous Party. *We* have had our own pleasure—and not the merriest were merrier than we on Christmas day when we drank a bottle of Cowslip wine to the healths of Father and Mother, Aunt Sarah and all absent friends—with a single toast to me, being mistress of the ceremonies on my own Birth-day. Your short note gave me very great pleasure and no less for the handwriting—it only occupied me a little longer in the reading, and if I were better used to your hand I should get

[1] This letter was probably written on the 5th, and certainly not later than the 12th, since W. W. and M. W. left London for Coleorton on Monday, 19th. (See *MW* 16, p. 32.)

[2] Betty and Jonathan Youdell, the quarryman and his wife from Hackett.

[3] Daughter of Mrs. Juliet Smith, of Tent Lodge, Coniston.

on better; so I hope you will take the pen again if Mary happens to be writing when you are in the house and at leisure.—I thank you, one and all, for remembering me so kindly; and I assure you when I have an opportunity of meeting the same party again assembled at Rydal Mount I will not be out of the way.—How much do I wish that Thomas and Mary Hutchinson could have gone to London at this time! I do not rejoice at the purchase of their estate, cheap though it be, for I fear it will bind them for Life to Wales. It gives me much concern to hear that your Brother had taken home with him a very bad cold. Give my love to Mr Tillbrooke, Mrs Ellwood, Mr George Sutton,[1] and believe me yours very affectionately

D Wordsworth

William Crackenthorpe intending to offer himself for the County!!! Surely he can have no hope of success, therefore where is his motive? For my Part I wish not success to any opposers of the House of Lonsdale; for the side that house takes is the good side! The acquittal of Hone[2] is enough to make one out of love with English Juries.

467. W. W. to LORD LONSDALE

MS. Lonsdale MSS., Record Office, The Castle, Carlisle. Hitherto unpublished.

48 Mortimer Street
Saturday Noon
Jan[ry] 18th[3] 1818

My Lord,

I feel much honored by your Lordship's communication received on Thursday the moment I was setting off for Windsor;[4] but I thought it best to leave it locked up here till my return when I could give it that attentive perusal which its importance demanded.—

[1] M. W.'s nephew, son of John Hutchinson of Stockton-on-Tees. He had inherited money on condition that he took the name of Sutton.

[2] William Hone (1780–1842) was put on trial in Dec. 1817 for publishing parodies of the Litany, the Athanasian Creed, and the Catechism. He conducted his own defence and was acquitted, despite the efforts of the Lord Chief Justice, Lord Ellenborough.

[3] Saturday was 17 Jan.

[4] Presumably to visit his uncle, Dr. William Cookson.

Your determination was a natural product of rectitude and patriotism, and as such was nothing more than they whose opportunities have rendered them competent to judge of your Lordship's mind would have expected; but, for my own part, I cannot sufficiently admire the dignified mode in which the disapprobation of the proposition was conveyed.

Both Mr B's[1] *inquiry,* (as he prettily terms it) and Mr W.'s[2] accompanying Letter are open to numerous comments beyond what either of the Parties, from very different causes probably, appear to have been conscious of. Was *this question asked* (I like to use Mr B's own language) do you think, my Lord, *before* or *after* his proposal to Mr Fox, to contest the County with the aid of Government,[3] an offer the modesty of which used to provide so much entertainment to the Duke of Norfolk?[4]—Mr B.—eleven or twelve years ago, describes himself as 'attached to no party exclusively', he seems to have been pretty much in the same lax state of feeling and mind ever since; and, as sooner or later it always happens with such men, they who act with him know as well as his opponents how little he is to be trusted.

I am glad that the accounts from the Country are so favourable, more especially as it is desirable that these people should be taught to feel early, from the strength put forth, how *little* they have to hope. Strongly as I am attached to your Lordship's interests, personal and family, I should not feel to the degree that I do upon this occasion, were I not assured that this attempt is no common affair of county Politics, but proceeds from dispositions and principles, which if not checked and discountenanced, would produce infinite mischief not to Westmoreland only, but to the whole kingdom.

Upon reflection, I thought it best to wait Mr Ramshay's answer

[1] i.e. Henry Brougham.

[2] i.e. William Wilberforce. In 1806 Brougham had induced Wilberforce—with whom he laboured in the anti-slavery cause—to approach Lord Lonsdale (Lord Lowther as he then was) with the suggestion that Brougham might represent the county with his Lordship's support. But Brougham had recently attacked the foreign policy of Pitt's government, and Lord Lonsdale turned down the proposal with some asperity. See Hist. MSS. Com., *Lonsdale MSS.*, pp. 182–4; A. Aspinall, *Lord Brougham and the Whig Party*, 1927, p. 14. W. W. believed that the whole incident could be used to discredit Brougham, and frequently returns to this theme in later letters.

[3] Brougham's proposal (which, he claimed, had Fox's support) had been that the government should assist the Lowther cause in Carlisle in return for Lowther support of Brougham as a government candidate for Westmorland. See Chester N. New, *Life of Henry Brougham to 1830*, 1961, p. 35.

[4] i.e. the 11th Duke, a lifelong opponent of the Lowthers, who died in 1815.

in London, as he might still be averse to a communication with me by *a Letter*,

With the highest respect
I have the honor to be
my Lord
Your Lordship's
obliged and faithful Ser^{nt}
Wm Wordsworth.

I shall not be able to quit town till next Wednesday or Thursday.[1]

468. W. W. to LORD LONSDALE

MS. Lonsdale MSS., Record Office, The Castle, Carlisle.
K (—). *MY ii. 598, p. 804* (—).

Coleorton Hall
Jan^{ry} 21st 1818.

My Lord,

The two Letters with which your Lordship has honored me have given me great pleasure; the former places in the clearest point of view the nature and character of this attempt, and the relation you stand in to the Parties who are making it. Your Lordship's second Letter (of the 17th which did not reach Coleorton till yesterday, the day of our arrival here) was very acceptable. Everything looks bright as one could wish, and the Party are manifestly confounded. Lord Lowther,[2] on whom I called the last thing before I left Town on Monday, thinks that Mr B. is only 'flirting' with the Committee and the affair will shortly fall to the ground, altogether. This is not unlikely, but I know that they still talk big, giving out that Mr B. is to be supported by Lord Thanet,[3] the Duke of Devonshire, Lord Darlington[4] and Lord Derby.[5] As to Lord Darlington, (if I may

[1] In fact, W. W. and M. W. left London the following Monday.

[2] William, Viscount Lowther (1787–1872), elder son of Lord Lonsdale. M.P. for Cockermouth, 1808–13: subsequently represented Westmorland until 1841. He succeeded to the title in 1844.

[3] Sackville Tufton, 9th Earl of Thanet (1767–1825), a prominent whig, who was frequently attacked by the Lowthers for the covert support he gave to Brougham during this election. As hereditary High Sheriff of Westmorland, he presided at the Poll at Appleby Castle.

[4] Brougham had been sitting for Lord Darlington's borough of Winchelsea since 1816. For Lord Darlington's relationship to the Lowthers, see *EY* 168, p. 347.

[5] Edward Stanley, 12th Earl of Derby (1752–1834), more notable as a sportsman than as a whig politician, but an influential figure in the north-western counties by virtue of his numerous estates and family connections.

WILLIAM, VISCOUNT LOWTHER, M.P.
by James Ward, from an engraving by W. Ward
in the British Museum

speak so of one so nearly connected with your lordship) after subscribing for Mr Hone, there is no act of folly or indecency of which he may not be deemed capable. My own accounts from the neighbourhood of Ambleside, are as favorable as possible, and from Kendal I learn that, though certain democratic Zealots speak in such a tone as might be expected, no cool-headed Person thinks a Contest can take place. But many will wish to see money spent, many will take delight in a stir of this sort for the mere pleasure of bustle, others will be gratified with the thought of opposition from that envy which power and influence are apt to create in the minds of those by whom the power and influence are not supported; party attachments will sway some in opposition to your Lordship's interests; and some conscientiously from narrow views in matters of Government will be glad to unite with our Antagonists. I have said from *narrow* views, less with reference to the public measures which you have supported, than from a firm conviction in my own mind, that if there did not exist in different parts of the Island that sort of political Power and Influence which your Lordship as a great Landholder possesses, the Government would be immediately subverted, and the whole Country thrown into confusion and misery. What else but the stability and weight of a large Estate with proportionate influence in the House of Commons can counterbalance the democratic activity of the wealthy commercial and manufacturing Districts? It appears to a superficial Observer, warm from contemplating the theory of the Constitution, that the political power of the great Landholders ought by every true lover of his Country to be strenuously resisted; but I would ask a well-intentioned native of Westmorland or Cumberland who had fallen into this mistake if he could point out any arrangement by which Jacobinism can be frustrated, except by the existence of large Estates continued from generation to generation in particular families, with parliamentary power in proportion. We have a striking proof of the efficacy of this state of things on the present occasion, where we see such a large body of all that is conspicuously respectable in Westmorland or connected with it rallying round your Lordship on the first alarm.—And should our adversaries proceed in their attempt, on application from any respectable quarter, I have no doubt that of the Individuals in London connected with that County, who have risen in the world by their talents and merits, or who are distinguished for property character or station, almost the whole would readily, in like manner, side with your Lordship and the present members, at this crisis. You will have the goodness to excuse my writing at such length, but I could not resist the temptation, as your Lordship had honoured me with such unreserved communications on the subject.

Fresh engagements in my late Brother's affairs started up and prevented me leaving Town. On Friday I heard again from Mr R.[1] He proceeds with caution and would not communicate with me except through his Friend,[2] and till I had pledged my honor to secrecy. This I did, stipulating only that your Lordship must be made party to all that passes. He still cleaves to the plan of a sum of money as first proposed by him, having fears about security for an Annuity.—Having no means of my own of granting such security, I presumed upon a kind expression of one of your Lordship's late Letters so far as to say that he need have no apprehension on that subject. I wrote him by return of Post, last Friday, offering an Annuity of £350;—and begging his answer addressed to me here.

When I receive his answer, I shall have the honor of communicating it to your Lordship; I fear it will not be favorable, as he seems to regard the whole amount of his profits in the light of an unencumbered annuity; not being disposed to make allowance for his sureties, or for trouble, or contingencies.—His situation is at present considerably better than mine; which is in a great measure owing to his profit on the collection of Coach Duties; a source apparently not to be depended upon.

I am very anxious to get down into the North, and particularly to ascertain on the Spot the temper of people's minds at Kendal. Sir George and Lady Beaumont are both remarkably well, in most excellent spirits, and enjoying themselves much. I never saw Sir George in such high condition; whose nerves are nevertheless irritable.

I had learned from Lord Lowther that Lady Mary[3] was better, and your account of her improvement gave us all here the utmost pleasure, though we could not hear of her suffering and weak state without deep concern. In this, and every other object near your Lordship's heart as far as known to me, be assured of my sincere sympathy.

I have the honor to be
my Lord, your Lordship's
faithful friend and Ser^nt
W Wordsworth

Our Friends here kindly considering my wish to be in the North,

[1] Mr. Ramshay. [2] Mr. Maugham.
[3] Lady Mary Lowther, Lord Lonsdale's second daughter.

allow us to quit there on the 27th. On the 29th and 30th I shall be at Mr Cookson's, Kendal.

469. W. W. to LORD LONSDALE

MS. Lonsdale MSS., Record Office, The Castle, Carlisle. Hitherto unpublished.

Coleorton Hall
near Ashby de la Zouche
23rd Jan^ry^ 1818

My Lord,

Yesterday I received the enclosed (No. 1) from Mr R.[1] It is decisive, and a hard bargain on his part; nor could by me be carried into effect without assistance from your Lordship. Had I been able to give security from an Annuity to the amount required, it would have been imprudent to do so, the uncertainty of my *own* life being considered.

But when I reflect that Mr R. is 71 years of age, and that this arrangement for my benefit, may thus be completed in a manner more easy and satisfactory to your Lordship than if the office should become vacant by the death of the present Holder; and also that if he should outlive me, the disposal of the united offices would in all probability still rest with your Lordship or your Heirs, and that the Annuity might continue to be paid out of the profits by my Successor, I am reconciled to the terms, if approved by your Lordship, though subjecting you to the obligation of becoming surety for a payment so considerable.

I shall wait your Lordship's reply before I answer Mr R's letter.

With regard to carrying this affair to a conclusion, I earnestly request that no wish on your Lordship's part to place me in this situation, may induce you to proceed, either as to the mode or the time, otherwise than as may be most agreeable to your feelings, and most suitable to your convenience.

With sincere gratitude
and the highest respect
I have the honor to be
My Lord
your Lordship's faithful Friend
and Servant
Wm Wordsworth.

[1] i.e. Mr. Ramshay.

P.S. The consideration on which I expected (as stated to Mr R.) that he might deem an annuity of £350 sufficient were—'That himself or somebody else must always be on the spot (to this he allows weight and to no other) that the Coach Duties and advertisements from which he states that £180 per ann of his 600 is drawn, are subject to great fluctuations—that the rate of poundage was once 5 per cent and has been reduced to four, and may be still further reduced; and that as hath been before done, some portion of the Collection of duties now allotted to Stamp-Distributors may be assigned to others—and lastly, that his Sureties would be relieved from responsibility, and be protected from loss through misconduct of his Agents.'

All the above considerations and several other contingencies were acknowledged by Mr Parry to be of great weight, and would readily have been so by Mr R himself had he been in my place.

I send Mr R's former Letter also—for your Lordship's perusal.

I leave this place early on Tuesday morning—your Lordship will judge whether it is best to direct to me here or to Mr Cookson's Kendal, where I shall remain till Friday morning.

470. W. W. to LORD LONSDALE

MS. Lonsdale MSS., Record Office, The Castle, Carlisle. Hitherto unpublished.

[*c.* 25 Jan. 1818][1]

My Lord,

Do not think of me at this crisis. The opposition will go forward, I fear, though Mr B. has not declared himself. It would grieve me to the heart, should your Lordship be prejudiced by any act or exertion of Patronage at this moment. Farewell. I conclude in great haste, having this moment learned, that my Letter will save a post, if put into the office this night.

with best wishes
I remain
Your Lordship's faithfully
Wm Wordsworth

[1] This letter was written from Coleorton after 23 Jan. (on which date the negotiations with Mr. Ramshay were still proceeding—see previous letter), but before 26 Jan., when Brougham's adoption was officially announced at a meeting in Kendal.

471. W. W. to LORD LONSDALE

MS. Lonsdale MSS., Record Office, The Castle, Carlisle. Hitherto unpublished.

Kendal 29th [Jan.] 1818

My Lord,

I have been induced to send the above,[1] collected from good authority, by recollection of an expression in one of your Lordship's letters, 'that all the Attornies of the County had been returned except two.'

I do not like the appearance of things in this Town. Your Lordship's Friends of the Committee are numerous, most respectable, zealous and active. But with the exception of Col. Maude,[2] Mr Daniel Harrison, a Wine Merchant, and Mr Long,[3] to whom may be added Mr James Gandy Junr,[4] they do not seem to have that popular character, which will sway much with those in inferior situations, who have not already a bias towards the present members. Mr Wilson of Abbot Hall,[5] though very wealthy, is not liked.

The Quakers, who have votes are about sixteen in number, all with the exception of 3 or 4, against us.

The present members are likely to be much hurt by the practise of splitting votes, every exertion ought to be made to prevent this. A caution from the Committee would have a good effect. I have taken care that their attention shall be directed to it.[6]

[1] The List of Attorneys that follows this letter. As this was the first contested election for some forty-four years, there was no up-to-date record of all freeholders entitled to vote: titles to freeholds were often disputed, and lawyers were indispensable on both sides to prevent abuses. Eligibility to vote finally rested on the Land Tax Assessment, and the Lowthers were later accused of manipulating this to their own advantage: see W. W. Douglas, 'Wordsworth in Politics: The Westmorland Election of 1818', *MLN* lxiii (1948), 437–49.

[2] Thomas Holme Maude, W. W.'s contemporary at Hawkshead School and St. John's College, Cambridge: banker, Mayor of Kendal in 1800 and 1814, and a Proprietor of the new Lowther paper, the *Westmorland Gazette*, launched later in the year. As a Vice-President of the local Lowther Committee, he seconded Col. Lowther's nomination when the Poll opened at Appleby.

[3] James Hoggarth Long, of Mint House, Skelsmergh, near Kendal: member of the Central Committee.

[4] A woollen manufacturer: member of the Central Committee.

[5] Christopher Wilson (1765–1845), of Abbot Hall, Kendal, and Rigmaden Park, near Kirkby Lonsdale: banker and landowner, and another of W. W.'s contemporaries at Hawkshead School: Mayor of Kendal, 1799. Chairman of the local Lowther Committee, and a promoter of the *Westmorland Gazette*, he seconded Lord Lowther's nomination at the Poll. Abbot Hall, his elegant eighteenth-century residence beside the parish church, is now an art gallery.

[6] This was the theme of W. W.'s first contribution to the *Kendal Chronicle*. See next letter.

If your Lordship fails, it will be owing to the hostility of little people; blind in their prejudices and strong in their passions.

It is confidently affirmed that Lord Thanet has subscribed 4,000.

At what period it will be advisable for your Lordship or Col. Lowther to appear in the County I cannot presume to say; but a most judicious Friend of your Lordship's said to me today, that if Mr Brougham appears before them, much mischief will be done.

From the Country I have heard little but good accounts.

As far as my ability extends, I will endeavour to open the eyes of people to the real character of this Contest, which those of your Lordship's Friends with whom I have hitherto conversed, do not seem to be aware of.

Very faithfully
Your Lordship's
Wm Wordsworth

Private

Attornies in Kendal

[*In D. W.'s hand*]

Messrs. Fell and Johnson[1]—Very active and zealous, but their influence appears to be principally among persons of consideration, that do not require being solicited—with the smaller yeomanry and Freeholders they do not seem to have much connexion, nor are they popular among them, being deemed *high*.

Messrs. James Wilson and Son (the Father Deputy Recorder) Solicitors for the Dallam Tower Family,[2] persons of great respectability and weight; but the Father much offended at being put down as one of the Committee without having been previously consulted (as was inconsiderately done in another instance, perhaps more). I have it from good authority that he will be an opponent.

Mr Isaac Wilson—a man of very considerable talents, and great assiduity, rising in business, very generally known among the small Freeholders and Yeomanry and of proportionate influence among them. The opposite party have strenuously urged him to accept a Retainer, but having been advised to stand neuter, he adopts that plan. He would have been glad to have been retained for your Lordship's interest in the first instance and from what I learn, it is much to be regretted that this was not done. A person

[1] Solicitors to the Lowther Committee.

[2] i.e. to Daniel C. Wilson (1746–1824), of Dallam Tower, Milnthorp, a Vice-President of the local Lowther Committee. James Wilson (1742–1818), the Deputy Recorder, died in May.

for whose judgement I have a high respect, said to me 'he would have been a Help[?]'—Johnson and he are not Friends.

Mr Edward Tatham—A young man of abilities respected and well connected, a Friend of Mr Wilson of Casterton[1] and of great influence among the party of Saints.

Mr Berry—The Town Clerk, his Father Alderman of the Town, canvassing for Mr Brougham.

Mr Thomas Pennington—A young Man who has been six or eight months in business—a Relation of Mr Fell.

Mr Barrow—has interested himself much in favour of the Lowther family—a clever man but not caring about business, having an independent fortune.

Mr Reveley—A respectable young man, well connected but not of shewy talents, nor of much business.

Of the above eight separate Offices of Attornies, only two I understand are retained, Messrs Fell and Johnson, and Mr Pennington.

472. W. W. to LORD LONSDALE

MS. Lonsdale MSS., Record Office, The Castle, Carlisle. Hitherto unpublished.

Kendal. Jan^ry 31st [1818]

My Lord,

The Committee are so convinced of the influence of Mr Isaac Wilson,[2] that they have been exerting themselves to induce him to accept a Retainer. I have just had an interview with him myself,—on finding that he was somewhat piqued at having been overlooked. I hope I did not do wrong in stating to him that your Lordship had been under a mistake with regard to the number of Solicitors retained. This assurance gave him great pleasure; and he expressed his regret at not having known the fact sooner, but having been earnestly solicited by the opposite party, and having declined accepting a Retainer from them, giving an assurance that he would remain neuter, he thinks that he cannot in honour act otherwise. There appears to be no way in which his scruples can be removed except one which I fear is not practicable, his being at liberty to declare publicly what I confidentially imparted to him, that your

[1] W. W. Carus Wilson (1764–1851), of Casterton Hall, near Kirkby Lonsdale, nominated Col. Lowther at the Poll: he was M.P. for Cockermouth, 1821–7. See also L. 394 above.

[2] See List of Attorneys in previous letter.

Lordship supposed a greater number of Solicitors to have been retained than actually have been so. But here is a matter of great delicacy. This, as every other cause, will suffer from its adherents not sacrificing personal feelings to general interests. Mr Johnson is most hearty, zealous and active but he is jealous of Mr Wilson and dislikes him. Should a declaration be made by your Lordship to the chairman of the Committee that you were mistaken as to the number of Solicitors retained, this would subject Messrs Fell and Johnson to unpleasant imputations. They are both highly respectable men; but, alas, not superior to those injurious influences which I have alluded to. Your Lordship will consider this matter;—not less than forty Freeholders have voluntarily consulted Mr Wilson how he would advise them to vote; so he says.

The Editorship of the Kendal paper has passed into other hands, those of Mr Harrison a Dissenting Minister.[1] He is inwardly against us, which is much to be regretted. The bias of his mind sufficiently appears, in the paper of this day, in the account he has given of Mr James Brougham's[2] reception. I am upon very friendly terms with Mr H. and could influence him, I believe, to a certain extent; but my situation requires a degree of caution which diminishes my power.[3]

The enclosed[4] was written by me yesterday, and got into the Kendal Paper by the exertions of Mr Johnson; I could not appear in the matter myself.

I am obliged to go to Rydal this day; but I have communicated with Mr Wilson of Abbot Hall, and can return hither at short notice.

[1] The Revd. John Harrison (1761–1833), Unitarian Minister of the Market Place Chapel, where James Patrick—original of the Wanderer in *The Excursion*—was buried. W. W. sometimes attended services there when staying with Thomas Cookson, a Trustee of the Chapel, and so came to know Harrison. See *Papers, Letters, & Journals of William Pearson*, ed. his widow, 1863, p. 13; F. Nicholson and E. Axon, *The Older Non-Conformity in Kendal*, Kendal, 1915, ch. xxix.

[2] James Brougham (1780–1833), brother of Henry Brougham and his staunch supporter at elections: first M.P. for Kendal after the Reform Bill. According to the *Kendal Chronicle* for 31 Jan., he arrived on 26 Jan. to announce his brother as the new candidate, and was chaired along the Highgate to the accompaniment of music and the ringing of church bells.

[3] As holder of a government office, the Distributorship of Stamps, W. W. was precluded from taking an open part in the election campaign, but his activities behind the scenes soon became known. See L. 485 below.

[4] A letter in the *Kendal Chronicle* for 31 Jan. signed 'A Friend to Consistency', dated Westmorland, 30 Jan. 1818: reprinted a week or so later as a handbill. It appealed to freeholders not to split or 'plump' their votes between one or other of the Lowther candidates and Brougham, as this would give a disproportionate advantage to the new candidate.

I have written this day to Lord Lowther, at some length.[1] Be so good as to inform me of the state of Lady Mary's health.

With best wishes
I have the honor to be
faithfully your Lordship's
Wm Wordsworth.

473. W. W. to J. KINGSTON[2]

Address: J. Kingston Esqre.
MS. Harvard University Library,
MY ii. 599, p. 804.

[*In John Carter's hand*]

Rydal Mount, Ambleside
2nd Febry. 1818.

Dear Sir,

I have this day received a Letter from the Stamp Office, from which it appears that inconvenience had been sustained in your Department by the want of my Quarterly and Annual Accounts. I regret this much and beg leave to state that when I was in Town I called at your office, and on representation that it was very inconvenient to me to leave London, I was informed by one of your Clerks, that the Office would not require my Accounts till the end of the Month, in consideration of what I stated.

The Accounts would have been in London on the 31st had it not been for the neglect of the Proprietor of the Kendal Coach, by which they had been sent from my office, to meet me at Kendal, on the 26th.[3] Though repeatedly called for, it was denied that the Parcel had been received: and it was not till several days that it could be found, having been mislaid.

I should take it as a great favour, if this could be explained to the Board, so that I might stand free of any change of negligence or inattention.

I am, Dear Sir, respectfully yours

[*signed*] Wm Wordsworth.

[1] This letter does not seem to have survived.

[2] A Comptroller of Stamps, and W. W.'s immediate official superior, whose 'phrenological development' had been examined by Lamb at Haydon's 'immortal dinner' on the previous 28 Dec., much to W. W.'s embarrassment. See *Autobiography and Journals of B. R. Haydon*, ed. Malcolm Elwin, i. pp. 316–19; and, for Keats's version of the incident, Rollins, i. pp. 197–8.

[3] See *MW* 16, p. 33.

The Accounts (sent by the Manchester Mail) would reach London on the 2nd Inst.

474. W. W. to LORD LONSDALE

MS. Lonsdale MSS., Record Office, The Castle, Carlisle.
K (—). MY ii. 596, p. 802 (—).

Rydal Mount
[Feb.][1] 3rd 1818

My Lord,

I am truly sensible of your Lordship's goodness in enabling me to close with Mr R.[2] but I cannot stir further in this business, till I have your sentiments on the apprehensions expressed in my last.[3]

On referring to that Letter of your Lordship in which mention was made of the Attornies, and which I could not get at when at Kendal, I find that the expression differs materially from my recollection of it. It is, 'We have engaged all the Attornies in the County, whom we knew; I have only heard of two engaged on the other side.'—I shall immediately set the matter right. I spoke of the subject to remove an unpleasant impression from the mind of an Attorney[4] whom I wished to conciliate, knowing that he could materially serve the Cause; and it is rather fortunate, that this unfaithfulness of memory, which I much regret, was on the side favorable to my purpose.

I am not sure that the enclosed[5] is of sufficient importance to justify me in troubling your Lordship with it. I send it on account of the first sentence; premising that Col: Maude whose name is mentioned below, has been (as the Writer knows) eminently active and serviceable. He is very popular with the lower orders, which unluckily Mr Wilson of Abbot Hall (though warm in the Cause) is not. Mr. Jackson tells me that nobody can surpass in zeal Sir Daniel le Fleming;[6] he lives in a parish where Mr J. says there are

[1] W. W. wrote *January*.

[2] Mr. Ramshay.

[3] i.e. L. 470 above.

[4] Isaac Wilson. See L. 472 above.

[5] W. W. enclosed a letter of 2 Feb. from Thomas Cookson with a note in his own hand: 'This is from a Dissenter, a Freeholder, strenuous for your Lordship.' Cookson's first sentence referred to dissensions within the Lowther Committee, and he went on to deplore the fact that all the attorneys had not been retained (—'he means Wilson and Son, Tatham, and Isaac Wilson', W. W. noted).

[6] Brother of Sir Richard le Fleming, the 'inhibited' Rector of Grasmere. Sir Daniel lived at Hill Top, a few miles east of Kendal, and was a Vice-President of the local Lowther Committee.

no less than 80 Freeholders, and Mr J. thinks that he will have influence over the lower class. It is this sort of influence that is wanted.—If property, situation in life, character etc. could ensure success, our triumph would be complete. But every man of weight overrates his own importance, till it is fairly tried, and this error seems as much owing to want of reflection, as to personal vanity. Our indolence bribes us, also, into a belief that ordinary influences are equal to extraordinary occasions; and we trust accordingly to passive qualities and circumstances, when every nerve ought to be strained and every power put into action.—But this of which I see instances on every side of me would be better said to the public.

Grasmere is staunch as far as appears, with only two exceptions, both Strangers; but what shall I say of my neighbours in Langdale, where are upwards of 20 votes all of whom except one were confidently relied upon; and it now appears that 8 or 10 hang back, complaining that the licence was taken from the only Public House in the Dale, some time ago, and that they cannot get it restored.—But this *pretext*, for I cannot regard it as anything more, may easily be removed—and I have urged Mr Jackson to set about it immediately.

Mr Curwen[1] (this is certain) when he passed through Ambleside the other day, finding that there was a crowd in the Kitchen of the Inn took his tea there, and commenced agitator among them. At Kendal he appears to have been still busier, and in a more obnoxious way; Having had an interview with the then Editor of the Kendal Chronicle, as I was assured, for the purpose of inserting in his paper, the most personal and inflammatory address which has, perhaps, hitherto appeared.[2] It is to be found in the paper of the 24th Jan[ry], dated Askham.[3]—If this be true, and my authority is from a Lad in the printing office, through a third Person, one cannot but deeply regret that conduct so contemptible should have anything mischievous in it.

Mr Brougham's own address[4] has just reached me. His reliance

[1] John Christian Curwen of Workington Hall: the agriculturalist and Whig M.P., first for Carlisle, and, from 1820 onwards, for Cumberland. He was a member of Brougham's Committee and a freeholder of Westmorland by virtue of his property at Windermere.

[2] *To the Freeholders of Westmorland*, signed 'An Independent Freeholder'. It accused Lord Lowther, a Lord of the Treasury, of living off government sinecures at the expense of the taxpayer, and questioned whether Col. Lowther had really earned his military rank. For W. W.'s replies to these charges, see L. 479 below.

[3] A village near Lowther.

[4] Dated London, 29 Jan. 1818, and printed in the *Kendal Chronicle* for 7 Feb. In the course of it, Brougham wrote: '. . . I know that my only recommendation

is on 'the *honesty* of his public Conduct'—Your Lordship could supply a startling comment on this Boast.

I fear that the length of my Letters trespasses inexcusably on your time at this busy period—impute it to the interest which I feel in the struggle, and have the goodness to bear with it, believing me to be

My Lord
gratefully and faithfully
Your Lordship's
Friend and Servnt
W. Wordsworth

475. W. W. to LORD LONSDALE

MS. Lonsdale MSS., Record Office, The Castle, Carlisle.
K (—). *MY ii.* 600, *p.* 805 (—).

Rydal Mount
10 Febry 1818

My Lord,

The Committee have now entered into the thing in earnest, and begin to understand the business, in which they were unavoidably inexperienced, at first. Everything looks brighter. The day after I had the honor of your Lordship's of the 4th Inst, I went over to Kendal, and on a suggestion of Lord Lowther, that I would consider if the Editor of the Kendal Paper could not be induced to deal fairly with our cause,—I saw him, and represented to him how ill his promises of impartiality had been kept;[1] and entered so fully into every branch of the subject, that I trust good will result from the Interview, as he acknowledged the reasonableness of what I said. He engaged to publish a notice to correspondents that nothing defamatory or personal should be admitted from either side; and that the accounts of proceedings, to the best of his judgement, should be fair.[2] He pleaded hurry (having only just entered on his

to your notice is the honesty of my public conduct; and you may rely upon my NEVER deserting your cause until we shall have obtained for ourselves the free choice of an independent Representative.'

[1] The *Kendal Chronicle* for 7 Feb. had reported at length no less than three speeches hostile to the Lowther interest: James Brougham's address at Appleby on the 5th defending his brother's political record, and two recent speeches in the House of Commons, one by Sir Francis Burdett in favour of Parliamentary Reform, and the other by Henry Brougham himself on the Repeal of the Suspension of *Habeas Corpus*.

[2] This promise of neutrality, published in the *Kendal Chronicle* for 14 Feb., was not kept for long.

COL. THE HON. HENRY LOWTHER, M.P.
by Sir Thomas Lawrence (1831) from an engraving by G. H. Phillips in the British Museum

office) for what I complained of; and said that no paper in support of the Lowther interest had been refused admittance.—Much of the abuse, which to my knowledge has done great mischief, found its way into the Paper, under the shape of Letters, often inserted for mere want of matter to fill the Columns. Being a dissenter the present Editor has naturally a strong bias to opposition, and complaint; but he is no approver of Mr Brougham, deems him unfit to represent any county, and regards him as a trading Publican. He has refused Mr B. his vote, and means to vote on neither side, unless (a reservation which is suspicious) he is provoked by the Intemperance of either Party.

In consequence of what I gathered, concerning the difficulty of filling the Paper, I have urged our friends to write, and shall write myself, were it only to keep others out.—I have prepared two addresses to the Freeholders,[1] one of which is left for publication in the paper, and the other shall follow next week, at least part of it.

As the Com. have struck off another thousand of the paper signed, a Friend to Consistency,[2] I presume they have found it serviceable notwithstanding my fears; indeed, I was told so, but I begged they would look carefully to the subject.

Not to exclude or give offence to Dissenters, who are very powerful in Kendal, I recommended 'King and Constitution' in preference to 'Church and King' as the latter part of the Lowther motto.[3]

I saw Mr Isaac Wilson,—his report is favorable; but many inwardly well-inclined hang back through fear that by a too hasty shew of strength, they should be disappointed of a journey to Appleby, and the riotous pleasure of an Election.

I should have met Lord Lowther and the Col: at Kendal,[4] but as

[1] Part of the first of these Addresses, signed 'A Freeholder', duly appeared in the *Kendal Chronicle* for 14 Feb. The second Address was withheld, as W. W. was evidently still uneasy over the editorial policy of the paper, and parts of it came out at the end of the month in the form of a broadsheet, which was reprinted in the *Carlisle Patriot* (see L. 481 below). Both Addresses were eventually published in full in early April as the *Two Addresses to the Freeholders of Westmorland* (see L. 490 below). For a full discussion of the textual history of the *Two Addresses*, see J. E. Wells, 'Wordsworth and De Quincey in Westmorland Politics, 1818', *PMLA* lv (1940), 1080–1128.

[2] See L. 472 above.

[3] In the *Kendal Chronicle* for 7 Feb., a correspondent signing himself 'Commonsense' had attacked the motto 'Lowther and Loyalty—Church and King' for associating Church and Monarchy with a particular party interest. One third of the population of Kendal were said to be Dissenters.

[4] The two candidates were already in the district, though they did not make their grand entry into Kendal until the 11th.

the pretext of this outcry is Independence, I thought it better, considering the office which I hold, by Your Lordship's patronage, to keep out of the way. I wish much for half an hour's quiet conversation, with either of the Members; and will wait upon them at their convenience.

Mr B's correspondence with Mr W.[1] may be turned forcibly against him; but your Lordship's dignified reply ought to go along with it, to give the thing its full effect.

I rejoice to hear that Lady Mary is better.

I have the honor to be
with highest respect
My Lord
Your Lordship's
faithfully and truly
W Wordsworth

476. W. W. to LORD LONSDALE

MS. Lonsdale MSS., Record Office, The Castle, Carlisle. Hitherto unpublished.

Kendal Friday noon
13th Febry 1818

My Lord,

Three times have I begun to write to your Lordship, since Wednesday afternoon, and have thrown the sheets into the fire, lest if I wrote with due regard to truth, I should alarm you and your family unnecessarily. Things seem now settled long enough to remove all apprehension.[2] Lord Lowther has been walking about the Town without anything occurring to his annoyance. On the frightful subject of the conduct of the Mob, I shall not enter at present. Thanks to a merciful Providence no lives were lost; the persons most severely hurt belonged to their own Party, with the

[1] i.e. Brougham's correspondence with Wilberforce in 1806. See L. 467 above.

[2] The *Kendal Chronicle* for 14 Feb. carried a full account of the Lowthers' grand entry on the 11th, the turbulent behaviour of the mob, and the clashes that broke out between rival factions as the procession moved through the town. Each side subsequently blamed the other for these incidents. The Broughamites were accused of exciting the populace with drink and inflammatory handbills; and they in turn charged the Lowthers with overcrowding the town with their supporters and dependants, and bringing in canal workers to cause trouble.

exception of Mr Fleming of Rayrigg,[1] whom I have seen this morning; and I am sorry to say he remains confined to his bed and Sofa at the King's Arms, suffering considerably.—A Stone, the size of a Man's hand struck him on the back, and caused a spilling of blood; but which appears to have ceased.

I came hither on Wednesday at the request of Lord Lowther, to try what could be done with the Editor of the Kendal Paper. I am glad for a more urgent reason that I was sent for, as from my knowledge of the characters of the leading people in this Town, I was enabled to point out those whose opinion was more worthy to be attended to, and in particular Mr Harrison the Surgeon, who was Mayor two years back.[2] He is an able, experienced, and judicious man;—but nothing can be more deplorable than the incapacity of the leading people in general. I know not how far it is prudent to speak in a Letter; but the facts explain themselves, in a great measure.

I have this moment heard that Lord Lowther is peacefully canvassing the Town, in Stramongate, the Votes much in his favour so far.

The account which you will see in the Kendal paper, was drawn up under Lord Lowther's directions, as being better than stating the facts in their naked deformity. It takes no notice of Mr James Brougham, and his harangue to the populace. I have been with the Editor this morning and he has promised to insert it, as sent. Five shares out of eight of this paper are in the hands of our enemies; therefore it would avail nothing could we get the *Editor* over to our side. He would be immediately dismissed, and a worse person put in his place. I do not see that anything can be done but making it a point of character with him to keep as near to his promise of impartiality, as possible.—The Paper might have been easily purchased a few weeks ago; now, if the Contest goes forward, they will not part with it. It has done great harm; and ought to be under your Lordship's command, as soon as it can be got hold of. To set up another on different principles would at present be of no use, as the People would only read that which flattered their passions.[3]

[1] The Revd. John Fleming, W. W.'s schoolfellow. See *EY* 166, p. 343. An active member of the Central Lowther Committee, he played a spirited, if injudicious, part in the campaign, engaging in acrimonious newspaper controversies under his own name.

[2] Thomas Harrison, Mayor in 1806 and 1816: author of *An Impartial Narrative of the Riotous Proceedings which took place in Kendal on Wed. Feb. 11th, 1818, collected from the Observations of Eye-Witnesses*, published early in March.

[3] It proved impossible for the Lowther party to purchase a majority of

Lord Lowther has called upon Mr Wakefield[1] this morning, I have been invited to dine at the House of Mr John Wakefield, and mean to go.—His son, who has canvassed actively for Mr Brougham, is a very amiable young Man; whose acquaintance I shall cultivate. I have already had a long conversation with him on the merits of this Contest, in which I omitted nothing that I could think of as likely to open his eyes to its true character. He was manifestly staggered; but he acknowledged that his Father is very violent.—The Young Man is going away for a month, and said that he is heartily glad of it, being sick of the business. Neither he nor the Editor of the Paper think that Brougham has any chance; and both deem him a person quite unfit to be a County Member, any where.—I suspect that his Kendal Committee are very poor; they refuse paying the Bill the Kendal Paper has against them, alleging they have no money. I know not what is doing on the other side of the County; but judging from the aspect of things as far as known to me, your Lordship is not only secure of victory, but of a complete Triumph.

The doctrine of our Adversaries is, in fact, this; where there is least property let there be most weight, where there is least knowledge let there be most sway. It is worthy of your Lordship to stand forward with all your might, against measures supported by such opinions.

Sat. Morn.

Here I was called off yesterday; I have since received your Lordship's of the 7th.—You will have heard the state of the Canvass in this Part. Nothing but firmness and activity are wanting, I am persuaded, to carry us through, triumphantly. I shall spare no pains in making known your Lordship's sentiments on the point of no other Gentleman's coming forward. But we must not think of giving way after what has passed. I have this moment seen the Kendal Paper of today. This sort of impartiality will in some quarters do the present Members great mischief.[2]—I shall be at the Editor again this morning, and will spare no pains in attempting to get the majority of the shares into yr. Lordship's hands; but the difficulties appear almost insurmountable.

shares in the *Kendal Chronicle*, and W. W. was soon supporting schemes already under way to establish a new paper, the *Westmorland Gazette*.

[1] i.e. Jacob Wakefield. His brother John was Chairman of Brougham's Committee and a Quaker. The Wakefields were woollen manufacturers and owned the Bank in Stricklandgate.

[2] Lord Lowther's version of the events of the 11th was in fact printed in the *Kendal Chronicle* for 14 Feb.—but along with renewed attacks on the Lowthers' ascendency in Westmorland politics and their network of patronage.

Lady Mary's observation is most just; but She is little aware of the imbecility that Lord Lowther has had to complain of. On Thursday night it was determined that the Town should be canvassed next morning. When the morning came the Committee were daunted, to a Man; and had it not been for Lord Lowther's firmness no attempt would have been made. He behaved nobly—I breakfasted with him and the Chairman.[1] Mr W. wished the sense of the Com. to be taken—Lord L. said no—'I take it upon myself.'—I observed that it was the point of honour, in the case and *must* be attempted. Mr W. pleaded fear for their houses and Families;—not being an Inhabitant I could go no farther. Lord L. required no support—he proceeded to canvass and did not meet with the slightest interruption. In almost everything Lord L. has had to act against the sense of the Comm. This is deplorable.

Yesterday, we put into Circulation a Paper, headed, Brougham an approver of the Corn Bill—an Extract from his Speech on Mr Western's Motion.[2] This has done great service, and proves that it ought to be followed up by things of the same kind.—Every thing consistent with honor must be done to impair the credit of his political character.

I dined at the Wakefields yesterday. Mr John W. senior broke out on the dependent and enslaved State of the County etc. I said that I had accepted his Son's invitation, to testify my respect for his family, and my personal regard for his Son; and this subject must be waived; only I begged to state that as to the fact of the County being represented by two of the Family of Lowther no person lamented it more than your Lordship. I then read part of that sentence in your Letter where you speak of it as a misfortune—and I added that it was your Lordship's earnest desire that some respectable Gentleman of the County, of sound Politics, would have come forward long since. He said in a fiery manner, the County still would have remained dependent. But that a public proposition should have been made, and the leading people in the County fairly consulted. I speak, said I, to the point of unjustifiable, and indelicate family ambitions, and on the part of Lord L. I utterly disclaim it; as to consulting the

[1] i.e. Christopher Wilson of Abbot Hall.

[2] The Lowthers had been accused of forcing up the price of grain by voting for the Corn Bill of 1815; yet Brougham himself, though not an M.P. at that time, was not hostile to this measure. On 7 Mar. 1816, Charles Callis Western, Baron Western (1767–1844), M.P. for Essex and a leading promoter of the Bill, had moved that the House of Commons go into Committee to consider the distressed state of agriculture; and in his speech on this motion on 9 Apr. (*Speeches*, 4 vols., 1838, i. pp. 503 ff.), Brougham explicitly supported the Bill.

Gentlemen in the way you propose, there were probably most weighty objections against that measure, at the time.—We then dropped local politics, and treated for a short time the general state of Representation in England. Which he attacked in the Old Bardellite way, and I defended. His Brother Jacob appears a moderate and sensible Man, and strongly expressed his disapprobation of the Conduct of Brougham's Committee in circulating that inflammatory handbill[1] on the morning the Members entered. The Young Man in whom the property of this worthy family will center, is naturally of mild and gentle disposition; and might most easily be conciliated; but at present this very gentleness of temper makes him the Instrument of others.

You are very good in saying that my Letters cannot be too long. I wish my pensmanship were better, as I am sure you must often have had great difficulty in making it out—

[*cetera desunt*]

477. W. W. to THOMAS MONKHOUSE

Address: Thomas Monkhouse, Esq., Queen Ann Street, Cavendish Square, London.
MS. Jonathan Wordsworth.
LY iii. 603a, p. 1371.

[14 Feb. 1818][2]

My dear Friend,

The latter member of the sentence in Mr A's letter begins with a 'Perhaps'. I cannot consent to be in uncertainty as to this point: my wish is to stand as a *specially credited* [ ][3] against the Estate, as far as I incur responsibility respecting this Mortgage. Be so good as to show Mr Addison this. Under that circumstance, I shall thank you to advance the money, and I will be co-security with my Brother to you.

We have had frightful doings here—I send you the Kendal papers—it is a very softened account—at some other time you shall hear particulars. One Address to the Freeholders in the Ken. P. is by me, but don't mention it.

[1] This repeated the charge that Lord Lowther was a placeman living at the taxpayer's expense. For W. W.'s reply to this accusation see L. 479 below.

[2] This letter was almost certainly written on the day W. W.'s *Address to the Freeholders* appeared in the *Kendal Chronicle* (see L. 475 above), and the day following Lord Lowther's tour of Kendal, mentioned in the previous letter.

[3] *Word omitted.*

I have been here since Wednesday. Lord L [w]as addressing the Town yesterday without meeting any obstruction.

If the other side of the county is as staunch as this, we shall beat them hollow—notwithstanding their success in this Town they have no chance whatever.

Be so good as to send back this Letter[1] when you can get a frank. I return this day to Rydale my dear Friend ever faithfully yours

W. W.

478. W. W. to LORD LONSDALE

MS. Lonsdale MSS., Record Office, The Castle, Carlisle. Hitherto unpublished.

Febry 18th Rydale Mount
[1818]

My Lord,

I am honored with your Lordship's of the 14th. The outrages committed at Kendal, will surely be of great use to our cause.—I am inclined to think that we shall gain ground in Kendal, though there is great want of the talent required for these occasions. I took much pains with the Editor of the Kendal Paper, and not without effect; but he is constantly under the influence of the opposite Party, and as a Dissenter has a bias against existing things, so that what appears to him impartiality would wear a very different aspect to one of another Persuasion. Nevertheless the last Paper, is certainly, upon the whole, in a much better spirit.—

The more I see of this Contest the more I regret that circumstances should have thrown the representation upon both your Sons. This is unpalatable to many respectable people wellwishers to your Lordship's Family; and forces them to acknowledge a shew of reason in the opposite Party which they would otherwise deny. 'Two Brothers, and these Sons of a Peer, for one County!' is a frequent exclamation from quarters entitling it to regard. Your Lordship is aware of the considerations which prompt me to speak thus without reserve. I am fully persuaded that this unfortunate circumstance is the only tenable ground of the enemy.—Notwithstanding the clamor from some despicable quarters, your Lordship is loved honored and respected throughout Westmorland, and your influence is looked up to with satisfaction and pleasure by a vast majority of what is respectable in all ranks of the County.—I have everywhere stated though with proper caution, your sentiments on

[1] i.e. Mr. Addison's letter.

the present state of the representation, and invariably except in the instance mentioned in my last with good effect. I have the strongest reason for believing that an intimation to this purpose made yesterday by a Friend of mine prevented a Vote of a most worthy Person being promised to Mr James Brougham who has been canvassing Ambleside this day, accompanied by Mr Curwen Jun.[1] and his left-handed Brother, Mr Bird. But it is not so much the number of Votes that will be *directly* influenced by the knowledge of your Lordship's sentiments on this subject as the *respectability* of the Voters, whose example will carry others along with it. It is now I think too late to propose a change in this particular were it possible, or even to hint it; it would seem that it was extorted by fear, and the hostile Party would rise in insolence accordingly. Every art is used, and all kinds of falsehoods are told to debauch the minds of the ignorant Freeholders; and this creates apprehensions because it is impossible to guard against such Attacks.

Mr Henry Brougham has been writing to Mr Clarkson,[2] who has promised, I doubt not, to exert his influence for him among the Westmorland Quakers. Your Lordship sees what a strange medley of opponents you have to contend with. Mr Clarkson in his simplicity, persuaded himself that Mr B. is an advocate of pure Whiggism—It is my honest opinion that well-intentioned Enthusiasts, (like my Friend Mr C.) with much talent and little discernment, are of all men living the persons who are most likely to do mischief when they meddle with legislation or Politics.—I am glad that Mr C. is not in the Country. He is an intractable man, deservedly noted for his integrity; and his countenance would, among a certain class, have strengthened the opposite Party. Besides he is of incredible activity, and unwearied perseverance in whatever he undertakes. We want such a Man on our side.

Unless the Opposition make a Party matter of it, and subscribe large Sums, Mr B. must, I think, very soon retire from the field for want of money. Mr Wakefield is the only wealthy adherent of his whom I have heard of in our neighbourhood, and he will be sparing of his cash.

I entirely agree with your Lordship, and Lord Lowther (for we conversed upon the subject) that the time is not yet come, when

[1] Henry Curwen (1783–1861) of Belle Isle, Windermere, whose daughter Isabella was to marry W. W.'s son John in 1830. Henry Curwen and John Bird of Hawkshead were both members of Brougham's Committee.

[2] S. H. was staying at Playford Hall when Brougham's letter arrived (see *SH* 40, pp. 121–2). For Clarkson's intervention later on in the election, see L. 486 below.

Mr Brougham's communication through Mr W.[1] is to be turned against him. Could it not be managed that he could be taken by surprize at some public meeting with his Supporters about him?— Believe me my Lord

Ever faithfully yours
Wm Wordsworth

479. W. W. to LORD LONSDALE

MS. Lonsdale MSS., Record Office, The Castle, Carlisle.
K (—). *MY ii. 601, p. 805* (—).

[?19][2] Febry 1818

My Lord,

In answer to the accompanying Letter,[3] I urged Mr Isaac Wilson, as previously agreed upon between us, with the approbation of Lord L., to renew his efforts to purchase a majority of shares in the old paper. I recommended this plan as much the best; because it would *immediately* put an end to all that was injurious in a most formidable opponent, and convert him into a powerful supporter. The Subscribers to the new paper are animated by very honourable feelings; and they hope to destroy the old paper, by withdrawing advertisements from it. But this would require time and we have none to spare; and while there continues to be a choice between two, the People whom we have most interest in keeping and setting right will only read what flatters their worst passions.

The difficulty in procuring shares, lies in three being in the hands of Jacob Wakefield; another belongs to one Swainson,[4] a fierce Democrat; and a fifth is under the power of one of the Wakefields as Executor to a Mr Swale. The remaining three are with your Lordship's friends of whom Alderman Pearson[5] is one.

Mr Isaac Wilson was unknown to me when I first mentioned him to your Lordship as promising, from his character, to be useful in no small degree. I do not doubt that he will continue to prove so.

The Handbill[6] you require is enclosed; pray be so kind as to

[1] Mr. Wilberforce.

[2] Date cut away.

[3] W. W. enclosed a letter from Isaac Wilson, dated 18 Feb. This stated that Christopher Wilson and others had started a Subscription for the new paper, even though Lord Lowther and W. W. were still hoping to gain control of the *Kendal Chronicle*.

[4] Robert Swainson of Brigsteer, a firm Broughamite.

[5] John Pearson, Mayor of Kendal in 1810 and 1819: a member of the Central Lowther Committee.

[6] The handbill which accused Lord Lowther of being a sinecurist. See L. 476 above.

preserve it. Compare it with the advertisement at the foot of 2nd Column of the 3rd page of last week's Chronicle;[1] and judge of Mr B's Kendal Committee.—This week I have addressed two Letters signed A Friend to Truth[2] to the Editor of the Chronicle which, if he inserts I shall have some hope of him;—if he does not I shall publish them elsewhere, to expose the character of these proceedings.

Lord L. was here[3] yesterday, and successful to his highest wishes. A *very* few still hang back, but I believe that in the end my desire and hope will be fulfilled, and *every* man amongst them will vote for the present Members, every one I mean of the old native Freeholders. The New Settlers are not above six—and one of these is favourable, one not now in England; another resides at a distance, and his sentiments are unknown to me. I speak of Grasmere and Langdale and Ambleside.

The only difficulty we have had to encounter in this neighbourhood has been caused by the misrepresentations and falsehoods of the Press, and especially of the Kendal papers.

I am obliged to be very guarded (Mr James B. said in Ambleside that he could fine me £100 for having intermeddled).[4] But these calumnies force me to write, and occasionally to speak—had I free use of my tongue every obstacle of this kind should be removed both here and in other parts of Westmorland. It is shocking that the whole of Long-Sleddale should be against us, through the influence of a single village orator.—

I have the honour to remain

my Lord
your Lordship's
faithful Servnt
W W.

[1] This reiterated the accusation as nothing short of the 'Truth'.

[2] These contributions, dated Orton Parish, 16 Feb., were both published in the *Kendal Chronicle* for 21 Feb., and refuted charges made against the Lowther candidates in handbills and in the anonymous *Chronicle* article by J. C. Curwen (see L. 474 above). The first letter upheld Lord Lowther's character and standing as a Lord of the Treasury: the second defended Col. Lowther's military career, and rebutted the charge that he had purchased rank by family interest. Both contributions are reprinted in full by Wells, op. cit., pp. 1085–90. Orton, a moorland village near Appleby, was a Lowther stronghold, and W. W. must have spent a day or two there on his way home from Kendal.

[3] i.e. Rydal.

[4] W. W.'s intervention in the election was already a talking-point in London, according to Thomas Clarkson. He wrote at this time to his wife, D. W.'s friend, 'to warn William lest he was ignorant of the predicament in which he stood . . .' (*SH* 41, p. 125).

480. W. W. to VISCOUNT LOWTHER

Address: The Lord Viscount Lowther, Lowther Castle.
Stamp: Kendal Penny Post.
MS. Lonsdale MSS., Record Office, The Castle, Carlisle. Hitherto unpublished.

[*c.* 25 Feb. 1818][1]

My dear Lord Lowther,

The Revd Wm Jackson of Queen's Coll: Oxford writes his father that B. has written to all the Freeholders of that University, and as Letters from the present Members have not been received he is afraid offense may be taken.

I wrote yesterday, enclosing what you requested.

Has Mr Myers[2] of Pow House Millom been written to? He is a person who rates his own importance rather highly—and as he was not applied to to sign the Declaration, if his Vote has not been asked for he will be piqued.

My eyes are considerably better but the weather still terrifies me; the ground here is covered with snow.

Ever my dear Lord Lowther
most faithfully yours
W. W.

Mr Gee has been requested by Sir Thomas Lethbridge[3] to go and manage the Poll for him but he is determined to stick to Westnd.

For a version of B's famous London Tavern speech see opposite page.

If money I lack
The Shirt on my back
Shall off—and go to the hammer;

For though with bare skin*
By G—I'll be in,
And raise up a radical clamor!

Placard for a Poll bearing an old Shirt.

*Or better perhaps Though I sell shirt, and skin,[4]

[1] This letter was written *after* the Dinner given for Brougham at the City of London Tavern on Saturday, 21 Feb. (reported in the *Kendal Chronicle* for 28 Feb.), but *before* Lord Lowther left for London at the end of the month.

[2] John Myers, W. W.'s cousin. See *EY* 2, 36, pp. 7, 122. He later owned a freehold at Grasmere.

[3] Sir Thomas Buckler Lethbridge, 2nd Bart. (1778–1849), of Sandhill Park, Somerset, a prominent ultra-Tory: M.P. for Somerset, 1806–12 and 1820–30. Gee owned property in that county and eventually lived there (and at Hendon) when his lease of Ivy Cottage expired.

[4] This election squib was presumably copied from a handbill, though the suggested emendation is probably W. W.'s.

481. D. W. to THOMAS MONKHOUSE

MS. Jonathan Wordsworth.
K. MY ii. 602, p. 806.

Kendal, March 3^{d}, 1818.

My dear Friend,

Knowing that you do not grudge a shilling that pays for tidings of old friends, and that if you can get a little sound good-government doctrine into the bargain, you will think the shilling well bestowed, I send you this paper;[1] which I think you will say is pretty well done. There is nothing comes out on the other side of the question worth reading, though every day brings out something fresh on both sides. The Broughamites evidently abate in their hopes, and the opposite party has *well grounded* hopes of success; but the misguided mob, including almost all of the lower classes who have no votes, cry aloud for Brougham, expecting that if he is but returned for Westmoreland, meal will be reduced to fifteen shillings a load. So they cry out! and no lady would venture to appear in a yellow[2] ribband in Kendal streets, though you cannot walk thirty yards without meeting a dirty lad or lass with a blue one! and the *ladies* of that party also have no fear of displaying their colour.

I am detained at Kendal by bad weather. I came in the coach on Thursday, and shall return upon Neddy to-morrow, if the day be fine. All are well at home. We often wish you had a vote to bring you down at the election. H. Brougham is expected about Easter, when it is much to be feared that there will be fresh disturbances.

I am called to dinner, so excuse this scrawl, and if you put this paper into any one's hands, pray erase all my scrawling. God bless you!

Ever your affectionate,
D. W.

I should have sent you the last Kendal paper, but it contained nothing but the London tavern dinner and some villainous writing in which there was no sense, on the other side.

[1] This letter was written on a copy of the broadsheet *To the Freeholders of Westmorland*, by a Freeholder, 28 Feb. 1818, which consisted of part of the second of the two Addresses referred to in L. 475 above. The text of this broadsheet, with a few variations, was reprinted on 7 Mar. in the *Carlisle Patriot* (the Tory paper, founded in 1815), and it eventually formed part of the second of W. W.'s *Two Addresses to the Freeholders of Westmorland*.

[2] Yellow was the Tory and blue the Whig colour.

482. W. W. to LORD LONSDALE

MS. Lonsdale MSS., Record Office, The Castle, Carlisle.
K (—). MY ii. 603, p. 807 (—).

Rydale Mount
11th March 1818

My Lord,

I am most happy to learn from your Lordship's Letter of the 3rd Inst^{nt} that the Report of the Canvass is so satisfactory. There appears to be no ground of apprehension with respect to the Issue. But I hope none of our Friends will be tempted to relax in their exertions on this account.—Mr B's Kendal Comm. give out, I do not mean publicly, but to some of their own party on whom they depend, that they have 900 *fast* Votes, and not less than ten thousand pounds subscribed.—This would not be worth mentioning, had it not come to me from a Person of too much importance for them to trifle with.—Mr Clarkson, I am pleased to find, is not inclined to be so active as I feared.[1] He, and all the Slave trade abolitionists, consider themselves as under obligation to Mr B. for having brought in the Bill by which the Traffic in Slaves was made felony. This disposes him to favor Mr B.—though he regrets much that he should have opposed your Lordship for whom he has the highest respect. Mr C. cannot have exerted himself much, or he would not have held the opinion which I am told he does, that the Quakers will not vote. This at least does not appear to be the opinion in Kendal, with respect to the greatest part of them.

I do not hear of any progress being made towards the purchase of the Kendal Chronicle. It will not be easy to meet with an Editor for the new Paper. At the request of the Subscribers, I applied to Mr Street[2] of the Courier, but he cannot assist them; for those who are qualified, he says, are all of bad principles. I have applied to the Editors of the Sun[3] and New Times,[4] also, but I do not expect much better success.—The Kendal Paper having renounced its professed neutrality, it seems to me advisable that your Lordship's Friends should not offer anything to it;—For the Party would only admit just enough to season their hostility.

The things in the Courier were good—some of them have been

[1] He confined himself to writing a letter of support to the Chairman of Brougham's Committee. See L. 486 below.

[2] T. G. Street and Daniel Stuart were joint proprietors of the *Courier*.

[3] John Taylor (1757–1832) edited *The Sun*.

[4] Begun in 1817 by Dr. (later Sir) John Stoddart in opposition to *The Times*.

reprinted in Handbills at Kendal.[1] But the Writer is much mistaken when he represents this Contest as an attempt merely to set up Lord Thanet's interest against your Lordship's. This view of the subject may answer for London[2]—but what could Lord T's purse or interest have done of themselves? A mere nothing.—The moral stamina of this *out-break* are misguided good intention—party spirit—dissent—disaffection—envy, pride, and all the self-conceited pretentions which absurd ignorance can be incited to by headstrong Reformers, and Revolutionists.—Such being my view of the subject, even if attachment to your Lordship's person and interests and those of your Family, had not moved me, a sense of duty to the public would not have suffered me to remain inactive. It is highly gratifying to me to know that your Lordship and the two members think so obligingly of my endeavours—Be so good as to mention Lady Mary's health when you write again—

With the highest respect your Lordship's
faithful Serv[nt]
W. W.

483. W. W. to LORD LONSDALE

MS. Lonsdale MSS., Record Office, The Castle, Carlisle. Hitherto unpublished.

14th March 1818

My Lord,

The anxiety which I feel respecting the state of things in West[nd] must plead my excuse for troubling your Lordship with this Letter. If you continue to read the Kendal Chronicle you must be greatly concerned to see that the Liberty of the Press should be so grossly abused. This Paper as now conducted reminds me almost at every sentence of those which I used to read in France during the heat of the Revolution. Notwithstanding the satisfactory result of the

[1] Several recent articles in the *Courier* had attacked Brougham's character and motives in this election. One was reprinted as a handbill entitled 'DINNER *of the Independent Electors in* LONDON' (i.e. the Dinner of 21 Feb.). Another, entitled '*Independence of Election*', which W. W. goes on to refer to, represented the contest as a struggle between Lord Thanet and Lord Lonsdale for the right of nominating members for the county.

[2] Because it tried to implicate Brougham in Lord Thanet's alleged discourtesy to the Princess Charlotte. She had visited Maidstone to receive a Loyal Address on the occasion of her marriage, and Lord Thanet had absented himself from the ceremony.

Canvass, there is a *ferment of disaffection* in the County—excited by these Libellers and others who talk as prompted by them; and I am convinced, at this moment there is such a hostility among the lower Ranks, including servants, day-labourers, handicraftsmen, small shopkeepers, to whom must be added many who from education and situation in life ought to know better, that if it went by counting heads Mr B. would sweep all before him, and be triumphant to a degree which I fear to contemplate. I will go farther and express my belief that if the Power of incitement which these seditious doctrines have derived from the events now pending in West^nd^ were spread all over England the Government would be in imminent danger. Mr B. may at this moment be regarded as the most prominent Demagogue in the Kingdom. His visit to West^nd^ is anxiously looked for by his adherents.[1] I submit, but with due deference, to your Lordship's consideration, whether *this* would not be an eligible time to make known his former advances[2] to turn the Lowther interest to his own profit. Pens not easily counted, and tongues without number are busy in extolling him at the expense of your Lordship's Family. I look earnestly to the return of Lord Lowther,[3] and his Brother.—If it be in the power of truth to humiliate this Pretender, it may and will be done. But I know of no means that bear so directly upon the case as those in your Lordship's possession.

The other day I had a long and interesting Letter from Mr Stuart one of the Proprietors of the Courier, and its quondam Editor, on the subject of the new paper in Kendal.[4] He is decisively of opinion that the old Paper ought not to be bought—but I think on mistaken grounds, from not being fully acquainted with the circumstances. I forwarded his Letter to the Kendal Committee appointed to manage the new Journal, for their guidance.

I have the honor to be
my Lord
ever faithfully your Lordship's
W.

[1] Brougham arrived in Kendal on 23 Mar. to canvass in person.
[2] i.e. his overtures through Wilberforce in 1806. See L. 467 above.
[3] Lord Lowther returned from London on 18 Mar.
[4] Stuart's letter of 9 Mar., which throws much light on the contemporary state of the press, is among the *WL MSS*.

484. W. W. to VISCOUNT LOWTHER

MS. Lonsdale MSS., Record Office, The Castle, Carlisle. Hitherto unpublished.

Rydale Mount
March 16th 1818.

My dear Lord Lowther,

I thought you did not mean to be so long absent from Westnd, or I should have written to you immediately on the Receipt of your two obliging Letters.

I hope you will not disapprove of the use I made of the information the latter conveyed respecting the amount of your Salary. I wrote to the Editor of the Ken: Chron: and he inserted my letter in his last Paper.[1] By the bye never was the Press more atrociously abused than in that journal at present: Every sentence almost in it reminds me of what I used to read in France, in the year 1792, when the Revolution was advancing towards the zenith of its horrors. I had an obliging Letter from Street, and another from Stuart, on the subject of the New Paper;[2] the Latter, I forwarded to Kendal for the guidance of the Proprietors. I wish the Paper were afloat—the enemy have a tremendous advantage over us, notwithstanding the excellent things that appear in the Carlisle Patriot. But a Carlisle Paper can never be expected to circulate in Westnd like a Native. I think the good cause would be much benefited, if Extracts were made of the best things that have appeared in its favor, and collected into a small pamphlet, printed in the least expensive form possible, to be distributed, or sold. The Yeomen and their families are fond of reading; and on wet days, they might take down this bundle of good things, from the shelf, and be amused and benefited at the same time.—I know no way in which a given sum of money could be better employed; newspapers are seldom recurred to if once read, even when they are at hand, which must be rarely. It is the succession,—the repetition of the blow which enables them to do so much mischief.

Grand preparations are making at Kendal for the entrance of the great Demagogue. Would not this be the time to bring forward the facts in Lord Lonsdale's possession which prove that Mr B. had no objection to the preponderance of the Lowther interest when he had

[1] This was the third of W. W.'s letters signed 'A Friend to Truth', and his last contribution to the *Kendal Chronicle*, which had now openly come out against the Lowthers. This letter, printed in the issue for 14 Mar., merely stated the gross amount of Lord Lowther's salary under Government.

[2] i.e. the proposed *Westmorland Gazette*. See previous letter.

a hope that he himself might profit by it. I wrote to Lord L. yesterday on this subject. Do consider it.

I congratulate you on the result of the Canvas; we shall be triumphant, I trust, but nothing can be worse than the spirit of the multitude in this country. They are ripe for any mischief. They expect to intimidate the Voters. Everyone is to be mobbed who does not vote for B. Such is the report in Ambleside—some are afraid, and more pretend to be so. Eagerly do I wish for your return and your Brother's.

My youngest Son is a complete Yellow, having got the jaundice, poor Lad, so that he has no *occasion* for Ribbons, though he wears them. The Daffodils are anxiously looked for that the *young* Ladies in Rydale, may adorn their bonnets with them. Excuse this trifling —and believe me my dear Lord Lowther, with most anxious wishes for your complete success,

ever faithfully yours
W Wordsworth.

485. W. W. to LORD LONSDALE

Address: The Earl of Lonsdale, Cottesmore, Greatham, Grantham.
Stamp: Kendal Penny Post.
MS. Lonsdale MSS., Record Office, The Castle, Carlisle. Hitherto unpublished.

[24 Mar. 1818]

My Lord,

The enclosed Account[1] of Mr B's speech at Kendal yesterday, hastily written by my Sister, imperfect as it is, may be amusing to Lady Lonsdale, and Lady Mary, of whose improved health I was most glad to hear. In regard to the correspondence[2] the copy of which is in Lord Lowther's possession, I am anxious to see his Lordship open this subject as I cannot but think that a beneficial use may be made of it. And it seems that no time ought to be lost—as several undecided Votes may by the present Canvass be given in Mr B's favor. Upon the temper of the people I shall request the honor of being permitted to write my opinion to your Lordship at some length. One naturally expects an anti-ministerial candidate to have more popularity than his Opponents. But there is no struggle between Ministry and opposition, as far as the multitude are con-

[1] D.W.'s eyewitness account of Brougham's arrival in Kendal on the 23rd was posted to Rydal Mount on the same day.

[2] Between Brougham and Wilberforce in 1806.

cerned. Do not let me tax your Lordship's civility with replying to every Letter I am urged to write.

I have the honor to be
W. W.

Kendal Mar: 23rd—4 oclock.

Copy

Half an hour ago we came home after seeing the procession, hearing the speech etc. etc. etc. Long before which time we were waiting at Mrs Strickland's,[1] a heavy shower of snow and hail came on, which continued during the whole of the harrangue. As to the *order* of the Procession, I can give no account of *that*. Except the flying Flags (and they were very gay) all is much prettier laid down in the hand-bill and the Kendal Chronicle,[2] which no doubt have reached you ere this. But the multitude of heads, fearless of the storm, one condensed line in motion wedging in the Horsemen and Carriages, which all slowly streamed on together, was grand. If the cause had been better, my feelings as a Spectator would have been really sublime. But when you looked at the Individuals who composed it, you could hardly single out a gentleman. Blackguards by the score—and multitudes of young Lads. The halt was made at the Bank, God Save the King, and other tunes played—and a short while after, Mr B. and his Brother had entered Mr Wakefield's drawing-room. 'Silence' was proclaimed, and the Candidate for the favour of that precious mob-assembly made his appearance at the centre window. But I should first have told you, that the Thompsons,[3] Wybergh,[4] and our Cousin Crackenthorpe[5] had been for some time stationed at the windows—and C. and I exchanged a friendly greeting in which the Misses Thompson joined. But now the Horsemen were gone, and the People condensed—at each end pressing up and down—so as to get as near as possible to the Orator. Of course *when* he appeared at the window, he was hailed by a tremendous shout—and when anything fell from his lips that particularly took their fancies, the cry of applause was repeated with more or less vehe-

[1] Probably Mrs. Cookson's mother, who lived opposite the Wakefield Bank in Stricklandgate.

[2] The order of Procession announced in the issue for 21 Mar.

[3] Probably the family of John Thompson, a manufacturer of Stricklandgate and a Dissenter, who voted for Brougham.

[4] Thomas Wybergh (1757–1827), of Isell Hall, near Cockermouth, who nominated Brougham at the Poll. He owned the ancient hall at Clifton, near Penrith, but the estate itself was mortgaged to the Lowthers.

[5] Crackanthorpe had been actively campaigning for Brougham both in London and Westmorland.

mence. His dress was a dark coat, yellow waistcoat and a very large blue silk Handkerchief tied round his neck—the streamers hanging down to the bottom of his Waist. I assure you he has nothing of a Westmoreland Countenance. I could have fancied him one of the French Demagogues of the Tribunal of Terror at certain times, when he gathered a particular fierceness into his face. He is very like a Frenchman. He opened his speech with *most humble* thanks to that goodly assembly—not of Freeholders and indeed you would have supposed he was ashamed of the word—ashamed of the *support* of Freeholders; for he never once addressed them—never *but* once used the word Freeholders and that was merely incidental, speaking of them as having some thing to do at the Election. He was most grateful for the reception he had met with—he had nothing to lament but the bad weather—which was the only unfortunate circumstance attending this meeting. What a contrast to the memorable 13th!—here he was admonished by his good Friend William Abbot,[1] or some other—it was the *11th*,[2] which rather put him out. 'I was going to say Gentlemen—that the only circumstance in favour of our opponents was the weather! how much are all other circumstances in our favour!' Loud applause. He then asserted that the Riots were occasioned by the conduct of the other Party—and not a little more of the like in the lowest style of Mob oratory. It was despicable—the only merit he had as an Orator was, that he uttered his words distinctly and had plenty of them at command. He did not intend to detain the Gentlemen long, but he would say a few words respecting the Arts used by the other Party. Among these were writings poured out daily—and now begins his Battery against *you*.[3] One of these vassel underhand anonymous writers had taunted him with Poverty. He was the first who had descended to personalities in the contest, a Man who held a Sinecure in this County and who had no other property besides—or very little. This Man whose writings etc. etc.—and so he went on abusing them. 'I do not speak of his poetry, but his laboured compositions in prose—which would be far harder work for his Readers than the *duties* of his place furnish *him* with.' After a great deal more of this, of which not a single word as applied to you, was understood by any of his hearers except the Faction around him, and our cousin C. who at the beginning of it gave a significant and good-humoured look to me, and,

[1] John Harrison's predecessor as editor of the *Kendal Chronicle*.

[2] i.e. 11 Feb., the day the Lowther candidates arrived in Kendal.

[3] Brougham had clearly recognized W. W.'s hand in the two Addresses in the *Kendal Chronicle* and *Carlisle Patriot*. He attacked the poet even more openly later the same day, during a speech at the Dinner given in his honour.

Miss C. says, retired from the window, I was determined to keep my place till he had finished with that subject.—From which he turned to the Lowthers and L. *Castle*—which, with eloquence well-adapted to his audience, he reminded them used to be called Lowther *Hall*[1]—He did not accuse the Lowthers of the falsehoods and calumnies so busily uttered—no—he knew my Lord Lonsdale was a man of far too much sense.—he then turned to the arguments used in their favour of their great wealth—of which you may guess what use he made, and how he was applauded. Again and again adverted to the reproach against his own poverty, and the poverty and smallness of Westnd—using your very words. His next subject was Lord Thanet and the Courier—Lord T. who disdained to use his wealth and power for electioneering purposes!—and in the course of this part of his argument he said, that if he, (B) had one tenth of the wealth of Ld L——e he would not let one of his Sons receive £11 or 1200 a year from the People. 'It comes out of *your* pockets'—and in another part of the speech you cannot conceive the bitterness with which he said 'They *have* great Riches, but how did they *get* their riches!'—Oh! he looked ready to lead a gang of Robespierrists set to pull down Lowther Castle and tear up the very trees that adorn it. He then—in illustration of what points I have really forgotten, bungled out a quotation from our 'immortal Poet'—not, as he said 'that Poet (pointing towards the Ambleside road) you are not to suppose I mean him whose writings I have just been alluding to.' No—the language intended to be uttered no doubt was Shakespeare's, but his memory here seemed to fail him; and as Mrs Strickland said, 'he put in some words of his own.' Whatever it was he meant to say, I could not hear distinctly what he *did* say, and I heard every word in all other parts. Before concluding, he addressed the Mob feelingly—concerning his pretentions to represent them—he had been taunted for poverty, but if he had a penny it did not come out of their pockets. 'Do you recollect my first address?'—'Oh yes, Oh yes!' 'In that I rested solely upon my public conduct.' 'Yes, yes,' And he assured them, he had a fortress as impregnable (clapping his hands on his breast) as Lowther Castle, even if it were as Brougham Castle, and others of the Castles of the Ancient Barons had been, a fortified Hold. He had been charged with being a Party man—he was not so—but he should not detain them, the weather being so bad, by detailing the course of his political conduct—but he assured them, in a great many words, that he had been labouring hard for the

[1] Lowther had been elaborately reconstructed in the Gothic style by Robert Smirke between 1806 and 1811.

repeal of one tax—and he trusted his object would be accomplished, That was the *Leather* tax, and he would never let it rest.[1] With this promise ended all the Information which he had to give. He concluded with his fervent thanks, 'Thanks! no it is not for me to thank you—the cause is yours—not mine and you ought rather to thank me!'—(Oh no—his important communications did not end so). He told them 'the name of a Westmorland Man in distant parts was hailed with triumph. It was esteemed an honour to belong to that County and in all parts a West^nd^ Man was looked up to.' Here he paused. I suppose that the Mob did not quite understand *where* they were held in such high respect—so he explained 'I mean in the South, in *Lunnon*.' Now, I have done—but I have not given and cannot possibly give you an idea of the manner in which all this was said, and an important part I have omitted. Towards the end of the harrangue, he told the Mob that among other calumnies it had been asserted that his Opponents had said he intended to withdraw from the Contest. 'Do you see anything about me *like* withdrawing?' (and he fiercely looked defiance) 'No, no'—'This is but a field day—and we shall meet again at Appleby, and then you will see *who* is the first to give out.' In the course of his peroration—his thanks, his leave-taking—he again bitterly lamented the bad weather, but hoped they would not catch cold and concluded that part of his subject with proud congratulations that they were not afraid of a storm.[2] Now I *have* done . . . It is plain they have yet a hope of carrying the day by *talk* on the Hustings. They expect to make a figure there; but they evidently do not expect to go thither prepared with Voters.

486. D. W. to SARA HUTCHINSON

MS. British Museum.
K (—). MY ii. 604, p. 807.

Easter Tuesday. [24 Mar. 1818.]

My dearest Sara,

I have had two days and a half of exertion and bustle, and now I take the pen not satisfied with the time that is before me for writing to you, to Mrs Luff and to Mrs Clarkson, three offices with which I was charged when I left Rydal on Sunday morning with your

[1] Brougham had associated himself with Whig efforts to repeal the Leather Tax, which pressed hard on the Kendal tanners. The Bill for Repeal was narrowly defeated on 5 Apr.

[2] In her account of Brougham's speech, D. W. includes much that was either toned down or omitted from the *Kendal Chronicle* report on 28 Mar.

brother Henry. I had set my heart upon seeing the People and the stir on Brougham's entry and should have come by the Coach on Saturday, but there was no room for me; and the weather had long been so very stormy, that I had not a thought of walking. However on Sunday morning the sun shone, and as Henry was at R, and willing to accompany me I resolved to come, though the wind blew fiercely but fortunately from the North, therefore except by the Lakeside where cross winds assailed us we were rather pushed forward than retarded by the blast. We left R at precisely ¼ past 12—halted ¾ of an hour at Stavely—and reached Kendal at ¼ before 5. I give you these particulars for the sake of our dear Friend, Mrs Luff, who will be glad to hear that at 46 I can walk 16 miles in 4 hours and ¾ with short rests between on a blustering cold day, without having felt any fatigue except for the first ½ hour after my entrance into the house at my journey's end when my Body remembered the force of the blast, and I was exhausted. It is now past 6 o'clock, Tuesday evening, and I have scarcely time to save the post with all my letters. What do you say to my being a turn coat? For the joke's sake I got this Frank—Crackenthorpe asked us this morning if we would have any; I replied 'No, I'll have none of your franks,' and then I recalled my words, recollecting that I wanted to write to *you*, and had had by me a long time a letter from the dead letter office, which I wrote to Miss Malcolm just after Wm and M went to London, and which I want to send to her to prove that she had not been neglected by us. But now for the events of yesterday. Truly thankful we were that all went off with the most perfect quietness;—but indeed how could it have been otherwise? Unless they had been guilty of the folly with which they charged the Lowthers, namely that of instigating a mob to endanger their own lives! Whatever Friends the Lowthers may have among the mob of Kendal, none appeared yesterday to disturb the peace, and the heads of the Lowther side used their best endeavours to preserve good order. At ½ past 6, the Clubs with all their flags assembled and all persons who wished to go to Burton to meet B. What right the Clubs had to be summoned to make a show, I know not. Probably there were not 10 votes among them. Elizabeth[1] and all the young ones of the Family saw the motley group depart—They declared there was not one except Towers the Apothecary who looked in the least like a gentleman. Allan Harden[2] and Mr King[3] were among the most

[1] i.e. Elizabeth Cookson.

[2] Son of John Harden of Brathay Hall.

[3] Thomas King of Grasmere (see *EY* 283, p. 636), a member of Brougham's Committee.

respectable (A. is a Blue, his Father a Yellow).—At a little after one we stationed ourselves at Mrs Strickland's windows and at about two, in the midst of a bitter snow shower, B. and his attendants with music and banners halted before the Bank. Among his precursors was Crackenthorp, who with the Misses Thompson, Mr T, the Wakefields, William Abbot and Wybergh was stationed in the windows right opposite us. The Hero of the day had been dragged by a set of ragamuffins in blue Ribbands from within 3 miles of Burton and when he drew up towards the door with music, Banners, horsemen, music and the immense multitude on foot, all joining in one huzza fearless of the driving storm the spectacle was grand. To my feelings it would have been sublime if the cause could have been a good one. The Candidate for the favour of that mob assembly was distinguished by a large blue handkerchief which hung from his neck to the bottom of his waist. He appeared at the window—face to face with us. Silence was proclaimed and the oration began, but if such be house of Commons eloquence, commend me to a good mountebank Doctor. Mrs Strickland, whose ears and whose faculties are as lively as they were at 20 years of age, says that when Dr Green[1] used to speak it was something like. He appeared like a gentleman and what he said was far better worth listening to. But Mr B's Speech was addressed *to* a mob—intended *for* a mob; and that mob he invited to meet him at Appleby. He never once addressed himself to the Freeholders, never but once used the word (and he spoke ¾ of an hour) and that was incidentally. In short you might have thought he was ashamed of claiming any connexion with that respectable body. But I have already once written down the substance of his speech[2] for Rydal and cannot set about doing it again. So you must be contented with one part of it. But first conceive John and me stationed side by side in the window right before him, E. Cookson's head above mine, Henry's above John's; and cousin Crackenthorp and two or three of the Thompsons at the next window to Brougham. His first words were words of gratitude to that goodly assembly—next of lamentation and sympathy on account of the bad weather which was indeed a contrast to the weather on the memorable 11th, a day which none of them could forget if they were to live a hundred years, but in all other respects how much the contrast was in *their* favour! (Loud applause) and here he impudently styled them the Lowther Riots and in plain language charged the Lowther party with being the Authors of them (which by interpretation was saying

[1] A notorious quack. See W. W. to Southey, [May 1833] (in later volume).
[2] See previous letter.

that they were so silly as to incite a mob to do its best to destroy themselves!) Then he began to describe the Arts used by the party to mislead the people. Their agents were anonymous writers—or writers under false names. One of these, the first who descended to personality in this contest, had taunted him with his poverty and the county of Westmorland with a like charge (he quoted the words of a friend of yours about Westmorland). '*That* man held a *sinecure* in the county and he had nothing else or very little else to live upon. He was the most active of the secret agents of the cause, and to be sure it was much harder work to read his writings—understand me I do not mean his *poetry*, but those other writings which he now pours out, than any of the duties of his office impose upon *him*.' There was much more of the like, and I determined to face it out. In the beginning of this part of the harangue Crackenthorp cast a good-humoured and significant look at me, which I returned and a short time after the end of this part of the subject I pushed E. Cookson to my place and took hers. No doubt he expected that the mob would at once understand whom he alluded to and looked for a triumphant laugh of sympathy; but no, it fell a dead weight upon the ears of all except the Faction at his elbow. However not daunted by this rebuff he turned to the subject again. 'In the words of our immortal Poet—you are not to suppose I mean that poet of whom I have spoken to you before (pointing towards the Windermere road), no, in the words of our immortal poet'—and here, poor Man, his memory failed him, and he blundered out some garbled lines which I could not hear distinctly—no doubt they had been *intended* for the words of Shakespear—but enough of this. The speech had not even the merit of producing much effect even upon the mob to whom it was solely addressed, and I must say that I could perceive no merit in the man as an Orator, except words at will when he did not pretend to quote from others—and a very distinct utterance. The utmost attention was paid by the auditory; but when all was over they looked heavy and stupid as if they had expected something which they had not found. Crackenthorp stole away from the dinner at 8 o'clock and stayed with us till past 12 and we had a very merry and pleasant evening, and he was very agreeable. This morning he called again—and just before he was setting off with B on his canvass ran down to us in out-of-breath haste to read us a letter just received from Mr Clarkson[1] to Mr Wakefield 'a letter worth a host

[1] Clarkson's temperate letter was printed in the *Kendal Chronicle* for 28 Mar. He argued that the Lowthers could not count on his public support just because he had received private favours from them, and maintained that, although Lord Lonsdale had supported the anti-slavery movement, Brougham's presence in

of votes'—and indeed it was a feather in their caps,—a beautiful—a delightful letter. Nothing has ever yet issued from their press that, compared with that letter, is worth looking at. No doubt they will publish it—but after he had read the letter he hurried off and we had no talk, and Elizabeth and I soon after saw him dragged at Brougham's side by a set of dirty lads and vagrant-like men preceded by music and banners, through the town. The mob was small to-day, and there was no joyousness in it but a great deal of odious coarseness. They are gone to Ambleside. C. will most likely sleep at Rydal. The Lowthers are expected here on Thursday and we *hope* quietness will be maintained; for unruly as they are, they yet have heads and leaders amongst them, and have agreed amongst themselves, under these leaders, not to commit further outrages. Such at least was certainly the arrangement yesterday, but they had no provocation. You will think, dearest Sara, that my head is turned with this election, that I can think of nothing else, and true it is, the tendency of all these proceedings is evidently so dangerous, that we are interested far more than it is even possible for *you* to conceive at a distance. I had intended writing to Mrs Luff to-day, but I shall not be able to save the post if I do. We were very happy to receive a letter from her from the quiet harbour of our Good Friend's house.[1] I am afraid she will feel this terrible cold very severely, she must take care not to expose herself rashly, and I hope in time she may get seasoned to the climate, but it is much to be feared that she will never be able to stand the fickleness of the Seasons in the North of England. I shall write to Mrs Clarkson to-morrow. We had a most affecting account from her of poor Tom's sufferings and fortitude. It has indeed for parent and child been a sad visitation. When we last heard from Joanna she complained of rheumatic pains; but she had not been so ill as when she wrote to you. It is very distressing. I hope the Middleton Bath which you recommend may be of use to her,[2] and that she may be able to come with Betsy; but until the weather is warmer there is no thinking of Betsy's coming, and we wish her visit to be rather early in the spring on account of others. After Betsy we are bound to invite Mrs Coleridge and Sara. Mrs C. proposed coming in April or May; but we told her we could not fix a time on account of Betsy. Then poor

Parliament was necessary for its continued progress. For the full text, see A. L. Strout, 'Thomas Clarkson as Champion of Brougham in 1818', *NQ* clxxiv (4 June 1938), 398–401.

[1] Mrs. Luff had now returned from Mauritius, and was staying with Mrs. Clarkson.

[2] See *SH* 44, p. 132.

Mrs Rd Wordsworth and Johnny must be wedged in at some vacancy. Mary Hutchinson wrote not very long ago and she did not say she was *not* coming, nor did she talk in such a manner as to make us think that she much expected to be able. In answer I replied that M and I did not see any force in objections urged; for you must know that we think her pregnancy is not of sufficiently long standing to make it unfit or uncomfortable for her to travel. Mary W. says that she is of opinion that Mary H. would not like to leave your Aunt without either Joanna or you, and Joanna, poor thing, is not likely to be fit to take much care upon her shoulders, and indeed I think with Mary that it would not be a desirable thing that your Aunt should be left sole housekeeper. Dorothy and Mrs. Gee's pupils were to have a merry holiday yesterday and I dare say the most of this week will be a holiday as I am away, and there is so much canvassing, and at a time when everybody has a holiday.

D. is certainly much improved in many important points—but she sadly wants thought, especially in application to her Latin. French she likes very well and is exceedingly quick in applying the rules of the Grammar. We are going to make a school-room to be ready against Betsy comes, and a very nice one it will be. The saddle room —above the stable. Without such accommodation I should dread the entrance into the house of one staying visitor—I am sure you will rejoice at this contrivance.

I need say no more concerning Miss Dowling[1] than what I said in my last which crossed yours, except that certainly if she had immediately succeeded Miss Fletcher her advantages would have been much greater. She would have had all her scholars. But even yet I have no doubt it wd answer and will. No time for more—a sad letter it is and hard work for you to read, but take a good will for a good deed and be thankful.

Kindest regards to Mr C and Mrs L and believe me ever, my dearest Sara, your affectionate D. W.

Is the tooth-ache better. All well here and at Rydal. Mr Cookson will return [the] week after next. No time to correct blunders.

Brougham has been galled by nobody's writings but William's, and they have cut to the quick, Depend on it. Henry returned to Rydal yesterday, John here still. William walked with us on Monday, dined with Mr Fleming, drank tea at Calgarth. Mr. Fleming much better. Mr. Rhodes[2] of Halifax—a good man he was—died

[1] Miss Dowling, formerly governess in Lord Galloway's family, was about to take over Miss Fletcher's school in Ambleside.

[2] John Rhodes, jun., son of the Marshalls' friend of the same name. See *EY* 7, p. 23.

lately from mis-swallowing a crumb of bread, which brought on a coughing fit and the Rupture of a blood vessel. He has left his sister 8000£ his Nephew 5000 and each of his Nieces, daughters of the same sister, 1000. His wife is to have, as they say, all the rest of his property for her life. This is placing great confidence in her, for he left a daughter, and report says the property amounts to 80,000£. One half of that sum would have made Hannah Gibson[1] of Newcastle think herself in strange luck!

487. W. W. to VISCOUNT LOWTHER

MS. Lonsdale MSS., Record Office, The Castle, Carlisle. Hitherto unpublished.

[27 Mar. 1818]

My dear Lord Lowther,

I have this moment yours of the 27th (this day). I am anxious to confer with you both on the general character of the Contest, and on some particular points; and for this purpose I will assuredly meet you at Kendal, on Tuesday next—if I do not see you before. I should at this moment determine to go over to Lowther tomorrow, did I not think that I may be more useful to the cause, by remaining at home for the purpose of preparing an answer to a Letter of Mr Clarkson to the Kendal Comm: of Brougham, which will appear in the Chronicle tomorrow;[2] and which I am sure will injure your interests with a certain set, principally the Quakers. The original of the Letter I have seen, but could not procure a copy.—It was shewn me by Mr Crackanthorp with the high-flying expression, 'We reckon it as good as 50 votes!'

We have had B. among us. He has done some injury, but I do not think much; if his personal presence does not do more for him elsewhere than it has done here, we shall beat him hollow. He tells the people of this neighbourhood that he means to come among them, when he returns into the Country, and will stay with them some days. He made four harangues, in this neighbourhood; two at

[1] Perhaps a younger daughter of Henry Gibson of Newcastle. See *EY* 140, p. 299.

[2] Clarkson's letter provoked many replies from the Lowther side in the *Carlisle Patriot* and (later) in the *Westmorland Gazette*, but none can be confidently attributed to W. W. He may well have thought better of engaging in public controversy with an old family friend. De Quincey was at this time trying to regain W. W.'s good opinion by espousing the Lowther cause, and W. W. probably left it to him to refute Clarkson's arguments in print. See Jordan, p. 317.

Ambleside, one at Grasmere, and one at Skelwith Bridge. At Grasmere, without mentioning names, he fell upon the Rector, and Mr John Green the Butcher,[1] concluding his lampoon with this elegant witticism that the Spirit and the Flesh were both against him.— I heard his 2nd harangue at Ambleside, in which he kept more within the bounds of decency; I cannot doubt that he knew I was present. He dwelt at great length on the pains he was taking to meet his opponents in the presence of the Freeholders; intermingling many insolent taunts, and haughty boasts, such as you can easily guess at.—

His mode is, when he cannot get any encouragement for himself, to attempt to cajole or entrap the freeholders into a promise that they will give a *plumper* to you. This, when he speaks to them in private and individually. It is therefore necessary to be *very explicit* in requiring a promise for *both members* on your side, whenever you come up.

The subject on which I particularly wish to converse with you is the *correspondence* between Mr W.[2] etc., a copy of which I understand from Lord Lonsdale is in your possession.

You must do a little violence to your own feelings, in getting up a commonplace harangue, for the freeholders; they are imposed upon by the readiness of this Mountebank; and they say among each other, 'What is a Member of Parliament good for that cannot talk'—so that you must try to humor them a little, if you happen to have any number of them together.

I have the honor to be
my dear Lord Lowther
ever faithfully yours
W W

If you do not mean to oppose the repeal of the Leather Tax, pray let the Kendal Tanners know this immediately; they are well inclined to the Yellows, but my Sister who is now at Kendal informs me that they are going over to the enemy, being determined to vote for no one that supports this tax: This she reports from 'good authority'.

[1] The Greens were an old and respected Grasmere family who had lived for generations at Pavement End, at the head of the lake. See *The Excursion*, vii, ll. 636–94 (*PW* v, pp. 251 and 466–7).

[2] Wilberforce.

488. D. W. to CATHERINE CLARKSON

Address: Mrs Clarkson, 16 Earl Street, Blackfriars, London.
Postmark: [?Mar.] 1818. *Stamp*: Kendal.
MS. British Museum.
MY ii. 605, p. 813.

'Sunday—I believe the 30th March'[1] [1818]

My dear Friend,

A week ago I left home, and brought your letter with me, intending to answer it the very next day; and do not think I was unfeeling or unkind because I did not do so, yet found time by snatches to write letters, and long ones, to others. In truth it was because I was so much distressed at the thought of your past sufferings, and of what you may yet have to go through (though I trust that all cause of fear is gone by) that I could not bring my mind to write to you the first, while I was so eager to disburthen it of the observations and excitements of this eventful week. I felt no disposition to detail the history of Mr Brougham's entry to *you*; and for others it *must* be done. Accordingly I have written sheets and sheets as the children say. There has been no letter from Sara since I left Rydal, therefore no news of you or your poor son; but bad news, if there had been any, would have reached us, so I trust he is gradually amending. What a dreadful visitation! I cannot conceive a more sickening anguish than you must have felt when you first beheld that Boy, who had parted from you strong, vigorous, active and comely lying upon his sick-bed so deformed in features, so helpless in body, so oppressed with pain! But a sustaining consolation must have followed when you witnessed his fortitude, and were assured that the danger was over. I cannot hope that the plague of boils will be speedily removed; they are very tedious in general, but always salutary after severe illnesses of this kind. I hope with you that Tom's constitution may be benefited by having gone through this terrible struggle—It often happens so.

I came to Kendal, not you may be sure, to do honour to Mr Brougham, but to see him, the man, and to hear him speak (I never before heard a parliament man), to speculate upon a Kendal mob and to note the stirrings in all ranks. The mob was very great, but we had no confusion. The heads of the Lowther party took the utmost pains to prevent any interference so that if there *had* been quarrels, the Friends of independence must have fought against each other. Oh! that is a mischievous word. It is the motto of the

[1] It was the 29th.

servants, of the Girls working at trades, comb-makers, straw-hat-makers etc, and really walking Kendal streets in the evening of one of these bustling days of Easter week the numbers of disgusting females shouting Brougham and independence were so great you might have supposed the whole of the female populace were turned out. I could not have believed it possible that so many impudent women and girls were to be found in Kendal. Crackenthorp who attends Brougham on his canvass often stole away from the bustle and sate for many hours with Mrs Cookson and me and to be sure we were the most good-humoured disputants that ever met. Many a plain truth did I tell him and poured out some shameful lies which I heard uttered by Brougham. He calls himself a *native* of this county. Henry Hutchinson, Mary Wordsworth, myself and others well acquainted with Penrith about the time when he was born, know that Burdnest was not then occupied by his Family, and we believe he was not born in the County.[1] I stated this to C. and he confessed that his mother did not *think* he was, but oh, replied C, a man may say he is a Westmorland man if he lives there, if his estates are there. 'True, in common conversation an Inhabitant of the county attached to it and proud if it *might* say so; but not that he was *born* there—if B. used the expression in the sense you would attribute to it, it looks as if he neither understood Latin nor English.' He replied, 'well I must give him a hint of it' and so I suppose he has done; for in the report of his speech in the Kendal Chronicle he is not made to call Westmorland his native county. I cannot but lament that Mr Clarkson has thought it right to lend his help to such a cause. He is little aware of the rebellious spirit stirred up in this county, or I am sure he would not have done it. The majority of the populace of Westmorland are ready for revolution, I firmly believe, and that they would be set to work before many years are over, if a majority of county members such as Brougham in political conduct and principles were returned to parliament. Crackenthorp ran down to us in an out-of-breath haste when the horses were ready to go out of town with B. and him to read us a letter just received by Mr Wakefield from your good Husband, and well may he be proud of his prize. They never *had* such a Feather in their caps before and never will have again. 'Oh', said he 'it is better than forty votes,' and indeed I felt that so it was. A beautiful letter and it presents

[1] Brougham Hall, popularly known as 'Birdnest', because the Manor of Brougham originally belonged to the Bird family, was purchased in 1726 by Brougham's great-great-uncle. Brougham was born in 1778 at Edinburgh; he does not seem to have lived at the Hall before 1792. (Note by de Selincourt.)

a noble picture of the firmness, the purity and simplicity of Mr Clarkson's mind. But with respect to the two grand arguments that Brougham *must* be in the house of commons, and that private obligations should give way to public considerations, it may surely be answered that there would be no difficulty in getting B into the house of C. The Opposition would do that—and the other argument except to the enlightened is a dangerous one. The Tenant has been accustomed to look up to a good Landlord, and accordingly Mr Crackenthorp told me that none of his tenants and [? not] many of his neighbours would promise their votes till they had heard what *his* opinion was. He gave it them supported by his best arguments and they vote for Brougham. Could they do better? But I do not believe that it was through the free use of their understandings convincing them that it was for the general good; but they were swayed by many motives—gratitude, personal respect—a belief that *he* knew better than they, and the like. Mr Clarkson's letter was published in yesterday's paper; and I have read it with delight, as an admirable letter and a faithful picture of his noble mind, but I feel assured that it will serve a cause which he would not wish to serve if he were acquainted with all its bearings. But I am leaving no room for private affairs. I was in hopes of getting a frank from Lord L. but he will not be here till Tuesday and there is no large paper in the house, so I must be brief. Miss Dowling has been at Rydal, since I left home, making arrangements for the establishment of a school in Miss Fletcher's place; and I trust nothing will happen to prevent the execution of her plan. Mary approves highly of Miss Dowling (I have never seen her) and William frankly promised her his daughter as a scholar, with which promise I am as much pleased as if any body had given me a thousand pounds. D. under the discipline of a school conducted by so sensible a woman as Miss Dowling will be as fine a Girl as ever was born. She only wants steadiness and a softening in her manners, her carriage etc, etc, and habits of application which our numerous interruptions in [?] make it very difficult for so lively a girl to acquire, and how very much better for her to be placed in a good school so very near to her own home, where she will, whenever she comes, pick up some random knowledge, while we shall at the same time have an opportunity of seeing what she *does* learn and giving her other instructions which will produce far more effect occasionally given than when she was always under the Parents' Roof. Sara's letter advertising Miss D. of the vacancy at Ambleside met her at Penrith on her way to London. This was very lucky. She stayed two days at Rydal, has set her agents at work, and is now gone to London where I hope she will meet you. Poor Mrs Luff is very desirous that Miss Dowling should settle at Ambleside, but I fear she will not have much benefit from her society there, as it is too probable that Mrs Luff will not be able to bear the changeable climate of the North, and, between ourselves, I think Mrs L would be much happier if she were placed near the Farquhars[1] where there would be greater variety of company, and more of such indulgences as she has been accustomed to while under their Roof. In solitude her sorrows would come back upon her. She would want employment, having no family and she would brood upon her loss. So I think; and it is plain that her mind is so formed that she can be amused with the common goings-on of easy life, lively company—and a change of scene. But she will not, I hope, decide hastily upon any plan, and perhaps if her health will permit her to live in Westmorland, by having a little garden, teaching a little school, or such occupations she may divert her mind, and keep off gnawing regrets; and I know it will be a great comfort to her to be near our family. Dear Sara gives us a very pleasant description of the goings-on at Playford, but they must have a sad want of you, and heartily do I wish that your dear Tom and you were with them again. Pray write as soon as you can. Do not mind a long letter. I only want to know how you go on, and a dozen lines with good news [?] What a sad scrawl I have made of it! Can you decypher it? I hope so for you are very clever in that way, and have now, I trust, leisure enough. Give my kind love to Tom and believe me,

Your affect.

D. W.

Pray tell us Mrs Kitchener's cure for children's heads. A little girl of Mrs Cookson's has been under the doctor a long time and no cure can be found.

Do not fail to send Mrs Kitchener's receipt.

I guess Coleridge will *not* call upon you.

[1] Sir Robert Townsend Farquhar (1776–1830), Governor of Mauritius from 1812, was at this time on leave with his family. Mrs. Luff had returned to England in their company.

489. W. W. to DANIEL STUART

Address: Daniel Stuart Esq., 9 Upper Harley Street, London.
Postmark: 30 Mar. 1818. *Stamp*: Kendal Penny Post.
MS. British Museum.
S. K (—). *MY ii. 606, p. 817.*

Rydal Mount, March [30, 1818]

Dear Sir,

I sit down with pleasure to give the best answer I am able, respecting your Brother's intended College engagements.[1] First, for the *time* of his going to College. Supposing him respectably prepared, which can only be ascertained by some qualified person examining him, or taken upon the report of his Master, (the propriety of trusting this report will depend, entirely, on the grounds you have for deeming him a competent judge, and an honest and honourable man) if your Brother has shewn that his talents and character are such as make it probable that he would apply to the severe study of the law, it would then be best that he should be admitted forthwith, with intention of going to reside next October. But if it were more likely that he should prove unfit for the law, then college Patronage would become a most important object to him; and, in this case, I should not recommend his going to College till the age of 19, provided I could ensure a rational probability of his making a good use of the intermediate time. It is, every day, becoming more and more difficult to obtain that degree of superiority which will ensure a man a Fellowship at College. And, unless he be made a Fellow he has nothing to look for from his College, and nothing that can be an object from the University. Now the longer a youth puts off going the better he may be prepared to outstrip his Rivals. There is another important point to be considered. If he looks to make his fortune from the University, the Church will be his profession—now he cannot get into orders before 23; and, should he enter at 17 with a view to the Church, there is an awkward period between the age of 20 and a few months, when he would take his degree of B.A., and three or 4 and twenty, during which he would scarcely know what to do with himself. Indeed if one could be *sure* that he would apply, so as to render it most likely that he would get a Fellowship (which is generally obtained, if at all, after a man has been four or five years at the University, and can rarely be had after six) this would be of less consequence. But, as the thing is uncertain and difficult to procure, he who *goes* best qualified,

[1] The future career of Stuart's brother-in-law was still under consideration.

and with the most fixed habits of application, is most likely to succeed. I know not whether this long explanation is to you perfectly intelligible. The sum of my opinion is that, if I had strong reasons for believing my Son would apply to the law, I should send him to college at 17—if I thought he must be obliged to take up with the Church, I should not send him till 19, unless I knew that he was so far advanced in his Studies, as to encourage a strong persuasion in me that he would distinguish himself, even if sent at 17. As to his College, the advantages of a large College are, that he may *chuse* his Company, and is more likely to be rouzed by emulation; and the public Lectures are more likely to be good, and every thing carried forward with more spirit—the disadvantages are that, seeing so many clever men and able scholars he may be disheartened, and throw up in disgust or despair. Also much more distinction is required to obtain a fellowship among so many competitors. But it very often happens that distinguished men educated at large Colleges, when there are not fellowships for them there, are elected into *small Colleges*, which happen to be destitute of persons properly qualified. The chief advantages in a small College are the much greater likelihood of procuring rooms and in the end, college Patronage; but there is danger of getting into lounging ways from being *forced* among idle People, and the public lectures are rarely carried on with such spirit. Of the smaller Colleges, Emanuel is, at present, likely to have the greater number of fellowships, owing to the few admissions lately there; but then the reason of this is that the Tutors and Lecturers, at present, are not in repute. I have a friend, a very worthy man and great Scholar, who is one of the tutors of Peter-House, (his name, Tillbrook, a clergyman) one of the smaller Colleges. There are only two large ones, St. John's and Trinity; but that is very full. He naturally is partial to small Colleges, and to his own in particular, which, no doubt, must be well managed, else it would not be so crowded. But one knows not what to recommend; so much depends upon the disposition of the Party. But there cannot be a doubt, that the noblest field for an ambitious, industrious, properly qualified, and clever, youth is Trinity Coll. As to Trinity Hall, I know little about it, because it is a College that makes little figure in the University. It is as you say appropriated mainly to the Civil Law. Its *Lay*-fellowships must be good things. There are lay-fellowships also at Pembroke, and a few I believe at every College; but the principal thing to look at is a spirited education. With that, a man may turn himself in the world and, on this ground, I should prefer Trinity Coll.; bearing in mind that if a Student there should be surpassed by others, so far as to be excluded from a fellowship, he still might be distinguished in a way that would recommend him to be chosen for some smaller College. When you determine where, and in what year, you will send your Brother, write to the Tutor of the College, and he will give you advice as to the mode of admission, and every other particular. As to Rooms, the earlier in the year he is admitted, the better chance but the great Colleges are not able to contain one-half of their Students. In many of the smaller, there is room. I think a private Tutor an advantage, but the expense is considerable. His education will be forwarded chiefly by his own habits of application; but that sort of attainment which is most likely to shew off to advantage in the University, is far more sure of being procured at the great public Schools. I mean in classics.

I have left myself no more room. Ever yours,

W. W.

I overlooked one advantage belonging to a smaller Coll., viz., the Tutors know better how the men are conducting themselves as to morals, expenses, etc.—what company they keep and so forth; and if requested, would make report to Parents and Friends; especially, if the Party belonged to some of their own friends, they would be less scrupulous, in such a case, about speaking unfavourably, if they had reason to do so.

490. W. W. to VISCOUNT LOWTHER

Address: The Lord Viscount Lowther.
MS. Lonsdale MSS., Record Office, The Castle, Carlisle. Hitherto unpublished.

Kendal April 4th [1818]

My dear Lord L.,

Be so kind as to look over this;[1] and if you think it will not hurt the cause, I shall put it as soon as I have the honor of your answer, into immediate circulation.

A Brief advertisement,[2] alluding to B's recent Perambulations, will be added

Ever faithfully
your Lordship's
W. W.

[1] W. W. had been busy during March revising the full texts of his two Addresses (see *MW* 18, p. 36), and these were now ready to be published as the pamphlet *Two Addresses to the Freeholders of Westmorland*, signed A Freeholder, and dated by the 'Advertisement' 26 Mar. 1818. (Grosart, i. pp. 213 ff., *Prose Works*, ed. William Knight, ii. pp. 279 ff.)

[2] i.e. 'To the Reader', dated 4 Apr. 1818.

491. W. W. to THOMAS HUTTON

Address: Thomas Hutton Esq, Penrith.
Franked: Lowther. Kendal. April four 1818. *Endorsed*: Mr Wordsworth and his Education.
MS. WL.
MY ii. *607, p. 820.*

Kendal, April 4th 1818

My dear Sir,

A press of engagements put your last Letter out of my recollection for several days. In answer to your proposal in regard to the education of the Child, I have to say that I shall chearfully assist Mrs W. as far as necessary. At the same time, I would observe, that in the course of a few years that education, if conducted suitably to his connections, and to the *wishes* of my Brother and myself, must prove so expensive, that any prospects in life which I have do not justify me in contracting to supply my portion of that expense, upon the supposition that I or my heirs are not to be remunerated from the Minor's Estate when he comes of age. Whatever sums I may advance on this account I should wish a *discretionary* power, for requiring repayment of the same, if the condition of my own family should demand it, to the full extent. Therefore I cannot *covenant* to relinquish such right; nevertheless I know Mrs W. will give me credit for every possible good wish towards my Nephew and for readiness to advance my portion of what may be required to procure him a suitable education. But she must clearly see, that I cannot in justice to my Wife *and Children* bind myself and my executors to a conduct, which might raise him at their expense. I will do my duty towards him.

I am very sorry I could not get over to Penrith when at Lowther, the other day.

ever most faithfully yours
W. Wordsworth

P.S. I have no objection whatever to *covenant* for my proportion of the support of my nephew's Education, upon the condition that the money advanced for that purpose, or as much of it as I or my Executors think proper, shall stand upon the same footing in respect to the Minor's Estate, as the sums advanced by me to keep down the interest.

W. W.

492. W. W. to LORD LONSDALE

MS. Lonsdale MSS., Record Office, The Castle, Carlisle.
K (—). *MY ii.* 608, *p.* 821 (—).

Rydal Mount
April 6th 1818.

My Lord,

I have desired half a dozen Copies of a Pamphlet,[1] which but for unavoidable engagements of the Printer would have been ready for Publication many weeks ago, to be forwarded to your Lordship. May I beg the favor that you would peruse this Tract, and if you, Lord Lowther and the Col. think that it contains nothing which would prejudice the cause, it shall be put into general circulation; otherwise it may be confined to a few Friends. My object in writing this work, was to give the *Rationale* of the Question, for the consideration of the upper Ranks of Society, in language of appropriate dignity.—It shall be followed up with brief Essays, in plain and popular language illustrating the principles in detail for the understanding of the lower orders. But I have not much confidence in truth and argument, when opposed to passion, and falsehood, after these latter are in previous possession of the ground.—

Had the Correspondence[2] been published on Mr B's first appearance in the Country, I think it might have done much service—at present there is no *especial* urgency; nevertheless it should seem that the *sooner* it sees the light the better. With Lord L's approbation I have glanced at it, in a passage added to some able Comments on Mr B's first speech at Kendal, by a Friend of mine, which are about to appear.[3] I presume that Mr Wilberforce can have no objection; the other Party does not seem entitled to any consideration, whether the correspondence is to be published, or when.

You will have learned from Lord L. how things are going on in Westnd. Upon one point Lord L. and I differ most materially as to the influence of opinion, independent of that of Property upon the

[1] *Two Addresses to the Freeholders of Westmorland*, Kendal, 1818.

[2] Between Brougham and Wilberforce in 1806. See L. 467 above.

[3] De Quincey's *Close Comments on a Straggling Speech*, published at Kendal in mid April in answer to Brougham's speech of 23 Mar. attacking W. W., included (p. 6) the following passage: 'With how little ceremony Mr Brougham treats his own consciousness, when he would raise his reputation as a public man at the expense of that of Lord Lonsdale, and what especial breach of decency is involved in the attempt, will appear when certain political tamperings in Westmorland . . . shall be divulged.' (For full text of the pamphlet and discussion, see Wells, op. cit., pp. 1096–1110; Jordan, pp. 303 ff.) For De Quincey's more open reference to the same incident in 1828, see Stuart M. Tave, *New Essays by De Quincey*, 1966, p. 366.

lower order of Voters. Lord L. thinks that there are not 160 Votes in the County that will not be determined by property. How can the Blues then muster so strong; knowing as we do that we have the property of the County on our side, in the proportion of 4 probably 5 to one? Either they must far surpass us in zeal, or in skill in managing the influences of property, or some other powers must be acting on their side, to account for the strength which they possess. Is it to be supposed that Mr B. can be followed from Township to Township by hundreds and hundreds, and that the lower order of Freeholders will not participate the sentiments of this clamourous Rabble, from whom they differ in nothing but the accident of possessing a 40 shillings or 5 pound Freehold?—There are instances in which Mr B. has harangued to hundreds, and not above three or four Freeholders there; in Patterdale there was only one. Yet his words were not thrown away; if the Father was not there, two or three of his Sons were, the Mother also, probably;—these catch the infection, and uniting their forces they become too strong for the old Man. I do not say that many votes have been lost to us in this way, but to my certain knowledge some have, and the work is going on. —Mr B. tells them, that whether Freeholders or not, they must come to Appleby; for though they cannot vote, they may back and encourage their Friends.—It is not to be doubted that when the Election draws near, every attempt will be made to *intermeddle* the Lowther voters. But to this it would not be prudent publicly to advert, at least at present. Fear and popular infection will both befriend the Blues, when the day of trial draws near; but I trust that with due exertion, both may be in a considerable degree counteracted; while on the other hand the influence of property will be more actively displayed, and more feelingly perceived by those whom they are brought to bear upon, when the time comes which requires them to decide one way or the other.—It is earnestly to be desired that Col. Lowther would make his appearance among us as soon as he can.—

Mr B's Speeches, especially the Kendal ones, were much softened in the public Reports; and some of the most offensive passages wholly omitted. Your Lordship would observe that his harangue at Penrith was intended principally to excite disturbances in Cumberland.[1] Mr B. is a man of desperate Fortunes, ungovernable passions, and prepared for any mischief. He would be well content to be a party man provided he could be a Leader; but a Leader of some sort or other he will attempt to be, at any expense of the peace and

[1] Brougham had attacked Lowther influence in Cumberland during a speech at Penrith on 31 Mar.

liberties of the Country;—if the People in power are not aware of this, their want of knowledge is much to be regretted.—

I congratulate your Lordship most sincerely on the recent addition made to the family of Lowther.[1]

and with the highest respect
I have the honor to be
my Lord
your Lordship's
devoted ser[vnt]
W. Wordsworth

493. W. W. to VISCOUNT LOWTHER

Postmark: 14 Apr. 1818. *Stamp*: Kendal Penny Post.
MS. Lonsdale MSS., Record Office, The Castle, Carlisle. Hitherto unpublished.

Sat Ev. April 11th [1818]

My dear Lord Lowther,

I am happy that my Addresses are honoured with your approbation. I sent half-a-dozen to Lord Lonsdale, but I do not yet know whether they have been received.

Dispose of the Matter of the Pamphlet in whatever way you think will best serve the Cause. But through what vehicle would you present it to the world? The Carlisle Patriot has by no means sufficient circulation in West: And the new Paper cannot make its appearance for some time. This puzzles me—I submit it altogether to your decision. There is one point, which the Kendal Chronicle of [to]day boldly asserts, that neither the Freeholder (meaning me) nor any other Writer on the Lowther side, has dared to insist upon, or even discuss, viz, the interference of Peers in Elections; now this point I have met, and openly defended that practise as indispensible. On that account, I could wish, what I have written to be put into speedy circulation, if approved by Lord Lonsdale and the Col: as it has been by yourself. *Many* of the opposite party consider this position of theirs as impregnable, and rest the merits of their cause upon it.

What do you think of printing the pamphlet in the way you propose in the Courier? Be so kind as to let me know your opinion—

[1] Lady Eleanor Lowther (1792–1848), Col. Lowther's wife, eldest daughter of the 5th Earl of Harborough, had just given birth to her first child, Henry, in London. As Lord Lowther died unmarried, this boy eventually became 3rd Earl of Lonsdale.

if you approve printing in the Courier do not scruple to do so immediately, *without* further communication with me.[1]

I shall at all times be glad to hear from your Lordship. I shall not fail to write if anything important occurs. Brougham appears to be confident—from what I hear of his private Letters.[2]

I remain my dear Lord Lowther
faithfully yours,
W W—

494. W. W. to VISCOUNT LOWTHER

Address: Lord Viscount Lowther.
MS. Lonsdale MSS., Record Office, The Castle, Carlisle. Hitherto unpublished.

[*c.* 14 Apr. 1818]

My dear Lord Lowther,

As Lord Lonsdale and yourself approve of the *doctrines* and Spirit of the Addresses, I will set them afloat in their present shape in such directions as seem most likely to make them serviceable; which need not prevent their being given piecemeal according to the plan recommended by you, in the Carlisle Patriot.[3]

The notes upon Brougham's Speech, I have not seen, unless they be those from the pen of Mr De Quincey of Grasmere, which, in your hurry, you may have forgotten that we read together at Kendal,—and that a passage was interwoven by me, at that time. It related to facts.[4]

Nothing material has lately occurred in this neighbourhood. I hear from Kendal that Brougham has hurt himself in several quarters, by the violence and jacobinical character of his late Speeches in Westmorland.

Calvert[5] thinks that they will not be able to carry on the Election for want of money. I did not hear this opinion from himself, but from good authority. He is likely to know what is the state of their funds.

The delay of the new Kendal Paper,[6] is much to be regretted.

[1] The *Two Addresses* were not reprinted in the *Courier*.

[2] Probably through S. H., who comments on Brougham's letters to Clarkson, *SH* 46, p. 137.

[3] This plan was never carried out.

[4] See L. 492 above.

[5] William Calvert of Greta Bank, Keswick.

[6] The *Westmorland Gazette* was still held up for want of a suitable editor. On 14 Apr. De Quincey solicited W. W.'s support in obtaining this post. See Jordan, p. 319.

Your Lordship's intention about the allowance for the Princes[1] is very prudent. It seems impolitic in the Ministers to bring things of this sort forward, on the Eve of a general Election.

James Brougham is expected in this neighbourhood, on Monday next. I have written to Col. Lowther, urging him to come among us as soon as possible.

I have the honor to be
my dear Lord Lowther
very faithfully yours
W. Wordsworth.

Be so good as to cast your eye over the Enclosed to Mr Wilkin.[2]

495. W. W. to LORD LONSDALE

MS. Lonsdale MSS., Record Office, The Castle, Carlisle. Hitherto unpublished.

April 23rd [1818]

My Lord,

A severe inflammation in my eyes, from which they have not yet quite recovered, had prevented me from expressing the satisfaction which I felt, upon learning that my endeavours to represent the West[nd] Contest in its true light had been honored by your Lordship's approbation. A dozen more Copies[3] were sent to Charles Street,[4] which I hope have been received.

As to Mr Curwen's abstinence from the concerns of the pending Contest, I can state, that the Revd. Dr Lawson,[5] Incumbent of Heversham, wrote not long since to Mr Strickland,[6] Parson of Crosthwaite, soliciting his Vote for Mr B. and adding that Mr Curwen had made application to him. The opposition ostensibly headed

[1] On 18 Apr. the Prince Regent had sent a message to both Houses of Parliament informing them of the impending marriages of the Dukes of Clarence and Cambridge, and requesting that a suitable provision should be set aside for them. The whole question of royal allowances was thereafter a matter of controversy both inside and outside Parliament.

[2] John Wilkin (or 'Mr. Pensioner Wilkin' as he was called in the *Kendal Chronicle* for 4 Apr.) was an official from the Tax Office in London who was brought in by the Lowthers to help with their canvass and advise on Land Tax Assessments. He apparently owed several other places under Government to Lowther influence, and was perhaps a younger relative of W. W.'s predecessor as Distributor of Stamps.

[3] Of the *Two Addresses*.

[4] Lord Lonsdale's London address.

[5] The Revd. George Lawson, M.D., fellow of Trinity, Cambridge, 1791; vicar of Heversham, 1798–1844.

[6] The Revd. James Strickland, a Lowther supporter.

by Mr B. is an attempt, by the grossest falsehoods, and by appeals to plebeian envy, pride and presumption, to incite the lower ranks of society against their superiors. Whenever, therefore, men of property, like Mr Curwen, Sir Frederic Vane,[1] or Mr Dykes,[2] step out of the line of their natural connections, to give *public* countenance, as these Gentlemen have done to such proceedings, they do an injury which renders their *private* exertions, be they what they may, of comparatively little importance. Mr Curwen cannot pass himself off with persons of discernment, for other than an enemy to the good cause, to the utmost of his ability.

Mr Clarkson's Letter[3] went far beyond the worst of my apprehensions. The purchase of his Estate of Eusemere, and the manner in which your Lordship dealt with him on that occasion, for I have often heard him speak upon the subject, were no doubt the events present to his recollection when he spoke of himself as being under obligations.[4] As to the Letter no terms which I could find would be equal to express my concern that it should have been written, and my condemnation of such a writing being published under such circumstances.

The Lowther interest will suffer greatly if Lord L. has voted for the additional allowances to the Princes.[5] His Lordship intimated to me that he did not mean it, and if he has not done so, no time ought to be lost in giving the fact publicity in Westmorland.

Col. L. has been among us. He has done well, though below what I once expected. But Mr Jackson says that in the end we shall be satisfied.

With the highest respect
I have the honor to be
my Lord
your Lordship's
faithfully
W. Wordsworth.

[1] See *EY* 118, p. 266. Sir Frederick Fletcher Vane owned property near Appleby, and was thus a freeholder of Westmorland as well as Cumberland. He unsuccessfully contested Cockermouth for the Blues in this election.

[2] Joseph Dykes Ballentine Dykes (d. 1830) of Dovenby Hall, Cockermouth, who owned land near Kendal: a member of Brougham's Committee.

[3] i.e. the letter supporting Brougham, published in the *Kendal Chronicle*.

[4] Clarkson apologized in the letter for his ingratitude to Lord Lonsdale, who had purchased his house when Clarkson left the Lakes in 1804.

[5] See previous letter.

496. W. W. to LORD LONSDALE

Address: The Earl of Lonsdale, Charles Street, Berkley Square, London.
Postmark: 5 May 1818. *Stamp*: Kendal Penny Post.
MS. Lonsdale MSS., Record Office, The Castle, Carlisle. Hitherto unpublished.

Rydale Mount
May 2nd 1818

My Lord,

Permit me to recur to Mr Curwen's declaration to Sir James G.[1] that he was *forced* upon the part he has taken in the Westnd Contest although I have no new evidence to bring forth upon the subject. He must allude, I suppose, to his public appearance at the London Tavern, as a supporter of Mr B.[2] He could not be *forced* to act as he did in passing through Westd—in his way to London. I mentioned[3] his harangue in the Kitchen of the Salutation Inn at Ambleside, his interview with Mr Abbot, the other Editor of the Kendal Chron,[4] the Paper he wrote for that journal in Mr Abbot's presence, and I specified what that paper was.—It has struck me since, that I ought to have been particular as to the Evidence on which I reported these things. Mr Jackson, our Rector, is my authority for the first, (and also for the Letter which Doctor Lawson wrote to Mr Strickland,[5] that Letter having been forwarded to Mr Jackson, by Sir Daniel le Fleming). As to the offensive Letter or Paper pretending to be dated from Askham; Mr Cookson of Kendal, informed me that he being in company with several Persons, one of the Party said that he had been with Abbot who was boasting what a clever Man Mr Curwen was, that he (Abbot) had been drinking wine with Mr C. who wrote in his presence a Paper for the Kendal Chronicle etc. A few days after, Mr Cookson's Son was informed by a Printer's Lad of the Office that Mr Curwen was the author of the Letter, dated Askham; so that Mr Cookson had not the least doubt that this obnoxious Letter was the Paper, which Abbot had spoken of as written in his presence. On the 21st Febry appeared two Letters in the Chronicle, signed, *a Friend to Truth* which I wrote; and in one I animadverted with some severity on a passage of the Askham Letter, reflecting on Col. Lowther. This was replied to, but *not till the 14th of March*; a plain proof that the writer, who continued to

[1] Sir James Graham, Bart. (1753–1825), of Kirkstall, Yorks.: M.P. for Cockermouth, 1802–5 and 1807–12, and thereafter for Carlisle.

[2] J. C. Curwen had presided at the Dinner on 21 Feb.

[3] See L. 474 above.

[4] i.e. William Abbot, editor before Harrison.

[5] See previous letter.

date from Askham, was not then Resident in the North; as, from the style of his Letter, it is evident that he was much nettled by my strictures, and would, of course, have replied to them immediately had his opportunities allowed him to do so.—I have already mentioned[1] that Mr Curwen's Son, and Mr Bird, were the only Persons that accompanied Mr James Brougham when he canvassed this neighbourhood. Mr H. Curwen addressed the Kendal Mob—and, with the exception of Mr Barton,[2] I know no Person about Windermere, over whom Mr Curwen can be supposed to have influence, or with whom he is intimate, who is not against the Lowther interest. —Your Lordship will have the kindness to excuse this tedious Review of my knowledge of the Case; but some years ago Mr Curwen courted my society a good deal; and I used to see him, as a neighbour, occasionally.—He took also some pains to recommend a Brother of Mrs Wordsworth's, who had been brought up to farming, to a situation under an agricultural Friend of his, Mr Champion Dymoke,[3] which I regarded as a favor done to myself. I would therefore be hurt, had I made any assertion to his prejudice on slight grounds of evidence, or without a justifying cause.—

I believe that we are gaining ground in *many* directions—you will smile at my illustration of this, by a dialogue which took place the other day at Ambleside, between an Apothecary's Apprentice, and a Chimney-Sweeper's Boy.—*Boy*, 'What, you have little to do with elections here?'—*Apprentice*, 'We have had a good deal—how are they at Kendal?'—*Boy*, 'We *were* all Blues, but they're turning; *My Master* promised his Vote to Brougham, but he'll give it to the Lowthers—he says, he doesn't like such black-guard work!'—Mr Brougham's rambles, I am persuaded, have not done him any service, upon the whole, but the contrary.

I have the honor of your Lordship's of the 28th, with the Bill concerning the public charities.[4] I am happy to hear from your Lordship that it is likely to be treated by Parliament as it deserves. Much credit is claimed for Mr. B. for his conduct in this matter; it

[1] See L. 478 above.

[2] The Revd. W. Barton of Windermere.

[3] Lewis Dymoke (1763–1820) of Scrivelsby Court, Lincs., hereditary Grand Champion of England, a title he claimed to inherit from the Lords Marmion. In July 1814 he unsuccessfully laid claim to this ancient Barony before the House of Lords.

[4] Since the appointment of his Select Committee on the Education of the Poor in 1816, Brougham had widened his investigations into abuses in the administration of educational charities. Early in 1818 he introduced a Bill to set up a commission of inquiry into all public charities, but the powers of this commission were drastically cut down by the Lords at the end of May. He returned to the attack in September. See New, op. cit., pp. 213 ff.

will be proper, therefore, that the character of the proposed Bill should be laid open to the West^{d} Yeomen and gentry, which, when the New Kendal Paper shall come out, I will attempt to do, unless some Person better qualified undertakes it. Mr Brougham is believed to have written in the Edinburgh Review those panegyrics on Mr Lancaster's system,[1] the ignorance folly and cruelty of which were most ably exposed by Mr Southey.[2] Those articles of the Review and this Bill may go together, as settling for ever the question of Mr Brougham's incompetence to legislate on such subjects. I am ashamed of the appearance of this Letter;

ever faithfully your Lordship's
friend and serv^{nt}
W. Wordsworth

P.S.

My eyes are much better.

Your Lordship's Friends in West^{d} are glad of your declining to support the proposed Grant for the Princes. There is scarcely any part of the conduct of Government which I have found so difficult to defend (or indeed which I have been so little inclined to defend) as the grant to Prince Leopold.[3] His former situation, his Youth, and his having no child to succeed to the Crown, makes the annuity of so *large an* amount, a Thorn in the Loyalty of the Country. But Mr Brougham has here no advantage over us, for he both voted and spoke in favor of that settlement.

It is much to be regretted that Mr B. should have meddled with the Reform of Charitable Schools etc.—there are great abuses in this department; but the correction of them must be set about very differently.

[1] 'Education of the Poor', *Edinburgh Review*, Nos. xxxiii and xxxvii (Nov. 1810 and Nov. 1811). See New, op. cit., pp. 200 ff.

[2] 'Bell and Lancaster's Systems of Education', *Quarterly Review*, No. xi (Oct. 1811): republished as *The Origin, Nature, and Object of the New System of Education*, 1812.

[3] Prince Leopold of Saxe-Coburg (1790–1865), uncle of Queen Victoria and King of the Belgians from 1831, had been granted an annuity of £50,000 for life on his marriage to the Princess Charlotte, the heiress presumptive, in 1816; and he continued to draw this after his wife's death in childbirth a year later.

497. W. W. to VISCOUNT LOWTHER

MS. Lonsdale MSS., Record Office, The Castle, Carlisle. Hitherto unpublished.

May 6th 1818

My dear Lord Lowther,

I cannot forbear writing to you upon the Conduct of the Carlisle Patriot. Every Friend of the Lowthers in the neighbourhood, is indignant at the last number. Mr Clarkson's Letter at full length![1] And a flaming account of the dinner of Mr Curwen's Friends![2] with only two short Articles tending to support the Lowther interest!

I know not what power Lord Lonsdale, and your Lordship and the Col: have over this Paper,[3] and therefore I cannot presume to advise what ought to be done, but I am sure you will not take it ill when I express a strong apprehension that there is double-dealing in the management of this Journal; at all events it is obvious that the Editor cannot be heartily in our cause. Do think about this and keep your eye upon the Contents of the Paper.

My Addresses[4] were forwarded to the Editor immediately upon my being acquainted with your wish that they should be published piece-meal but he has taken no notice of them.

An answer, which I wrote to a Portion of the Yeoman's address has been published.[5] I will forward a copy as soon as I can procure one.

[1] Clarkson's letter in support of Brougham was reprinted in the *Patriot* for 2 May at the request of 'Civis' who wrote in defence of Clarkson's intervention.

[2] This was in the *Carlisle Journal* for 2 May, not the *Patriot*.

[3] Lord Lonsdale and Lord Lowther were keeping an eye on the policy of the *Patriot* at this time. (See Aspinall, *Politics and the Press*, p. 361.) In March, T. G. Street of the *Courier* had agreed to contribute a weekly letter upholding Lowther politics.

[4] i.e. W. W.'s *Two Addresses*. Lord Lowther had proposed they should be reprinted in the *Patriot*.

[5] Almost certainly a handbill. When he wrote to the newspapers, W. W. usually supplied the Lowthers with full details so that they could look up the items for themselves; but on the assumption that this 'Answer' is identical with the 'Paper' mentioned in the next letter, it must have been written and published between 3 and 6 May, just when the local papers (including the *Carlisle Patriot*) were most hostile, and when a contribution from W. W. would be least acceptable. No such item can be identified in any of the papers. On the other hand, a handbill entitled *DECEPTION EXPOSED; Or, AN Antidote for the Poison of the Westmorland Yeoman's Address*, by ANTI-JANUS, was actually in circulation during the first week of May, according to the *Kendal Chronicle* for the 16th, and this is much more likely to be the 'Answer' referred to here. Furthermore, *DECEPTION EXPOSED* was reprinted as soon as possible—in two parts, on 23 May and 6 June—in the new Lowther paper, the *Westmorland Gazette*, which is precisely what one would expect if W. W. *was* the author. The Yeoman's *Address*, or to give it its full title, *AN ADDRESS TO THE YEOMANRY of the Counties of Westmorland & Cumberland, on the*

I am glad to hear so good account as is given in your last; everything I gather from other quarters concurs with it.

I have the honor to be
my dear Lord Lowther
ever faithfully yours
W Wordsworth

We were all gratified with your not voting for the Princes' grants.

498. W. W. to LORD LONSDALE

Address: The Earl of Lonsdale, Charles Street, Berkley Square, London.
Postmark: 11 May 1818. *Stamp*: Kendal Penny Post.
MS. Lonsdale MSS., Record Office, The Castle, Carlisle. Hitherto unpublished.

[*c.* 11 May 1818]

My Lord,

My sincere thanks are due to your Lordship; but considerations respecting time and circumstance, which add incalculably to the obligation, prevent me from even wishing to be appointed to the office in question. No hope of advantage to myself could tempt me to commit your Lordship's interests in the North, and to be an occasion of injuring a cause which I would do my utmost to support. There would be no limits to the clamour, if such a junction,[1] however reasonable in itself, should be made in favor of any of your friends at this crisis. For myself I have the honor of being distinguished by the especial hatred of the enemy;[2] and obloquy is showered upon me

Present State of THEIR REPRESENTATION IN PARLIAMENT, had first appeared in London and Kendal in the previous January (see G. H. Healey, *The Cornell Wordsworth Collection*, 1957, nos. 664 and 665), when the authorship was commonly attributed to Brougham (see *MW* 19, p. 39); and it was republished in the *Kendal Chronicle* for 9 May. In his *Two Addresses* W. W. had already considered the general arguments advanced by the Yeoman, but he had not dealt specifically with that 'portion' of the *Address* which attacked the Militia Laws, the taxation system, and the National Debt, and *DECEPTION EXPOSED* is concerned exactly with these matters. There is nothing in the style or contents of the handbill that would preclude W. W.'s authorship, and much that positively suggests it. For light on the author's choice of the pseudonym 'Anti-Janus', see perhaps *The Excursion*, ii. ll. 249–53 (*PW* v, p. 51).

[1] i.e. of his own territory as Distributor of Stamps with that of Mr. Ramshay.

[2] The authorship of the *Two Addresses* and of *Close Comments* was soon detected, and both W. W. and De Quincey were attacked in the *Kendal Chronicle* during April and May. W. W. may have in mind here a letter signed 'A Freeholder & Churchman' which appeared on 25 Apr. This described both pamphlets as 'hullets' —i.e. owlets—'being all feathers with very little flesh', and referred to W. W. as 'Bombastes Furioso' and De Quincey as 'an angry Giant' given to 'midnight rambles'. For further comment on W. W.'s electioneering, see Hazlitt, 'Mr Wordsworth & the Westmorland Election', *Examiner*, 5 July 1818 (*Works*, ed. P. P. Howe, 21 vols., 1930–4, xix, p. 213); and for Thomas

from the Rabble of all Quarters; though I have proceeded with as much caution as the duties I had to perform would allow.—

I have a strong reason, (an official one) for thinking that Mr Wm Spenser[1] was in Town in the 26th April last. As far as concerns the collection of the Revenue, with less trouble and less expense, the *re*union of the Districts is desirable; nor could, I think, the Commissioners have the slightest objection on that account. In things of this kind, are they not governed chiefly by the wishes of the Treasury? I have always understood so.—Could this arrangement have been made before the disturbance in West^{d} broke out, I should have been very thankful; I demurred as soon as the affair became serious; and it was under that impression I begged, on my return to West^{d}, that the business might be suspended; and not from apprehension that the Board of Stamps would be averse to the measure, at least to a degree, which by a hint from the superior Power might not easily have been got over. If preparation could be made privately for the fulfilment of your Lordship's kind intentions at a more favourable season this is all which the sense of what I owe to your interests and the welfare of my country, will allow me to desire.—

My information respecting the hopes of our opponents concurs with that your last Letter gives, but I know that Mr B. writes very confidently to a Friend;[2] his expressions being such as if he were *quite sure* of his Election; and the Person to whom he writes believes that this is neither policy nor mere boasting, but that he is sincere.—

The Editor of the Carlisle Patriot has disgusted our Friends in this neighbourhood by his last Number.[3] His conduct does not easily admit of favourable explanation. I have written to Lord Lowther on the subject.

I enclose a Paper which I wrote last week[4]—it will shew what falsehoods we have to contend with. Some of the facts were supplied by Mr Wilkin.[5]

Love Peacock's comments to Shelley, Peacock's *Works*, ed. H. F. B. Brett-Smith and C. E. Jones, 10 vols., 1924–34, viii, p. 199. Keats's reaction was equally irate when he paid his only visit to Rydal Mount towards the end of June and found W. W. away at the Poll. See Rollins, i, pp. 299–301.

[1] Of the Stamp Office.

[2] i.e. Thomas Clarkson. See *SH* 46, p. 137.

[3] W. W. must mean the last number but one, that of 2 May, which had reprinted Clarkson's letter in support of Brougham.

[4] Probably the handbill *DECEPTION EXPOSED* apparently referred to in the previous letter.

[5] See L. 494 above. As an expert on taxation, Wilkin would have been able to supply information about the horse tax and the property tax which Anti-Janus set out to justify in his handbill.

Your last account of Lady Mary was very favorable—I hope she continues to go on well.

I have the honor to remain very gratefully
your Lordship's Friend and Servant
W W—

The New Kendal Paper[1] will appear we hope on the 23rd Inst^{nt}

499. W. W. to ROBERT LUMB

Address: R. Lumb Esqre, Lowther.
Stamp: Kendal Penny Post. *Endorsed*: May 12 1818, Mr Wordsworth.
MS. Lonsdale MSS., Record Office, The Castle, Carlisle. Hitherto unpublished.

Rydal May 12 [1818]

Dear Sir,

The Widow of the poor man who along with his son was killed in the Quarry at Hartsop,[2] has just called upon me—and as I learned by a note from Dr Satterthwaite that he had requested you to put down Lord Lonsdale's name for the Sum of £20 to the Subscription, I have myself judged it proper to do this—thinking it desirable that his Lordship's benevolent intention should be made known in this neighbourhood as soon as possible. I have also put down £2–2 under the signature of a Clergyman, meaning Dr Satterthwaite—and acting according to instructions rec^{d} some time ago from him—so that you need not add any thing to this on his account. I did not pay the money, in either case.

With best wishes, I am Sir
very truly yours
Wm Wordsworth

500. W. W. to LORD LONSDALE

MS. Lonsdale MSS., Record Office, The Castle, Carlisle. Hitherto unpublished.

Rydale Mount
4th June 1818

My Lord,

There is certainly a very general disposition in those parts of West^{d} which I am best acquainted with to overawe the Freeholders

[1] The *Westmorland Gazette*.

[2] In Patterdale. On 11 Apr. a man named Leck and his son had been killed by a fall of slate. See Jordan, p. 321.

in the Lowther interest by boasts of the manner in which they will be handled by the immense members of their adversaries who will repair to Appleby. I mentioned to your Lordship some time since that Mr B. invited his audiences on many occasions, whether Freeholders, or not, to attend at the Election. This has not been without effect; our enemies are emboldened, and in this neighbourhood the Dalesmen friendly to your Lordship and the present members are not a little intimidated. Yesterday our Parish Clerk stopped me to mention that he had been that day an extensive round, and he found this generally to be the case. Mr Thompson, Minister of Patterdale, on Monday last told me the same. So that with respect to this quarter it cannot be doubted. I have not scrupled to say, that Soldiers will be placed, where the Law allows, to keep order; and I have done all in my power to remove the apprehension, and to let the Enemy know that they will not be able to behave as they did at Kendal; and that order *must* and *will* be kept. I have not *written* anything upon the subject, as I had not authority to do so; but certainly no pains ought to be spared to set the minds of our Friends at rest on this point.

Mr Jackson, our Rector, I am sorry to say is very much indisposed; so that he can do nothing.

The appointment of Mr Garnett to the Post Office at Penrith, as I learned when over there, last Thursday, has given very general satisfaction.—

Mr A. Harrison[1] cannot see the slightest ground for doubting that the issue will be as we wish; nor does Mr Matthew Atkinson,[2] whom I met by chance at Pooley; but certainly, though for what cause I do not know, indifferent Persons for the most part seem to think that we shall be beaten.[3] I have the honor to be

My Lord
Your Lordship's
Most faithfully
W. Wordsworth.

[1] Anthony Harrison, the Penrith solicitor.

[2] A notable Lowther supporter from Appleby.

[3] 'I have a desponding Letter from Mr Wordsworth. He says that they are endeavouring to keep up the Fears of the People in his Neighbourhood . . .' (Lord Lonsdale to Lord Lowther, 8 June—*Lonsdale MSS.*). This was apparently W. W.'s last letter before the Poll, 30 June—3 July, at which the Lowther brothers were triumphantly returned with 1211 and 1157 votes respectively, to Brougham's 889. W. W. was present at Appleby; but he did not vote though entitled to do so.

501. W. W. to VISCOUNT LOWTHER

MS. Lonsdale MSS., Record Office, The Castle, Carlisle. Hitherto unpublished.

Rydal Mount
18th July [1818]

My dear Lord Lowther,

Not having returned home till yesterday, I have been unable to reply earlier to your obliging communication of the 10th Inst.

For numerous and obvious reasons we cannot expect that the ferment of the Westnd Election will die away like that of a large City such as Westminster or even Liverpool.[1] If the Magistrates cannot contrive to organize a strong civil power that can be depended upon, of which there seems to be no prospect, a military force will be necessary in Kendal till the ensuing winter is passed.[2]—The populace vow vengeance against all who have been distinguished as opponents of the Blues, and, what is still worse, they are encouraged by several of their superiors.—Mr Harrison, the covert Conductor of the Kendal Chronicle, informed me the other day, that he had incurred the displeasure of some leading Zealots, by a paragraph inserted last week, in which the Magistrates were commended for calling in the Military to quell the late riot; and in which violence and disorder were reprobated.[3] I agree with you entirely as to the propriety of conciliatory measures for the future;[4] but I confess that I am at present utterly unable to recommend any course of parliamentary conduct which would appease, much less satisfy the different descriptions of Dissenters who have so much influence in Kendal. Oppose jobs, and lavish expenditure, and be as careful of the public purse as the carrying on of affairs will allow—this is a *duty* of a member of parliament, and with respect to the people of Westnd and of Kendal in particular, who are frugal and economical, it would be *politic*. Beyond this, and that degree of attention which I am sure you would bestow upon any suggestions from them respecting their interests and concerns, I see nothing at present which I can point out to your consideration. But I shall inquire and if I learn anything you shall be sure to know it.—It need scarcely be said how desirable it is that you and the Col: should be personally known in the

[1] Brougham had stood unsuccessfully for Liverpool in the General Election of 1812, and had tried to intervene at Westminster two years later.

[2] On 4 July, the day following the close of the Poll at Appleby, there had been riots in Kendal and troops were called in to restore order.

[3] See editorial for 11 July.

[4] 'This contest I hope being concluded—our next consideration should be to soothe the troubled tempers of our opponents', Lord Lowther had written on the 10th (*WL MSS.*).

County as extensively as your engagements will allow,—especially among the Yeomanry. I have not the *least doubt* that the enemy will return to the charge, on the first opportunity, if they can *raise money*. Since I left Appleby I have seen a good deal of different parts of the County, and every thing confirms me in this belief. But we need not be in the least discouraged—though it is any thing but pleasant to look forward to the expense and trouble of a 2nd contest.[1] We are *much* stronger, I am sure, than *before* the Election; many who *voted* for you with leanings the other way have been warned by the election and are become zealous Partizans, and Numbers have had their opinion of Brougham much lowered.—Nevertheless it seems indispensible, that the enemy should be met in their avowed intentions of purchasing and creating new freeholds.[2] But this must be done with the utmost care that no improper persons be accommodated or advized to purchase.—This subject is pressing and appears to be worthy of most serious consideration—but as I shall look for the pleasure of seeing you in West^nd^ erelong, I shall defer till that time anything that may have struck me upon this, and other parts of this interesting business.

Believe me my dear Lord Lowther
very faithfully yours
W Wordsworth

502. W. W. to JOHN MONKHOUSE

Address: Mr. Monkhouse, Stow, Hay, Brecon.
Stamp: Kendal Penny Post.
MS. WL. Hitherto unpublished.

Rydale Mount
July 23rd 1818

My dear Sir,

Understanding by a letter just received from S.H. that you are under some embarrassment in respect to a promise given that (on the request of some friends) you would indeavour to procure them

[1] At the close of the Poll, Brougham had announced his intention of forming an Association to secure 'the Independence of Westmorland', and of contesting every future election till this aim had been accomplished.

[2] Both parties now tried to strengthen their position by increasing the number of freeholds and distributing them among their firmest supporters. A freehold might become available either by purchase, or by the process known as 'enfranchisement', by which a customary tenancy might, with the consent of the landlord, be turned into a freehold. The Broughamites had been particularly incensed by the suspension of the Land Tax Assessments during the election, and claimed that this had lost them many votes.

permission to shoot on Lord L's Manors about Shap, I write to say that A. Harrison mentioned to me, when I saw him at Lowther some time since, that you had applied to him, with this view.—He seemed shy about meddling with the business in which I thought he was right. I ventured to tell him so, on which he said he would not interfere. My reason for giving such an opinion was partly founded on the general delicacy of the subject, and still more, on a consideration which you will appreciate and can mention to your Friends as a sufficient excuse; *viz.* the reluctance which one could not but feel in applying for favours at the time of the Election—when applications were so numerous, and when it might seem as if one was setting a price upon one's services. Independent of this consideration, I do not see how one could ask the permission required, unless one were acquainted with the general Rules adopted in such cases, and knew beforehand that such indulgencies were not universally granted—a particular of which both A.H. and myself were ignorant. It is now too late to obtain this information for your friends purpose; so that I can only express regret at our inability to fulfill your wishes. Lord Lonsdale, and his Sons, are all in London at this time.

I am glad to hear favorable accounts of your farm. We are all well—and unite in best love—I shall leave the rest of the Sheet for Mrs W.—My sister is at Kendal—

ever very sincerely yours
W. Wordsworth

503. W. W. to LORD LONSDALE

MS. Lonsdale MSS., Record Office, The Castle, Carlisle.
K (—). *MY ii. 601, p. 805* (—).

[*c.* 3 Aug. 1818]

My Lord,

I am much concerned that Lady Mary's health is not sufficiently reestablished to allow of her visiting the North—and earnestly hope that her recovery will continue to be progressive. I have communicated your Lordship's invitation to the Gentlemen of this neighbourhood[1]—none of them are likely to avail themselves of it before the 8th Inst^{nt}, for different reasons;—they all seemed much gratified by the mark of attention; particulars I shall mention when I have the honor of seeing your Lordship; at present I am in suspense,

[1] This invitation to Lowther Castle was conveyed in a letter to W. W. on 28 July (*WL MSS.*).

expecting Sir George and Lady Beaumont, who have engaged to stop two or three days with us in their way to Keswick; they were to leave Coleorton at the beginning of this month.—If it be in my power, I shall get over to Lowther before the 8th—Lord Lowther is to be at Kendal on the 6th to dine with the gentlemen educated at Cambridge.[1] I shall meet him there if possible, and proceed to Lowther on the 7th.—I wish much for your Lordship's opinion as to the propriety of precautionary measures, in augmenting the number of trust-worthy Freeholders—an offer has been made to me of an Estate[2] which would divide into *twelve* small freeholds; and with your Lordship's sanction I would purchase it, being able to redeem on as many persons, Gentlemen, my friends and relations, who could be depended upon. If it be found that your adversaries adopt the plan of encreasing the number in their interest, it will be necessary to keep pace with them; and I do not think that the matter can be safely left to casualties and the mere inclinations of your Lordship's friends, and those of your family; though, I find, that the wish, among such, to become freeholders is very general.—

The subscription has descended so low, I am told, as 1s. 6d. from servant Maids. Their advertisement shews that they depend much upon the folly of the fair sex.[3]

The Editorship of the new Kendal Paper has passed into the hands of a most able man;[4] one of my particular Friends: but whether he is fit, (I mean on the score of punctuality) for such a service, remains to be proved. *His* attainments and abilities are infinitely above such a situation.

Hoping for the pleasure of seeing you speedily

I have the honor to be

my Lord
your Lordship's faithfully
Wm Wordsworth

[1] This Dinner was reported in the *Westmorland Gazette* for 8 Aug.

[2] The estate of Hackett in Langdale. See L. 524 below.

[3] The *Kendal Chronicle* for 25 July had carried a notice appealing for subscriptions to defray Brougham's election expenses. 'The LADIES having already taken the lead in the Subscription, it is earnestly hoped, that the same liberality will be shown by those Female Friends to the Independent Cause, who may not have been apprized of the exertions of their fair Country women.'

[4] The first editor of the *Westmorland Gazette*, who was brought up from London, quickly proved unsatisfactory, and De Quincey was appointed in his place in July, probably on W. W.'s recommendation. He remained editor until Nov. 1819. See [Charles Pollitt], *De Quincey's Editorship of the Westmorland Gazette*, Kendal, 1890. W. W. continued to keep a close watch on the policy of the paper, and his fears about De Quincey's competence as an editor were, in the event, only too well founded.

504. W. W. to LORD LONSDALE

MS. Lonsdale MSS., Record Office, The Castle, Carlisle. Hitherto unpublished.

Greata Bank
near Keswick
August 23rd 1818

My Lord,

May I beg your Lordship would be so kind as to let me know whether it would suit you that I should go over to Lowther, Thursday next.—I am staying a few days here;[1] on Tuesday and Wednesday, if the weather permit, I go with Sir George Beaumont to Wastdale.—He is looking very well, and Lady B. is considerably improved. I have taken the liberty of proposing to Mr Southey to accompany me to Lowther, on Thursday,—which he would willingly have done, but he expects a Friend at that time. Mr Wilberforce is expected at Rydale on Tuesday[2]—his servants are arrived. We had a strange account yesterday from Ambleside; that one of the young Ladies of Calgarth had eloped with the Butler—

With respectful regards to Lady Lonsdale
I have the honor to be
My Lord
Your Lordship's
most faithfully
Wm Wordsworth

My address
Greata Bank
Keswick

505. D. W. to MR. WHITE[3]

Address: Mr White, Stamp Office, Whitehaven.
Franked: Wm Wilberforce. *Stamp*: Kendal Penny Post. *Endorsed*: Ambleside Septr seventh W. W.
MS. Cornell. Hitherto unpublished.

Rydal Mount, 4th September 1818

Sir,

I know you will excuse the liberty I am going to take in requesting that you will take the trouble to inquire at the Coach office at

[1] With William Calvert.

[2] Wilberforce and his family arrived at Rydal for a holiday on 25 Aug. and stayed until 15 Oct. See L. 506 below; and R. I. and S. Wilberforce, *The Life of William Wilberforce*, 5 vols., 1838, iv, pp. 388–97.

[3] Sub-distributor of Stamps at Whitehaven.

Whitehaven if an Umbrella is lying there, which was left at the Top of the Coach on Monday morning, by a little Boy who got on to the Coach at Rydal and went as far as Wytheburn, and when he dismounted forgot his Umbrella. If the Umbrella is found, pray desire that it may be brought by the Coach, directed for Wm Wilberforce Esqre,[1] Rydal, near Ambleside. If you hear nothing of it you need not trouble yourself to write.

I am, Sir,
Yours respectfully
Dorothy Wordsworth

turn over[2]

The Umbrella was a Gingham One with a black handle with an Eagle and a Motto under the Eagle carved on the handle—it had a contrivance of a Spring fastened on the handle and a hook answering to it in the [?hasp] by which the Umbrella opens, this Spring was similar to the common One which keeps Umbrellas open but its use was to keep this Umbrella shut when the Umbrella was closed.

506. D. W. to CATHERINE CLARKSON

Address: Mrs Clarkson, Playford Hall, Ipswich.
Franked: Ambleside, Sept. twenty, 1818, Wm Wilberforce. *Stamp*: Kendal Penny Post.
MS. British Museum.
MY ii. 609, p. 822.

Sept. 18, 1818.

My dear Friend,

By a note from Mrs Coleridge we heard of you yesterday; and of your having been engaged in the trying office of nursing your good Father during a dangerous illness; I am thankful with and for you that he has recovered and you have my earnest wishes that it may please God to prolong his life for many years to come, in that happy state in which I know him,—though in times suffering in body, yet not grievously—and always blessed with chearful spirits which made him enjoy the Happiness spread around him, yet ever looking forward to another state of being. I never think of your dear Father

[1] See previous letter.
[2] The description which follows is in another hand.

without sentiments of love and reverence. I saw him first at Eusmere, but did not then perceive what he was. To know him perfectly he should be seen at home, with his Family and long established connections around him. Do not think, my dearest Friend, that I only write to you now because I have chanced to hear of your Father's illness—I certainly should have written this very day. So far, last Monday—It is now Friday, therefore alter the word 'written' for 'begun to write'. How I was prevented from going on I do not recollect; ever since, however, we have been engaged in some way. But indeed, my dear Friend, I am hurt when I review the many months which have passed since we have had any communication with each other. It is like wilfully wasting means of comfort and happiness and of social intercourse of that best kind where true friendship and true love exist. At our time of life why be guilty of this folly? Old Friends must needs be diminishing year by year and new ones cannot now become like the old. We may value, esteem, admire them, but something is still wanting. To what does all this tend? You may well call it prosing, the truth, however, is that I want to make an *effectual* resolve never again to be so foolish, and to induce you to do the like. We talk of engagements, and of business—of domestic employments, and out of doors pleasures; but we all know very well that the fault is in ourselves.

You wrote to me last—this I know but *when* I cannot say, only it was some time before the West[d] Election, and that was three months ago. I really think that our Party have carried themselves with moderation on their triumph, and it may be hoped that private enmities are subsiding; though indeed they were very bitter in some instances at Kendal and even at Grasmere—as to us Rydal people some Friends we have gained—for instance the Norths who I believe formerly never looked upon us with a friendly eye give us always a cordial greeting—and Mrs North during the whole of the Election sent her own Son to me every day with the earliest intelligence of the state of the Poll. All the rest of the family except Dorothy, were at Appleby. As I say we gained some new Friends and I do not think we have lost any of our old ones—at least we have had no sparring and have met one another at all times with 'accustomed cordiality'. A few weeks ago Lord Lowther spent three days with us and my sister and I liked him much. He has very good sense and was pleasant and chearful in a quiet way. He is certainly very discerning in the characters of men and seems to have no *bitterness* in his judgments. This contest must have been of infinite use to him. If he did not know it before he must now perceive that much will be and is already required of him, and that rank and great professions must be upheld by personal character and a judicious attention to the interests of the people with whom he is connected, and indeed he seems disposed to give his mind to the acquirement of knowledge, especially in connection with these two Counties. Col[l] Lowther and his wife, Lady Ellinor, called on Tuesday. He is a fine brave Fellow and has seen much of active service abroad. He is painfully shy. The first time he spoke to Mary and me he seemed quite daunted—like a Rustic from one of our mountain vales, but on Tuesday we thought that he had gained courage during the late struggle for his shyness seemed to be much worn off. The Wilberforces[1] have been at Rydal rather more than three weeks and are delighted with the country. Their houses (for they have two) are at the bottom of the hill by the road-side, just opposite to the road turning up to Lady Fleming's house and ours. But these two houses (though we have borrowed a press-bed which is placed in a parlour) are not sufficient for their needs. They have no less than 5 beds at different houses in the village. The family amounted to 19 when they first came, but three are gone—two schoolboys and a Secretary. The arrangements were first begun by Letters between Mr W. and my Brother—but the business was soon given up by William to me and innumerable were the Letters which passed between me and Mr Wilberforce,[2] and no little contrivance was required to get together Beds for so many, the cottagers, though they had rooms, not having beds of their own. First of all I had to receive 7 servants (William and Mary were at Keswick at the time) and on their arrival I was a little out of heart. With 7 servants came 5 horses—and there was no provender for them—and the Inns at Ambleside could not take them in—and packages and servants upon a wet and dirty day seemed at once to fill the small rooms—and when I said 'the Family will I fear be sadly crammed!' I assure you I was not encouraged to dissipate my fears—'Aye, if you saw our house! the first floor would far more than hold both these two houses.' Add to this, the old Cook's observation upon my answering to one of her questions 'such and such things must be sent for to Ambleside', 'Our men

[1] Several of Wilberforce's six children, who are incidentally mentioned below, pursued notable careers in later life when the Oxford Movement was at its height. William (1798–1879), Robert Isaac (1802–57), Archdeacon of the East Riding and a distinguished theologian, and Henry William (1807–73), were all converted to Roman Catholicism: Samuel (1805–73) became Bishop of Oxford and afterwards of Winchester. Wilberforce's two daughters Barbara and Elizabeth both predeceased him.

[2] Two of these letters, dated 1 July and 10 Aug. 1818, are among the *WL MSS.*

don't like going errands, they are not used to it'—and her exclamation 'what an inconvenient place!' when she found they could not get 'a drop of Beer' nearer than Ambleside—besides objections of the housemaid and kitchen maid to sleep upon a Mattress, and you will not wonder I was rather afraid, that our good Friends might find themselves not a little uncomfortable on their arrival,—but I assure you it was a pleasing contrast when they *did* come, all joy, animation and thankfulness. The rooms were larger than they expected—and so *many* sitting rooms it was quite delightful, and as to the garden—the situation—everything was to their minds. I desired the servants to send for me when the Family came. I found all at dinner except Mr W. and his two youngest sons who were not come. Mrs W. looked very interesting, for she was full of delight and talked as fast as any of the young ones—but I must say that she has never since appeared to me to such advantage. Yet I like her very well—admire her goodness and patience and meekness—but that slowness and whininess of manner—tending to self-righteousness, I do not like. Not a particle of this was visible that first day when they were all rejoicing over their dinner of Mountain mutton and Westmorland Beef—and each telling,—and all at once—his or her separate feelings. Then came Mr Wilberforce himself and all ran to meet him—*I* must go to—and then indeed I was much affected, seeing his feeble body, which seemed to me completely worn out. This was the more affecting as I perceived at the same time that his mind was as lively as ever. Such were my first impressions. I soon however discovered with great satisfaction that he has yet no small share of strength; and it now seems to me that he *may* live many years.

The two daughters are very sweet Girls—remarkably modest and unaffected—lively, animated and industrious, in short just what well-educated girls ought to be. The weather has not been steadily fine, but they do not mind a few showers, and we have had many most delightful days, which they have made full use of—all except Mr W. who seems to have far too much to do.

We see each other very often—but have never eaten a meal together till yesterday, when my Br. dined with Mr W. and all came up to tea with us. The evening passed very pleasantly. Mr. Fleming of Rayrigg and his son were of the party. Thomas Monkhouse is with us, and we hope he will not be in a hurry to go away; for he is always happy at Rydal. He has brought a friend, Captain *Sertorius*,[1]—how he came by that name I know not. He is a natural son of

[1] Capt. Sertorius is mentioned from time to time in *MW* and *SH*, but nothing more is known about him than the details given here.

George Rose, and through his interest, I suppose, was made post Captain at an early age. He is a pleasant, brave Fellow, and has seen much hard service. Trade goes on as it *should* do and T. M. seems now to have decided that it is better not to give it up, and I cannot but think he does wisely. He is in no danger of being so wedded to gain as to shut out good affections. It is above three weeks since Joanna left us to go to Hindwell; but we have not yet heard from her. Perhaps she is waiting to tell us of Mrs H's confinement, but this is not well; for we have been anxious to hear of Joanna as the weather was damp when she left us, and not favourable for a rheumatic person. Poor thing! her health is sadly broken. We do not much expect Sara this winter—at least Miss Dowling told us she intended to spend the winter in Wales, but she has said nothing of it to us. It is now, I believe, six weeks since we heard from her. She was then well and in good spirits. We have had the most delightful summer ever remembered—weeks of uninterrupted sunshine, genial showers, again weeks of sunshine. Our fruits have ripened and the fields have been for ever green. Strange this may sound to you; but so it was. In May and a part of June the drought was excessive, but the abundant dews I suppose prevented the parching of the pastures, and that you know is the time when the fern springs and that is always green in summer. We never had such an abundant supply of vegetables in our garden, while from all other parts of England we hear of the scarcity. I am sure that you will be pleased to hear that we are, so far, highly delighted with Miss Dowling's school. Dorothy is perfectly happy, and we have no doubt that she will greatly improve. No hour of her day is unemployed. She was at home last Sunday; and on account of her Cousin Monkhouse is to come again next Sunday. We do not go to see *her* finding that, when we have done so, she has been disturbed by the expectation of our going again, and has been on the watch for us from the top of the hill where Miss D.'s house stands. She grows much but will not, I think, reach her mother's height. She will soon be taller than I am. William had a sad illness in spring; but is now well and *for him* strong. John is a very fine-looking Boy. All strangers are taken with him from his ingenuous countenance, and the mixture of hardness and modesty in his deportment and manners. And now, my dearest Friend, it is time that I inquire after you all. How is Mr Clarkson? and where is Tom? I hope that by this time he has not only wholly regained his health and strength but cast off the traces from his Countenance of that dismal disease. Tell us that you both think about coming to see us and, further, that you talk of the time when, and the means how.

This is a sad scrawl, I have been afraid of missing the post and now they come for my letter—God bless you, my dearest Friend,

Ever yours
D. W.

507. W. W. to VISCOUNT LOWTHER

MS. Lonsdale MSS., Record Office, The Castle, Carlisle. Hitherto unpublished.

Rydale Mount
Sept^br 22nd 1818

My dear Lord Lowther,

Your two interesting Letters, the Pamphlet,[1] and Sun and Chronicle, have been duly received, for which I heartily thank you. The Pamphlet I have carefully read; it is precisely in the same spirit as all the other performances of its Author. As the Kendal Chronicle has not *yet* made any extracts from it relating to the Lowther family, it seemed best not to notice it in the Gazette,[2] for it has always appeared to me bad policy to extend the circulation of injurious remarks, merely because one can expose their injustice; or to put objections in the way of people who might otherwise never have heard of them, because one is provided with sufficient answers. —I find that moderate Persons among my South-country Acquaintance regard the omission of Brougham's name among the honorary Comm^rs[3] as a proof of the indisposition of people in power to enter heartily into the inquiry. Should it appear that this opinion is prevalent among respectable persons in Cum^nd and West^nd it might be well to publish in the Gazette or elsewhere, a few remarks in opposition to Brougham's claims to that distinction. If anything on this subject strikes you be so good as to mention it.—

The Morning Chronicle shews that the Party are very angry; and that you have done right in no longer deferring to act upon the

[1] *A Letter to Sir Samuel Romilly upon the Abuse of Charities*, 1818 (*Speeches*, iii, pp. 17 ff.), in which Brougham described abuses in charities unconnected with education, and in educational charities which had special visitors. The House of Lords had expressly excluded both these categories from the terms of his commission of inquiry (see L. 496 above).

[2] De Quincey noticed Brougham's pamphlet in an editorial on 10 Oct., after extracts had appeared in the *Kendal Chronicle* for 26 Sept.

[3] The Government had refused to accept Brougham's offer to act as an honorary commissioner without pay.

offensive.[1] This ought to be followed up; especially when Parliament meets. Brougham has puffed up his Westnd supporters with the expectation that he will break out at that time in great force; and that he will be irresistible upon the appointment and management of the '*Bludgeon* Men' at the Election.[2] If you do not, yourself, mean to observe upon Brougham's allusion to the St Bees School[3] through some public channel, I should like to be provided with such facts as Lord Lonsdale and you might wish to have brought forward in refutation of his slanders; and also in regard to the Lowther foundation.—

I find that the Appleby Speeches have been very serviceable in this neighbourhood. John Green saluted me in great triumph—'Plenty of matter', said he, 'and all to the purpose'.—Practise in Committees, and you will soon be orator enough for one in your situation.

I much wish to have a brush at Brougham either in the Gazette or one of the London Papers; but I want more facts; and the most favorable time is not yet come.—I will forward the Chronicle to Southey. I see regularly no London Papers but the Observer[4] and the Courier.

I remain, my dear Lord Lowther,
ever faithfully yours
Wm Wordsworth

[1] At a public dinner given in Appleby on 10 Sept. to celebrate the Lowther victory, Lord Lowther attacked Lord Thanet for financing Brougham's campaign, and for abusing his position as High Sheriff by packing the Grand Jury at the recent Assizes with 'Blues'. On 19 Sept. the *Morning Chronicle*, the most influential of the Opposition papers, went to Lord Thanet's defence, but the charges were revived in the *Courier* for the 21st and *Westmorland Gazette* for the 26th.

[2] i.e. the army of 'special constables' enlisted by the Lowthers to keep order at the Poll. According to the Broughamites, they were there to browbeat the freeholders.

[3] In his pamphlet Brougham dealt with the conduct of the charity of St. Bees College, of which Lord Lonsdale was a benefactor, and accused the Trustees of serious irregularities. See L. 510 below.

[4] Founded 1791: at this time a Treasury paper.

508. W. W. to LORD LONSDALE

MS. Lonsdale MSS., Record Office, The Castle, Carlisle. Hitherto unpublished.

Rydale Mount
[*c.* 25] Sept[br] 1818

My Lord,

Mr Scambler, our Apothecary, reports to me that the Blues are active, in taking steps to encrease the number of Freeholders in their interest; and has stated to me his own earnest wish to be possessed of a Freehold, either by purchase or enfranchisement. He has a respectable customary property at Ambleside and in the neighbourhood, any part of which he would be glad to enfranchise (for the purpose of so far counteracting their plans); if it suited your Lordship's arrangements. I know him to be strongly attached to your cause, and could recommend him as confidently as any person whom I know, for a Man to be depended upon. If your Lordship thinks proper to enfranchise any part of his property, be so good as to let me know, and Mr Scambler may then communicate with Mr Lumb upon the subject.[1]—

Lord Lowther was so kind as to send me Mr D's Letter to Sir S.R.[2] It is in the same spirit as all that comes from him, and Lord L. says will be triumphantly refuted, and the author treated as he deserves. The Morning Chronicle is very angry with what was said at the Appleby dinner.[3] They dread our acting upon the offensive—and surely the forbearance of the Lowther Party has been unexampled.

With the highest respect
I have the honor to be
My Lord
most faithfully your Lordship's
Wm Wordsworth

[1] Richard Scambler succeeded in enfranchising his property and duly voted or the Lowthers in the 1820 election.

[2] Sir Samuel Romilly. See previous letter.

[3] See previous letter.

509. W. W. to VISCOUNT LOWTHER

MS. Lonsdale MSS., Record Office, The Castle, Carlisle. Hitherto unpublished.

Sept 29th
1818

My dear Lord L.,

I have had a conference with the Editor of the Gazette about a rascally Letter to you which appeared in the last Kendal C.,[1] and still more rascally notice of it by the Editor of that Journal. We have agreed upon the mode of noticing both, which he has undertaken to do.[2]

Ever faithfully yours
W. W.

P.S. The allegations in the Letter will not, of course, be repeated in our notice.

510. W. W. to VISCOUNT LOWTHER

Address: The Lord Viscount Lowther, Lowther Castle.
Stamp: Kendal Penny Post.
MS. Lonsdale MSS., Record Office, The Castle, Carlisle.
K (—). *MY ii. 610, p. 827* (—).

Rydale Mount
October 6th 1818

My dear Lord Lowther,

I have to thank you for yours of the 28th Septbr yesterday, also I had the pleasure of receiving the letter to Sir Wm Scott in reply to B's to Sir S.R.[3] The St Bee's case is treated at length; and in such manner that Extracts might, I think, be advantageously inserted in the Westnd Gazette—the other Paper having already laid before its readers the Charges upon this subject.[4] As I have said before, I

[1] A letter in the *Kendal Chronicle* for 26 Sept., signed 'Not Brougham but Birch, St. Bees School', sharply attacked Lord Lowther, and contrasted his conciliatory language about his opponents at the close of the Poll with the tone of his latest criticisms of Lord Thanet (see L. 507 above). An editorial in the same issue condemned the Lowthers for resorting to personal abuse.

[2] See next letter.

[3] *A Letter to the Right Hon. Sir William Scott &c. &c., in answer to Mr Brougham's Letter to Sir Samuel Romilly, upon the Abuse of Charities, and Ministerial Patronage in the Appointments under the Late Act*, dated 1 Oct. 1818. Sir William Scott, Lord Stowell (1745–1836), ecclesiastical lawyer, judge, and friend of Dr. Johnson, was M.P. for Oxford University, 1801–21.

[4] An editorial in the *Kendal Chronicle* for 26 Sept. accused Lord Lonsdale of retaining at a ridiculously low rent certain coal-mining rights at St. Bees which

do not think it politic to put accusations and charges in the way of those of our Friends who might never otherwise have heard of them merely because one is able to shew that they are either groundless or the facts grossly misrepresented; but unfortunately our Adversaries take care to disperse among the Yellows such numbers of the Kendal Chronicle, as they hope will best answer their purpose. At least such is their practise in respect to this neighbourhood; for I have ascertained, that the Paper containing that infamous letter signed, Birch,[1] has been sent to different persons of the Lowther Party.—This is a vile course. Two rules *we* ought to lay down; *never* to retort by attacking private character; and never to notice the *particulars* of a personal calumny; or any allegation of a personal nature proceeding from an anonymous quarter. We ought to content ourselves with protesting in the strongest terms against the practise, and pointing it out to indignation and contempt. What the Editor of the Gazette said in his last number upon this subject was not quite what I wished and we agreed upon,[2] but I hope it would do no harm.—There appear to be two weak points in the St Bees case; 1st a Trustee is Tenant of a Trust Estate; and 2ndly, a benefit might be derived from the Lease, by the power it gives of *excluding* others, though it might not be for the interest of the Party to work in the ground, himself. I mean to go over to Lowther shortly, when I shall probably see Dr Satterthwaite—in the meanwhile, use may be made of the Letter to Sir Wm Scott, and I shall take it to De Quincey, today.—

Sir James Lowther, in his capacity as Trustee, had granted to himself in 1742. It was alleged that Lord Lonsdale was being abetted in this dubious transaction by his fellow Trustees, who were mostly clergymen—like John Fleming and Dr. Satterthwaite—holding livings in his gift. In his editorial for 10 Oct., De Quincey promised to review the *Letter to Sir William Scott* the following week; but instead he published a sharp attack on the *Kendal Chronicle*.

[1] See previous letter.

[2] In his editorial for 3 Oct., De Quincey had deplored BIRCH's campaign of abuse. 'It may be expected . . . that the Lowther party will not descend from their present vantage ground to an arena of this sort, in which the Brougham party are likely to have a natural superiority, and in which we know they have the advantage of practice and veteran experience. If the Lowther party on their side once relax their austerity of forbearance on this point, and shew a disposition to entertain charges such as those of *Birch*, even for the purpose (laudable under other circumstances) of finally repelling them,—there is an end at once to the grandeur of a high constitutional contest pursued upon constitutional principles. The struggle will thenceforward present a field of petty malice and jacobinical rancor: all the old women in the county, of scandalous research, will be summoned to evacuate the contents of their memories: juvenile delinquences will be disinterred from the archives of nurses and pedagogues: and the character of the contest and the deportment of the combatants will drive all men of sense and dignity from the field.' De Quincey con-

As to the enlarging of my District[1] in which you are so good as to take interest, it is of no consequence, except in connection with the age of Mr Ramshay and the precarious state of his health. Should his death take place, and the enlargement not be made *then*, it would be unpleasant that it should happen afterwards at the expense of his Successor, unless he entered upon his office *prepared* for such a diminution of his prospects.—

I have lately had some disagreeable correspondence with the Board of Stamps, upon a representation from the Treasury respecting certain arrears in my Account,—unavoidable from the nature of our Currency, which, about Penrith and Appleby, particularly, consists almost exclusively of Scotch Notes for which no Banker will give Bills at less than six weeks or two months Rate. This I have frequently explained to the Commissioners; and have been much plagued about it; for the case admits of no remedy; for they cannot be unreasonable as to expect that *I* should be the loser by discounting these Bills.

Ever Faithfully yours
W. Wordsworth

Mr Gee was highly gratified with his Sport, and his reception at Lowther Castle.—He is gone to try his fortune again, at Ravenstondale, taking with him Mr Monkhouse, a Relation of Mrs Wordsworth, and a particular friend of mine. Mr Monkhouse will be here, I hope, when you come. I have seen a good deal lately of Mr Stanley[2] of Ponsonby; he improves upon familiar acquaintance.

511. W. W. to WILLIAM COLLINS[3]

MS. Indiana University, Oscar L. Watkins Collection.
MLN lxi (1946), 403–4.

Rydale Mount
Octbr 8th 1818

Dear Sir,

I hope that the arrival of your luggage before this reaches you will have set you at ease, and rendered explanations unnecessary.

cluded his remarks somewhat abruptly through shortage of space. His distance from the printing-office in Kendal was already proving inconvenient.

[1] See L. 462 above. North Cumberland was eventually added to W. W.'s district in 1831.

[2] Edward Stanley (1790–1863) of Dalegarth and Ponsonby Hall: M.P. for West Cumberland, 1832–52.

[3] William Collins, R.A. (1788–1847), visited the Lakes from Aug. to Sept. 1818, and while at Keswick painted the charming portrait of Sara Coleridge as

It arrived here by return of coach and on the following day was taken back by Mr Jackson's directions. On the arrival of your first letter, which did not reach us till Wednesday evening (Tuesday being a blank Post Day) we wrote to Mr Jackson desiring him to advize you by what coach and when it was forwarded from Kendal—This I hope was done, and that the valuable materials will duly reach you.

—We have had beautiful weather since you left us, and nothing can be finer than the foliage is at present—Wishing you every possible success in your meditated labours, I

remain dear Sir, with best regards f[rom]
Mrs W.—very truly yours, W. W.

512. W. W. to VISCOUNT LOWTHER

MS. Lonsdale MSS., Record Office, The Castle, Carlisle. Hitherto unpublished.

Octbr 10th
1818

My dear Lord Lowther,

A great dinner of the Blues, at which B. is to be present, takes place this day at Kendal; or I should have gone over in consequence of yours received last night. My presence in the Town would have been noticed; and it would have been thought that I had gone as a Spy upon their proceedings—a Compliment, I would not willingly give them an occasion of paying themselves. I therefore defer my visit till Monday. I do not expect to succeed, because every precaution would be used, in the case of an Article[1] so infamous.—I do not see how I could call upon the Editor (supposing him to be Mr Harrison) to give up the Author, unless I were prepared to say that the Paper would be prosecuted for a libel—and surely it is not worth while to deal with the article in that way, it would make it of too much importance. Nevertheless I feel with you that this infamous conduct must be checked; and that with that view it is

'The Highland Girl'. (See Stephen Potter, *Minnow among Tritons*, 1934, p. 67.) With Sir G. and Lady Beaumont, he visited Rydal and Ambleside, departing south on 5 Oct. At Kendal he found that his sketches, forwarded from Keswick, had been sent to Rydal. His inquiries produced this letter from W. W. Collins was the father of Wilkie Collins the novelist, whose *Memoirs of The Life of William Collins, Esq., R.A.*, 2 vols., 1848, give extracts from the artist's journal describing his visit to the Lakes, i, pp. 128–30, and his letter to Lady Beaumont describing the recovery of the sketches, i, p. 133.

[1] The letter signed BIRCH.

extremely desirable to find out the Author. I shall spare no pains—and unless I apprehend that it will tend to frustrate my purpose, I shall remonstrate with the high Priest upon the scandalous and senseless threat held out in the leading article of that same paper, that this mode of attack will be followed up. The Carlisle Patriot, I am told, contains a large portion of the evidence on the St Bees case, or an Extract from B's Pamphlet,[1] I am not sure which, without a hint from the Editor that it is an *ex parte* Statement. Surely this to say the least of it, is not a friendly course.—The West[nd] Gazette of today has a spirited article from the Editor;[2] a little too strong perhaps in the expression.

I quite agree with you on the St Bees case.

ever most faithfully yours

W. W.

P.S. You know how zealous Ladies are; Mrs W. takes upon her to be half displeased with Col. Lowther, that he was not at Carlisle Races,[3] to keep down the insolent.—James B. is one of the Stewards, I see, for next year!!—

I stick to the opinion of my last that no notice should be taken (I mean through the press) of the particulars of any *anonymous slanders or allegations*, and that nothing should provoke us to personalities of a private nature.

513. W. W. to VISCOUNT LOWTHER

Address: To Lord Viscount Lowther, London.
Postmark: 17 Oct. 1818. *Stamp*: Kendal Penny Post.
MS. Lonsdale MSS., Record Office, The Castle, Carlisle. Hitherto unpublished.

Rydale Mount

Oct[br] 14th [1818]

My dear Lord Lowther,

The results of my visit to Kendal has not been more favorable than I expected.—It does not appear to be known by any of the

[1] 'St. Bees School: Evidence taken before the Education Committee relative to this Establishment. From the Appendix to Mr Brougham's Letter to Sir S. Romilly', *Carlisle Patriot*, 10 Oct., etc.

[2] This discussed Brougham's pamphlet and the Bill he had introduced earlier in the year to set up his commission of inquiry. 'By the admission of all impartial men, for a grave act of legislature it presented a model and practical assertion unique and solitary of jacobinism without limit,—and tyranny without example.'

[3] 29 Sept.–1 Oct.

Lowther Party in Kendal, who wrote the Letter.[1] Suspicion falls on old Thomson[2]—but it is no more than suspicion—and I think on very slight, that is, little better than general, grounds.—I applied to Mr Surgeon Harrison; and he has promised to do all in his power; but he does not hope to succeed. I have also set another person to work. The difficulty lies chiefly in this, that one cannot procure *positive* evidence without a breach of confidence in some quarter or other—and one cannot attempt to put respectable people upon any service of that kind, if such could undertake it. So that all that I hope for is a concurrence of circumstantial evidence tending to fasten suspicion on somebody or other. People are much more upon their guard than in the beginning of the Contest, and the two parties mixing so much less with each other makes it more difficult for each to learn what its opponent is doing.

Saturday was a very stormy day so that Brougham's grand entree[3] was very inauspicious, and the sport in a great measure spoiled. He addressed however a short speech to the Mob, in which he bewailed as heretofore, the unfavourableness of the weather. Old Wakefield himself acknowledged that if it had not been for the wetness of the night there would most likely have been disturbances. Everyone else seems of the same opinion.

Young Wilson[4] of Abbot Hall, says that Mr Daniel Harrison assured him that the Blues in Kendal had made 30 additional Freeholds since the election. This, I hope, is an exaggeration, but I *know* that several have been made.

It seems best to take no further steps for the present in regard to the threats held out by the opposite Party, or to what has already been done upon this shameful principle. It is clear that they hope to *intimidate* us by slander and calumny. They will be disappointed. But, with submission to your feelings, I think we ought to wait a little, till we can see farther into what has been done, and what they mean to do.

I remain my dear Lord Lowther
very faithfully yours
W. Wordsworth

Brougham entered Kendal in a Gig. Mr Wilberforce attended

[1] Signed Birch.

[2] Probably Mr. Thomson of Ambleside, whose fervent support for Brougham is noted in L. 540.

[3] For the Dinner on 10 Oct., see *Kendal Chronicle* for the 17th. The grand procession beforehand was spoilt by rain. Brougham's arrival by gig was ridiculed in the *Westmorland Gazette* for the 17th.

[4] Edward Wilson (1796–1870), later of Rigmaden Park.

yesterday the Bible Society meeting[1] at Kendal, and spoke 40 minutes. Hardy,[2] your Council, was there also, and spoke an hour.

514. D. W. to JANE MARSHALL

Address: Mrs. Marshall, Hallsteads [*apparently delivered by W. W.*].
MS. WL.
K (—). *MY ii. 611, p. 827.*

[14] October [1818]

My dear Friend,

I have been very idle I must confess in not having written to you long ago in answer to your kind letter from Allonby, if I had had no other motive for writing; but I am sure you have wished to hear of us; and on that account alone I ought to have written, and, believe me, I have blamed myself not a little for my idleness.

Sir George and Lady Beaumont returned from Hallsteads inexpressibly delighted with the hospitality and kindness which they had met with under your Roof. They were never weary of talking of the kindness of one and all; and, as for you and Mr. Marshall, they were sure they had tried you to the uttermost by having kept dinner waiting hour after hour.

They often said that they hoped at some time to have the pleasure of seeing you at Coleorton on your way to London or Bath.

My Sister urged me to write while the Beaumonts were with us. She knew of my former negligence, and was desirous to return her thanks for the partridges which you were so thoughtful as to send with our Friends, and which you might then be sure were well-timed.

All the Wilberforces intend to leave Rydal tomorrow. Mr. W. and his eldest Son and youngest Daughter departed on Thursday week; and truly sorry were we to lose them. There never lived on earth, I am sure, a man of sweeter temper than Mr. Wilberforce. He is made up of Benevolence and loving-kindness, and though shattered in constitution and feeble in Body he is as lively and animated as in the days of his youth.

[1] Fully reported in the *Kendal Chronicle* for 17 and 24 Oct., but only briefly noticed in the *Westmorland Gazette*. In his speech Wilberforce attributed the success of the Bible Society to the fact that it united all sects and parties in pursuit of one grand object, whereas the S.P.C.K. was less effective in that membership was confined to the Established Church.

[2] John Hardy, Chairman of the meeting.

His Children very much resemble him in ardour and liveliness of mind; the two Girls are sensible and very amiable—and the youngest Boy is a very interesting and clever Lad.

Sir George and Lady B. left us on the Saturday, and I accompanied them to Keswick and on Monday morning I went into Borrowdale. The next day, Mr. and Mrs. Wilberforce, all their Family, and Sir George and Lady Beaumont came with store of provisions, Miss Barker having provided vegetables etc., and we all dined together. The next day, which was one of the finest of the year, I ascended Scaw Fell from Seathwaite with Miss Barker—and never before did I behold so sublime a mountain prospect. Our Guide, who is a Shepherd of Borrowdale, turning his eyes thoughtfully round when we were on the pinnacle of Scaw Fell, said 'I do not know that ever in the whole course of my life, I was at any season so high upon the mountains on so calm a day'. There was not a breath of wind to stir the very papers which we spread out with our food, when we ate our dinners on that commanding eminence. The next day I returned to Keswick and stayed with Lady B. till Saturday, a day of incessant rain, when I came home with our Neighbours, the Wilberforces.

My Brother will give you a good report of the health of all our Family and I hope, my dear Friend, that he will find your poor little Ellen quite recovered. It concerned us much to hear of her being suffering under one of her distressing attacks when Mr. Monkhouse and his Friend called at Hallsteads.

By your letter from Allonby I first heard of the full extent of your poor Sister Catharine's misfortune, and Lady Beaumont has since given me many particulars. Lady B. seemed to hope with you that she would gradually be restored to the use of her leg—she told us that you were all going to Bath early in the spring. Perhaps if the visit to Bath does not produce the wished-for benefit your Sister may be induced to put herself under Mr. Grosvenor's care at Oxford. It seems to be one of those cases in which Mr. G.'s mode of treatment is likely to be serviceable. Lady B. spoke much, and feelingly, of your Sister's chearfulness and patience, and of the tender attentions paid to her by every member of your Family. My Brother was very glad to meet with your Son John at Leeds, but was not so fortunate as to see Miss Pollards and Mary Anne. They had passed through Kendal. His young Friend and he had a very pleasant chat together.

I am going on Tuesday to spend a few days with Mrs. Calvert at Keswick. It is a visit which I have been urged to pay for several years, and something has always happened either to make me unwilling to leave home, or it has been inconvenient. My Brother has promised to call for me on his road from Lowther.

Mrs. Calvert has just parted from her only Daughter, whom she has placed under Miss Dowling's care; therefore I hope the company of a Friend may be more than at any other time acceptable.

Miss Dowling called here this afternoon with her Sister, who takes part with her in the duties of the school, and with her little Flock of Boarders, now amounting to six. Dorothy seems to be as happy as possible, and we have every reason to be satisfied with the improvement she is making—indeed all the Girls look chearful and contented—just as one would wish—not excepting Miss Calvert, who has left home a fortnight. Poor Dorothy had, I believe, at first a sad home-sickness, though she said nothing. Her eyes always filled with tears when she saw any of us; but it is now all over. Mary Calvert and she are great Friends, and well pleased at being under the same Roof together.

Two or three new scholars are expected after Christmas, so it is probable that Miss Dowling will soon have as many Boarders as she will wish for.

It is some time since I heard from Halifax; but the account of our good Friends was truly chearing. I have for some weeks been in daily expectation of a letter from Mr. Ferguson to whom I wrote, requesting him to purchase some stuff for Curtains. I suppose he is waiting till the stuff is dyed and sent off; for surely if any misfortune had been the cause of his silence I should have heard of it. We were much mortified (my Sister and I), that we happened to be from home when Mr. and Mrs. Stansfeld Rawson[1] called; and we only had two minutes' talk with them on the Road, as they passed in their carriage. My Brother was fortunate enough to be at home; but they only stayed half an hour, being in a hurry to proceed on their journey. Mr. R. looked very well.

I hope to hear a good account of your Sisters, that their journey has been of use to Miss Catharine. Lady Beaumont tells me that you have yet some trouble from your lame foot. It was indeed a grievous accident but, as you observe, compared with your Sister's it was as nothing, though it must have been a serious draw-back from your summer enjoyments; the weather has however been so very warm, that it has often been more delightful to sit and feel and enjoy than to make any exertion of limbs, and this has for you and her been a great blessing.

[1] William and Nelly Rawson's son and his wife.

Remember me kindly to Mr. Marshall and all of your Family who are at home.

My Sister begs her best regards. Believe me ever truly yours
D. Wordsworth.

515. W. W. to VISCOUNT LOWTHER

MS. Lonsdale MSS., Record Office, The Castle, Carlisle. Hitherto unpublished.

Thursday
[15 Oct. 1818]

My dear Lord Lowther,

Yesterday I received yours of the 12th, after I had sent off a letter giving a report of my Kendal Researches.—What I did was in so quiet a way that nothing amiss can come of it. Besides, I did not mention you to either of the Parties whom I spoke to. I represented it merely as a wish of my own to know who was the author of that Letter.[1]—

What you say of St Bees gives me great pleasure. The Editor of the Gazette is prepared to act as you wish in respect to private conduct.[2]

I find that the publication of the Poll[3] has excessively mortified many of the lower order of Blues. They were foolish enough to suppose that they could vote against you without its being generally known.

ever yours
W. W.

516. W. W. to LORD LONSDALE

MS. Lonsdale MSS., Record Office, The Castle, Carlisle. Hitherto unpublished.

October 20th 1818
Rydal Mount

My Lord,

Mr Wilberforce left this country on the 15th Insnt—But having occasion to write to him, and knowing that your message would give

[1] Signed Birch.

[2] i.e. not to descend to personal abuse of his opponents.

[3] *The Poll for Knights of the Shire, to represent the County of Westmorland, taken at Appleby, on Tues. 30th June, Wed. 1st, Thurs. 2nd, and Fri. 3rd Day of July, 1818,* Kendal, 1818.

him pleasure, I shall not scruple to report it. Mrs Wilberforce and some of her family are still here— for a few days. They are now at Patterdale but return this evening. Mrs W. will be made acquainted with Lady Lonsdale's invitation.

Official business (this being the week in which my Quarterly Account is prepared and sent off) and a visit from some friends, will prevent, I fear, my quitting Rydale, before Saturday next. Should I not be at liberty on that day, on Monday next I hope to have the pleasure of paying my respects to your Lordship, at which time I have reason to think Sir George and Lady Beaumont will not be gone. I hope that you found Lady Mary improved in health.

I have the honor to be
most faithfully
Your Lordship's
friend and Servant
Wm Wordsworth

517. W. W. to VISCOUNT LOWTHER

MS. Lonsdale MSS., Record Office, The Castle, Carlisle. Hitherto unpublished.

Rydale Mount
Oct[br] 20th [1818]

My dear Lord Lowther,

I have this day written to both the Parties;[1] desiring the inquiry to be dropped—which will, of course, be done.—I never hinted at any wish on *your* part to know the Author—but spoke entirely as from myself.

Lord Thanet is to be sure a troublesome enemy; but nothing but the creation of new Freeholds (in which the Party must be met) can enable them to gain their point, in the face of the Lowther interest and connection.

I shall be at Lowther during the chief part of the next week, so if you have occasion, or feel inclined to write, my address will be there.

ever faithfully yours
W. Wordsworth

I find that Col. Lowther *was* at Carlisle Races, so that Mrs W. need not have been in such a haste to find fault.

[1] i.e. Mr. Surgeon Harrison and the other person whom W. W. had approached with a view to finding out the identity of Birch.

518. D. W. to WILLIAM JOHNSON

MS. WL transcript [possibly in John Carter's hand].
DWJ i. p.425 (—). W. W. printed an adapted version of this letter in his *Guide to the Lakes* (ed. E. de Selincourt, 1926, p. 112).

October 21st, 1818.

. . . Sir George and Lady Beaumont spent a few days with us lately and I accompanied them to Keswick. Mr. and Mrs. Wilberforce and their family happened to be at K. at the same time, and we all dined together in the romantic Vale of Borrowdale, at the house of a female friend, an unmarried Lady, who, bewitched with the charms of the rocks, and streams, and mountains of that secluded spot, has there built herself a house, and though she is admirably fitted for society, and has as much enjoyment when surrounded by her friends as any one *can* have, her chearfulness has never flagged, though she has lived more than the year round alone in Borrowdale, at six miles distance from Keswick, with bad roads between. You will guess that she has resources within herself; such indeed she has. She is a painter and labours hard in depicting the beauties of her favorite Vale; she is also found of music and of reading, and has a reflecting mind; besides (though before she lived in Borrowdale she was no great walker) she is become an active climber of the hills, and I must tell you of a feat that she and I performed on Wednesday the 7th of this month. I remained in Borrowdale after Sir G. and Lady B. and the Wilberforces were gone, and Miss Barker proposed that the next day she and I should go to Seathwaite beyond the Black lead mines at the head of Borrowdale, and thence up a mountain called at the top *Ash Course*, which we suppose may be a corruption of *Esk Hawes*, as it is a settling between the mountains over which the people are accustomed to pass between Eskdale and Borrowdale; and such settlings are generally called by the name of 'the Hawes'—as Grisdale Hawes, Buttermere Hawes, from the German word Hals (neck). At the top of Ash Course Miss Barker had promised that I should see a magnificent prospect; but we had some miles to travel to the foot of the mountain, and accordingly went thither in a cart—Miss Barker, her maid, and myself. We departed before nine o'clock, the sun shone; the sky was clear and blue; and light and shade fell in masses upon the mountains; the fields below *glittered* with the dew, where the beams of the sun could reach them; and every little stream tumbling down the hills seemed to add to the chearfulness of the scene.

We left our cart at Seathwaite and proceeded, with a man to carry our provisions, and a kind neighbour of Miss Barker's, a statesman shepherd of the vale, as our companion and guide. We found ourselves at the top of Ash Course without a weary limb, having had the fresh air of autumn to help us up by its invigorating power, and the sweet warmth of the unclouded sun to tempt us to sit and rest by the way. From the top of Ash Course we beheld a prospect which would indeed have amply repaid us for a *toilsome* journey, if such it had been; and a sense of thankfulness for the continuance of that vigour of body, which enabled me to climb the high mountain, as in the days of my youth, inspiring me with fresh chearfulness, added a delight, a charm to the contemplation of the magnificent scenes before me, which I cannot describe. Still less can I tell you the glories of what we saw. Three views, each distinct in its kind, we saw at once—the vale of Borrowdale, of Keswick, of Bassenthwaite—Skiddaw, Saddleback, Helvellyn, numerous other mountains, and, still beyond, the Solway Frith, and the mountains of Scotland.

Nearer to us, on the other side, and below us, were the Langdale Pikes, then our own Vale below them, Windermere, and far beyond Windermere, after a long distance, Ingleborough in Yorkshire. But how shall I speak of the peculiar deliciousness of the third prospect? At this time *that* was most favoured by sunshine and shade. The green Vale of Esk—deep and green, with its glittering serpent stream was below us; and on we looked to the mountains near the sea—Black Combe and others—and still beyond, to the sea itself in dazzling brightness. Turning round we saw the mountains of Wasdale in tumult; and Great Gavel,[1] though the middle of the mountain was to us as its base, looked very grand.

We had attained the object of our journey; but our ambition mounted higher. We saw the summit of Scaw Fell, as it seemed, very near to us; we were indeed, three parts up that mountain, and thither we determined to go. We found the distance greater than it had appeared to us, but our courage did not fail; however, when we came nearer we perceived that in order to attain that summit we must make a great dip, and that the ascent afterwards would be exceedingly steep and difficult, so that we might have been benighted if we had attempted it; therefore, unwillingly, we gave it up, and resolved, instead, to ascend another point of the same mountain, called *the Pikes*, and which, I have since found, the measurers of the mountains estimate as higher than the larger summit which bears the name of Scaw Fell, and where the Stone Man is built which we, at the time, considered as the point of highest

[1] i.e. Great Gable.

honour. The sun had never once been overshadowed by a cloud during the whole of our progress from the centre of Borrowdale; at the summit of the Pike there was not a breath of air to stir even the papers which we spread out containing our food. There we ate our dinner in summer warmth; and the stillness seemed to be not of this world. We paused, and kept silence to listen, and not a sound of any kind was to be heard. We were far above the reach of the cataracts of Scaw Fell; and not an insect was there to hum in the air. The Vales before described lay in view, and side by side with Eskdale, we now saw the sister Vale of Donnerdale terminated by the Duddon Sands. But the majesty of the mountains below and close to us, is not to be conceived. We now beheld the whole mass of Great Gavel from its base, the Den of Wasdale at our feet, the gulph immeasurable, Grasmere[1] and the other mountains of Crummock, Ennerdale and *its* mountains, and the sea beyond.

While we were looking round after dinner our Guide said that we must not linger long, for we should have a storm. We looked in vain to espy the traces of it; for mountains, vales, and the sea were all touched with the clear light of the sun. 'It is there', he said, pointing to the sea beyond Whitehaven, and, sure enough, we there perceived a light cloud, or mist, unnoticeable but by a shepherd, accustomed to watch all mountain bodings. We gazed around again and yet again, fearful to lose the remembrance of what lay before us in that lofty solitude; and then prepared to depart. Meanwhile the air changed to cold, and we saw the tiny vapour swelled into mighty masses of cloud which came boiling over the mountains. Great Gavel, Helvellyn, and Skiddaw were wrapped in storm; yet Langdale and the mountains in that quarter were all bright with sunshine. Soon the storm reached us; we sheltered under a crag, and almost as rapidly as it had come, it passed away, and left us free to observe the goings-on of storm and sunshine in other quarters—Langdale had now its share, and the Pikes were decorated by two splendid rainbows; Skiddaw also had its own rainbows, but we were glad to see them and the clouds disappear from that mountain, as we knew that Mr. and Mrs. Wilberforce and the family (if they kept the intention which they had formed when they parted from us the night before) must certainly be upon Skiddaw at that very time—and so it was. They were there, and had much more rain than we had; we, indeed, were hardly at all wetted; and before we found ourselves again upon that part of the mountain called Ash Course every cloud had vanished from every summit.

[1] i.e. the peak of Grasmoor.

Do not think we here gave up our spirit of enterprise. No! I had heard much of the grandeur of the view of Wasdale from Stye Head, the point from which Wasdale is first seen in coming by the road from Borrowdale; but though I had been in Wasdale I had never entered the dale by that road, and had often lamented that I had not seen what was so much talked of by travellers. Down to that Pass (for we were yet far above it) we bent our course by the side of Ruddle Gill, a very deep red chasm in the mountains which begins at a spring—that spring forms a stream, which must, at times, be a mighty torrent, as is evident from the channel which it has wrought out—thence by Sprinkling Tarn to Stye Head; and there we sate and looked down into Wasdale. We were now upon Great Gavel which rose high above us. Opposite was Scaw Fell and we heard the roaring of the stream from one of the ravines of that mountain, which, though the bending of Wasdale Head lay between us and Scaw Fell, we could look into, as it were, and the depth of the ravine appeared tremendous; it was black and the crags were awful.

We now proceeded homewards by Stye head Tarn along the road into Borrowdale. Before we reached Stonethwaite a few stars had appeared, and we travelled home in our cart by moonlight.

I ought to have described the last part of our ascent to Scaw Fell Pike. There, not a blade of grass was to be seen—hardly a cushion of moss, and that was parched and brown; and only growing rarely between the huge blocks and stones which cover the summit and lie in heaps all round to a great distance, like skeletons or bones of the earth not wanted at the creation, and there left to be covered with never-dying lichens, which the clouds and dews nourish; and adorn with colours of the most vivid and exquisite beauty, and endless in variety. No gems or flowers can surpass in colouring the beauty of some of these masses of stone which no human eye beholds except the shepherd led thither by chance or traveller by curiosity; and how seldom must this happen! The other eminence is that which is visited by the adventurous traveller, and the shepherd has no temptation to go thither in quest of his sheep; for on the Pike there is no food to tempt them. We certainly were singularly fortunate in the day; for when we were seated on the summit our Guide, turning his eyes thoughtfully round, said to us, 'I do not know that in my whole life I was ever at any season of the year so high up on the mountains on so calm a day'. Afterwards, you know, we had the storm which exhibited to us the grandeur of earth and heaven commingled, yet without terror; for we knew that the storm would pass away; for so our prophetic guide assured us. I forget to tell you that

I espied a ship upon the glittering sea while we were looking over Eskdale. 'Is it a ship?' replied the Guide, 'A ship, yes, it can be nothing else, don't you see the shape of it?' Miss Barker interposed, 'It is a ship, of that I am certain. I cannot be mistaken, I am so accustomed to the appearance of ships at sea.' The Guide dropped the argument; but a moment was scarce gone when he quietly said, 'Now look at your ship, it is now a horse'. So indeed it was—a horse with a gallant neck and head. We laughed heartily, and, I hope when again inclined to positiveness, I may remember the ship and the horse upon the glittering sea; and the calm confidence, yet submissiveness, of our wise Man of the Mountains, who certainly had more knowledge of clouds than we, whatever might be our knowledge of ships. To add to our uncommon performance on that day Miss Barker and I each wrote a letter from the top of the Pike to our far distant friend in S. Wales, Miss Hutchinson. I believe that you are not much acquainted with the Scenery of this Country, except in the Neighbourhood of Grasmere, your duties when you were a resident here, having confined you so much to that one Vale; I hope, however, that my long story will not be very dull; and even I am not without a further hope, that it may awaken in you a desire to spend a long holiday among the mountains, and explore their recesses.

519. W. W. to VISCOUNT LOWTHER

MS. Lonsdale MSS., Record Office, The Castle, Carlisle. Hitherto unpublished.

Rydale Mount
October 23rd 1818

My dear Lord Lowther,

I entirely concur with you in your observations on the West^nd Gaz: and on the desirableness of letting its election politics subside. The Editor I am sure would treat with deference any observations coming from me on this subject and still more would he be inclined to do so, when made acquainted (which he shall be immediately) with your sentiments. But Mr F.[1]—though one of most upright of

[1] John Fleming had published in the *Westmorland Gazette* for 17 Oct. the first of what turned out to be a long series of weekly tirades against Brougham in which he defended his own character, and the conduct of the Lowthers, in the St. Bees affair. Lord Lowther's apprehensions were roused at once, and he wrote to W. W. on the 22nd suggesting that De Quincey should get more material from the London papers. 'Really if he puts in all that is sent to him, every clergyman and schoolmaster in the county will become an author. If this scurrility could be dropped it would be far better for both parties.' (*WL MSS.*)

men, and most strongly attached to your family, is very quick in taking offence, and somewhat headstrong and unmanageable. The Editor has several times expressed to me his embarassment in respect to communications from that quarter, and knowing Mr F., he much fears that he must make great sacrifices on his account or break with him altogether, which for many reasons he is unwilling to do. It is already too late for anything said by me to be of use for tomorrow's paper; but I will take care to see the Editor before I depart for Lowther, where I mean to be on Monday.

As to any private Anecdotes to the prejudice of the Leaders of the opposite Party it is well to be possessed of that sort of information and that they should have reason to know you possess it—it will keep them in check—but as I took the liberty of saying some little time ago, I would on no account be tempted by any aspersions or threats of theirs into a newspaper warfare of this sort. I think you ought not to condescend to it. Be assured my dear Lord Lowther, that I shall ever be ready to support your cause to the utmost of my power, and to give proofs of the sincere regard with which I am

most faithfully yours
W Wordsworth.

P.S. The number of their votes is certainly encreasing, and not slowly, by new Freeholds. This must be met.

520. W. W. to WASHINGTON ALLSTON[1]

Address: To Mr Alston [*delivered by George Ticknor*].
MS. Cornell.
Jared B. Flagg, Life and Letters of Washington Allston, 1893, p. 133. LY iii. 1184 n. Broughton, p. 98.

[*c.* Nov. 1818 or early 1819]

[Sent with a copy of W. W.'s poem *Composed upon an Evening of extraordinary Splendour and Beauty*]

Transcribed by Mrs Wordsworth for Mr Alston, in gratitude for the pleasure she received from the sight of his pictures, in particular, The Jacob's Dream.[2]

Wm Wordsworth

[1] This note was written soon after Allston returned to America permanently in Sept. 1818, and either just before or during the visit of George Ticknor (1791–1871), the American author, on 21 Mar. 1819. Allston's reply of 15 Nov. 1819 is among the *WL MSS*. See also W. W. to R. H. Dana, Oct. 1843 (in later volume).

[2] Painted in 1817, exhibited at the British Institution two years later, and

N.B. The author knows not how far he was indebted to Mr Alston for part of the 3d stanza.[1] The multiplication of ridges in a mountainous country, as Mr Alston has probably observed, are from two causes, *sunny* or *watery* haze or vapour; the former is here meant. When does Mr Alston return to England.

W. W.

521. W. W. to LORD LONSDALE

MS. Lonsdale MSS., Record Office, The Castle, Carlisle. Hitherto unpublished.

Rydale Mount
November 6th 1818

My Lord,

I rode over to Storr's Hall yesterday, but as I had not heard from Mr Bolton,[2] announcing your arrival, my disappointment was less in not finding Your Lordship and Lady Lonsdale there. On Wednesday I went to Coniston. On stating to Mr Knott[3] the object of my visit, he said, with a due sense of the respect shewn him by your Lordship on this occasion, that he was already in the Commission for Lancashire;—that he had not qualified, because no professional Gentleman lived in this neighbourhood to consult in case of a difficulty, and the neighbouring Country Gentlemen had been disinclined to qualify also;—but that lately several had proposed to qualify along with him, having been sensible of the want of Magistrates in that part of Lancashire;—that, if this intention was carried into effect, he thought it would be beneficial that he himself should be enabled to act for Westmorland also, living upon the edge of

purchased by Lord Egremont for Petworth House, Sussex, where it has remained ever since. 'The subject is very sublimely and originally treated, with a feeling wholly distinct from the shadowy mysticism of Rembrant, and the graceful simplicity of Raphael. Instead of a ladder or steps, with a few angels, he embodied the idea of a glorious vision, in which countless myriads of the heavenly host are seen dissolving into light and distance, and immeasurable flights of steps rising, spreading above and beyond each other, vanish at last into infinitude.'—Anna Jameson, 'Washington Allston', *Athenaeum*, 1844, p. 16.

[1] W. W.'s poem (see *PW* iv, pp. 10–13 and *app. crit.*) was, according to the original title, 'Composed during a sunset of transcendent Beauty, in the summer of 1817'; but he could not have seen the picture at Allston's studio until his visit to London in the December. He is presumably referring here to the revised version of ll. 41–49, inspired by the memory of Allston's picture, and incorporated into the text as published in 1820.

[2] John Bolton, 'the Liverpool Croesus': a prominent Lowther supporter.

[3] Michael Knott of Waterhead House, formerly owner of Rydal Mount.

that County as he did; and that in the mean time his being put upon the Commission for Westnd would be acceptable to him; but that he could not engage to qualify for that County, unless he should do so for Lancashire also. The above answer seems judicious; and I may add that I was much pleased with Mr Knott.

I have inquired further into the subject of the trespasses on manorial rights in this neighbourhood—and do not see how they can be prevented or checked except by the appointment of Gamekeepers, for your Lordship's manors, and for Rydale. If some *gentleman* would undertake the office, his interposition might be effectual. A Person of inferior rank is too apt to be afraid of giving offence. These practises are certainly very hurtful to good order.—I am also persuaded that if the Lords of Manors in the adjoining part of Lancashire would unite with your Lordship in opposing such courses, it would tend greatly to prevent the settling of objectionable characters among us; and might drive some of the higher rabble, by whom we are infested, out of the Country.—I am well aware of the handle which the opposite party would make of the measure which I have taken the liberty of submitting to your Lordship's consideration.—Regretting that I have not had the pleasure of seeing your Lordship and Lady Lonsdale again before your departure, I have the honor to be

My Lord
most faithfully yours
Wm Wordsworth

Mr Southey's appointment is from the Lord Chamberlain.[1]

522. W. W. to VISCOUNT LOWTHER

MS. Lonsdale MSS., Record Office, The Castle, Carlisle. Hitherto unpublished.

Rydale Mount
Nov^{br} 8th 1818

My dear Lord Lowther,

I hope you have less occasion to find fault with the Gazette; but I much fear that the Editor will hurt the character of his paper by making too many promises, and then failing frequently to perform

[1] Francis Seymour, 2nd Marquess of Hertford (1743–1822): Lord Chamberlain, 1812–21. W. W. is perhaps referring to some document connected with the Laureateship.

them.—He assured me that when Mr Fleming's present Letter is finished, nothing more of the kind will be admitted.[1]

I hear of nothing new in this neighbourhood except that Mr Bolton means to give a dinner[2] to a numerous assemblage of the Freeholders in this neighbourhood.

Having been from home for some time I did not receive your last till long after its date.—How are things going on at Paris?[3] Romilly's defeat[4] is shocking—but probably you will think, as I do, that he was an unsafe Man.

I found everyone well at Lowther; and was happy to see Lord Lonsdale's looks daily improve.

with sincere regard
I am
my dear Lord Lowther
truly yours
Wm Wordsworth

523. W. W. to LORD LONSDALE

MS. Lonsdale MSS., Record Office, The Castle, Carlisle.
K (—). MY ii. 612, p. 830 (—).

Rydale Mount
28th Novbr 1818

My Lord,

I have just learned that a Mr Barber,[5] of the Temple, who has a small fancy-property in Grasmere, is about to have himself set Tenant upon it, with a view to enfranchisement. This Gentleman is of my acquaintance, and I think it proper to mention to your Lordship, that he is much connected with the Dissenters, and I know

[1] John Fleming's embarrassing articles were still continuing to appear every week. Writing to W. W. on 29 Oct., Lord Lowther had expressed himself as thoroughly ashamed of the *Westmorland Gazette*: 'I cannot think it very good taste of Mr Fleming in addressing B[rougham] *in propria persona* . . .' A day later, he wrote: 'I wish you could make the Editor superintend and do not let us place the Enemy on the advantage ground of good breeding . . .' (*WL MSS.*)

[2] The Dinner at Storrs Hall on 17 Nov. was described in the *Westmorland Gazette* for the 21st.

[3] Lord Lowther was spending the rest of November in France, where elections were in progress after the withdrawal of all foreign troops.

[4] W. W. must mean Sir Samuel Romilly's *death* by suicide on 2 Nov.

[5] Samuel Barber, the eccentric bachelor of Gell's Cottage, Silver Howe, who was quizzed by M. W. and S. H. for the fantastic alterations he made in his house and garden. See L. 540 below.

that his general Politics are of an objectionable cast, and that he is hostile to the principles upon which your Lordship's family stood during our late Contest. May I take this occasion of suggesting that, as I know other customary Tenants of this neighbourhood have the same views, unless indiscriminate enfranchisement is to take place, it would be adviseable to meet the wishes of no one in this particular, unless his character and principles were vouched for by some of his Neighbours, Friends to your Lordship. It is not easy to know whom we trust, but Mr Jackson or myself would do our best for this neighbourhood.—Looking at this subject generally I cannot but be of opinion that the feudal Power yet surviving in England is eminently serviceable in counteracting the popular propensities to reform which would unavoidably lead to revolution. The People are already powerful far beyond the encrease of their information, or their improvement in morals.

This neighbourhood, I am sorry to say, continues in an agitated and disorderly state, which is not a little owing to Mr King and Mr Dixon.[1]—I much regret that political circumstances are such as to render this an unfavourable time to adopt the plan adverted to in my former Letter.[2] But it would have been most happy for this district if your Lordship had been less indulgent. For many years we have been infested with persons whose chief motive for settling among us was the facilities they find for sporting over the adjoining Manors.—Since I wrote last, I myself was insulted, in the public road, in the night, with a cry of 'Brougham for ever,' by a party of these lawless Sportsmen returning from their day's amusement, with the above-named Mr Dixon at their head. With the highest respect I have the honor to remain

Your Lordship's faithful Friend and Serv^{nt}

Wm Wordsworth

[1] John Dixon, a Grasmere farmer, who had given a 'plumper' to Brougham at the Poll.

[2] i.e. to appoint gamekeepers. See L. 521 above.

524. W. W. to THOMAS MONKHOUSE

Address: Thomas Monkhouse, Esqre, 21 Budge Row, London.
Postmark: 7 Dec. 1818. *Stamp*: Kendal Penny Post. *Endorsed*: W. W. to T. M. Dec. 4. 1818.
MS. WL. Hitherto unpublished.

4 December 1818

My dear Friend,

Many thanks for the trouble you have taken on John's account; I thought it proper to call on his present Master,[1] and the result is that I am determined to send him to the Charter-House next Sunday, anxiously hoping that he may be admitted[2] into the House of the most approved Master. I think however that it will be proper first to consult Dr Wordsworth—and I beg therefore that you would have the goodness to seek an interview with him (as speedily as possible) which will be accomplished with the least trouble to yourself if you write a note begging to know when you can find him at home. It is possible that Dr Wordsworth may know some objectionable particulars; at all events I should like to have the sanction of his experience. If he approves, lose no time in entering him if possible under the Master named by you, if you are satisfied he is the best. The Papers inform us that there has been a mutiny in the school—how is this? And be so good as to be particular as to the length of the several vacations and the time when they begin. We shall be truly happy in John's being a week with you before he enters the School; and learn for us also how he will be best equipped with clothes; for instance Can he wear country woollen stockings this winter?

I have been disappointed with respect to Southey joining in the purchase[3]—though anxious to do so he cannot spare the money at this time, and is resolved not to borrow. I am however to look out for him on a future occasion. At present the associates are Mr Gee, John and Henry Hutchinson and yourself: it was mentioned to Thos. Hut:[4] but we have not received an answer yet. Under the present circumstances therefore it seems advisable that we should select a trusty Yellow or two amongst your friends. The Estate will give 7 handsome Freeholds to co-purchasers[5] united in one street. Mary

[1] At this time the Revd. John Dawes of Ambleside.

[2] John W. was refused a place at Charterhouse owing to the standing rule of admitting no boy over 14 years. See L. 530 below.

[3] Of the Ivy How estate in Little Langdale. See *MW* 20, 24, pp. 40, 49.

[4] i.e. Thomas Hutchinson.

[5] The syndicate finally seems to have consisted of eight members (see L. 538 below): C. W., M. W.'s brothers John and Henry Hutchinson of Stockton-on-

thanks you for your last interesting letter which she would have answered before; but that she waited for Southey's final reply. Mr Westall[1] has been here, and from him you will receive a Proof of his Caves which Mr Gee has paid for.

I am truly happy to hear so favorable an account of Haydon; say to him from me everything that is kind. I hope to write him ere long—To Charles Lamb also and his Sister remember me very affectionately—Farewell—I am going to write to my [Brother] to prepare him for your call.

I remain your faithful and affectionate friend
Wm Wordsworth

[*M. W. writes*]

Have you paid Mrs Bradley for the chairs?

[*D. W. writes*]

My Brother has given me his letter to look over and I cannot but add a word—Your account of the School has put his mother and me into heart. I trust he may do in time not as a great Scholar but a respectable one—God grant that he may preserve his ingenuous dispositions! It will be a sad parting—and most anxious shall we be till the first month is over. I am glad you were all so happy in Wales. We shall hope to see you when John comes home in summer. Mind to state exactly the time of the several holidays. God bless you and believe me ever yours

D. Wordsworth.

Tees and Thomas Hutchinson of Hindwell, her cousins Thomas Monkhouse and John Monkhouse of Stow, Eldred Addison (see *MW* 41, 72, pp. 83, 149) son of R. W.'s partner, and Mr. Gee. C. W. agreed to become a freeholder in a letter to W. W. of 6 Feb., in which he described a recent encounter with Brougham at a Speaker's Dinner: 'We were mutually civil . . . and got on very tolerably—not the less so, I dare say, for the close fighting in Westmorland. Having good opportunities for observing, I was much struck with the disagreeableness of his countenance—and remarked that his left cheek, and his nose was in a sort of *convulsive* twitch, the whole of the afternoon. I do not know whether this is habitual to him; or that he may be in a greater degree of irritable excitement than usual,—but the effect was exceedingly unpleasant.' (*WL MSS.*)

[1] William Westall, the artist (see L. 436 above), stayed at Rydal Mount several times in 1818, 1819, and 1820. His *Views of the Caves near Ingleton, Gordale Scar, and Malham Cove in Yorkshire* had just appeared, and inspired three sonnets from W. W. (see L. 530 below).

525. W. W. to VISCOUNT LOWTHER

Address: Lord Visc[t] Lowther, M.P., London.
Postmark: 9 Dec. 1818. *Stamp*: Kendal Penny Post.
MS. Lonsdale MSS., Record Office, The Castle, Carlisle.
K (—). *MY ii. 613, p. 831* (—).

Rydale Mount
Dec[br] 6th [1818]

My dear Lord Lowther,

I have at last resolved to call upon Mr Fleming.—I was in hopes that this week would have concluded his lucubrations;[1] and knowing his character I wish to spare him the pain of the communication which you authorised me to make. I called several times lately on De Quincey before I could see him, to learn whether Mr Fleming's letter was upon the point of closing and to urge him to make in his character of Editor a strong public declaration against personal and retrospective Politics. Something of this kind he has done in his last number;[2] today I begged him to announce his determination not to tolerate long winded controversies, nor even to admit discussions upon points where there was nothing new to be said.

I fear that from one cause or another the Gazette is sinking.[3]

Our Opponents are very active in procuring Freeholds, so much so that we must exert ourselves with the view of preserving the balance. This necessity is much to be regretted—but it is to me so obvious, that I purchased the other day a freehold Estate in Langdale[4] which will divide into 7. Of these 5 are already disposed of, one to Mr Gee, and the other four to my own Relations. I recollect you were afraid of too much being done by our friends. I have not yet seen any excess to confirm the apprehension.

[1] His last article appeared on 12 Dec.

[2] In his editorial for 5 Dec., De Quincey stated that the trivia of local politics were only of interest when they threw light on national issues. 'In his personal capacity Mr Brougham is no object of notice or regard to us: we know him, we speak of him, simply as the depository of certain principles, the advancer of certain pretensions, the accuser of certain men and institutions, and the champion of certain innovations.'

[3] De Quincey was not only having difficulty handling awkward contributors: he was also by nature dilatory, and his personal habits hindered the efficient running of the paper. On 21 Nov. he inserted the following NOTICE TO THE PUBLIC: 'The Editor of the "West. Gaz." has to lament that a painful indisposition for some weeks past, which has made the act of composition very distressing to him, has prevented him from fulfilling many engagements heretofore contracted to the Public generally, or to particular correspondents. In other respects (especially in the selection and preparation of the articles) he has not allowed any personal consideration to interfere with the laborious discharge of his duty to the Public.'

[4] See previous letter.

Your account of France interested me much.[1]—The People are likely to be too strong in every country, for the information they possess.

You shall hear from me again as soon as I have seen Mr Fleming which I hope will be tomorrow.

Ever my dear Lord Lowther
faithfully yours
Wm Wordsworth

526. W. W. to VISCOUNT LOWTHER

MS. Lonsdale MSS., Record Office, The Castle, Carlisle. Hitherto unpublished.

Rydal Mount
Decr 8th 1818

My dear Lord Lowther,

I have seen Mr Fleming, and told him every thing you wished,—adding a good deal from my self. I read him a considerable part of your last Letter—he says that he has now finished;—the *conclusion* of his Letter being sent for publication next week. I asked him if there was any part of it not yet published which he wished to alter in consequence of the communication I had made; he said, no; and that the Public would hear no more of him unless he were personally attacked. Now this he must expect and so I said to him; and endeavoured to persuade him that the most dignified mode of proceeding was to treat the assailants with silent contempt. But of this it is impossible to convince him; so that after all I fear there will be no way of keeping him quiet but by a resolution on the part of the Editor not to admit matter of this obnoxious character. I have frequently urged De Quincey to adopt this plan; he acknowledges the propriety of it; but he has no firmness.—I shall be at him again upon the subject.

It is some satisfaction to learn that you think tranquillity may be preserved in France, for some time at least. I was afraid of a speedy explosion.

You will not think I am taking a liberty when I say that it would be well if an opportunity should occur for your paying some atten-

[1] Lord Lowther had written to W. W. from Paris on 30 Nov.: 'The people are wild to imitate England, and you may guess how far this Country is fit for a Representative Govt. It is the nature of the French to be active and to like mischief or change, and though all will remain quiet for a few years, it is to be feared that the Revolution is not at an end.' (*WL MSS.*)

tion to young Wilson the eldest Son of Mr Wilson of Abbot Hall; I understand he thought himself neglected by you at Appleby. I know nothing of the Young Man, but from his situation in the County, it is reasonable and politic that he should not be overlooked.

Ever faithfully yours
Wm Wordsworth

527. W. W. to C. W.

Address: To the Rev^d Dr Wordsworth, Rectory, Lambeth.
Postmark: 4 Jan. 1819. *Stamp*: Kendal Penny Post.
MS. WL.
MY ii. 614, p. 831.

Jan^ry 1st 1819

My dear Brother,

Mr Monkhouse will probably have shewn you the copy of Mr Russel's[1] Letter, as I learn he has already done of mine to him.—As mine was perhaps longer than necessary or expedient his is concise enough.

If I understand the Madras system, one of its fundamental principles is; that so far from want of quickness being an objection, the efficiency of the new system is chiefly shewn in the treatment of slow Boys.—One Boy advances *more rapidly* than another, but *all* are made to advance according to their talents.—I conclude then, either that Mr Russel does not perceive this principle of the system, or he is content to have his school managed with as much of the new scheme as suits his fancy, and to fall below the point of its characteristic excellence, or that not questioning but my Son might benefit to a certain degree, he apprehends that striking a balance between loss and gain, the account would be against the Boy. This supposing him to judge conscientiously; if he be determined by selfish notions grounded upon the great name of the School, then, he must submit to the charge brought against most Masters of Public Schools, viz., that of indifference concerning the mass and the slower Boys provided a few at the top can make a brilliant figure.—It is difficult to give a just account of John's powers of mind—the darker side has been laid before you—the brighter is of less interest to a *school* master. His judgement is excellent, [h]is memory good, his command of words extraordinary, his love of knowle[d]ge striking, but

[1] The Revd. John Russell, D.D. (1786–1863), headmaster of the Charterhouse, 1811–32, and Canon of Canterbury from 1827.

his difficulties in attaining it such as I have described. He is never weary of listening to interesting and instructive conversation, catches at it from all quarters, when the trouble is not imposed upon him of seeking it *himself* in books—not that I can say that he is *idle* now, or wanting in zeal; but he is so long in finding his words in his dictionary, and so inaccurate in reading that he meets with difficulties often where his Aunt would not have found them at 4 years of age.—I'll give you a slight specimen of his way of reading English, exhibited two or three days ago—'Oh! that', (he read '*On* that') 'requi[te]' he read rightly—the *same* word in the next line he read '*require*'; three or four lines lower, 'meagre stores of verbal gratitude', he read *stories*—and so on. In his spelling he is much improved, but it continues very bad for his years.

His distinguishing himself at the University, educate him where you will, appears out of the question; he is nevertheless a promising Youth, with whom every body is pleased; his character is so manly, modest and dignified.

I have had an offer of £30 for the House at Cross Cannonby the Title deeds are lost—do you think it worth our while to guarantee the purchase as Trustees, otherwise it cannot be sold—pray let me know.—I sent you long since a Copy of the Address to the Freeholders, by an acquaintance; who took it [to] London and said she had forwarded it to you—a few other small things were sent at the same time. The Wordsworths are too poor to print at their own cost for the gratification of others—many thanks, however, for your good intentions and wishes—ever most affectionately yours W W

If you think it would be possible to get my younger Son on the foundation at Charter House I should like to try. Tell me how to set about it. My *income* is far short of what is necessary to educate three children as I could wish—I must dip into the principal of our little; so that such a situation for Wm. would be very acceptable.

[*M. W. writes*]

What a deplorable scrawl this is!—Accept the joint good wishes of us all to you and the dear Boys. M. W.

528. W. W. to VISCOUNT LOWTHER

MS. Lonsdale MSS., Record Office, The Castle, Carlisle. Hitherto unpublished.

Rydale Mount
January 2nd 1819

My dear Lord Lowther,

I should have thanked you for the kindness of your Note announcing your return, immediately, had you not given me reason to expect a Letter next day.—Mr Fleming did *not* take my communication well;[1] I knew that he would not, and deferred making it from a hope that it would prove unnecessary. You know my respect for his character; I believe him to be a most honourable man;—but his feelings are far too acute and his temper too irritable to deal with. He wrote to Lord Lonsdale on the occasion; and fortunately the answer he received was such as set his mind at rest.—He was anxious to be at work again upon the subject of the Bible Society, and sent to the Editor a long communication upon it—to be *continued.* The agitation of this Question through the Westnd Gazette, I think, is much to be deprecated; as we have numerous friends who are zealously attached to that Society. I cannot but be of opinion, therefore, that Mr Fleming had better publish what he has to say upon this subject in a separate pamphlet, as the discussion in the Gazette would tend to sow dissension among us; which we cannot afford,—having a most formidable enemy to contend with. Never lose sight, my dear Lord Lowther, of these facts, that 40 shillings a year is a qualification; that less will suffice where the conscience is not very nice; and that incessant pains are taken to persuade the lower orders that the Yellows are their oppressors; that they flourish at their expense, and that could they have men of their own chusing, meat and drink would be at half the price, and every thing to their mind. With what is going on at Kendal, and my own neighbourhood I am well acquainted, and can assure you, that we must not sleep at our posts. Several here are looking out for Freeholds in Cumberland also—Edmonds[2] has purchased one, and Mr Crump[3] will do so also on the first opportunity.

I received under cover from Mr Beckett[4] a pamphlet on the

[1] i.e. to abstain from newspaper controversies.

[2] An Ambleside attorney who presided at the Dinner of Brougham's supporters, mentioned in the next letter.

[3] The Liverpool attorney who in 1805 built Allan Bank.

[4] Right Hon. Sir John Beckett, 2nd Bart. (1775–1847), who had married Lady Ann Lowther, Lord Lonsdale's third daughter, in 1817. M.P. for Cockermouth, 1818–21, for Hazlemere, 1826–32, and for Leeds, 1835–7; Judge Advocate General, 1826–30 and 1834–5.

subject of Brougham's misrepresentations concerning Winchester School.[1] A summary of the grossest of his offences in this way, shall be laid before the Public (through the Gazette) at a proper time.

Many thanks for your interesting intelligence from France.—Be so good as let me know how Lady Mary is in health. I remain my

Dear Lord Lowther
ever faithfully yours
Wm Wordsworth

529. W. W. to VISCOUNT LOWTHER

MS. Lonsdale MSS., Record Office, The Castle, Carlisle. Hitherto unpublished.

Jany 10th [1819]

My dear Lord Lowther,

I was much gratified by your last interesting Letter. Dr. Ireland's Pamphlet[2] will be of use to us when we review Brougham's conduct through the whole of this business, which will be done during the sitting of Parl[nt]. I scarcely know what to say of Mr Fleming's feelings. I do not fear that any shyness between us will take place in consequence, but I am sure that I stand lower in his opinion, from not seeing some things in the light he does, and from not sharing several of his sentiments.—He was hurt also at your not writing *directly* to himself, and has dwelt much upon it. But do not take any notice of this ground of offence; what I regret most is, that he has spoken to many of my conversation with him, in consequence of which it is now noised (by means of the Chronicle[3]) through West[nd], that an extinguisher has been put upon him. I am much hurt, for he is both an able and excellent man; but it is entirely his own un-

[1] *Vindiciae Wykehamicae, or A Vindication of Winchester College. A Letter Addressed to Henry Brougham, Esq. occasioned by his Letter to Sir Samuel Romilly on Charitable Abuses.* By the Revd. W. L. Bowles. Extracts were published in the *Westmorland Gazette* for 12 and 19 Dec. 1818, and 2 Jan. 1819.

[2] *A Letter to Henry Brougham Esq., M.P.* [in reply to certain statements respecting charitable funds connected with the parish of Croydon made in Brougham's *Letter to Sir Samuel Romilly M.P.*], dated 21 Dec. 1818. John Ireland (1761–1842), Dean of Westminster and benefactor of Oxford University, had been vicar of Croydon, 1793–1816. In a letter to W. W. of 5 Jan., Lord Lowther described this pamphlet as 'a severe flagellation' of Brougham (*WL MSS.*).

[3] An editorial in the *Kendal Chronicle* for 2 Jan. hinted that the editor of the *Westmorland Gazette* was being embarrassed by a contributor who refused to be silenced.

governable temper which has brought this, which will be proved an additional vexation upon himself.

I cannot but look with some apprehension at a passage in your last, which coincides with Reports current in Westnd, that some person will be brought forward not of your family.[1] The wishes of the Gentry must, if they take that direction, be attended to; but, as I mentioned to Lord Lonsdale, I am decisively of opinion, that unless the Gentry require the change, we shall lose greatly by it.—The Yeomanry and lower order of Freeholders who have already voted for you and your Br[other] care nothing for the objection of two members from one Family; and that being so they naturally attach themselves with most zeal to those whom they have heard the most about, and who have the most power, that is the Lowthers. Take away one of this name, and *substitute* a Person little known, and I am sure that the zeal of many would be exceedingly damped. Besides, many will consider such a step as giving way to the enemy, while the rest will feel that it is the same power acting covertly instead of openly.

Last Saturday was a great day at Ambleside; Wakefield's medals[2] were distributed, and Mr Curwen made one of his long speeches; in which without enlightening the understanding of his audience he considerably inflamed their passions. One of his topics, was the Corn Laws, and he dwelt much upon the misgovernment of the country as manifested by the difficulty which a Labourer finds in maintaining himself and his family. Lord Liverpool has not courage enough to govern this country in time of Peace. What you say of the Westminster election[3] I entirely concur with; and as far as I am qualified to judge in respect to French affairs also. I remain dear Lord Lowther

very faithfully yours
Wm Wordsworth

[1] See L. 542 below.

[2] At a Dinner on 9 Jan. (reported in the *Kendal Chronicle* for the 16th) some of these medals, which had been struck at John Wakefield's expense to commemorate Brougham's intervention in the Westmorland Election, were presented to 'the Independent electors' of Ambleside.

[3] i.e. the pending by-election, caused by the death of Sir S. Romilly. Brougham, who was still sitting for Winchelsea, apparently declined an invitation to come forward (see Aspinall, *Lord Brougham and the Whig Party*, p. 94). For the result, see L. 538 below.

530. D. W. to CATHERINE CLARKSON

Address: Mrs Clarkson, at W. Buck's Esqre, Bury, Suffolk.
Stamp: Kendal Penny Post.
MS. British Museum.
K (—). *MY ii. 615, p. 833.*

Tuesday 12th Jan. [1819]

I hesitated for a moment before I ventured to open your *little* letter—Because it was a little one a fear rushed in that some thing amiss might have happened; and believe me, my dearest Friend, that I felt very happy, not only in finding that my apprehensions were unfounded, but that you were even happier than usual. Above all it is matter of rejoicing that your dear Son is now likely to settle into habits of steadiness. If he is fond of his profession he cannot but do well as there has never been a doubt in any quarter of his abilities. I hope this letter will find you at Bury—You cannot think the pleasure it gives me to be so affectionately remembered by your excellent Father. What delight he must take in his little Grandson! I fancy I see the benevolent smile in his eyes when he is caressing that child. Your letter came on Saturday evening. On Sunday I could not write—was engaged all day yesterday—and now it is (on Tuesday) within half an hour of post time and I resolved to put off writing till to-morrow, when I recollected that to-morrow I am engaged to go with a party of young ones to visit Betty Yewdale in Langdale, the good woman recorded in The Excursion, who received the Pedlar in her cottage and walked backwards and forwards with her light upon the hill to direct her Husband's homeward steps from the Quarry.[1] I wanted to write to you at length and thoughtfully; in my present hurry I shall forget more than half of what I ought to say. I wish I could be useful to the young Man who wishes to improve himself in the North, but there is only one possible chance that occurs to me or any of us. Mr Dawes is quite out of the question for various reasons which I need not detail; but the schoolmaster of Barton, we think not unlikely, and through Thomas Wilkinson you might apply. He is very steady, sensible and a good schoolmaster. He is a curate at some one of the Churches in that neighbourhood, is, I believe, married and has a nice comfortable house. I have conversed with him at his own door and was much pleased. His name is Thompson.[2] He has, I believe, had one or two young men in his house for the purpose for which you apply, and I

[1] *The Excursion*, v, ll. 728–71 (*PW* v, p. 175).

[2] The Revd. John Thompson (1777–1861), rector of Patterdale for fifty-seven years: mentioned in L. 500.

believe several big Boys have gone to him in the holidays. Upon the whole I think your Friend may succeed by applying to him. Since I last wrote to you we have gone through all the anxiety and agitation of determining to send John Wordsworth to the Charterhouse. Shirts were made, journey arranged, and every thing ready, and a letter came from Mr. Russell the head master which put a stop to his going. My Brother wrote frankly and with most tender solicitude describing John's age, attainments, and dispositions. Of the last he *could* not speak too favourably. Mr. R's reply was that the standing rule of his school was to admit no boy after 14 and from what my Br. had said he thought it not advisable to depart in this case from the general rule. This was a great disappointment to us. My Brother would not for the world send him to any other *public* school; but the Charter H. being conducted on Dr Bell's plan he had great hopes that John might do well there. I have much more to say on this subject but time will not allow. John is to stay at home for a while under his Father's sole tuition and he intends him for Cambridge—with no hope of his making a figure there; but I trust he has well-grounded expectations that he will not disgrace himself. John now takes great pains. His understanding is very good; yet his slowness inconceivable. Dorothy has been at home 3 weeks, returns to school tomorrow week. She is greatly improved and we have every reason to be delighted with Miss Dowling and her sister. Miss D. will have nine Boarders after the holidays, and it seems likely that the school will go on increasing till she has as many as she wishes for, or can manage, everything being taught by herself or her sister. Mrs Coleridge is here, with Sara and Edith,—two sweet Girls,—and you may be sure we have mirth and merriment enough, with such jinglings of the Pianoforte as would tire any but very patient people. We had a grand Ball last Thursday. The house turned inside out. Ballroom decorated with evergreens, a happy employment with hard labour for the Girls. Two whole mornings were so engaged, and who should come in unexpectedly but Dr. Bell? The Lasses' Friend, he was detained for the Ball, and only left us yesterday. He tutored Miss Dowling, carried her Girls with D. to form a Class, visited the Trinket shop, spent four guineas for them, and left every one a guinea at parting. Mr. Johnson from the Central School is to be here on Saturday; but alas, only for two days. On that day Mrs. C. leaves us—and the girls are woe be-gone. Hartley has done excellently at Oxford[1]—has had high compliments from the Tutor,

[1] Hartley Coleridge, who had been at Merton College, Oxford, since 1815, had just been awarded a Second Class *in literis humanioribus* (see *Letters of*

is now with his Father—writes thoughtfully—resolves to do his utmost in the beaten road, has got the promise of two pupils. We have great hopes that Derwent will get to one of the Universities;[1] but it is not yet so far settled that I can say anything further than that Grosvenor Lloyd has offered to allow him 30£ per ann out of his living. This is noble and affecting, and his Mother[2] rejoices at it. *She*, poor woman, is at Birmingham struggling with law-suits and family quarrels,—her husband at Ambleside in a wretched state—he lies in bed all day—and lies or sits up in bed all night awake, his imaginations are horrid. William has written some beautiful sonnets lately.[3] That is all he has done. His giving so much time to John will be a sad thing and glad should I be if a private situation could be found for John where he might be well-instructed. No time for more—no room. All well at Hindwell—all well here. Give my kind love to Mr Clarkson, your Father and Sister. Remember me to your Brothers and Mrs Kitchener. God bless you, my dear good Friend—Believe me evermore your affectionate D. Wordsworth—I cannot look over what I have written.

531. W. W. to LORD LONSDALE

MS. Lonsdale MSS., Record Office, The Castle, Carlisle.
K (—). *MY ii. 616, p. 835* (—).

Rydale Mount
Jany 13th 1819

My Lord,

Is it worth while to mention to your Lordship that on Saty last Mr Wakefield's medals[4] were distributed at Ambleside? There was an attendance of Demagogues from Kendal; and Mr Curwen made

Hartley Coleridge, ed. Griggs, pp. 18–19). In April he was elected fellow of Oriel.

[1] Derwent Coleridge, who had taken employment as a tutor, eventually went up to St. John's College, Cambridge, in the autumn of 1820.

[2] D. W.'s statement as it stands is confusing: 'his Mother' clearly refers to Mrs. Coleridge, while '*she*' is Mrs. Charles Lloyd; but the mention of Grosvenor Lloyd has led her mind from the one to the other. Grosvenor, Charles Lloyd's eldest son, was now working in his grandfather's bank in Birmingham. See *Minnow Among Tritons*, pp. 73–4.

[3] See *MW* 21, p. 41. These sonnets included three 'Suggested by Mr W. Westall's Views of the Caves, etc., in Yorkshire' (*PW* iii, pp. 36–7), published in the January issue of *Blackwood's Magazine* (see L. 532 below) and in the *Peter Bell* vol. in April; and nineteen on the River Duddon, published in 1820 (see *PW* iii, pp. 505–6).

[4] See L. 529 above.

one of his long harangues. Among other topics he dwelt at length upon the last Bill;[1] and declaimed against the Government of the Country for having made it so difficult for a labouring man to maintain his family. Your Lordship knows what kind of hearers this discourse must have been addressed to and will infer (what was really the case) that their passions were not a little inflamed, without any addition being made to their knowledge.—

It was lately notified to me that my name has been inserted by the Lord Chancellor in the Comm^{n} of the Peace for Westnd.[2] As an additional proof of Your Lordship's favorable opinion, this official communication of an event which your last Letter led me to expect could not but be gratifying to me. I wish I could add that I feel myself properly qualified for the undertaking, and that I could get rid of those apprehensions which they who know me better than I know myself are perpetually pressing upon me, that my literary exertions will suffer more than I am aware of from this engagement. They ground their opinion upon an infirmity of which I am conscious; *viz*, that whatever pursuit I direct my attention to, is apt to occupy my mind too exclusively.—But why should I trouble your Lordship with these personal considerations?—I am anxious to discharge my obligations to society, and if it should continue to be thought proper for me, in the failure of other eligible Persons, to attempt to be serviceable in this way, I must be upon my guard to suffer as little injury as possible.

Have the goodness when you write to let me know how Lady Mary is in health.

With the highest respect
I have the honor to be
my Lord
Your Lordship's
most faithfully
Wm Wordsworth

[1] i.e. the Corn Bill of 1815.

[2] As Lord Lieutenant, Lord Lonsdale had the responsibility of submitting nominations. 'You will easily prepare yourself for the office of Magistrate . . .', he wrote encouragingly on 22 Jan. (*WL MSS.*); but in April W. W. was still hesitating whether to qualify (see L. 540 below). In the end he seems to have decided against it, for the reasons he goes on to give.

532. W. W. to THE EDITOR OF THE *WESTMORLAND GAZETTE*

MS. untraced.
Westmorland Gazette, 6 Feb., 1819. Pollitt, op. cit., p. 25.

Rydal Mount, Feb. 3rd, 1819.

Sir,

Having observed three original Sonnets of mine[1] announced as making part of the contents of the last number of Blackwood's Edinburgh Magazine, you will oblige me by reprinting them in your journal from my own M.S. in which they have undergone some alteration since they were presented by me to Mr Westall,[2] with liberty to make what use of them he thought proper.

I am, Sir, respectfully yours,
William Wordsworth

533. W. W. to FRANCIS WRANGHAM

Address: The Revd. F. Wrangham, Hunmanby, Bridlington.
Stamp: Kendal Penny Post.
MS. Henry Huntington Library.
Grosart (—). K (—). MY ii. 620, p. 840.

Rydal Mount, Febry 19th, 1819.

Dear Wrangham,

I received your kind Letter last night, for which you will accept my thanks. I write upon the spur of that mark of your regard—or my aversion to Letter-writing might get the better of me. Rogers read me his Poem[3] when I was in Town about 12 months ago; but I have heard nothing of it since. It contained some very pleasing passages, but the title is much too grandiloquent for the performance, and the plan appeared to me faulty. I know little of Blackwood's Magazine, and wish to know less. I have seen in it articles so infamous that I do not chuse to let it enter my doors. The Publisher sent it to me some time ago, and I begged (civilly you will

[1] 'Suggested by Mr W. Westall's Views of the Caves, etc., in Yorkshire.' See L. 530 above.

[2] See L. 524 above. Much to W. W.'s annoyance, Westall must have sent the sonnets straight off to John Wilson, editor of *Blackwood's*, which was still banned at Rydal Mount (see next letter). W. W. now took the opportunity of adding a fourth sonnet 'Composed During a Storm' (*PW* iii, p. 27), which had only just been completed.

[3] *Human Life, A Poem*, published in spring, 1819.

take for granted) not to be troubled with it any longer. Except now and then, when Southey accommodates me, I see no new Books whatever, so that of course I know nothing of Miss Aikins' Queen Elizabeth.[1] I ought to have mentioned that the three Sonnets advertised in Blackwood's Magazine as from my pen were truly so, but they were not of my sending.[2]

As to the St Bees case you will see that no doubt as well as all others, in the report from the Committ[ee] which will soon be laid before Par[liament]. It will prove that all Mr B's allegations are unfounded.

I am glad to hear you are engaged with Dr. Zouch.[3] I find it difficult to speak publicly of good men while alive, especially if they are persons who have power; the world ascribes the eulogy to interested motives, or to an adulatory spirit, which I detest. But of Lord Lonsdale I will say to you that I do not think there exists in England a man of any rank more anxiously desirous to discharge his Duty in that station of life to which it has pleased God to call him. His thought and exertions are constantly directed to that object, and the more he is known the more is he beloved and respected and admired.

I ought to have thanked you before for your versions of Virgil's Eclogues,[4] which reached me at last. I have lately compared it line for line with the original, and think it very well done. I was particularly pleased with the skill you have shewn in managing the Contest between the Shepherds in the third Pastoral, where you have included in a succession of couplets the sense of Virgil's paired hexameter. I think I mentioned to you that these Poems of Virgil have always delighted me much; there is frequently in them an elegance and a happiness which no translation can hope to equal. In point of fidelity your translation is very good indeed.

You astonish me with the account of your Books,[5] and I should

[1] Lucy Aikins, *Memoirs of the Court of Queen Elizabeth*, 2 vols., 1818. In his letter to W. W. of 15 Feb. (*WL MSS.*), Wrangham pointed out that she had rejected the tradition W. W. followed in *The White Doe of Rylstone*; *or, The Fate of the Nortons* that the Nortons, father and sons, had been executed. For the ballad W. W. relied on, see *PW* iii, p. 538. See also L. 114, pt. i, p. 237.

[2] See previous letter.

[3] Thomas Zouch, D.D. (1737–1815), uncle of Lord Lonsdale, divine and antiquary, and Prebendary of Durham from 1805. He published an edition of Isaac Walton's works, 1795–6. Wrangham's edition of Zouch's works appeared in 2 vols. in 1820.

[4] Fifty copies printed in 1815: published in Valpy's *Family Classical Library*, 1830.

[5] 'Does your passion for old Books continue?', Wrangham had inquired. He claimed to have 14,000 vols. in his own library.

have been still more astonished if you had told me you had read a third (shall I say a tenth part) of them. My reading powers were never very great, and now they are much diminished, especially by candle light. And as to buying books, I can affirm that on *new* books I have not spent five shillings for the last 5 years. I include reviews, magazines, Pamphlets, etc., etc. So that there would be an end of Mr. Murray, and Mr. Longman, and Mr. Cadell etc., etc., if nobody had more power or inclination to buy than myself; and as to old Books, my dealings in that way, for want of means, have been very trifling. Nevertheless (small and paltry as my Collection is) I have not read a fifth part of it. I should however like to see your army.

> Such forces met not, nor so wide a camp,
> When Agrican, with all his *Northern* powers
> Besieged Albracca as *Romances* tell.[1]

Not that I accuse you of romancing. I verily believe that you have all the books you speak of—believe, and like the Devils, *tremble*! Dear Wrangham, are you and I ever likely to meet in this world again? Yours is a *corner* of the earth; mine is not so. I never heard of any body going to Bridlington, but all the world comes to the Lakes. Farewell. Excuse this wretched scrawl. It is like all that proceeds from my miserable pen. Be assured I shall be glad to hear of you at any and all times; but literary news, except what I get occasionally from Southey, I have none to send you in return. Ever faithfully yours

Wm. Wordsworth.

As to the Nortons the Ballad is my authority, and I require no more. It is much better than Virgil had for his Aeneid. Perhaps I ought to have mentioned that the articles in B's *Magazine*[2] that disgusted me so, were personal,—referring to myself and friends and acquaintances, especially Coleridge.

[1] *Paradise Regained*, iii. ll. 337–9.

[2] W. W. would be thinking particularly of the 'Observations' on his *Letter to a Friend of Burns* in *Blackwood's Magazine* for June, Oct., and Nov. 1817 (i. 261–6; ii. 65–73, 201–4). The Oct. issue (ii. 3–18) had also contained a highly derogatory review of Coleridge's *Biographia Literaria*. John Wilson had subsequently made some amends in two 'Essays on the Lake School of Poetry' in July and Dec. 1818 (iii. 369–81; iv. 257–63), which showed real sympathy for W. W.'s aims and methods. But more recently still—in the January and March issues for this year (iv. 396–404, 735–44)—there appeared the 'Letters from the Lakes: Translated from the German of Philip Kempferhausen: written in the summer of 1818', which reported personal conversations with Southey and W. W. As a result of this, *Blackwood's* remained under a cloud throughout the year (see *SH* 52, p. 152).

534. W. W. to ROBERT LUMB

Address: To Mr Lumb, Lowther.
Endorsed: Feb. 27. 1819. Mr. Wordsworth.
MS. Lonsdale MSS., Record Office, The Castle, Carlisle. Hitherto unpublished.

Rydal Mount Febry 27th [1819]

Dear Sir

Herewith I enclose a Deed of William Park late of Ivy How little Langdale—who, you will find, has purchased part of Mathew Spedding's Estate called Walthwaite in Gt. Langdale and as he is a Friend, Mr Jackson joins me in wishing him to be admitted Tenant *immediately*, in order to enable him to enfranchise.

Edward Park, brother of the said William, is also very steady, he has a small customary parcel in Great Langdale and wishes to purchase the *Intack*,[1] but nothing more free, to enable him to Vote at the next Election.—Pray let me know, at your earliest convenience, what will be the expense of these two enfranchisements.

I wish to see you *as soon* as you come into this neighbourhood, having some particulars to mention.

You will be glad to hear that there are good dispositions for strengthening the Lowther Party in this Parish—though I cannot say that our Opponents abate of their hostility.

I am dear Sir
Yours very truly
Wm Wordsworth

535. W. W. to JOHN SPEDDING[2]

MS. Cornell. Hitherto unpublished.

Rydal Mount
Ambleside March 1st [1819]

Dear Spedding,

I am about to write to you upon a small concern of my own, which you will probably hear of through Mr Losh of Newcastle.

I understand from my Subdistributor of Stamps at Ulverstone that certain considerable duties due under the Will of my old Friend

[1] A local word signifying a mountain-enclosure, or piece of ground taken in from a moorland. Cf. *An Evening Walk* (1793), l. 65 (*PW* i, p. 8.).

[2] Of Ormathwaite Hall, near Keswick, W. W.'s old schoolfellow (see *EY* 38, pp. 114 ff.): father of James Spedding, the editor of Bacon.

John Baldwyn[1] are going to be paid, and as your Cousin Mr Church is one of the Ex[rs], it is to be feared that the money may be paid through him, directly to the Head-Office in London. Now I presume upon your kindness so far as to request that you would beg of Mr Church and the other Ex[or] Mr Bailey if he acts, to allow the duties to be paid through the Ex[rs] who live in or near Ulverstone, one of whom, I know, is willing and desirous that they should be paid, upon the request of my Subdistributor residing there. It is proper to mention that the Estate of a Testator, derives no benefit by duties being paid into the Head off.—Our lamented Friend Godfrey Sykes, while Solicitor of Stamps, paid through my Office duties due under a Will to which he was Co-executor with a person living in my District.—But I will say no more; I am sure you will do your best to serve me with Mr Church.

My Wife and Sister join me in kind remembrances, and believe me Dear Spedding

Faithfully yours
Wm Wordsworth

536. W. W. to ROBERT LUMB

Address: To Mr Lumb, Lowther, Penrith.
Stamp: Kendal Penny Post. *Endorsed*: March 16, 1819. Mr W. Wordsworth.
MS. Lonsdale MSS., Record Office, The Castle, Carlisle. Hitherto unpublished.

Rydal Mount
March 16th [1819]

Dear Sir,

I could not write sooner from not being able to see the Parties.[2] We wish William Park's Special admittance to be executed immediately, and after that be so good as to forward his Enfranchisement if it can be done at an expense under £10. Edward Park, for the Intack and Knopsdale has consented to go to the expense of from £5 to £6 his object only being to Vote. He is an elderly Man without children and his Estate will go to one of his Brother's two Sons. Both the above appear to be as trust-worthy Persons as can be found. We shall add several more to the list of friends in this neigh-

[1] Of Aldingham Rectory near Ulverston, son of Dr. Roger Baldwin (see *EY* 50, p. 145), and brother of Cecilia Baldwin who married James Losh (see *EY* 85, p. 213). He had died on 25 Aug. 1818.

[2] See L. 534 above. Both William and Edward Park became freeholders as a result of these transactions, and duly voted for the Lowthers at the 1820 election.

bourhood.—But we get slowly forward. On some of the cases I wish to confer with you. Hoping to see you at Sockbridge on the last day of this Month or the 1st of April—

I remain with thanks for your obliging Letter

Yours very truly

Wm Wordsworth

Mr Jackson talks of going over to Sockbridge with me, hoping to see you.

537. D. W. to SARA HUTCHINSON

MS. WL. Hitherto unpublished.

[*c.* 17 Mar. 1819]

My dearest Sara,

Your letter of wonders arrived last night and I hasten to tell you that we are very grateful to Mary Hutchinson for her enthusiastic kindness in proposing to take such a journey for the love of us—and that we shall be ready to receive you all whenever it suits you to come[1]—only you must beware of the dangers of cold weather: for young children—cutting winds are more dangerous than even wet weather, as you will travel under cover. Last year we had most pleasant weather in May. It was the time when Mrs Ellstob and Betsy[2] were here; and often it was so warm that we suffered the fire to go out in the middle of the day. I know not when Easter falls; but that time will make no difference with respect to Dorothy, as Miss Dowling makes no holidays except at Midsummer 6 weeks, and at Xmas 4 weeks—not even a single day; but the indulgence of coming to tea on a Saturday afternoon, or to dinner on a Sunday does her no harm now that she is completely reconciled to school. She meets us with delight, and parts from us cheerfully and without agitation.—You *must* halt at Mr Cookson's; for Mrs C. we are sure will be very earnest that you should do so, therefore you had best propose it to her yourselves, which will please her the better. Their house is very much enlarged by taking in those rooms (formerly let) above the Dye-house; and I believe they will not even have occasion to borrow a bed; but there would be no difficulty in this for a night

[1] S. H. had been staying at Hindwell, and was planning to bring her sister-in-law on a visit to Rydal Mount early in May.

[2] Elizabeth Hutchinson, M. W.'s invalid sister, in the care of Mrs. Ellstob.

or two—Strickland[1] could sleep at Mr Wilson's,[2] where he is Clerk—or at Mrs Strickland's. We shall be able to manage very well. The front kitchen will make an excellent nursery and the middle kitchen must be used for cookery.—I am sorry to hear that Joanna has not begun to throw off or cut away some of her coverings—Pray tell her that Mr Scambler lays more stress upon this than any thing else. I am afraid that Tours is not sufficiently to the South for winter's warmth; but it must be a delightful place for summer; and if she should find that it was not likely to be warm enough in winter she might easily go southward. The length of the Voyage is a great advantage for her. My first thought was what a nice opportunity for me to go with her and how useful I should be for a few weeks till she was settled! but then came in the objection to me of the length of the voyage and the great expence of so much travelling—besides that we have no money to spare for me to spend in France. I really hope that Joanna may receive great benefit from the voyage, and change of scene and climate. As to poor Henry *he* will bring forward no obstacles. If he can be of use to Joanna he will be sufficiently happy at Tours or anywhere provided he is not forced into company.—We are of your opinion precisely respecting Betsy—that she can nowhere be so well as with Mrs Ellstob, provided she will keep her; and this I believe she will not consent to do unless she is well assured that she can hold her in security—but she had said she *could* not do it, and Mary is afraid that she could not accommodate a servant in her house. A letter came from John[3] last night enclosing a copy of one from Coleridge, promising to pay a half of the money in 4 weeks and the other half by a Bill at eight months or more. He objects

[*cetera desunt*]

[*written across first sheet*]

March [?18th]. Sir G. Beaumont says that Coleridge was so enchanted with his Daughter's picture[4] painted by Mr Collins that he could not help giving it him. I think it very like her and such a sweet picture.

Give my kind love to your Aunt and everyone else. God grant that dear Mary and her children may be the better for their journey. Yours ever

D. W.

[1] i.e. Strickland Cookson, later W. W.'s solicitor.
[2] One of the Kendal attorneys: probably Isaac Wilson.
[3] John Hutchinson. The origin of Coleridge's debt to him is unexplained.
[4] See L. 511 above, and Griggs, iv. 1147, 1158, pp. 878, 891.

538. W. W. to VISCOUNT LOWTHER

Address: To Lord Viscount Lowther.
MS. Lonsdale MSS., Record Office, The Castle, Carlisle.
K (—). *MY ii.* 622, *p.* 846 (—).

[early Apr. 1819]

My dear Lord Lowther,

Knowing how pressing your engagements must be at this time, I am greatly obliged by your last interesting Letter, and presume so far upon your kindness as to beg you would keep in mind your promise of writing if anything important in public affairs should occur.—The manner in which the abandonment of West^{r} to the Jacobins first, and then to the Whigs,[1] is taken by the supporters of the present administration, does them great credit. Cannot the Whigs be kept out by an union with the Grenville party, or that headed by Lord Wellesley[2]—or can these two parties be brought to act in concert, if the accession of one to those who support the principles of the present administration should not promise to be sufficient? I confess I dread the Whigs. There is not much perhaps in toasts at public dinners; but what shall we say to men who on such occasions drink the health of the Bishop of Norwich?[3] The possession of Place makes a great change in men's conduct; but still the Whigs are to be feared from their countenance of every species of Dissent; for this, if for no other reason.—Do you suppose that Tierney[4] is really sincere in his declaration that he adopts the positions of the Report of the Bullion Committee of which Horner[5]

[1] At the Westminster by-election in February, the Hon. George Lamb (1784–1834), brother of the 2nd Lord Melbourne, had been persuaded to stand in the Whig interest against the radicals John Cam Hobhouse and Major Cartwright. The radical Henry Hunt (1773–1835), who had unsuccessfully contested the seat in 1818, now supported Lamb and he was elected after a fifteen-day contest, having polled 4,465 votes to Hobhouse's 3,861 and Cartwright's 38.

[2] Richard Colley Wellesley, Marquis Wellesley (1760–1842), brother of the Duke of Wellington. Governor-General of India, 1797–1805, and Foreign Secretary under Perceval. With Grenville, he had supported the Government's recent repressive measures; and later, when some of Grenville's supporters took office under Lord Liverpool, he accepted the Lord Lieutenancy of Ireland.

[3] Henry Bathurst (1744–1837), who succeeded Manners-Sutton as Bishop of Norwich in 1805. He supported Catholic Emancipation and the Reform Bill, and was said to be unorthodox.

[4] George Tierney (1761–1830), M.P. for Appleby, 1812–18, and then for Knaresborough: at this period the recognized leader of the Opposition in the House of Commons, and a leading authority on finance.

[5] Francis Horner (1778–1817), the friend of Brougham and one of the founders of the *Edinburgh Review*. He entered the House of Commons in 1806, and in 1810 moved that a committee should be formed to inquire into the true causes of the high price of bullion and the state of the exchange. Their Report established the principle that the value of paper money could only be

was chairman? If he does he has studied political economy to little purpose.—For instance, what an assertion that gold had not risen in value, it was only that paper had fallen!—This is Theory trampling upon fact;—upon a consequence arising from the State of Europe obvious, one would have thought to a child.

If you will send down the Report of the Com: on public charities,[1] when it appears, I will take care to transfer it to the Editor of the Gazette, for the purpose of making extracts. No West^nd petition! You can hardly conceive how blank are the looks of some of B's supporters in this neighbourhood. Had B. no appearance of a case? or would he have really been sorry to be called to try his fortune again?—The Estate I purchased in Langdale has furnished votes for 8 gentlemen of my connection and Friends,[2] among whom is my brother Dr Wordsworth. Mr Myers reports that you are quite well.—The enclosed which I beg you would direct your Ser^nt to put into the 2 penny Post, is to a friend of mine connected with these Counties, who wishes together with some of his friends, natives of West^nd, to support the principles of your family by procuring freeholds. I shall trouble you with the kindest regards of Mrs Wordsworth and my Sister, who will be happy to see you again under our quiet roof. Ever

dear Lord Lowther
most faithfully yours
Wm Wordsworth

maintained as long as it was immediately convertible into gold. W. W.'s friend Sharp was a leading member of the Committee, and advocated the protection of the currency by law. The findings of the Committee were naturally unpopular with the government and the banks. On 2 Feb. 1819, Tierney moved the appointment of a committee to inquire into the effects produced on the exchange with foreign countries by the restriction on payments in cash by the bank, and to report what reason existed for continuing the restriction. In his speech he affirmed his adherence to the views of Horner and the Bullion Committee. (Note by de Selincourt.)

[1] This report appeared in late April, or early May, but De Quincey made no use of it in the *Westmorland Gazette*. He was preoccupied with political economy and with schemes for extending the literary side of the paper.

[2] See L. 524 above.

539. W. W. to MR WHITE[1]

Address: To Mr White, Stamp Off. Whitehaven.
Stamp: Kendal Penny Post.
MS. Cornell. Hitherto unpublished.

Rydale Mount
April 3d 1819

Dear Sir,

I learn that a fresh Coach is on the point of starting to run between Kendal and Ambleside. That which now runs, has been always licensed by me and the duty paid at my office here. As the whole space between the two places may be said to lie in my district, it is just that the duty should be paid to me; which is not likely unless it be licensed by me. I have therefore to request that you would wait on the Person to whose House at Whitehaven it runs, and try to prevail upon him to express a wish to the proprietors to that effect, if you find that it is not to be licensed here.

I presume so far upon your wish to serve me; though it is my desire that the duty as is the Case at Carlisle with the Coaches in Mr Ramshay's district should be paid direct to my office.

I am dear Sir
very truly yours
Wm Wordsworth

Since the above was written, I learn that the Coach is to start from Whitehaven in about a weeks time; and that it is connected with a Manchester Coach which may cause a difficulty, as it is too probable that the Coach will be licensed at Manchester for the whole way to Whitehaven—which could be very unreasonable. If you find that this is likely to be done, you will have the kindness to urge the Whitehaven Proprietor to object to it.

540. W. W. to LORD LONSDALE

MS. Lonsdale MSS., Record Office, The Castle, Carlisle. Hitherto unpublished.

Rydale Mount
April 7th 1819

My Lord,

Having occasion to go to Sockbridge along with our Rector, Mr Jackson, I begged of Mr Lumb to meet us there. He did so—he shewed us a List of Applicants for Enfranchisement; as far as we

[1] This letter illustrates W.W.'s careful administration of his Distributorship. As no regular salary attached to the office, it was necessary to see that the various licences and stamp duties which came under its jurisdiction were preserved and extended as far as possible, or the Distributor's income would suffer.

knew, they were all unexceptionable but two; a person named Thomson[1] of Ambleside who bore the flag before Mr B. and a violent agitator during the late Contest. The other case was that of Mr Barber,[2] which I took the Liberty of mentioning to your Lordship some time ago.—It had been represented to Mr Lumb that Mr Barber, being a Man of Fortune, could easily purchase a Freehold, and that if enfranchisement were refused he might make a case of it among his Friends, and induce several of them in London and elsewhere to purchase Freeholds, when they would otherwise have been quiet. I replied, "Grant all this; first we must bear in mind, that as far as is known this enfranchisement was never applied for, till it became an object to Mr Barber for the express purpose of voting against Lord Lowther and his Friends. It is therefore indelicate in Mr Barber to apply to his Lordship for this purpose, as he (Mr B.) must know that Lord Lonsdale cannot not grant his wish without prejudicing his own political interests, and, above all the cause, which, for the sake of public good, he has so strenuously supported. Now that such injury would ensue, I am certain. Votes in this neighbourhood have been procured, or are procuring to the amount of at least 20, for the purpose of supporting the present members, and many of these entirely on public grounds; now I ask whether such persons would not be greatly discouraged if they found that his Lordship was enfranchising persons in decided hostility to his interests and his cause. If Mr Barber wants a Freehold let him purchase one, and not call upon his Lordship to do what the supporters of the Lowther cause cannot but complain of." The above, my Lord, was the sum of what I said to Mr Lumb on the subject, in all which Mr Jackson agreed, as also Mr Gee, my neighbour, to whom I reported the conversation.

I do not look for any observation from your Lordship on this delicate subject, but I cannot be easy without informing you of the grounds of my opinion.

I presume much upon your Lordship's candor and kindness, and I rely upon your knowledge of the interest I take in this great question, or I should fear being condemned for officious interference.—

I have consulted some Friends in this neighbourhood whether I ought to qualify for the Magistracy.[3] Mr Barton has expressed a

[1] Vice-President at the Ambleside Dinner on 9 Jan., when Wakefield's medals were distributed.

[2] See L. 523 above.

[3] W. W.'s relatives were beginning to deplore the readiness with which he allowed these outside activities to consume his time. C. W. voiced the general

wish that I would, and offered his assistance; others recommend waiting a little, on the ground that the measure would, then, seem less connected with political considerations, in the minds of the ill-disposed. I have not seen Mr Knott, since he has been of the Commission.

I hope Lady Mary continues to improve in health.

With the highest respect
I have the honor to be
my Lord your Lordship's
most faithfully
Wm Wordsworth

Whitehaven is about to have another Newspaper.[1]

541. W. W. to J. FORBES MITCHELL[2]

Address: J. Forbes Mitchell Esq re, 40 Gloucester Place, London.
MS. WL.
Mem. MY ii. 621, p. 843.
[*In M.W.'s hand*] Rydal Mount, Apr. 21st 1819.

Sir,

The letter with which you have honoured me, bearing date the 31st of March, I did not receive until yesterday; and therefore could not earlier express my regret that, notwithstanding a cordial approbation of the *feeling* which has prompted the undertaking, and a genuine sympathy in admiration with the Gentlemen who have subscribed towards a Monument for Burns, I cannot unite my humble efforts with theirs in promoting this object. Sincerely can I affirm that my respect for the motives which have swayed these gentlemen has urged me to trouble you with a brief statement of the reasons of my dissent. In the first place, Eminent poets appear to me to be a Class of men who, less than any others, stand in need of such marks of distinction, and hence I infer that this mode of

feeling in a letter of 17 Apr.: 'I long to hear of your getting on with the Recluse—and grieve therefore to think of your time being taken up in Executorship business and in Justice Business (but this I hope is a premature report), and above all, I hope that (as you do not mention it) you have not persevered in the plan of instructing John yourself. Really your time is too valuable for such occupations.' (*WL MSS.*)

[1] The *Whitehaven Gazette*. See L. 547 below.

[2] John Forbes Mitchell (1786–1822) of Thainstone, near Aberdeen. At a meeting in Edinburgh on 24 Apr., he was elected Treasurer of the fund for building a national monument to Burns on the Carlton Hill.

acknowledging their merits is one for which they would not, in general, be themselves solicitous. Burns did, indeed, erect a monument to Ferguson;[1] but I apprehend that his gratitude took this course because he felt that Ferguson had been prematurely cut off, and that his fame bore no proportion to his deserts. In neither of these particulars can the fate of Burns justly be said to resemble that of his Predecessor, his years indeed were few, but numerous enough to allow him to spread his name far and wide, and to take permanent root in the affections of his Countrymen: in short he has raised for himself a Monument so conspicuous, and of such imperishable materials, as to render a local fabric of Stone superfluous, and therefore comparatively insignificant. But why, if this be granted, should not his fond admirers be permitted to indulge their feelings, and at the same time to embellish the Metropolis of Scotland? If this may be justly objected to, and in my opinion it may, it is because the showy Tributes to Genius are apt to draw of[f] attention from those efforts by which the interests of Literature might be substantially promoted; and to exhaust public spirit in comparatively unprofitable exertions, when the wrongs of literary men are crying out for redress on all sides. It appears to me that towards no class of his Majesty's Subjects are the laws so unjust and oppressive.— The attention of Parliament has lately been directed by petition to the exaction of copies of newly published Works for certain Libraries;[2] but this is a trifling evil compared with the restrictions imposed upon the duration of Copyright, which in respect to Works profound in philosophy, or elevated, abstract, and refined in imagination, is tantamount almost to an exclusion of all pecuniary recompense for the Author, and even where Works of imagination and manners are so constituted as to be adapted to immediate demand, as in the case of those of Burns, justly may it be asked what reason can be assigned that an Author who dies young should have

[1] Robert Fergusson (1750–74), a poet to whom Burns often acknowledged his debt. For his tombstone in the Canongate Churchyard, Edinburgh, Burns wrote the inscription:

> No sculptur'd Marble here, nor pompous lay,
> 'No storied Urn nor animated Bust';
> This simple stone directs pale Scotia's way
> To pour her sorrow o'er her Poet's dust.

(Note by de Selincourt.)

[2] This petition was laid before the House of Commons on 17 Apr. 1818. Sir Egerton Brydges, M.P. for Maidstone, 1812–18, had introduced a new Copyright Bill just before this, but his proposal lapsed with the dissolution. W. W. had probably read Southey's review of the whole question in the *Quarterly Review*, No. xli (Jan. 1819).

the prospect before him of his Children being left to languish in Poverty and Dependence, while Booksellers are revelling in luxury upon gains derived from Works which are the delight of many Nations.

This subject might be carried much further, and we might ask, if the course of things insured immediate wealth, and accompanying rank and honours, honours and wealth often entailed on their families to Men distinguished in the other learned professions, why the laws should interfere to take away those pecuniary emoluments which are the natural Inheritance of the posterity of Authors whose pursuits, if directed by genius and sustained by industry, yield in importance to none in which the Members of a Community can be engaged.

But to recur to the proposal in your letter:—I would readily assist, according to my means, in erecting a Monument to the memory of Chatterton, who with transcendent genius was cut off by his own hand while he was yet a Boy in years; this, could he have anticipated the tribute, might have soothed his troubled spirit; as[1] an expression of general belief in the existence of those powers which he was too impatient and too proud to develop. At all events it might prove an awful, and a profitable warning—I should also be glad to see a monument erected on the banks of Lochleven to the memory of the innocent, and tender-hearted Michael Bruce,[2] who, after a short life spent in poverty and obscurity, was called away too early to leave behind him more than a few trustworthy promises of pure affections and unvitiated imagination.

Let the Gallant Defenders of our Country be liberally rewarded with Monuments: their noble Actions cannot speak for themselves as the Writings of Men of genius are able to do; gratitude in respect to them stands in need of admonition; and the very multitude of Heroic competitors, which increase the demand for this sentiment towards our Naval and Military defenders considered as a Body, is injurious to the claims of Individuals.—Let our great Statesmen and eminent Lawyers, our learned and eloquent Divines, and they who have successfully devoted themselves to the abstruser Sciences, be rewarded in like manner; but towards departed Genius, exerted in the fine Arts and more especially in Poetry, I humbly think, in the present state of things, the sense of our obligation to

[1] *Written* and.

[2] Michael Bruce (1746–67), born on the banks of Loch Leven, the son of a weaver—educated at Edinburgh, he became a schoolmaster. His poems were edited in 1770 by John Logan: he is said to have been the real author of Logan's *Cuckoo*. (Note by de Selincourt.)

it may more satisfactorily be expressed by means pointing directly to the general benefit of Literature.

Trusting that these opinions of an Individual will be candidly interpreted, I have the honour to be,

Your obedient servant
[*signed*] Wm Wordsworth

542. W. W. to VISCOUNT LOWTHER

MS. Lonsdale MSS., Record Office, The Castle, Carlisle. Hitherto unpublished.

Rydale Mount
April 25th 1819

My dear Lord Lowther,

Your Letter and the accompanying account of the Dinner[1] were very acceptable. I should have thanked you for both, immediately, but I waited thinking something might occur in West^nd^ worth mentioning.—We are all very quiet; I have the satisfaction to say that the Lowther interest is greatly strengthening and consolidating itself in this neighbourhood, and elsewhere; so that unless the opposite Party are active in the East Ward (which your account of Lord Thanet's dispositions does not render probable) we may consider ourselves as gaining very considerably upon them. I cannot learn that more than eleven Blue Votes have been, or are likely to be made, about, and in Ambleside; I trust *we* shall shortly have upwards of 20.—It is evident from the dinner Speeches in London, that they are greatly discouraged. It is remarkable that not a word was said about the famous Association.[2] Are they ashamed of the thing? Or has its Founder discovered the impolicy of his scheme?—It requires assuredly no small degree of confidence in Mr B. to talk so openly of other People's ill temper, he who managed his own so wretchedly through his exertions in West^nd^.

Knowing young Graham's[3] hostile dispositions, I was not chagrined to see him in open array.—His object is Cumberland. Is

[1] The London Dinner of the Friends to the Independence of Westmorland was held on 13 Mar., with J. C. Curwen in the chair (see *Kendal Chronicle* for 20 Mar.). Brougham and William Crackanthorpe were among the speakers.

[2] Brougham's Association for securing the Independence of Westmorland.

[3] Right Hon. Sir James Robert Graham, 2nd Bart. (1792–1861), of Netherby. At this time Whig M.P. for Hull, he later represented Carlisle and then Cumberland, 1827–37. First Lord of the Admiralty, 1830–4, he was one of the four who prepared the first Reform Bill. He lost his seat in 1837 on going over to the Tories, but was Home Secretary under Peel in 1841.

it not probable that he spoke on the late motion of Sir M. W. Ridley[1] not without a hope of indirectly casting some disparagement on you for having filled the office of a junior Lord?—It is *unparliamentary* to impute discreditable motives; but I have heard enough of this Person to make me apprehend that he is not above the influence of such feelings.

I am truly glad that the Whigs are disappointed in the results of the Westminster Election, as a test of their popularity.[2] But let me return a moment to the Westmorland Dinner. Much was said of Mr Hasell;[3] the younger, I suppose, being the person meant. It is certainly to be regretted that two Lowthers were proposed; but that having been got over, it is to be hoped that some time will elapse before another election takes place; otherwise, you will probably agree with me, that it would look like an acknowledgement of inferiority, neither pleasant nor creditable if such a change should be made in the *Persons* while the *principle* continues the same. The county of West^nd is decidedly favorable to those measures of Government which the Lowther family have supported, and [as] long as they retain the same confidence in the Lowther family, the discerning part of the County will not complain of their influence, they will rather feel it a benefit to West^nd and to England at large.—As to young Hasell he is a very deserving Person, but could a Candidate equally eligible from this side of the County have been found, our cause would have derived much more support from such a one; in case a change *is* intended; which, I confess, *I should be sorry for*.

A word upon France—the principle of augmenting the number of Peers[4] is probably good, but Europe and America will feel the

[1] Sir Matthew White Ridley, 3rd Bart. (1778–1836), of Heaton Hall, Northumberland: M.P. for Newcastle upon Tyne. On 18 Mar. he had moved a reduction in the number of junior Lords of the Admiralty, and Graham supported his proposal in the interests of economy.

[2] See L. 538 above.

[3] i.e. Edward W. Hasell (1796–1872), son of Edward Hasell (1765–1825) of Dalemain, near Penrith. The latter was acknowledged leader of the Lowther party in his district, and had been mentioned as a possible candidate in the 1818 election before the adoption of both the Lowthers. In his speech at the Dinner, Graham had insinuated that they would not both be proposed again: 'They were now to have some undergrowth from the eavesdropping of Lowther Castle, some *Hazle*, some sapling, a hireling imposed upon the County of Westmorland as one of its Representatives.' An editorial in the *Kendal Chronicle* for 20 Mar. drew attention to rumours that one of the Lowthers would be withdrawing from Westmorland in order to stand for Cumberland.

[4] Louis XVIII had recently decided on the creation of fifty-four new peers, which, with the recall of twenty-two more, who had been struck off the list by the ordinance of 24 July, 1815, would secure his ministers a majority in the Chamber of Peers. Some of the new peers were to be chosen from those who had

selection of *Persons* operate as an injurious example to the latest period. It is a perfect whitewashing of vile tergiversations; again, what a reflection does it cast upon the proceedings adopted towards Ney[1] and others. I pity poor Lewis. The Kendal Chronicle is delighted with these measures.

Ever yours most faithfully

Wm Wordsworth

543. W. W. to LORD LONSDALE

MS. Lonsdale MSS., Record Office, The Castle, Carlisle. Hitherto unpublished.

Rydale Mount
May 1st 1819

My Lord,

This severe east wind, after a little too close application on my part, produced an inflammation in my eyes, which has hindered me from earlier expressing my thanks for the two last Letters with which your Lordship has honored me.—I am truly glad that my view of Mr Barber's case[2] and others similarly situated meets with your Lordship's approbation.—The Lowther interest is gradually strengthening and consolidating in Westnd—but I cannot say that in this neighbourhood I have yet heard of one Freeholder having gone over, though I have reason for believing that several are sorry for having taken the opposite side.—But we are gaining, I believe, greatly upon the enemy, notwithstanding their exertions.

The observations on the Article in the Quarterly Review[3] I have not seen; if they are in the Edinburgh Rev: I shall get a sight of them. I wish anxiously for the Report of the Committee; trusting that the St. Bees case will then be set in its true point of view.

distinguished themselves during the Revolution, and the *Kendal Chronicle* for 13 Mar. saw this as a blow to the ultra-Royalists.

[1] Marshal Ney (1769–1815), the most distinguished of Napoleon's generals, had been made a peer at the first restoration of Louis XVIII; but he had renewed his allegiance to Napoleon during the Hundred Days, and after Waterloo he was arrested, court-martialled, and shot.

[2] See L. 540 above.

[3] W. W. is referring either to the pamphlet *A Vindication of the Inquiry into Charitable Abuses, with an Exposure of the Misrepresentations contained in the Quarterly Review*, 1819, or to the discussion of this pamphlet along with others in the *Edinburgh Review*, No. lxii (Mar. 1819), which was based on information supplied by Brougham. The *Quarterly Review*, No. xxxviii (Dec. 1818), had briefly defended the Lowthers' good name over the St. Bees affair during a long discussion of the Charities question, parts of which were probably written by John Wilson Croker (1780–1857) and Canning. See New, op. cit., pp. 219–23.

Mr B. *knows* perfectly well that all the reports he had been the means of circulating concerning the immense advantages derived by the House of Lowther from the Leases, are monstrous fabrications!

When I go to the Continent, it will be with my Friend, Mr Monkhouse,[1] according to an engagement, which has existed for several years; so that of course I do not accompany Sir George and Lady Beaumont as your Lordship had heard. Such a trip, I feel would be of service to me; but my present ties will scarcely allow it.

I find that Mr Barton's wish that I should qualify for the magistracy, rose principally from Mr Maud's[2] absence, and the troublesome conduct of a little intermeddling Attorney of the name of Edmonds who lives at Ambleside, and of whom, Mr B. says, all the respectable people in Ambleside are afraid. There is something ludicrous in the notion of *my* descending from my situation on Parnassus, be it where it may, to combat this Pettifogger.

Lady le Fleming appears little improved by her travels. If she should have an accession of dignity and take out a new Coat of Arms, her waiting Maid and her Butler ought to be recommended to the Heralds, as Supporters.—They attended her on her travels, and their dominion is confirmed. She literally walks or rather steals out of church leaning on the arm of her Abigail, without the least attention paid to any part of the Congregation. It is pitiable—for she will be deceived—plundered—and, though it be a harsh word to use, despised.

I hope Lady Mary liked "Peter Bell".[3] It has cost me a good deal of pains at one time or another, and one does not like to labour in vain. As you do not mention Lady Mary's health, I trust, it is improved.

This Letter, I fear, will scarcely repay the trouble of reading it; but I am happy on all occasions to assure your Lordship of the high respect with which I have the honor to be

faithfully yours
Wm Wordsworth

[1] i.e. Thomas Monkhouse. The projected tour took place a year later.

[2] Probably T. H. Maude of Kendal. See L. 471 above.

[3] *Peter Bell, A Tale in Verse* (*PW* ii, p. 331), composed in 1798 and subsequently much revised, was published in Apr. 1819. The dedication to Southey (dated 7 Apr.) reiterated W. W.'s conviction that 'the Imagination not only does not require for its exercise the intervention of supernatural agency, but that . . . the faculty may be called forth as imperiously, and for kindred results of pleasure, by incidents within the compass of poetic probability, in the humblest departments of daily life.'

The Catholic Question is indeed momentous, may the wisdom of our ancestors preside over the decision!—As to the Bank restriction Bill,[1] why do not the Ministers declare that the Resumption or rather continuance of cash payments, at least upon the old principle, is neither profitable nor desirable?—This declaration must come at last.

544. W. W. to VISCOUNT LOWTHER

MS. Lonsdale MSS., Record Office, The Castle, Carlisle. Hitherto unpublished.

[*c.* 8 May 1819]

My dear Lord Lowther,

I sit down a moment to thank you for your Speech on the C. Q.[2] It is just what it became you to say: and has given your Friends *here* great satisfaction, and at Kendal also.—The business came on many days earlier than I had been prepared to expect. What a rhapsody is Grattan's speech as reported in the Courier! Is he prepared for a Catholic Sovereign on the British throne? If not, to what purpose tell us that the unfavorable opinions which Protestants hold of the Catholic religion are a reflexion on Christianity, and, through that, upon Divine Providence; and that exclusion upon such grounds is an impeachment of the Gospel. Have we not History to warrant these unfavorable opinions?—But the Religion is improved in modern times; grown mild and tolerant. So we may believe were we [to] take our notions from individuals of liberal minds, who profess it. But to know the *real* character of a religion we must observe its effects on the *great body of the People* among whom it prevails. Look at Austria and the Irish for genuine Catholicism.—

I have received a Pamphlet of Sir Wm Congreve's[3] upon Cash

[1] The Committee on the Resumption of Cash Payments, under the chairmanship of Robert Peel (1788–1850), at this time M.P. for Oxford University, had just reported in favour of further temporary restrictions, and a Bill to this effect had been introduced on 5 Apr. See L. 549 below.

[2] The Catholic Question. On 3 May Henry Grattan (1746–1820), M.P. for Dublin, had presented a petition in favour of Roman Catholic claims, pleading that Catholic and Protestant should coexist under the same Constitution (see *Courier* for 4 May). Lord Lowther had opposed further concessions as contrary to the principles of the Constitution in Church and State, and dangerous in the light of experience and unanswerable historical facts. Grattan's motion was lost by only two votes.

[3] *Of the Impracticability of the Resumption of Cash Payments*, 1819. Sir William Congreve, 2nd Bart. (1772–1828), was comptroller of the Royal Laboratory at Woolwich, and M.P. for Plymouth, 1820–8.

payments—am I obliged to you for it? It contains excellent matter —and is, I think, in the main, right but with some important errors.—Does the Charity Report notice the St Bees case?—I hope so, being anxious to have it placed in a true point of view.

The Quarterly Review, 2 edition, I have received under cover from Mr Beckett, sent by Lord Lonsdale.

Ever my dear Lord L.
faithfully yours
Wm Wordsworth

545. W. W. to LORD LONSDALE

MS. Lonsdale MSS., Record Office, The Castle, Carlisle. Hitherto unpublished.

Rydale Mount
22nd May [1819]

My Lord,

I have deferred thanking your Lordship for your kind attention in sending me (through the hands of Col: Lowther) the Q. R.,[1] till I could give it an *attentive* perusal. This I have now done, and been much gratified. The subject is treated in a masterly manner; I had, however, to regret that want of information has disqualified the Writer from doing justice to the St Bees case; and I regret it the more, because this case, I understand, has not yet come under the notice of the Comm[rs]. As far as your Lordship is personally concerned enough is said, but it is fit that the public should know, under what circumstances leases in question were granted; and that the grossest misrepresentations have been circulated (in connection with this enquiry) respecting profits derived therefrom.—

The Reviewer extols Mr B.[2] for his intense application. In this I think he is wrong. Diligence is indeed praiseworthy, when it is directed to the *thorough* understanding of those subjects upon which a man undertakes to write and speak. But this is not the case with Mr B.: he divides his attention to far too *many* subjects; and consequently being *master* of *none*, his desultory industry only makes him more mischievous.—It seemed to me also that the Reviewer would have done well if he had oftener quoted the *very* words of the

[1] The *Quarterly Review* for Dec. 1818, which discussed the Charities question. See L. 543 above.

[2] Brougham.

Report,[1] and above all of the Bill[2] in the different shapes it took. With these two exceptions I found nothing in the Review, but what was quite to my wishes.

I hope the County of West[nd] or some considerable part of it at least will feel it to be its duty to petition against further concessions to the Catholics, if the affair should be resumed, as no doubt it will, next session.—We were all much gratified by Lord Lowther's speech on the occasion.[3] It became him not to give a silent vote on so momentous a Question.

The Bank restriction Committees still cleave to the notion that the Bank has it in its power, to regulate, by its paper issues, the price of gold. When one sees what *great* errors practical men do *avowedly* fall into upon these points; no speculative man who is conscious that he has studied the subject, need be afraid of a charge of presumption, if he differs in opinion from those who have had the most experience in the management of money concerns. This opinion of the Report, will I venture to say, in a few years be acknowledged universally to be a mistake; it has already done much injury—and nothing but more mischief seems likely to spread conviction of its fallacy.

My Bookseller will in a few days break in upon your Lordship with another little Piece[4] in verse of mine. The subject is slight—but the Poem was written con amore, and in the opinion of my friends with Spirit.—Peter Bell has furnished abundant employment to the Witlings and the small critics, who have been warring with me for more than 20 years, and seem more bitter than ever.[5]

[1] The reviewer discussed, along with the other pamphlets, the first five *Reports of the Select Committee appointed to Inquire into the Education of the Lower Orders in the Metropolis* . . . 1816–18.

[2] Brougham's Bill to set up his Commission of Inquiry.

[3] See previous letter.

[4] *The Waggoner* (*PW* ii, p. 176), written in 1805 and later revised, appeared in late May or early June. It was dedicated, much to his delight, to Charles Lamb, who recalled hearing W. W. read it aloud many years before: '. . . Benjamin is no common favorite—there is a spirit of beautiful tolerance in it—it is as good as it was in 1806—and will be as good in 1829 if our dim eyes shall be awake to peruse it.' (*Lamb*, ii. 322, p. 249). W. W. was probably prompted to publish the poem now by the hostile reception given to *Peter Bell*. (See *SH* 53, p. 154).

[5] The campaign of abuse, which was largely politically inspired, began as soon as *Peter Bell* was advertised. John Hamilton Reynolds's highly successful parody *Peter Bell, A Lyrical Ballad*, which at once aroused the anxiety of S. T. C. (see Griggs, iv. 1191, 1195, pp. 934–5, 938–9), was given further publicity by Keats's ambivalent remarks in the *Examiner* for 25 Apr.; so that by the time the real *Peter Bell* appeared, curiosity and prejudice had been thoroughly excited and the poem was assured of a stormy reception. Leigh Hunt's review in the *Examiner* of 2 May spoke of 'another didactic little horror' of Wordsworth's,

Somebody, however, must have been pleased, for the Edition was sold in a few days.

With the highest respect and thanks for your Lordship's obliging attention

I have the honor to be
My Lord,
faithfully yours
Wm Wordsworth

546. W. W. to LORD LONSDALE

MS. Lonsdale MSS., Record Office, The Castle, Carlisle.
K (—). *MY ii. 623, p. 846* (—).

Monday
24 May 1819
Rydal Mount

My Lord,

Allow me to add a few words (by way of Postscript to my Letter of Saturday) respecting the management of the Quarterly Review. Wishing that what I cannot but think the errors of the Bullionists should be laid open, I wrote to Mr Southey begging his interest with the Editor of the Q.R. to procure the Reviewing of the Pamphlets on this subject for Mr De Quincey, editor of the West^nd^ Gazette.[1]

Mr Southey writes in reply: 'I fear the Q.R. would be closed against De Q's opinions upon the Bullion question, as it is against *mine on the Catholics*' (Mr Southey is an enemy to further concession); 'and indeed more certainly because some years ago it took the

and complained of its 'half-witted prejudices', and its 'philosophy of violence and hopelessness'. Further parodies followed (see G. L. Marsh, 'The Peter Bell Parodies of 1819', *Modern Philology*, xl (1943), 267–74). The ridicule of the London wits pursued W. W. to Westmorland: the *Kendal Chronicle* (1 May) reprinted parts of Reynolds's skit with Keats's review of it, and (15 and 22 May) the hostile review of W. W.'s poem from the *St. James's Chronicle*. The crowning insult was a public recitation of another parody during festivities at the house of Thomas King, the local Broughamite (reported on 12 June). Notoriety was not without its compensations, however; for a second edition of *Peter Bell* was called for within a fortnight. W. W.'s own friends were not entirely happy about the poem. Lamb called it 'one of the worst of Wordsworth's works' (see *HCR* i, p. 230).

[1] In a notable editorial on 6 Feb., De Quincey had already argued against the resumption of cash payments on the ground that a metallic currency was not the test or appropriate product of national wealth; and he followed this up with a series of articles on 'Paper of the Bank of England', which appeared on 6, 17 Feb.; 20, 27 Mar.; 3, 10, 17 Apr.; and 22 May.

wrong side upon that subject;[1] and consistency in a political error is the only kind of consistency to be expected in a journal of this kind. This I am sorry for, because if De Quincey could bring his reasonings before the public through a favorable channel I think he would go far towards exploding a mischievous error.' From this extract, may be seen that these Reviews value above everything, the keeping up the notion of their own mysterious infallibility. It is probable that the Q.R. is closed against the opponents of the Catholic claims, in consequence of its having espoused the other side, through the influence of Mr Canning over the Editor.[2] The great circulation of the two Reviews the Quarterly and the Edinburgh, has been very injurious to free discussion, by making it almost insurmountably difficult for any writer not holding a public situation, to obtain a hearing if his opinions should not suit either of these periodical publications.

I was truly glad to see the majority by which the House of Lords expressed their opinion of the Cath. Q.[3]

I have the honor
to remain
My Lord
most faithfully yours
Wm Wordsworth

547. W. W. to LORD LONSDALE

MS. Lonsdale MSS., Record Office, The Castle, Carlisle. Hitherto unpublished.

Rydal Mount
16th June 1819

My Lord,

It must be mentioned to your Lordship that my Neighbour Mr Gee, and myself, have thought it right to give Mr Lumb, such

[1] i.e. after the publication of the Bullion Committee's Report in Aug. 1810. The *Quarterly Review*, Nos. viii and ix (Nov. 1810 and Feb. 1811), had included no less than four articles discussing the Report and related topics, and all of them were in general agreement with the Committee's conclusions. For the evidence for Canning's hand in these articles, see F. W. Fetter, 'Economic Articles in the Quarterly Review & their Authors, 1809–50', *Journal of Political Economy*, vol. lxvi (Feb. and Apr. 1958). For Southey's own view of the Bullion question, see Warter, iii. p. 136.

[2] i.e. William Gifford. Both Canning and Croker had come out in favour of concessions to the Catholics.

[3] The Catholic question had been debated in the House of Lords on 17 May: a motion in favour of relief was lost by forty-one votes.

information respecting the political opinions, conduct and connections of certain Persons in this neighbourhood, who have applied for enfranchisement, as we hope will be serviceable to the cause.—An opportunity has fortunately occurred for coming to an explanation with some on this point; persons with whom we were in habits of intercourse. Without presuming to say a word as to what course your Lordship would take upon their applications, they were told, that we felt it our duty to state what their opinions and political connections were, and should do so in respect to all those, who, with similar views, would make the same applications.—The business now stands upon a footing satisfactory to our minds; for it was not pleasant to be instrumental in opposing favorite objects of those with whom one is living in habits of neighbourly communication, without their knowing it. I attended at Grasmere, and Mr Gee attended at the other Courts holden at Low Wood and Bowness. No one can be more zealous and active than he is.—On looking over Mr Lumb's list of new freeholders in this neighbourhood, I was sorry to find that half a dozen whose names I expected to see were not there—owing, principally to delays at Kendal in executing the deeds—which Mr Lumb would take care to get done speedily.

Many thanks for your Lordship's exertions and intentions on behalf of Mr De Quincey's introduction to the Quarterly Review. I am afraid it is improbable on account of the view he takes of the subject.[1] I have seen the Article in the E.R.[2]—it is as your Lordship describes, feeble and false; and, what one would scarcely have expected, manifestly depressed and heartless.

Mr Ware of the Cumberland Pacquet[3] may thank his own supineness for the Opposition paper in Whitehaven.[4] I was lately in the neighbourhood of Ravenglass and learned that several persons who had taken in the new Paper on account of the flatness of the Pacquet, were disappointed and meant to return to their old acquaintance.

I have not heard from Sir George Beaumont since his departure.—The Kendal Chronicle has been taking great pains, in no less than four numbers, to persuade my neighbours that I am a very bad Poet;[5] from which I conclude that they do not much like me as a

[1] i.e. the Bullion question. See previous letter.

[2] The *Edinburgh Review* for Mar. 1819, which discussed the Charities question. See L. 543 above.

[3] *The Cumberland Pacquet and Ware's Whitehaven Advertiser*, the oldest of the Cumberland papers, first appeared on 20 Oct. 1774.

[4] *The Whitehaven Gazette and Cumberland Advertiser*. The first number had appeared on 19 Apr.

[5] See L. 545 above.

Politician. At Keswick I saw the other day both Mr Southey and Mr Calvert both well, and Calvert a determined enemy to the plans for resuming Cash payments. He *was* a good deal of an Admirer of young Graham of Netherby; but his public attack upon the Hasell family[1] has sickened him a little.

I was rather surprised that young Hasell did not demand an explanation of one of the offensive terms used by Mr Graham on that occasion.

Knowing how much your Lordship is engaged I ought to apologize for troubling you so long.

I have the honor to be
my Lord
faithfully yours
Wm Wordsworth

548. W. W. to HANS BUSK[2]

Address: To Hans Busk Esq[re], 31 Nottingham Place, London.
Postmark: 9 Jy. 1819. *Stamp*: Kendal Penny Post.
MS. Henry Huntington Library.
MY ii. 624, p. 847.

Rydal Mount, Ambleside
July 6th 1819

Dear Sir,

Your writings are not to be hurried over; this must plead my excuse for not having thanked you earlier for the 'Vestriad'; which, though detained upon the road, by a fault of some of Mr Longman's people, in directing the parcel it was enclosed in, reached me some time since. The plan is more extensive than that of your former poems; and the execution equally good—I was particularly pleased with the descents into the submarine regions, and the infernal. These two Cantos I liked best; and the 'Council' is perhaps the least happy: in all councils there is something too quiescent—The serious passages, everywhere so gracefully interspersed, will excite a wish in many as they did in me, that you would favor the world with something in downright earnest—Your Portrait of Silene is

[1] See L. 542 above.

[2] Hans Busk (1772–1862), scholar, poet, and country gentleman with an estate in Radnorshire, and thus a neighbour of T. Hutchinson at Hindwell. His *Vestriad*, a Mock Epic in three books, was published in 1819. Busk had written to W. W. on 29 Apr. and 24 June in praise of *Peter Bell* and *The Waggoner* (*WL MSS.*)

eminently happy; and throughout the whole of your productions is an air of lively novelty that most honourably distinguishes you among the multitude of candidates for poetic celebrity—Your two obliging Letters require especial acknowledgement. If you have erred at all in the movement of your couplets it is surely on the right side.—You seem to understand my opinions on this subject perfectly:—I have, indeed, a detestation of couplets running into each other, merely because it is convenient to the writer;—or from affected imitation of our elder poets. Reading such verse produces in me a sensation like that of toiling in a dream, under the night-mair. The Couplet promises rest at agreeable intervals; but here it is never attained—you are mocked and disappointed from paragraph to paragraph. In regard to monosyllabic lines, I do not think that there lies any objection to them merely as such; I mean any objection on musical considerations. For the words, if well *chosen* and suitably united, blend into each other upon the ear, as readily almost as if the feet of the verse were composed of polysyllables.—

I noticed in your Vestriad with particular pleasure, your flight in the Balloon. Rich in bold fictions as your Poem is, you were not called upon to make more of that vehicle than you have done—Judgement is shown in nothing more than the power to resist temptations of Fancy, especially where, as in your case, the gratification lies within easy reach.—

The 'Waggoner' was written con amore, and as the Epilogue states almost in my own despite; I am not therefore surprized that you read it with pleasure; composing wide[ly] as you do from unborrowed feelings—The critiques to which you allude I have not [seen] and if, as is probable they be such, as so[me] good natured person forwarded to me, in the Literary Gazette,[1] I should indeed thorough[ly] despise them. It is now 20 years since the 'Duncery' of the periodical Press first declared war against me; and they have kept it up with laudable perseverance; I wish I could praise any other quality which they have evinced—Farewell—and, dear Sir believe me with sincere thanks for your kind attentions

most respectfully yours
Wm Wordsworth—

[1] A weekly, founded in 1817 and edited for thirty-three years by William Jerdan (1782–1869).

549. W. W. to VISCOUNT LOWTHER

MS. Lonsdale MSS., Record Office, The Castle, Carlisle. Hitherto unpublished.

July 18th 1819

My dear Lord Lowther,

I trusted to a Kendal Friend who was here at the beginning of the week to send me word when the Cambridge dinner takes place.[1] He has neglected to do so—and I have inquired in vain in this neighbourhood. Tonight I shall write to Kendal and you shall hear as soon as I receive an answer. This disappointment has vexed me; but I hope the information may reach me in time to prevent your being inconvenienced by the want of it. I am told also that the meeting is annually advertised in the Kendal Paper which will of course be the Gazette.

Your account of the Majorities is pleasant to hear of—but I should have liked some of them better if the Ministry had shown less conformity to the principles of their opponents. I cannot say that I am an admirer of that sort of candor of which Mr Peel gave so signal an example in the Debate on the Bank Restriction Bill.[2] It is not politic, I think, in public men holding such high office, to acknowledge having been in the wrong in measures of such importance and their adversaries right, especially in cases, like the present, where it is very probable, that, after all the first opinion may be the sound one. Time will shew; for my own part I cannot but think that what is proposed will be found impracticable. There surely must be some secret history belonging to the last Session, which probably you can explain.

On recurring to the file of Kendal Papers, I find that the meeting took place last year, July 6th.—Probably the time for this year is not yet fixed.

We are going on well in Westnd.
Ever yours
Wm Wordsworth

[1] See L. 551 below.

[2] In 1811 Peel had voted against Horner's resolution, based on the Report of the Bullion Committee of 1810, recommending the resumption of cash payments. But by now he had become convinced that the system of paper currency followed since 1797 had brought about a fall in the foreign exchange rates and a rise in the price of gold. In a memorable speech on 24 May, he introduced a Bill which provided that the Acts restraining cash payments should finally cease on 1 May 1823.

550. W. W. to HENRY PARRY

Address: H. Parry Esq, Stamp Office, Kirby Lonsdale.
MS. untraced.
MY ii. 625, p. 849.

Rydale Mount July 20th 1819.

My dear Sir,

I shall be truly glad to see you. On the other side[1] you have the needful. The Subs—have been written to—

ever faithfully yours
Wm Wordsworth

551. W. W. to VISCOUNT LOWTHER

MS. Lonsdale MSS., Record Office, The Castle, Carlisle. Hitherto unpublished.

Rydale Mount
Wednesday [28 July 1819][2]

My dear Lord Lowther,

I have just learnt from Kendal that the dinner of the Cambridge men takes place the first Thursday in August. I hope to have the pleasure of meeting you there; but it happens unluckily that the Inspector from the Stamp Off: London will be with me for a couple of days, at the beginning of the month. These Gentlemen make the Distributors a biennial visit; I will be at Kendal, if possible.

Our dinner at Ambleside[3] went off very well; the attendance far above what was expected, considering that the tickets were as high as 10s. 6d. which kept a great many small 'Statesmen' away. Observing the quantity of wine drank I waited on Mr North[4] the next day, to propose that the deficiency should be made up by subscription, which he declined, taking the whole surplus expense very handsomely upon himself

Mr North is a determined enemy of Brougham; and declared at the meeting that notwithstanding his vaunts, he would not offer for Westnd again; having never shewn his face twice at the same place.

[1] The 'other side' has been torn off the manuscript (Note by de Selincourt.)

[2] This letter was written after W. W. had found out the date of the Cambridge Dinner, mentioned in L. 549 above. As it is unlikely that he could have got the information by Wednesday 21st, the letter can fairly certainly be dated to the 28th.

[3] A Dinner on 5 July on the anniversary of the election of Lord Lowther and his brother.

[4] Ford North of Ambleside, occupant of Rydal Mount before the Wordsworths. He presided at the Dinner.

A Mr Beck[1] of Hawkshead appeared at the meeting: he is a young man, not a Freeholder, but possessed of a handsome Estate, as good I am informed, as £2000 per ann: he never declared before for either party; though no doubt he has been courted a good deal by the Curwens and Sandys's.[2]

The indecent attack of young Graham upon the Hasell family[3] has done him no little harm in Cumberland.—It was much better commented upon by Hasell at Appleby[4] than it appears to have been at Carlisle.

Mrs Wordsworth and my Sister would be glad to see you here, as I should be—at any time of the Summer.

Ever faithfully yours
Wm Wordsworth

552. D. W. to CATHERINE CLARKSON

Address: Mrs. Clarkson, Playford Hall, Ipswich.
Stamp: Kendal Penny Post.
MS. British Museum.
K (—). *MY ii. 626, p. 849.*

Sunday August 1st [1819]

My dear Friend,

I trust that the thought of the possibility that you were neglected or forgotten by us, or that we did not feelingly sympathize with you in your affliction has never once crossed your mind; but that you have wished for a letter from us—have looked to it as a comfort I do indeed believe—and you have been disappointed perhaps grieved that no letter came. Is not this, my dearest Friend, a sufficient cause for the self reproaches which do now torment me? I can only say for myself the truth that I have been cowardly. The act of writing being a voluntary act, a thing that may be done to day as well as to-morrow, I have put it off—and am utterly inexcusable. Sara would have written long ago, but she knew that I intended it—and she wished too that I should write—You know how I reverenced your excellent Father and though I knew that happy as he was in

[1] Thomas Beck of Esthwaite Lodge.

[2] Myles Sandys (1761–1839) of Graythwaite Hall, Newby Bridge: a collateral descendant of Edwin Sandys (1516?–88), Archbishop of York, founder of Hawkshead School.

[3] See L. 542 above.

[4] At the anniversary Dinner at Appleby on 5 July the elder Hasell had defended the Lowther cause and his own political consistency against Graham's attacks.

his pious life, and useful to all around him, the thought of death brought neither dismay nor sorrow to him—that to him it was peace and joy, I could not write or think of your loss without distress;—and feeling that no consolation could be given by others—that all must proceed from yourself and from the remembrance of what your Father was, I shrunk like a coward from the expression of my own feelings. You must forgive me. It was very kind in you to write so particular an account of your Father's last moments. It comforts me to read your letter; therein I see that you are happy when you think of him; and I trust by this time even *chearful*, but the loss can never be made up in this world. That I know. Mrs Luff came to Miss Dowling's, our house being quite full. She is now at Mr. Crump's and will not come to stay at Rydal till towards the end of next week. We met her at Church this morning, and she told me she had had a letter from you, with a distressing account of Mr. Clarkson's having been very ill, and you from home! I join with you in joy and thankfulness for his recovery. Long may you be spared a sorrow like that which you have lately gone through! I do not wonder at your resolution not to leave him again; but let us hope that out of this resolve another may arise, namely to go from home *together* oftener; and to come into this country. You will need a little change more than you have hitherto done. There is repose and comfort in the thought of your deceased Father—but when he was alive and you had him within a day's journey of you, there was an invigorating power in that thought. Think how years go by, how the children are coming forward to take their place in active life, and we are going down the hill. Thank God, your health being amended you are stronger than you were years ago, and perhaps not one of *us* is very much failed in point of strength; and for my part I have as much enjoyment in walking as when I first came into Westmorland twenty years ago, yet you will be surprized when you see me, in face a perfect old woman. I have only eight teeth remaining—two in the upper jaw, the rest below and of those two or three are on the point of coming out. Sara is very well. She has got a nice pony and she and her nephew John ride out together. She is going to Patterdale tomorrow with our neighbours, the Gees, to meet William who is now at Lowther. William is quite well, preserves his teeth, and does not look older for his years than formerly. Mary too is well. Dear Dorothy is just gone back to school. We have a sad missing of her, yet are thankful for the loss as she is as well placed for general improvement, and for the correction of her peculiar faults as it is possible for a girl to be. She is as lively as ever—not yet quite steady, but in due time I think she will be so. Her health is good and she grows regularly in height—and is sufficiently stout, though as yet she has no womanly breadth, indeed we are glad (seeing others of her own age perfect women) that she continues a child so long. She will be 15 on the 16th of this month. John is a very good Boy; but he grows a man almost—and it is far too soon; for his attainments are much behind his years—yet he does now improve for *him* even rapidly, considering the disadvantages he labours under, having only his Father for an instructor. We wish very much that a Tutor could be had in the house, or that we could hear of some clergyman who could receive him as a pupil. When you see Mr Tillbrooke talk to him on the subject. Perhaps together you may hit upon some plan; but we shall see Tillbrooke again on his way from Scotland. He paid us a very short visit and stayed a few days at Allan Bank. Have you seen *Peter Bell* and *The Waggoner*? William has done nothing lately except a few Sonnets, but these are exquisitely beautiful. Poor Mrs Luff has set her heart upon furnishing a cottage; but no cottage is to be had—and indeed I think she is much better without one, though I believe that for a few months it would make her as happy as she could be after her great loss. I wish her mind were such that she could content herself in lodgings where she might be quite independent when at home, and have the power of moving at will. She has an excellent heart, and is only too generous and unsuspecting. I wish I could see how she could be made happy—but I fear without someone to lean upon she will never be so. When she is under our Roof we can judge better what to advise, and what is possible. Mrs Luff delighted me today with your account of Tom. I trust, my dear Friend that henceforth you will derive uninterrupted comfort from him. Give my kindest love to him. Are we likely to see him in the North? The hay harvest is almost concluded, and never were there finer crops or a more delightful season. The weather is very hot. The Hutchinsons left us a fortnight ago. They are now at Stockton. Mrs. H. is a sweet creature. She is an example for all mothers. She is playful and tender with her children, yet resolutely guards against all foolish indulgence. We were very sorry when they left us. The house was quiet even to dullness. Rydal Mount is the nicest place in the world for children. You will almost long to be young again, as I do, when you see it; for the sake of trotting down the green Banks, running and dancing on the Mount etc. You must come and see us indeed you must before it is too late for you and for all of us. —I am sure when you come to the end of this letter you will feel as if I had told you nothing. So I feel myself; and it is always so with me after a long silence—I trust we shall hear soon from you again; and that I shall have no more to reproach myself, and then I will think of all that I have to tell you. Farewell, my dear Friend, Give my best love to your Husband and believe me ever your affectionate D Wordsworth.

553. W. W. to VISCOUNT LOWTHER

MS. Lonsdale MSS., Record Office, The Castle, Carlisle. Hitherto unpublished.

Monday 23 August 1819
Rydal Mount

My dear Lord Lowther,

I shall be at liberty and glad to receive you here, having no engagement in prospect but a conditional one at Lowther.—If you could let me know the *day* when I may expect you, it would be better, as I would take care to be on the spot, when you arrive.—I do not yet know the day of the Book Club dinner.[1] The enclosed is from my friend Mr Cookson of Kendal. It relates to certain Freeholds he wishes to dispose of. I should apprehend that the same circumstances which induce him to wish to part with them would render them ineligible purchases for friends not on the spot. I ought to mention that Mr Cookson was in treaty for this enfranchisement if it was not actually effected, some time before the political stir in West^nd and that the number of his Sons is 7: for whom he means to reserve freeholds.

I hear nothing of B's proceedings in this neighbourhood, except that a few days ago a barrel of Ale arrived to be drank by his Friends in Grasmere, on the occasion, as was given out, of his marriage.[2]

I much fear that there may have been some mismanagement, at Manchester,[3] on the part of the supporters of Government, and

[1] The Annual Venison Feast in Kendal on 7 Sept., attended by Lord Lowther and many of his supporters.

[2] Brougham had recently married Mrs. Spalding, a widow with two children. She was a niece of the 1st Lord Auckland.

[3] At the famous meeting held by 'Orator' Hunt at St. Peter's Fields, Manchester, on 16 Aug. to petition for Parliamentary Reform and repeal of the Corn Laws, the Yeomanry had charged on the crowd, killing several people and wounding hundreds of others. The *Westmorland Gazette* for 21 Aug. exonerated the magistrates; but the *Kendal Chronicle* held them responsible to some extent for the 'massacre', and later opened a fund for the victims.

particularly if it be true that several special Constables were cut down or trampled on by the Cavalry while charging the Mob. A Manchester paper has been sent me from some unknown person; but it is all on the side of the Reformers—a mischievous publication!

With best Compts from Mrs W. and my Sister who charges me to say how happy they shall be to see you.

I remain dear Lord L.
very faithfully yours
W Wordsworth

554. D. W. to JOANNA HUTCHINSON

Address: To Miss Joanna Hutchinson [*delivered by hand?*]
MS. WL.
MY ii. 627, p. 852.

Sunday September 5th 1819

My dear Joanna,

Sara is gone to Church on horseback with Tom Monkhouse—and the rest of the family on foot with Lord Lowther. After making a pudding and giving a few directions for dinner I sit down in my own Room, with an open window, viewing the sunshine upon the green fields, a great treat to us now, for, after the finest season of hot and dry weather that ever was known we have had, with little intermission since last Sunday, torrents of rain, and the corn cut and *un*cut, especially the latter, must be greatly injured. My lover, as you call him, has a crop of the grandest oats ever seen in Grasmere now standing in the sheaf, which he assures us has received 'six punds' damage. We have passed our time very pleasantly since T.M.'s arrival, and I trust he has also, for he has been in excellent health and spirits. Lord Lowther arrived on Friday to dinner at 5 o'clock. We were not quite in such a bustle as on that ever memorable day when you, dear Joanna, left us. The rain was almost as heavy, and many a time I thought of you, and of our unhappy cook's misery. We have got a delightful young woman in her place, who is always chearful, tidy and good humoured, and in the management of her fires, that never ending plague when Jane was here, she is exactly the opposite of Jane, and cooks well with less fuel than any servant we ever had. Yesterday the two Mr Jacksons and Mr Gee dined with us upon venison and partridges from Lowther. We have been very comfortable and without the least bustle till last night when before the Gentlemen had left the dining room our loquacious Friend Mr Myers arrived half tipsy. He produced a letter he had received from Mr Crump and his own answer to it, four sides of a folio sheet which he deputed Mr Monkhouse to read to the gentlemen, and his own comments upon it were loud and long, with stamping and gestures; but not content with this when he came into the study he gave *me* the two letters for my own reading. After a careful perusal he called upon me for a discussion of the merits of his dispute with the people of Grasmere respecting the inclosure of an Intake, and when this was done, he himself, for the benefit of Ladies and Gentlemen, (all except Lord L. who luckily happened to be in his own Bed-room) read the two letters aloud, Mr Crump's in a hum-drum voice with many comments upon errors in style, and his own with all the pomposity of an Actor—Then came on his third discussion. In short he talked all—and every body was miserable, and it is a real fact that he made me quite ill—I am sure I ailed nothing before his arrival, and before he went away I was as uncomfortable—all over—as possible. Delighted we were when he left us saying that he was engaged all this day; but judge of our vexation when he came in to breakfast when we had half finished—all dirt and snuff. In the course of the Breakfast he pulled a pair of old white yarn stockings out of his pocket, displayed them at full length threw them on the floor and desired me to take charge of them. Then came on an harangue concerning his wardrobe—and after all he began with the old story of the blue and buff, which no doubt Mary H. well remembers. I am sure I have been compelled to hear [it] a score of times. Breakfast ended all were assembled on the front and Mr. M. found that *he* should be too late to dress and go to Ambleside Church as he had 'promised Julia Rachel'[1] he should do, therefore he proposed to bring her hither. This we positively declined, stating William's particular engagements with Lord L. Luckily he was not affronted, for he promised to come again to-morrow. The Venison Feast at Kendal is on Tuesday, and the Ball, I believe, on Wednesday. Lord L. leaves tomorrow, and William will meet him at Kendal if his eyes are well enough. They are now distressingly inflamed. Mr. Gee will dine with us to-day and perhaps Mr de Quincey. He has been invited, but we never see him now. The Hiltons[2] are in Mr Gee's old house. We are to meet them at Mr Gee's tomorrow. Mrs Luff left us when Lord L. came.

[1] Thomas Monkhouse's love-affairs were causing some amusement in the Wordsworth circle. See *SH* 56, pp. 160–1. He eventually married Jane Horrocks of Preston.

[2] See *SH* 54, p. 156.

She will return on Tuesday, and thinks of taking lodgings for a while at Ambleside, as Mrs Hilton's house at the foot of the hill will not be vacant till the end of October. We have not seen Henry since his first arrival, but T. M. Wm John and Sara were at Coniston on Thursday in quest of fish. He is well and quite happy to find himself again at Coniston. Unfortunately they did not see him—he was out fishing. Tom M. goes to Penrith from the Kendal dinner and Ball, but will return before the Races whither John W. is to accompany him. After all, I trust that Willy is to go with him to London (Mary H will be delighted to hear this) to be under Mr Johnson's care till he is old enough to be entered at the Charter House. This seems at present to be fully resolved on, and I hope the resolution will not fail at last as the *necessity* of a change is now fully perceived by all parties. I think John will be placed at Sedbergh School; but this is not certain. Dorothy grows very fast, and looks well and healthy—much better than when Mary left us. Miss Dowling thinks highly of her application and consequent improvement. We expect her this afternoon—

Now for the business which I have to write about—namely Mr Baudouin's reply to my inquiries respecting lodgings in or near Paris. His answer is such as entirely to quash any hopes from that quarter, the price of board being upwards of 100£ per annum, lodging above 30£ and with other expenses—according to Mr Gee's calculation it was dearer than in England. The precise sum I cannot state, having forgotten, and as I do not know the exact value of French money I cannot, by referring to Mr B.'s letter, make a calculation. I trust however that you will have no occasion to leave your own country. I had a letter from Miss B.[1] lately. Her uncle and Family were going to leave Boulogne. She did not know whither they were going; but if to Paris she seemed to think she would take lodgings in Boulogne. She had been poorly; but was in good spirits at the time of writing. I fear she will be forced to remain in France many years unless some one leaves her a legacy, and that is not very probable. Mary and Mrs Luff have talked of going into Borrowdale for a few days; but I think they will not get off at all, having delayed till the evenings are likely to be cold, and short days and long nights do not suit Borrowdale. We were very much grieved that the dear children were poorly on their arrival at home. No doubt it had been owing to the heat. Give Aunt Dorothy's very best love to them. I hope George thrives apace now, and has had no more of those

[1] Miss Barker, their old Keswick friend, who was now living in Boulogne. See *SH 55*, p. 159.

frightful bowel complaints. D. is just arrived. She sends her tender love to her dear little cousins. We often talk of them and their goodness and I am sure I am grateful to their dear Mother for the exertion she made to bring them to see us. It was a great undertaking. D's love to you all severally, and to her God-Mother. It is time to dress for dinner so I must stop, and indeed I think I have not any more news for you. Yes, Mrs Lloyd is at young John Green's house with her little girls, and will stay a while. She is as well as one can expect. Her husband is in London. We have had no remarkable persons this summer, but the Bishop of London[1] and his Lady. They dined with us. The Bishop is a very delightful man and his wife is a pretty pleasing woman. God bless you! dear Joanna, I hope you continue pretty well—clothe yourself as light as possible and use exercise in the fresh air whenever it is dry. This is Mr Scambler's advice. Give my best love to Tom and Mary. I hope your Aunt is now quite well again. Remember me kindly to her, and do not fail to give my love to John Monkhouse when you see him. Believe me ever, dear Joanna,

Your affectionate Friend
D Wordsworth.

I cannot read over what I have written—excuse scrawling. I hope you will not be very busy when you receive this that you may have time to decypher it.

555. W. W. to LORD LONSDALE

MS. Lonsdale MSS., Record Office, The Castle, Carlisle. Hitherto unpublished.
[*In M. W.'s hand*]

Rydal Mount
Septr. 19th [1819]

My Lord,

I had confidently expected, till within the last few days, that I might have had the honour of accepting your Lordship's invitation to Lowther on the 23rd but at present, I am sorry to say, I have little or no hope that such a gratification will be allowed me. The inflammation in my eyes, which was much abated, has returned, and obliges me to employ an Amanuensis to express my regret upon this occasion.

[1] William Howley, D.D., Bishop of London, 1813–28, and then Archbishop of Canterbury.

A change for the better may take place in three days, if so, I shall have much pleasure in joining the Party selected by your Lordship, to pay their respects to a Prince,[1] whose virtues, and amiable qualities render still more impressive the lesson which his elevation, and his afflicting losses afford to the world.

Mr Brougham, I understand, has in vain attempted to muster a meeting to express in West^nd^ public disapprobation of the conduct of the Manchester Magistrates. I also learn from the same authority, Mr Monkhouse, that several of the Blues have joined the Corps of Yeomanry to be raised in the neighbourhood of Penrith. I expressed to Lord Lowther, when I had the honour of seeing him here, an anxious wish that a sufficient number of them should unite themselves with this Body to prevent its having the appearance of a Party Corps, and I was sorry to learn that at *that* time there was not a prospect of such a union. But the revolutionary projects of the most active Reformers are becoming every day more manifest; and the respectable part of our Opponents in West^nd^ whatever be the course of their outward conduct, cannot but, in their hearts, incline to the principles which the Lowther Family have so strenuously supported.

With best regard to every part of your Lordship's family, and with the highest respect, I have the honour to be

My Lord
most faithfully yours
Wm Wordsworth

556. W. W. to VISCOUNT LOWTHER

MS. Lonsdale MSS., Record Office, The Castle, Carlisle. Hitherto unpublished.
[*In M.W.'s hand*]

Rydal Mount
Sept 19 [1819]

My dear Lord Lowther,

This disorder in my eyes has proved a tedious business of better and worse, and I regret to say that they are at present in that state which allows me little hope of being at Lowther on the 23rd—if I can appear I will.

[1] Prince Leopold stayed at Lowther Castle 25–29 Sept. during a tour of the north of England. He had previously visited Scott at Abbotsford.

Mr Monkhouse tells me that Mr B.[1] has in vain attempted to raise a meeting to express disapprobation of the Manchester Magistrates—and he assures me that several of the Blues are prepared to join the Yeomanry Corps—you know how anxious I was that this should be.

Mrs W. being my amanuensis, I do not scruple to say that I have heard your speech at the Kendal dinner,[2] much commended, both for matter and manner.

I shall greatly regret if I have not the pleasure of seeing you again before you quit Westnd.

I enclose you a Copy of the Paper which I had from a Gentleman of the Stamp Office. I remain, with kindest regards from this Family, who recollect your late visit with much pleasure my dear Lord Lowther

most faithfully yours
Wm Wordsworth

557. W. W. to LORD LONSDALE

MS. Lonsdale MSS., Record Office, The Castle, Carlisle. Hitherto unpublished.

[*In M. W.'s hand*]

Rydal Mount
Sept 22nd [1819]

My Lord,

Prince Leopold may be inclined to visit Keswick from Lowther: should this be the intention of his R.H:, allow me, in the absence of Mr Southey, to suggest that the Lake is seen to great advantage from General Peachey's[3] House upon the Island, and also from Friar's Crag on the opposite shore.—Mr Gray's[4] account of the lakes printed as an Appendix to Mr West's Guide, is the best. Treating of Keswick Vale, he speaks in high terms of the view from the Hersing-block close to the Vicarage. Plantations made since his time have hindered a just proportion of the lake being seen from

[1] Brougham.

[2] The Book Club Dinner on 7 Sept.

[3] Major-General William Peachey (1763–1838), of Derwent Isle, Southey's friend and correspondent: M.P. for Yarmouth, 1797–1802, and for Taunton, 1826–30.

[4] Thomas Gray's 'Journal of a visit to the Lakes in Oct. 1769'—from a letter to Dr. Wharton published in Mason's *Life*—was reprinted in *A Guide to the Lakes, in Cumberland, Westmorland, and Lancashire*, by the author of *The Antiquities of Furness*, i.e. the Jesuit topographer Thomas West (1720–79).

this point. The view is now much better from the neighbourhood of Ormathwaite and from the *new road* close under Skiddaw by Applethwaite—proceeding towards Bassenthwaite less than ½ a mile and returning the same way. Lowdore and Borrowdale as far as Bowder Stone are well worth visiting returning to Keswick by the opposite side of the Lake. In the Vale of Grasmere, if there should be 10 minutes to spare, when the Swan Inn is reached enquire for a small Hill called Butterlip How, it commands a panorama view of this celebrated Vale—thence proceeding by the Church to rejoin the road, leading to Ambleside by Rydal. The Valley of Ambleside is perhaps nowhere better seen than from the Terrace at Rydal Mount —the grounds of Rydal Hall with their Waterfalls are known to everyone. Your Lordship will infer from this letter that I am not much relieved. Greatly regretting my inability to be with you to-morrow I have the honour

My Lord, your faithful
Friend and Servt
Wm Wordsworth

558. W. W. to WALTER SCOTT

Address: Walter Scott Esqre Abbot's Ford, near Melross.
Stamp: Kendal Penny Post. *Endorsed*: Wordsworth 22 Sept.
MS. National Library of Scotland.
MY ii. 627a, p. 915.

[*In M. W.'s hand*]

Rydal Mount Septr 22nd [1819]

Dear Scott,

An inflammation in my eyes obliges me to employ an Amanuensis, for the performance of a melancholy office with which your friend Mr Erskine[1] has charged me, and which he himself, from the state of his feelings, is unequal to.—It is to communicate to you the painful intelligence that his Wife is no more. My own confinement to the house has prevented me from seeing Mr E. but I learn from his Apothecary, the Bearer of this wish respecting you, that the Lady's illness, though tedious, was attended with little pain and that she was carried out of this world, to all appearance as gently as possible.

[1] William Erskine, spoken of by Lockhart as Scott's 'dearest friend'. In 1822, largely through Scott's influence, he was made a Judge at the Court of Sessions. He took the title of Lord Kinnedder, but died the same year. (Note by de Selincourt.)

She expired at Low-wood Inn on the banks of Windermere on Monday morning.—On the Tuesday preceeding it was evident that unless the tap which was wasting her away could be stopped her constitution would sink under it—on Saturday there was no hope. Mr E. I understand is by this time as tranquil as could be expected —His Wife's Mother arrived yesterday and the Body is to be removed to Scotland.

I greatly regret that I have not seen your Friend, it is possible that I might have been of some service to him during his long detention in this neighbourhood—several weeks elapsed before I learned who the Stranger was—*upon learning* I called immediately, but did not find him at home—he was then at Grasmere preparing to leave it for Low-wood. I have since that time been myself unable to leave the house, and as Mr E's melancholy condition, I suppose, prevented him from communicating with me, his silence made me fearful that a visit from Mrs W. might be an intrusion. This consideration however would not have prevented her calling had we been aware of the dangerous situation of Mrs E.

I have heard with great concern, from several quarters, that your own health has been much deranged, and it added to my disappointment in not seeing Mr Erskine that I missed the opportunity of making enquiries from him upon this subject. Do be so kind as to let me know how you are and have been.[1] For myself I am happy to say that my general health is good, but my eyes have been for some time unequal to the service to which I could wish to put them. My Family are well and join in every kind regard to yourself and yours of whom we should be glad to have the like good account. I hope Southey will have seen you before his return from Scotland.[2] Believe me, d^r^ Scott, to be affectionately and faithfully yours

Wm. Wordsworth

[1] For Scott's reply, describing his friendship with the Erskines and his recent illness (during which he had dictated *The Bride of Lammermoor*), see *Letters of Sir Walter Scott*, ed. H. J. C. Grierson, 12 vols., 1932–7, v, p. 491.

[2] Southey was touring Scotland 17 Aug.–1 Oct. with Thomas Telford (1757–1834) the engineer and John Rickman (1771–1840) the statistician; but he does not appear to have seen Scott. See *Journal of a Tour in Scotland in 1819*, ed. C. H. Herford, 1929.

559. W. W. to JOHN EDWARDS

Address: Mr Edwards, Derby.
MS. Cornell. Hitherto unpublished.

[Autumn 1819]

My dear Sir,

Many thanks for your obliging Letter. I was glad to see a Son of yours, and have been as helpful to him as I could. Your Sonnet is pleasing. The verses I shall deal with as you desire. They are not without merit.—

I am pleased you think so highly of Peter Bell.—Remembering what you liked in the Waggoner, I was rather surprized you overlooked the Epilogue, which is much admired among those who have a feeling for these things. I received some little time ago a Derby paper for which I have to thank you.—If you had been a frequent Correspondent of that Journal which I find is not the Case, I should have suggested that you might have served the cause of Literature, by a word or two in commendation of what I have lately published, through that channel—You may perhaps have noticed [?that] there is a pretty general combination at this time to write me and my poems down—it fails altogether and produces a contrary effect.—

I shall publish one or two poetical pamphlets[1] next Spring—by way of completing a third volume to match with the two which you possess. I mention it that you may reserve what you have—viz. the Thanksgiving Ode, and Peter Bell, and Waggoner, to bind up with these.[2] Adieu.

ever yours,
W. W.

560. W. W. to LORD LONSDALE

MS. Lonsdale MSS., Record Office, The Castle, Carlisle. Hitherto unpublished.

Thursday 14th Oct. 1819
Rydale Mount

My Lord,

Mr Monkhouse returns to Rydale Mount on Saturday or Sunday next, to take along with him my younger Son (under ten years of

[1] i.e. *The River Duddon* and *Vaudracour and Julia*, which were so printed that they could be bound together with *Peter Bell*, *The Waggoner*, and *Thanksgiving Ode* to form a third volume to be added to the 2-vol. *Poems* of 1815.

[2] For an example of this procedure, see *Cornell Wordsworth Collection*, no. 56.

age) to be placed under the care of Mr Johnson at the Central School, London, previous to his being sent to the Charterhouse. Mr M. speaks of remaining here only two or three days at the utmost, so that I trust I shall be able to join your Lordship and the Ladies at Whitehaven on Tuesday next, or Wednesday: but if your Lordship's stay at Whitehaven should not be prolonged till towards the end of the week, it will be better perhaps that I should defer the pleasure of seeing you till your return to Lowther. Will your Lordship be so good as to direct me in this respect?

The Blues will have everything in their own way at Kendal I suppose, on the approaching public meeting.[1] The Government and the Nation at large, will, I hope, be made acquainted that this meeting does not speak the sense of the County of West[nd] but of a Party.

My feelings have been much gratified by the kind concern expressed by your Lordship on account of the late disorder in my eyes. The lid of one still remains swoln, but I am able in some degree to resume my employments, and my general health is very good.

I have the honor to be
My Lord
Your Lordships
faithful friend and Servant
Wm. Wordsworth

561. W. W. to VISCOUNT LOWTHER

MS. Lonsdale MSS., Record Office, The Castle, Carlisle. Hitherto unpublished.

Rydal Mount
27th October 1819

My dear Lord Lowther,

Your Letter followed me to Whitehaven. I don't think any of your Friends wished you to attend the meeting[2] at Kendal—and for my own part I am glad you did not appear. It certainly was a County meeting *legally convened*, but why at *Kendal*? assuredly for the sake of the support of the Kendal Mob, to drown the voices, and perhaps

[1] At the request of Brougham and his followers, Lord Thanet had agreed to summon a county meeting at Kendal on 21 Oct. to consider petitioning the Prince Regent for a recall of Parliament to inquire into the Manchester 'massacre'.

[2] The county meeting on 21 Oct., at which it was decided to petition for the recall of Parliament. For a full account of the speeches, see *Kendal Chronicle* for 23 Oct.: the *Westmorland Gazette* dismissed the gathering as unrepresentative.

break the heads, of the supporters of Government, and of the Lowther party in general. I do not deny that Kendal is a more convenient place than Appleby; but this is the first time, I believe, that any such meeting was ever holden there.—I learn from good authority that the Kendal meeting has done much disservice to the Blue cause. Brougham was not half violent enough; and the abuse of the Radicals from Crackanthorpe and Mr Christian[1] was very unpalatable to the Fell-siders; and to the lower orders in general.

I cannot but think that there may be exceptions to the general rule for the attendance of County Members at County Meetings when convened according to the forms of Law. If a large majority of Constituents do not wish for such attendance, but are averse to it, certainly a Representative cannot be blamed if he should stay away; on the other hand he clearly has a right to attend if he himself thinks proper. But looking at it as a question of expediency, into which all government resolves itself, and all conduct in public affairs, many cases might occur, (and I think the recent ones of Cumberland and Westnd are of that character) in which it is better to leave the opposite Party to themselves.

I have not yet seen the Westnd address.[2] I understand it is drawn up by Mr Carus Wilson. Some confusion was occasioned in parts of Cumberland, by *two* addresses appearing;[3] the former having been withdrawn on account of its not being agreeable I understand to Mr Wallace,[4] and to some others, who thought it too strong. It was in a great measure composed by Mr Southey, at the request of Mr Calvert. S. meddled very unwillingly in the business and is extremely sorry that he should have been the occasion of anything unpleasant. I believe the allegations of the former address are true;

[1] John Christian (1776–1857), a barrister, J. C. Curwen's son by his first marriage and heir to Ewanrigg Hall, Maryport, and the other 'Christian' properties in the Isle of Man.

[2] A Loyal Address to the Prince Regent, expressing general confidence in the Government while deploring the hardships of the poor. For full text, see *Westmorland Gazette* for 20 Nov., where W. W.'s name appears among the signatories.

[3] At the Westmorland county meeting Brougham had attacked the Cumberland Address as first published; accordingly, after a meeting in Whitehaven under the chairmanship of Lord Lonsdale, a second Address, apparently composed by Wallace, was substituted (see *Cumberland Pacquet* for 26 Oct.). In this amended form, the Address lamented recent events in Manchester, but refrained from apportioning the blame for what had happened. For Southey's authorship of the original Address, and the text, see Warter, iii, pp. 148–50; Curry, ii, pp. 202–3.

[4] Right Hon. Thomas Wallace, Lord Wallace (1768–1844): M.P. for Cockermouth, 1813–18, and then for Weymouth. He was Vice-President of the Board of Trade, 1818–23, and was raised to the peerage by Wellington in 1828.

nevertheless the Result has proved that it was not suited to the purpose; though as to Mr Wallace himself, it is probable he opposed it from pique. Calvert and a good number of independent persons signed the former address without scruple. In the substituted address, is an expression which I *very* much disapprove,—the the sentence runs thus—'We entertain no apprehension of the result of a Contest (*come when it may*) between the friends and enemies of the Constitution' etc.—The above parenthesis is surely very objectionable, as it admits the idea of such a Contest being probable. In the Cumberland Pacquet of yesterday,[1] you will find a defence of the former address, from the pen of its author. My eyes are much better, nearly quite well.

With best regards from this family I remain dear Lord Lowther

very faithfully yours

W Wordsworth.

The address of Governor Farquhar is 38 Conduit Street; should you have leisure and inclination to see him on Mrs Luff's affair;[2] he will explain everything.

562. W. W. to LORD LONSDALE

MS. Lonsdale MSS., Record Office, The Castle, Carlisle. Hitherto unpublished.

Rydale Mount

Nov[b] 11th 1819

My Lord,

The sale of Thos. Ellis's[3] Land concluded satisfactorily,— the whole passing into the hands of friends, without any necessity for Mr Jackson's bidding on the part of your Lordship.

I was at Kendal last week and found the Radicals intent upon getting up a meeting there—but the attempt was dropped, none but the very lowest of the Rabble being likely to attend.

Mr Stephens,[4] Master of Sedburgh School is in a dying state.

[1] In a letter signed 'A. B.' in the *Cumberland Pacquet* for 26 Oct. (reprinted in *Westmorland Gazette* for 6 Nov.), Southey reaffirmed his contention in the original Address that in so far as the Manchester meeting had constituted a threat to public order, the magistrates had been within their rights in breaking it up.

[2] Mrs. Luff was trying to obtain a pension. See L. 565 below.

[3] Thomas Ellis of Kendal, a freeholder of Ambleside and Lowther supporter.

[4] The Revd. William Stevens (1769–1819), fellow of St. John's College, Cambridge, and headmaster of Sedbergh from 1799. See L. 565 below. He was succeeded by another fellow of St. John's, the Revd. Henry Wilkinson (1792–1838), under whom John W. was entered in 1820.

This part of the Country would be greatly benefited if his Successor should prove an able Man, especially as the school at Hawkshead is quite neglected by the Master.

Mr Southey has addressed a Letter to Mr Brougham upon the unfair comments he chose to make at the County Meeting, Kendal, on the former Cumberland address. It will appear, I trust, in the Westnd Gazette of tomorrow, signed, Vindex.[1]

The Papers speak confidently of the Ministers giving up the Catholic Question—to conciliate new Friends; and for the general purpose of strengthening the Government. One would hope that this is a mere rumor. Such a measure might produce additional strength for the Ministry in Parliament; but it would tend greatly to encrease the disquiet of the Country. All the Dissenters, especially in the Corporate Towns would be set in motion; take Kendal for instance, where they are very powerful, and certainly more clever and intelligent for the most part than the Churchmen of that place. Among the Dissenters with whom I mix, I hear perpetual complaints of the ignorance incompetence and injustice of the Corporation.

Mr Dawes the Minister of Ambleside refused to sign the loyal address.—He is a perverse Man.

With most respectful remembrances to Lady Lonsdale and Lady Mary

I have the honor to be, my Lord,
Your Lordship's
faithful friend and Ser^{vnt}
W Wordsworth

[1] See *Westmorland Gazette* for 13 Nov. Southey had taken no part in the Westmorland election of 1818, and though attacked by Brougham on the eve of the Poll, he refrained from publishing the pamphlet which he wrote in reply (see Warter, iii, p. 94; Curry, ii, pp. 187–8). But now, Brougham's attack on the first Cumberland Address gave him a pretext for restating publicly his aversion to Brougham's methods: 'Wherever you obtain that fit audience which you lose no opportunity of seeking, it would not be easy for an opponent to gain a hearing; and certainly no person who regards his own character as a gentleman would expose himself to a personal altercation with one who cares so little in all his public conduct for the urbanities of life. There is one requisite of a demagogue, Mr. Brougham, which you possess in perfection: when you address the rabble you address yourself admirably to their humour, and cast aside every thing in feeling or manner by which they could possibly distinguish you from one of themselves. The press, however, is open to your antagonists, and in bringing you by this means before the tribunal of sober minds, they run no risque of being silenced by the clamour of your friends, or the brickbats of your partizans . . .'

563. W. W. to LORD LONSDALE

MS. Lonsdale MSS., Record Office, The Castle, Carlisle. Hitherto unpublished.

Rydal Mount
Dec[br] 5th 1819

My Lord,

The enclosed I received some little time ago, from Mrs Barker, Sister to the late Captain Wordsworth;[1] and perhaps I have done wrong in not forwarding it earlier, but I was loth to intrude upon your Lordship knowing how much you were engaged about that time. It relates to the command of the Lowther Castle; and I have nothing to add upon the subject in furtherance of Mrs Barker's wishes, but that the command of a succession of Ships upon this interest would have continued in some branch or other of the Wordsworth family for more than 50 years, had it not been for the distressful circumstances which I need not particularize to your Lordship. Mrs Barker in her letter has overrated the Power which her late Brother possessed as Ship's Husband; but I hope she is not mistaken in the fact that Cap[tn] Mortlock is prepared for a change as holding the command conditionally. In respect to the qualifications of Mrs Barker's nephew I regret that I have nothing to say, never having had the pleasure of seeing him; but I know that he is a young man in whom his late Uncle took great interest.[2]

The Measures now taking by Parliament[3] cannot but materially contribute to check the bad disposition of the Times, and if equal pains be taken to remove as far as possible every just cause of complaint, I trust that England may yet hold up her head.

There was an eager competition for the land of the late Thomas Ellis; but it happened fortunately to be intermixed with property of your Lordship's Friends. Mr Wilson of Abbot Hall was obliged by an Agent of the opposite party to pay high for a parcel which he bought.

With the highest respect
I have the honor to be
My Lord
Your Lordship's faithful friend and Servant
Wm Wordsworth

[1] Capt. John Wordsworth, W. W.'s cousin: son of Richard Wordsworth of Whitehaven, and brother to Elizabeth Barker of Rampside.

[2] Lord Lonsdale replied on 15 Dec.: 'I return you Mrs Barker's letter—as one of the sharers in the Lowther Castle I presume I may have a vote in the appointment of a captain. . . . I shall always have the greatest pleasure in being useful to any one of your connections.' (*WL MSS.*)

[3] In the face of growing social unrest, the Government was pressing on with

564. W. W. to VISCOUNT LOWTHER

MS. Lonsdale MSS., Record Office, The Castle, Carlisle. Hitherto unpublished.

[mid Dec. 1819]

My dear Lord Lowther,

I entirely concur with you that no Government could stand against the continuance of such a Battery as the Press has for some time been making upon ours.—If the Bill[1] to the principle of which I feel so strong an objection be passed now without any provision for its being temporary, that need not prevent its being repealed in future should the state of things allow it. Our Cumberland and West[nd] oppressionists[?] in the House have begun to open their eyes; strange that the portion of common sense, small as it is, which some of them possess, did not enable them to foresee that the passions of the populace could not be wrought on and their opinions misled as they have been, without bringing on these desperate acts.

I was at Kendal two days ago. Mr Wilson of Abbot Hall says that there is an improvement in the behaviour of the lower orders there. But I *know* that in the public Houses, shocking wishes and notions are frequently uttered. The proprietors, Editor and Printer of the Chronicle are all by the ears together. The two latter have resigned. The concern is considerably in debt to the Bank, and Wakefield refuses to advance any more money. So that if party zeal does not save the Paper it may be considered as in a great measure ruined. But this perhaps you have heard from other quarters.

The Guardian[2] a loyal Newspaper has found its way here. It promises well but a weekly London Paper crowded with advertizements, is not likely to suit the Country. It is dated *Sunday*, also; this would prove an objection to its circulation in many houses in the Country, especially as I observe Quack medicines, etc. etc.—

legislation to curb the Press, and to forbid seditious meetings and the illegal possession of fire-arms. Lord Liverpool's notorious 'Six Acts' were all passed in December.

[1] The Newspaper Stamp Duties Bill, passed by the House of Commons on 22 Dec.

[2] The *Guardian*, under the editorship of the Revd. George Croly and others, ran from 12 Dec. 1819 until Apr. 1824. J. W. Croker, Secretary to the Admiralty, was now actively engaged in promoting it: see Croker's *Correspondence and Diaries*, ed. L. J. Jennings, 3 vols., 1885, i, pp. 138 ff.; M. F. Brightfield, *John Wilson Croker*, 1940, pp. 168–76. W. W. submitted (through Southey) a short poem entitled *Hints from the Mountains for Certain Political Aspirants*, which was published anonymously in the issue for 16 Jan. 1820. See *PW* ii, p. 151.

advertized. Our neighbour, Mr Gee, first opened out in the Courier upon Martin Bree, Greenough, etc.[1]

De Quincey has left the Gazette.[2]
I remain my dear Lord Lowther
ever faithfully yours
Wm Wordsworth

I have sent my little Boy to the Central School, Baldwyns Gardens, and I scruple not to beg that the enclosed for his Master there may be put into [the] twopenny post by one of your Servants. Mr Johnson, the Master, was formerly curate at Grasmere.

565. D. W. to CATHERINE CLARKSON

Address: Mrs Clarkson, Playford Hall, Ipswich.
Stamp: Kendal Penny Post.
MS. British Museum.
K (—). *MY ii. 628, p. 856.*

Sunday. Decr 19th [1819]

My dear Friend,

I am become one of the idlest, and seemingly the most ungrateful of correspondents; at least as far as you are concerned with me in that way. To my shame I speak it and with sorrow; but no more on this subject. You can more easily forgive me than I can forgive myself. Another year is drawing to its close. It has been to you a year of change, with affliction; yet such change as comes in the natural course of this life, and I trust that your late anxieties on your Husband's account are over, that he has wholly regained his usual good health; and that you still continue to receive hopeful and chearing accounts of your son. Thomas Monkhouse, who, I believe, sees him pretty often, gave us such reports of him—his conduct, manners, and the bent of his mind, as were highly satisfactory and confirmed

[1] Martin Bree (1771–1842), a notorious quack who had dabbled in medicine and then in mining ventures around Keswick along with George Bellas Greenough (1778–1855), the well-known geologist. On the death of his uncle Sir Martin Stapylton, 8th and last Baronet, of Myton Hall, Yorks., Bree assumed the name of Stapylton, inherited the estates, and set up as a country gentleman. His activities and pretensions were ridiculed at length in the first issue of the *Guardian*. See also Curry, ii, p. 208.

[2] De Quincey was asked to resign in November, but he had been doing very little for the paper since the summer. Among his last contributions was a brief article on 'Immanuel Kant and Dr Herschel' on 11 Sept. For some light on De Quincey's achievements as an editor as well as his shortcomings, see Pollitt, op. cit.

what you had said before of his attention to his profession and the studies connected with it. *We* have to look back on the past year with thankfulness; it has not brought any serious affliction immediately pressing upon this Family; and one resolve we have reason to rejoice at—the resolve to part with William. *I* had long been convinced that nothing but a removal from home could save the Boy from ruin; but his Mother could not be brought to this conviction till it was forced upon her; and long did the Father waver and despond from fears for his health; but happy am I to be able to tell you that his health and his looks have visibly improved; and this I believe to be solely owing to a chearful submission to unbending laws; and activity of mind *fixed*—not wandering, as it ever used to be. Mr Monkhouse says that the improvement in William's reading is marvellous—far beyond his most *sanguine* expectations; and Mr. Johnson says that no boy can behave better than he does—that he is getting rid of bad habits very fast, is as lively as a lark—very observant and very happy. He shews a talent for figures. Luckily for himself and his present teacher he had not been practised in that way at home. He is to spend his holidays (a fortnight) at Sundridge. Mr Hoare[1] has been very kind to him—So has Mrs Douglass the mother of a little boy (the nephew of the Marquis of Queensbury)[2] who was also with Mr. J. for a few weeks after William's arrival; but has been obliged to go home ill of the measles and hooping cough, of which complaints his younger Brother has died. Happily they were not caught at the Central School. We hope that my brother will send John to Sedbergh School after the holidays. He and my sister went over to Sedbergh that very week before Mr Stevens' death with intention to place him there, if circumstances had encouraged them; but no sooner did they see Mr Stevens than they perceived that he was a dying man, though he himself had no apprehensions, and when William said he would wait a little for an amendment in his health before he fixed respecting John, Mr S. replied 'the more he had to *do* the better for him'. Poor man! he placed his motherless Family side by side—produced their mother's picture—wept while he talked; and said that he trusted he should be able to give his Children good educations—'all he *had* for them'.

[1] Samuel Hoare, head of the banking firm of that name in Lombard St., and a Quaker. His wife was a churchwoman. The families of W. W. and C. W. often stayed with them at their house in Hampstead.

[2] The 6th Marquess (1777–1837). He was succeeded by his brother John Douglas (1779–1856) as 7th Marquess, and the only surviving son of the latter, Archibald William Douglas (1818–58), the little boy mentioned here, eventually became 8th Marquess.

William sent the Doctor to him from Kendal: he was *much worse* when he arrived; and in a single week he was dead. On the other side of my paper you will see a statement of the case of these 12 poor children, which has been circulated among Friends; and the subscription is likely to be a good one. I send it you not expecting or wishing that *you* should give anything. You have enough to do in your own neighbourhood in addition to other especial calls on Mr. Clarkson's humanity; but you have rich Friends, and the Father having been a Clergyman, a Schoolmaster, and a Fellow of a College, these children seem to have claims beyond the circle of a private acquaintance. Crackenthorpe was a pupil of Mr. Stevens and most affectionately attached to him and his wife. He has subscribed £50, a great Sum, considering his means. We expect Mrs. Coleridge and Sara next week on their way from Liverpool. Mrs C took Sara thither to get her fitted with steel stays or supporters for her Back. She has long had a weakness there; and the spine has been almost imperceptibly forming a slight curve in one part. The stays have been made under the direction of a Surgeon eminent for skill in such cases, and he entertains no doubt of a perfect cure provided her health is good. To attain this she ought to be allured from standing as much as possible and *must* lie on her back for at least two hours in the day.

Dorothy will be at home on Friday night; and we shall have her for one month. She, thank God! has at present no bodily weakness— She is almost twice as bulky as Sara, and considerably taller. I wish she were half as studious; and perhaps both would be the better for such a division of property. However we may be thankful for the good we have. Dorothy is affectionate, lively, has good sense; and is anything rather than listless or indolent. Derwent is to go to his Father after Christmas. This is a pity. Would you believe it possible, Coleridge expressed a wish that Sara could go to Highgate to be under the care of Mr. Gilman!! the cleverest medical man with whom he was ever acquainted!! Hartley is, I believe, at Ottery with his Uncles.

We have given up all hope of Mrs Luff's being able to procure a pension. Lord Lowther has taken infinite pains; but when my brother last heard from him, he gave us reason to fear that there was not the smallest chance for her. This will no doubt settle all her thoughts of house-keeping, except in a very small cottage; and I think she would be much happier in lodgings considering the liberty she would have in not being tyed to any house. Yet I am very sorry her income is so small; for even in lodgings, with her habits, her pleasure in giving, her pleasure in spending, she will find herself poor. She is a good creature; and I should have liked to have seen her a perfect Lady Bountiful in our neighbourhood. If John goes to school, my Brother will visit London in the Spring, and he will take me along with him—such at least is his wish and mine, but I consider the matter so uncertain that I think little about it and talk less. You say you intend to be there in the Spring, so I hope we may meet in London, and go together to the Central School—at all events I trust you will come into the North next summer—you have given us better hopes of this than ever before; and I think that Mr. Clarkson will not find it easy to refuse coming after his very long absence from this country. Sara sends her very best love. I do not know whether I ought to tell you that she is most eagerly and happily employed in knitting yarn stockings for Mr Clarkson. She knits and reads by the hour together. All well—Sara loses her teeth fast, but it makes no difference in her appearance or very little. Mine are *all* gone but three above and three below and I have now a true old woman's mouth and chin. My profile is seventy. Shall I get a set of new teeth? We talk of it. Yet I do not altogether like the experiment. Give my kind love to your Husband, in which all join, and to Tom. God bless you, my dearest Friend, Believe me ever your affectionate, D. Wordsworth. It is very chearing to me when I close this letter, so near the end of the year, to think that I have two chances of seeing you before the end of another year.

John is taller than his mother, indeed not above an inch shorter than his Father. At the time you wrote requesting me to recommend your friend at Bootle to Captain Wordsworth's notice; he, poor man, was too ill in mind and body for me to apply to him, and his dismal end, no doubt, you have heard of. I hope Sara will write soon —her letter will be better worth postage than this. We have had intense frost and deep snow; no stoppage of roads. Fine skating upon Rydal Water—for John and his Father. The eyes quite well again.

[*A Copy of Notice about the Revd. W. Stevens was attached to the letter.*]

566. W. W. to JOHN KENYON[1]

Address: John Kenyon, Esqre, London.
MS. untraced.
Transactions of the Wordsworth Society, no. 6, p. 77. *K* (—). *MY ii.* 629, *p.* 859.

[late Dec. 1819]

. . . Mrs. Coleridge and her daughter are now here, both well. Since you left us Mrs. W. and I have been over to Sedbergh, to see the orphan family of Stephens; we found their prospects brightening—the subscription is going on well, and situations have already been procured for several. To the honor of Liverpool, be it mentioned that Mr. Bolton, sometimes called the Liverpool Crœsus, has contributed £50. You speak of this great commercial place as I should have expected. In respect to visual impression, nothing struck me so much at Liverpool as one of the streets near the river, in which is a number of lofty and large warehouses, with the processes of receiving and discharging goods.

I am truly thankful for your travelling directions. The ladies unite

[*cetera desunt*]

567. W. W. to VISCOUNT LOWTHER

MS. Lonsdale MSS., Record Office, The Castle, Carlisle. Hitherto unpublished.

Rydale Mount
Friday 31st Dec^{br} 1819

My dear Lord Lowther,

The persons who object to Sunday Newspapers, are fortunately those who stand least in need of the admonitions which, I hope, the Guardian will give. They are already well disposed.

In the last Kendal Chronicle[2] appeared a most malignant mis-

[1] John Kenyon (1784–1856), the friend of many of the literary men of the time, including Southey, Landor, and later the Brownings, had made the acquaintance of the Wordsworths at the beginning of December, though, as S. H. tells T. Monkhouse, 'he had been as he says ever since his residence at Keswick [fifteen years before] . . . *bit* by Wms Poems—and indeed he seems to have a better verbal knowledge of them than the Author himself' (*SH* 58, p. 167). This letter was sent with a copy of the second of W. W.'s poems entitled 'September, 1819' (*PW* iv, p. 99).

[2] A letter in the *Kendal Chronicle* for 24 Dec., signed 'A Westmorland Inhabitant and Freeholder', attacked Lord Lowther for having had Westmorland included within the operation of the Seizure of Arms Bill, and insinuated that his action was prompted by 'a fit of spleen and revenge' against the county for daring to put up an independent candidate against the Lowthers at the last election.

representation of the words you used upon the searching for arms Bill. I am in the habit of despising things in this spirit, deeming it politic for the most part to let them go unnoticed. But I was requested to animadvert upon this Letter, which indeed I had felt some disposition to do when I first read it. Accordingly I wrote a Letter to the Editor of the Gazette (which I expect will appear today) signed 'an Enemy to Detraction'.[1] I am not sure but that you may think I had better have left the slander to its natural death.

The Ministers do not appear to me to have cleared themselves from the charge of not having made the best use of the previously existing laws for the punishment of Libel.[2] The failure of the prosecution of Hone, furnished no sufficient reasons why other offenders of that description should not have been indicted. I cannot but think that the Law officers were remiss. It is well however that the Bills are passed; but after all it is probable that the additional severity of punishment will indispose Juries to convict. There lies the great difficulty in legislating; moderate punishments are despised; and juries don't like that rigorous ones should be inflicted; and thus the interest of the State is compromized.

I was at Lowther the other day, when poor Lumb was dying. Dr Satterthwaite and I passed an hour in the Library; what a melancholy place is a great House when the family are absent!

With kindest regards from Mrs W. and my sister I remain

my dear Lord Lowther
very faithfully yours
Wm Wordsworth

[1] See *Westmorland Gazette* for 31 Dec. W. W. defended Lord Lowther's action on the ground that Westmorland was close to Carlisle and other disaffected areas. 'The people of Westmorland, moreover, are aware of the dangers to which the Constitution is exposed, and they confide in the judgement and integrity of its Government. Our Representative may be assured that the discreeter part of the County will not deem it an insult, but an honor, that he has acted upon the belief that such were their feelings. The whole kingdom was wisely made subject to the bill for the regulation of public meetings; upon the ground, that the seditious, if prevented in one quarter, would transfer their operations to another. The same course, to a certain degree, might be adopted in respect to the accumulation of arms,—and it was obviously the interest of the County of Westmorland, that its character should not suffer, nor its quiet be disturbed by strangers resorting to it, with a liberty to act here as this law would prevent them from acting in the districts to which they belonged. Strictly is it true, then, that this bill will operate as a *protection* to the County of Westmorland, and our Representative did well to maintain this, in spite of the sneers of high-flying Patriots, whether in Parliament or out of it . . .'

[2] The new Blasphemous and Seditious Libels Bill was passed by the House of Commons on 24 Dec.

568. W. W. to UNKNOWN CORRESPONDENT[1]

Endorsed: 4 Jan. 1820. Rydale Mount nr Kendal. Wm Wordsworth Esq.
MS. Cornell. Hitherto unpublished.

Rydale Mount
near Ambleside
Jan^ry 4th 1820

My Dear Sir,

The enclosed from some foolish Person in America arrived during my Absence. I beg leave to repeat, in respect to it, the request you were so obliging as to comply with on a former occasion, viz, that you would authorize Mr Fenton to repay me the amount of the Postage, if it appears to you proper to do so.[2] I have some scruples about troubling you on this occasion as the Letter, preposterous as it is, is not designed as an insult; yet I am inclined to think you will not deem it right that a Man should be compelled to pay at this rate for the senseless impudence of others. At all events I am pleased with the occasion of renewing the assurance of the respect with which I have the honor

to be very sincerely yours
Wm Wordsworth

569. W. W. to VISCOUNT LOWTHER

MS. Lonsdale MSS., Record Office, The Castle, Carlisle.
K (—). MY ii. 632, p. 863 (—).

[mid Jan. 1820]

My dear Lord Lowther,

Allow me to ask your advice about a little private business of my own. You are well acquainted with French affairs; do you think it would be prudent to lodge money in the French funds; I mean for one like myself who cannot afford to lose any thing. By the sale of an Estate[3] I have about [£]2,000 to place somewhere or other: encrease of interest is an object, as the education of my children is now reaching its most expensive point; and if without much risk as

[1] This letter was almost certainly addressed to the postmaster at Kendal. Myles Fenton, who is mentioned below, became postmaster himself at a later date.

[2] Postage was paid by the recipient of a letter until the introduction of postage stamps in 1840.

[3] Probably part of the Place Fell property which Lord Lowther's father helped him to acquire in 1806.

to regular payment of the interest, or loss upon the principal, I could profit by placing it in the french funds, I should like to do so. And upon this subject I know no one whose opinion I should value so highly as yours.

James Brougham has been on a short visit to our neighbour Edmonds. The heads of the Party met him there, and at Dixon's. The Chronicle being a losing concern, has past into the hands of Lough the Printer, an ignorant fellow; who cannot possibly conduct it without assistance.[1] The new paper at Whitehaven gains ground upon Ware's,[2] in advertizments, very much. It is conducted in a mischievous spirit.

I remain my dear Lord Lowther
very faithfully yours
Wm Wordsworth

570. W. W. to UNKNOWN CORRESPONDENT

MS. Colby College, Maine.
Colby Library Quarterly, 1:5, pp. 80–1 (Jan. 1944).

Rydale Mount
Monday 16th [Jan.] 1820

Dear Sir,

I do not like to let the land[3] at the rent proposed by [Bewsher],[4] because I think it would affect the letting of the whole next year.

I prefer its being retained in my hands, and let as meadow when the grass is fit to cut. As the crop will be taken off those fields the incoming farmer shall have an allowance accordingly.

I am afraid the Blacksmith's shop is likely to lie idle.

I remain, dear sir,
Very sincerely yours
Wm Wordsworth

[1] The change of proprietor was announced in the *Kendal Chronicle* for 8 Jan.
[2] i.e. the *Cumberland Pacquet*.
[3] Probably part of W. W.'s Broad How estate in Patterdale.
[4] Perhaps Thomas Bewsher, wheelwright and joiner, of Pooley Bridge.

571. W. W. to BENJAMIN ROBERT HAYDON

Address: B. R. Haydon, Lisson Grove north, London.
MS. untraced.
Haydon (—). *MY ii. 630, p. 860.*

Rydale Mount near Ambleside. 16th January, 1820

My dear Friend,

Mr Monkhouse has probably informed you how far I have suffered under the same malady as yourself.—I am better so far as to be able to use my eyes by day; but I neither write nor read by Candle light.—I do most sincerely rejoice in *your* recovery—and congratulate you with all my heart on the completion of your Picture;[1] of which I hear from our common Friends the Beaumonts the most excellent accounts. Indeed they speak of it in the highest terms.—Your most valuable Drawing[2] arrived, when I was unable to enjoy it as it deserved. I did not like to employ an Amanuensis to thank you for it; as I hoped for a speedy recovery:—a hope I shall not indulge in again as I am convinced that the organ of sight is with me in a precarious state; that is very irritable and subject to inflammation. Under these circumstances as I was sure of your painful sympathy I ran the risk of incurring your displeasure, as the less evil of the two—Your drawing is much admired as a work of art; some think it a stodgy[3] likeness; but in general it is not deemed so—for my own part I am proud to possess it as a mark of your regard, and for its own merits.

I purpose being in London in the Spring; when I trust I shall find you well and prosperous. Do you ever hear of John Scott—pray how is he? and where; if you are in communication with him let him know that I am much interested in his welfare.—Mr Monkhouse, I understand, you see occasionally, and through him we hear of you; always with lively interest. Now that you have recovered your eyes, paint, and leave writing to the dunces and malignants with which

[1] *Christ's Entry into Jerusalem*, in which W. W. appears as a spectator 'bowing in reverence and awe', while Keats, Voltaire, and Newton stand near by. Haydon had been at work on the picture for several years. For his own interpretation of it, see *Diary of Benjamin Robert Haydon*, ed. W. B. Pope, 5 vols., 1960–3, ii, pp. 258 ff.; and for a full history, Blanshard, op. cit., pp. 147–8.

[2] The chalk drawing of W. W. made for M. W. during their visit to London in Jan. 1818 (see Haydon's *Diary*, ii, p. 182; and *SH* 36, p. 115), and left with Thomas Monkhouse until it could be safely sent to Rydal Mount. For full details, see Blanshard, op. cit., pp. 149–50. Haydon had written to W. W. on 12 Sept. 1818: 'With respect to the Drawing I did of your head, I am happy to tell you, it met with universal public approbation—and was considered by a great many as the best sketch I had ever made of any one . . .' (*WL MSS.*)

[3] *Written* stogy.

London swarms—You have taken too much trouble about them.—How is Keates, he is a youth of promise too great for the sorry company he keeps.[1] You perhaps have heard from Mr Monkhouse that my younger son is at the Central School, Baldwyns Gardens. I should like to know what impression your picture makes upon him, and shall beg of Mr Monkhouse to take him to see it. Do you skate, we have charming diversion in that way about our lakes. I wish you were here to partake of it. The splendor of the snow-clad mountains, by moonlight in particular is most charming; and the softness of the shadows surpasses anything you can conceive; this when the moon is at a particular point of elevation. I never saw any thing so exquisite; though I believe Titian has; *and* so, therefore, perhaps may you.—Let me hear from you at your leisure, and particularly how far you are pleased with your own performance. If I could see your Picture, I think it would inspire me with a Sonnet; and indeed without seeing it I do not lack matter for so slight a tribute to your merit.—Mrs Wordsworth and Miss Hutchinson join me in most hearty congratulation, and sincerest regards; and believe me, my dear Haydon,

Your faithful friend
and sincere admirer
Wm. Wordsworth

571a. W. W. to HENRY CRABB ROBINSON

MS. untraced.
K (—). Morley, ii. p. 850. *LY i.* 780a, *p.* 254 (—).

[late Jan. 1820]

My dear Sir,

Dr. Satterthwaite was to leave Lowther about this time, for London; but I think your best way would be to address him at Lowther, to be forwarded, if gone, as he would certainly order his letters to be sent after him.

I distinctly remember the day I passed at Mr. Hammond's;[2] but have, as I regret, a much stronger recollection of Pollock[3] the

[1] Haydon replied on 28 Apr.: 'Keats is very poorly, and I think in danger . . .' (*WL MSS.*).

[2] Elton Hamond, a London tea-merchant and close friend of H. C. R.'s who had committed suicide on New Year's Eve. See Sadler, ii, pp. 141–57.

[3] Sir Frederick Pollock, Bart., F.R.S. (1783–1870), at this time a rising young lawyer. He was elected to Parliament in 1831, served as Attorney-General in Peel's first and second administrations, and was appointed Chief Baron of the Exchequer in 1844.

Lawyer than of my Host. Pollock is a forward person, talking much like most Lawyers; Hammond said little. There was also present a Mr. Miller, Brother of a gentleman who acquired some distinction at Oxford. Hammond was a great admirer of Joanna Bailey.—As I purpose, if possible, to go to Switzerland this summer, my journey to London will be deferred till May; so that I cannot hope for the pleasure of accompanying you. You will probably see Gifford, the Editor of the Quarterly Review; tell him from me, if you think proper, that every true-born Englishman will regard the pretensions of the Review to the character of a faithful defender of the institutions of the country, as *hollow*, while it leaves that infamous publication Don Juan[1] unbranded; I do not mean by a formal Critique, for it is not worth it; it would also tend to keep it in memory; but by some decisive words of reprobation, both as to the damnable tendency of such works, and as to [the] despicable quality of the powers requisite for their production. What avails it to hunt down Shelley, whom few read, and leave Byron untouched?

I am persuaded that Don Juan will do more harm to the English character, than anything of our time; not so much as a *Book*;—But thousands who would be afraid to have it in that shape, will batten upon choice bits of it, in the shape of Extracts. I could tell you an anecdote to this purpose which I heard the other day. . . .

[*cetera desunt*]

572. W. W. to LORD LONSDALE

MS. Lonsdale MSS., Record Office, The Castle, Carlisle. Hitherto unpublished.

Feb 2nd 1820

My Lord,

I sincerely condole with your Lordship, on the lamented death of our most gracious and venerable Sovereign.[2] We were prepared for the shock, having heard previously that the King was not expected to live three days. Your Lordship will feel much on this occasion; the best consolation of us all, lies in the reflection that George the Third will be ranked by posterity among the best and wisest Kings that ever sate upon the throne of England.

The same Paper, the Times, which has brought us this Intelligence, has agitated my Family and myself much by containing, in

[1] The first two cantos of *Don Juan* had appeared in July 1819. Gifford was very closely associated with Byron at this time.

[2] George III died on 29 Jan. at the age of eighty-one. See *PW* iii, p. 40.

a most conspicuous part of it, an advertisement declaratory of Mr Brougham's intention once more to disturb the County of Westnd.[1] It may not appear so to the world, but to us it appears a shocking indecency—we have felt it such—not to leave the people of Westnd one moment of undisturbed regret upon this awful occasion!

My Lord, can any of your Friends be of service to frustrate this coarse-minded Man's attempts? I speak especially in the name of Mr Gee, Mr Jackson and myself—but I have no doubt that *every one* will do their utmost, should this prove more than a threat as empty as it is indecent!

Sincere thanks for your Lordship's kind offer in respect to the command of the Lowther Castle.[2]

Lady Lonsdale and Lady Mary will accept of my sincere respects.

I have the honor to be
my Lord
most faithfully your Lordship's
friend and Ser^{nt}
Wm Wordsworth

Mr James Brougham was staying some few weeks since in this neighbourhood, and had interviews with the principal persons of that party;—but with what views I do not know.

I have sent a short paragraph to the Kendal paper, upon Mr B's Advertisement.[3]

[1] The first version of this advertisement is dated 30 Jan. Brougham later modified it slightly, in order to straighten out the ambiguity W. W. complains about in the next letters. 'The approaching Dissolution of Parliament affords another opportunity to you of asserting your Independence, and to me of redeeming my solemn pledge never to desert you in this noble struggle. This event is, on every account [except the melancholy occasion of it] a subject of sincere congratulation. [It is unnecessary to add that I feel as deeply as any man the melancholy event in question, but I am quite incapable of making a parade of feelings, which are common to the whole nation for electioneering purposes.]' In spite of these concessions to his opponents, however, Brougham made a point of denigrating the achievements of the previous reign at a meeting in London on 19 Feb.

[2] See L. 563 above.

[3] This paragraph appeared in the *Westmorland Gazette* for 5 Feb., since Lord Lonsdale wrote back on 9 Feb., 'Your observations on B's Address are admirable . . .' (*WL MSS.*). But no copy of this issue of the paper seems to have survived.

573. W. W. to LORD LONSDALE

MS. Lonsdale MSS., Record Office, The Castle, Carlisle. Hitherto unpublished.

Rydale Mount
4th Feby 1820

My Lord,

Pray excuse me for breaking in upon you again. It is to state what I have learned of the feelings of this neighbourhood, respecting the Westnd Representation.[1] They are *decisively* in favor of your Lordship's Sons being proposed again. I need not trouble you with names, for the feeling is *universal* among our friends. Mr Calvert, of Keswick, says 'two Lowthers will keep out B. but one not.' I am not of his opinion exactly; but with an anxiety which your Lordship will pardon, I state my firm conviction, that if a change takes place we shall fight under deplorable disadvantages. Great numbers will be slack and several will with difficulty be brought to vote at all.

I *know* also, that such hopes as the Blues have, are chiefly founded on the expectation that someone else will be brought forth. Everyone appears shocked with B's advertisement;[2] it is slightly *altered* in the Times I have received to-day but it is dispersed over Westnd in a handbill as *first* written, dated the 30th, which was the sabbath day. His Friends admit that he is rash and wants judgement, but plead in his excuse that the Yellows had the start the last time, and he was determined to have it now.

I have the honor to be
my Lord
most faithfully your Lordship's
friend and servant
Wm Wordsworth

Not knowing Col. Lowther's address I have taken the liberty of enclosing a note to him, merely to state the wishes of this neighbourhood respecting him as a Candidate.

[1] The Lowther party in Cumberland was having difficulty in finding a suitable candidate for the approaching election. John Lowther (1759–1844), Lord Lonsdale's brother, later Sir John Lowther, Bart. of Swillington, Yorks., who had been M.P. for Cumberland since 1796, was reluctant to stand again, and it was rumoured that Col. Lowther was to be withdrawn from Westmorland to take his place. In the end, however, John Lowther overcame his scruples, and remained M.P. for Cumberland till 1831. For the younger Hasell as a possible alternative to Col. Lowther in Westmorland, see L. 542 above, and *SH* 61, p. 178.

[2] See previous letter.

574. W. W. to VISCOUNT LOWTHER

MS. Lonsdale MSS., Record Office, The Castle, Carlisle.
K (—). MY ii. 633, p. 863 (—).

Rydal Mount
4 February 1820

My dear Lord Lowther,

Sincere thanks for your letter; it has determined me to trust £2,000 to the French Funds.[1]

Mr Calvert of Keswick says that two Lowthers will keep out B.—one *not.* I am not of his opinion exactly but depend upon it, my dear Lord L., that you will suffer deplorably if any other candidate be substituted. I *know* that such hopes as the Blues have are mainly founded on the expectation that some one else will be brought forward. I cannot forbear to state this. I am aware of the difficulty you mentioned respecting Cumberland; but if it be possible let you and your Brother meet this audacious Man again. They have not the least hope of beating you; but should a change take place in the persons proposed, they will exult—they will cry out 'you see how their power is shaken, they have given way, and the struggle after this will drive them out of the field altogether, if even they should beat us now.'

B's advertisement has shocked almost every Body, seeming to exult as he does in the King's death and coming out immediately after that event. I sent a short paragraph to the Kendal Gazette on this subject.[2]

If you can find a moment's leisure do write me a word—I am so anxious to hear what is intended.

Ever my dear Lord Lowther
most faithfully yours
W Wordsworth

P.S. I have written to Lord Lonsdale to the above effect. The enclosed is for the twopenny post.

[1] See L. 569 above.
[2] See L. 572 above.

575. W. W. to VISCOUNT LOWTHER

MS. Lonsdale MSS., Record Office, The Castle, Carlisle. Hitherto unpublished.

Rydale Mount
5th Febry 1820

My dear Lord Lowther,

Not one of your friends has the least fear of a *triumphant* result; now that it is determined that the Col: is to come forward again. This family is rejoiced, as indeed are all your Friends. Everything possible shall be done to promote an object in which we are all so deeply interested.

What is to be done in Cumberland? Can I possibly be of use there; do not spare me—ever yours most faithfully

W Wordsworth

It may be proper to mention the residences of a few new Voters whose freehold[s] lie in this neighbourhood—[1]

John Hutchinson Esq., Stockton upon Tees
Henry Ditto Ditto Esq., Greatham near Stockton
Thomas Ditto Ditto Esq., Radnor
John Monkhouse Esq., Stow, Hay, Brecon
Thomas Ditto Esq., 28 Queen Anne Street, Cavendish Sq
Eldred Addison Esq., London, but Mr Monkhouse knows his address
George Gee Esq., Rydale
Rev. Dr Wordsworth Lambeth
John Myers Esq., Pow House near Broughton, Lancashire
Rev. Wm Jackson Queen's College Oxford
Mr Scambler Ambleside
—Partridge Esqre,[2] India House

[1] The list which follows records principally the membership of W. W.'s Ivy How syndicate. See L. 524 above.

[2] William Henry Partridge of Battersea, probably a friend of Thomas Monkhouse.

576. W. W. to LORD LONSDALE

MS. Lonsdale MSS., Record Office, The Castle, Carlisle. Hitherto unpublished.

Rydale Mount
6th Febry 1820

My Lord,

We are overjoyed at the Colonel's determination to come forward again.—A thousand thanks to him and to your Lordship; I speak in the name of all your friends in this neighbourhood; and no doubt our feelings are participated by every Yellow in the County.

Supposing that your Lordship might be called to Town, I have lately addressed you there twice; my second Letter is now happily superseded—but it will show how anxious we were.

I have seen Mr North and Mr Gee since I received the Colonel's Letter this morning. The Freeholders will immediately be waited upon; and every step taken to promote an object in which we are all so deeply interested.

The Colonel's address is as excellent as Mr B's was unfeelingly timed, and incautiously worded.[1] But, no doubt, the phrase '*This event*' etc., was meant by him not to refer to the King's death but the dissolution of Parliament; it is one of the grossest errors in expression ever committed; and would not have been *possible* had he shared the feelings natural to a Briton upon such an affecting occasion.

Again my Lord accept my thanks, as an Englishman and as a friend to your Lordship's family for this determination.

Ever yours
W Wordsworth

577. W. W. to LORD LONSDALE

MS. Lonsdale MSS., Record Office, The Castle, Carlisle. Hitherto unpublished.

Rydale Mount
Febry 14th 1820

My Lord,

Mr Gee writes at length to Colonel Lowther today, giving an account of his late Excursion. His report is most favorable in every

[1] Col. Lowther's Address, dated 1 Feb., drew attention to the ambiguous wording of Brougham's original Address, which appeared to imply that the King's death was 'a subject of sincere congratulation'. See L. 572 above.

particular, except that it appears that the object of the Declaration[1] had been as little explained in the East and West Wards as here, and in consequence the signing of it had not at all been pushed. In fact till the receipt of your Lordship's last Letter, we had not the least notion that it was intended as a manifestation of strength:— and it is now too late to do anything more with it in this Quarter. I am sorry also to say that there has been a remissness in *execution*, I mean framing the legal Instrument for 'Deeds of Gift', etc., for the Creation of new freeholds, so that we have not gained as much accession of strength in that way, as might easily have been effected. In Grasmere four Voters have thus been prevented, and about Bowness *many* more. It seems, therefore, politic to conceal the exact number of new freeholds as much as may be; for the imaginations of our opponents will naturally swell them beyond the actual amount; and this will make them more afraid of a Contest. I have therefore taken the liberty of desiring Mr Gee who has just seen Mr Nicholson[2] to write to him with a request that he would keep this as much as possible to himself.

As to Cumberland, it seems impossible to raise even a fourth part of the money, required to contest that County.[3] The dispositions are no doubt in many quarters as bad as possible; all your Lordship's friends, nevertheless, seem to think the attempt will fall to the ground, for want of funds to support it.

Mr Jackson, I am sorry to say, continues very unwell; but he is notwithstanding as zealous and active as possible. I have not seen Mr North since I received your Lordship's letter.

I have the honour to be
most faithfully
your Lordship's
Friend and Servnt
W Wordsworth

P.S. I have just learned that there is some dissatisfaction among the Voters in Patterdale, but not the particulars.

[1] The *Declaration* of the freeholders of Westmorland in support of the Lowthers, dated 5 Feb., published with list of signatories in the *Westmorland Gazette* for 19 and 26 Feb.

[2] William Nicholson, who succeeded Robert Lumb as agent at Lowther.

[3] i.e. by bringing forward another candidate, in addition to John Lowther, to stand against George Howard, Lord Morpeth, later 6th Earl of Carlisle (1773–1848), who had been the other M.P. for Cumberland since 1806. At the General Election in March, John Lowther in fact stood alone and was returned unopposed; for the Whigs showed their dissatisfaction with Morpeth's politicial conduct by putting up J. C. Curwen (who had already been returned for Carlisle), and Morpeth was forced to retire at an early stage of the Poll.

578. W. W. to LORD LONSDALE

Address: The Earl of Lonsdale, Cottesmore, Greatham, Grantham.
Stamp: Kendal Penny Post.
MS. Lonsdale MSS., Record Office, The Castle, Carlisle. Hitherto unpublished.

Febry 23rd 1820

My Lord,

There cannot be a doubt that Miss Parker's purpose is to supply her Brothers[1] out of the requested Enfranchisement with Freeholds. They are all Blues, and are all her near connections, except her Brother-in-Law Mr Gell,[2] who signed the Declaration. Under these circumstances no judicious Friend of your Lordship in this neighbourhood would advise the Enfranchisement. Mr Barton, whom I have seen since I received your Lordship's Letter, and who knows all the Family thoroughly, is decidedly against it. One of her Brothers, is expected to be canvassing this neighbourhood today against the present Members.

A Freeholder of Kentmere whom I have seen to day, and who voted for Lord L. and the Col. last Election, says that he shall stay at home. I should not have thought it worth while to mention this, had not his reasons been partly of a public nature. He says, that he voted for the present Members, as representing the landed interest; which according to his opinion is neglected. He means to sell his land; for with all his pains he cannot keep his property from wasting.

Upon this subject and the state of the farming world, I have received some particulars, connected with most respectable persons, relations of Mrs Wordsworth, which I shall mention to Lord Lowther.[3] This matter requires the most serious attention of Government; as disaffection will keep pace with distress.

I should have enclosed a Letter to Lady Mary with thanks had I not been engaged all the morning.

I have the honor to be
your Lordship's
faithful Servnt
Wm Wordsworth

I am concerned to hear that the venerable President[4] is about to be

[1] Charles Parker, R.N., of Parknook, and Simpson Parker of Urswick, near Ulverston.

[2] J. Sherbrooke Gell of Troutbeck, a solicitor, who later resided in Nottingham.

[3] See *SH* 61, p. 175.

[4] Benjamin West (1738–1820), who succeeded Reynolds as President of the Royal Academy in 1792, died on 11 Mar. 1820.

removed. This severe winter has taken away many old people. Mr Jackson continues to be confined by illness; but nothing can exceed his anxiety to serve the cause.

579. W. W. to MRS. ROSE LAWRENCE[1]

MS. untraced.
MY ii. 634, p. 863.

Rydal Mount, 7 March 1820

My dear Madam,

Your Letter has this moment reached me, having been detained at Ormskirk whither it got by some blunder of the Liverpool Post-master; Kendal it should seem is a safer direction to me than Ambleside.

I am truly sorry to hear of your severe illness—and the more so as your convalescence may be retarded by the return of this severe weather.

This morning our hills and vale were white with snow—it has disappeared from the Vale already, but the air as probably with you is very ungenial.

I have seen Mr Southey—I spent three days with him and returned only the day before yesterday. I did purpose to write to you—but I am sorry to say he does not appear inclined to meddle with Cervantes. Navarete[2] he has not seen; but his first observation was, when I mentioned your wish, that the life would be best done by a Spaniard. Besides Mr. S'-s hands

[*cetera desunt*]

[1] Miscellaneous writer and friend of Mrs. Hemans. Wife of Charles Lawrence, of Wavertree Hall, near Liverpool, who owned estates in Jamaica. He was mayor of Liverpool in 1823.

[2] Juan Fernandez Navarrete (1526–79), surnamed El Mudo (the Mute), Spanish painter of the Madrid school who studied under Titian in Venice. At the time of his death he was occupied with a series of paintings for the Escorial.

580. W. W. to MATTHEW SMITH[1]

Address: Matthew Smith Esqre, Cockermouth.
Franked: Lonsdale, Penrith West, first April 1820. *Endorsed*: April 1820 William Wordsworth Esq. from Lowther Castle about the House at Crosley.
MS. WL. Hitherto unpublished.

Lowther Castle Wednesday.
[29 Mar. 1820]

My dear Sir,

I cannot sufficiently thank you for the trouble you have taken in my late Brother's affairs. I have heard from Mr Wood, with great concern that you were severely indisposed some time ago; and I assure you it gives me sincere pleasure to learn that you are so much better. Nothing should have prevented me calling upon you in passing and repassing through Cockermouth, had I been Master of my own movements; but as you would learn I was in the Carriage of the Earl of Lonsdale. When I passed through Cockermouth last Autumn I wished much to pay my respects to you but it was not in my power.

My late Brother's tenant has paid his half years arrears of Rent—deducting, I think for seven years Rates; as I had no means of ascertaining that an allowance on this account had ever been made by my Brother I did not feel justified in refusing this demand.

I hope Mr Wood will succeed in procuring the Arrears from Mr Satterthwaite, (half a year I believe is the amount) and the interest from Mr Senhouse, upon the £100 left on account of the customary part of the property he purchased.

As we cannot give a title to the House of Crosley, I think much the best way would be to *let* it, for such Rent as could be procured, and I shall feel truly obliged if you would effect the letting of it.

I did not receive your Letter till I came to Keswick yesterday on my return to this place.

I remain, dear Sir
very respectfully
your obliged Servant
Wm Wordsworth

[1] Almost certainly the partner of William Wood, the Cockermouth attorney.

581. D. W. to THOMAS MONKHOUSE

Address: To Thomas Monkhouse Esqre, No. 38 Queen Anne Street, Cavendish Square.
Postmark: 25 Apr. 1820. *Endorsed*: 25 Ap. 1820. D. W.
MS. WL.
MY ii. 635, p. 864.

Lambeth. Tuesday [25 Apr. 1820]

My dear Friend,

I hope I may see you at dinner today, but in case of disappointment I write to tell you the result of my deliberations with my good Brother[1] this morning. Last night I was so completely jaded that I determined to dismiss all thoughts that did not lead to composure and sleep, and was accordingly rewarded by a good night's rest, and am this morning fresh for business, yet I am resolved to spend the whole day in quietness. I cannot make up my mind to give Dumergue 50 guineas without first satisfying myself as to the prices of other Dentists; and should I hear that Cartwright's or Fox's prices are much lower I should then wish to make inquiries respecting their comparative success in putting in whole sets of teeth. I settled with Mrs Stoddart that in case I determined on Dumergue we should go together on Thursday; but as I want to inquire further I cannot so soon fix with him, therefore I now write to her to that effect, and I hope that through your help I may tomorrow be able to gather such information as will satisfy me. I was thinking of writing to William Allen[2] to inquire after Fox, and perhaps *he* also may know something of Cartwright. My Br. seemed to approve of this; but thinking again, he advised me rather to go to Wm. Allen and proposed that Miss Lamb should go with me. This cannot be as Miss L. is out of town. Miss Stoddart also is engaged. But *you* I think may be able to help me. I only want to know the prices in the first instance.

If it be possible, then, I wish you would meet me at Mr Lloyd's[3] lodgings tomorrow morning—I will be there at twelve o'clock; and the sooner after that time the better. If you cannot, pray send me a line there, No. 11 Charing Cross.

It vexes me to give so much trouble; but I cannot in conscience go to such a price without due consideration.

[1] i.e. C. W. W. W. did not proceed south until the end of May.
[2] The Quaker philanthropist and scientist. See L. 360 above. He was Lecturer at Guy's Hospital, 1802–26.
[3] Charles Lloyd, somewhat restored in health, was now living in London. See *Lamb*, ii. 349, pp. 267–8.

25 April 1820

Do ask about Cartwright if you see any one who can tell you. This evening or tomorrow morning. God bless you.

Yours most truly
D. W.

582. W. W. to LORD LONSDALE

MS. Lonsdale MSS., Record Office, The Castle, Carlisle. Hitherto unpublished.

April 27th, 1820

My Lord,

I am honored by your's of the 25th. Your Lordship would learn by mine of yesterday all that at present I can ascertain from Mr and Mrs Gee; but I had already requested them to procure further particulars. If Mr Green[1] has actually circulated such [a] Pamphlet there will be no difficulty in getting at the fact, and procuring the work. Of his hostility there can be no doubt;— that it is of a most marked disposition I have heard from several quarters. It is also well known that Mr G. is a dabbler in Pamphlets. Through Mr Monkhouse, to whom I take the Liberty of enclosing a Note, I shall probably come at the Pamphlet, if it has ever existed.[2]

Mr Brougham asserts that 100 votes have gone over to him:[3] if this statement be false, as I hope it is, we must have it contradicted in the most public manner.

I am truly glad that Mr Beckett has demanded an explanation of Mr C. Mr Beckett assured me, immediately after the conversation in question, that Mr C. having proposed, as a condition of Mr Brougham's relinquishing the Contest, that Mr Beckett should acknowledge that the Lowther Votes were exhausted, he (Mr Beckett) utterly rejected such acknowledgment, and expressed his

[1] Andrew Green of Cockermouth, mentioned in Lord Lonsdale's letter to W. W. on 25 Apr. as the author of a pamphlet attacking the Lowthers (*WL MSS.*). He contested Cockermouth in the radical interest in 1832, but came out at the bottom of the poll.

[2] W. W.'s conclusion was that no such pamphlet could be definitely attributed to Green. See L. 588 below.

[3] The Poll had been held at Appleby on 15–22 Mar., and Brougham had secured 1,349 votes to Lord Lowther's 1,530 and Col. Lowther's 1,412. In his speech at the London Dinner of the Friends of the Independence of Westmorland on 22 Apr., Brougham claimed that 100 out of the 460 new votes cast for him had come from former Lowther supporters (see *Kendal Chronicle* for 29 Apr.).

astonishment that Mr Crackanthorpe should have made such a proposition.[1]

It is to be hoped the Clergy will not be cajoled by Mr B's encomiums;[2] those of Westnd cannot have forgotten that it is the same Mr B. who reviled them in almost every township where he harangued, in 1818.

I remain
my Lord
ever faithfully
your Lordship's
W. Wordsworth

583. W. W. to LORD LONSDALE

Address: The Earl of Lonsdale, London.
Postmark: 29 Apr. 1820. *Stamp*: Kendal Penny Post.
MS. Lonsdale MSS., Record Office, The Castle, Carlisle. Hitherto unpublished.

Rydal Mount [28 or 29 Apr. 1820]

My Lord,

I have delivered your Lordship's message to Mr North, Mr Newton,[3] Mr Jackson and Mr Gee. Each is inclined to do his utmost; but I find it impossible to proceed as expeditiously as I could wish.

Mrs Gee says, that Mrs Andrew Green[4] forced upon her Sisters printed papers reflecting upon your Lordship's public character; and did her utmost to impress them with injurious notions of the same; and that they had no doubt that these were derived from her husband, as Mrs Green has no connection with these Counties but through him. Mr Gee also says, that he has been told (but does not recollect by whom) that Mr Green had put into circulation a tract or paper to the same purpose.

I should not have thought it worth while to mention this subject

[1] On the last day but one of the Poll the Lowthers, though only a few votes ahead, had called on Brougham to concede defeat, claiming that they had 100 more votes unpolled. Brougham agreed to withdraw, but only on the terms mentioned here; and polling continued for another day. Brougham afterwards alleged that these last votes were cast by paupers and coal-miners brought in by the Lowthers for the occasion. For full account, see *Westmorland Gazette* for 18 and 25 Mar. and *Kendal Chronicle* for 1 Apr.

[2] In his second speech at the London Dinner, Brougham paid tribute to the clergy for their help in the inquiry into the education of the poor.

[3] Either William Newton of Ambleside or Robert Newton of Grasmere. Both were Lowther supporters.

[4] See previous letter.

to Dr F[1] or to allude to it now, were it not that Mr Green has been recommended as a fit person to act as a Magistrate for Cumberland.

The belief gains ground that Mr Wakefield is offering Leases upon his own life to all who will apply; some say for £10 and some for a trifle more.

Mr Jackson says we shall require a 1000 new Votes; I mention this Estimate merely to shew the prevailing opinion of the extreme activity of our opponents.

Yesterday I was conversing with an intelligent Yeoman, a Friend. 'The right of voting' said he, 'goes far too low'. Our Friends are deeply sensible of this truth.

Yesterday I forwarded to Mr Wilson[2] an application from Mr Horrocks[3] (Member for Preston) for freeholds, for himself, his Son, and his Partner.

Your Lordship perhaps has already received a Publication of mine.[4] The account of the Revd Robert Walker,[5] in the Notes to the 1st Poem, will I think interest you; as probably will some parts of the Description of the Lake Country at the end of the vol.

We hear that Mr Parker[6] of Browsholm has sold that Place—the last, probably, of his Acres.

I have the honor to be
most faithfully
your Lordship's friend and Servnt
W Wordsworth

The enclosed is this moment received from Mr Wilson—It shews how things are going on. Mr Cookson writes me word that Mr Wakefield is granting freeholds for his life, for ten Pounds—I suppose Leases, otherwise they must be registered and we shall be able to learn the amount.

Will your Lordship allow one of your Servants to put the enclosed into the two penny post offce.

[1] William Fell, the Ambleside surgeon.

[2] Isaac Wilson, the Kendal attorney, or Christopher Wilson of Abbot Hall.

[3] Samuel Horrocks (d. 1842), cotton manufacturer, and M.P. for Preston, 1807–26. His sister Jane married Thomas Monkhouse.

[4] *The River Duddon, A Series of Sonnets: Vaudracour and Julia: and other Poems. To which is Annexed, A Topographical Description of the Country of the Lakes, in the North of England*, 1820. This was the first appearance of the *Topographical Description* under W. W.'s name. It was published separately two years later as *A Description of the Scenery of the Lakes in the North of England . . .*, but it was not till 1835 that it appeared under its final title, *A Guide through the District of the Lakes in the North of England, with a Description of the Scenery, etc. for the Use of Tourists and Residents.*

[5] See *PW* iii, pp. 510 ff.

[6] Probably Isaac Parker of Langdale.

584. W. W. to BENJAMIN ROBERT HAYDON

Address: R. B. Haydon Esq[re], Lisson Grove-north, London.
MS. untraced.
MY ii. 631, p. 861.

Rydale Mount Near Ambleside
Friday [? late Apr. 1820]

My dear Friend,

I am sure you are little aware of my pecuniary resources, or you could never have thought of me in your difficulties; which I do earnestly wish I could remove.—But it is some time since I have been impelled to lay down a rule, not to lend to *a Friend* any money which I cannot afford *to lose.*

My income has at no period of my life exceeded my wants; within this last year it has been considerably reduced, while the education of my children is reaching its most expensive point.—It sounds paradoxical, but the fact is strictly true; that I have too great an admiration of your talents, and too much regard and respect for you to comply with your request: for I could not be easy were you to repay the money to your own inconvenience and I could not at the same time spare it without embarassment. I have for several years been obliged to defer my trip to the Continent because I could not afford it; and if it be executed next summer as I have promised, the engagement was incurred altogether in consequence of the offer of a friend to supply the cash if needed.—It avails little to repeat how much this inability hurts me on the present occasion,—Had my literary labours brought me profit, it would have been otherwise—but I shall say no more.—

I wrote to you a day or two before the Receipt of yours.—Your account of Scott gives me great pleasure,—I shall look for his book on Italy[1] with impatience—as to his Magazine what is its Title? I never heard of it [2] Scott and I disagree about many very important points; but I greatly admire his Talents, and respect him highly. ——I hope your Picture[3] is not much hurt by my Presence in it, though heaven knows I feel that I have little right to be there. As to the clamour of the London infidels, you despise it as I do. I am sending to the press a collection of poems, that conclude the third

[1] John Scott's *Sketches of Manners, Scenery in the French Provinces, Switzerland, and Italy,* published posthumously in 1821.

[2] *The London Magazine* first appeared in Jan. 1820. For some account of John Scott's editorship, see T. N. Talfourd, *Final Memorials of Charles Lamb,* 2 vols., 1848, ii, pp. 1–9.

[3] *Christ's Entry into Jerusalem.*

and *last* Vol: of my miscellaneous pieces.[1]—In more than one passage their publication will evince my wish to uphold the cause of Christianity.—My industry has often been as much as my health could bear, since I saw you, but with a product by no means proportionate![2]—But with God's blessing I shall be remembered after my day.—

Ever faithfully yours
Wm Wordsworth.

Your Letter arrived the day before our [? black] day; this is the very earliest opportunity for answering it.

585. W. W. to JOHN WILSON

MS. untraced.
K. MY ii. 636, p. 865.

Rydal Mount, May 5th, 1820.

My dear Sir,

Of the particular fitness of any one to fill the chair of Moral Philosophy, in the University of Edinburgh,[3] I am an incompetent judge, having only a vague notion of the duties of the office. But if the choice is to depend upon pre-eminence of natural powers of mind, cultivated by excellent education, and habitually directed to the study of ethics in the most comprehensive sense of the word; upon such powers, and great energy of character with correspondent industry, I have no hesitation in saying that the electors, the university, and Scotland in general, must be fortunate in no common degree if among the competitors there be found one more eligible than yourself.

[1] *Poems by William Wordsworth: including The River Duddon; Vaudracour and Julia; Peter Bell; The Waggoner; A Thanksgiving Ode; and Miscellaneous Pieces*, vol. iii, 1820.

[2] Haydon had written on 12 Sept. 1818: 'I hope these abominable politics will no longer interfere with your poetry.' (*WL MSS.*)

[3] Wilson had written somewhat formally to W. W.: 'The Election lies with the Magistrates and Town Council, who have declared their determination to elect the person who produces the most satisfactory certificates of his abilities from literary men. I am, accordingly, now collecting them—and I apply to you for such a Certificate as you may think yourself justified in giving me. It may either be in the form of a letter to myself, or in that of an attestation . . .' (*WL MSS.*). For S. H.'s comment on Wilson's subsequent election, see *SH* 66, p. 188: she described W. W.'s letter of recommendation as 'Jesuitical'.

Wishing you, cordially, success in the pursuit of this honourable object of ambition,

I remain,
My dear Sir,
Very faithfully yours,
Wm. Wordsworth.

586. D. W. to MARY HUTCHINSON

Address: Mrs. Hutchinson, Hindwell, Radnor.
Postmark: 9 May 1820. *Franked*: London, May Ninth, 1820. S. Horrocks.
MS. WL.
MY ii. 637, p. 866.

Thursday morning
concluded Friday evening 5th May [1820]

My dearest Mary,

Since we parted at Rydal Mount I have often thought of writing to you, but Sara was writing—or Mary—or they were going to write, and as I was never a *set* correspondent of yours so I put it off; and thereby I have not done justice to my own feelings; for few people have been so much in my thoughts as you and your dear little ones, and sometimes—with a twitch of pain—I have fancied that you might call me forgetful or ungrateful.—I congratulate you both on the birth of your second Daughter.[1] The news was quite unexpected when your brother Tom greeted me with it.—I should have been very glad to have heard of a fine Boy to match with my delicate pretty nursling George; but as a Girl it is, one may be allowed to rejoice over *that* in comparison, and I am sure I was better pleased than if I had heard that a Boy was born. We little thought that the time was so near when Thomas was at Rydal, where notwithstanding his very bad cold, he was very contented, and seemed to enjoy himself. Not so, I understand, at Appleby—and no wonder: for it was truly provoking to be confined there helpless in a crowd. Thomas gave but a chearless account of farming, and I tried all I could to persuade him that it would be best to give over and come and live on your means in the North. Surely better live without *attempting* to gain any thing, than to labour in the attempt with anxiety, and after all to reap loss instead of gain.

[1] Elizabeth, b. 3 Apr. 1820.

I cannot endure to hear you talk of emigration. I hope, my dear Mary you will accept me as God-mother to your little Girl. Your Husband has consented, and probably you have sent me a message to that effect; but I have not been in the way of receiving it.—I am exceedingly comfortable and happy at Lambeth, and glad that I had the resolution to come away unprepared. I had new sets of cloaths (petticoats shifts etc) ready for making and I intended coming with William and Mary; these I put into my trunk and thought I should easily get them done here; but I found that London is no place for working, and if I can get Willy's clothes repaired in the holidays it will be as much as I can do, with my own little jobs that are perpetually rising up. It will be three weeks this very night at eleven o'clock since I reached Lambeth.—Your dear and kind good Brother came to see me the next morning with Willy—You can judge of the joy of our meeting. It was wholly unexpected on Willy's part, and he was completely overcome with pleasure. We walked out together; and till last Monday my time was completely filled up,—with inquiries after dentists, gazing about the streets, seeing Panoramas—pictures—Exeter change etc etc, your brother Tom being my companion most daily—sometimes my Brother Christopher for a short way: but *his* occupations are constant and except once, he has never been able to go out with *me*. I have gone with *him* on his round to other places—only one day we dined at Hampstead—stayed all night at Mrs Hoare's and did not come home till the next day at dinner time (5 o'clock). There we met Miss Joanna Baillie[1] who is one of the nicest of women—very entertaining in conversation, without the least mixture of the literary Lady. I spent one whole day with Miss Lamb; Willy was with us and the next day, he and Henry Hutchinson dined here, and Henry having two days holiday dined the two following days. Henry is very little changed except in his speech. He is a fine hardy good natured Lad who will make his way, and I doubt not be a credit to his Father and Family. Willy is very sweet and interesting—in all respects wonderfully improved—no better Boy can be—and he will take care of himself amongst the 400. I was next him. I went once to him at school. The Boys were at play without hats, and he and I wandered about the large Square like two forlorn things—nobody noticing us—but I doubt not he is quite at home there when he is playing with the rest. Willy's school breaks up on the 12th and he is to go again

[1] The Scottish dramatist and poet, whom W. W. had met some years before. See L. 246 above. W. W. spoke of her as 'the model of an English gentlewoman'.

to Mr Johnson; but we shall have him here at least once a week. Tom and I thought it better that we should deny ourselves at present for fear of unsettling him now at his first going to the C. house;[1] and I assure you I have no disposition to spoil him, much as I should enjoy seeing him oftener. Tom and I went with him last Sunday but one to the opening of a handsome Chapel given by a Mr Watson[2] to the National Society. The Bp. of London preached, Mr Johnson read prayers, and Mr William Coleridge[3] (who is appointed morning preacher) read the Communion Service. All the duty was admirably performed, and the Bishop's sermon excellent. The children have the whole Gallery allotted to them, the Girls in the centre—the Boys down each side—(Willy was amongst them) —and it was an affecting sight. The children sang very well. As I told you much of my first fortnight was employed in seeking after Dentists, and your Brother and I took infinite pains. A Mr Dumergue was recommended to me; but when he told me his price (50 guineas) I could not resolve on him: and infinite pains I have taken: but after all I fixed on him, Dumergue, not being satisfied with any other and believing him to be the best in England—and now I am glad I did so. He drew all my remaining teeth (8 in number including stumps) on Monday—all but one sound one, which is left to steady the new set for the time it will last; and when it goes I can have a false one in its place. The tooth-drawing was not half so bad as I expected, though bad enough. He is certainly a delightful operator; and I hope my gums will be sufficiently healed by next Thursday to be measured for the new set. If they should not answer —but every body encourages me to expect they will—I shall only have the 50gs to regret, for I rejoice in having got rid of my old teeth. My mouth has not been so comfortable for many months, and I wish that poor Sara, whose mouth is for ever growling, were in exactly my state.—I confined myself to the house two days in which I was fully employed in writing. I had a mantua maker in the house too; but as to sewing with her it was completely out of the question —glad I was that I could get any one to do the work for me. I now walk out for my health's sake; but see none but particular friends. On Wednesday Tom dined with us, and Mrs and Miss Hoare sat a

[1] Willy was about to enter the Charterhouse. He was not happy there, and eft in 1822.

[2] Joshua Watson. See L. 590 below.

[3] William Hart Coleridge, D.D., S. T. C.'s nephew, at this time secretary to the S.P.C.K. and preacher at the National Society's chapel in Ely Place: later Bishop of Barbados, 1824–41, and then Warden of St. Augustine's College, Canterbury.

long while in the morning. Mrs H is a charming woman—a particular friend of Tom's and she is a mother to my three nephews and very kind to Willy. Yesterday morning I began this letter to you, and you will see where I stopped. Miss Lamb came in from the country, where they have a lodging, and intend to spend most of the summer. After we had sate comfortably for an hour—who should come in but Mrs Clarkson and her son Tom? Miss Lamb left us at 2 o'clock, and I accompanied Mrs. C. on foot to Charing Cross at 3. We had most interesting discourse together, and you will be glad to hear that she looks much better than 11 years ago, and I think, scarcely a day older. She makes no complaint except that she cannot walk much, from uneasiness and swelling in her legs. She tells me I am not so much changed by the want of teeth as she expected; but how this should be I know not: for now my mouth is drawn up to nothing, and my chin projects as far as my nose; but I look healthy enough, though I have lost 8 lbs since I was last weighed, being now only 6 stone 12 lbs: Miss Lamb is quite well and has been so for above a year. She is little altered in the face except from the loss of a tooth, but is sadly too fat; and she dresses so loose that she looks the worse for it and cannot walk so well; yet she is still a very good walker. I have forgotten Southey—He called on Wednesday morning, and agreed to breakfast with us today, and your Brother Tom, who dined here the same day promised to meet him this morning; and when I took up the pen they had just left me. T. and my Brother are gone to visit the White Chapel Schools and I hope to see him again tomorrow and that he will bring an account of Willy whom I have not heard of since my visit to him. Southey is quite well, and as pleasant as can be; he intends to breakfast with us very often. My brother Chris^{r} is as kind a Brother as can be; and I am very much at my ease here. He has a library below stairs and I have a nice drawing room above which looks into the Archbp's grounds—a beautiful green field with very fine trees—and not a building to be seen except one rustic cattle shed; he breakfasts in the study after prayers—usually at 9 o'clock—I then leave my Brother—His callers go to him and we come upstairs. All the morning he is busy; but comes up now and then to say 'how do you do?'—If it suits we go out together, dine at 5 or half past—and he sits with me till tea is over—goes to his study with candles, and comes up again at 10—reads prayers and we sit together till bed-time, and often do not part till twelve o'clock. I have not yet seen any of his sons. We are to go to Sundridge for a day or two as soon as my teeth are in; but he intends not to remove thither till the Boys' holidays at Midsummer.

This is the better for me, though I should have liked to have spent these 10 days, when I cannot shew myself, at Sundridge. The Marshalls are in town; but I have not seen them—Mrs M. wrote to say she would call on me on Monday to dine and go to see King Lear at night; but *that* was the day of my trial. They are coming to our Church on Sunday and will call on me at noon—I, of course, cannot shew myself at Church. I left my writing to take a solitary walk—solitary though in a crowd, for I came up the Strand having crossed Waterloo Bridge. The river was most beautiful today and beyond Vauxhall Bridge all was as clear and bright as among the Lakes. It is delightful weather for London; but the winds are cold and blighting. This reminds me of an afflicted family of whom I hear much, they being intimately connected with Mrs Hoare. You have seen Mr Brompton's[1] name among the *benevolent* members of the house of commons. When my Brother was in the North he was informed by Mrs Hoare that Mr B's eldest son a remarkably fine hopeful Boy ten years of age had died of an inflammation of the Bowels and that all the rest of the children except an Infant at the breast were ill of the measles and hooping cough—and since we came to Lambeth, three of those children have died one after another and there is yet another in the last extremity of weakness. The Baby is a sweet little thriving creature, and as it has not carried the disease from its mother's house I trust it will escape. Mrs Hoare has had it with the Nurse ever since the beginning of the over-whelming affliction.—Though I walked in the morning, I must go out again to look at the sunset. The trees are casting their long shadows over the green field, and the sparrows are making no unpleasant chirping—and I do assure you that I sometimes hear the notes of the Thrush and blackbird from these trees. My Brother is going out to dinner, and I have dined alone and have not seen anyone else today, for a wonder, since Tom left me in the morning. I have had a letter from Miss Barker—she is gay and chearful, for cares never press on *her*; but cheap as Boulogne is, she says she cannot save enough there, and must go to a more retired place. What a dull and quiet house there must now be at Rydal Mount, poor John being gone away. I at a distance felt all the sadness of his parting and have been very anxious about him; but thank God the accounts are most chearing. He is quite satisfied with his Master; and this I think is a sure sign that he is in the way of improvement: and I am sure we have every reason to be thankful for his removal from home. D. grows very

[1] Unidentified (there was no one of this name in the House of Commons at this time), unless D. W. really means Samuel *Crompton*, M.P. for Retford.

much—is happy, and I doubt not goes on improving—I am exceedingly glad my dearest Mary that George has got a situation at a little distance from you. It will give him time to decide upon emigration to some place or other—there is nothing for him; and if he had a grain of independence of mind or of honorable spirit—(do not say or think I speak harshly) he could not endure any other thought, and I would not rest day or night till he had hit upon some place. It grieves me that Joanna should fret so much about him—She had no reason for comfort before; and perhaps it is now better that it has come to the worst (if Tom can escape loss) as it will necessarily force him into a new, and perhaps a better course. I hope you have ere this got your own dear little Thomas cured, and that the notable Mary and sweet George are together enjoying their infant pleasures in this sweet season. I often think of them and their several ways, and fancy them playing on the steps or the grass-plot before the door—Give my kind love to Miss Cookson and tell her I thank her for her letter which gave me great pleasure, and that I hope to answer it when I have anything new to tell you. I believe I owe Joanna, too, a letter—I rejoice in her recovery—tell her so with my kindest love. I am truly sorry that she cannot pay the promised visit to Miss Lowden[1] while I am in Town, and still more for the cause. My dear Mary I hope I shall hear from you when you have leisure. This is a true gossiping letter, and seems very dull to me; but I hope it will read better both as to matter and penmanship when it reaches the end of its Travels. Give my love to your Brother John and tell him that Tom has a copy of the new Poems for him to be sent the first opportunity, which I hope he will accept from me, and place on his book shelves beside the other two. Give my Goddaughter a kiss with all the rest of the young ones—and kind remembrances to your Aunt. How does her School go on. Best love to Thomas—I hope he is now quite well—Believe me, dear Mary, ever your affect. D. Wordsworth.

Concluded on Friday Evening 8 *o'clock*, 5th *May*. I am just [returned] from walking in a little garden of the Archbp's which [*seal*] with the water garden—it is about 50 yards long or more—close to the Thames, being only separated from the water by a wall down which you look upon the water, which is for ever varying with boats perpetually enlivened—the Abbey is right before us, and we look down to Westminster Bridge and up to Vauxhall—and are shut out behind from all houses except the Palace Towers which overtop the garden wall—and from all passengers and [*seal*] in complete

[1] A London acquaintance.

seclusion, yet looking out on the busy scene [?]. There I have walked before and since sunset,—and only wanted some Friend by my side for perfect enjoyment. Before, I treated my self with a shilling's worth upon the water. I am delighted with the water and often tempted to extravagance. Whenever my walk is likely to be too long I take a Boat preferring it greatly to paying the same money or more for a Coach.

587. D. W. to THOMAS MONKHOUSE

Address: To Thomas Monkhouse Esqre, 28 Queen Anne Street, Cavendish Square.
Postmark: 9 May 1820.
MS. WL.
MY ii. 638, p. 872.

[9 May 1820]

My dear Friend,

I cannot express my mortification on my return home to find that you had called and were gone—if you had but stayed half an hour we should have met; but I think you would not have gone if you could have dined with us, therefore I reconcile myself to the disappointment in some measure; but the less willingly because I cannot dine with you on Wednesday. I had forgotten that the Lloyds were to be here to dinner on that day when I engaged myself to you, but I will call in Queen Anne Street either on my way to Mrs Marshall's or from thence—I have been looking in the Map and shall find no difficulty. It is very plain—through the Park and along the Bond Streets—and if I do not hear from you that it will suit you better to see me only later I will call in going. I shall set off the moment breakfast is over. Should it suit you better to see me at 2 o'clock I will be with you at that hour; but should much prefer the former plan, as at 2 Mrs M. will be with me.

I am much concerned at Willy's cough. I hope he will be with you when I call; but whether or not I shall be obliged to you if you will send him to me on Thursday morning, the sooner the better—if to breakfast so much the better—and I will keep him all day, and if you do not come to us (but I hope you will) I shall send to attend him home to you at night.

I have a letter today from Sara which you shall see—very natural and very intelligible; and now I can go on plainly with my directions and intend to proceed alone to Longman's[1] tomorrow

[1] W. W.'s *Miscellaneous Poems* in 4 vols. were now in the press. See next letters.

morning as soon as breakfast is over. You may guess when I shall be there; and I will wait by the watch one hour in the hope that you may call in upon me, as I believe Longman's is not very far from Budge Row.

Derwent came this morning, and I went with him in a boat to the Temple, called on Tom Clarkson and thence to his Mother—sate with her till ½ past 2, called on Mr Johnson—and on this side of Black Friar's Bridge was compelled to shelter in a coach, which brought me home less tired than I should otherwise have been. My Brother and I met at the gate. He had been riding and was much pleased with his pony. I think he is better today, and though tired with his ride I hope it will have done him good.

I drank tea with Mrs Stoddart and had a pleasant walk home on Sunday.

I called on Mr Johnson this morning—He is very busy for the examination. God bless you my dear Friend—I could thank you a thousand times for all your kindness to me; but that I know you would not like it. It does me good to think that I have such a kind friend near me—Ever yours

D. Wordsworth.

Thursday evening.[1]

Sara does not say a word but about the poems—therefore I conclude there is no intention of setting off on Monday—so I still keep that obscure passage in Mary's letter to myself.

I have not yet got Mr Whelpdale's[2] packet.

I am much amused with John Hutchinson's easy way of treating his Friends!

588. W. W. to LORD LONSDALE

MS. Lonsdale MSS., Record Office, The Castle, Carlisle. Hitherto unpublished.

Rydal Mount
10th May 1820.

My Lord,

I deferred writing in reply to your Lordship's of the 1st Inst^{nt}, having reason daily to expect an answer to inquiries concerning the Pamphlet.[3]

Mr Monkhouse says 'that he cannot learn from Mr G's Relations that any such Pamphlet was ever published by him. But they know

[1] 9 May was a Tuesday.

[2] A. Whelpdale of Penrith, a friend of the Wordsworth circle and a recent visitor at Rydal Mount. See *SH* 63, p. 181.

[3] See L. 582 above.

very little of his proceedings, and one of them quarelled with him some years ago on account of his democratic principles and strange notions in religion. He is decidedly hostile to Lord Lonsdale's political interests. He is a scribbler and has written Pamphlets, and is reckoned an odd eccentric Person by everyone.'

One of Mrs Gee's Sisters writes thus 'The impression she (Mrs Green) gave us was of being one of a Party decidedly hostile to the Lowthers; of whom she spoke in terms of strong disapprobation and dislike; mentioning several instances of injustice and tyrannical abuse of Power on their part, respecting St Bees, the *Bridge* etc., at Carlisle.' This latter subject, my Lord, was represented so offensively that I cannot bring myself to repeat it. The Writer adds, 'whether Mrs G. imbibed her opinions and prejudices from her husband we cannot say, but we think it most probable that she did, as she had gone but a short time before an entire Stranger into the Country. In support of what she advanced she sent us some newspapers, but we never read them.' Mr Monkhouse will continue his inquiries, with the necessary caution.

The above circumstances, which are at present all we can collect, include the answer to your Lordship's question whether the conduct of Mr G. may be mentioned. Nothing, in respect to these calumnies, is *brought home* to *him*. It seems, upon the whole, probably that Mr Gee's Informant must have been mistaken as to the Pamphlet; and the story might have risen from the Articles in those Newspapers being possibly written by him. It is most likely that the Newspaper was the Carlisle Journal which was at one time stuffed with slanders of this sort.

It gives me much satisfaction that those little Poems[1] have afforded your Lordship so much pleasure.

On Monday week Mrs W. and I start for the South, meaning to halt three or four days in Oxfordshire.

It is reported in Kendal that the notorious Mr John Thomson[2] applied upwards of a month ago for the situation of Land Steward at Levens, just become vacant by the death of Mr Harriman. Mr Beckett has acted as became him.

Ever most faithfully your Lordship's
friend and servant
W. Wordsworth.

[1] Lord Lonsdale had written on 1 May: 'I have read the Sonnets on the Duddon, and the notes annexed to them with great Pleasure,—any opinion of mine on the merits of the former would be of no value—but I can only say the perusal of them afforded me infinite satisfaction. The account of Mr Walker is very interesting . . .' (*WL MSS.*).

[2] Of Ambleside.

589. D. W. to THOMAS MONKHOUSE

Address: Thomas Monkhouse Esqre., 28 Queen Anne Street, Cavendish Square.
Postmark: 16 May 1820.
MS. WL.
MY ii. 639, p. 874.

Lambeth Tuesday ½ past 12 o'clock
[16 May 1820]

My dear Friend,

I know you have been engaged, or I should have seen you this morning—I now write to tell you how I go on that we may not miss each other when you can come. I was yesterday at Kensington with Willy. We set off at ¼ past 7 and walked all the way, very delightful in the parks and Gardens.—W. spent a happy day with the little Girls, running about continually and was just as much of a Baby as the very youngest; but I was well pleased to see that he has got rid of all the disagreeable part of babyism—he was neither restless nor troublesome; but all joy and happiness. Mr L.,[1] who is quite well, walked with us into Oxford St, and we took a coach there to Greys Inn Lane. W. expressed a strong and natural wish to come home with me last night to sleep; but much against my own inclination I refused, thinking it better that he should begin the morning at school and he did not murmur—but when we got to the door of Mr J's house he said 'You'll go in to see Mr Johnson' and the tears could no longer be kept in. He sobbed aloud; but though my very heart was melted I checked his grief and we parted chearfully. He is to come on Friday afternoon, as Mr Johnson is going out —I was sadly tired when I reached home at ½ past 8, having lost my way in Lambeth and walked fruitlessly at least two miles.

My Brother[2] is worse again—which grieves me very much. I have had a note this morning from Mrs Clarkson, asking me to go to her this morning. The rain prevents me, and I am not sorry for this, as I wish only to have a *short* walk today having had so much fatigue yesterday. I have proposed to her to come tomorrow; but I shall be at liberty till one o'clock so if you can come tomorrow morning we might see something together or if you can come at any time in the course of the day you will find me at home—unless Mrs Clarkson should rather chuse me to go to *her*, which I have said if she cannot come hither, I will—but that I prefer her coming. If she is engaged tomorrow I have given her the offer of Thursday, but in that case also, I shall be at liberty till one o'clock, for she will not be here before. I wish I had got my teeth, and I would have gone to the

[1] Presumably Charles Lloyd.

[2] i.e. C. W.

Central School examination tomorrow. Perhaps you will be there? Mrs Hoare *will.* I hope to have the teeth on Thursday—but perhaps even then they may not be useable. Pray write and tell me what you are doing and fix as early a morning as you can—for us to walk about together. Remember Miss Lamb's invitation for Thursday evening. I shall call on her on Thursday morning after breakfast so perhaps you may meet me there but I think you said you were engaged on that day. But do write and tell me your engagements upon paper—then I can guess when to expect you. I am sure I feel as if I were a great plague to you—but without seeing you now and then I find such a want of you as I can hardly give you a notion of.

Two letters of corrections from Rydal! but no proofs yet from Longman—I am going to sit down to hard work at correcting the printed copy to print *from.* They will not set off till Whitmonday—so they will be a week later.

When is it that you can join us at Paris? William says he had understood that if we set off about the 5th July you could join us in ten days—I hope you may be able to set off before the end of the month; and I cannot see how we can do better than spend the three weeks at Paris.

There is no need to fix about Lodgings for Wm and M. as they can certainly be here the first fortnight. If Mr. Lloyd comes he will be gone again when they arrive.

God bless you!
Believe me ever, my dear Friend,
yours affectionately
D. Wordsworth.

590. D. W. to JOSHUA WATSON[1]

Address: To Joshua Watson, Esqre.
Endorsed: Miss Wordsworth, 20 May 1820.
MS. Jonathan Wordsworth. Hitherto unpublished.

Lambeth 3 o'clock Saturday
[20 May 1820]

Dear Sir,

My Brother has requested me to say to you that he begs you will accept his best thanks for your kind note; and that he feels himself

[1] Joshua Watson (1771–1855), philanthropist and a leading figure in the high-church party; active in the S.P.C.K. and Church Building Society, and a member of Lord Liverpool's Royal Commission on Church Building. In 1811 he had joined with C. W. in founding the National Society for the education of the poor. See Edward Churton, *Memoir of Joshua Watson*, 2 vols., 1861.

much better this morning. D[r] Maton was here at 5 o'clock yesterday with Mr Morgan; and I think that the Doctor's prescriptions have been of considerable use. My Brother slept in the course of last night, which he had not done for four nights before; and his pulse is, I believe, much slower than it had hitherto been; and he seems more comfortable and less languid than yesterday. I trust therefore that he may be now considered as convalescent. I shall be happy to inform you, by note, how he goes on, as I am sure that you will be anxious to know that he continues to amend. Quiet, and a perfect withdrawing from all business are strictly enjoined.

My Brother has desired me to send the enclosed papers for your consideration.

I am very sorry that it has not yet been in my power to call upon Mrs and Miss Watson, for whose kind attentions I feel myself much obliged.

I am, dear Sir,
respectfully yours
Dorothy Wordsworth.

591. D. W. to JOSHUA WATSON

Address: To Joshua Watson, Esq[re].
Endorsed: Miss Wordsworth, 23 May 1820.
MS. Jonathan Wordsworth. Hitherto unpublished.

Lambeth Tuesday—May 23rd [1820]

My dear Sir,

I hoped when I had the pleasure of seeing you yesterday morning, that I should have been able to tell you today of my Brother's progressive, though slow, amendment; but I am sorry to say that he is certainly, not better—perhaps rather worse—this morning than when you called. He had a fresh access of fever in the evening, and passed a disturbed, and almost sleepless night.

The enclosed Resolution of the Vestry Meeting troubled my Brother. He says you will sufficiently understand why; and he desires me to add, that he will, to the utmost of his power, abstain from all thoughts connected with these, or any other matters of business.

My Brother bids me assure you of his most kind remembrances. As soon as it is fit for him to see anyone, he will be anxious to see you; and truly rejoiced shall I be when I can tell you that *it is* so. I will write, from time to time, to inform you of his progress—but I fear, indeed, that the amendment will be very slow.

I am, dear Sir,
Yours most respectfully
Dorothy Wordsworth.

592. D. W. to JOSHUA WATSON

MS. Jonathan Wordsworth. Hitherto unpublished.

Rectory, Lambeth—
Thursday Morng. 25th May [1820]

My dear Sir,

I am happy to inform you that my Brother has again passed a much more easy night, with some hours of sleep; and he appears to be tolerably comfortable this morning; though the pain in his head never goes away; and continues, at times, to be very distressing. He bids me tell you however, that 'he trusts he is getting on; but very slowly;' and that is what we must expect.

Mr Morgan has just seen him, and he tells me that his pulse is now below a hundred (which I suppose it was *not* yesterday) for he added 'I think him better this morning than yesterday.'

You do not mention Mrs Watson, therefore I hope she is going on well.

I am, dear Sir,
With great respect,
yours faithfully
Dorothy Wordsworth

593. W. W. to VISCOUNT LOWTHER

Address: The Lord Viscount Lowther, London.
Postmark: 27 May 1820. *Stamp*: Kendal Penny Post.
MS. Lonsdale MSS., Record Office, The Castle, Carlisle. Hitherto unpublished.

[26 or 27 May 1820]

My dear Lord Lowther,

Your Letter was truly acceptable. Knowing how much you are engaged your Friends can readily excuse your occasional silence.

I regret that I have nothing particularly interesting to communicate. Your Friends here are well disposed, and something respectable will be done though too slowly. Persons acting on the defensive are always less prompt than Assailants.

I was pleased to hear of what you had done in respect to the

Cumberland Pacquet.[1] I have yet learnt nothing of the Editor. The expression 'lucre of gain', pretty much such a one as 'gratis for nothing', occurred two or three weeks back in the leading Article,[2] and though in itself of no importance, one would be tempted to infer from it, that he is not a regularly educated Man.

A late Clerk of the Proprietor of the Whitehaven Gazette told Mr De Quincey that his Master had lost a great part of his business since he engaged in that undertaking.

Brougham is manifestly thirsting for Place, and ready to make any sacrifice for it. When something to this effect was observed to an old Woman, one of his Kendal Friends, she replied 'Odd love him, he'll do good wherever he is.'

Your Friends will be happy to see you in this neighbourhood. I regret much that I shall be absent; that is, if the irritable state of my eyes will allow.

Mr Myers reports very favorably of the dispositions of the Millom People to come forward as freeholders for West[nd].

Mr Gell has just been over in the East and West Wards. He says that the Blues are there more active than the Yellows. Among other things they have just purchased at Bolton a property that with a small additional expense will make 40 Votes.

One knows not what to think of the public distress. I fear nobody sees their way clearly through it. As far as my knowledge extends the Agriculturists bear their hardships more patiently than the Manufacturers, but each party complains loudly of the selfish spirit of the other.

In a day or two I hope to set off for London; but I have two or three visits to make which will detain me on the Road. I shall find you out as soon as I arrive in town. Till then adieu

believe me my dear Lord Lowther

ever faithfully yours

Wm Wordsworth

The enclosed for the twopenny post. Thanks for several franks which my Sister has had.

[1] Lord Lowther had appointed Kendall, a London journalist, as editor in succession to Ware who had just died. A few weeks later Kendall was arrested for debt, but he continued to write his weekly articles in Carlisle gaol. Later he was dismissed, but given enough money to release himself from gaol. (See Aspinall, *Politics and the Press*, pp. 362–4.)

[2] The editorial on 9 May had appealed for the support of readers in upholding the traditional policy of the paper: 'That this earnest support is needful must be manifest to all; for, in the day in which we live, and from the causes we have just described, it is not difficult to know by what means a Newspaper may be best made to secure to itself the greatest number of friends, and best minister, on the part of its publisher, to the mere lucre of gain.'

594. D. W. to JOSHUA WATSON

Endorsed: Miss Wordsworth 27 Mar. [May?] 1820.
MS. Jonathan Wordsworth. Hitherto unpublished.

Saturday 27th [May 1820

My dear Sir,

I trust my Brother is going on as well as we have any right to expect, though it is so very slowly as to be scarcely perceptible; and I needed the chearing report of Mr Morgan this morning, before I could be quite satisfied that my Brother was as well as yesterday, on account of an appearance of more than usual languor. Mr Morgan's words, however, were, 'he is decidedly better.' and I can further add that he had a pretty good night.

We have not yet seen Dr Maton today.

My Brother begs you will be so kind as to present one of the two Books (which you will receive by your servant, who is waiting while I write) in his name to your Daughter; and the other to your Niece, your Brother's eldest Daughter. I will explain further when I have the pleasure of seeing you—

I remain, dear Sir,
most truly yours
D Wordsworth

595. D. W. to THOMAS MONKHOUSE

Address: Thomas Monkhouse Esqre. Queen Anne Street, Cavendish Square.
Postmark: [?] May 1820.
MS. WL.
MY ii. 640, p. 876.

8 o'clock Tuesday night [late May 1820]

My dear Friend,

When I came home this evening the enclosed letter was put into my hands—Southey had left it for me to see—he says it is utterly impossible for him to hunt out this Mortimer. In the first place he has no *time* to spend in that way; and in the second, if he had, he would not know which way to turn. If Mr. M were found, and if his report were such that it should seem desirable for T. Hutchinson to inquire further, I have no doubt that if Southey has any knowledge of Mr Howard[1] (and I suppose he has, or why apply to *him*?) he would do his utmost to recommend Thomas to the situation. My Brother and I have been talking the matter over together and we see no way of rendering the least help in this matter except through you. Perhaps you may be able to inquire out this Mr. Mortimer—My Brother thinks it is much more likely that he is a Solicitor than a Barrister. Perhaps Henry Robinson might help you—or Tom Clarkson—or T. Clarkson's Master—whose name is Hammond, I believe. Tom Clarkson, however, lives in Paper Buildings—near the top of the Row of houses. It is [a] strange and unaccountable thing to me that Sara should put Tom upon such an application to Southey.—I shall be at Dumergue's at ½ past 3 tomorrow and will call on you; but I fear I shall not find you at home—but if you can let me see you here tomorrow evening or in the course of Sunday, I shall be at Whitechapel with my Brother; and shall go after church to Mrs. Clarkson and return home by about 5 o'clock. Perhaps you might meet me at Mrs. Clarkson's—I want to settle with you about meeting Willy. Perhaps it would be best for him to come hither on Sunday night—I have no doubt Sophy can make up a bed for him without much trouble—unless you think we can conveniently meet on Monday morning. In that case we must have all settled. Miss Lamb called this morning, went with me to the Dentist's——got a mould made—but wanted again tomorrow—a letter from William Jackson this morning—He is coming to Town for one day—asked me to fix an hour for meeting—I have fixed breakfast tomorrow—My cousins Cr and Wm. Cookson came in my absence. They are to breakfast here tomorrow.

No proofs from Longman. I wish you would call at Longmans and tell them I have been disappointed and am very anxious to get on.

My Brother is better—I am very desirous to know what you think of this application of T. H.'s—I think you will see it in the light I do—I could fancy half a dozen more rational modes of proceeding. I heartily wish he may get the place if it is worth having; but have little hope on account of the great number of applicants in such cases——I write in the dark—

Yours ever D. Wordsworth.

[1] Probably Henry Howard (1757–1842), of Corby Castle, near Carlisle. Thomas Hutchinson had not been prospering lately, and was apparently seeking a position as farm manager or land agent.

596. D. W. to DORA W.

Address: Miss D. Wordsworth, Rydal Mount, Kendal.
Postmark: 23 June 1820. *Franked*: London June twenty three 1820. Lowther
MS. WL.
LY iii. 640a, p. 1372.

[23 June 1820]

My dearest Dorothy

Your Father and Mother brought me your nice letter this evening. They came to tea, and you will find by my letter to your Aunt, I expected them. It was a great pleasure to me, and though it is now past eleven o'clock and the Watchman has twice gone his rounds I cannot be easy to go to bed without telling you my dear Girl, how happy your letter has made me, and that I am pleased to find that you take pains to improve yourself, and are a good girl; and therefore growing in the love of all your Friends. May God bless every good resolution that you form! and may you, in this happy season of your youth, lay up stores for contentment and comfort through life!—I am very glad that you obtained the French prize; this proves to me that you have taken great pains; for Miss Dowling would not have adjudged it to you had you not deserved it. Your Father and Mother were both in good spirits this evening—Your Father's eyes a little better. He has consulted a Physician; and on Tuesday he is to see him again, and he will then he says be able to decide whether travelling is likely to be injurious to his eyes or not. I did not finish my sentence last night, being anxious to go to bed, when, however, I did not lie down till half past twelve o'clock. I am very solitary here much more so than if I were alone at Rydal Mount, having neither care, business nor anxiety in the house beyond the room where I sit. I walked with your Father and Mother last night by moon and lamp light to the square of Westminster Abbey where we parted, and they went home. We talked about you when we stood under the trees of the Palace gardens by the water side, which your Aunt will remember, and looked upon the brilliant moonlight water scattered over with Boats and adorned with hundreds of golden pillars—the reflection from the lamps. It was most beautiful indeed—and I have no fear of walking alone in London at that time of the night, as nobody has ever spoken to, or even seemed to look at me. To-day I am going to Sir G. Beaumont's to meet your Father and Mother at a Family dinner. Tomorrow I shall be in Queen Ann Street with Willy—and on Sunday they will all dine with me—[ ] will go to school with Willy in the evening, and your Father and Mother will sleep here, and we expect Mrs Clarkson to spend

Monday with us; but in the morning we intend to look over your poor Aunt's clothes and pack up a trunk or box. On Tuesday I am to breakfast with Mrs Richard Twining[1]—your Father and Mother will call for me to go to the Charter House—and at night will sleep here; and if the Bp. of London will be at home on Wednesday, we shall go by water to Richmond and call at Fulham and Twickenham in our way. I shall probably, at the end of next week, go again to Hampstead to see your good Uncle;[2] and if he is much better than when I last saw him shall then prepare for our long journey; but if he is not, I cannot think of leaving England; and will go with him to Sundridge. When I next go to Hampstead I expect to see my Nephew Charles. All these Boys are very fond of William, as indeed is every one else. I am glad he has got to school again; for though I humoured him as little as possible he now and then, before his departure, was rather difficult to manage. By taking no notice of him, however, at these times, and by never yielding in the smallest degree I always conquered him. He was delighted at Hendon where he played among the Girls[3] as carelessly as if they had all been his sisters—They ran after him and he jumped out of the window and seriously declared that he could not find a quiet place from[4] them in all the House. The young Ladies who were in the North were truly rejoiced to see us, and all inquired most kindly after you. Miss [Lockier?][5] and Mrs Prince[6] will be in town on Saturday, we hope, and we shall see them. This is a delightful summer's day, and for the first time I have been without a fire, but strange to say, after breakfast I was obliged to put on my Bonnet to walk ¾ of an hour to warm myself—and am now quite warm for the day; but not hot—It is time to turn to the commissions left for me last night. You must give your Father's kind regards to John Carter, and tell him that Maryport, Cockermouth, and Workington are to be added to his District—and that he will write to J. C. as soon as it is settled.

Are John's pony and the Bank[7] sold? Is your Father's great coat come back from Kendal? Has your Aunt got the Applethwaite and Patterdale Rents? Mrs Wheelwright[8] has, unfortunately, been ill, and will go by another road, so, probably, you will not see the party, but no doubt they will send the shoes.

[1] Wife of the senior partner in the firm of R. G. and J. A. Twining, tea merchants in the Strand.

[2] C. W. was staying with the Hoares.

[3] Probably relatives or connections of the Misses Lockier, friends of the Gees, who lived at Hendon.

[4] *Written* for.

[5] *MS*. obscure.

[6] A Hendon acquaintance: her husband was a bookseller. See *SH* 157, p. 416.

[7] This word might be 'Bark' or 'Buck'.

[8] Wife of Thomas Monkhouse's business partner. The Wheelwrights

On Monday night I am going to Miss Kelly's[1] Benefit with Mr and Miss Lamb, and I shall not wish to go to another play unless (which your Mother wishes) we go with Willy on Saturday night—

And now, my dear Dorothy you must excuse me if I write no more at this time; for I have to write a most unpleasant letter to Miss Barker. Tell your Aunt Sara that I did not give Miss B. any of *her* comments upon Pearson's[2] conduct, I only transcribed that part of her last letter which related simple facts.

I have also two or three other letters and notes to write before I dress to go out.

My dear Dorothy, this is a very nice quiet place and there is plenty of amusement out of doors. I often wish I could have had you here: but I hope you are better employed and are preparing yourself in mind, manners, and good principles to be a comfort to your Uncle when you *do* visit him—I often think what a pleasure it will be for me to spend a while with you and your cousins and William at Sundridge.

Give my kind Love to John—I think much of him and am glad he goes on so well at school.

My best Love to Betty and Mary Bell, and Mary Anne[3]—I shall send them each a piece of black *Mode*[4] (Aunt Sara will tell you what it is) to make them a Bonnet—Go down to Mrs Gee's when you have read and *re*-read this letter, so that you have made it thoroughly out, and read such parts as will interest her and all the rest aloud to them. You must not give them the letter it is so sadly penned—and take it as an example of what is to be avoided yourself.

My love to Miss Smith and Miss Anstie.[5] I shall have much talk with them of Hendon when I return, but that will not be till Christmas, I think, if I go abroad, as I shall most likely spend a few weeks with Mrs Clarkson at my return.

You must tell Mr Gee that your Father[6] has nothing new to say

frequently visited the Lakes and in 1817 were looking for a residence there. See *SH* 33, pp. 109–10.

[1] Frances Maria Kelly (1790–1882), a popular actress at Drury Lane: 'neither young nor handsome, but very agreeable', according to H. C. R. Charles Lamb unsuccessfully proposed to her in 1819. (See *Lamb*, ii. 323–5, pp. 253–6.)

[2] See *MW* 29, pp. 58–59. The reference is not, apparently, to W. W.'s friend William Pearson of Borderside; but rather to a servant of Miss Barker's, or perhaps a tenant of her house in Borrowdale.

[3] Maids at Rydal Mount.

[4] *Mode* = Alamode, a thin glossy black silk (*O.E.D.*).

[5] A London friend of the Wordsworths and Coleridges.

[6] W. W. and M. W. had followed D. W. to London at the end of May. *En route* they had stayed with the Revd. Robert Jones at his rectory at Souldern, near Banbury (see *MW* 29, pp. 55–59), and visited Oxford (see *PW* iii, p. 39).

of politics. The fact is, that he, like all of us, think of those matters much less than in the North. He will write when his eyes are a little better.

My love to Miss Eliza,[1] and tell your Aunt that her letter was delightfully interesting. How you must be enjoying yourselves on this beautiful day! *My* walk to Grosvenor Square will not be very delightful; but I have never once been distressed with heat since I left home.

God bless you both! and believe me ever my dear Dorothy

Your affectionate Aunt

D. Wordsworth

597. W. W. to C. W.

Endorsed: My Brother June 28.
MS. Jonathan Wordsworth.
Charles Wordsworth, Annals of My Early Life, 1806–1846, 1891, p. 8.

[June 28, 1820][2]
Wednesday Noon Lambeth

My dear Brother,

Lord Lonsdale informs me that Lord Liverpool assured him yesterday that the M-ship of T-[3] would not be disposed of without consulting the Archbishop of C.

ever your aff^{t}. Br
W. W.

598. W. W. to S. T. COLERIDGE

Address: S. T. Coleridge Esq, Gilman's Esq, Highgate.
MS. untraced.
MY ii. 641, p. 877.

Saturday [8 July 1820]

My dear Coleridge

Last Wednesday I purposed to have been at Highgate, but a return of my complaint upon the sudden change of the weather on

[1] i.e. Miss Dowling; or possibly Miss Elizabeth Crump.

[2] Date and brackets added by C. W.

[3] Shortly after this, C. W. was made Master of Trinity and Rector of Buxsted with Uckfield, Sussex, on the recommendation of his patron Charles Manners-Sutton, the Archbishop of Canterbury. According to Charles Wordsworth, it was rumoured that Monk, then Greek Professor, was to have the mastership, and the Duke of York had actually congratulated him upon his appointment. The previous Master, William Lort Mansel, had died on 27 June.

Monday prevented it.—I am now considerably better. Dr [?Faire] I believe thinks favorably of my case, which is Lippitudo. My last attack was a Stye (do I spell right?) with bloodshot.—I am truly grateful to Dr[?Faire] for his most friendly attentions; I shall see him again tomorrow. On Monday we start for Switzerland. To-morrow afternoon I shall be at Lambeth Rectory, and shall dine there at two. I regret very much having seen so little of you; but this infirmity and my attendance at Chantry's,[1] for my Bust, and numerous other engagements have stood in my way. I hope to be more lucky on my return.

Tell Derwent, with my best love, and kindest wishes, that I have ordered Mr Longman to send him the new Edition of my Poems next week.

Be so good as to thank also Mr Gilman for his kind recommendation of me to Dr[?Faire]

ever my dear Coleridge
most faithfully yours
W. Wordsworth.

599. M. W. and D. W. to SARA HUTCHINSON and DORA W.

Address: To Miss Hutchinson, Rydal Mount, Kendal, Westmorland, Angleterre
Postmark: 21 July 1820.
MS. WL.
MY ii. 642, p. 878 (—).

Dunkirk July 13th 1820,[2] the 9 o'clock Drum beating and Father saying I must off to bed.

[*M. W. writes*]

My dearest Sarah and darling Dorothy

I must begin a letter to you however before I follow, be it merely to say that we have wished and wished again that we had you with

[1] Sir Francis Leggatt Chantrey, R.A. (1781–1842), sculptor and founder of the 'Chantrey Bequest'. Sir George Beaumont commissioned this bust, which was regarded as highly successful. W. W. himself said that he wished to be known to posterity by it, and S. T. C. remarked that 'it was more like W. than W. himself'. This letter fixes the date of its execution, which was uncertain. See Blanshard, op. cit., p. 151.

[2] The long-awaited visit to the Continent commenced on 11 July, and the party consisted of W. W., M. W., D. W., Thomas Monkhouse and his bride Jane Horrocks, and her sister Miss Horrocks. H. C. R. joined them at Lucerne on 16 Aug. See *Journal of a Tour on the Continent, 1820, DWJ*, vol. ii; *HCR* i, pp. 243 ff. M. W.'s unpublished *Journal* is among the *WL MSS*. W. W.'s *Memorials of a Tour on the Continent, 1820* (*PW* iii, p. 164) were composed

us—and dear Willy also—*him, especially* when we drove off in our 2 voitures with each 3 horses from the Inn yard at Calais, this morning—Monsieur le Postilion cracking his whip over his head with all his might through the streets—making such an uproar! this, instead of a Horn to clear the way I suppose—and the same ceremony is repeated in passing the villages and approaching the Towns where we change horses. We arrived here just as the Party were sitting down to Table d'hote (all but 2 I think English, a long table full) had a delightful journey tho' but thro' a dreary country, in general very like the worst parts of Scotland—but I must not go on to tell you more to night than that we are all well and have enjoyed ourselves. Mrs. M. who, D would report, perhaps yesterday, was unwell, better and gone to bed, in the resolution to be up in time—so good night I dare not stop another minute.—Friday on Board the Packet to Ghent—having left the most beautiful City of Bruges not half satisfied, for a month would not be sufficient to study its magnificent Architecture, stately Houses,—Public buildings—Churches—Graceful quiet, interesting People—Such a change since we left France—not so *amusing* perhaps—but far better than that. Were I the Crumps I should fix for some time at Bruges. D. is a most industrious Journalist so, tho' I should not injure her report were I to do my best I will not flatten by anticipation. We are now sailing in a Packet boat between Elmtrees—little children playing, linen bleaching on the banks. I have been making a few memoranda sitting in our carriage.—D. has joined me and W. just gone to join the Company who now seem so merry that I believe I must quit you—he has been the very reverse sonneteering,[1] but it is now written out and as our affairs have suffered by his remissness I trust he will now cease. Slept at Dunkirk, at Fernes—at Bruges—great variety of country—barren—Scotch like at first. Now luxuriant and rich beyond everything I have seen—heavy crops—large cows—Horses, Sheep—Pigs immense but none to be seen in the fields—only in one instance for many miles past have I seen cattle in the fields. Our friends enjoy themselves—but we have all been too busy—hope to be better—to have less trouble in our settlements etc as we gain more experience—we think of you perpetually and wish and wish for you—if ever

some time later, in Nov. and Dec. 1821, while D. W. was writing up her *Journal* of the tour.

[1] *A Parsonage in Oxfordshire, PW* iii, p. 41, written to commemorate his recent visit to Robert Jones at Souldern. Jones had been invited to join the party, and in a letter to W. W. of 21 Feb. 1821, he wrote that 'it would have been a singular and memorable incident in our lives to have gone over the same ground again together after an interval of thirty years' (*WL MSS.*).

we are rich enough depend upon it I shall come again with you and my children! Tell Miss Charlotte[1] that her bag rests on my knee. Yesterday I tore out the lining and it is not so smart, it is still the most useful thing I possess. We learn that it is festival at Bruges and that if we are there on Sunday as we had intended to be we shall have 5 guineas to pay for each bed—this will be one of our disappointments. I am not in a humour to write now so must depend upon another opportunity, but I must tell you that we have 2 nuns and a Priest on board——the nuns in black petticoats and white woollen gowns these pinned up with great care—a pure white cap first of all—then a white stiff front which covers the forehead—square at top—a black silk hood closed under the chin flat over the top and hanging all over the shoulders and waist—then from the top of the back to the feet a black silk scarf fastened round the waist—the dress is not becoming, but they are intelligent looking women and very merry—I must go and see more of them.—I have just returned from dinner left D. upon deck with the Ladies and a shower coming on made everyone look after guarding their property, all the canvas is spread out, and I came to take care of the exposed part of our carriage and mostly liking solitude, remain to get on with this letter as I think you will be expecting to hear *directly* from us before this reaches you—you will have heard of our safe landing at Calais from Mrs. Hoare, therefore we have been the less anxious—poor little Willy, he will be thinking himself left alone in the world. I trust my dear D. has written him a nice letter before now. When shall we hear from you! I only wish if M. Bell is to come to London that she had arrived before our departure. Our corner at the dinner Table has been a silent one—but at the other end was plenty of chat—all english, and it was amusing enough to listen to them. Miss H. and Mrs. M. met with a young man who knew many of their acquaintances—some who live at Ghent. The nuns with their attendant Friar did not dine at our table, which I was sorry for. The trees are now rustling in a brisk breeze which made me look up thinking it was raining heavily—but it does not come yet—only we have just had enough to prove to us that they have rain in the Netherlands. These barges are gay things—where the Passengers sit forms are ranged round, and across like as in a Playhouse a gay glittering flounced dome overhead and farther into the barge over the luggage they have hung canvas to shelter it from the threatened rain—The Carriages below, from which I see all the company myself screened

[1] Charlotte Lockier of Hendon, who spent some time in the Lakes this summer.

by Mr M's which stands before me—and thus we pass on—one thin elm tree, appearing on each side in succession after another. Amongst the company have just come up from below a *very pretty young* woman dressed in a yellow figured muslin bordered and flowered—a french green silk hand kerchief and a pretty mob cap gaily decorated with artificial flowers—an elderly old woman laden with rings, a muslin dress, a red silk handkerchief tied on with her belt—a large yellowish bonnet made of a thin sort of material—sits by her side. Near to me a party of men gibbering Flemish and smoking their pipes—this is a slight specimen—I do not mention the Dandy and others all pleasant in their way. The cocked hat Priest is come up and I perceive now that he is in the open air that his coat is brown and not black—he wears a waterloo blue ornament that turns over his waistcoat. We expect to be at Ghent at 4 o'clock but though we hear great praises of the beauty of the place, I never expect to see anything like Bruges again. We do so lament that we might not have stayed longer. You would above all things have delighted in it. W. never was in the churches at all—and we not half long enough, but he went up the town after D. and I had left with Tom's ladies—which we might as well have done and which we ought to have done. The rain does not come—I wonder what you are doing all of you—and whether you have had any acct from the Stamp off.—and when you will receive the book and fifty things. By the bye the great box was sent off upon the day of our departure per canal—You must enquire how long it ought to be on the road and if it does not appear in reasonable time write a letter p.p. to Mr. Bates 28 Queen Ann's St. and he will enquire after it. T.M. has just come up to enquire what I am about, he sends his best love. You must tell M.[1] about us for T. says he will not write yet awhile to her. I trust she is getting better—We had just such a letter from her as I expected about her going with us. I never thought she would possibly make up her mind to leave those little Darlings—that is that she could not feel herself sufficiently free absent from them, to be likely to derive benefit from the journey. God grant that we may have good accounts of her. Tom wrote to her about going the day after I had done so—and we all should have been very glad if she had gone—passing by a Hamlet. It would only have been dull if we had not partly employed ourselves—for it is too hot always to be making oneselves agreeable. Yet many of them do so. I do not think W. has come from the cabin yet—Yes, I hear him laughing—glad am I that he is not murmuring below. A boat just past laden—

[1] Mary Hutchinson.

faces thick as they could stand—Here I stop till I fill up at Ghent where I shall post my letter. Saturday, Ghent ½ past 5 o'clock. Dressed and waiting for our Attendant to conduct us to the sights—we were out and with him as long as we could see last night—W. in bed, D. ready. Poor W. is no longer the active traveller he used to be, and I greatly question that the journey will do him any good—but I must not despair yet. This city is very grand—more picturesque much larger but not so fine to the *imagination* as Bruges. A greater variety of interest certainly—here is more business, and more than in proportion to its size. The people far inferior in all respects—Children impudent as in great English towns—Houses very spacious, this which we are in immensely large—Our bedrooms (D and ours) such a distance from the rest and from the sitting room, that after a fagging day it is wearisome to get to it. Its furniture consists of the Bed small (we often have 2 in the room) a heavy wooden stock wooden valence like the pannel in a wainscoat—high frame, standing up at the head and foot—stuffed and covered with woollen at the feet—the hangings are framed by an iron bar stuck into the wall near the ceiling of the very high room—a golden ball at its end—this reaches across the bed and over it is thrown 4 breadths of white calico, one half spread over the frame at the top, the other the bottom. This is different from the hangings we have hitherto seen—with the curtains suspended from a circular frame, gaily ornamented, at the top—these if the rooms were not very lofty would come too near to the face and be uncomfortable—but in these they are very nice and look beautiful. Marble tables to wash upon and leather ones to write upon. You generally find an inkstand and pen prepared, but not that supply of water I expected and no sope but there is a chest of drawers, chairs etc.—an Abelard and 2 pictures of french cottage children—the room, as they all are, hung with a handsome Paper, Large mirrors., tho' in this room there is only one—always against the wall—

[*D. W. writes*]

My dearest Dorothy—What I have to say will suit you particularly and to you I must address myself; this Sunday morning at Brussels I have no place to sit but your Father's Bedroom—and he is only half dressed. We came to B. expecting to lodge in our carriages. It is the very grandest fête that has been for 50 years—At the City gates at 12 o'clock last night your mother rouzed me from a sleep—We were going over a drawbridge—and were stopped to give an account of ourselves—then the massy gates were opened—the effect very grand of light and shade and the entrance to the city most striking—We flashed through the streets—and they are decorated with garlands for miles—just such only far finer, as at our Ball. It was most beautiful; but will no doubt look paltry enough by day—but the City is grand and picturesque as possible and in the brilliance of light, with the contrast of occasional gloom, it was delightful—a scene of Romance or Fairy land. We drew up to a large Hotel where in three apartments we could be lodged. Could you be brought hither in a moment how you would be astonished! The entrances to these great Hotels are as big as to Castles—The very passages are covered with paintings and the apartments with marble chimnies, a time piece—elegant hangings to the walls—with these are clumsy doors, and locks that would almost disgrace a new built English cottage—you can have no idea of the buildings here. We drove through long streets of lofty houses—like the finest of Glasgow or Edinburgh—only much richer in ornament, and more varied. It is now 10 o'clock. Your Father and Mother and Mr. M. are gone about passports. This is not one of the pleasures of continental travelling. The country we passed through yesterday is like the very richest parts of England, but the trees are not so fine—hedge rows—trees innumerable—thatched cottages with gardens very pretty—and such crops as my eyes never saw. Harvest beginning—It is however miserable to contrast the ragged and wretched appearance of women and children with the bountiful richness of the produce of the earth. The people too are impudent and uncivil by the way—laughing at you. How different from Bruges! that place has left a most delightful impression—of cloistral quiet and dignified gravity—with great kindness and civility of manners—Ghent all bustle and business—Brussels all flash and splendour. In this very square there are 9 or 10 Buildings as grand as the finest of our palaces in London. Groups of people going to church—or walking almost for pastime—a woman at the door has just given me a bouquet—a waiter comes into your room—with 'excusez moi' and pushes forward though you are but half dressed. We have yet seen nothing but the garlanded streets with their ever varying lofty houses revealed by flashes of strong light and the square of the hotel. At Ghent we saw some very fine pictures—and one church the most beautiful that I ever saw—almost made of marble within—and adorned with fine pictures and statues—such as made you disregard the Tinsel of the full dressed Jesuses and the Lady Mother. At Bruges we saw hundreds kissing the Bottle in which is contained the 'Blut von Jesus' which our guide assured us with great earnestness had been happily preserved through all revolutions. Dorothy,

I have bought a little Image for you at Bruges—for six sous. People here are in English dresses—and dresses of all kinds—so they were at Ghent—but the two nuns and the Priest in our boat from Bruges gave an unspeakable effect of the Group. Near them was a beautiful Flemish girl, elegantly dressed with a French Mob and a Bunch of Roses—But nothing have I seen that has left an impression so interesting as Bruges.—The City is as quiet as a convent—yet people are for ever walking about—the women are very graceful in long black cloaks and caps as white as snow. The caps of the country are much more becoming to them than the French or English caps. Bruges continually reminds me of Oxford—We often wished we could convey thither one of its spacious squares. Your Father has written a beautiful sonnet—so much the worse for us; for we rather mismanaged Bruges in consequence of that—but he has done and I hope finally—otherwise *he* will be no better for the journey. This morning he is well and all alive and ready to plan for the best. We intend to stay here till tomorrow; but shall most likely have to change our lodgings as others will probably arrive who will pay more. These French windows are delightful—wide and open from top to bottom. The paper of this room is in oils—very gay like India paper—and well painted. It is 40 years old yet as fresh as if put up only yesterday. Here I write looking out of the noble windows—past 3 o'clock. Miss Horrocks and I went to the grande Eglise—so full of people that we could only see heads. The music is at times in gushes tremendously sublime—heat excessive—we then walked thro' squares and streets of palaces—and through public gardens—adorned with statues—shady avenues—arbours—everything you can conceive—scattered over with gaily dressed—and gorgeously and quaintly dressed people. Found our Friends in a Garret stationed to see the Procession of the Host. This was preceded and followed by military in the most gorgeous habits—You see nothing like it but in Flemish pictures—and the streets and garlands are beautiful by day-light. Oh! this is a wondrous place. There stands a girl of the country in the Balcony of a palace house opposite to my window—and there goes a sweet creature in black and green with a Guitar—Her ears are hung with golden drops and her hair is as black as jet—I never saw a beautiful procession till to-day. The priests and choristers sang as they passed in most solemn voices—The military were attended with *their* band. We have seen the gay Ballroom where our heroes danced before the day of Quatre Bras—and heard details from the mouths of living witnesses of the horrors of the return of sick and wounded——If I were but to go round this Square and describe all I might fill a sheet. We have been obliged to throw off our cloth dress and are now in white—Your Father and Mother and M [?rs Monkhouse drove] in a carriage round the City.

Your Mother just come in from her Ride [ ] I will tell you she has been taken for a Duchess. A Frenchman stopped her Carriage and begged her pardon, but took her for the Duchesse of ——.

The shops are open—but people seem to have no thoughts of business.

The heat today has affected my Bowels, so I cannot go out again till evening. I have been quite well till yesterday—when we walked rather too far. But I am now well—and so is your Mother—and we are the best travellers of the party and enjoy ourselves very much—though our wishes for you and Aunt Sara are at times painful. I fear you cannot read this part of the letter I am in a great hurry to finish. When I write to you again I will do it by degrees. We shall leave Brussels tomorrow evening. To night we see grand fireworks, shall dine at the Table d'Hote at 4. God bless you dearest Sara and dear Dorothy.

Finished Monday

Observe we have an elegant sitting Room but Mr. Monkhouse slept there, and when I began to write he was not dressed. All the Rooms are *superbe* and fit for Dukes.

600. D. W. to CATHERINE CLARKSON

Address: Mrs Clarkson, Playford Hall, Ipswich, Angleterre [*readdressed to*] Miss Sara Hutchinson, Rydal Mount, Kendal, Westmorland.
Postmark: 1 Aug., 1820.
MS. WL.
MY ii. 643, p. 885.

Coblentz 23rd July [1820]

My dear Friend,

I begin to write to you at Coblentz having just returned from the heights which overlook the City and the splendid vales of the Rhine and the Moselle. It is impossible to conceive any more delightful prospect of the kind than we have just beheld—but it is not for me to describe it—still less in the small compass of a letter such as can be written in the snatches which we take of rest—and no doubt your husband has been here—he will tell you how elegant—how beautiful looks the city of Coblentz with its palaces and spires and its purple slated roofs situated as it is at the junction of these majestic rivers on a plain formed into an angle by the rivers. Yesterday we travelled up the Rhine from Cologne, having spent a day there, and we came along the Meuse from Namur—the most enchantingly interesting and varied country that ever I travelled through. The Rhine is stately, rich, and for ever changing, but the Meuse is romantic beyond expression from the variety of the Rocks fortifications chateaus and cottages and the *trees* of the Meuse are superior to any we have seen elsewhere on the continent. They are not so fine as those in South Wales but very much like the trees of the North of England, though not the best of those. The woods on the Rhine are greatly inferior. But let me not disparage this majestic wealth-giving glorious river—its plains of corn, vines, fruit-trees—its stately convents—churches, villages. We were indeed through almost the whole of our ride yesterday in a perpetual state of excitement. Yet I think and more, if possible, delight in the memory of the Meuse, though I was unfortunately on that day so very unwell that I could hardly speak at all—and—from pure exhaustion, was obliged to sleep in the carriage even for miles of the most interesting parts of the road. The heat had become excessive two days after our arrival at Calais and I had been tempted at Ghent to walk so much that I was quite overcome. My Bowels were much affected, this brought on weakness.—At Brussels again I fatigued myself—There we stayed two nights—At Namur I did not go out as much as others but went slowly up to the Citadel, where I saw a beautiful view and the junction of the Sambre and the Meuse. This was too much for me and I was as I said overpowered and exhausted. Thence to Liège a miserable city of poverty and splendour enchantingly situated—forming a crescent on the hillside—with convents, spires, towers. Others walked before breakfast, but I took mine in bed, though I rose at 5 o'clock. It is my way now not to be able to sleep in the mornings—but my legs ached so from the state of my Bowels that I was forced upon the bed again. At Aix la Chapelle I took rest in the same way only went to view the Chair of Charlemagne etc. Rested in the carriage, and at Cologne did not stir out all day, while others were walking, only at night I viewed the magnificent Cathedral which has never been finished and the tower now stands as a majestic Ruin yet just as the workmen left it I believe every stone remains. The quire is perfectly beautiful and quite finished; but many of its painted windows are gone. The next day I rose quite well, but resolved to spare myself. The charming ride on the Banks of the Rhine seemed to give me strength as I went along—and I trust that (being resolved now to do always less than I *can* do) I shall know no more suffering. Today I have been the strongest of the Females yet I have resisted my inclination to take several tempting walks in the environs of this singularly happily situated city. I certainly am not so strong as I was twenty years ago. This I am now obliged to confess and I must manage myself accordingly. Five years ago I used to say I felt no difference. My Sister is an excellent traveller—all alive and full of enjoyment. So indeed am I —and, with a little better arrangement, I expect that I shall not be obliged to give up any important gratification in the delightful countries whither we are bound. William's eyes are much better— and except during two days when nothing would serve but he must write poetry, he has been perfectly well. The young people are, as you may suppose, very happy—Mrs Monkhouse is a sweet good modest and amiable young woman, but she is not strong and is therefore unable to walk about like her sister and Mr Wordsworth, but not enjoying things in the same sort and degree that I do the privation is not so great for her as it has been for me. It is now Sunday the 23rd of July. How different from an English Sunday! but this is a quiet place and there is nothing unpleasing to me in the pleasuring of the sober people here. It is, however, painful to see labour going on on the sabbath day and the shops open. But at Brussels (which is of itself a gayer town) it was a time of Festival. One of the grandest of the Fêtes and lucky we were in seeing it— but at Brussels there was so much flash and bustle—and noise of carriages—so much finery—and everyone seemed so intent on pleasure—I was very glad at the end of the day that we had not another to spend there and longed for the stillness of an English Sabbath. In the morning was the procession—military and sacred music. In the square all day through rattling of carriages—the public walks for ever crowded—at night illuminations—and after all fireworks. We in the evening went in the string of carriages to the Hyde Park of Brussels and on the outskirts of the public place there was a fair and thousands of people—drinking—walking— what noisy laughing. But it is time to turn to England, where I hope you are all as well as we left you. It will be yet a fortnight before we reach Berne and till we are there we can have no letters, and this thought sometimes comes suddenly upon me and raises momentary fears. I cannot give you any other address than à la poste restante à Berne; for we do not know what our movements will be; but at Berne we shall desire that our letters may be sent after us—and pray my dear Friend, write immediately. When this letter reaches you our little darling William will I hope be under your care. He is no doubt in most of his leisure moments of rest from school studies and play, employed in planning his journey and thinking of the pleasures of it. That was a very hasty note which I wrote to you just before we left London, and I am afraid I did not half express the satisfaction which the Father and Mother felt when I first named to them your wish to have William at some of his holidays. I then said 'what if he can be received at the next (for it cannot be convenient for my brother Christ. to have him)' and they snatched at the idea greedily. William must put a word or two in your letter and give our kindest love to him and tell him that when we come home again we shall have a great deal to tell him of what we have seen. Journals we shall have in number sufficient to fill a Lady's bookshelf, —for all, except my Brother, write a Journal. Oh! Mine is nothing but notes, unintelligible to any one but myself; I look forward however to many a pleasant hour's employment at Rydal Mount in filling up the chasms. But it is grievous to pass through such a country as this only glancing at the objects in the broad high-way and leaving so many entirely unseen. I think of you all, of every Friend I have in England at night when I am in bed—often till I am obliged to endeavour to forget you and to keep down the strong wish which I and all of us have to hear from you all again. True it is that for months together no important changes trouble us—often so it is—but on the other hand how dreadful and how sudden are the changes that [?happen] in fancy and *have* happened three times in our [ ]. But I must not think of it. Trusting for good [?news] I entreat you to write. It is near ten o'clock (and tomorrow morning we are to depart at 6 o'clock). We go up the Rhine to Schaffhausen stopping a li[ttle on] the way.—I have written with perpetual [interrup]tions. William's and Mary's room is through this [and we] have eaten our meals in the common Room and dined at the Table d'hote, and as is the custom have all sate in our own bedrooms, and partaken of other customs of the country. In this room has been [ ] I have [?] each and all over and over [?] talk on all questions, or to ask me to interpret and it seems though I have scribbled so much I have told nothing when there is so much to tell of. This is a delightful inn so clean and comfortable in comparison with that at Cologne where we were assaulted by stenches at every turn. But on the other hand, the situation at Cologne was so amusing that I, who was a prisoner, was delighted with it. I sate at an open window all day mending my ragged cloaths and watching the immensely large Ferry boat which was emptied and re-filled every

¾ of an hour close to me. It has a square platform for passengers, and is covered with so many and so varied groups that it is like a piece cut out of a Market place. Fruit women with their Baskets, peasants with their rakes baskets etc. Gentlemen with carriages young ladies, children, soldiers, perhaps a cart laden with calves—a few sheep, a calf tied to a string. In short every thing comes and goes—and there are all the gay colours of the Rainbow. This Inn is the posthouse and is in a narrow street. The Landlord speaks good English and is a most sensible and intelligent man. The servants are clean and respectable. Every thing good in the house, and a quietness which I have seen in no other German Inn. I am going to give you a troublesome office. I must beg you to write a line to Mrs Hoare telling her that we are well and happy. You may say that I have been a little poorly, but am now quite well. I am anxious to hear of my brother Christopher, and Mrs H. kindly promised to write to me. Tell her that I have no other address to give than Berne, and that letters will be forwarded from that place to us. Say also that I have not forgotten my promise to write to my nephew John[1] but that must not be till we get into Switzerland, we have so little time for writing. Also I beg you will write to Miss Lamb and give my kindest love to her and her Brother, and say to them I will write from Switzerland. There we hope to meet Henry Robinson. After you have read and digested this letter (and less than one day, I think, will not serve for this, it is so badly written) pray forward to Sara Hutchinson. I wonder whether Mary Bell goes to our Brother or not and very much do we long to hear every thing concerning Sara and Dorothy and John. And now my dearest Friend may God bless you and yours and preserve you till we meet again! My kind love to Mr Clarkson and Tom, and I pray you read this sad scrawl with indulgence. The fine-toned clock warns me it is time to pack for tomorrow. Ever your affectionate and faithful friend D W.

[1] John Wordsworth, C. W.'s eldest son: at this time about to enter Winchester along with his younger brother Christopher.

601. D. W. to HENRY CRABB ROBINSON

Address: a Monsieur. Monsieur Henry Robinson, a la Poste Restante Geneve.
Stamp: Bern. *Endorsed*: 6 August 1820. Miss Wordsworth. The Itinerary, by Wordsworth.
MS. Dr. Williams's Library.
K (—). *Morley, i, p. 95.*

Berne.
Aug. 6th [1820]

My dear Sir,

We arrived here yesterday all in good health and spirits, and very much pleased with our travels. We intend to depart tomorrow morning for Thoun, and shall proceed by Interlachen, Grindlewald etc, to Lucerne, making little tours and turnings by the way. I hope it will not be long before you find us out somewhere; and to assist you in so doing we shall take care to leave notices at the inns of our route. We intend to go as far as Milan—but further than Milan I think we shall not attempt to go, seeing by the way all that time and strength will permit. Often and often have we wished for you while we have been in Germany. At the time of bill-paying you would have saved us great trouble, and sometimes no little vexation.

My Brothers eyes are better, though not strong. My Sister makes a very good traveller, and I, though not the stoutest of the three, have done pretty well, and we have all enjoyed ourselves. Mr Monkhouse is quite well, and his Wife and Miss Horrocks are also in good health; but I am sorry to tell you that Mrs M. is not strong enough to cross the Alps with us, or to make any very fatiguing excursions, therefore, we shall part from her and her Sister at Lucerne; and they will wait for us at Geneva.

They have a maid-servant, and will be very comfortable. Mr Monkhouse will be of our party over the Alps. I think I have no more to say, except that we shall all rejoice to see you, and that I am your faithful and affectionate Friend

Dorothy Wordsworth

We were delighted with Heidelbergh, and with the kindness and hospitality of your Friend Mr Pickford,[1] and his Family.

Berne August 6th
Crown Inn

From Lucerne to Brunnen, Schwytz-Altdorf Lugano Como etc etc.

[1] See *DWJ* ii, pp. 63–67; *MW* 31, p. 62.

OUR INTENDED ROUTE.

Thoun
Interlachen
Lauterbrun
Grindelwald
Over the Brunick to
  Lucerne
Brunnen
Schwytz
Altorf
Over the St. Gothard
  To Bellinzone
To Locarno
Lugano
Portezza

Menaggio on the Lake of Como
Como
Milan
Varese
Laveno
Boromean Islands
Domo D'ossola
Cross the Simplon into the Valais

We shall leave a Letter at Lucern Altorf at Bellinzone at Como-Milan etc.

10th left Grindelw Lauterbrun
11th wd be at Meiringen
12th at Lucerne
14th Eagle

[*pencilled note. By H. C. R.?*]

602. D. W. to SARA HUTCHINSON

Address: Miss Hutchinson, Rydal Mount, near Kendal, Angleterre.
Postmark: 26 Aug. 1820. *Stamp*: Lucerne.
MS. WL.
MY ii. 644, p. 890.

Interlacken—8th August—Tuesday.

My dearest Sara,

I begin to write after an afternoon spent upon the hills of the valley of Interlacken,—on one side overlooking the first reach of the beautiful Lake of Thun, and between that lake and the Lake of Brientz the short level plain or vale scattered over with the finest walnut trees ever beheld—near one end as it appears at the plain is the little town of Unterscale, at the other the village of Interlacken. On one side of us, as I say, we beheld these beautiful objects and on the other the Jungfrau terminating a lovely valley scattered over with brown deserted summer huts embosomed in fruit trees—chiefly walnut—indeed the whole vale is scattered over with them—and there is one little chapel where an Englishman who died here, of the name of Elliot, is buried.—The Jungfrau is so called from having never been conquered by man. It is covered with snow (except where the rocks will not permit the snow to lie) for a space as high as the whole height of Skiddaw—and tonight we have seen these mountains tinged with rosy light.—But I must not attempt to describe any thing. This vale is wonderful, it is overpowering from its loveliness, but except the Alps themselves every thing that is most beautiful in this country reminds us of our own. I believe Mary wrote to you from Schaffhausen before I had returned to them. You will be glad to hear that Mrs M. was much amended by her rest, and that we females had a very pleasant journey together. To be sure the trial was a short one; but I should not fear to travel through Germany France and Switzerland without any companions but females—Not that I do not prefer male society, but as to protection you need none. Females find protectors wherever they go in a strange land; and I believe they would also find less of a disposition to impose upon them than the men do, and one reason is that they are not so much inclined to suspicion, and men and women are equally weak against fraud in the territory of the foe. We were highly gratified at Schaffhausen—There and there alone we saw the famous waters of the Rhine in their purity, of a greenness between the emerald and sea-green, and clear as crystal—rushing on stately yet impetuous. The town is beautifully situated—Of the Falls I say nothing. Next day to Zurich an interesting place—the banks of the Lake very populous, and all white houses—trees around them. If grandeur were the characteristic of the shores of Zurich it would be spoiled by so many houses; but it is not—I gladly gave up the picturesque and the simply rural for the pleasing fancy that hundreds and hundreds of families were enjoying at leisure the beautiful scenes of that Lake. From Zurich to Leinsberg, a town with a castle nobly situated on a lofty eminence much higher than Stirling. That afternoon we had part seen the snows of the Alps—and early the next morning Mary and I beheld from the castle roof the grandest spectacle we had yet seen—the distant snowy Alps bright with sunshine. Opposite to them the range of the Jura—a sea of mist below us and all round—and islands of wood, bare hill—castles rising out of the mist. We could have lingered till all was cleared away by the sun but time would not allow, and after three quarters of an hour's stay with regret we descended the hundreds of steps to the vale below. Opposite to the Inn was a [?] Garden which you would have delighted in. Exquisite flowers—clipped hedges—clipped trees—statues—and a fountain. For your sake Mary looked at it so attentively that I believe she has it all off by heart—and will tell you every angle and turning when we meet again. Next day dined at

Murgenthal (you must look at your maps) and slept at Hertzergeboscher but not all in our beds, for the Landlord had the rapacity and impudence to ask 6 livres for each bedroom. Mr M. took one room for his wife, Miss H. and the Maid, and William and Mr M. packed themselves up in one carriage, Mary and I in the other, after we had taken bread and milk under the shed of a cottage. (Here every cottage has a spacious shed for out-of-doors comfort—except the very small huts in these Alpine vales). The day had been very hot—and at about 12 a tremendous storm of thunder and lightning came on with torrents of rain. Think of our situation—In a street nearly opposite to the Inn—large houses—Galleries—every thing strange in buildings—Watchman with his grand voice at intervals—a fountain close at hand tearing out its waters—A Dog howling—house clocks striking all round the quarters and the hour—and the Church clock the like. The lightning incessant—thunder very loud—We were awe-struck but had no fears. At ½ past 4 in heavy rain we departed, breakfasted Kirchenberg, and dined at Berne—a noble city—and grandly situated. There we stayed from Saturday noon till Monday morning. Next day to Thun, a delightful spot—It is a small town at the foot of the Lake. Thence we departed at 7 this morning in a Boat. Landed at an Inn at the head. There got into a long cart with seats swung across that hold two—and thus we 7 and the driver rode merrily along about two or perhaps rather more miles past Unterseen along the flat valley to Interlaken. All are in bed but me. It is eleven o'clock and I must go. Tomorrow I shall speak of other matters—God bless you my dearest Friend. How I wish you were with us! and not less do I wish that Dorothy were here also. Give my tenderest love to her.

6 o'clock Wednesday morning. I have just called William and Mary. The sun shines upon that lily-white Jungfrau and all the green or rocky mountains round Oh! that you could see the walnut trees which grow before the house!

My dearest Sara, Before we arrived at Berne we had many fears that no letter might be there for us, as we had fixed too late a time for your writing. Wm. either thought we should be longer on the road, or that letters would come more speedily! accordingly there were no letters for us, yet for every one else, and the same directions were given to their friends as to you. It was a sad damping—but we were prepared for it! On Sunday came a letter from Mrs Hoare, thank God with good news of my Bro. Christ. and of William—and we flatter ourselves that all is well at Rydal or the contrary tidings would have reached us. Tom M's letters were all on business—

and his Wife's and Miss H.'s brought *us* no comfort. William has desired letters to be sent after us and we hope to meet them at Lucerne, where we shall arrive in a few days, and God grant that all may be well. We have particular reasons to be anxious at this time, as your comforts had been so upset by the loss of poor Mary Bell, and the unprincipled conduct of John Carter and Mary Anne. I wish we could have a letter from John W. When you write to him pray tell him to give our kind regards to his Master with best thanks for his most clear and sensible directions for our Tour. They are now of very great use to us. Mary is very well and very stout,—but she is even thinner than when she was in London—and no wonder; for she makes so poorly out in the eating way. T. M. is well—and his wife also—but it will be quite impossible for her and Miss H. to go further with us than to Lucerne. There we part. They will return to Berne, where they have kind friends in the relations, whom they found out, of their French Master—also in our Inn-keeper and his wife at the *Crown*, and they will stay there a few days and proceed to Geneva to wait for us. We have found the Inns in Switzerland generally very comfortable and no imposition in the established and known places—They have delightful open Balconies for tea and other refreshments—At Zurich we took coffee by candlelight on one of these places—a spacious and long shed or gallery close to the Lake. Here at Unterlaken also is a delightful one—But I must go on with the party. William's eyes are certainly much better; but subject to variations. He is obliged to screen himself from strong lights both of the sun and candles, and he has frequent threatenings of swellings in his lids; but by proper applications inward and outward we stave it off—and if he could take his *business* more quietly he would receive great benefit from this journey. He *does* now manage that better, and when our party is smaller I think he will do perfectly well. No people can be more amiable than Mrs M. and Miss H. but it cannot be denied that our party is too large for such a country as this. It is in vain for me to attempt to describe our future route, for I do not know it myself—only from Lausanne we make to the Alps touring about as we go—and when we come back from Italy we shall have more touring in Switzerland. You must direct to Geneva till you hear again.—I am now quite well; but you never saw me so thin in your life. I have had a disorder in my Bowels twice; but neither time, though I hardly had strength for the walking up and down the stairs while the disorder was on me, did it leave me in the least degree weaker. I am as strong now as ever I was in my life; and having discovered the proper diet, and ascertained also, the sort of hurry which upsets me, I trust I shall have nothing more to complain of. When I talk of walking up and down stairs you must not fancy the stairs of an English house. To our bedrooms at Frankfurt we had to ascend above eighty steps. I expect every moment to be summoned to breakfast, and when that is over we are to set out upon our rambles among the mountains and shall go upon the Lake of Brientz. The morning air is most refreshing in these vales—and it is felt even till 9 o'clock from the height of the mountains—and as to the mid-day heat, you know of that *I* am not likely to complain. I ought to write both to Mrs Hoare and to Miss Lamb, but really I have not time at present, and perhaps shall not for two or three weeks to come, therefore be so good as to write to Miss Lamb telling her that we are [in] good spirits going on well, and hoping to meet our kind friend Henry Robinson when we reach Lausanne at the latest. He was to set off about the first of the month. I must beg you also to write either to Mrs Hoare or to my Brother Christopher—You will probably prefer writing to him, but there is one objection, that I know not where he may be. But it would be I think best to direct to Lambeth. Say to Mrs Hoare that her letter arrived the day after we reached Berne, and that we were all very grateful for it, the more so as it was our only letter. You will tell her our address, Geneva, and say that it made me very happy to hear so good an account of my Brother after his great exertions, and also to hear that nothing worse than ten days abstinence had befallen the dear Boys. (They were inoculated for the small-pox two days before we left London.) Poor Mary Bell! I wonder whether we shall see her in London or not! and our good friend Mr Jackson how glad would it make us to hear of his perfect recovery! I should also be glad to hear that he had wrapped up his affairs with my Lady,[1] but that will never be while he has a leg to crawl on. I hope the Gees are at Rydal and will not leave it all this summer—indeed I think they will be little inclined to go away when all is in full perfection and beauty around them and they will not like to leave you. Give my kindest love to each of the Family. I hope Miss Charlotte is as well as when you last spoke of her. We expect to meet Misses Rebekah and Louisa[2] somewhere. Give our very kind love to Betty and Jonathan —God grant that we may find them and you as we left you all— well and happy! But it is grievous that we must lose those good

[1] Probably Lady le Fleming.

[2] Rebecca and Louisa Lockier of Hendon, who were touring Italy and Switzerland.

creatures as neighbours. For my part, after this unworthy conduct to Mary B. I can never more have any pleasure in J. C.[1] and I wish William could muster courage to part with them. Conceit or any other fault I cared not for—but this is unendurable. I should not however venture either to advise, or express a wish for a change, knowing how little William is fitted to struggle with extra business and how important to him it is to have leisure and quiet.—Wednesday morning 7 o'clock Lucerne 16th August—Dorothy's birthday and her Mother's. God Grant that the Daughter may be as well as the Mother! But we have had no letters. We stopped at the post office last night as we came along. You may judge of our grief and disappointment. Write directly to Geneva. From Interlacken to Lautterbrunnen. Thence over the Wigern Alp to Grindelwald. Thence over the Sheidak pass to Meerigen—thence up the enchanting vale to the Fall of the Aar at Hendrik,—back to Meirighen. On Sunday travelled by the little lovely English-like lakes Lugern and Sarnen—down past Saxland to Sarnen. Thence to Engelberg where there is a convent among the Alps—very grand—slept there —saw the celebration of the feast of the Virgin—procession of priests and peasants—beautiful and affecting in that place. Maidens in their Swiss hats large and flat, all decked in Ribbands and flowers —their holiday best. From Ingleberg to Lucerne where we arrived last night. We have not travelled over a foot of uninteresting road since I took up this letter. It was illegible enough at Unterlacken; but after travelling in the crown of my bonnet ever since and after the wetting of two thunder showers, it is worse than ever, and will, I fear, give you some trouble. After making a few turns and spending a week hereabouts we shall begin the Pass of St Gothard. All are well. I am growing fatter and am, I think, the strongest of the Party,—climbing the Passes of the Alps is not near so fatiguing as our mountains. We reckon nothing of what we have hitherto done in that way.—The air is delightful here. No letter from Mrs Clarkson—Oh! that we had but one from somebody. We have only seen the view from the Bridge in this town, and the cleanly suburbs. It is a charming country. Would that you and D. were here! God bless you! write to Geneva. I think I have no more to say. There is so much that *should* be said.

We have had charming weather for Switzerland—clear air— only a few thunderstorms in the afternoon and at night.

I will write to Mrs Hoare today so you need not trouble yourself with that.

[1] Mary Bell had been jilted by John Carter.

603. W. W. to LORD LONSDALE

MS. Lonsdale MSS., Record Office, The Castle, Carlisle.
Mem. Grosart.

Lucern August 19th 1820.

My Lord,

You did me the honor of expressing a wish to hear from me during my continental Tour; accordingly I have great pleasure in writing from this place where we arrived three days ago. Our Route has lain through Brussels, Namur, along the banks of the Meuse to Liege,—then to Aix la Chapelle, Cologne, and along the Rhine to Mayentz, to Frankfort, Heidelberg (a noble situation, at the point where the Necker issues from steep lofty hills, into the plain of the Rhine) Carlsruh[e], and through the black Forest to Schaffhausen, thence to Zurich, Bern, Thun, Interlacken. Here our Alpine Tour might be said to commence; which has produced much pleasure thus far; and nothing that deserves the name of difficulty; even for the Ladies. From the valley of Lauterbrunnen we crossed the Weigern Alp to Grindelwald, and thence over the grand Sheide to Meyringen. This journey led us over high ground, and for 15 leagues along the base of the loftiest Alps which reared their bare or snow-clad ridges and Pikes, in a clear atmosphere, with fleecy clouds now and then settling upon and gathering round them. We heard and saw several Avalanches. They are announced by a sound like thunder, but more metallic and musical; this warning naturally makes one look about, and we had the gratification of seeing [them] falling in the shape and appearance of a torrent or cascade of foaming water, down the deep-worn crevices of the steep or perpendicular granite mountains. Nothing can be more awful than the sound of these cataracts of ice and snow thus descending unless it be the silence which succeeds. The elevations from which we beheld these operations of nature, and saw such an immense range of primitive mountains stretching to the East and West, were covered with rich pasturage, and beautiful flowers, among which was abundance of the Monkshood, a flower which I had never seen but in the trim borders of our gardens, and which here grew not so much in patches as in little woods or forests, towering above the other plants. At this Season the Herdsmen are with their Cattle in still higher regions than these which we have trod, the herbage where we travelled, being reserved till they descend in the Autumn. We have visited the Abbey of Engelberg, not many leagues from the borders of the Lake of Lucern. The tradition is that the Site of this Abbey was pointed by Angels, singing from a lofty mountain that rises from the plain of the valley, and which from having been thus honoured is called Engelberg, or the hill of the Angels.[1] It is a glorious position for such Beings; and I should have thought myself repaid for the trouble of so long a journey by the impression made upon my mind, when I first came in view of the vale in which this Convent is placed, and of the mountains that enclose it. The light of the sun had left the valley, and the deep shadow spread over it heightened the splendour of the evening light spread upon the surrounding mountains, some of which had their summits covered with pure snow, others were half-hidden by vapours rolling round them, and the rock of Engelberg could not have been seen under more fortunate circumstances, for masses of cloud glowing with the reflexion of the rays of the setting sun were hovering round it like choirs of spirits preparing to settle upon its venerable head.

To-day we quit this place to ascend the Mountain Rhigi. We shall be detained in this neighbourhood till our Passports are returned from Bern signed by the Austrian Minister, which we find absolutely necessary to enable us to proceed into Milanese. At the end of five weeks at the latest we hope to reach Geneva, returning by the Simplon pass. There I might have the pleasure of hearing from your Lordship, and may I beg that you would not omit to mention Westmorland politics. The diet of Switzerland is now sitting in this place. Yesterday I had a long conversation with the Bavarian Envoy, whose views of the State of Europe appear to me very just. This Letter must unavoidably prove dull to your Lordship, but when I have the pleasure of seeing you I hope to make some little amends, though I feel this is a very superficial way of viewing a country, even with reference merely to the beauties of Nature. We have not met with many English; there is scarcely a third part as many in the Country as there was last year. A Brother of Lord Grey[2] is in the house where we are, and Lord Ashburton[3] left yesterday. I must conclude abruptly with kindest remembrances to Lady Lonsdale and Lady Mary and believe me my Lord most faithfully

Your Lordship's
Wm Wordsworth

[1] See *Engelberg, the Hill of Angels*, *PW* iii, p. 174.

[2] Charles, 2nd Earl Grey (1764–1845), the distinguished Whig statesman. It is impossible to determine which of his brothers is referred to here.

[3] Richard Barré Dunning, 2nd Lord Ashburton of the first creation (1782–1823): son of John Dunning, the celebrated lawyer.

604. W. W. to JOHN CARTER and SARA HUTCHINSON[1]

Address: To Miss Hutchinson, Rydal Mount, Kendal, Westmorland, England.
Postmark: 16 Sept. 1820.
MS. WL. Hitherto unpublished.

Milan
Sept. 3 [1820]—Sunday

Dear John Carter,

This day we turn our course towards England; but it is not probable that I shall be in London in time to sign the Quarterly Account. Be so good therefore as to direct it when due to the Head Office; stating that Mr Wordsworth (this is the form) having gone abroad for the benefit of his health has directed you to forward the Account which he will sign on his return to England, which he hopes will be in a short time. Miss Hutchinson will tell you how we all are, and how we have been amused—ever sincerely yours

Wm Wordsworth

Dearest Sarah, one word merely to let you know I am alive, though I was present at the Destruction of Troy last night, when there was a prodigious conflagration, from which, through the influence of my good Stars I only escaped. I long to hear how you are, we expect a letter at Geneva, and another at Paris. The first letter we hope to find at Sion. Say all that's kind to Mr Gee, and Mrs Gee, and Miss Lockyer, not forgetting the young Ladies. Finding my scrawl takes up so much room I conclude. I hope Mr Jackson is better. Give Dorothy a kiss for me and love to dear John. Adieu dear Sarah ever faithfully and affectionately your W. W.

[*M. W. adds*]

We do not hear that the Poems[2] are yet published—indeed from what we can judge they are not. A letter from Mrs Hoare told us that Dr. W. had heard nothing from Longman's since we left the country—at that time all the proofs were corrected—and one sheet only was wanted for Dr. W. to give in corrected, which when Mrs. H. wrote was not rec^d.—If the book is yet neglected write to Longman's and tell him that Wm. is aware of the delay and does not understand it—We saw the *Literary Advertiser* for Aug. yesterday and no mention is there made of the appearance of the work—We brought a copy with us. I hope you go to see Miss Knott.

[1] Written at the end of a letter from M. W. to S. H.
[2] The *Miscellaneous Poems* of W. W. in 4 vols.

605. D. W. to CATHERINE CLARKSON

Address: Mrs Clarkson, Playford Hall, near Ipswich, Suffolk, Angleterre.
Postmark: 16 Sept. 1820.
MS. British Museum.
K (—). *MY ii. 645, p. 896* (—).

Sunday Sept. 3rd [1820]. Milan.

My dearest Friend,

You may have some faint notion of the value of your letter to us when I tell you that, except one written on the 18th of July by our kind friend Mrs Hoare, yours is the only letter we have yet received from England. I may truly say that in the whole course of the 18 years since my Brother's marriage we have never received a letter which has brought so much comfort, contentment and pleasure. We have sadly mismanaged the matter, but I will not take up your time or my own with the how and the when. It is enough to say that, though you did not even name Rydal Mount or Sara H, except incidentally, we were quite satisfied that all was well there,—and Willy's own account of himself with your own delightful additions to it made us perfectly happy—and there was no drawback—for what you say of yourself and Mr Clarkson and Tom is just what one would wish for. How admirable and to me astonishing the ardour and industry of your good husband—to think of writing a sermon to be read to his Family on the same evening! I wish he could even now return to his office in the Church; I know no one whose figure and manner would have a more impressive effect in the pulpit! But I forget that I am writing to you from Italy. This is a fête day, and our quiet English Sabbath. Mary and I are returned to our bedrooms, after a long walk through the streets to see a military exhibition. 4000 soldiers, Bohemians and Italians with laurel twigs in their caps, were assembled at Mass, a temporary altar being erected for the occasion. The spectacle, with the music, sacred and military, was very splendid. The jingling of bells never done. We wait here to be summoned by the gentlemen to go to Mass at the Cathedral, which is certainly on the outside the most splendid and *beautiful* Building I ever beheld; yet wanting the solemnity and massiveness of a place of worship. In those respects how inferior to our Cathedrals! It is all of polished marble, exquisitely wrought, and the statues are not to be numbered by the gazer, but I believe their number is more than 2000 thousand [*sic*]. Every small pinnacle supports a statue, the airy figure lifted up to the sky. The inside is very imposing, the pillars very fine, but there are many faults to be found in the architecture. One of Buonaparte's works was the finishing of this Cathedral, and I wish he had never done anything worse. The Italians always call him *Napoleone*, and he seems to be a great favourite here, and the people being what they are, and having no dignified government of their own to be attached to, it is no wonder. The weather is clear and very fine, hot enough as you may suppose in the sunshine; but the Italians contrive their houses so nicely for excluding the sun and admitting the air within doors you suffer much less from heat than in *every-day* houses in England, and even in the streets which though generally so narrow as to exclude air except there is a current, the houses being so high you generally have a shady side, and even there (in the streets) *I* am very seldom overcome by heat. I wish I could say the same of Mary. *She* often suffers much from it and so she does in England. But I must tell you where we have been—and what we have seen in as few words as I can. Willy will have left you or I would have written to him on this sheet. I wish however that you would take the trouble of writing him a letter which will make him both proud and happy and tell him that we are all well and were very much pleased to hear from him. No! on second thoughts, I wish you would write to Miss Lamb, and tell her how we are going on, and that I beg she will forgive me for having broken my word, but that really I have had no time for writing except when I needed rest both of body and mind. *She* will, I am sure, be so good as to write to William by the two penny post (paying the postage) and will deliver the messages to him. I wrote to you from Coblentz. Thence to St. Goar on the Rhine (where we dined) and to Bingen (where we slept). It was a most delightful day's journey, mostly between the steep banks of the Rhine—towns, villages, ruins upon the slopes at every bending of the river—Convents—Churches—Villages—Vineyards—and every plot of ground cultivated—but still in general a want of fine trees. Next day dined at Mayence, slept at Frankfurt, next night at Dormstadt—all palaces, immense houses, squares with nobody to walk in them, streets desolately wide, and soldiers, gardens, and dullness. Yet the gardens very hilly, not flat country. On to Heidelbergh, a city gloriously situated, rich in hill and dale—woods, corn, fruit, and green hills.—Romantic walks—with every enticement of seats and bowers to linger in the shade—Next day to Carlsruhe and Baden. By the bye, what I have said of Dormstadt applies still more to Carlsruhe—though they are both places of the same kind and I thought of Carlsruhe when I described Dormstadt. Thence to Hornburg—a Romantic town in a long Romantic vale. Thence to Schaffhausen and thence to Zurich to another Baden and to Leinsburgh. This little town with a Ruined Castle upon a lofty eminence, commanding a noble view terminating on one side by the snowy Alps, on the other by the mountains of Jura. In that day's journey we first saw the higher Alps—and in the morning before our departure ascended the castle hill and beheld the grandest exhibition I had ever seen of mist and sunshine, ample space and clear distant mountains —Castles rising below us as from a sea on different eminences like Islands—thence by Murgenthal and Herzegeboshie (I know I spell these names wrong, for I write by the ear but you may perhaps trace them on the map), to Berne, a handsome town, nobly situated, surrounded by fine walks commanding magnificent views. Next day 20 miles to Thun along a spacious rich vale scattered over with small villas, comfortable large wooden houses—and pretty villages and happy industrious looking people—and no beggars! a great treat—nor had we yet had many beggars in Switzerland—but further on they were intolerable especially in the Canton of Uri. Thun is a small old town—Castle and Church on an eminence near the foot of the beautiful Lake. Here I had the last remains of the indisposition, which at the beginning of the journey occasionally troubled me; but since we left Thun I have been perfectly well. Next day down the Lake and through Unterseen, a romantic town on the River Aar, about a mile further to Interlachen,—a village situated in a most enchanting vale. We stayed two days at an Inn, standing on a little open space of turf—(a *green* we should call it) embowered in the finest Walnut trees—indeed every village is so embowered—almost every house—from Interlachen up the valley of Outterbrünnese to that village and thence over the Wangern Alps—an eight hours journey—to Grindelwald. This pass carries you close to the snows of the Mountain Yung-frau—and there we first heard and just saw an Avalanche—one and many more after it—but one greeted us and stayed our course instantly, listening in the clear air to a sound like thunder just at the point where we were descending into a hollow before the last stage of our ascent. We dined upon cheese, milk, bread, and delicious cream in a miner's hut—on one side of this hollow;—green and flowery—for flowers were always to be found, where we were on the Alps. The other side at an equal height snow and ice.—Cattle on the green height above, and close to us—Downwards to Grindelwald and its Glaciers. Thence over the Sheidach Mountain to Meeringhen—a lovely vale—an eight hours journey. On this day, my Brother, Mary and I had one Mule amongst us—and observe that during a great part of the day we could not ride—These journies we performed without fatigue and with perfect delight. From Meeringhen up the tumultuous River Aar to Handele then a fine waterfall—and the vale as interesting as possible—back again to Meeringhen. Next day over the hills to Sarnen by the sweet Lakes of Lugern and Sarnen—very much like the Lakes of our own country. Most of this days journey (18 miles) we walked. Next day to Englebergh—a convent among mountains sublimely situated. This is a glorious [*seal*] We had a sort of cart which they call a Char-a-banc but could only make use of it for a part of the journey—the rest we walked—thence back again by the same road and by Stanz and Stanzstadt across a branch of the lake of the 4 Cantons to Lucerne. Here we stayed 3 days and here Henry Robinson joined us. We had a most joyful meeting and have found him as pleasant a companion as possible and very useful on all occasions as a spokesman where German was the language of the Country. Thence along two branches of the Lake to Kûsnach, and thence (a 4 hours climb) to the top of Mount Rhigi—where we slept and had an awful thunderstorm. Thence on foot through the desolated Vale of Lauerz—and over the ruins of the mountain to a village at the foot of the beautiful little Lake Lauerz—thence by Schwytz to Brunnen, beside that division of the Lake of the 4 Cantons called Uri, 'By whose unpathway'd margin still and dread, was never heard the plodding Peasants tread' (see Descriptive Sketches).[1] Thence up to the lake and to Altorf—and from Altorf to Amsteg by carriage, and carriages can go no further than Amsteg.—here begins our ascent towards St Gothard. At ½ past 5 o'clock the next morning we set off on foot—I will not attempt to describe the pleasure of that day—we walked 18 miles crossed the Devils Bridge and slept in the Vale of Urseren. The next dined at St Gothard and slept 3 leagues on the Italian side of the Alps at Airolo. Next day walked 12 miles and went 24 in a carriage to Bellinzona—Thence 9 miles on foot to Locarno—then to Lugano—thence having travelled almost the whole length of the Lake in a boat, to the most magnificent and most beautiful of all the Lakes—Como. There we spent 3 nights and days and are now at Milan. To-morrow we turn our faces towards the Simplon pass, which we hope also to cross on foot, having never felt any fatigue that deserved speaking of in crossing St. Gothard, and having found fresh delights spring up at every turning. Let no one speak of fatigue in crossing the Alps who has climbed Helvellyn—It is nothing in point of exertion to that ascent. Would you believe it? I am grown fat in the journey and we

[1] Lines 285–6. (*PW* i, p. 58).

are all perfectly well—William's eyes certainly, though weak much better. Write to me I pray you immediately à la Poste restante à Paris—We shall be at Geneva in less than a fortnight. Our journey has been delightful even beyond my expectations and we have had very fine weather—have only been once wet. Thunderstorms frequent, but when we were housed in the evening. Mary writes to Sara today so you need not send her this letter

Monday Morn.

I have not patience to read over my letter—to correct it is impossible. It is a sad letter and will be hard work for you.

I wish you would write to Miss Lloyd with our best love

Yours ever

D. Wordsworth.

Last night we saw such a sunset as I never saw in England—after that, magnificent fireworks—how busy every one is here in quest of pleasure!

Tell Miss Lloyd I should like to write to her but [?] is wanting. Tell her I shall be obliged if she will send my Manuscript of the Greens to Mrs Hoare to be forwarded by her to Misses Lockier, Hendon.—Mrs Hoare will send it.

606. W. W. to LORD LONSDALE

MS. Lonsdale MSS., Record Office, The Castle, Carlisle.
Mem. (—). *Grosart* (—). *K* (—). *MY ii. 646, p. 901* (—).

Paris, October 7 [1820], 45 Rue Charlot,
Boulevards du Temple.[1]

My Lord,

I had the honor of writing to your Lordship from Lucerne, 19th of August, giving an account of our movements. We have visited, since, those parts of Switzerland usually deemed most worthy of notice, and the Italian Lakes; having stopped four days at Milan, and as many at Geneva. With the exception of a couple of days on the Lake of Geneva, the weather has been most favorable, though frequently, during the last fortnight, extremely cold. We have had no detention from illness, nor any bad accident, for which we feel more grateful, on account of some of our fellow-travellers,

[1] For W. W.'s meetings in Paris with Thomas Moore and Canning, which are not mentioned in the next letters, see *Memoirs, Journal, and Correspondence of Thomas Moore*, ed. Lord John Russell, 8 vols., 1853–6, iii, pp. 159 ff.

who accidentally joined us for a few days. Of these, one, an American gentleman,[1] was drowned in the Lake of Zurich, by the upsetting of a boat in a storm, two or three days after he parted with us; and two others, near the summit of Mount Jura, and in the middle of a tempestuous night, were precipitated, they scarcely knew how far, along with one of those frightful and ponderous vehicles, a continental Diligence. We have been in Paris since Sunday last; and think of staying about a fortnight longer, as scarcely less will suffice for even a hasty view of the Town and neighbourhood. We took Fontainebleau in our way, and intend giving a day to Versailles. The day we entered Paris we passed a well-drest young man and woman dragging a harrow through a field, like cattle; nevertheless, working in the fields on the Sabbath Day does not appear to be general in France. On the same day, a wretched-looking Person begged of us, as the Carriage was climbing a Hill; nothing could exceed his transport in receiving a pair of old Pantaloons which were thrown him from the carriage. This poor mendicant, the Postilion told us, was an *ancien Curé*. The churches seem generally falling to decay in the country. We passed one which had been recently repaired. I have noticed, however, several young persons, men as well as women, earnestly employed in their devotions, in different churches, both in Paris and elsewhere.—Nothing which I have seen in this city has interested me at all like the *Jardin des Plantes*, with the living animals, and the Museum of Natural History which it includes. Scarcely could I refrain from tears of admiration at the sight of this apparently boundless exhibition of the wonders of the creation. The Statues and pictures of the Louvre affect me feebly in comparison. The exterior of Paris is much changed since I last visited it in 1792. I miss many antient Buildings, particularly the Temple, where the poor king and his family were so long confined. That memorable spot where the Jacobin Club was held, has also disappeared. Nor are the additional buildings always improvements; the *Pont des Arts*, in particular, injures the view from the *Pont Neuf* greatly; but in these things public convenience is the main point.

I say nothing of public affairs, for I have little opportunity of knowing anything about them. In respect to the business of our Queen, we deem ourselves truly fortunate in having been out of the

[1] Frederick William Goddard of Boston, a student at Geneva, who was drowned on 21 Aug. while touring with a friend named Trotter. See *Elegiac Stanzas*, *PW* iii, p. 193 (with introductory note by H. C. R.); and *MW* 32, p. 67.

country, at a time when an inquiry at which all Europe seems scandalized, was going on.[1]

I have purposely deferred congratulating your Lordship on the marriage of Lady Mary with Lord Frederick Bentinck, which I hear has been celebrated. My wishes for her happiness are most earnest.

With respectful compliments and congratulations to Lady Lonsdale, in which Mrs. Wordsworth begs leave to join, I have the honour to be, my Lord

Your Lordship's
obliged and faithful friend and servant,
Wm. Wordsworth.

PS

I am at a loss whither to direct, but I risk Lowther Castle, thinking that your late arrival there may detain you beyond your usual time.

607. W. W. to MISS WILLIAMS[2]

Address: Madme Williams, Rue Hauteville, Fauxbourg Poissonières.
MS. Amherst College.
Amherst Wordsworth Collection, 1936, p. 62. MY ii. 649, p. 907.

44 Rue Charlot Wednesday morning [11 Oct. 1820]

Mr. Wordsworth regrets, that owing to conditional engagements he could not reply to Miss Williams obliging note before

[1] In June 1820 Queen Caroline, whose name had been omitted from the Prayer Book and who was denied recognition at foreign courts, returned to England and was received at Dover by huge crowds who regarded her as a persecuted woman. In July Lord Liverpool introduced the 'Pains and Penalties' Bill, to deprive her of her title and annul the marriage, and the country was deluged with the squalid details of the case. In October Brougham opened her defence; in November the Government majority dwindled to nine, and Liverpool dropped the measure. (Note by de Selincourt). W. W. seems to have had some sympathy for the Queen, though he abused *The Times* for its articles in her favour (*HCR* i, pp. 242–3); and on his return to London he took the trouble to attend the last day of her trial, on 10 Nov. For the painting of the scene in the House of Lords by James Stephanoff, in which W. W. appears along with Sir George Beaumont, see Blanchard, op. cit., pp. 64–65, 152.

[2] Helen Maria Williams, whose poems had influenced W. W. in boyhood. They had failed to meet when W. W. was in France in 1791–2 (see *EY* 20, p. 69), but now at last an introduction was effected through H. C. R., who had been helping her to find a publisher for her latest work, *Letters on the Events which have passed in France since the Restoration in 1815*, 1819. (See her manuscript letters to H. C. R., *Dr Williams's Lib.*). She had written to W. W. on 10 Oct.: 'Miss Williams was led by Mr Robinson to expect the honor of seeing

this morning. He is now happy to say that it will be in his power to wait upon Miss Williams on Friday Evening, and to bring Mrs and Miss Wordsworth, his Sister, along with him.

608. D. W. to CATHERINE CLARKSON

Address: Mrs Clarkson, Playford Hall, Ipswich.
Postmark: 27 Oct. 1820.
MS. British Museum.
MY ii. 648, p. 904.

Saturday 14th October [1820]

My dearest Friend,

Mr Monkhouse and his wife and sister-in-law intend to leave Paris on Monday or Tuesday;[1] and though I think we shall follow them in ten days, I am glad of the opportunity of sending a few lines by them which I should not think worth foreign postage; but I know you will gladly pay the English price, merely for the pleasure of knowing that we are all well, and I do not grudge it for you. We arrived here tomorrow fortnight—entered upon our lodgings the day following (Monday) which are taken for a month; we shall certainly not enter upon another week, and it is probable that we shall depart a few days earlier—but you shall hear as soon as we get to London.[2] Poor Mary Lamb is again ill. Thus we have lost one of our strongest inducements to linger in London, therefore I think our stay there will not exceed a week. My Brother will have some business with Chantry.[3] From London we go to Cambridge Wm and M will halt there a few days, and I shall make my way

Mr Wordsworth on Tuesday last, and felt greatly disappointed at his not coming—she flatters herself that the departure of their mutual friend will not deprive her of a visit which she will know how to value—altho' the greatest part of her life has been passed abroad, she has not lost her sensibility to the charm of english poetry—Mr Wordsworth will therefore easily believe how deeply she has felt the power of his compositions and how much she would regret losing an opportunity of being introduced to him . . .' (*WL MSS.*). According to M. W.'s *MS. Journal*, the Wordsworths visited Miss Williams on Friday, 13 Oct. and again on Friday, 20 Oct.

[1] H. C. R. had already left for home on 9 Oct.

[2] W. W., M. W., and D. W. left Paris for Boulogne on 27 or 28 Oct. and stayed with Miss Barker for a few days while awaiting places on the channel pacquet. On 2 Nov. they were shipwrecked while putting out from Boulogne harbour, and were unable to sail again until 7 Nov. They finally arrived in London early on the morning of 9 Nov. and stayed there a fortnight, seeing much of the Lambs and Samuel Rogers and something of Haydon and Coleridge. W. W. dined at Holland House on 16 Nov. On 23 Nov. the party moved on to Cambridge, where C. W. was now installed in Trinity Lodge.

[3] See L. 598 above.

from Cambridge to Playford. I am unwilling to give up the pleasure of being at Cambridge with Wm and Mary, though I shall have to make a considerable circuit in getting to you instead of going directly from London. Besides, when I leave you my Brother Chris may possibly not be at Cambridge.

I am very sorry to tell you that Wm and M will feel themselves obliged to give up the pleasure of visiting Playford—indeed I did not think (as you remember I told you) that they would afford the time to go so far out of the direct road. After our parting from Willy they will be very anxious to get home—not only for the sake of home—but because of the Stamp office, where new arrangements have been made in our absence. Coleorton lies in the way and they will stop there a few days. They had made a promise the last[1] time they were in town and broke it in their anxiety to be at Rydal.

In answer to a question which you are no doubt putting to me while you have this scrawl in your hands 'How do you like Paris?' I know not what to say. It is certainly a most amusing place though we are too late in the season for garden gaieties, yet the weather has been perfectly clear since we entered Paris which was on a thoroughly rainy day and to be sure our first impressions were not very favourable. We were set down in a cold hotel—our rooms high up—and out of doors nothing was to be seen but open shops without purchasers—and men and women picking their way through the mire, the Bourgeoises heart and soul intent upon their petticoats and stockings—we went out and dined in the Palais Royale—there the shops were half shut—no gaiety. Next day things wore a different aspect, the sun shone and with the exception of 3 days it has shone ever since and we have not had another drop of rain. We have seen a great deal, though we have never had a Voiture but to take us to Versailles. Today we go to Vincennes. Our lodgings are very pleasant—close to the Boulevard du Temple. The only inconvenience is our distance from the Louvre etc, but *I* am so strong that to me it is nothing. I have never but once been tired since I came to Paris.—Last Sunday night we were on the Boulevards. I cannot express the melancholy feelings which the mis-named gaiety exerted on my mind. More on that evening in contrast to our Sabbath of quiet and rest.—The Arabian splendour of Coffee houses and theatres—the laughter—the eagerness—the fierceness—the happy seeming never tranquil—but I must haste to conclude. We have heard of poor Willy's illness, but not till it was over. We are very thankful that he had been given the care of so tender a Friend

[1] last *written in text,* former *written above the line.*

though grieved that you should have had the awful anxiety. Thank God it is [*seal*] and we can never be sufficiently grateful.

John Wordsworth of Lambeth had told us Mr C's alarms respecting the Sportsman—dear good man! I long to see you all. We shall call upon Tom as soon as may be.

I possibly may stay a little while at Cambridge after Wm and M are gone, but I suppose that you can receive me at any time. You shall hear from us both from London and Cambridge. We have had great satisfaction at Paris in seeing our Friends[1] whom I have mentioned to you. Of this when we meet. Last night we drank tea at Miss Williams. She is a very sweet woman and we were much pleased with our visit. I think we shall go again. We talked much of you and I believe her nephew will send a letter.

God bless you my dear Friend ever yours D. W.

Breakfast waits and then for Vincennes.

609. M. W. to MISS WILLIAMS

Address: Madme Williams, 10 Rue Hautville, Faubourg Poissoniere.
MS. untraced.
MY ii. 647, p. 903.

Sunday—12 o[clock] [15 Oct. 1820]
45 Rue Charlo[t]

My dear Madam,

I had the honour of receiving your letter yesterday Evening, together with the several copies of your tender and beautiful Verses—for which my Sister joins me in offering you our best thanks. Allow me this opportunity of expressing the pleasure I shall have in possessing this little tribute from yourself—as also, the gratification which the perusal of both the Poems has afforded me.—The 12 lines towards the conclusion of 'The Charter'[2] have most parti-

[1] i.e. Annette Vallon and the Baudouins who lived in the Rue Charlot. The Wordsworths had apparently taken lodgings there with a view to seeing as much of them as possible; but very little was committed to writing about the meetings that took place. D. W. is completely silent about these days in Paris, and M. W. only offers the briefest notes in her *MS. Journal*. Under 2 Oct. she records: 'W. and D. went to Mrs Baudouins. I wished to write in my room, so Mr R[obinson] left me to pay *his* visits, we are all to meet at the Louvre at 1 oclock.' And then under 5 Oct.: 'Churches etc. with M[adame] B.' But H. C. R., who was of course in the secret, adds a few more details to the scanty picture, including a description of Caroline herself: '. . . a mild amiable little woman . . . I liked everything about her except that she called Wordsworth "father", which I thought indelicate' (*HCR* i, p. 248).

[2] 'The Charter; addressed to my nephew Athanase C. L. Coquerel, on his wedding day, 1819', *Poems on Various Subjects*, 1823, p. 266.

cularly affected me—I mean those beginning 'For not alone with blooming Youth'—they have dwelt upon my tongue ever since I read them—The Couplet 'For then the hand' etc to my mind is exquisite.

It will not be from want of inclination, if we do not avail ourselves of your kind wish, to repeat our visit to you next Friday Evening.—I will take care that you shall be informed in time if we are not able to wait upon you—I am dr. Madam your obliged St.

M. Wordsworth.

turn over

Mr. Wordsworth begs me to offer you his thanks for the elegant Translations, the originals of which were intimately known to him —He will have great pleasure in taking the Work to England.

The message in Mrs Clarkson's letter was simply what your Nephew understood it to be—to give him an opportunity of forwarding letters by us to England.

610. W. W. to LORD LONSDALE

MS. Lonsdale MSS., Record Office, The Castle, Carlisle. Hitherto unpublished.

Master's Lodge, Trinity Coll.
4th Decbr 1820

My Lord,

If the Newspapers are not mistaken in stating that your Lordship waited upon his Majesty a few days ago, I shall not be premature in offering my congratulations on your recovery. Lady Anne[1] was so kind as to send me welcome news, to this place, of the great improvement of your Lordship's health, and therefore I trust, that it will soon be entirely reestablished.

When I was in Town, Dr Stoddart, Editor of the New Times mentioned to me that he was preparing a Tract upon the State of the Press,[2] the abuse of it, and the means of applying a remedy. He purposed, by way of giving more weight to his mode of treating the subject, to adopt the form of Letters, to be addressed to your Lordship. This intention was mentioned to me the night before I left Town. It struck me that the thing might not be agreeable to your

[1] Lady Ann Beckett, Lord Lonsdale's third daughter.

[2] Untraced: if written, perhaps left unpublished. Stoddart had lately been attacked by William Hone under the character of 'Dr Slop'. A highly successful satire, *A Slap at Slop*, appeared in 1821.

Lordship, and I stated to the Doctor that it seemed to me proper that your dispositions in respect to it should be known, especially as he did not purpose to subscribe his name to the Letters. The State of your Lordship's health prevented me from mentioning the matter earlier, but if you would honor me with your opinion, I should be happy to communicate it immediately to Dr S.

I am much gratified with what I have seen of this University. There is a great ardour of Study among the young Men. The Masters, Tutors and Lecturers appear for the most part, to be very zealous in the discharge of their duties; and, judging from what one sees here, one cannot but augur well for the rising generation.

There were only two voices opposed to the late address,[1] one a person scarcely reckoned in his senses. The Chancellor,[2] as probably your Lordship will have heard, does not mean to go up with the Address. It is said that the Bishop of B.[3] does not purpose to go —which reminds me of an observation of your Lordship, upon the early political connections of this Prelate, made to me at the time he was raised to the Bench. At all events, if he be prevented by engagements, it is unfortunate.

On Wednesday we go to Coleorton, where we shall stay at least a week.

I have the honor to be
my Lord
most faithfully your Lordship's
Wm Wordsworth

It may be mentioned to your Lordship's *private* ear that some young men of the University have manifested dispositions in respect to the Queen, which it is hoped may not be carried into effect. The spirit among them is nevertheless good, upon the whole.

[1] A Loyal Address to the Throne from the University of Cambridge, presented by C. W., the new Vice-Chancellor, on 7 Dec.

[2] William Frederick, Duke of Gloucester (1776–1834), Chancellor of Cambridge University from 1811.

[3] Probably Dr. John Kaye (1783–1853), the newly appointed Bishop of Bristol, who continued to be Master of Christ's College until 1830. He became Bishop of Lincoln in 1827.

611. D. W. to THOMAS MONKHOUSE

Address: To Thomas Monkhouse, Esqre, 21 Budge Row, London.
Postmark: 5 Dec. 1820.
MS. WL.
MY ii. 650, p. 907 (—).

Begun on Sunday—Finished Monday morning
Playford Hall near Ipswich. [5 Dec. 1820]

My dear Friend,

My wanderings have now brought me to Playford Hall, where I arrived this morning at a little past 9 o'clock, having walked from Ipswich (four miles) with a Boy for my Guide. I was not the less joyfully received because my coming was unexpected. Circumstances had prevented me from fixing the day of my departure from Cambridge till Friday morning when it was determined that I should set off the next day. You have heard from Mary the cause of this sudden determination, and I now write to request that you will be so good as to send William hither. He tells his Mother that Mr Chapman[1] said that he might depart from London on Monday or Tuesday. Now I think it probable that you may have fixed for his spending Sunday with you, in which case it may be most convenient for him to go from your house; and, if [Dr. Russell?][2] and Mr Chapman have no objection we should prefer Monday to Tuesday, as allowing him one more day to stay at Playford, it being inconvenient to keep him here more than a fortnight as Mr and Mrs Clarkson are expecting company about the end of that time.—Mrs C. tells me that there is a Safety Coach by which he came from, or went to, London the last time, and we think that if the weather is fine, (as at present) he might come on the outside of that Coach, as he has a good great Coat and may be well wrapped up—but if you think otherwise let him come in the Inside, and in that case perhaps his place had better be taken in another Coach, as Mrs C tells me that the *In*side of the Safety Coach is particularly disagreeable. I leave all these arrangements to your consideration, only be so kind as to write me a line to be at Ipswich next Saturday, telling us when and how we may expect the Child. You must be so good as to pay his Fare in London and entrust him to the care of the Coachman, and he must have especial charges not to eat apples, or any thing that is likely to disagree with him, on the road. At the end of a fortnight all danger of infection

[1] William Herbert Chapman (1783–1861): assistant master at Charterhouse, 1812–38.
[2] *MS. obscure.*

from communication with Charles W.[1] will have passed away; and there is another great advantage in his spending a fortnight of his holidays here; namely that the time will be shortened at Cambridge, which, on his Uncle's account is desirable, he having already a sufficient weight of care and business. To this may be added that it will be a good thing for Willy to have a free run in the fresh air of the Country. It is impossible to give you an idea of the tenderness with which the poor child is thought of here. He won his way so into Mrs Clarkson's affections that it seems if he had been brought up under her own eye she could hardly have loved him more, and her own Maid seemed delighted when she heard he was coming. His patience during his illness, they say, could not have been exceeded.

I have asked you to write me a *line*; but I shall not be contented with that.—You must tell me particularly how your Wife is going on—if she grows stronger, is able to go out, and whether Miss Horrocks is still with you, how she is and when she will leave London. I believe it was about this time that Mr Horrocks was expected. If my Friend Miss Alice[2] comes with him pray remember me kindly to her. When you see Mr Robinson tell him, with my best regards, that I spent above an hour with his Sister, on my way through Bury, and had the good fortune to meet with Mrs Corsbie[3] at her house. Mr Robinson was not at home when I arrived, but I had the pleasure of seeing him before the Coach took me up. Nothing could exceed the kindness with which I was received at Mr Robinson's, and I was very sorry that it was not in my power to stay all night, which they had expected, and seemed much to wish me to do; but I was bound to make all possible haste, William and Mary being determined not to leave Cambridge till the manner of Willy's spending the Holidays should be decided; and as my Brother Chr. will be going to London on Tuesday afternoon or Wednesday morning with the address to his Majesty they have no motive to wish to stay longer at Cambridge. I wish you and my Brother may get a sight of each other; but unless you can seek him out (and I am sorry to say I do not know where he will be, for I never thought of asking him) there will be no chance of it, as he is obliged to hasten back to Cambridge as fast as possible, his duties there at present occupying him every day, and almost all the day through.—It is

[1] Charles Wordsworth, C. W.'s second son: at this time a schoolboy at Harrow.

[2] Alice Horrocks, later Mrs. Master.

[3] Catherine Clarkson's sister.

very unlucky that he is Vice-Chancellor this first year; but his health, I trust, is quite reestablished, and except when two or three things are pressing on his thoughts at once he does not seem to be *put out of the way* by his new occupations—*hurried* he never is—and I think no one can be better fitted for the regular duties of Master of a College. It will be a nice jaunt for your wife and you at some time, to go and see Cambridge. We very much enjoyed our visit—a strange contrast to the bustle of Oxford Street, and the evenings of talk at Charles Lamb's etc.[1] All is so quiet and stately both within and without doors. We were very fortunate in the weather, and walked the groves through and through many a time, besides visiting all the curiosities. The FitzWilliam Museum is a delightful place to go to—the pictures in general are excellent, and there is a noble collection of prints. The discipline of the University appears to be admirable; and the deportment of the young men when you see them walking about is just what you would wish in such a place. *Rows* no doubt they have now and then, but we saw none of them, and all agree in the opinion that there has been a great reformation in the manners of the young students within the last twelve years. Derwent Coleridge appears to be very happy, and congratulates himself on being placed at Cambridge[2] rather than at Oxford. He is studious, and I hope studious in the right way. Tillbrooke intends to go to London at Christmas, and no doubt he will soon seek you out. He is in good health and spirits but we fancy that his lameness grows upon him. He talks of the Ivy Cottage with great pleasure and seems resolved to take it into his own hands at the end of Mr Gee's lease.—Mr and Mrs Clarkson have inquired much about you and your Wife, and beg their kind regards to both of you. Mr C is certainly much aged in appearance; but he seems to enjoy better health than formerly, and is less nervous, I am sure, and well contented with his present situation. This is a nice comfortable old house—newly fitted up, surrounded by pretty gardens and gently sloping fields, and every thing is in the best order. Mrs C's health is wonderfully improved. She is able to rise at eight o'clock and sit up the whole day, and takes an interest in every thing around her; but, seeing how heartily she enjoys company, and

[1] According to M. W.'s *MS. Journal*, the Wordsworths visited the Lambs on 13 Nov. and again on the evening of 21 Nov., when they met Bryan Waller Procter, better known as 'Barry Cornwall' (see *Lamb*, ii. 368, p. 286), Dr. Stoddart, Miss Kelly the actress, and Talfourd (see *HCR* i, p. 257). They also accompanied the Lambs on two visits to Thomas Monkhouse's new residence in Gloucester Place, and the Lambs visited the Wordsworths at least three times at their lodgings.

[2] Derwent was now at St. John's College.

knowing, as we all do, how well she is fitted for giving pleasure to others, I cannot but lament that she should be stationed in so lonely a place. She is going to drive me to the post-office this morning in her little gig. When I parted from you I thought it possible that I might see you again before my return into the North, as I might have been induced to accompany William to London if he had returned to school from this place, but even had he done so I should have suffered him to depart alone as I want to see my other three Nephews once again before I go home. I intend to leave Playford a few days before the end of William's holidays. I shall find him at Cambridge, and shall go to Rydal so as to meet with John before his return to Sedbergh. When you see the Lambs give my Love to them. I often thought of them at Cambridge, and delivered their message to Mr Henshaw,[1] who shewed us the Trinity Library. He was glad to hear of them—Adieu my dear Friend, with grateful remembrances of your kindness to me for the last seven months believe me ever yours affectionately D. Wordsworth.

My best love to your Wife. I hope we shall meet in the North early in the summer.

Miss Horrocks was so kind as to ask me to halt at Preston on my way homewards. That will not be in my power, as I shall go to Penrith. Pray give my kind love to her and tell her so.

The Safety Coach goes from the Golden Cross, Charing Cross.

612. W. W. to LORD LONSDALE

MS. Lonsdale MSS., Record Office, The Castle, Carlisle. Hitherto unpublished.

Coleorton Hall
11th Dec^{br} 1820

My Lord,

We all under this roof sincerely rejoice in your Lordship's rapid advances towards recovery of health and strength; to which fortunately the present season continues favorable.

I have communicated to Dr Stoddart your Lordship's sentiments concerning his proposal. His long experience will enable him to be a competent judge of the advantage which his Publication[2] must derive from your Lordship's countenance and name; and he will be

[1] Aldous Edward Henshaw (1781–1837), librarian of Trinity, 1804–37: probably a relative of William Henshaw, Lamb's godfather.

[2] See L. 610 above.

highly gratified by the favorable manner in which you speak of him.

I understand that the Cambridge address was most highly approved of, and that it was delivered by the Vice-Chancellor in the most impressive manner.

I ought not to omit mentioning that Dr *Wood*[1] is not a little dissatisfied with the present state of the University. *I* spoke of what I saw, and heard of, and may confess that the average of attainment is very much higher than some years back. Men are also much more temperate in respect to drinking. The Masters of the large Colleges must naturally have their attention directed to what is amiss, and in their anxiety to suppress it may magnify the evil, in their estimation.

Sir George and Lady Beaumont are quite well, and unite with Mrs Wordsworth and myself in best wishes and kindest remembrances to your Lordship and Lady Lonsdale.

and believe me
my Lord,
most faithfully
your Lordship's
friend and servant
Wm Wordsworth

May I beg a direction for the enclosed to
Miss Hutchinson
Rydal Mount
Kendal.

613. WILLY W. and D. W. to THOMAS MONKHOUSE

Address: To Thomas Monkhouse Esqre, 21 Budge Row, near the Mansion House, London.
Postmark: 18 Dec. 1820. *Endorsed*: 14 Dec. 1820. D. W. & W. W. Junr.
MS. WL.
MY ii. 651, p. 910.

Playford Hall Dec 14th, 1820.

My dear Cousin,

I write to you a few lines as my Aunt has desired me. I had rather a wet journey for the first 3 or 4 hours, and then it became fine, and I got upon the outside of the Coach when we came to

[1] Dr. James Wood, mathematician. Master of St. John's, 1815–39, and a generous benefactor of the College: Vice-Chancellor, 1816–17. He had been W. W.'s tutor at Cambridge: see *EY* 199, p. 427.

Colchester because I grew sick in the inside. I had a very pleasant journey the last part of the way.

I found my Aunt and Mr and Mrs Clarkson very well.

It was not Mr Clarkson that sent you the Pheasants and Rabbits.

I hope Mrs Monkhouse and Miss Horrocks are quite well.

I remain Your obedient Cousin.

W. Wordsworth

Saturday Eveng, 16th

My dear Friend,

I have not much to say to you; for this is not a place for novelties and adventures; but I feel sure that you will not grudge the postage though you might have gathered from our silence almost as much as from what we have to communicate, *no news*, in such cases as this, being wisely taken for *good* news. Your dear little charge delivered your and Miss Horrocks's kind notes to me after the first ten minutes' bustle and joy of meeting was subsided, and I can not express the pleasure with which I read your account of him. You and your dear Wife are very good to him, and especially in wishing for his company during the whole length of the holidays in *London*, where so much of it must inevitably have been forced upon you within doors; but I need not say that his Mother would have had no hesitation in asking this kindness of you for the first part of the holidays if we had not particularly wished him to be in the country if possible during the whole of them; and I hope that his fortnight's run here will be of real use in hardening him against colds when he returns to London. I trust there will be no danger of infection from his cousin Charles; but we shall not venture to send him to Cambridge till we hear that the three Brothers are suffered to be together, or till we have an assurance from his Uncle that he thinks he will be safe. It gives me great satisfaction to observe how much William is beloved, how tenderly he has been remembered by this Family. He was a model of patience during his illness, and gave as little trouble as possible, except to his good friend Mr Clarkson, who was, I believe, very anxious and unhappy, though Mrs C. never apprehended danger. He now perceives such an alteration in Willy's looks, and he is in such high spirits, and so strong and active, that since the first day Mr C. has ceased to look alarmed, and to put in his sudden questions 'What's the matter with that child? Is that child ill?' I am sorry that you did not see my Brother Christopher in London, especially as Mary tells me he was not to return to Cambridge till the Monday—M. writes in good spirits.

They intend to leave Coleorton on the 20th, so I calculate on their arrival at home on the 23rd. They expected to find John at Kendal. What a joyful meeting when all three reach Rydal Mount. No doubt Sara and her Niece Dorothy have already counted the hours.—This is a very comfortable place, the country is soft and pretty, and the gardens are very pleasant—and Mrs Clarkson and I are very happy by the fire-side, or in our *walks* among the cottagers, and *rides* in the gig when the weather permits, (which has been almost daily) for we have had remarkably mild weather till yesterday, when Willy and I walked to Ipswich. He was a most entertaining companion, and walked with such spirit! I was quite delighted with his vigorous appearance compared with last June, when he seldom walked without fatigue.

The news from Hayti[1] has grieved Mr Clarkson very much, as you may suppose. He is anxiously expecting private accounts, having at present heard nothing but through the Newspapers. Mr Clarkson is just as doleful about farming as our Friends in Wales—not that he complains on his own account, for he holds his farm at so very low a Rent that he cannot lose much, but he says that it is utterly impossible for Farmers to go on in the sad way in which they are at present.

I was particularly sorry, (after the pleasing accounts of your first letter) to hear that your Wife had again been unwell; she must be very careful during the severe weather, of which we seem now to have got a beginning. The wind today is terribly cold. We expect snow—William played out of doors more than two hours this morning and his activity was such that he felt nothing of the cold. He is perfectly happy here—quiet and tractable—and sufficiently industrious at his lessons; but he seems yet to have little or no satisfaction in reading *alone*. He draws and writes of himself but never takes up a Book except when I require it [of him]. I must say he always does it chearfully.

In reckoning up all the money I have expended since I left home (a black account) I am reminded of the last 10£, which I desired you not to set down in your account with Mary; and which I suppose you did not. Pray be so good as to tell me; and also, if it is not

[1] The people of Haiti had revolted from their king, Henri Christophe, and established a republic. On 8 Oct. Christophe shot himself; he had been cruel and despotic, but was an energetic and enlightened ruler. He had instituted marriage in the island, and established schools on the Lancastrian system, where French and English were taught. His widow and daughters came to England and stayed with the Clarksons at Playford. See D. W. to C. C. 24 Oct. 1821 (in next volume). (Note by de Selincourt.)

too much trouble, I shall be much obliged if you will send me an account of the different sums you were so kind as to let me have when I was in London. I hope before the end of another year to scrape up ten pounds to discharge my debt, I shall have no temptation to extravagance, for at least one twelvemonth to come, as I shall certainly not renew my travels in the course of that time. So it will be a time for *saving*.—In looking back upon my expenses in London I cannot point out any one extraordinary extravagant expense yet the sum of the whole surprizes me—and I think I shall profit by experience and contrive better another time.—Pray burn this when you have read it. I am not a little flattered by your Brother's wish to see me; and I assure you, if my motives for going home were not so very strong, I should be greatly inclined to turn aside into Herefordshire. I could be right happy for a month or so at Stowe, for there are not many people whom I like better than your Brother John. This however is not the time; I have now travelled my span, and to be sure it is ridiculous enough to go by Herefordshire from Suffolk into Westmorland—something like going by Edinburgh to Whitehaven. I hope to reach home before John returns to school. No doubt both he and his sister must be greatly changed during my absence. I long to see them. Tom Clarkson is expected on Thursday or Friday—Mr and Mrs C expressed themselves as very grateful to you for your kind attentions to him. My best love to your Wife—Pray let me hear from you as soon as you have leisure. Excuse this stupid scrawl and believe me ever your affectionate Friend,

D. Wordsworth

If you have nothing else to write about pray let me have an answer to my queries and add a particular account of your Wife's health. Remember me to Mr Robinson and to Charles and Mary Lamb. Many happy Christmasses may you both enjoy! Adieu again!

D. W.

614. W. W. to LORD LONSDALE

MS. Lonsdale MSS., Record Office, The Castle, Carlisle. Hitherto unpublished.

Coleorton Hall
18th Dec^br 1820

My Lord,

Yesterday I received a Letter from Dr Stoddart, of which the following is an Extract:

'I beg that you would present to Lord Lonsdale my best acknowledgements for the very flattering manner in which his Lordship is so kind as to speak of me. When I have finished the Work of which I spoke I will submit it to his Lordship's inspection; and if he thinks fit, it shall be addressed to him; otherwise not.'

Dr S., apologising for not having written sooner, says 'that he has been occupied with a scheme which he considers of great importance; viz., the formation of a general Society to oppose the progress of disloyal and seditious principles' and its chief object will be to watch and counteract the efforts of the licentious Press. Dr S. adds that your Lordship has been made acquainted with the foundation of this Society.[1] The objects of this Association must be deemed of prime importance by every reflecting mind. If its regulations be found judicious, I need not say, my Lord, that I shall be happy to do all in my power to carry them into effect as far as my influence extends, and to receive any directions from your Lordship to that purpose.

The other day I went into a Bookseller's Shop in the neighbouring Town of Ashby, and found, among a very small Collection of Books, 'the Koran' and the famous Pamphlet, 'Killing no Murder.' These Books were not on sale, but had been borrowed for the perusal of the Master of the Shop and his Visitors. I afterwards learned that this person was a notorious Jacobin and Incendiary, and Usher of a School in the Town, the Trustees of which (Tradesmen of the Place) had turned out a loyal Schoolmaster, and put in his place one of opposite principles, who had given the 'Manchester Massacres' as a Theme for his Boys. What are we to expect from children educated by such Teachers?

On Wednesday we quit our kind Friends for Westmorland. They

[1] The Constitutional Association, nicknamed the 'Bridge Street Gang'. It was active in prosecuting publishers of what was judged to be radical or seditious material.

are well and unite with Mrs Wordsworth and myself in best regards to your Lordship and Lady Lonsdale.

Ever my Lord
sincerely and faithfully yours
Wm Wordsworth

If your Lordship has occasion to write be so kind as to mention your health, which I hope has suffered no relapse. The snow is lying here pretty thick.

615. D. W. to JOHN KENYON

Address: John Kenyon Esq[re], at Mrs Dunn's, Montague Square, London, *and readdressed to* at Thomas Hall Esq, Holly Bush, near Litchfield.
Postmark: 21 Dec. 1820.
MS. untraced.
Transactions of the Wordsworth Society, no. 6, p. 80. K. MY ii. 652, p. 914.

Playford Hall, near Ipswich,
December 19th, 1820.

My dear Sir,

I received your letter dated Bracebridge this morning, and have written to Miss Rogers[1] to request that she will do me the favour to permit you to see the little Sarcophagus which you mention if it is in her possession. To prevent loss of time I have desired Miss Rogers to be so kind as to address a note to you at Mrs. Dunn's, Montagu Square.

I had a letter from my Sister a few days ago. She and my Brother were well, and had fixed upon the 20th as the day of their departure; so I calculate that they will reach home two days before Christmas day.

My Nephew William is here in high health and spirits. He is to go to Cambridge on Saturday, where I shall join him a few days before the end of his holidays; and about the 20th of next month I intend to set off for Rydal, so if you are able to procure the candle-shade before that time, I can take charge of it.

Hoping that before you again quit England your wanderings may lead you into the North, where we shall again have the pleasure of meeting you, I remain, dear Sir,

Yours sincerely
Dorothy Wordsworth.

[1] Samuel Rogers's sister Sarah.

ADDENDA

103a. W. W. to LADY HOLLAND

Address: To Lady Holland.
Endorsed: Wm Wordsworth 1808.
MS: *British Museum. Hitherto unpublished.*

Grasmere, April 11th, 1808

My dear Madam

I have taken the liberty of sending you the enclosed Paper,[1] containing an account of a melancholy event which occurred in this vale a few weeks ago, for the purpose of soliciting your Ladyship's benevolent assistance.—I well know how many claims you must have upon your bounty in these times of general distress, and I only think the application, which I am now making, justifiable upon the extraordinary circumstances of the case, both with respect to the worth of the parties concerned, and the nature of the distress.—

I am very sorry that I had not the pleasure of seeing you, when I lately did myself the honour of calling upon your Ladyship and Lord Holland, in Pall-Mall. I should have called earlier and oftener but I had several visits to pay, one of a week's length, to friends in the neighbourhood of London, and the short time I was in London I was confined chiefly to Mr. Coleridge's sick room, the sole object of my journey to Town having been to see him.

I am, dear Madam,
with great regard,
your Ladyship's
obedient Servt
Wm Wordsworth

[1] For the enclosure, 'George Green and Sarah his wife 'etc., see pt. i, p. 213.

Addenda

221a. W. W. to CAPTAIN PASLEY

Address: To Captain Pasley, Royal Engineers, to the care of Mr. E. Lloyd, Bookseller, Harley Street, London. To be forwarded.
Postmark: Apr 2 1811. *Stamp*: Keswick 398.
MS. British Museum. Hitherto unpublished.

My dear Sir, see for the beginning of this letter the last page; I write so bad a hand that you could not I found have decyphered it, and therefore was obliged to employ a Friend, to make the copy which I send you.

W. Wordsworth.

[*The letter, which is in the hand of De Quincey, follows, beginning at* 'Now for your book', (see L. 221, pt. i, p. 474). *At the end, Wordsworth transcribes the first paragraph* ('I address this . . . you never received', as pt. i, pp. 473–4) *with a note*: '(for the continuation of this Letter, copyed [*sic*] by my Friend's hand, see Page 1 etc.)' *and then continues*:]

As I have some blank Paper before me, I will employ it in transcribing 2 Sonnets, which may be more acceptable to you as they relate to an Event noticed in your Essay.

Upon a celebrated Event in the History of Greece.[1]

A Roman Master stands on Grecian ground:
And to the Concourse of the Isthmian Games,
He, by his Herald's Voice, aloud proclaims
The Liberty of Greece!—the words rebound
Untill all voices in one Voice are drowned,
Glad acclamation by which air was rent
And Birds, high-flying in the Element,
Dropp'd to the earth,—astonished at the sound.
A melancholy Echo of that noise
Doth sometimes hang on musing Fancy's ear:
Ah that a Conqueror's Words should be so dear!
Ah that a *boon* could shed such rapturous joys!

[1] The two sonnets, with the titles *Upon a celebrated Event in Ancient History*, and *Upon the same Event*, were published in *Poems, including Lyrical Ballads* in 1815, among the *Sonnets dedicated to Liberty, Part II*. See *Oxf. W.*, p. 312. Their appearance in this letter helps to date their composition, which probably followed W.'s reading of Pasley's *Essay*. There are several variations from the text of the printed version.

A gift of that which is not to be given
By all the blended powers of earth and heaven.

Upon the same subject

When far and wide, swift as the beams of Morn,
The tidings went of servitude repealed,
And of that joy which shook the Isthmian Field,
The fierce Aetolians smiled with bitter scorn.
''Tis known', they cried, 'that He, who would adorn
His envied Temples with the Isthmian crown
Must either win through efforts of his own
The prize, or be content to see it worn
By more deserving brows. Yet so ye prop,
Sons of the brave who fought at Marathon,
Your feeble spirits. Greece her head hath bowed
As if the wreath of liberty thereon
Would fix itself as smoothly as a cloud
Which, at Jove's will descends on Pelion's top.

234a. W. W. to DR. ANDREW BELL[1]

MS. untraced.
C. C. Southey, *The Life of the Rev. Andrew Bell*, 1844, ii, pp. 399–400.

[January 1812]

Dear Sir,

I was much gratified by your obliging letter, which I received this morning; I showed it immediately to Mr Johnson,[1] and am happy to find this evening that he has determined to propose himself for the office or offices which are about to be instituted. I need scarcely here repeat what I said upon the character of Mr Johnson when I had the pleasure of seeing you at Grasmere. As a moral man he is eminently conscientious; as a Christian he is humble-minded, pious, and zealous; and as a schoolmaster we have found him active, intelligent, and fond of his employment. . . .

It may be proper for me to state, that I learn from Mr Johnson that, having made an accurate calculation, he finds that his present situation, as curate and schoolmaster of Grasmere, brings him in between L.90 and L.100 per annum; so that certainly, in a pecuniary point of view, (the expenses of living here and in London being compared,) he would be no gainer by being appointed to the office of master of the central school, unless an appointment to that of

[1] See Letters, 126, 223, and 230, pt. i..

chaplain, with an additional salary, were likely to follow. I have thought it necessary, in justice to Mr Johnson, to make this representation; and, in other respects, he would make much more considerable sacrifices, as he must leave very valuable friends here, and in the neighbourhood, and give up the peace of a country life in a beautiful district, to which he is much attached. . . .

I am happy to hear that the great work goes on so well; it is some consolation to think, in the present afflicted state of Europe, that there is at least one small portion if it where men are acting as if they thought that they lived for some other purpose than that of murdering and oppressing each other. With many thanks and good wishes, I remain your obedient servant, W. Wordsworth.

236a. W. W. to DR. ANDREW BELL

MS. untraced.
C. C. Southey, *The Life of the Rev. Andrew Bell*, ii, p. 402(–).

[March 1812]

. . . Every thing will be done here to enable Mr Johnson to depart as soon as he receives the bishop's permission. I have a pleasure in repeating my opinion, grounded upon a year and a half's knowledge, that the institution will find in Mr Johnson a most excellent servant. I know you will esteem it a strong recommendation of him when I say, that he is extremely fond of teaching, and much attached to his pupils, and they in their turn to him. I believe many, I may say most, of the boys will shed tears at his departure. And I assure you, such is my sense of the good which he has done in this place, that I deem the availing myself of this opportunity to recommend him to your kindness as one of the most disinterested acts of my life. For besides his general usefulness to the parish, I feel how much my own children will lose in him. . . .

[*cetera desunt*]

250a. W. W. to CAPTAIN PASLEY

Address: Captain Pasley, Chatham.
Postmark: G 20 JU 181[2]. *Stamp*: Radnor.
MS. British Museum. Hitherto unpublished.

Hindwell near Radnor
June 18th [1812]

My dear Sir,

A domestic distress, viz. the sudden death of a sweet little girl of 4 years of age has hurried me from London hither, to afford such consolation as I am able to Mrs. Wordsworth, the afflicted Mother, who is now staying here. Coleridge and I had intended to go down to Chatham together to pass a couple of days with you; and I have relinquished this hope with great regret; wishing that at some future time I may be more fortunate.

I had the pleasure of travelling a few days [a]go, 40 miles, with a most excellent and interesting Person, a Cousin of yours, Mr. Malcom[1] [*sic*] who is going to his living in Gloucestershire. He is a particular Friend of my Brother Dr. Wordsworth, and I was highly gratified by this accidental meeting with him.—

I shall be very happy to hear from you at any time, and trust you will occasionally let me know what progress you make in your important occupations.—I was pleased to find on your account that Lord M.[2] is not displaced—

Wishing you health and success and happiness, I remain

Your affectionate friend
W. Wordsworth

411a. W. W. to C. W.

MS. WL.
Hitherto unpublished.

Sunday Morning
June 2nd 1816

My dear Brother

Having received from Mr. Hutton[3] a Copy of my Brs will, and a Letter, in which to my great regret, he declined acting as Trustee; I came over to Sockbridge immediately, and had an interview with Mr. H. He strenuously recommended that Thomas Wilkinson of Yanwath[4] should be applied to, and requested to act as Trustee in his place. I was on

[The rest of the sheet is filled with a summary of R. W.'s debts and assets, in the hand of W. W.]

[1] Gilbert Malcolm. See L. 250, p. 27, n. 1.

[2] Henry Phipps (1755–1831), Lord Mulgrave; later Earl of Mulgrave and Viscount Normanby. He had been First Lord of the Admiralty 1807–10, and was at this date (1812) Master-general of the Ordnance. He was a patron of David Wilkie and a friend of Sir George Beaumont. See L. 43, pt. i, p. 79.

[3] See L. 415, p. 328, n.

[4] See L. 11, pt i, and n. and L. 416, p. 329 above. From the latter it appears that T. W. did not become the third trustee.

Addenda

463a. W. W. to JOHN PAYNE COLLIER[1]

MS. untraced.
J. Payne Collier, *Seven Lectures on Shakespeare and Milton, by the late S. T. Coleridge*, 1856. pp. lv–lvi. T. M. Raysor, *Coleridge's Shakespearean Criticism*, 1930, ii, pp. 53–4.
LY iii. 595a, p. 1371.

Wednesday [Dec. 1817 or Jan. 1818][2]

My dear Sir,

Coleridge, to whom all but certain reviewers wish well,[3] intends to try the effect of another course of Lectures in London on poetry generally, and on Shakespeare's poetry particularly. He gained some money and reputation by his last effort of the kind,[4] which was, indeed, to him no effort, since his thoughts as well as his words flow spontaneously. He talks as a bird sings, as if he could not help it: it is his nature. He is now far from well in body or spirits: the former is suffering from various causes, and the latter from depression. No man ever deserved to have fewer enemies, yet, as he thinks and says, no man has more, or more virulent. You have long been among his friends; and as far as you can go, you will no doubt prove it on this as on other occasions. We are all anxious on his account. He means to call upon you himself, or write from Highgate, where he now is.

Yours sincerely,
W. Wordsworth.

[1] 1789–1883. Antiquarian, critic, and editor of Shakespeare, whose works he published in an 8-volume edition in 1842–4. At the date of this letter he was a reporter on *The Times*.

[2] Wordsworth was in London from the end of Nov. 1817 until 19 Jan. 1818. He met Coleridge twice at social gatherings on 27 Dec. and 30 Dec. (*H.C.R.* i, pp. 214–15) but also probably called on him in Highgate. This letter would seem to be the result of such a visit, which is more likely to have taken place in Jan. 1818 than Dec. 1817.

[3] Wordsworth refers chiefly to Hazlitt, who 'reviewed' the *Statesman's Manual* by anticipation in the *Examiner* in Sept. 1816, and again after its publication both in the *Examiner* and the *Edinburgh Review* Tom Moore had also reviewed *Christabel* unfavourably in the *Edinburgh Review* in Sept. 1816, and William Gifford, editor of the *Quarterly*, refused to allow *Christabel* to be reviewed at all.

[4] Coleridge's first set of lectures on Shakespeare were given in the winter of 1811–12 to the London Philosophical Society. He was now about to give his second series, 'On the Dramatic Works of Shakespeare', and other English writers. These lectures were delivered on Tuesdays and Fridays from 27 Jan. until the end of March 1818.

INDEX

PRINTED IN GREAT BRITAIN
AT THE UNIVERSITY PRESS, OXFORD
BY VIVIAN RIDLER
PRINTER TO THE UNIVERSITY